A DICTIONARY OF CONTEMPORARY HISTORY
1945 TO THE PRESENT

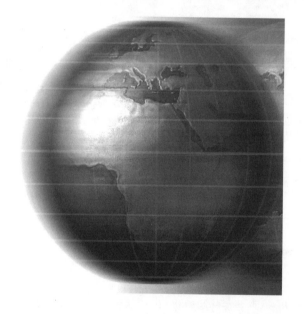

DUNCAN TOWNSON

BLACKWELL
Publishers

The right of Duncan Townson to be identified as author of this work has been asserted in accordance with the Copyright, Designs and Patents Act 1988.

First published 1999

2 4 6 8 10 9 7 5 3 1

Blackwell Publishers Ltd
108 Cowley Road
Oxford OX4 1JF
UK

Blackwell Publishers Inc.
350 Main Street
Malden, Massachusetts 02148
USA

British Library Cataloguing in Publication Data

A CIP catalogue record for this book is available from the British Library.

Library of Congress Cataloging-in-Publication Data

Townson, Duncan.
    A dictionary of contemporary history, 1945 to the present / Duncan
Townson.
        p. cm.
    Includes bibliographical references.
    ISBN 0–631–20016–9 (hb: alk. paper).—ISBN 0–631–20937–9 (pb:
alk. paper)
    1. History, Modern—1945—Dictionaries. I. Title.
D842. T69 1999
909.82′5—dc21   98–21835
                                                 CIP

Typeset by Pure Tech India Ltd, Pondicherry
http://www.puretech.com
Printed in Great Britain by TJ International Ltd, Padstow, Cornwall
This book is printed on acid-free paper.

For Nigel, Nicola and Rowena

Contents

Introduction

This book covers the period from the end of the Second World War to the beginning of 1998. It is primarily a dictionary of political and economic history and of international relations and does not include entries on scientists, artists, musicians or literary figures, except for people (such as SAKHAROV, SOLZHENITSYN) whose importance extends beyond their professional life. The dictionary aims to do more than give a bald recital of facts by looking at the origins and significance of events as well as their course. It is therefore analytical as well as descriptive and covers the whole world. The dictionary includes treaties, world organizations and movements which cut across national boundaries (e.g. GLOBAL ECONOMY). Extensive cross-referencing enables the reader to link one entry with another: words in SMALL CAPITALS indicate that the subject has an entry of its own. There are bibliographies for most entries, so that the reader can pursue any topic in depth. Entries are arranged alphabetically, according to the key word in the title: US raids on Libya appears as LIBYA, US RAIDS ON. Pinyin, the official romanization system in the People's Republic of China, has been used for Chinese names (Beijing rather than Peking), but where the Wade–Giles system is more familiar to readers (notably in the case of Chiang Kai-shek rather than JIANG JIESHI), a name is first given in pinyin followed by the Wade–Giles equivalent. Accents have been used only for European languages.

I am particularly grateful to my son Nigel, who took time off from his own research to write all the entries on Spain and Portugal and some on Latin America and who provided a considerable amount of material on other topics; to Dr Rex Haigh, who wrote the entry on the INFORMATION REVOLUTION; and to Prof. David Killingray, who once again has been a mine of information on Africa. I also want to thank my agent, David O'Leary, for placing the book and Tessa Harvey at Blackwell, who has seen the dictionary through all its stages from gestation to final draft with great efficiency. My wife Lesley has done all the typing and has been involved in the preparation of the dictionary from its earliest stages. Without her constant support and encouragement it would never have been written.

Duncan Townson

A

Abacha, Sani (1943–98)   President of Nigeria (1993–8). A Hausa, born in northern Nigeria's largest city Kano, he entered the army in 1962 and was trained in military academies in Nigeria, Belgium, Britain and the US. He became a major-general in 1984 and was a member of the ruling Supreme Military Council from 1984–5. A close colleague of General Babangida (see NIGERIAN MILITARY RULERS) he supported his military coup in 1985 and was made Chief of Staff, becoming Minister of Defence in 1990. In the presidential election of 1993 Babangida was defeated by Chief Abiola, a Yoruba from the south-west, so the military annulled the election. Abacha forced Babangida to step aside in August and became President himself in November.

When Abiola declared that he was the elected President, he was tried for treason and put in jail, where he remained in 1997, in spite of a personal plea for his release by President MANDELA of South Africa. Abacha meanwhile began the most brutal dictatorship Nigeria had seen. He skilfully bought off many politicians, including Abiola's vice-presidential candidate, Chief Baba Kingebe, who accepted the post of Foreign Minister. This discredited the politicians, who were too compromised to pose a threat to Abacha. Those he could not bribe he persecuted. In April 1985 between 60 and 80 army officers were executed for alleged plotting and in July 40 more, including General Obasanjo, were sentenced to death or life imprisonment by a secret military tribunal. There was such an international outcry at these sentences that Abacha commuted the sentences.

Abacha faced criticism for his handling of the economy and particularly for the exploitation of Nigeria's major resource, oil, by MULTINATIONAL CORPORATIONS. Ken Saro-Wiwa, a human rights activist on behalf of the Ogoni people, condemned the pollution of the area by the Shell Oil Company. In November 1995 Abacha had Saro-Wiwa and other activists executed. International alarm at events in Nigeria led the US and the European Union to announce military sanctions against Nigeria in 1993, but they had little effect as Nigeria's main export, oil, was unaffected. After the execution of Saro-Wiwa Canada, New Zealand and Jamaica proposed tougher measures against Nigeria but the British government blocked them. Abacha's incompetent rule (in spite of its large oil reserves Nigeria's average annual income was one of the lowest in the world) therefore continued. He died from a heart attack in June 1998.

Abdul Rahman, Tunku (Prince) (1903–90)   Prime Minister of the Federation of Malaya (1957–63) and of Malaysia (1963–70). A son of the Sultan of Kedah, he was an anticommunist Anglophile. He graduated at Cambridge University in 1925 and then studied law at the Inner Temple in London but failed his bar exams. On returning to Malaya in 1931 he was a district officer in the civil service. After the Second World War he returned to London and qualified as a barrister in 1949. He was a founder of the United Malays National Organization (UMNO) in 1945 and its President in 1951, forming the Alliance Party from a coalition of UMNO with the Malayan Chinese

Association and the Malayan Indian Congress. The Tunku wanted all races (Malays 53 per cent, Chinese 36 per cent, Indians 11 per cent) to support demands for independence. He led the negotiations with the British which produced an independent Federation of Malaya in 1957 with himself as Prime Minister and Foreign Minister. Independence would have come sooner but for the MALAYAN EMERGENCY (1948–60), when a communist revolt was put down.

Abdul Rahman wanted to redress the situation in the colonial period, when Malays were far behind the Chinese in education, in control of businesses and in the civil service. He therefore bitterly disappointed the non-Malays by the new constitution: the head of state was to be one of nine Malay sultans elected by themselves; Malay was to be the official language and citizenship laws excluded 41 per cent of the Chinese population. The head of state could allocate quotas for Malays in the civil service. The Tunku saw the economic advantages of joining with Sabah (North Borneo), Sarawak and Singapore in a Federation of Malaysia, which came about in 1963. This produced a confrontation (1963–6) with Indonesia, which ended (abruptly) when General SUHARTO replaced SUKARNO as the dominant figure in Indonesia. Improved relations with Indonesia enabled Abdul Rahman to be a founder of ASEAN (1967). Rivalry between the Tunku and LEE KUAN YEW, Prime Minister of Singapore, led to Singapore withdrawing from the Federation in 1965. This tipped the racial balance further in favour of the Malays (the population of Singapore was almost wholly Chinese) and ensured their leadership of the Federation but it increased the fear of the Chinese community. Chinese resentment exploded in riots in Kuala Lumpur, the Malaysian capital, in 1969, in which 2,000 (mainly Chinese) were killed. The government declared a new state of emergency and suspended all political activity. A year later Abdul Rahman retired. He came out of retirement in 1988 to condemn the government of MAHATHIR for repressing its opponents.

Abdullah Ibn Hussein (1882–1951)

First King of Jordan (1946–51). Born in the holy city of Mecca where his family, descended from the Prophet Muhammad, had been local rulers for a thousand years, he took part in the Arab revolt against the Turks in the First World War. As a reward Winston CHURCHILL, the British Colonial Secretary, made him Emir of Transjordan in 1921, an arid area with only 300,000 inhabitants, mainly nomads. In 1946 Transjordan was given independence with Abdullah as king.

When it was clear that there would be war between Arabs and Jews as the British mandate of Palestine came to an end in 1948, Abdullah negotiated in secret with the Zionists. He proposed to keep out of the fighting, accept the existence of Israel and annex for himself the parts of Palestine allocated to the Arabs by the UNITED NATIONS partition plan of 1947. In the end he did not make such an agreement, because he was convinced that the Arab armies would win. When the first of the ARAB–ISRAELI WARS began, his Arab Legion captured East Jerusalem, including the Old City, and the West Bank of the Jordan. These were annexed by Abdullah when he proclaimed the Kingdom of Jordan and trebled the population of his kingdom. The ARAB LEAGUE condemned the annexation and expelled Jordan. Israel had won the war, so Abdullah again made discreet contacts with it to negotiate a non-aggression pact between the two countries in 1950. He also granted Jordanian citizenship to all in the annexed territories, including PALESTINIAN REFUGEES. In July 1951 he was assassinated in the Al Aqsa mosque in Jerusalem.

Collusion Across the Jordan: King Abdullah, the Zionist Movement and the Partition of Palestine, A. Shlaim (1988)

King Abdullah, Britain and the Making of Jordan, M. C. Wilson (1988)

King Abdullah and Palestine, J. Neva (1996)

Acheson, Dean Gooderham (1893–1971)

US Secretary of State (1949–53). The son of a bishop, educated at private schools and élite universities (Yale and the Harvard Law School), Dean Acheson was rich, well-connected and an archetypal figure of the Eastern Establishment. A secretary to Supreme Court Justice Louis Brandeis, he was appointed Undersecretary of the Treasury by President Roosevelt in 1933 but soon resigned as New Deal economic policies were too liberal for him. FDR recalled him as Assistant Secretary of State (1941–5), but it was under President TRUMAN that he exercised his greatest influence as Undersecretary (1945–7) and then Secretary of State. Acheson was a leading figure in the conduct of foreign policy in 1946–7, as Secretary of State James Byrnes and then George Marshall spent much time abroad.

He was contemptuous of communism and thought there was little point in negotiatng with the Soviet Union. The US, he believed, must act firmly to stop the spread of communism, so he formulated the TRUMAN DOCTRINE, which committed the US to supporting anti-communist regimes throughout the world. He was closely associated with Kennan's policy of containment by building up the economic and military strength of America's West European allies through the MARSHALL PLAN and NATO and by promoting the revival of former enemies Germany and Japan, though these measures intensified the COLD WAR. Acheson was blamed for the 'loss' of China when the communists won the CHINESE CIVIL WAR (1946–9) by not adequately supporting JIANG JIESHI (Chiang Kai-shek), though he maintained that the US could not have stopped a communist victory in China without committing millions of American troops. He considered recognizing the communist government in China until the KOREAN WAR (1950–3). Acheson was accused of help-ing to bring this about by giving the wrong signals to KIM IL SUNG, when he said in January 1950 that the US defence perimeter in the Pacific excluded Korea and that areas excluded would have to rely on self-defence and the UN. He then sought to make Japan a US outpost in Asia by ending the OCCUPATION OF JAPAN in the SAN FRANCISCO TREATY (1951), while retaining US bases there in the JAPAN–US SECURITY TREATY. He robustly and disdainfully rejected MCCARTHY's assault on the State Department in what he called 'the attack of the primitives'. When EISENHOWER became President Acheson reverted to his law practice, though he became a foreign policy adviser again to Presidents KENNEDY and JOHNSON, calling for an air strike on Cuba during the CUBAN MISSILE CRISIS of 1962 (advice Kennedy rejected) and helping to persuade Johnson to seek negotiations to end the VIETNAM WAR.

Dean Acheson, D. Smith (1972)
Dean Acheson and the Making of US Foreign Policy, D. Brinkley (ed.) (1993)

Adenauer, Konrad (1876–1967)

Chancellor of the Federal Republic of Germany (FRG) (1949–63). The son of a clerk in the Rhineland, he studied at several German universities before practising law in Cologne, where he was Mayor from 1917–33. A prominent member of the Centre Party during the Weimar Republic, he was President of the Prussian State Council (1920–33) until he was dismissed from all his offices by the Nazis because of his opposition to their regime and was twice imprisoned by them (in 1934 and 1944). His public career seemed at an end until the British made him Mayor of Cologne again in 1945, though they soon dismissed him for insubordination. He then formed the political party the CDU (Christian Democratic Union), and chaired the Parliamentary Council which drew up the BASIC LAW (the West German constitution). In the 1949 elections the CDU did not gain an overall majority, so Adenauer had to form a coalition with minor parties and was elected Chancellor by one vote. At the age of 73 he was expected to be Chancellor for only a short time but held this office for the next 14 years, being popularly known as 'the old man' (*der Alte*). He won the 1953 election but his greatest triumph was in 1957, when the CDU was the first party in German history to win an absolute majority with 50.2 per cent of the vote, a feat never repeated since.

The popularity of the CDU and of Adenauer was largely due to the WIRTSCHAFTS-WUNDER (economic miracle), for which his Economic Minister Ludwig ERHARD was mainly responsible. The policy of *Mitbestimmung* (co-determination) gave the trade unions an important role in determining economic and social policy and helped to create industrial relations in which consensus rather than confrontation was the norm. A WELFARE STATE, with generous benefits such as family allowances and pensions linked to the general rise in incomes, also helped to consolidate Adenauer's hold on power. The Chancellor was anxious to make peace with the Jews and in 1952 gave three billion marks in goods and services to Israel because of the Nazi genocide of the Jews in the Holocaust. He also compensated individual Jews in the FRG but he did not resume de-Nazification. The personnel in the civil service, judiciary and universities were very much the same in the FRG as under the Nazi regime.

Adenauer decided foreign policy himself. He did not appoint a Foreign Minister until 1955 and even then he took all major decisions. After GERMANY was DIVIDED in 1949 he had no illusions about a speedy reunification, though he was convinced that the communist system would ultimately fail. The integration of the FRG into a democratic Western Europe would be strong enough to deter the Russians and provide security for the FRG. In 1949 the FRG joined the OEEC, which distributed MARSHALL PLAN aid. The first major step towards European integration, which Adenauer welcomed, was the Schuman Plan to 'pool' the coal and iron industries of France and Germany, which led to the formation of the ECSC with Italy and the BENELUX countries.

The biggest crisis he had to face arose from the proposal that the FRG should contribute militarily to Western defence. When the KOREAN WAR began Adenauer offered to join a multinational force but it was not until 1955 that the FRG became a member of NATO. Unlike other members, it retained no forces outside NATO and had no General Staff of its own. Adenauer had to agree not to manufacture atomic, bacteriological or chemical weapons or to change existing frontiers by force, but in return most of the restraints imposed on Germany by the Allied occupation authorities were abandoned. The FRG was now an equal partner with the Western democracies and in 1956 introduced conscription: by 1961 it had an army of 350,000. In 1957 the Saar, after a referendum, joined the FRG, thus finally settling its Western frontiers. In the same year Adenauer continued the FRG's integration into the West by signing the TREATY OF ROME, which created the EEC (European Economic Community). His relations with the communist bloc were less cordial (though the Soviet Union recognized the FRG in 1955), largely owing to the Hallstein doctrine, which prevented the establishment of diplomatic relations with countries which recognized the German Democratic Republic (communist East Germany).

In the 1961 election the CDU lost its overall majority. Adenauer remained as Chancellor, at the head of a coalition government but, strong-willed and authoritarian, his popularity fell with his inaction when the BERLIN WALL was built. His final achievement was the Franco-German Treaty of Friendship in 1963, which established the frequent summit meetings between the French and German heads of state which have continued to be an important feature of European politics. After his coalition partners insisted on his resignation as Chancellor in 1963 he remained head of the CDU until he stepped down in 1966 at the age of 90.

Konrad Adenauer, T. Prittie (1983)
German Politics, 1945–1995, P. Pulzer (1995)
Konrad Adenauer, vols 1 and 2, H.-P. Schwarz
(1996)

affirmative action   A means of eliminating racial prejudice in hiring workers in the US to comply with the CIVIL RIGHTS ACT of 1964. In 1968 the Department of Labor requested federal contractors to submit a 'written, affirmative action program' for the hiring of non-whites. A year later President NIXON went much further with the Philadelphia Plan. Construction companies in Philadelphia were to set 'goals and timetables' for the hiring of blacks and in 1970 this was applied to all federal hiring (to a third of the national labour force). He did this to improve race relations after the BLACK GHETTO RIOTS, to split blacks from the unions (which opposed affirmative action) and to attract them to the REPUBLICAN PARTY. Originally only African-Americans were to receive preferential treatment because of the disadvantages they suffered from slavery, but soon women were added and minorities such as American Indians and Hispanics.

The Supreme Court at first supported such measures. Chief Justice Burger ruled in 1971 in *Griggs v Duke Power Company* (which had used intelligence tests for applicants) that 'The Act proscribes not only overt discrimination but practices that are fair in form but discriminatory in operation'. The government extended affirmative action programmes to colleges and universities, which fixed specific quotas for admitting non-whites. Such practices were condemned as reverse discrimination against whites, as hiring or admission was according to racial quotas regardless of the merit of the applicant. The Supreme Court ruled on this in 1978, when it declared that it was illegal for colleges to set a fixed number of admissions for minor-

ities and deny whites the chance to compete for those places on merit.

Affirmative action was also applied in South Africa after the victory of the ANC in the 1994 elections.

In Defence of Affirmative Action, B. R. Bergmann (1996)
The Ironies of Affirmative Action: Politics, Culture and Justice in America, J. D. Skrentny (1996)

Afghan civil war (1978–)   The war began when a communist coup in Kabul overthrew and killed the Afghan President, Daud Khan. Communist reforms, such as the emancipation of women, deeply offensive in a conservative Islamic society, spread the rebellion throughout Afghanistan. The revolts were sufficiently serious for the communist leaders to call for the SOVIET INVASION OF AFGHANISTAN in 1979, but rebel activities were not co-ordinated. Soon there were six Pakistan-based SUNNI Afghan rebel groups, three of them ISLAMIC FUNDAMENTALIST and three traditional religious parties who wanted a return to the old monarchy, which had ended when King Zahir Shah was deposed in 1973. The strongest were the *Hizb e Islami* (Islamic Party) led by the radical lay Muslim Gulbuddin Hikmatyar and the *Jamaat e- Islami* (Islamic Society), whose leader was Borhanuddin Rabbani, a graduate of al-Azhar University in Cairo and respected by the *ulama* (religious scholars). SHII Hazaras were also in revolt in the central highlands. The *Mujahidin* ('holy warriors' – guerrillas) controlled the countryside, the Afghan army and the Russians the towns and main roads. When the last Soviet troops withdrew in 1989 it appeared that the communist government of Muhammad Najibullah could not survive but the guerrillas had no central military command and failed to capture the important town of Jalalabad, on the road from Pakistan to Kabul.

After his fall in 1992 the war between Islamists and Marxists, which had begun in 1978, ended. The Islamic State of Afghanistan was proclaimed and was readmitted to the Islamic Conference Organization (ICO). Gambling and alcohol were banned, the veil made compulsory for women and co-educational made into single-sex schools. The *Sharia* (Islamic law) became the sole source of law. The civil war, however, did not end, as the *Mujahidin* alliance fell apart with the defeat of the common enemy. There were ethnic conflicts as well as personal rivalries of the guerrilla leaders: Hikmatyar was a Pushtun (40–45 per cent of the population), Rabbani a Tajik (20 per cent), Abdul Rashid Dostum an Uzbek (10 per cent), the Hazaras being 15 per cent of the population. Kabul was controlled by Tajiks, Uzbeks and Hazaras. Hikmatyar began a continuous and devastating barrage on the capital, hitherto unscathed during the civil war. The violence was not confined to Kabul but affected the provinces too. Dostum controlled nine provinces in the north. In 1994 the ICO and UNITED NATIONS made unsuccessful attempts to bring about a negotiated settlement and a new faction, TALIBAN, appeared, demanding the total seclusion of women in society. By early 1995 it controlled six provinces and captured Herat in the west in September. It went on to take the capital Kabul in September 1996 and executed Najibullah. The last major city outside Taliban control, Mazar i-Sharif in the north, fell to them with the aid of local Uzbeks in May 1997. It seemed that the civil war was over, but Taliban attempts to disarm its allies led to renewed fighting in which the Taliban were forced out of Mazar i- Sharif, so the war continued. It is estimated that of the 15.5 million people in Afghanistan when the civil war began, a million have been killed, two million permanently disabled and two million displaced. The UN estimated in 1988 that there were 3.15 million Afghan refugees in Pakistan, 2.35 million in Iran.

Afghanistan, Soviet invasion of (1979–89)

In 1978 there was a communist coup in Afghanistan in which Daud Khan, the Pre-sident, was overthrown and killed. The coup, which surprised Moscow, was followed by reforms (such as the end of arranged marriages) which were unpopular in a conservative Muslim society and risings which marked the start of the AFGHAN CIVIL WAR. SHII rebels, aided by mutinous troops of the Afghan army, briefly seized Herat, so in March 1979 the communist leader, Muhammad Taraki, appealed for Soviet troops. Soviet leaders were unenthusiastic. In September Taraki was himself toppled by his hard-line deputy Hafizullah Amin. The KGB in Kabul reported that this coup would lead to 'harsh repression'. On 12 December 1979 the Politburo decided to use Soviet troops to overthrow Amin and install a more broadly based communist government. Amin was killed and Babrak Karmal, in exile in Moscow, was made head of state. Soon there were 50,000 Russian troops (later to rise to over 100,000) in Afghanistan: they were to remain there for ten years.

Soviet aircraft and fire-power, particularly the use of helicopter gunships, brought enormous destruction among the *Mujahidin* (holy warriors) and in the villages which succoured them. Yet this was a war Soviet forces could not win. The mountainous terrain was ideal for guerrilla warfare and enabled the *Mujahidin* successfully to attack Soviet convoys and cut their supply lines. The Soviet and Afghan armies controlled the towns and the major roads, the guerillas the countryside. 15,000 Soviet troops lost their lives. The US and Saudi Arabia poured in arms to the guerrilla bases in Pakistan and in 1986 the US supplied them with British Blowpipe and US shoulder-held Stinger anti-aircraft missiles, which were very effective.

A change in the Soviet attitude to the war, which was deeply unpopular in the Soviet Union, came when GORBACHEV became First Secretary of the CPSU (Communist Party of the Soviet Union) in 1985. He wanted the government to reach an agreement with the Islamic opposition and when he realized that their leaders would not negotiate with Karmal, he secured his replacement by Muhammad Najibullah in May 1986. The UN played a key role in mediating the Geneva agreement, signed in February 1988 by the Soviet Union, the US and Pakistan, which provided for the withdrawal of Soviet troops by February 1989. This was duly achieved, though the civil war continued, as the USSR and US continued to supply their allies with arms.

Afghanistan Under Soviet Domination, 1964–83, A. Hyman (1984)
Afghanistan: The Soviet Invasion in Perspective, A. Arnold (1985)

Alfonsín, Raúl (1926–)   President of Argentina (1983–9). Born near Buenos Aires, he studied law at university, having joined the Radical Party (Unión Cívica Radical, UCR).

Under the military regime of 1976–83, Alfonsín was noted for his outspoken criticism of human rights violations by the security forces. Chosen as the Radicals' presidential candidate in the first elections held since military rule ended after defeat in the FALK-LANDS WAR, Alfonsín triumphed in October 1983 over the Peronists, in large part because of his record on human rights. The Radical Party also defeated the Peronists in the legislative elections. Alfonsín's declared aim was to end the constant cycle of military intervention and political instability.

As president, Alfonsín faced a terrible dilemma: the rule of law had to be re-established for the credibility of the new democracy, but this had to be done without triggering a coup by the aggrieved armed forces. Alfonsín promptly retired half the military high command. In December 1985 five high-ranking military leaders were jailed and, six months later, the three-man Junta that led Argentina into the Falklands war. However, in May 1987, following an attempted coup, all but the top-ranking officers were amnestied.

The stability of the new democratic regime required that the devastating economic legacy of the military dictatorship – a foreign debt of $43 billion and inflation at over 1000 per cent – be surmounted. In 1985 Alfonsín introduced an austerity programme. The concessions to the military in 1987 and the continuing demands of the austerity package greatly eroded Alfonsín's popular support. They also undermined the consensus that had been originally established in 1983 between the Radicals and their traditional rivals, the Peronists, to ensure the survival of democracy.

The watershed for Alfonsín was the provincial and legislative elections of September 1987. The Radicals not only lost 16 of the 21 provinces to the Peronists, but also their overall majority in the Chamber of Deputies. Alfonsín tried to rule in harness with the Peronists, but they blocked his reforms. Alfonsín's authority was further damaged by two abortive coups in 1988 and an upsurge in terrorism from both left- and right-wing groups. Lacking the support of the Peronists, and in particular the Peronist-controlled trade unions, to apply the necessary measures, the Radicals were overwhelmed by economic problems as inflation once again soared back over 1000 per cent. The May 1989 presidential election was won by the Peronist Carlos MENEM, though Alfonsín had to step down five months earlier than planned because of the fast-deteriorating economic situation.

Elections and Democratization in Latin America, P. Drake and E. Silva (eds) (1986)
The Penguin History of Latin America, E. Williamson (1992)

Algerian war of independence (1954–62)
The French government regarded Algeria, with its *colon* (European settler) population of nearly a million, as part of France and was not prepared to grant independence. The FLN (*Front de Libération Nationale*) therefore, encouraged by the French defeat at DIEN BIEN PHU by the VIET MINH, began

a rising on 1 November 1954. Too weak to hold a base area, they avoided frontal attacks on the French army, concentrating on guerrilla warfare, attacking *colon* estates and Muslim loyalists. The terrain in the north (large mountains with few roads), where most of the war was fought, was ideal for this type of warfare. From the start the FLN indulged in a reign of terror, disembowelling, castrating or slitting the throats of their victims. The French replied in kind, burning down villages (sometimes with the inhabitants inside) and shooting whole communities as a reprisal for the killing of French soldiers, thus providing almost total support of the Algerian peasants for the FLN. The FLN, supported by the ARAB LEAGUE, trained their troops in Egypt, Morocco and Tunisia and in 1956 extended the war west to the Moroccan border and into the major cities. They controlled the *casbah* (with a population of 80,000) in Algiers, where a battle took place from mid-1956. General Massu and the parachute regiment waged a ruthless campaign there, arresting 24,000 (of whom 3,000 died in prison), systematically using torture. The information gained was used to wipe out the FLN in Algiers by October 1957, though the methods used were roundly condemned in France and elsewhere. The Moroccan and Tunisian frontiers were effectively closed off by electrification, minefields and radar and over a million Muslims were herded into overcrowded and insanitary resettlement villages, where they could give no aid to the FLN.

In May 1958 *colons* seized government buildings in Algiers, while General Salan, in open revolt against the government of the FOURTH REPUBLIC, which he felt was not sufficiently determined to hold on to Algeria, called for DE GAULLE to take over. De Gaulle, fearing that France would slide into anarchy or a military dictatorship, said he would assume power if invited to do so; the French Prime Minister resigned and President Coty invited de Gaulle to become Prime Minister. The FLN was almost destroyed by 1959 but French military success did not solve the political problems. De Gaulle had come to see France as divided as in 1940 and near to civil war. The Algerian war was also an enormous burden on the French economy (there were 550,000 French forces there in 1959, of whom 120,000 were local Muslims). In November 1960 he proposed a referendum in France and Algeria on self-determination for Algeria: in both countries there was a resounding yes vote. Opponents of an independent Algeria founded the OAS (*Organisation de l'Armée Secrète*) in January 1961, attempted to seize power in Algeria and when that failed began a terrorist campaign, which spread to France. This made de Gaulle determined to pull out of Algeria quickly, so in March 1962 he made the Evian agreements with the FLN for an immediate cease-fire and an independent Algeria.

The most sober estimate is that 300,000 were killed during the war, of whom 17,000 were French soldiers and 3,000 European civilians, though more were killed after the cease-fire (including between 30,000 and 150,000 Muslim loyalists). About one and a half million people, mainly *colons*, left Algeria, most of them settling in France. The war brought the Fourth Republic to an end and speeded up DECOLONIZATION in the rest of Africa. The Evian agreement allowed free movement of people between Algeria and France: controls were later imposed but the number of Algerian immigrants continued to rise, a valuable safety-valve in a country with a very high birth-rate but a source of conflict in metropolitan France.

A Savage War of Peace: Algeria, 1954–62, A. Horne (1977)
The War Without a Name: France in Algeria, 1954–62, J. Talbot (1980)
The Wars of French Decolonization, A. Clayton (1994)

Allende Gossens, Salvador (1908–73)

President of Chile (1970–3). Born in the northern port town of Valparaíso into a well-to-do family (his father was a lawyer), Allende was expelled from university for his political activities, but later returned to graduate in medicine in 1932.

Allende was a founder member of the Chilean Socialist Party (Partido Socialista, or PS) created in 1933. Four years later, he was elected a deputy, before being appointed Minister of Health for the Popular Front government in 1939. As minister until 1942, Allende introduced accident cover and health insurance for workers as well as social benefits for working mothers. A year after leaving the ministry, he was made secretary general of the PS. After three failed attempts to become President Allende finally triumphed in 1970 as the candidate for Popular Unity (Unidad Popular, UP), a coalition dominated by the socialists and communists. Having failed to secure an overall majority, he had to be confirmed as President by parliament with the grudging support of the Christian Democrats.

The UP faced a redoutable series of obstacles if it was to achieve its revolutionary programme, ranging from the lack of a majority in both the Chamber of Deputies and the Senate to the hostility of the media, the judiciary, the civil service, and the foreign companies in Chile, especially the US corporations. Moreover, the US government was determined, following Fidel CASTRO's conversion to communism and the imbroglio of the VIETNAM WAR, not to let a Latin American nation 'go communist'.

A sweeping series of reforms was introduced by Allende's administration, ranging from agrarian reform (the break-up of the large estates) to the nationalization of the banking and other sectors, including Chile's leading industry, copper. However, the reforms triggered an economic crisis, with a slump in production and investment, while inflation, accentuated by the slashing of US aid and investment, had rocketed by the end of 1972 to 180 per cent, the highest level in Chilean history. The state-engineered redistribution of wealth towards workers and peasants provoked the mounting protest of the middle classes, as reflected above all in the strikes and lockouts of the lorry drivers, shopkeepers, students, and professionals. Allende's authority and public support for his government was rapidly eroded by the economic crisis.

By 1973 the government was under siege from its own supporters as well as the opposition. The left, both within and without the UP, forcefully urged the President, unsuccessfully, to deploy extra-constitutional means. Although Marxist in outlook, Allende always defended the constitutional order, convinced that socialism could be realized by democratic parliamentary means.

By contrast, the right, aided and abetted in its destabilization campaign by the US government and corporations, had begun plotting Allende's downfall even before he had assumed office. The economic crisis grew steadily worse as foreign investment continued to be withdrawn and the trade unions took to the streets, while Allende wavered between compromise and confrontation. The initiative was seized by the right. The army, led by General PINOCHET and backed by the US, overthrew the government by force on 11 September 1973. Allende, who had refused safe passage, died in his presidential palace, probably through suicide. The Allende years, together with the Frei administration of 1964–70, demonstrated that radical change could not be achieved by the left or the centre alone. On the contrary, their rivalry debilitated the democratic state and facilitated the triumph of the right in alliance with the armed forces.

Chile at the Turning Point: Lessons of the Socialist Years, 1970–1973, F. Gil, R. Lagos and H. Landsberger (eds) (1979)
The Last Years of Allende, N. Davis (1985)
Crisis in Allende's Chile: New Perspectives, E. Kaufman (1988)

Alliance for Progress   A treaty proposed by President KENNEDY and signed in 1961 by all Latin American states except Cuba. It was seen by some as a MARSHALL PLAN for Latin America and was designed to counter the appeal of communism after Fidel CASTRO's seizure of power in Cuba. The US promised $20 billion over ten years in aid and investments to promote land reform, cheap housing, better health services, more literacy and economic growth. Latin American companies were to invest $80 billion from their own resources. The US kept its word and provided $18 billion in loans and grants (directly and through the WORLD BANK) and three billion more of commercial investments but Latin American countries, deeply in debt, were unable to invest much. In fact, 90 per cent of new aid was used for debt servicing. Economic growth in the 1960s in Latin America was 1.5 per cent a year, much less than the Alliance target of 2.5 per cent and little improvement on the 1950s.

The Alliance That Lost Its Way: A Critical Report on the Alliance for Progress, J. Levinson and J. de Onis (1970)

American Federation of Labor–Congress of Industrial Organizations (AFL–CIO)

The organization to which most trade unions in the US belong. The AFL (founded in 1886) was based on the worker-aristocracy of craft unions and concentrated on gaining economic benefits for its members: higher pay, shorter hours and better working conditions. Its political involvement was limited. The CIO (founded in 1935) represented workers of different types, including the unskilled and semi-skilled, in particular industries such as steel. It was more politically active than the AFL, more committed to liberal causes such as the CIVIL RIGHTS MOVEMENT and was more closely attached to the DEMOCRATIC PARTY. Both organizations were strongly anti-communist: the CIO expelled 11 communist-dominated unions in 1949–50 and cut its ties in 1953 with the Longshoremen's Association and other unions riddled with corruption and racketeering.

The AFL and CIO were traditionally hostile to one another but merged in 1955 in order to combat the TAFT–HARTLEY ACT. In that year the AFL consisted of 109 unions with 10.9 million members, the CIO of 32 unions with 5.2 million members. George Meany, head of the AFL, became President of the new organization with Walter REUTHER, head of the CIO, as Vice-President. The AFL–CIO included 90 per cent of unionized workers and a third of non-agricultural labourers. It expelled the largest union, the Teamsters (and other unions) for racketeering in 1959 (it was readmitted in 1987). Reuther's disagreement with Meany led to his taking the 1.3 million United Auto Workers out of the AFL–CIO in 1968: they came back in 1981. The AFL–CIO was an important political pressure group, hawkish on foreign policy and a consistent supporter of US involvement in the VIETNAM WAR almost to the end. It supported liberal domestic politics and helped to secure approval for the CIVIL RIGHTS ACTS of 1964–5 and the creation of Medicare. It was not, however, able to stop the decline in union membership: 35 per cent of non-agricultural workers were trade union members in 1945, 27 per cent in 1970, 24 per cent in 1980 and 16 per cent by 1990. This was partly because of structural changes in the workforce. Manufacturing jobs disappeared with automation and the relocation of some industries abroad (see MULTINATIONAL CORPORATIONS) and were replaced by jobs in the service sector, where union organization was much more difficult. Some industries moved to the South and West, hostile areas for trade unions. Meany made little attempt to halt the decline by expanding union membership in the South and had little interest in mobilizing the unskilled. By 1990 the AFL–CIO was less important in American politics that at any time since its foundation.

Unions in American National Politics, G. K. Wilson (1979)
The Decline of Organized Labor in the United States, M. J. Goldfield (1989)

Amin Dada, Idi Oumee (1925–)   President of Uganda (1971–9). A Kakwa from the West Nile province, he had little education. He began his military career in the King's African Rifles in 1946, and served in Kenya during the MAU MAU emergency. Amin rose from the ranks to become an officer before Uganda became independent in 1962 and led the attack on the Kabaka of Buganda's palace in 1966. Obote, the President of Uganda, was confident that he could control the apparently jovial and rather stupid Amin, so he made him Chief of Staff of the armed forces. While Obote was in Singapore attending a COMMONWEALTH Conference, Amin seized power in a military coup in 1971.

Heavyweight boxing champion of Uganda, a polygamist and a charismatic figure, Amin promptly made himself a Field Marshal and established a dictatorship, dissolving the national assembly, suspending most civil rights and political activities, assuming the power to rule by decree and declaring that he was Life-President. As he was from a minority ethnic group (which extended into Sudan and Zaire) Amin consolidated his position by massacring thousands of police and soldiers from the Acholi and Langa tribes (Obote was a Langa) and throwing their bodies into the Nile and Lake Victoria. They were replaced by people from his own province, from Sudan and Zaire. During his reign of terror the whole educated élite was murdered, fled or disappeared, including the Chief Justice and the Anglican archbishop. Amin placed the armed forces above the law by giving them the power to arrest and try civilians and to do anything they wanted to preserve public order. The result was anarchy: it is estimated that 300,000 Ugandans were killed. Amin carried out some popular measures, though they were disastrous for the economy. He nationalized British businesses without compensation and in 1972 expelled 40,000 Ugandan Asians (most of whom came to Britain), who controlled the wholesale and retail trades. As transport broke down and there was drought in the north, many starved

in a fertile land and by 1979 industry was working at only 15 per cent of its capacity. Amin therefore looked abroad for help. He received military assistance from the Soviet Union and as a Muslim was given aid by Libya and Saudi Arabia. When an Air France aircraft *en route* to Tel Aviv was highjacked by the PLO and forced to fly to Entebbe in 1976, Amin connived in the passengers being taken hostage. He was humiliated when Israeli commandos freed all but three hostages and killed the terrorists. From this time his regime began to break down. As the economy deteriorated further with the collapse of world coffee prices in 1977, Amin sought to restore his fortunes by invading Tanzania in 1978, the base of many Ugandan exiles. His troops were soon driven back and as NYERERE ordered the Tanzanian army to invade Uganda, Amin's army, decimated by the purges, broke up into lawless bands. Some 1,500 Libyan troops were flown in to support him but were defeated at Kampala and Amin fled, first to Libya and then to Saudi Arabia.

Amin and the Tradedy of Uganda, S. Kiwanuka (1979)
Politics and the Military in Uganda, 1895–1985, A. Omara-Otunnu (1987)

Amnesty International   An organization, founded in 1961 and based in London, to inform the public of the violation of human rights and of the imprisonment and torture of political dissidents. It also provides support for the families of political prisoners. Awarded the Nobel Prize for Peace in 1977, it has extended its activities to cover social issues such as rape and the persecution of homosexuals. In the US, where it has over 400,000 members, branches have led protests at the death penalty. It had a million members in 150 countries in 1996.

ANC (African National Congress)
South African political party. The South African Native National Council was founded

in 1912, the first African political organization which covered the whole country, and changed its name to ANC in 1923. Its leaders were from the small group of highly educated Africans with Christian mission education, who rejected revolution and an appeal to the masses and wanted to persuade the white parliament to reduce racial discrimination and extend civil rights to Africans. In the 1930s the ANC was small, disorganized and ineffectual and was not revitalized until a younger and more militant generation founded the ANC Youth League in 1944. Its first President, Anton Lembede, a Catholic intellectual, rejected the 'language of supplication' and put forward the idea of Africa for the Africans, who would have to liberate themselves. After MALAN's government came to power in 1948, the ANC adopted the ideas of the Youth League with its Action Programme of 1949, which committed it to strikes, boycotts and civil disobedience, but radicals, led by Robert Sobukwe, disillusioned by the ANC President's moderation, broke away to form in 1958 the PAC (Pan-Africanist Congress). In 1955 the ANC and other organizations produced the Freedom Charter, which declared that 'the rights of the people shall be the same regardless of race, colour or sex' and demanded that 'all *apartheid* laws and practices shall be set aside'. The government reacted by arresting 156 of its leaders: in the Treason Trial (1956–61): all were acquitted.

The PAC rather than the ANC was responsible for the demonstrations which ended in the SHARPEVILLE massacre (1960), but following it both organizations were banned. Consequently, the ANC had to go underground. A group led by Nelson MANDELA decided that the non-violence advocated by the ANC President Albert Luthuli had failed and that sabotage and guerrilla warfare should be organized, so they formed a military wing, *Umkhonto We Sizwe* (Xhosa: Spear of the Nation). This was responsible for several acts of sabotage from 1961–3, when its leaders were arrested, tried and sentenced to life imprisonment. For a decade the ANC was demoralized. The BLACK CONSCIOUSNESS movement owed little to the ANC, which had only a small involvement in the Soweto riots (1976), though it benefited from them as many of the 4,000 young people who fled from Soweto joined ANC military training camps in Angola, Mozambique and Tanzania. From 1978 armed guerrillas infiltrated into South Africa to attack government offices and police stations, although this 'armed struggle' had little impact. There was a great increase in support for the exiled ANC with the BLACK TOWNSHIP REVOLTS of 1984–6, so that delegations of South African business, church and trade union leaders visited ANC headquarters in Lusaka (Zambia).

The ANC was widely regarded by Africans as the South African government-in-exile, an attitude encouraged by DE KLERK when he lifted the ban on the ANC in 1990 and released Mandela. In December 1991 the ANC took part in a Multiparty Convention for a Democratic South Africa, to discuss a new constitution which was to be followed by a multiracial interim government. After protracted delays, during which there was fighting between ANC and Inkatha supporters (the ANC accused the security forces of supporting Inkatha), there were elections in April 1994 for a Constitutional Assembly, in which the ANC gained 62 per cent of the vote, just short of the two-thirds which would have allowed it to draft a new constitution without consulting other parties. Mandela became President of South Africa with Thabo Mbeki of the ANC as Vice-President. The ANC had therefore become the dominant political force in South Africa.

In power for the first time the ANC, aware that it needed foreign investment, pursued a pragmatic policy. It abandoned socialism, Mandela announcing that 'PRIVATIZATION is the policy of the ANC'. To counter the fall of the rand, the South African currency, the ANC adopted a conservative economic policy, though this put a great strain on its relations with its allies in the Communist Party and

COSATU (the Congress of South African Trade Unions). The local elections of 1996 confirmed the results of the 1994 election: although the ANC share of the vote fell by 2–3 per cent, it remained dominant everywhere, except in the Western Cape and KwaZulu-Natal.

Black Power in South Africa, G. M. Gerhart (1978)
Black Politics in South Africa since 1945, T. Lodge (1983)
State, Resistance and Change in South Africa, P. Frankel, N. Pines and M. Swilling (eds) (1988)

Andreotti, Giulio (1919–)   Prime Minister of Italy seven times between 1972 and 1992. Born in Rome (his father was an elementary school teacher) he studied law at Rome University and rose rapidly in the CHRISTIAN DEMOCRATIC PARTY (DC) as a protégé of DE GASPERI. Elected to the Constituent Assembly in 1946, he remained in the Chamber of Deputies until 1992, when he became a life Senator. In 1947, at the age of 28, he held the key post of Cabinet Under-Secretary to De Gasperi and thereafter sat in 33 cabinets, holding at one time or another all the important posts (finance, defence, foreign affairs, industry). His main stronghold was in Lazio (round Rome), where he built up such a formidable clientistic network that his support was indispensable to any government.

A devout Catholic who attended mass every morning at 6 a.m. and was a friend of four popes, he was a great manipulator, who spent much of his time arranging deals to keep his party in power. 'De Gasperi', he said, 'was against exacerbating conflict. He taught us to search for compromise, to mediate'. By the mid-1970s he accepted 'the opening to the left' and formed centre–left governments which included socialists. He went even further and was Prime Minister during the historic compromise with Berlinguer and the PCI (Italian Communist Party), an informal agree-ment by which the PCI (the largest opposition party) would not oppose the government in return for having some influence on government policy. He was Prime Minister when Aldo MORO was kidnapped by the RED BRIGADES. Andreotti's refusal to free terrorists in prison led to the murder of Moro by his captors. In the mid-1980s, when the socialist Bettino CRAXI was Prime Minister, Andreotti was Foreign Minister, pursuing a pro-Arab policy in the Middle East and an integrationist one in Europe. He was Prime Minister again in 1989.

The DC collapsed in the early 1990s amid scandals in which he was accused of being deeply involved. The imperturbable Andreotti found himself indicted in two trials: for protecting the MAFIA in return for the support of parliamentary deputies which it controlled and for ordering, or consenting to, the murder of an investigative journalist in 1979.

Andropov, Yuri Vladimirovich (1914–84)   General Secretary of the CPSU (1982–4) and President of the Soviet Union (1983–4). The son of a railway worker from the Stavropol region of the North Caucasus, he worked on Volga riverboats and as a seaman before beginning a career in the Komsomol (Communist Youth League). He joined the CPSU in 1939 and in 1951 moved to Moscow as a member of its Secretariat. Soviet ambassador to Hungary (1953–7) at the time of the HUNGARIAN RISING (1956), he played a key role in suppressing it. As a secretary of the Central Committee of the CPSU he brought in young, intelligent people (such as GORBACHEV), who were later to be prominent reformers. However, he was no liberal and as head of the KGB (1967–82) persecuted dissidents as well as corrupt officials.

When he succeeded BREZHNEV in 1982 he was an unusual General Secretary in that he spoke excellent English, loved jazz and modern Western literature. He also became, in 1983, Chairman of the Defence Council and President of the USSR and so acquired in seven months posts it had taken Brezhnev 13 years to obtain. He waged campaigns against corruption, alcoholism and absenteeism and began some economic reforms, giving greater autonomy to local enterprises, without fundamentally changing the command economy. His foreign policy was more adventurous and showed a genuine desire for DÉTENTE and for arms control. He suggested a non-aggression pact between NATO and the WARSAW PACT, who would agree not to use force against any third country, or against members of the other alliance or its own. President REAGAN's response to this repudiation of the BREZHNEV DOCTRINE was to talk of the 'evil empire' and to begin the SDI programme. Andropov was effective ruler for only a few months as he had renal, cardiac and diabetic problems. He wanted Gorbachev to succeed him but his wishes were ignored when Chernenko was appointed instead.

Andropov, Z. Medvedev (1983)
Andropov in Power, J. Steele and A. Abraham (1983)

Anglo-Irish Agreement (1985)   Signed by the British Prime Minister Margaret THATCHER and the Irish Taoiseach (premier) Garret Fitzgerald, the agreement involved the government of the Republic of Ireland in the affairs of the North for the first time since independence.

The Agreement gave the Irish Republic the right 'to put forward views and proposals' about the government of the North. An intergovernmental conference was to consider security, the administration of justice and cross-border co-operation. The Irish government recognized, for the first time since the creation of the Republic, that Northern Ireland was part of the United Kingdom. 'Any change in the status of Northern Ireland', it said, 'would only come about with the consent of the majority of the people of Northern Ireland [and] the present will of a majority . . . is for no change.' The Republic

undertook to adhere to the 1976 European Convention on the Suppression of Terrorism, which made extradition between North and South easier of those accused of terrorist offences.

The Agreement was widely welcomed in Britain, Ireland, the US, the EEC and the COMMONWEALTH. It was meant to reassure the Unionists but most condemned it, as they saw it as the first step towards British withdrawal. The new role of the Irish government in Northern affairs appeared irreversible and for many this implied that eventually there would be a formal system of joint authority for the North.

The Road to Hillsborough: The Shaping of the Anglo-Irish Agreement, A. Kenny (1986)
Northern Ireland Since 1968, P. Arthur and K. Jeffery (1988)
Under Siege: Ulster Unionism and the Anglo-Irish Agreement, A. Aughey (1989)

Angolan civil war (1975–)   The independence of Angola was assured by the PORTUGUESE REVOLUTION of 1974 but it was not achieved until November 1975. Before that date a civil war began between the three liberation movements, each of which was supported by foreign troops, Cubans and South Africans acting on behalf of their COLD WAR sponsors, the Soviet Union and US. The agreement between the liberation groups broke down in March 1975, when the FNLA (National Front for the Liberation of Angola), based on the northern Bakongo people and helped by the Zairean army, attacked the MPLA (Popular Movement for the Liberation of Angola), an urban-based Marxist movement in and around Luanda, the capital, which formed the first Angolan government after independence. In the south, UNITA (National Union for the Total Independence of Angola), supported largely by the Ovimbundu people, also fought against the MPLA. Both the FNLA and UNITA were supported by the CIA, the MPLA by the Soviet Union.

In 1975 there was a multiple attack on the MPLA government: South African troops invaded the south from Namibia, Zairean troops attacked in the centre of Angola and the FNLA in the north. The success of these attacks prompted the MPLA to call on Cuba: 10,000 Cuban troops were flown in, held up the South African advance in January 1976, drove the Zaireans and FNLA out of the country and UNITA into the bush. This was the end of the FNLA as a serious participant in the civil war. KISSINGER, who was behind the invasion, had his policy repudiated by the US Congress: fearing another VIETNAM WAR, it vetoed aid to participants in the war.

In the south Angola provided SWAPO (South-West Africa People's Organization) with bases in its bid for the independence of Namibia, so South Africa continued its undeclared war on Angola. There were frequent and large-scale South African attacks from 1981, in which they advanced up to 300 kms inside Angola. When the US Congress lifted its ban on aid to UNITA in 1985, the US provided it with arms. Battles between Cuban and South African troops culminated in a South African defeat in 1988 but UNITA controlled wide rural areas in the centre. In December 1988 an agreement was signed by Angola, Cuba and South Africa, which provided for the independence of Namibia, the withdrawal of Cuban troops by July 1991 and the end of South African support for UNITA. At the end of 1990 the Soviet Union and the US told the MPLA and UNITA that they would no longer provide military aid.

Peace negotiations to reconcile UNITA and the Angolan government began in 1989 and there was eventual agreement for a ceasefire in 1991. Elections, which the UN said were free and fair, were held in September 1992, but when it was clear that the MPLA had won, Jonas Savimbi, UNITA's leader, accused the government of fraud. Civil war broke out again and spread throughout Angola. Savimbi, though condemned by the UNITED NATIONS, who imposed an arms embargo on UNITA, had considerable suc-

cess and at one time controlled nearly two-thirds of the country. A peace treaty (the Lusaka Accords) was signed in November 1994, which left Angola effectively divided into areas controlled by Savimbi (the diamond-rich areas of the north and north-east) and those in the hands of the government. Since 1992 Savimbi's strategy has been to delay every step of the peace process, such as the demobilization of his troops, so that the UN Security-General accused him of 'totally unacceptable' practices. The attempt to form a government of national unity was deadlocked when Savimbi turned down the job of Vice-President in August 1997. As he receives an estimated $400 million a year from the sale of diamonds he can buy all the arms he wants, in spite of the UN embargo. Peace therefore remains fragile, with Savimbi able to restart Africa's longest civil war at any time.

The civil war has been disastrous for Angola. A potentially rich country with oil, diamond deposits and a productive peacetime agriculture, it had to import vast quantities of food and had a huge burden of foreign debt. Its communications were destroyed (the Benguela railway to the Atlantic port of Lobito had been closed since 1975 by UNITA) and two million people suffered from starvation. The administration collapsed as the government could not pay civil servants, teachers and doctors, so it was unable to provide water, electricity, education and health care. It will take years to recover from the war.

Destructive Engagement: Southern Africa at War, P. Johnson and D. Martin (1986)
Confrontation and Liberation in Southern Africa, I. Msaboka and T. Shaw (eds) (1987)
Revolution and Counter-Revolution in Africa, G. Nzongola-Ntalaja (1987)

ANZUS Treaty (1951) A defence pact signed by the United States, Australia and New Zealand. Since the end of the Second World War Australia had wanted the United

States to guarantee her security but President TRUMAN was unresponsive until the KOREAN WAR. The US then wanted a peace treaty with Japan (later signed at SAN FRANCISCO), which Australia would not consider without an American alliance. The result was ANZUS, in which 'each Party recognizes that an armed attack in the Pacific area on any of the Parties would be dangerous to its own peace and safety and declares that it would act to treat the danger in accord with its constitutional processes'. This fell short of guaranteeing US military help if Australia or New Zealand was attacked but it was the basis of the foreign policy of those countries until 1985, when the New Zealand Prime Minister, David LANGE, refused to allow US nuclear-powered ships into New Zealand ports. The US then effectively excluded New Zealand from ANZUS. The impasse ended in 1992 when the US announced that its warships would no longer be nuclear carriers. Normal contact between the two countries was restored in 1994, returning the ANZUS pact to its original status.

apartheid (Afrikaans: apartness)   A word first used in the Cape newspaper *Die Burger* in 1943, which meant the separation of Europeans from other races in South Africa but with the white minority dominant. Strijdom (Prime Minister 1945–8) said: 'Call it paramountcy, *basskap* or what you will, it is still domination ... Either the white man dominates or the black man takes over'. It was the slogan of the National Party in the 1948 election but there was nothing new about the idea. The Act of Union of 1909 excluded the black majority from political power; the Natives' Land Act (1913) allocated 7.5 per cent (increased to 13 per cent in 1936) of the land in South Africa to blacks, who were 70 per cent of the population; from 1923 blacks were not allowed to live in 'white' areas, their movements were controlled by Pass Laws and they could not enter white hotels or beaches. Most skilled jobs were reserved for whites. Blacks could not vote for members of parliament, who were all whites.

Apartheid simply continued these segregationist policies, which were approved of by nearly all whites, but applied them more rigorously, beginning with MALAN. He was followed as Prime Minister by the architect of *apartheid*, VERWOERD, who turned the native reserves into partly self-governing BANTUSTANS (homelands), some of which were granted a nominal independence. All rights could therefore be withdrawn from Africans in South Africa, as they were supposed to enjoy full citizenship rights in the *Bantustans*. *Apartheid* began to collapse when P. W. BOTHA was Prime Minister. He abolished most of the 'petty apartheid' restrictions, but was determined to maintain white supremacy, an increasingly untenable position as there were BLACK TOWNSHIP REVOLTS (1984–6) and international sanctions began to bite. Many Afrikaners had come to see that *apartheid* was no longer viable and forced Botha to resign as Prime Minister in favour of DE KLERK in February 1989. He dismantled the rest of the system of separate development, which finally ended in 1993, after white South Africans had approved of its abolition in a referendum a year earlier.

The Political Economy of Race and Class in South Africa, B. Magubane (1989)
The Making of Modern South Africa: Conquest, Segregation and Apartheid, N. Worden (1995)
Segregation and Apartheid in Twentieth-Century South Africa, W. Beinart and S. Dukow (eds) (1995)

Aquino, Benigno (1932–83) and Corazon (1933–)   Corazon Aquino was the first woman to be President of the Philippines (1986–92). Benigno was a brilliant, charismatic journalist–politician who married Corazon in 1954. He qualified as a lawyer, became the youngest mayor in the town of

Tarlac, the province's youngest vice-governor and governor (at the age of 27) and in 1967 was the youngest Filipino senator. As the leader of the opposition Liberal Party he was the main challenger to President MARCOS, who declared martial law in 1972 and imprisoned Benigno and other opponents. He was allowed to go to the US in 1980 for heart surgery but on his return to Manila in 1983 was murdered at the airport.

His death severely undermined the legitimacy of the Marcos regime, which collapsed three years later, when Marcos fled to the US and Corazon became President. She came from a wealthy and prominent political family in Luzon, where her father was a Filipino Chinese businessman. Educated in Catholic schools in Manila and the US, where she graduated, she had not taken a prominent public role before her husband's assassination. She disliked intensely the corruption of the political system and saw her main tasks as restoring democracy, protecting human rights, recovering the Marcos fortunes for the state and reviving the economy. She appointed a commission which produced a new Freedom Constitution, which aimed to make the abuses of the Marcos era impossible in the future. There was to be a presidential system but the President could not serve for more than one term of six years and could not impose martial law for more than 60 days without the approval of the bicameral parliament. However, she lacked the experience to deal adequately with the deep-seated problems inherited from the Marcos regime, particularly the foreign debt of $29 billion, servicing which used up 40 per cent of the budget in 1990. Landlords in parliament prevented land reform and, disliking patronage, she saw her coalition government fragment. Military factions were a serious threat to political stability: there were six unsuccessful coups by officers loyal to Marcos between 1986–9, the most serious of which was in December 1989, when she was saved only by US military intervention. Seeking conciliation, she was accused of weakness when she

tried to persuade the communists, whose New People's Army (NPA) had been engaged in guerrilla warfare since 1969, to stop fighting by releasing prisoners and offering an amnesty and cease-fire. This annoyed the army and had little effect, so the government began a major offensive against the NPA in 1989 which had considerable success. She negotiated an end to US military bases in the Philippines, which were evacuated in 1992.

Aquino and the People of the Philippines, C. A. Buss (1987)
The Philippines in Crisis: Development and Security in the Aquino Era 1986–92, W. Scott Thompson (1992)
Corazon Aquino and the Bushfire Revolt, R. H. Reid and E. Guerrero (1997)

Arab League   The League was formed in March 1945 and consisted of seven Arab states: Egypt, Iraq, Saudi Arabia, Yemen, Syria, Lebanon and Transjordan. Membership was open to any independent Arab state and eventually included 22 members. It aimed to promote co-operation between members and defend their interests. Each member retained its sovereignty and decisions taken were binding only on those who had voted for them. Since 1948 the League has imposed an economic boycott on Israel.

The League has not been very successful in settling disputes among its members. The organization was paralysed in the late 1950s by the dispute between Egypt and Iraq over the latter's membership of the BAGHDAD PACT. Attempts to mediate in the Yemen Civil War failed, as did calls for arbitration between Jordan and the PLO in 1970. Plans to end the fighting in the LEBANESE CIVIL WAR were never put into practice. In March 1979, following the CAMP DAVID ACCORDS, Egypt was suspended from membership and the Secretariat moved to Tunis. In 1982 Saddam HUSSEIN sought military support from the League in the IRAN–IRAQ WAR but failed to get it, as he had started the war and some

League members (Syria, Libya) supported Iran. Egypt, readmitted in 1989, joined with Saudi Arabia in a resolution that condemned Iraq's invasion of Kuwait and authorized Arab League forces to co-operate with British and US forces in the GULF WAR. This decision split the League and the Secretary-General resigned. In 1990 ten nations, led by Iraq, boycotted a meeting that approved the return of the Secretariat to Cairo.

The Foundation of the League of Arab States,
   A. M. Gomaa (1977)

Arab–Israeli wars   See ISRAEL, BIRTH OF; SIX DAY WAR (1967); SUEZ CRISIS (1956); YOM KIPPUR WAR (1973)

Arafat, Yasir (1929–)   Chairman of the PLO (Palestine Liberation Organization) (1969–). Born in Jerusalem, he was educated in Egypt, where he was influenced by the MUSLIM BROTHERHOOD and Arab nationalism. After graduating as a civil engineer at Cairo University in 1956 he went to work in Kuwait. There, with others, he founded al-Fatah (Palestine National Liberation Movement). In December 1964 he persuaded his colleagues to begin an armed struggle against Israel, as the FLN had done in the ALGERIAN WAR OF INDEPENDENCE (1954–62). He left his job to work full-time for al-Fatah and in 1965 organized the first guerrilla warfare in Israel from across the Jordanian border, though this had little impact in Israel.

In 1969 the Palestine National Council elected him Chairman of the PLO but the PLO's armed forces were forced out of Jordan in Black September (1970). Arafat then moved to Lebanon to continue guerrilla attacks on Israel and supported international terrorism aimed at Israel. In 1974 the ARAB LEAGUE recognized the PLO as the 'sole legitimate representative' of the Arab people and a year later Arafat addressed the UNITED NATIONS, the first non-governmental official to do so. He became involved in the LEBA-

NESE CIVIL WAR and after the Israeli Invasion of Lebanon in 1982 was forced to leave Beirut for Tunis. He then adopted a diplomatic rather than a terrorist strategy, gave up all hope of defeating Israel and began a process of conciliation aimed at establishing a Palestine state (with himself at the head) in the Israeli OCCUPIED TERRITORIES of Gaza and the WEST BANK. In 1988 he accepted Israel's right to exist and renounced terrorism. His support for Saddam HUSSEIN in the GULF WAR because Saddam tried to link Israeli evacuation of the West Bank and Gaza with his evacuation of Kuwait, was a serious error of judgement, as the wealthy GULF STATES withdrew their subsidies from the PLO, which produced a financial crisis for that organization. There was a danger for Arafat that he would be sidelined and cease to be an important player in the Middle East PEACE PROCESS, but his fortunes revived when secret negotiations with Israel produced the Oslo Accords in 1993. The PLO was to take control, in a series of stages, of Gaza and Jericho. Arafat called for an end to the INTIFADA, violent demonstrations against Israeli occupation, but he had plenty of troubles of his own in Gaza, where he moved in July 1994 as President of the Palestinian Authority to administer the Gaza Strip and Jericho. There his authoritarian and sometimes brutal rule was increasingly unpopular and he was regarded by many as an Israeli puppet. Consequently HAMAS, an ISLAMIC FUNDAMENTALIST movement, eroded the support which Arafat had long enjoyed in the occupied territories. He shared the 1994 Nobel Peace Prize with Yitzhak RABIN and Shimon PERES.

Behind the Myth: Yasser Arafat and the Palestinian Revolution, A. Gowers and T. Walker (1991)

Arbenz Guzmán, Jacobo (1913–71)
President of Guatemala (1951–4), the most populous country in Central America with 9 million inhabitants, over half of them Indians. The son of an immigrant Swiss pharmacist,

he took part in a revolution led by university students and young army officers to overthrow the dictator Jorge Ubico and establish democracy in 1944. The freest elections in the country's history then made Juan José Arévalo the President, with Arbenz as his Minister of War. The revolution under Arévalo (1944–50) and Arbenz, who was elected to succeed him in 1950, abolished forced labour, granted minimum wages and gave workers and peasants the right to strike and form trade unions. Arbenz legalized the Communist Party, whereupon the US ordered the international agencies it controlled to stop aid to Guatemala. He then passed a radical Agrarian Reform Law in 1952. His was the most progressive regime in Guatemala's history. Arbenz intended to expropriate unused land on the great estates and hand it over to peasants. 100,000 peasants received 1.5 million acres, including 1,700 owned by the President himself.

One of the companies affected, the United Fruit Company (UFCO) of the US, which owned 42 per cent of the nation's land, was to give up 234,000 acres of unused land. It complained and was supported by the US State Department. President EISENHOWER, who regarded Arbenz as 'merely a puppet manipulated by the communists', though there was no evidence to support this assertion, ordered the CIA to plan a counter-revolution. Guatemalans were trained by the US in Honduras and invaded in 1954. They made little progress until the US provided air support. Arbenz then made the mistake of trying to supply worker and peasant militias with arms; the army would not tolerate a rival force and defected. Arbenz resigned and spent his later years in exile in Cuba. A brutal dictatorship quickly reversed all the reforms and replaced the democratic regime: UFCO recovered its land and in return gave the government a 30 per cent tax on its profits instead of the 10 per cent it had paid previously. US aid was resumed.

Guatemala: A Nation in Turmoil, P. Calvert (1985)

Asad, Hafiz al- (1930–)   President of Syria (1971–). Asad came from the Alawi minority, a SHII Islamic sect, which is 11 per cent of the Syrian population but dominates the armed forces. He joined the Ba'th Party in 1947 and trained as an airforce pilot in the 1950s. Asad took part in the military coup of 1963, which gave the Ba'th control of Syria, and from then his rise was rapid: Commander of the Airforce in 1964, Minister of Defence in 1966, Prime Minister and Secretary-General of the Ba'th in 1970 and President of Syria in 1971. Calculating and ruthless, he saw himself as the successor to NASSER, one of his heroes, as leader of the Arab world.

The constitution of 1973 enhanced his power, as the President decided policy, appointed the Prime Minister and members of the cabinet, selected senior judges and could veto legislation. Asad has been elected every seven years as President, as the constitution requires. His power base is in the army and security services: Asad is army commander and controls all senior appointments (over half the officers are Alawis). In addition to the army, which expanded from 60,500 in 1968 to 500,000 in 1986, there are special security forces, also mainly Alawi. Opposition came from outside the regime, particularly from Muslim organizations. The MUSLIM BROTHERHOOD, a mainly urban movement with support from bazaar merchants and middle-class professionals, wanted an Islamic state and rejected the secularism of the Ba'th. The Brothers called for a jihad against the regime in 1976 when Asad intervened in the LEBANESE CIVIL WAR on behalf of the Christians. In 1979 merchants in Aleppo organized a general strike, while national syndicates of lawyers, engineers, doctors and academics demanded the lifting of the state of emergency, in force since 1963, and the release of political prisoners. This was the most serious challenge yet to Asad, who saw them as an ISLAMIC FUNDAMENTALIST movement like that which had brought Ayatollah KHOMEINI to power in the IRANIAN

REVOLUTION. In April 1980 he sent 11,000 special troops to Aleppo, who cordoned off the city, executed several hundred Islamists and put thousands in detention centres. After an assassination attempt on Asad in the same year, he decided to smash the Muslim Brotherhood. A hundred imprisoned Brothers were executed and membership of that organization was made a capital offence. Street courts were set up by the security forces to carry out executions instantly. Muslim opponents of Asad formed the Islamic Front, which was responsible for violent riots (1980–2) in Aleppo, Homs and Hama, culminating in their take over of Hama in February 1982. Asad sent to Hama 12,000 troops who bombarded and almost destroyed the city, killing as many as 20,000 in the two weeks it took them to regain control. From that time the opposition was in disarray. Unrest in the towns was also fomented by economic decline. Most Syrian industry had been nationalized before Asad came to power but the state sector was corrupt and inefficient with a bloated bureaucracy. Growth in the 1970s, when Asad partially liberalized the economy, was rapid because of petro-dollars and foreign aid. When these declined in the late 1970s growth fell sharply, adding to the problems of an economy in which over half the budget was spent on the armed forces.

Asad's foreign policy was dominated by the conflict with Israel. On three occasions he went to war with Israel – in the SIX DAY WAR in 1967, when he lost the GOLAN HEIGHTS, in the YOM KIPPUR WAR of 1973 and during the Lebanese Civil War in 1982 – and on each occasion he was defeated. From 1967 his paramount aim was to recover the Golan Heights. Asad talked a lot about Arab unity but his relations with Arab states were generally poor. His alliance with Egypt in the Yom Kippur war ended when SADAT made a separate peace treaty with Israel in 1979. Diplomatic relations with Egypt were not restored until 1989. Since the mid-1970s Asad has been a bitter opponent of Iraq, whom he saw as a rival for leadership in the Fertile Crescent. His support for Iran in the IRAN–IRAQ WAR (1980–8) was condemned throughout the Arab world. His hostility to Iraq was shown again in the GULF WAR (1991), when he provided troops for the international force to resist Saddam HUSSEIN's occupation of Kuwait. Intervention in the Lebanese Civil War from 1976 did make Syria the dominant power in that country but the cost, financially, was great. Asad used the COLD WAR to make Syria a major power in the Middle East by obtaining military and diplomatic support from the Soviet Union in his struggle against Israel. After GORBACHEV came to power relations with the USSR changed, as Soviet support was reduced. By 1990, with the Soviet Union an unreliable ally, Syria sought better relations with the US, the only country who could persuade Israel to withdraw from the Golan Heights, in return for a peace settlement with Syria and Asad's undertaking to prevent HIZBULLAH attacking Israeli settlements from southern Lebanon and to stop supporting Yasir ARAFAT's opponents in Damascus, where the Rejectionist Front (which opposes the Palestine state being set up in Gaza and the WEST BANK) is based. In October 1991 he agreed to take part in the Middle East Peace Conference, intended to lead to talks based on UN Security Council Resolution 242, between Israel and its Arab enemies. Asad disapproved of the Oslo Accords and the Jordanian–Israeli Peace Treaty but did nothing to undermine them.

Asad of Syria, P. Seale and M. McConville (1988)
Asad, the Sphinx of Damascus, M. Ma'oz (1988)
Syria: Politics and Society, 1945–86, D. Hopwood (1988)

ASEAN (Association of Southeast Asian Nations)   Formed in 1967 by Indonesia, Malaysia, Singapore, the Philippines and Thailand. Brunei joined on becoming independent in 1984 and Burma, Cambodia and Laos in 1997. There was a feeling that regional organizations (such as SEATO) were run by foreigners and reflected their interests. Southeast Asian nations wanted an organization controlled by people from the region, which would be concerned solely with their own problems, particularly economic development and security. As the VIETNAM WAR was escalating and China was in turmoil during the CULTURAL REVOLUTION, non-communist states felt that co-operation would provide them with their best chance of survival. The end of the confrontation of Indonesia and Malaysia when SUHARTO and the army took control in Indonesia made ASEAN possible, though it was very difficult to get the members to co-operate economically, as they had different economic philosophies: Singapore was in favour of free trade, Indonesia of state direction of the economy. They traded more with Japan and the US than they did with each other, their inter-regional trade rising from only 14.7 per cent in 1975 to 22.5 per cent in 1983. Little progress was made in reducing trade barriers until 1992, when all members agreed to move in the next 15 years to an Asian Free Trade Area in manufactured goods. ASEAN countries in the late 1970s began to copy the NEWLY INDUSTRIALIZING ECONOMIES (NIEs), starting with labour-intensive industries such as textiles, to take advantage of their cheap labour. All except Indonesia (which benefited from its oil revenues) suffered from the sharp fall in commodity prices in the 1980s, increased their debts and had a new regional competitor in the SPECIAL ECONOMIC ZONES in China. In 1989 ASEAN joined with Japan, Australia, New Zealand, South Korea and Canada to form a Council for Asia–Pacific Economic Cooperation. ASEAN did not form a military alliance to protect its members but used its influence to end the VIETNAMESE OCCUPATION OF KAMPUCHEA in 1989.

The ASEAN Success Story, L. Martin (ed.) (1987)

A New Regional Order in South–East Asia: ASEAN in the Post-Cold War Era, A. Acharya (1993)

Regional Cooperation and Growth Triangles in ASEAN, Toh Mun Heng and L. Low (1993)

Attlee, Clement Richard, 1st Earl (1883–1967)

British Prime Minister (1945–51). Unusually for a leader of the LABOUR PARTY, Attlee came from a prosperous middle-class family (his father was a successful City solicitor) and went to a public school, Haileybury, before reading history at Oxford. In 1905 he helped with a boy's club in Stepney and spent the next seven years among the London poor. This experience changed his whole career. Instead of practising as a barrister he did social work, joined the Stepney Independent Labour Party in 1907 and five years later gained a lectureship at the London School of Economics. When the First World War began he enlisted in the army, rose to the rank of major and took part in the Gallipoli campaign, where he was severely wounded. After the war he returned to Stepney, became mayor and in 1922 was elected as MP. He served in both of MacDonald's Labour governments: in 1924 as Under-Secretary at the War Office, in 1931 as Postmaster-General, the only time he ran a department. In the 1931 election most Labour leaders were defeated and Attlee found himself one of only 46 Labour MPs. A dull speaker, he did not impress, as his talents for running committees with quiet efficiency were unobtrusive. It was a surprise, therefore, when he was elected as leader of the Labour Party in 1935. BEVIN and Dalton rather than Attlee were responsible for the Labour Party abandoning appeasement and disarmament, and it was not until the Second World War that Attlee really made his mark. Patriotic in the fight against Hitler, he pressed for the removal of Chamberlain as Prime Minister. When Winston CHURCHILL formed a coalition government in 1940, Attlee entered his War Cabinet and remained a member till the end of the conflict, being officially recognized as Deputy Prime Minister in 1942. The CONSERVATIVE PARTY was expected to win the 1945 election owing to Churchill's popularity but Labour won comprehensively, taking 393 seats (with 48 per cent of the vote) to the Conservatives' 213 (with 40 per cent of the vote). This was the first time Labour had a majority: previous Labour governments in 1924 and 1929–31 had been minority administrations.

Attlee was Prime Minister of a government in which many members had gained valuable experience as ministers in Churchill's coalition government during the war. Taciturn and enigmatic, his great strength was as a team leader who had no real enemies and plenty of courage. The programme of legislation he put before parliament was more ambitious than that of any previous government: the nationalization of major industries, the establishment of a National Health Service and of a WELFARE STATE, the repeal of the Trades Disputes Act (1927) and the building of more houses. The Conservatives were prepared to accept much of this as the centre of politics had moved left, in what was later called BUTSKELLISM.

Herbert Morrison saw the nationalization bills through the House: the Bank of England, civil aviation, coal, telecommunications, transport and electricity all by 1948 (iron and steel, the most contentious issue, was not nationalized until 1951). In total, 20 per cent of industry was taken over by the state but there was no cohesion, as there was no overall planning. The National Insurance Act of 1946 provided benefits for those who were sick, disabled or unemployed and was paid for by contributions from wage-earners, employers and the state. An old age pension was available to all, for men at 65, women at 60. The National Health Service, set up by Aneurin BEVAN, gave free medical and dental services to everyone. Education reform was based on R. A. BUTLER's Education Act of 1944, which established secondary schools for all children, with selection by examination at

11 for grammar, technical or secondary modern schools. Warmly welcomed at the time, this Act reinforced the class division, as the vast majority of pupils in the grammar schools came from the middle class, nearly all working-class children going to the secondary modern schools (there were few technical schools). The school leaving age was raised from 14 to 15. There were also some modest constitutional changes: the delaying power of the House of Lords was reduced from two years to one, university representation in parliament was abolished and so was the business premises vote.

Attlee had to face two crises in 1947, when there was the worst winter for a century and a big freeze from January to March, causing an energy shortage which in effect shut down industry for weeks. To make matters worse there was a run on the pound when it was made convertible in July. Hugh Dalton, the Chancellor of the Exchequer, had to suspend convertibility in August and in November introduced a budget which began a period of austerity: imports were cut, taxes raised and food rations reduced. The popularity of the government dropped and Attlee faced a leadership challenge from Sir Stafford Cripps. Supported by Ernest Bevin he survived but he did not give a clear lead and it was Cripps, who replaced Dalton as Chancellor, and MARSHALL PLAN aid which rescued the government. There was a further crisis in 1949 when a recession in the US made a devaluation of sterling necessary. Once again Attlee, silent and remote, gave no lead and it was left to younger ministers such as Hugh GAITSKELL to convert his colleages to the necessity of devaluing the pound by 30 per cent.

Attlee had a close relationship with Bevin, whom he consulted on most matters. 'My relationship with Ernest Bevin', he wrote, 'was the deepest of my political life'. For most of the time he allowed his Foreign Secretary to deal unhindered with foreign policy but occasionally played a decisive role, as he did when he decided to speed up the

INDEPENDENCE OF INDIA and of Burma, as he wanted to avoid anything like the INDO-CHINA WAR OF INDEPENDENCE. He successfully kept both India and Pakistan in the COMMONWEALTH. Attlee had a far-sighted and radical view of Britain's commitments. In a memorandum of 1945 he noted the pointlessness of an East of Suez defensive strategy and the diminishing importance of outposts in the Persian Gulf and Eastern Mediterranean but he could not convince Bevin. In 1951 British military expenditure was higher per capita than in the US.

After the 1950 election, in which Labour received more votes than ever before but saw its majority reduced to five, Attlee seemed to lose his way. Dalton had noted in 1950 that 'We are all stale, uninspired and uninventive'. Dissension within his government, which had been kept under control, came to the surface when he appointed Gaitskell as Chancellor of the Exchequer instead of Bevan. Attlee accepted his 1951 budget which provided for increased defence expenditure Britain could not afford and also introduced changes in the National Health Service. Bevan and Harold WILSON, President of the Board of Trade, resigned and so brought about a split in the Labour Party which kept it out of office for the next 13 years. Attlee knew Bevan would resign on this issue but did nothing to dissuade him or bring about a compromise. An unexpected balance of payments crisis in 1951 prompted Attlee to call an election in October. Labour still had the largest share of the vote (48.8 per cent to the Conservative 48 per cent) but the Conservatives had 321 seats to Labour's 295. Attlee therefore became leader of the opposition, doing nothing to heal the breach between Bevan and Gaitskell. He had lost all his drive and retired when Labour was defeated again in 1955, becoming the first Labour leader to accept an hereditary earldom.

Labour in Power, 1945–51, K. O. Morgan (1984)

The Attlee Years, N. Tiratsoo (ed.) (1993)

Labour's High Noon: The Government and the Economy 1945–51, J. Fyrth (ed.) (1993)

Clem Attlee, F. Beckett (1997)

August coup (1991)

The attempt by conservative communists in the USSR to seize power and reverse the reforms of Mikhail GORBACHEV. Leading members of the CPSU, the police and the army strongly disapproved of the market reforms which, they said, were impoverishing the Soviet people; of the declining influence of the CPSU, which had lost over four million members in the 18 months to July 1991; and of the independence movements which threatened the break-up of the Soviet Union. The trigger for the coup came in April 1991 when Gorbachev made the 'Nine Plus One' agreement with the leaders of nine republics of the USSR, giving them more autonomy. In July a new Union treaty was proposed, delegating even greater power to the republics, such as the right to collect taxes and hand over only a part to the central government. The plotters thought that the Union would collapse unless decisive action was taken and so began the coup on 19 August, the day before the Union treaty was due to be signed.

They sent a delegation to Gorbachev, on holiday in the Crimea, demanding that he should resign or sign a decree establishing a state of emergency. He refused, so the KGB put him under house arrest and isolated him. As tanks rolled into the centre of Moscow and surrounded the White House (the seat of the Russian parliament), the conspirators, who included Kriuchkov (the head of the KGB), announced that a State Emergency Committee had taken power, as Gorbachev was ill. A state of emergency was declared in Moscow and Leningrad and press freedom suspended but, as Yazov the Defence Minister later admitted, 'There was no conspiracy with a plan. . . . We had not thought anything through, either for the short or the long term'. They failed to arrest their key opponents, particularly Boris YELTSIN and did not jam Western broadcasts, which kept the Soviet citizens informed of what was happening in Moscow. Yeltsin, showing great determination and courage, seized the initiative by climbing on to the top of a tank to encourage the defenders, as large crowds gathered outside the White House and barricades were set up. The coup leaders were incompetent and inhibited, as they wanted to give the appearance of a legal takeover and to avoid bloodshed. They took no military measures outside Moscow, Leningrad and the Baltic states and relied on the army to obey them in the rest of the country, but the forces were split. Some tanks outside the White House went over to Yeltsin and when Kriuchkov ordered his élite Alpha group to attack the Russian parliament his orders were ignored. On 21 August the coup collapsed. Troops were ordered back to barracks, the Supreme Soviet of the USSR declared the actions of the Emergency Committee illegal and the leading conspirators were arrested. Three people only had been killed.

The effects of the coup were precisely what its leaders had sought to avoid. Yeltsin was now considerably more powerful than Gorbachev who, on his return to Moscow, was heckled as he addressed the Russian parliament and tried to defend the CPSU, whose Central Committee was silent during the coup and condemned it only when it was clear that it would not succeed. He was publicly humiliated when Yeltsin forced him to read out before the television cameras the Cabinet minutes of 19 August, which showed that of 20 ministers, 18 had either approved of the plot or not opposed it. Yeltsin brought about a real revolution by banning the Communist Party in Russia on 23 August. On 29 August the Supreme Soviet suspended CPSU activities throughout the USSR. Another result of the coup was the speedy COLLAPSE OF THE SOVIET UNION. The Baltic republics had already declared their independence: the rest of the Soviet republics now did so. In December 1991 the three Slav republics (Russia, Ukraine and Belarus) formed the CIS (Commonwealth of Independent States), soon joined by most of the other former Soviet republics, so the USSR ceased to exist.

Moscow Coup, M. Sixmith (1991)
'The August Coup' in *The Demise of the USSR: From Communism to Independence*, V. Tolz and I. Elliot (eds) (1995)

Aung San Suu Kyi (1945–)   Burmese opposition leader. Daughter of the leader of the Burmese independence movement, Aung San, who was assassinated in 1947, she left Burma when she was 15 to study abroad. She took a degree at Oxford University, married a British Tibetologist, Michael Aris, and had two sons. Suu Kyi did not return to Burma until April 1988, to look after her dying mother. This was a time when popular unrest at the military dictatorship of NE WIN reached its peak, with demonstrations in August being brutally crushed with the loss of many lives. The army then promised free elections. Suu Kyi and her followers formed the National League for Democracy (NLD), which attracted considerable popular support. Highly intelligent and articulate she addressed tens of thousands in rallies, but in July 1989 she was placed under house arrest for 'endangering the state' and thousands of her party members were arrested. This did not stop the NLD from gaining a stunning victory in the May 1990 election. SLORC (State Law and Order Restoration Council) would not accept the election result and offered to release Suu Kyi only if she left the country, never to return. She had an agonizing choice to make, as to remain in Burma to lead the democratic movement meant being separated indefinitely from her husband and sons. Suu Kyi rejected SLORC's offer and in 1991 was awarded the Nobel Peace Prize for her non-violent struggle for democracy and human rights. In July 1995 she was released from house arrest but was still denied freedom of movement. Her requests for countries to boycott Burma until democracy is restored there have had only a limited success.

Austrian State Treaty (May, 1955)

The treaty was signed by Austria and war-time Allies (the USSR, USA, Britain, France) who had occupied Austria since 1945. It was a surprising product of the DÉTENTE which followed STALIN's death, as Stalin had consistently refused to make such an agreement, by which Austria recovered her independence. Allied occupying forces were to be withdrawn, Austria was to be permanently neutral, renounced major offensive (including nuclear) weapons and agreed that she would never be united with Germany. This was a major Soviet concession.

Ayub Khan, Mohammad (1907–74)

President of Pakistan (1958–69). A Pathan, he studied at the Aligarh Muslim University in India and then did military training at Sandhurst, being commissioned in the Indian army in 1928. During the Second World War he commanded a battalion in Burma. After the INDEPENDENCE AND PARTITION OF INDIA in 1947 he was appointed the first Commander-in-Chief (1951–8) in Pakistan. In 1958 the President, Iskandar Mirza, dismissed the cabinet, abolished the legislature and political parties and proclaimed martial law, with Ayub Khan as martial law administrator. Ayub soon removed Mirza to become President himself and so began a period of military rule, promoting himself to be a field-marshal. He produced a new constitution in 1962 which provided for a presidential system of government: all executive power was in the hands of the President, who could veto any legislation. 'Basic Demo-

crats' (there were 40,000 each in West and East Pakistan) were elected at the local level and they elected the President and the provincial and central legislatures, whose powers were restricted. Industrial and agricultural production grew rapidly in the 1960s as the GREEN REVOLUTION increased grain yields and as Ayub favoured a capitalist, market-oriented economy, but the main beneficiaries were a small élite: 22 families owned two-thirds of industry, four-fifths of banking and nearly all insurance services. Senior civil servants, military officers and the small middle class also did well under the new regime.

Ayub was involved in the INDO-PAKISTANI WAR of 1965, during which the Indian army advanced to within a few miles of Lahore. A UNITED NATIONS cease-fire was agreed in September and at Tashkent in 1966 both sides agreed to withdraw their forces to positions they held before the war. Zulfikar Ali BHUTTO, his Foreign Minister, then left the government and in 1967 formed the Pakistan People's Party (PPP) in opposition to the President. There was opposition to Ayub in East Pakistan too, from Mujibur Rahman's Awami League, which was demanding autonomy for the East. In 1968 Ayub arrested both Rahman and Bhutto, the latter for 'inciting the masses'. By 1969 there was mass civil disobedience, strikes and demands for a restoration of parliamentary rule. Ayub, who had a heart attack in 1968 which put him out of action for several months, promised to hold elections and then handed over power to General Yahya Khan.

The Military and Politics in Pakistan 1947–86, H. A. Rizvi (1986)
The Political Economy of Pakistan 1947–85, O. Norman (1988)

B

Baader–Meinhoff group   Left-wing terrorists in the Federal Republic of Germany (FRG: West Germany). The Red Army Faction (RAF), as the group called itself, was led by Andreas Baader (1943–77) and Ulrike Meinhoff (1934–76). Established in 1970, it opposed the capitalist organization of the German economy and the presence of American troops in the FRG. Most members were middle class (Baader was the son of a professor) and well-educated and began with attacks on property (the arson of department stores) and bank robberies. The three main leaders were arrested in 1972, the year in which the chief wave of terror began with the kidnapping of leading politicians and industrialists. Between 1970 and 1978 the RAF killed 28 people and took 162 hostages, the climax coming in 1977 when the President of the FRG Employers' Federation, Hans-Martin Schleyer, was kidnapped and a Lufthansa jumbo jet was hijacked and taken to Mogadishu, Somalia. The terrorists demanded the release of 20 of their imprisoned members in return for freeing Schleyer and threatened to kill all hostages on the plane. Chancellor SCHMIDT rejected their demands and staged a spectacular commando raid which freed the hostages. The RAF promptly murdered Schleyer, whilst Baader and two other members of the RAF committed suicide in prison (Meinhoff had already done so). The methods of the RAF had by this time alienated most of its original sympathizers. Youthful protest now took up peaceful causes, such as those supported by the GREEN PARTY. By 1980 most RAF leaders had been caught and imprisoned, though sporadic violence continued. In 1989 the RAF linked up with other terrorist groups in Europe to attack NATO installations. Many RAF members had fled to the GDR (East Germany), where the Stasi (secret police) welcomed them and gave them false identities. Deprived of its logistical support in the GDR with GERMAN REUNIFICATION, the RAF declared a ceasefire in 1992.

Hitler's Children, J. Becker (1977)

Baghdad Pact (1955–9)   After the KOREAN WAR (1950–3) the EISENHOWER administration in the US developed the doctrine of containment, a scheme of collective defence against communism. The Baghdad Pact was part of this plan, though the US did not become a member. Originally, it was a military agreement of Iraq and Turkey, which Britain, Iran and Pakistan joined. NASSER was strongly opposed to it as, with its NATO links (both Britain and Turkey were members of NATO), he saw it a means of continuing Western dominance in the Middle East and succeeded in preventing Jordan from joining, though King HUSSEIN wanted to do so. The pact collapsed when Iraq withdrew after Qasim had overthrown and killed the royal family and Iraq's pro-Western Prime Minister in a military coup. The remaining members changed the name of the alliance to the Central Treaty Organization (CENTO), but this too broke down when Iran pulled out after the IRANIAN REVOLUTION (1979), followed quickly by Pakistan.

Balewa, Alhaji Sir Abubakar Tafawa

(1912–66) Prime Minister of Nigeria (1959–66). A Muslim from the north, he qualified as a teacher and studied education at London University (1945–6). He began his political career in the Central Legislative Council (1947–52) and in 1951 helped to make the Northern People's Congress (NPC) into a political party. Balewa held various government posts in the 1950s and after the 1959 pre-independence elections, in which the NPC did well in the Northern Region but did not win a majority in the federal parliament, he formed a coalition with the National Council of Nigeria and the Cameroons (NCNC). He was Prime Minister and led Nigeria to independence in 1960, as a member of the COMMONWEALTH.

As the leader of Africa's most populous state Balewa had considerable international prestige and was respected in the West as a moderate and pragmatic leader. Yet he faced formidable problems, as Nigeria was torn apart by regional and ethnic rivalries. In each of Nigeria's three regions an ethnically based party controlled the regional government: the NPC in the Hausa–Fulani Northern Region; the NCNC in the Igbo Eastern Region; the Action Group (AG) led by Chief Awolowo in the Yoruba Western Region. The unity of the country was precarious, with the Christian Eastern and Western Regions fearing domination by the more populous Muslim North. After a violent struggle between two factions of the AG, Balewa stepped in, declared a state of emergency, arrested Awolowo and charged him with plotting to overthrow the government. He was sentenced to ten years imprisonment but this was widely regarded in Nigeria as a political decision to crush a rival. The corruption of Balewa's government, rising rents and food prices and the widening gap between rich and poor led to general strikes in 1962 and 1964. Revelations of fraud in the 1964 federal elections discredited Balewa. The final blow to his government came from the Western Region, where rigged elections in 1965 were followed by violence in which over 2,000 were killed. Unable to restore law and order, Balewa was assassinated in a military coup in January 1966 (see NIGERIAN MILITARY RULERS)

Nigeria's Modernization and the Politics of Communalism, R. Melson and H. Wolfe (eds) (1971)
A History of Nigeria, C. Isichei (1983)

Banda, Hastings Kamuzu (1906–97)

President of Malawi (1966–94). The son of a peasant in Nyasaland, he was educated at mission schools before working as a clerk in a South African gold mine. He then went to the US, where he lived for 12 years qualifying (he was a brilliant student) and practising as a doctor. After continuing his medical studies in Edinburgh, he was in the 1940s and early 1950s a much-respected doctor in the north of England and in London, where his home was a meeting place for radical African nationalists. While working in Ghana (1953–8) he was persuaded to return home, after 40 years abroad, to lead the Nyasaland African Congress (NAC) in its struggle against the CENTRAL AFRICAN FEDERATION (CAF). The colonial government responded by declaring a state of emergency in 1959, banning the NAC and imprisoning Banda and other African leaders. His followers immediately founded the Malawi Congress Party (MCP) and continued the struggle. The British Colonial Secretary, Iain Macleod, realized the strength of African feeling against the CAF, so in 1960 he released Banda and ended the state of emergency. Banda then led the MCP to victory in the 1961 elections and self-government in 1962. The Federation was dissolved in 1963 and Nyasaland became the independent state of Malawi in 1964, with Banda as Prime Minister. When Malawi became a republic in 1966, Banda took office as President and in 1971 as Life President.

Malawi was made a one-party state, in which Banda chose all the candidates at elections, who were returned unopposed. All adult Malawians were ordered to join the MCP. An elder of the Church of Scotland, Banda imposed many of his puritanical ideas on Malawi. Films, books and magazines were rigorously censored. Opponents, or possible rivals, were ruthlessly despatched and hundreds of political opponents were detained without trial. 'Anything I say is law', Banda told the directors of Lonrho. In 1992 Western countries cut off aid to Malawi because of the gross violation of human rights. A cult of personality accompanied the dictatorship: he had to be addressed as *Ngwazi* (conqueror).

Banda's foreign policy infuriated neighbouring countries (and was much admired in the West) as his was in 1967 the first African state to establish diplomatic relations with the APARTHEID regime in South Africa. His reward was South African financial and technical help. Banda enjoyed friendly relations with Portugal's rulers SALAZAR and Caetano, and when Mozambique became independent allowed Renamo, the resistance movement to the Marxist government, to use bases in Malawi. He refused to help the Popular Front in Rhodesia in its struggle against Iam Smith's white minority regime and refused to attend Zimbabwe's independence celebrations. Banda rejected African socialism in favour of private enterprise and set an example to his ministers and party officials by owning a major group of companies, which made him the richest man in Malawi. Yet while an élite became very wealthy, Malawi remained one of the poorest African countries. Banda was forced by international pressure to allow multiparty elections in 1994, which the MCP lost. He was later charged with the murder of three of his ministers but was acquitted in 1995.

Malawi: The Politics of Despair, D. T. Williams (1978)

When Silence Rules: The Suppression of Dissent in Malawi, Africa Watch Report (1990)

'Kamuzu's Legacy: The Democratization of Malawi', *African Affairs* 94 (1995), pp. 227–57

Bandaranaike, Sirimavo Ratwatte Dias (1916–)

Prime Minister of Sri Lanka (1960–5, 1970–7). The daughter of a Sinhalese landowner, she married Solomon Bandaranaike in 1940 and succeeded him as head of the Sri Lanka Freedom Party (SLFP) when he was assassinated in 1959. She won a decisive victory in the 1960 general election and so became the first woman Prime Minister in any country. She carried on her husband's nationalist and socialist policies, replaced English by Sinhala as the language of government and secularized education to bring all schools under state control, thus antagonizing the Roman Catholics. Many foreign and indigenous economic enterprises were nationalized. As most overseas trade was dominated by foreigners and Sri Lankan minorities, this was seen as a means of changing the balance in favour of the majority Sinhalese. As ethnic conflict mounted she moved to the left and formed a coalition government with a Trotskyite party in order to stabilize her regime, but this was unpopular and she lost the election of 1965.

She returned to power in 1970 as head of a United Front of SLFP and Marxist groups but was faced by severe economic problems: unemployment, inflation and food scarcities. There was opposition too from some of her former supporters. The Janata Vimukti Peramuna (JVP: People's Liberation Front), a radical left-wing organization dominated by educated but unemployed youth, began a rising in 1971 which was put down ruthlessly. A year later she introduced a new constitution to remove alien British elements. Ceylon became Sri Lanka, the Senate (the upper house of parliament modelled on the British House of Lords) was abolished. The state was declared to be secular but with a duty to 'protect and foster Buddhism'. The new constitution was unpopular with Tamils, so communal conflict increased, some Tamils wanting a separate state in the north and east. She had some success in improving race relations when about half a million Indians were granted the citizenship they had been denied since independence. The OPEC PRICE RISE of 1973 hit Sri Lanka hard, forcing the government to cut food subsidies and welfare. Tea (mainly British owned) and rubber plantations were nationalized in 1975 but this did not improve the economic situation. There were the worst strikes for 20 years in 1977, the year in which the SLFP was comprehensively defeated in the general election, winning only 9 out of 168 seats in the National Assembly. In 1980 Sirimavo Bandaranaike was found guilty by a presidential commission of misuse of power, deprived of her civil rights for six years and expelled from parliament. In 1988 she contested the presidential election but lost to Premadasa.

A History of Sri Lanka, K. M. da Silva (1981)
Politics in Sri Lanka 1947–79, A. J. Wilson

Bangladesh, independence of (1971)
East Pakistan was economically underdeveloped and impoverished 20 years after independence in 1947. It contained 55 per cent of Pakistan's population and earned most of Pakistan's foreign currency with its export of jute, yet less was invested in East than in West Pakistan. Many in the East regarded it as a colony of the West, administered mainly by civil servants from Punjab who spoke Urdu, not Bengali. East Pakistan was kept under control by an army and air force, which was almost completely dominated by Pathan, Baluch and Punjabi officers.

Sheikh Mujibur Rahman, the Bengali leader of the popular Awami League, decided to end the dependence of the East on the West. In 1966 he put forward a Six-Point Programme, which called for the autonomy of East Pakistan and a separate militia. AYUB KHAN charged Mujibur and eight others with treason in 1968 and flew West Pakistan troops into Dhaka, the Eastern capital, a few days before he declared martial law in 1969. General Yahya Khan, who replaced Ayub as President in 1969, announced that parliamentary elections – the first since independence –

would be held throughout Pakistan in October 1970, after which he would hand over power to elected representatives. In the 1970 elections the Awami League won 160 out of the 162 seats allotted to the East in Pakistan's National Assembly, Zulfikar Ali BHUTTO winning a majority in the West. Yahya, however, would not step down and Bhutto would not accept Mujibur as Prime Minister. When Bhutto demanded that the National Assembly, due to meet in March 1971, should be postponed and Yahya agreed, Mujibur declared that East Pakistan was now Bangladesh. As West Pakistani troops fired on students and crowds, Mujibur was arrested. The Indian government of Indira GANDHI appealed to the UNITED NATIONS, as a million Bengalis fled from the East (by December there were ten million starving refugees in India).

Pakistani planes attacked Indian airfields in the West on 3 December 1971. In response Indian troops invaded Bangladesh and so began the third INDO-PAKISTANI WAR. Indian forces fought in West Pakistan as well as the East, where their rapid advance towards Dhaka resulted in the Pakistani army surrendering on 15 December. India then unilaterally declared a cease-fire. The war deprived Pakistan of over half its population and left its economy and army on the point of collapse, with the myth of Muslim unity, on which the creation of Pakistan had been based, destroyed. On 20 December Yahya resigned, handing over to Bhutto, who released Mujibur from jail.

The Genesis of Bangladesh, S. R. Chowdhury (1972)
The Foundations of Bangladesh, H. O. Rashid (1992)

Bantustans   'Homelands'   for   black South Africans in the native reserves. These had existed since the Natives' Land Act of 1913, which allocated 7.3 per cent of the land in South Africa (increased to nearly 14 per cent in 1936) as reserves. At that time blacks were 72 per cent of the population: they could not own any land outside the reserves. The Bantu Authorities Act (1951) gave some limited administrative powers to government-appointed chiefs in the reserves, but at this time the architect of APARTHEID, VERWOERD, had no intention of making the reserves independent. By 1959 he had changed his mind, as he hoped he could gain international respectability by giving political rights to Africans in the reserves and, at the same time, strengthen white supremacy in the rest of the country. The Promotion of Bantu Self-Government Act (1959) set up eight (later ten) *Bantustans* in existing reserves, each with some self-government. Africans were divided into 'nations', which were the basis of the *Bantustans*: KwaZulu for the Zulus, Transkei and Ciskei for the Xhosa, Bophuthatswana for the Tswana. In 1963 Transkei was the first *Bantustan* to be given self-government and a legislative assembly, extended to other 'homelands' in the Bantu Homelands Citizenship Act in 1970. This also deprived Africans of South African citizenship and made them citizens of their 'homeland', even if they had been born outside it and had never been there – under 50 per cent of blacks lived in the homelands. The next stage was to grant 'independence' to the *Bantustans*, the first being Transkei (1976), followed by Bophuthatswana (1977), Venda (1978) and Ciskei (1981). A blow to this strategy was the rejection of independence by the most powerful 'homeland' leader, Chief BUTHELEZI of KwaZulu.

The *Bantustans* were never economically viable. They were overcrowded, far from the main road and rail routes, lacked mineral resources, and suffered from overgrazing and erosion of land. They were dependent on the money sent back by migrant workers in South Africa. Verwoerd did not allow white investment in the reserves. Instead, industries were set up in South Africa near the *Bantustans* border, so they could draw on the cheap labour there. Only one of the *Ban-*

tustans consisted of a single block of land: Bophuthatswana had numerous segmented territories, one of which was 150 miles from the closest part of the 'homeland'. The *Bantustans* became rural slums, sources of cheap labour for white South Africa and dumping grounds for the blacks no longer needed there. Africans were relocated from 'white' areas to the *Bantustans* on an enormous scale: 3.5 million from 1960–83. In most cases they were moved to barren areas without resources, infrastructure or employment. Most of the government income of the *Bantustans* came directly from the South African government. The *Bantustan* system began to break down after the release of Nelson MANDELA in 1990: they were gradually reintegrated into South Africa, a process completed in 1994, a move strongly opposed by the black leaders of the *Bantustans*, who would lose their privileged positions.

Move Your Shadow: South Africa Black and White, J. Lelyveld (1986)
Uprooting Poverty: The South African Challenge, F. Wilson and M. Ramphele (1989)
The Making of Modern South Africa, N. Worden (1995)

Basic Law   The constitution of the Federal Republic of Germany (FRG: West Germany). It was drawn up by a parliamentory council, formed from representatives of the *Land* (regional) parliaments and was approved by the Allied military governors of the Western zones in May 1949. There were two houses in the federal parliament. The Bundestag was the most important and was popularly elected every four years. The method of election was not laid down in the Basic Law but was designed to avoid the mistakes of the Weimar Republic, when proportional representation encouraged the formation of a large number of parties and weakened government. 60 per cent of the candidates were elected by a simple majority in local constituencies: 40 per cent were elected by proportional representation by voting for a party list of candidates. To prevent a vast number of parties, each party had to win at least 5 per cent of votes in the FRG as a whole, or three seats in any region, to qualify for seats in the Bundestag. Each voter had therefore two votes: one for a local candidate and one for a party list. The second chamber was the Bundesrat, to which governments of the *Länder* sent delegates: it could not initiate legislation but could delay or amend legislation concerning states rights.

The President was the head of state but, because of the part played by President Hindenburg in the destruction of the Weimar Republic, he was given only a ceremonial role. He was not popularly elected but appointed by a Federal Assembly, consisting of Bundestag members and representatives of state parliaments. The President held office for five years and could serve no more than two terms. The Chancellor, as head of the government, was the most powerful figure. He could not be removed by a vote of no confidence in the Bundestag, unless there was at the same time a majority vote in favour of a successor. This did not take place until 1982, so the Chancellor provided stability. The federal government was reponsible for foreign and military affairs, immigration, monetary policy and communications. Other matters were normally dealt with by the *Länder*. A Bill of Rights, which guaranteed freedom of conscience, of speech and of assembly and the security of private property, was attached to the Basic Law, as was a Constitutional Court, which dealt with the compatibility of state with federal laws, and infringements of the rights of citizens. Its rulings were binding on the government. The Basic Law was regarded as provisional but was so successful in providing the FRG with strong, stable government that it has survived, with some amendments, to the present.

Batista, Fulgencio (1901–73) Dictator (1933–40) and President (1940–4 and 1952–8) of Cuba. A mulatto of humble origins, he

rose from the ranks in the army and was a sergeant when he led other NCOs in a rising in 1933 and soon established a dictatorship, with himself as Chief of Staff of the armed forces. In 1934 the Platt Amendment (1901) which had given the US the right to intervene in Cuba, was annulled as part of F. D. Roosevelt's 'Good Neighbor' policy. Backed by the US and Cuban businessmen, Batista also appeared as a populist leader by passing social welfare legislation, building houses for workers and creating employment through large public works projects. In the countryside he redistributed some land and began a programme of rural education. By the late 1930s he was confident enough to allow elections for a constituent assembly, which his Social Democratic Coalition (formed with the Communist Party) won. The new constitution of 1940 granted universal suffrage, state direction of the economy and workers' rights such as a minimum wage, pensions, social insurance and an eight hour day. This began a period of democratic government, though corruption and political violence continued. Batista won a fair presidential election in 1940 but lost that of 1944. Batista retired to the US, returning to Cuba in 1948. The rule of the Auténticos (1944–52) was marred by corruption, violence and intrigue, so that Batista's bloodless coup of 1952 received much support.

The second Batistato (1952–8) marked the end of democratic government and the 1940 constitution. Cuba was among the top three or four Latin American countries in education (with 80 per cent literacy), health and welfare but Batista condoned vice and corruption and Havana became the gambling and prostitution centre of the Caribbean. The torture and murder of opponents was commonplace. Opposition grew, particularly after the brutal treatment of captives after Fidel CASTRO's quixotic attempt to overthrow Batista by attacking the Moncada barracks in 1953. Fidel was more successful in the Cuban Revolution (1956–9), which ended with the flight of Batista first to the Dominican Republic and later to Spain, where he died.

72633

Bay of Pigs invasion (17–19 April 1961)

The most serious attempt by the US CIA (Central Intelligence Agency) to overthrow Fidel CASTRO. His seizure of power in Cuba aroused American fears of communism in the region. President EISENHOWER had allowed the CIA to train and equip a force of Cuban exiles in Guatemala but his presidency ended before any decision was taken as to when they would be used. President KENNEDY therefore inherited the problem of what to do with them. He was unwilling to support them directly with US forces, as this would be most unpopular in Latin America and would adversely affect his ALLIANCE FOR PROGRESS there. As a member of the OAS (Organization of American States) the US had pledged not to interfere in the internal affairs of member states. CIA director Allen Dulles said that an invasion of Cuba must go ahead as the invaders, if brought back to the US, would make clear American involvement. Moreover, the Soviet Union would regard Kennedy as soft on communism and would stir up communist takeovers throughout Latin America. Many of Kennedy's top military advisers opposed the invasion but the President allowed it to take place.

The plan was for the invasion force to land, with US air support, on the south coast of the island near the Escambray mountains, move into the hills and rally the Cuban people, who were expected to rise against Castro's dictatorship. The aim was to repeat the successful invasion of Guatemala in 1954 which overthrew President ARBENZ GUZMAN. The plan was constantly changed right up to the time of the invasion: the landing site was moved west to a flat, swampy area far from the mountains and offering no cover or a way of escape. The bombing attacks on Cuban airfields were reduced, so that Castro's air force was not destroyed and at the last minute Kennedy refused to supply American air cover for the landing. Cuban jets sank the ammunition ship on which the invaders depended and when the invasion did take place there was no popular anti-Castro rising and it was crushed in three days: 1,100 of the 1,400 invaders were captured and flown to the US in 1962 in return for $53 million of medical aid.

President Kennedy later accepted full responsibility for the fiasco. There were anti-American demonstrations in Latin America and the stoning of US embassies in Tokyo, Cairo and New Delhi. Castro's popularity in Cuba increased and he moved closer to the Soviet Union: in July 1961 there was a Soviet–Cuba alliance and in December Castro declared that he was a Marxist. Perhaps the most important short-term effect was to convince KHRUSHCHEV that Kennedy was weak and indecisive, so he decided to put nuclear missiles on Cuba, so precipitating the CUBAN MISSILE CRISIS of 1962.

Bay of Pigs: The Untold Story, P. Wyden (1979)
The Perfect Failure: Kennedy, Eisenhower and the CIA at the Bay of Pigs, T. Higgins (1987)

Begin, Menachem (1913–92)

Prime Minister of Israel (1977–83). Born in White Russia, he took a law degree at the University of Warsaw. When the Nazis invaded Poland in 1939 he escaped to Lithuania, occupied by the Soviet Union. He was arrested and sentenced to eight years in a Siberian labour camp. Released in 1941, after the Nazi invasion of the Soviet Union, he reached Palestine in 1943 as a member of the Free Polish forces and was made commander in Irgun Zvai Leumi, a Jewish terrorist organization. He declared an armed struggle against the British in January 1944. Anti-British, owing to the restrictions Britain placed as the mandatory power on Jewish immigration into Palestine, he was deeply involved in illegal Jewish immigration. In 1946 Irgun members blew up the King David Hotel in Jerusalem, the British headquarters, killing 91 people. In 1947, after some Irgun members had been hanged as terrorists, Irgun hanged two British sergeants and booby-trapped their bodies. Irgun's activities helped to convince Ernest BEVIN, the British Foreign Secretary, that the mandate should not continue and prompted Britain to withdraw from Palestine. After the state of Israel was proclaimed in May 1948 Irgun was responsible for the massacre of Arab civilians at DEIR YASSIN, an act which Begin described as 'heroic'. In the same year Irgun was disbanded as BEN-GURION, the Prime Minister, who loathed Begin, would not allow separate armed groups.

Begin founded the right-wing Herut (Free-dom) Party in 1948, which wanted a Jewish state on both sides of the River Jordan and was, with 12 per cent of the vote, the largest opposition group in the Knesset (Israeli par-liament). In 1967 he joined the Government of National Unity on the eve of the SIX DAY WAR as Minister Without Portfolio but this broke up in 1970. Three years later Herut joined two other rightwing parties to form Likud (Unity), with Begin as leader. After the early disasters of the YOM KIPPUR WAR (1973) public opinion moved away from the Labour parties which had dominated the Knesset since independence.

Likud won the election of 1977 and Begin became Prime Minister. Surprisingly for a hawk he decided that Sinai (which was not part of the biblical land of Israel) should be given up in return for the added security of a peace settlement with Egypt and, aided by President CARTER, made the CAMP DAVID ACCORDS with Anwar SADAT in 1978, for which he was awarded the Nobel Peace Prize. The Accords led to the conclusion of a peace treaty with Egypt. In 1982 he began the ISRAELI INVASION OF LEBANON to strike at the PLO bases there. He was con-demned universally for the Sabra and Shatila massacres by Christian militia in the Beirut refugee camps, which the Israeli army did nothing to stop. The heavy Israeli casualties in Lebanon and inflation of 400 per cent a year produced a political crisis in Israel and the resignation of Begin in 1983.

Benelux   A customs union of Belgium, the Netherlands and Luxembourg. Its name comes from the first syllables of the names of the member states. Their governments-in-exile had agreed in London in 1944 to form a customs union, which was set up in 1948. It provided a free market of goods, services, capi-tal and labour between the three states and was a model for the wider integration of Western Europe, which came with the TREATY OF ROME and formation of the EEC (European Economic Community) in 1957. Benelux was then largely absorbed in the bigger commun-ity, though it continued to exist. It aimed at common social services, monetary union and a single currency. These were not achieved but Benelux did abolish internal customs barriers and established a common tariff for imports before the EEC. It also pioneered a passport-free area, which was extended to France and West Germany in June 1985 by the Schengen Agreement.

Ben-Gurion, David (1886–1973)   Prime Minister of Israel (1948–53, 1955–63). He was a leader of ZIONISM and of its labour movement in Palestine for over 40 years, of the *Yishuv* (Palestine Jewish Community) and then of Israel, whose political life he domi-nated for the first 15 years of its existence. Born David Gruen in Russian Poland, he emigrated to Palestine in 1906 as a farm worker. In 1912 he went to Constantinople (Istanbul) University to study Turkish law but returned to Palestine when the First World War began and was deported by the Turkish governor in 1915. He went to the US, where he joined the Jewish Legion of the British Army. Returning to Palestine (now a British mandate) after the war, he changed his name to the Hebrew Ben-Gurion ('son of a lion cub') and when the *Histadrut* (General Organization of Jewish Workers in the Land of Israel) was formed in 1920 he soon became its General-Secretary (1921–35). Through it he built up his own power base. By the 1930s his socialist party Mapai (Workers' Party of the Land of Israel) was the dominant political movement in the *Yishuv*.

From 1935–48 Ben-Gurion was Chairman of the Jewish Agency Executive, a cabinet responsible for the *Yishuv's* affairs.

When the Second World War began he had divided loyalties. He was anti-British because the White Paper of 1939 limited Jewish immigration to Palestine, yet he was pro-British in wanting an Allied victory in the war against Nazi Germany. 'We will fight the war', he declared, 'as though there were no White Paper and we will fight the White Paper as though there were no war': 130,000 Palestine Jews volunteered to fight against Germany. He opposed the terrorism of Irgun under Menachem BEGIN, as it would make Britain hostile to the formation of an independent Jewish state. From 1945 he bought arms in Europe and built up a professional army in preparation for the establishment of the state of Israel. On 14 May 1948, the day the British mandate ended, Ben-Gurion proclaimed the independent state of Israel and became its first Prime Minister. On the next day President TRUMAN recognized the new state. Ben-Gurion successfully led Israel in the first ARAB–ISRAELI WAR (1948–9) and so played a major part in the BIRTH OF ISRAEL.

As Prime Minister the short and stocky Ben-Gurion was a difficult colleague to work with. He had few close friends, did not find personal relations easy and did not seek a consensus. When he had come to a decision he would not change it and so gave the impression of being self-righteous and stubborn. Yet his tremendous will power was appreciated and was much needed, as he had to deal with massive immigration. In the first decade there were over a million immigrants, many poor and uneducated, who needed homes and jobs. In providing these he was helped by the reparations he obtained from Chancellor ADENAUER of West Germany. As the COLD WAR developed he took the side of the West but in 1952 he abruptly resigned and retired to a desert *kibbutz*, where he led a simple and austere life. In 1955, when Israel was threatened by an alliance of Egypt, Syria and Jordan, he returned as Prime Minister

and vigorously prepared for war with his Chief of Staff, Moshe DAYAN. They colluded with Britain and France to attack Egypt in the SUEZ CRISIS and in five days defeated the Egyptian army, seized Sinai and the Gaza Strip and ended the ten-year blockade of the Gulf of Aqaba. Though Ben-Gurion was forced by the UNITED NATIONS and US to return the conquered territories, the Gulf of Aqaba remained open. After his second retirement in 1963 Ben-Gurion formed a new party Rafi (Israel Workers' List) but it did badly in the 1956 elections and so merged with the left-wing parties to form the Israeli Labour Party in 1968. He opposed the retention of the OCCUPIED TERRITORIES after the SIX DAY WAR (1967), as he believed that hanging on to them might ultimately destroy the Jewish state. Old and in declining health he finally gave up politics in 1970.

The Armed Prophet, H. Bar-Zohar (1967)
The Modern History of Israel, N. Lucas (1977)
Ben-Gurion and the Palestinian Arabs, S. Teveth (1985)

Berlin blockade (24 June 1948–12 May 1949)   The US, Britain and France introduced a new Deutschmark (in effect a devaluation of the old one) in their occupation zones of Germany in order to bring about economic stability. The Russians objected, as they said that the Potsdam agreement required the unanimous approval of the occupying powers for such a move. When the Western powers introduced the Deutschmark into their sections of Berlin, the USSR closed land access routes (railways, roads, canals) to West Berlin, which was 120 miles (192 km) inside the Soviet zone. They also cut off electricity supplies from their zone on which the Western sectors depended. The US decided not to call STALIN's bluff by forcing a way through but to use an airlift instead. The 2.4 million inhabitants of West Berlin faced starvation, as they had food for only 36 days and no one believed that an airlift on the scale required could be mounted successfully. Yet this was done: there were 277,000 flights, with a plane reaching West Berlin every 30 seconds at the height of the airlift, until Stalin lifted the blockade. Stalin had hoped to prevent the formation of a West German state, or at least to force the Allies to withdraw from West Berlin. He failed and speeded up the process he was trying to prevent, as he convinced the Western powers that they must strengthen their zones of Germany by uniting them. West Germany was now regarded as a bastion of democracy rather than as a threat to Allied security, a role which the USSR had assumed. The blockade also reduced German hesitations about creating a government for the Western zones.

The US and the Berlin Blockade, 1948–9, A. Shlaim (1983)

Berlin Wall   It was built to separate West Berlin from East Berlin and the surrounding German Democratic Republic (GDR). The frontier of the GDR with West Germany (the Federal Republic of Germany: FRG) had been closed since 1952, but East Germans could move to the West by going to Berlin and crossing from the eastern (Soviet) sector of the city to the western. Three million had done so from 1945–61, an intolerable drain on the economy of the GDR, as many were skilled and highly educated. ULBRICHT, therefore, obtained the permission of KHRUSHCHEV to seal off the east of the city from the west. On 13 August 1961 barbed wire separated the two parts of the city, to be followed by the building of a wall, 25 miles long and 20 feet (6 metres) high in places. Searchlights, towers with armed guards, and land mines deterred people from crossing the wall. Over 200 people were to lose their lives in attempting to do so.

The building of the wall was a humiliating recognition that the democratic FRG was more attractive and economically successful than the repressive communist regime of the GDR, yet it served its purpose. The exodus to the West ended and this made the government of the GDR more stable and secure. The reaction in the FRG was dismay that its Western allies had done nothing. Politicians there decided that they would have to devise their own policy towards the East. Willy BRANDT later recalled how the building of the wall affected him: 'it was against this background that my so-called OSTPOLITIK – the beginning of DÉTENTE – took shape'. The wall was opened unexpectedly in the EAST GERMAN REVOLUTION OF 1989, which marked the collapse of communism in the GDR and led to the REUNIFICATION OF GERMANY.

The Ides of August: The Berlin Wall Crisis of 1961, C. Cate (1978)
The Berlin Wall, N. Gelb (1986)

Berlusconi, Silvio (1937–)   Italian Prime Minister (1994). From school he went to work for a Milan construction company and became its general manager at the age of 23. In 1961 he founded his own construction company and ten years later moved into television. He set up a private station Tele-Milano and soon expanded into Canale 5, Italy's first private nationwide television network, which ended the monopoly of RAI, the state television and radio. By 1985, after he added a third station, 44 per cent of prime-time viewers were watching his channels, 40 per cent watching RAI. Television attracted advertising: in 1990 60 per cent of all advertising revenue in Italy went to his Fininvest company. Berlusconi is also a publisher, who owns a Milan daily newspaper, many periodicals, a chain of cinemas and the football team AC Milan.

His commercial interests had been protected by his socialist friend Bettino CRAXI, Prime Minister from 1983–7, but by 1994 the PSI (Italian Socialist Party) had collapsed, so he founded *Forza Italia*, which was more a series of supporters', clubs than a political party. It was run by his television managers, who used marketing techniques. 'Focus groups' were formed in different regions to find out what voters wanted and then *Forza* would promise to provide it. In the election campaign Berlusconi had more television coverage than anyone else and was able to distance himself from the TANGENTOPOLI scandals which affected most of the other political parties. In order to have a majority Berlusconi had to form an alliance with the NORTHERN LEAGUE and with the neo-Fascists (renamed the National Alliance – AN) in Rome and the South. As these parties loathed each other, Berlusconi made agreements separately with each of them. The 1994 election produced an extraordinary result: his coalition won 46.4 per cent of the vote and 366 seats to give it a majority in the Chamber of Deputies, though it did not have a majority in the Senate. Starting from scratch Berlusconi had won an election after a three-month campaign and without a coherent political programme, as the electorate was totally disillusioned by the endemic corruption in the parties which had dominated Italian politics since the war. He had promised a million new jobs, depicted the left as communist and with the collapse of the CHRISTIAN DEMOCRATIC PARTY *Forza* was the only centre-right party to whom the electorate could turn.

Little seemed to have changed. Berlusconi spent six weeks of horse-trading before he could form a government, the various factions squabbling about the spoils of office as in the past. There was little chance of stable government as the Northern League wanted spending cuts, PRIVATIZATION, more power to the regions and lower taxes. The AN, on the other hand, with its base in the impoverished South, wanted an increase in welfare spending and in subsidies to state industries and strong central government. Berlusconi was soon in trouble when he issued a decree, without consulting parliament, to free 2,000 accused of corruption from pre-trial detention, as he appeared to be protecting the corrupt ruling class he had been elected to replace. When he tried to diminish the public

debt by reducing pensions he antagonized all state employees, but it was the judges who created his greatest difficulties. The Constitutional Court ruled that no one could own a quarter of the nation's television channels (Berlusconi owned 3 out of 12). This ruling was followed by the resignation of the popular investigating magistrate Antonio Di Pietro, who alleged political interference in his work. In December the Northern League said it was joining the opposition, proposed a vote of no confidence and Berlusconi resigned. His government, unable to pass any controversial legislation, had lasted seven months, in which time unemployment had risen by 400,000 and the value of the lira had fallen by 13 per cent against the Deutschmark.

Italy: The Unfinished Revolution, M. Frei (1996)
Modern Italy, 1871–1995, M. Clark (1996)

Betancourt, Rómulo (1908–81) Provisional President (1945–7) and President (1959–64) of Venezuela. He took part in student protests against the dictatorship of General Gomez in 1928 and in the abortive April rebellion, after which he escaped to Colombia. Back in Venezuela in 1941 he founded Democratic Action (AD), a radical party which, in alliance with young army officers, led the coup in 1945 which began the period known as the *trienio*. As Provisional President and head of the seven-man ruling junta, he increased taxes on the rich and did a deal with foreign oil companies which gave the government 50 per cent of their profits. A new constitution in 1947 provided for a secret ballot and the vote for all over 18, including illiterates. The first direct elections in Venezuela were held the same year and gave AD a landslide victory but the short democratic episode came to an end in 1948 with another military coup, which resulted in ten more years of dictatorship. Betancourt again went into exile.

After the 1958 revolution which brought down the military dictatorship, Betancourt returned to Venezuela. He and the leader of the Social Christian Party (COPEI), Rafael Caldera, made the pact of Punto Fijo, which is seen as ending the cycle of military coups. Divisive issues were removed from the political agenda and support for a common programme of reforms agreed. The first presidential candidates committed themselves to a national unity coalition, in which all parties would have seats in the cabinet irrespective of who won the election. Since then all Venezuelan Presidents have been elected in fair, direct elections. The stability of Venezuelan democracy owes much to the pact of Punto Fijo. It established a two-party political system. AD and COPEI moved from the left and right wings respectively towards the centre and between 1973 and 1993 shared 80 per cent of the vote for the legislature and 90 per cent of the presidential vote. Their hold was broken in 1993 when Rafael Caldera became President with a new coalition party.

Betancourt won the presidential election in 1959 but was soon at odds with members of his own party because of his strong anti-communist and pro-US line. At home he laid the basis for economic growth, which benefited from the oil industry, as it provided 90 per cent of Venezuela's exports and over 50 per cent of government income and gave Venezuela the highest per capita GDP in Latin America. Venezuela was one of the five founding members of OPEC in 1960. After his presidency Betancourt was an elder statesman and adviser to later AD governments. He died in New York.

Venezuela: Politics in a Petroleum Republic, D. E. Black (1984)
Venezuela: The Democratic Experience, J. D. Martz and D. J. Myers (eds) (1986)

Bevan, Aneurin (1897–1960)   British Minister of Health (1945–51). Born in South Wales, one of 13 children of a miner, he went down the pit himself at the age of 13. Self-educated by voracious reading, he was elected to parliament in 1929 for Ebbw Vale, a constituency he represented for the rest of his life. He was expelled from the Labour Party in 1939 for advocating a Popular Front with the communists against Fascism but was readmitted the following year. During the Second World War he was a persistent critic of CHURCHILL and of the LABOUR PARTY's subordination to him in the coalition government.

ATTLEE boldly made him Minister of Health after the labour victory in the 1945 election, a position in which he took a pragmatic approach to become the great reconciler. His greatest problem in setting up a National Health Service (NHS), in which everyone would get free medical, dental and opthalmic treatment, was the strident opposition of the doctors in the British Medical Association. Bevan knew that without their support the scheme would not work, so he made concessions to consultants, who were given the right to continue their private practice in NHS hospitals. By the time the NHS came into operation in 1948, 90 per cent of doctors took part and 93 per cent of the population. Bevan had nationalized the hospitals in order to ensure that equal treatment was available everywhere and paid for the NHS mainly out of general taxation rather than through national insurance contributions. For the first time women, children and the elderly received free medical treatment, a move that remained immensely popular 50 years later, in spite of the escalating costs of the service. The success of the NHS received international acclaim.

Bevan was also responsible for housing. He was anxious that most new houses should be council houses, rented by those on low incomes, but progress was slow until 1947, as there was a shortage of raw materials. Not till MACMILLAN was Prime Minister were 300,000 houses built in one year, but Bevan built over 200,000 a year from 1947–51 and insisted on quality. New houses had to contain three bedrooms, with indoor bathroom and lavatory. Rent Control Acts in 1946 and

1949 protected the tenants of private land-lords by controlling rents. The environment benefited as planning authorities were given the right to control advertisements and preserve historic buildings, National Parks were set up and there was an Access to the Countryside Act. The New Towns Act of 1946 set up development corporations to build new towns, such as Stevenage and Hemel Hempstead, to take the overspill from London.

Bevan, with his mastery of detail and eloquence, was the main architect of the WELFARE STATE in Britain but Attlee did not promote him. When Cripps and BEVIN resigned owing to ill-health. Attlee made GAITSKELL Chancellor of the Exchequer and Morrison Foreign Secretary. Bevan was bitter and was unhappy with his move to the Ministry of Labour. The rivalry of Gaitskell and Bevan came to a head with the KOREAN WAR. Gaitskell introduced a budget which vastly increased defence expenditure and sought some minor cuts in the health service. The cuts were trivial (£ 13 million in a budget of £ 4 billion) but the principle of a free service was at stake and Bevan resigned.

The split in the Labour Party did enormous damage to its electoral prospects for the next 13 years. Bevan emerged again as a rebel, was briefly expelled once more from the Labour Party in 1955, the year in which Gaitskell won the contest to become leader of the party after Attlee's retirement. There was a partial reconciliation with Gaitskell when Bevan joined the Shadow Cabinet as Colonial Secretary and made a blistering attack on EDEN's conduct during the SUEZ CRISIS, but relations with his colleagues remained uneasy. His promotion to Shadow Foreign Secretary produced a row with his left-wing allies. Bevan, appalled by the CZECH COUP and BERLIN BLOCKADE, had become virulently anti-Soviet and told the party conference in 1957 that Britain should retain her nuclear weapons so that she did not go 'naked into the conference chamber'. In 1959 he became deputy leader of the Labour Party but, suffering from cancer, died shortly afterwards. When he died the *British Medical Journal* described him as 'the most brilliant Minister of Health this country ever had'.

Labour People, K. O. Morgan (1987)
Nye Bevan and the Mirage of British Socialism, J. Campbell (1987)
The State of the Nation: The Political Legacy of Aneurin Bevan, G. Goodman (ed) (1997)

Bevin, Ernest (1881–1951)   British Foreign Secretary (1945–51) and trade union leader. Illegitimate, Bevin lived in poverty with his mother until she died in 1889, and then lived with a half-sister. He left school at 11 and had several poorly paid jobs before he became involved with the TRADE UNION movement. Known as 'the dockers' KC' for arguing their case before wage tribunals, in 1922 he planned the amalgamation of 18 unions into the Transport and General Workers Union (TGWU), which continued to absorb smaller unions until it was the largest in the country. As its General Secretary Bevin was the most powerful trade union leader in Britain. In 1921 he had called for a General Council of the Trade Union Congress (TUC) and with Walter Citrine dominated that body in the 1920s and 1930s. He was a national leader of the General Strike (1926) and a member of the General Council which ended it. A strong supporter of the League of Nations and collective security, Bevin was opposed to Fascism but refused to collaborate with the Communist Party in a United Front against it. From the mid-1930s Bevin had heart trouble and was considering retirement when Winston CHURCHILL invited him to join his coalition government in 1940. He therefore became an MP at the age of 59 and served as Minister of Labour from 1940–5, greatly expanding the labour force and persuading the trade unions to accept 'dilution', the use of unskilled labour in skilled jobs.

Bevin was the dominant personality of ATTLEE's Labour government (1945–50). A lonely man with few friends and no hobbies, he was a forceful and skilled negotiator, who showed a fierce loyalty to Attlee, particularly when Cripps and Dalton tried to remove him as Prime Minister in 1947. The only manual worker in the cabinet, he was indispensable in securing the support of the trade unions. When Attlee made Bevin Foreign Secretary he gave him a free rein, except in India. According to Lord Listowel, Secretary for India, Bevin 'was at heart an old-fashioned imperialist, keener to expand than contract the Empire'. Yet he realized the need to prepare for the transfer of power to native leaders. The main thrust of DECOLONIZATION did not take place until the 1960s, but Bevin granted independence to Burma and Ceylon in 1948, and made a determined attempt to assist colonies economically by setting up the Colonial Development Corporation and the Overseas Food Corporation. He maintained British commitments East of Suez, signing defence treaties with Arab states in the Persian Gulf to protect the route to India as in the past and began a campaign in the MALAYAN EMERGENCY (1948–60) to crush communist rebels.

These moves were a corollary of Bevin's belief that Britain was still a world power, with commitments to the COMMON-WEALTH. When the US ceased to co-operate in helping Britain to produce its own atomic bomb, Bevin and Attlee decided to go it alone, without consulting the rest of the cabinet. This caused deep dismay in the Labour movement, where there was a strong anti-nuclear faction. Conscription, introduced for up to two years, kept Britain with armed forces of over 750,000 and a defence expenditure it could not afford. Events in Palestine soon made clear that Britain was over-extended. Britain was the mandatory power there but when Bevin failed to persuade Arabs and Jews to compromise, he referred the matter to the UNITED NATIONS in February 1947 and in September announced that Britain would withdraw in May 1948. This was a humiliation, brought about by Jewish terrorism and the cost of peace-keeping, as Bevin

withdrew without any successor state being established and amid growing chaos. Britain's weakness was evident too in the GREEK CIVIL WAR (1944–9), when Bevin informed the US in 1947 that it could no longer defend Greece and Turkey against communist subversion. Australia and New Zealand both realized that they could no longer rely on Britain for their defence and so concluded the ANZUS TREATY (1951) with the US: Britain was excluded.

Bevin's main concern in his foreign policy was to tie the US to Europe, so that it would reject its interwar isolationism and retain troops on the Continent to defend it against any possible Soviet attack. An enthusiastic supporter of the MARSHALL PLAN, which he called 'a lifeline to a sinking ship', he and Georges BIDAULT coordinated the European response to it and in April 1948 formed the OEEC. The British and American zones of occupation in Germany joined to form Bizonia, a prelude to the unification of West Germany and when the Russians imposed the BERLIN BLOCKADE Britain made a major contribution to the airlift which fed the population of West Berlin. To defend Western Europe after the CZECH COUP of 1948 NATO was formed in April 1949. Bevin insisted that the Mediterranean should be protected as well as the North Atlantic, so Italy and Portugal (and later Greece and Turkey) were included. The Foreign Secretary regarded this as his greatest achievement, as it finally tied the US to the defence of Europe. When the KOREAN WAR began Bevin faithfully supported the US.

His attitude to Europe was ambivalent. He played a leading part in forming the Brussels Treaty with France and the BENELUX countries to create an integrated defence system but he, like the rest of his colleagues, had no intention of giving up any British sovereignty. Bevin declined to take part in the discussions which led to the formation of the ECSC (European Coal and Steel Community). He had a series of minor heart attacks after the war but his work was not seriously affected until late in 1950. Ill-health forced him to resign in 1951, only five weeks before he died.

The Life and Times of Ernest Bevin, 3 vols, A. Bullock (1960, 1967, 1983)

Bhopal disaster (2–3 December 1984)

The worst industrial disaster so far. At Bhopal, the capital of Madhya Pradesh state in India, 45 tons of toxic gas escaped from a storage tank at a pesticide plant run by a subsidiary of the US Union Carbide Corporation (UCC). The safety system at the understaffed plant did not work as the gas drifted over the densely populated neighbourhood, killing many instantly and causing panic as thousands fled. 3,500 died as a result of the accident and another 60,000 were left with serious health problems: many were permanently disabled, while others suffered from psychological disorders. Between 150,000 and 250,000 people were affected.

The disaster illustrated the problems developing countries meet in their relations with MULTINATIONAL CORPORATIONS (MNCs) as they try to expand economically. The Indian government of Rajiv GANDHI was in a dilemma, as it wanted to protect the victims without frightening off MNCs from investing in India. It settled out of court in 1989. Despite the Bhopal disaster and the closure of the plant there, the Gandhi government continued its policy of reducing controls on MNCs in order to attract foreign investment.

The Bhopal Tragedy, W. Morehouse and M. A. Subramaniam (1986)

Bhutto, Benazir (1953–)

Prime Minister of Pakistan (1988–90, 1993–6). The daughter of Zulfikar Ali BHUTTO, she was educated at Harvard and Oxford universities. After her father's execution she was under house arrest (1979–84) before she went into exile (1984–6) in England. She returned to Pakistan when President ZIA UL-HAQ lifted martial law and

was rapturously welcomed on her four-week tour of the country. After Zia's death in a plane crash the military allowed elections to take place in November 1988. The Pakistan People's Party (PPP), founded by her father and now led by Benazir, won the largest number of seats in the National Assembly, so she became Prime Minister of a coalition government at the age of 35, the first woman to hold such a post in an Islamic country.

She freed political prisoners, restored civil rights and rejoined the COMMONWEALTH in 1989 but she faced formidable problems. There was a vast budget deficit, violent conflict between ethnic groups in Sind and the destabilization of the Northwest Frontier Province in the wake of the AFGHAN CIVIL WAR, during which three million refugees had flocked into Pakistan. Taxation and inflation increased as the army was called in to restore order in Sind and her government was accused of corruption. Her husband Asif Zardari was known as Mr Ten Per Cent, as he had to approve all big industrial contracts and import–export transactions. In 1990 President Ghulam Ishaq Khan, who had the right to overrule the Prime Minister according to the 1985 constitution, dismissed the government, dissolved the National Assembly and called for new elections in October. In these elections the Islamic Democratic Alliance (IDA) won 105 seats, the PPP 45: there were similar results in provincial elections. Benazir Bhutto therefore was leader of the opposition until 1993, when new elections were held and she became once again the Prime Minister of a coalition government.

A feud in the Bhutto family in 1993 badly damaged Benazir's reputation. Her mother Nusrat, who had been ousted as co-chairman of the PPP, leaving Benazir as sole chairman, resented the way she had been treated and saw her son Murtaza rather than her daughter Benazir as her husband's rightful heir. Ethnic violence in Sind often brought pitched battles between SUNNI and SHII Muslims in which many were killed. There was trouble too abroad, as the Rabbani government in

Afghanistan accused Pakistan of interfering in its internal affairs by supporting TALIBAN, a group of extreme Islamists. This led to a deterioration in relations with Iran, which supported Rabbani. Benazir's worst and most pressing problem was the economy, which was in ruins. Defence and debt servicing took up 81 per cent of total government expenditure, social services 2.7 per cent. A third of textile mills (textiles formed 60 per cent of Pakistan's exports) were closed in 1995, when the IMF suspended a loan of $1.5 billion because the economy was not being liberalized quickly enough. As she was Minister of Finance, Benazir was blamed for much of the mismanagement of the economy.

In November 1996 Benazir Bhutto was removed from office for the second time by the President in the fourth government dismissal since 1988. President Leghari, who had been a leader of the PPP, accused her of a lack of accountability and interference in the independence of the judiciary. A friend of her estranged brother Murtaza, who had been shot dead by police in September, he had the full support of the army. New elections were held in February in which (with a turnout of only 26 per cent, an indication of public disillusionment with politicians) Nawaz Sharif's Pakistan Muslim League won a landslide victory with over 130 seats in the 217 seat National Assembly. Bhutto's PPP won only 19 seats and was reduced to the status of a regional party in her native province of Sind.

Bhutto, Zulfikar Ali (1928–79)   President (1971–3) and Prime Minister (1973–7) of Pakistan. From an aristocratic Rajput family who owned large estates in Sind, he was educated at the universities of Bombay and California, Berkeley before studying law at Oxford and Lincoln's Inn London, where he qualified as a barrister. He was a lecturer in international law at the University of Southampton before returning to Pakistan to practise and teach law at the University of Sind (1953–8). In 1958 he held the first of several

ministerial posts under President AYUB KHAN and was his Foreign Minister from 1963–6. A year later he founded the Pakistan People's Party (PPP), denounced Ayub Khan as a dictator and was imprisoned (1968–9).

When General Yahya Khan replaced Ayub as President in 1969, Bhutto was released and became Yahya's Foreign Minister and deputy Prime Minister. Yahya promised to hold elections in 1970, after which he would hand over power to a civilian government. When elections were held Bhutto's PPP won most seats in West Pakistan but the Awami League, led by Mujibur Rahman, won 160 out of 162 seats in East Pakistan. This would give it a majority of seats in the National Assembly, something that neither Yahya Khan nor Bhutto was prepared to accept. Bhutto asked for the meeting of the Assembly to be postponed. Yahya agreed, so Mujibur now declared the INDEPENDENCE OF BANGLADESH (East Pakistan), thus helping to bring about the third of the INDO-PAKISTANI WARS which ended with the defeat of Pakistan and the loss of its eastern province. On 20 December 1971 Yahya handed over as President to Bhutto, the first civilian to hold this position in Pakistan. He took for himself the posts of foreign affairs, defence and the interior. Agreement was reached on a new constitution after discussions with the leaders of all parties. This marked a rejection of the presidential system in favour of a parliament in which the chief executive would be the Prime Minister, answerable to the lower house. The President would be elected by both houses voting together. With power now in the hands of the Prime Minister, Bhutto gave up his post as President and became Prime Minister.

He soon lost much of the support he had enjoyed, as he became increasingly authoritarian. The government of Baluchistan was dismissed in 1974 for inciting the people to rebel against the central authorities. An amendment to the constitution gave the government the right to declare any political party illegal for 'operating in a manner prejudicial to the sovereignty or integrity of the country', and was used to ban the National Awami Party, the only effective opposition to the PPP. It appeared that Bhutto intended to make Pakistan a one-party state. The lower classes, who had played an important role in the PPP's victory in 1970, expected social reform to limit the power of the landowners, but Bhutto sought the support of big business and the landed aristocracy. The funds promised for free education and health care did not materialize, though Bhutto did benefit the urban poor by raising wages and imposing protective labour laws.

Bhutto took Pakistan out of the COMMON-WEALTH when Britain, Australia and New Zealand recognized the independence of Bangladesh. Strongly opposed to India, he cultivated good relations with China and antagonized the United States by beginning to develop a nuclear bomb. His main problems, however, were at home, particularly as the 1977 elections approached. Nine opposition parties formed the Pakistan National Alliance (PNA) to oppose the PPP and did well in the election campaign, but when the results were declared the PPP was awarded 155 seats, the PNA 36. The PNA alleged massive fraud and launched a civil disobedience campaign. Law and order broke down in several towns, and the army was called in to restore order. With the country on the verge of civil war Bhutto agreed to new elections in October but they never took place, as the army seized power in July under General ZIA UL-HAQ. Bhutto was charged with having instigated the death of a PPP dissident in 1974, was sentenced to death by the Lahore High Court in March 1978 and, after the Supreme Court confirmed the sentence, was hanged in April 1979.

Pakistan Under Bhutto 1971–7, S. J. Burki (1980)

Biafran war (1967–70)   An attempt by the Eastern Region of Nigeria to become an independent state. The origins of the war go back to the division of Nigeria at independence (1960) into three regions: the Muslim Northern Region of Fulani and Hausa, the Western Region where the Yoruba were dominant and the Eastern Region where Igbos were in the ascendant. The predominantly Muslim Northern Region had a larger population than the other two combined and so was likely to dominate the federation permanently. This was unacceptable to the southerners, particularly to the civil servants and army officers in the east. In January 1966 young, mainly Igbo, officers staged a coup in which the federal Prime Minister Sir Abubakar Tafawa BALEWA, who was a northerner, was murdered, as were the Prime Ministers of the Northern and Western Regions. A military government was set up under General Ironsi, who had not taken part in the coup but was an Igbo. Northerners now feared domination by the Igbos, so in July northerners in the army killed Ironsi and other Igbo officers. Military discipline was restored by General Gown, a Christian northerner, but he could not prevent attacks on Igbo merchants and civil servants in the Northern Region. Many were killed and a number fled to the safety of the Eastern Region. On 30 May 1967 the military governor of the Eastern Region, Colonel Ojukwu, declared the secession of the east as the independent state of Biafra.

Biafra was recognized by only four African states (Tanzania, Zambia, Gabon and the Ivory Coast), but was supported by South Africa, Rhodesia, Portugal and France. Britain was loyal to the federal government, which, with its larger numbers and resources, was bound to win in the end: by mid-1968 most of the large towns and non-Igbo areas of Biafra were in federal hands. The war was prolonged for over a year by the aid France gave to Ojukwu and became a war of attrition. Biafra was blockaded and suffered terribly from famine before Ojukwu fled to the Ivory Coast in January 1970 and the Biafrans surrendered. About 100,000 had been killed in the fighting but between one and two million civilians had died from starvation and disease.

Gowon behaved with great generosity and was concerned with reconciliation rather than revenge. Igbo civil servants were reinstated in the federal administration and Igbo officers were allowed to go free.

The Nigerian Civil War, J. de St Jorre (1972)
'The Biafran Crisis and the Midwest', S. E. Orobatov, *African Affairs* 86 (1987), pp. 367–83

Bidault, Georges (1899–1983)

Prime Minister of the FOURTH REPUBLIC in France (1946, 1949–50). Educated at a Jesuit school and at the Sorbonne, he was a history teacher for much of the inter-war period. After the fall of France in 1940 he played a leading role in the Resistance and was a founder of the National Council of the Resistance, which brought different factions together. He became its head, arranged for it to support DE GAULLE and took part in the Paris rising. Bidault was Foreign Minister in de Gaulle's provisional government, a position he held for five years in the Fourth Republic (1944–8, 1953–4). He was also a founder and leader of the MRP (*Mouvement républicain populaire*), a Christian Democratic Party.

Bidault included communists in his first government and wanted a harsh peace imposed on Germany. This brought him into conflict with the United States. He had to moderate his stance, as he realized that US military support was essential for France. Bidault welcomed the MARSHALL PLAN and with the British Foreign Secretary Ernest BEVIN, coordinated the European response to it. They convened a meeting of 16 nations receiving aid which became the OEEC (Organization for European Economic Co-operation) and formed a military alliance, the Brussels Treaty, with the BENELUX countries to complement their economic co-operation. After the CZECH COUP of 1948 Bidault asked George Marshall for a military alliance which would include the US. This led to NATO talks which began while he was still Foreign Minister.

When Bidault was Prime Minister for the second time (1949–50) he made a major contribution to European integration. Jean MONNET with Bidault's strong support proposed the Schuman Plan, which led to the formation of the ECSC (European Coal and Steel Community), a forerunner of the EEC. Bidault was less successful when he was Foreign Minister again in 1953–4. A fervent colonialist, he believed that France would decline without her empire. He deposed the Sultan of Morocco, exacerbating the situation there, and persuaded the US to become more involved in the INDOCHINA WAR OF INDEPENDENCE (1946–54). This did not prevent the disaster of DIEN BIEN PHU, after which the government of which he was a member fell. Bidault, who had close ties with the *Colons* (European settlers), rejected any French withdrawal from Algeria. That brought him into conflict with de Gaulle. His links with the terrorism of the OAS (*Organisation de'armée secrète*) led to his flight into exile in Brazil in 1962. Granted an amnesty after MAY 1968, he returned to France.

Parliament, Politics and Society in France, 1946–58, D. MacRae (1967)
Crisis and Compromise: Politics in the Fourth Republic, P. Williams (1972)

Black Consciousness

A movement in South Africa in reaction to white racism and white liberal paternalism. African students in their segregated universities, who were frustrated by white domination of the National Union of South African Students (NUSAS), broke away in 1969 to form the all-black South African Students' Organisation (SASO). Its President from the medical school at the University of Natal was Steve Biko. Black Consciousness, with its emphasis on black pride and self- reliance, was strongly influenced by the American CIVIL RIGHTS MOVEMENT and BLACK POWER and by the writings of Frantz Fanon and Leopold SENGHOR. It followed the lead of the Pan-

Africanist Congress (PAC) in stressing that South Africa belonged to the blacks alone and in rejecting liberal and white-dominated organizations, but its economic and political programmes were vague: a belief in sharing wealth was combined with an acceptance of private property. Black Consciousness did not affect the working class or peasants and was criticized by the ANC for being too élitist and out of touch with the masses. It rejected the leaders of the BANTUSTANS and *Inkatha* as collaborators in white supremacy and when it greatly influenced the Soweto riots of 1976 the South African government decided to destroy it. All Black Consciousness organizations were banned and their leaders persecuted, Biko being tortured and killed in 1977. Yet the ideas of Black Consciousness remained influential in the struggle for equal rights for blacks in the South Africa of APARTHEID.

Black Politics in South Africa since 1945, T. Lodge (1983)
Bounds of Possibility: The Legacy of Steve Biko and Black Consciousness, N. Pikyana, M. Ramphele, M. Mpusalwana and L. Wilson (eds) (1991)

Black ghetto riots (1964–8) The most destructive riots and the most prolonged period of unrest in the US since the American Civil War. The riots began in Harlem and another area of New York City in 1964. A year later a week-long riot in the Watts district of Los Angeles (where three-quarters of adult males were unemployed) began the first of four 'long hot summers'. When Martin Luther KING walked the streets preaching non-violence he was ignored. 34 people were killed and over a thousand injured: property worth $35 million was destroyed. There were 38 riots in 1966, particularly in Chicago, and in 1967 the high point was reached with 164 insurrections, the worst being at Newark, New Jersey and Detroit. In five days' rioting at Newark 26 people were killed (all but two of

them black) and 2,000 injured. The riots at Detroit left 43 dead, thousands homeless and damage of $500 million. The disturbances did not involve pitched battles between the races, as they had done in Chicago in 1919 and Detroit in 1943, but took place within ghetto boundaries where shops (many white-owned) were looted and burned and firemen obstructed. Most riots, which were not organized and had no programme, followed incidents between white police and black residents. The assassination of Martin Luther King in Memphis, Tennessee in April 1968 set off a new wave of riots all over the country, including Washington and Chicago. The riots, which were influenced by the BLACK POWER movement from 1966, involved hundreds of thousands of people: 60,000 were arrested for arson and looting, 10,000 seriously injured and 250 killed. They were finally suppressed by using soldiers and National Guardsmen on a large scale: 32,000 in 1967, 60,000 in 1968.

Burn, Baby, Burn! The Los Angeles Race Riot, August (1965), J. Cohen and W. Murphy (1966)
Rivers of Blood, Days of Darkness, R. Conot (1967)

Black Muslims Black separatist religious movement in the US. It is the popular name for the Lost-Found Nation of Islam (which changed its name in 1976 to the World Community of Islam in the West), a sect founded in Detroit in 1930 by Wallace Fard (Wali Farad), who claimed that black Americans were descended from an ancient Muslim tribe. Followers adopted Muslim names and believed that Farad was an incarnation of God. There were 8,000 Black Muslims when Farad disappeared in 1934 and was succeeded as leader by Elijah Muhammad, who regarded all whites as 'devils who had enslaved the Black Nation'. He told his followers to avoid contact with whites and sought a separate state for blacks. Black Muslims had to adopt a strict moral code, avoiding 'white' vices such as drinking alcohol, drug-taking or fornication.

When he was imprisoned during the Second World War for telling Black Muslims to avoid conscription, membership of the sect dropped to 1,000, but it later rose sharply owing to the conversion of MALCOLM X and his activity on behalf of the Nation of Islam, which had 100,000 members by 1960. The rift between Elijah Muhammad and Malcolm X, who left the movement, threatened to reduce the popularity of the Black Muslims, particularly when Malcolm X was assassinated by three members of the sect in 1965. The conversion of the heavyweight boxing champion Cassius Clay (Muhammad Ali) enabled the Nation of Islam to recover and claim 250,000 members. After the death of Elijah Muhammad in 1975 his son Warith Deen Muhammad took over and made the sect conform to the orthodoxy of SUNNI Islam.

When he called on all Muslims to be patriotic Louis Farrakhan led a break-away group, the Nation of Islam (NOI). This returned to the original belief of the Black Muslims and added anti-Semitism to its anti-white views. Its theology regards the devil as embodied in the white man, who is responsible for all evils which have afflicted blacks, slavery, racial oppression and poverty. The white man has a temporary dispensation to rule the world but this will end in Armageddon, when the black nation will be redeemed. The NOI exercises considerable influence in the no-go areas of cities such as Washington and Los Angeles, where Farrakhan is idolized. Its 'Islamic patrols' of unarmed vigilantes are popular as they have brought safety to the streets. The NOI Security Agency has 'dopebusting' contracts in several cities and provides security for several corporations. The Million Man March on Washington organized by Farrakhan in 1995 showed the NOI's capacity for organization and its appeal to many African Americans.

Allah in the West, G. Kepel (1997)

Countdown to Armageddon: Louis Farrakhan and the Nation of Islam, M. Gandell (1997)

Black Power   A radical movement in the US which rejected the aims and methods of the leaders of the CIVIL RIGHTS MOVEMENT (CRM) like Martin Luther KING. He had promoted non-violent agitation to get rid of racial segregation and wanted the integration of white and black societies. Stokely Carmichael, who had worked for several years with the Student Nonviolent Coordinating Committee (SNCC, which organized sit-ins and freedom rides) demanded Black Power in 1966. Influenced by the ideas of the BLACK MUSLIMS and MALCOLM X, he believed that integration was 'a subterfuge for the maintenance of white supremacy'. Blacks should develop their own cultural identity and run their own communities, electing black officials, forming black businesses and consumer co-operatives and by taking control of black schools. Rejecting non-violence, he said that 'black people should and must fight back'.

The Black Power movement spread throughout the black community and influenced the BLACK GHETTO RIOTS. Both CORE (Congress of Racial Equality) and the SNCC adopted parts of its programme, while a militant minority (never more than 2,000), the Black Panthers, was involved in shoot-outs with the police. By promoting African-American values it affected black life-styles in theatre, dance, music and the taking of African surnames and created the demand for black studies at universities. It also spread a black nationalist theology, which presented Jesus as a black Messiah preaching black liberation. It did not, however, greatly affect mainstream political and economic institutions. As moderate CRM leaders (Roy Wilkins of NAACP and King) pointed out, blacks as a minority needed allies in the labour movement and in other ethnic groups to make any significant changes. After 1970, as the leadership split up (Carmichael went to live in Uganda in 1973), the Black Power movement declined in importance.

Making Peace with the '60s, D. Burner (1996)

Black township revolts (South Africa)

African students were greatly infuenced by the BLACK CONSCIOUSNESS movement and by the freedom movements in Mozambique and Angola (see PORTUGAL'S COLONIAL WARS). When the South African government declared in 1976 that half the curriculum in black schools should be taught in Afrikaans there was a protest in Soweto (South-west Township), near Johannesburg. As 15,000 students marched through Soweto, the police fired, killing several students. Africans responded by attacking the police and destroying schools, administrative buildings and beer halls. The conflict soon spread to other townships on the Rand and in the following weeks to Cape Town and the eastern Cape. Police encouraged migrant hostel workers to attack students, who wanted to close their government-owned beer halls. By the end of the year 575 people had been killed, 2,389 wounded (these government figures are probably an underestimate). The riots were not a serious threat to the government, as the students lacked organization and leadership and did not make any formal contact with workers. The police coped without the help of the army and no State of Emergency was declared. Yet, like SHARPEVILLE, Soweto became known throughout the world as a symbol of black resistance to white oppression. Instruction in Afrikaans in black schools was dropped.

More serious township revolts took place from 1984–6. There was a major rebellion in the Transvaal, partly in resistance to rent increases but also as a protest against the tricameral parliament, set up by P. W. BOTHA, which gave representation to coloureds (of mixed race) and Indians but not to blacks. There were attacks on police and government buildings and black councillors were killed, as

the revolt spread to the Orange Free State, the Cape and Natal. After the police fired on a funeral procession at Uitenhage, in the Cape, killing 20 Africans, there were clashes with police throughout the country and a State of Emergency was declared (it was not lifted until 1990). In many townships the normal administration collapsed and was replaced by organizations, often led by youths, calling for 'people's power'. This time there were links between students and workers and rent and consumer boycotts of white businesses in small towns, which had previously been unaffected by black militancy. In some areas youths set up 'people's courts' to punish those who ignored consumer boycotts and burned to death state collaborators by 'necklacing' (putting burning tyres around their necks). The government responded by using the army as well as the police in the townships and by detaining thousands. The army had crushed the rebellion by 1987. It also encouraged black vigilante groups, which arose in 1985 to protect black councillors but later attacked anti-APARTHEID activists. The South African media called it 'black on black' violence, which enabled the police to disassociate themselves from the excesses (though they had armed and organized many vigilante groups) and to claim to be the only guarantee of public order. There were other 'black on black' clashes on a larger scale, the fiercest of which took place in the Natal townships from 1987–90, in which 4,000 people were killed. They were not ethnic conflicts of Xhosa and Zulu, as most on both sides were Zulus, but struggles for power, between supporters of the ANC and of BUTHELEZI's Inkatha.

The township revolts had both economic and political effects. The rand (South African currency) collapsed, inflation soared and the government raised interest rates to 20 per cent. Shock-waves were felt throughout the white community, which came to realize that *apartheid* would have to be abandoned, political prisoners released and a democratic political system set up.

Year of Fire, Year of Ash: The Soweto Revolt,
   B. Hirson (1979)
Popular Struggles in South Africa, W. Cobbett
   and R. Cohen (eds) (1988)
*All, Here and Now: Black Politics in South
   Africa in the 1980s*, T. Lodge and B. Nasson (1991)

Black Wednesday (16 September 1992)

The day Britain was forced to withdraw from
the Exchange Rate Mechanism (ERM). Margaret THATCHER had agreed to enter only in
1990, when John MAJOR was Chancellor of
the Exchequer, at a rate of 2.95 Deutschmarks
(DM) to the pound. Many economists considered that Britain had entered at too high a
rate. As production fell and unemployment
rose there were demands for a lower exchange
rate and an expansionary policy but these
were rejected by the government.

Turbulence in the financial markets was
caused by Germany's high interest rates,
which were designed to control inflation
after the REUNIFICATION OF GERMANY.
Other countries felt bound to follow the German lead (Britain needed to borrow to cover
its large balance of payments deficit), though
high interest rates inhibited growth. On 13
September Italy devalued the lira and withdrew from the ERM, in spite of the Bundesbank spending DM 24 billion in a week to
protect the lira. Speculators then turned on
the pound, which had fallen to DM 2.79, on
16 September. The government spent £10
billion of its currency reserves to maintain
the value of the pound and in increasing desperation raised interest rates twice in the day:
first from 10 per cent to 12 per cent and then
to 15 per cent. All was in vain, so the Chancellor Norman Lamont had shamefacedly to
announce that Britain was withdrawing from
the ERM and that the pound would be
allowed to float: it fell to DM 2.65.

Black Wednesday destroyed the government's reputation for economic competence,
a reputation which had helped it to win the
1992 general election: immediately the
LABOUR PARTY's lead in the Gallup poll
doubled from 7.6 per cent to 16.4 per cent.
The economic effects, however, were beneficial, as exports were made more competitive, interest rates gradually fell, as did
unemployment, and there was a rise on the
stock market.

'Black Wednesday', B. Jones in *Talking Politics*, vol. 5, no. 3 (1993)

Blair, Anthony Charles Lynton ('Tony') (1953–)

Prime Minister of Britain
(1997–). Born in Edinburgh, he was educated at a Scottish private school and at Oxford
University. He qualified as a lawyer, was
called to the Bar in 1976 and became a Labour
MP in 1983. Affable, self-confident and lucid,
he rose rapidly in the LABOUR PARTY to
become the youngest member of the Shadow
Cabinet in 1988. Neil Kinnock appointed him
to speak on employment, a position in which
Blair combined support for the European
Social Chapter with acceptance of many of
Margaret THATCHER's measures on TRADE
UNIONS, such as ballots before strikes and
limits to secondary action. As Shadow Home
Secretary in 1992 he again stole the Conservatives' clothes by making Labour a strict law
and order party. His success on the front
bench was such that he became leader of the
Labour Party when John Smith died suddenly
from a heart attack in 1994.

Blair was convinced that the Labour Party
had lost the 1992 election because it was out of
touch with public opinion and had not
adapted quickly enough to changing circumstances. The working class, Labour's core
support, had contracted with the decline of
the old mass-production industries such as
steel and textiles. The Labour Party must
therefore appeal to the population as a whole
by shedding its image of a party dominated by
the trade unions and wedded to high taxation
and public expenditure. Tony Blair persuaded it to revise Clause IV, which committed the party to the common ownership

of the means of production, and to declare support for the market economy. He converted the Labour Party to European-style Social Democracy, which rejected KEYNE-SIANISM and the belief that the state could promote growth and employment by demand management. Low inflation would be a main economic objective of a Labour government, along with a strict control of social expenditure. The 1997 general election was a triumph for Blair and New Labour. The CONSERVATIVE PARTY suffered its worst defeat since 1906, losing 177 seats and ending up with 165. In the electoral landslide Labour won 419 seats.

Tony Blair became the youngest Prime Minister in Britain since Lord Liverpool in 1812 and began with a flurry of reforms, which included the most far-reaching constitutional changes since the First World War. Referenda approved of the election of a Welsh Assembly and of a Scottish Parliament with tax-raising powers (see SCOTTISH DEVOLU-TION). The European Convention on Human Rights was incorporated into British law and a Freedom of Information Act was promised, as was the abolition of the voting rights in the House of Lords of hereditary peers. In 1998 London will have an elected mayor. The Chancellor of the Exchequer, Gordon Brown, was determined to deal 'with the perception of Labour as the tax, spend, borrow party' and accepted the tight spending limits of his Tory predecessor, Kenneth Clarke, and guaranteed not to raise income tax for two years. He was innovative in handing to the Bank of England control over interest rates and in removing from the bank its regulation of the financial services. To protect the consumer from the abuse of financial services, such as the collapse of Barings Bank and the closure of the Bank of Credit and Commerce International after massive fraud, he set up the Securities and Investment Board. The new board was to bring together regulation of banking, securities and insurance and for the first time in its 300-year history Lloyd's came under an external regulator. The Chan-cellor's first budget used a windfall tax on public utilities to fund welfare to work schemes. For many of its economic policies the Blair government used the US as a model. There President CLINTON had imposed a public sector squeeze and a reduction in the budget deficit, which was accompanied by a fall in long-term interest rates, low inflation and an investment boom. The government's five-year deficit reduction programme was taken from the US, in the belief that a reduction of the deficit would lower inflation and long-term interest rates, and give scope for savings to finance private industry rather than public debt.

boat people   Migrants who fled by sea from Vietnam on a large scale from 1975, when the VIETNAM WAR ended and the communist North took over the South. Initially, they were political refugees, connected with the Saigon administration, who feared persecution by the communists. They sailed in unseaworthy, overcrowded boats with inadequate food and water and were the prey of pirates: many, perhaps a third, were lost at sea. Later, the boat people were mainly economic refugees, fleeing from starvation and the government's decision to close down private businesses and transfer many city-dwellers to the countryside. In the late 1970s, when Sino-Vietnamese relations deteriorated and China invaded Vietnam in 1979, boat people were ethnically Chinese from both North and South Vietnam.

They arrived in southern Thailand, Indonesia, Malaysia, Singapore, the Philippines and Hong Kong, some even reaching South Korea, Japan and Australia. They were generally not welcomed. In 1988 Hong Kong and a year later all ASEAN countries started screening to distinguish political refugees from the vast majority of economic migrants, whom they hoped to return to Vietnam. That country, however, did not want them back, as it had taken a large number of Vietnamese refugees from Laos. Many were held in disagreeable holding camps for long periods: the British and Vietnamese governments did not agree until 1992 on the forcible repatriation of 55,000 boat people in Hong Kong. About one and a half million were resettled in other countries, particularly the US, which took over 600,000 (420,000 from Vietnam, 100,000 from Laos and 78,000 Cambodians), and Australia 150,000. By 1994, when the US lifted its trade embargo on Vietnam, about 60,000 refugees remained in camps, mainly in Hong Kong.

Bolger, James Brendan (1935–)   Prime Minister of New Zealand (1990–7). The son of Irish Catholic immigrants, he left school at the age of 15 to work on the family farm. He entered parliament in 1972, held several posts in Muldoon's government and became leader of the National Party in 1986. In 1990 the National Party won an overwhelming election victory over the Labour government, so Jim Bolger became Prime Minister. He, and particularly his Finance Minister, Ruth Richardson, continued the policies of Robert Douglas in the LANGE Labour government which the electorate had rejected. As there was a large government deficit, public spending was slashed and the number of civil servants cut by more than half. The Employment Contracts Act of 1991 emasculated the trade unions by ending compulsory unionism and the right of collective bargaining and by limiting their ability to take industrial action. The WELFARE STATE, largely untouched by Douglas, still stood in the way of the free enterprise society, so Richardson proceeded to destroy it by what critics called 'ruthenasia'. Universal benefits were abolished, the automatic right to an old age pension being replaced by a means-tested pension. Unemployment, widows', sickness and single parent allowances were cut by between 9 per cent and 25 per cent. Health care was 'targeted' so that only those on low incomes received free health care. Most people paid the full costs of doctors' visits, prescriptions and out-

patient charges. Public housing rents had been limited to 25 per cent of a tenant's income: they now rose to market levels, so the poor could spend 35–50 per cent of their income on rent. The poorest were most badly affected, as their rents rose as their benefits dropped. The new policies increased the rate of economic growth (at 7 per cent in 1994 it was the fastest growing of all OPEC countries), unemployment fell from 11 to 7 per cent (1991–4) and inflation was kept at under 2 per cent. However, the increase in inequality has been more marked in New Zealand than anywhere else in the developed world and there has been a sharp rise in crime and in the prison population. The number of those in poverty (as defined by the 1972 Royal Commission) increased from 360,000 in 1990 to 510,000 in 1993, one in seven of the population.

Support for Bolger dropped sharply in the 1993 election, the National Party winning 50 seats (a loss of 17) and the Labour Party 45 (a gain of 16). Eventually he was able to form a coalition government but had even more difficulty after the 1996 election, a defeat for the right which held 53 out of 120 seats, the centre-left winning 50. The balance of power lay with New Zealand First, led by Winston Peters, a populist and nationalist party opposed to immigration and foreign investment. Bolger was able to continue in office only by making an unholy alliance with Peters, who became Deputy Prime Minister. Within a year there were financial scandals and the coalition was profoundly unpopular, leaving Bolger in a precarious position. Opposition to him grew within his party, too, and in November 1997 he was forced to stand down as leader of the National Party and as Prime Minister.

Botha, Pieter Willem (1916–)   Prime Minister (1978–84) and President (1984–9) of South Africa. The son of a wealthy Orange Free State farmer, he became a full-time organizer for the National Party in 1936. A member of the *Ossewabrandwag* ('ox-wagon guard'), a pro-Nazi organization, he entered parliament in 1948 and was appointed Minister of Community Development and Coloured Affairs (1961–6) by VERWOERD and Minister of Defence (1966–78) by VORSTER. When he became Prime Minister in 1978 he surprised many by telling white South Africans that they must 'adapt or die' and that APARTHEID was 'a recipe for permanent conflict'. Realizing after the Soweto riots that repression alone was not enough, he adopted the 'total strategy' of the French General Beaufre, who maintained that winning 'the hearts and minds' of the people was necessary to counter the appeal of guerrillas. Repression and reform must therefore be combined to sustain white domination. A government commission of 1979 pointed the way by recommending the recognition of black trade unions and the right to strike and the end of job reservation for whites. The pass laws were finally abolished in 1986 and many 'petty *apartheid*' constraints removed. The ban on 'mixed marriages' (of whites with other races) and on sexual relations of whites with blacks and coloureds was abandoned, as was the compulsory segregation of hotels, restaurants and beaches. These concessions to non-whites led to a split in the National Party, with Andries Treurnicht and some extremists breaking away to form the Conservative Party in 1982. The parliament represented only whites, so Botha gave some political rights to Indians and coloureds (of mixed race) in the tricameral constitution of 1983. This provided for two new parliaments, one for coloureds and one for Indians, which would control such matters as health and education for their own communities. All other matters would continue to be dealt with by the white parliament. At the same time a new office of State President, with wide powers, was created (Botha was the first President). There was no parliament for the Africans, 73 per cent of the population, as they were held to have their own representatives in the BANTUSTANS. This attempt to share power while retaining overall white control was a failure, as the elections for the new assemblies were boycotted by most Indian and coloured voters.

At the same time as he carried out some reforms at home, Botha sought to crush the guerrillas, who were operating from bases abroad, and the governments who supported them. He therefore raided ANC centres in Lesotho, Swaziland, Zimbabwe and Botswana and destabilized the neighbouring states of Angola and Mozambique by supporting rebel movements, Renamo in Mozambique and UNITA in Angola. He had some success in 1984, when Mozambique agreed to expel ANC guerrillas in exchange for South Africa ending support for Renamo, but South Africa suffered a severe military defeat in 1987 at Cuito Cuanavale in Angola. Botha had to agree to free elections in Namibia (which SWAPO won in 1989 with 57 per cent of the vote) in return for Soviet and Cuban withdrawal from Angola. Meanwhile, the economic situation deteriorated in South Africa: as the price of gold fell there was a balance of payments crisis, a reliance on loans from the IMF, inflation, unemployment and a fall in the standard of living for all South Africans. To add to Botha's troubles there were BLACK TOWNSHIP REVOLTS from 1984–6, in which the government's authority there collapsed, but in his 'Rubicon address' he rejected any idea of majority rule or of giving way to foreign pressure. The result was the collapse of the rand (the South African currency), the imposition of sanctions by the US, most COMMONWEALTH and EC nations (except Britain) and the visit of South African business leaders to the ANC in Lusaka. In February 1989 Botha's cabinet forced him to step down as Prime Minister in favour of DE KLERK, though he insisted on remaining President. In August KAUNDA announced that de Klerk would visit Zambia. Botha disapproved because of Kaunda's support for the ANC, but the cabinet supported de Klerk, so Botha resigned as President and retired. In 1990 he resigned from the National Party because of its political reforms.

The Apartheid State in Crisis, R. M. Price (1991)

Malan to De Klerk, R. Schrire (ed.) (1994)

Forty Lost Years: The Apartheid State and the Politics of the National Party, 1948–94, D. O'Meara (1996)

Bourguiba, Habib Ben Ali (1903–)
President of Tunisia (1957–87). The son of a Tunisian officer in the French army, he studied law in Paris and married a French-woman. In 1921 he joined the nationalist Destour Party but in 1934 broke away and formed with others the more radical Neo-Destour, which gradually took the lead in the campaign for independence. He was imprisoned from 1934–6, from 1938–43, and from 1952–4, until the government of MENDÈS-FRANCE decided that, after the disaster of DIEN BIEN PHU in Indochina and the outbreak of the ALGERIAN WAR OF INDEPENDENCE, Tunisia should be granted self-government. It was given autonomy in 1954 and, at Bourguiba's insistence, complete independence in 1956. The Bey included Neo-Destour members in his cabinet and made Bourguiba Prime Minister, but he did not want to share power and in 1957 deposed the Bey and declared a republic. A new constitution in 1957, which gave nearly all power to the President, made Bourguiba virtually a dictator in a one-party state.

A Francophile, he began to turn Tunisia into a Western, secular state, much as Kemal Atatürk had done in Turkey in the 1920s and 1930s. French, rather than Arabic, was the official language of government, higher education and élite society. Land held by religious foundations was nationalized, Quranic schools absorbed into the state system, *Sharia* (Islamic law) courts abolished and Zaytouna, a famous centre of Islamic learning, closed. Polygamy was forbidden, as was the wearing of headscarves by women; marriage and divorce became civil matters. His foreign policy, too, was pro-Western: he was aloof to the Arab cause in the SIX DAY WAR (1967),

regarding hostility to Israel as 'self-destructive and economically wasteful'.

The economy flourished in the 1970s as oil was discovered and produced half of export earnings and MULTINATIONAL CORPORATIONS invested in Tunisia, but it could not keep pace with the growing population and there were many unemployed. When there was a general strike in 1978 he ordered the army to crush it and dozens were killed. In the early 1980s a slump in oil prices and mounting INTERNATIONAL DEBT led to economic decline. The IMF insisted on austerity measures, which were unpopular. These provided an opportunity for the *Mouvement de la Tendance Islamique* (MTI) to appear as the greatest challenge to the regime. There had been an Islamic revival in Tunisia since 1978–9, promoted by the Egyptian MUSLIM BROTHERHOOD, the oil-rich states of Libya and Saudi Arabia and the IRANIAN REVOLUTION led by KHOMEINI. Bourguiba, who loathed ISLAMIC FUNDAMENTALISTS, said he would 'eradicate the fundamentalist poison' and accused the MTI of being an Iranian puppet. Thousands of opponents were imprisoned and in a major trial some MTI leaders were sentenced to death. By this time Bourguiba, isolated and intolerant, President for life since 1974, was in poor health (he had a stroke as early as 1967). He made General Ben Ali Prime Minister in October 1987: a month later the general deposed the 84-year-old President, claiming that Bourguiba was not physically or mentally able to rule.

The State and Social Transformation in Tunisia and Libya, L. Anderson (1987)

Brandt, Willy (1913–92)   Chancellor of the Federal Republic of Germany (1969–74). Born illegitimate with the name of Herbert Frahm in the Baltic port of Lübeck, he spent much of his youth in socialist activities. When the Nazis seized power in 1933 he fled to Norway, took Norwegian nationality and graduated at the University of Oslo. He moved to Sweden in 1940 when Germany invaded Norway. During his exile he adopted the name Willy Brandt and retained it after the war, when he returned to Germany as a correspondent for Scandinavian newspapers. He resumed his German citizenship in 1947 and was a member of the SPD (Social Democratic Party) in the Bundestag from 1949–57, when he became Mayor of West Berlin (1957–66). Brandt rallied the West Berliners when the BERLIN WALL was built in 1961, a stark contrast to Chancellor ADENAUER's indecision. In 1964 he became Chairman of the SPD and two years later formed a Grand Coalition with the CDU (Christian Democratic Union), taking the posts of Vice-Chancellor and Foreign Minister. In this capacity he established diplomatic relations with Romania (1967) and Yugoslavia (1968), thus abandoning the Hallstein Doctrine.

Brandt's greatest success came in 1969, when he changed coalition parteners, forming an alliance with the FDP (Free Democratic Party) and became Chancellor. He expanded the WELFARE STATE by increasing pensions for the old and disabled and in 1972 gave works' councils greater control over working conditions. Higher education was also extended: the 26 West German universities and polytechnics in 1964 had increased to 49 ten years later. His record on civil liberties was more ambiguous. He provided for abortion on demand in the first 12 weeks of pregnancy but when the Constitutional Court declared this illegal, as it contravened the 'right to life', he replaced it with a law allowing abortion on medical grounds only. Brandt was much criticized for agreeing with state governments on loyalty checks after a resurgence of urban violence: civil servants and teachers who opposed democratic institutions could be dismissed. The Chancellor faced severe economic problems. The public debt increased by 42 per cent from 1969–73, partly because of large wage increases in the public sector and greater spending on welfare, but also owing to events outside Brandt's control.

President NIXON had in 1971 ended the system of fixed exchange rates agreed at Bretton Woods in 1944: large amounts of capital flowed into Germany, adding to inflation. The OPEC PRICE RISE, which arose from the YOM KIPPUR WAR in 1973, also increased inflation, which trebled to reach 7 per cent. Growth fell to almost zero in 1974, when unemployment was nearing a million for the first time since the 1950s.

Much of the Chancellor's time was taken up with OSTPOLITIK, his determined attempt to improve relations with the communist bloc and particularly with the GDR (German Democratic Republic: East Germany). This was unpopular with many members of the FDP, who sided with the CDU in a no-confidence motion, which Brandt survived by only two votes. Brandt had been awarded the Nobel Peace Prize in 1971 for his *Ostpolitik* and fought the 1972 general election on this single issue. With 45 per cent of the vote the SPD for the first time outvoted the CDU, whose 44.9 per cent was its lowest since 1949. This electoral endorsement of *Ostpolitik* was a triumph for Brandt. Both the FRG and GDR were admitted as members of the UNITED NATIONS in 1973. A year later Brandt resigned when a leading aide, Gunter Guillaume, was exposed as a GDR spy. He then found a new career championing the poor throughout the world. A member of the European Parliament (1979–83), he chaired committees on the GLOBAL ECONOMY and in 1980 produced the Brandt Report. This dealt with the NORTH–SOUTH DIVIDE and recommended a change in trade relations, whereby the rich North would help the poor South. A second report in 1983 forecast 'conflict and catastrophe' unless more aid was given to South.

Germany from Partition to Reunification, H. A. Turner (1992)

A History of West Germany, vol. 2, 1963–91, D. L. Bark and D. R. Gress (1993)

German Politics, 1945–95, P. Pulzer (1995)

Brezhnev, Leonid Ilich (1906–82) First Secretary (from 1966 General Secretary) of the CPSU (Communist Party of the Soviet Union) (1964–82) and President of the USSR (1977–82). Trained as a land surveyor in the 1920s, he joined the CPSU in 1931, studied engineering and graduated in 1935. During the Second World War he was a political commissar in the Red Army and after it became Party boss in Moldavia (1950) and then in Kazakhstan (1955), where he implemented KHRUSHCHEV's 'virgin lands' scheme. In 1957 he became a full member of the Presidium (Politburo) and in 1960 Chairman of the Supreme Soviet (parliament). He led the group which forced Khrushchev to retire in 1964, replacing him as First Secretary of the CPSU in the collective leadership. Kosygin, the Prime Minister, was at first more important and took the lead from 1964–8 in economic and foreign affairs, but as General Secretary Brezhnev was able to put his supporters into positions of power and by 1971 was the dominant figure. Cheerful and sociable, he treated his colleagues courteously and had considerable charm but he was not as intelligent as Khrushchev. He had no original ideas and did not introduce any major economic or political reforms (GORBACHEV called the period 1965–85 'an era of stagnation'). The short, sturdy, beetle-browed Brezhnev was exceptionally vain and self-indulgent and, though not a charismatic figure, tried to build a cult of personality round himself.

'Stability of cadres' was his slogan in the 1970s, which meant that those in key positions held them for life: it was very popular among the NOMENKLATURA. Throughout his period of office GNP was growing at an ever-smaller rate, but Brezhnev was fortunate that as the Caspian oil-fields began to decline in the 1970s, new ones in Western Siberia came on stream and huge natural gas reserves were discovered there, too. The Stalinist system continued with central direction of the economy: Gosplan, the main planning ministry, expanded. Inefficiency and bottlenecks

proliferated but Brezhnev was lucky again with the OPEC PRICE RISE in 1973 and with the rise in the price of gold, too (the USSR was the world's second largest producer). Though agriculture languished (capitalization increased by 160 per cent) from 1965–80, output by 20 per cent and grain had to be imported, he was able to provide many benefits for Soviet citizens. Real wages doubled from 1960–80, there were more hospital beds, higher education and consumer goods (televisions, refrigerators, washing machines) and an improved diet (the consumption of meat, fish and fruit increased by 50 per cent). The minimum wage was raised, there was a five-day working week and longer holidays. Workers, with job security and an easy life, were satisfied with the communist system.

Brezhnev continued Khrushchev's policy of peaceful coexistence but this did not prevent him from competing with the US for influence in areas which the Soviet Union had previously neglected. The SIX DAY WAR (1967) was a serious set-back for the USSR, as its Arab allies were comprehensively defeated. Soviet intervention in Czechoslovakia in the PRAGUE SPRING (1968) and the BREZHNEV DOCTRINE to justify it was another embarrassment, though he had no further trouble with his East European satellites until 1980, when SOLIDARITY arose in Poland. On that occasion prompt action by General JARUZELSKI made any Soviet response unnecessary. DÉTENTE continued and reached its peak with the SALT agreement with President NIXON in 1972 to limit the spread of nuclear weapons and with the HELSINKI FINAL ACT (1975), which recognized all existing European frontiers and spelt out the human rights which signatories were to accept.

Soviet–US relations came under strain when the Soviet Union built an ocean-going navy, with guided missile ships and its first aircraft carriers. In the 1970s there was a Soviet naval squadron permanently in the Mediterranean and a smaller one in the Indian

Ocean. For the first time the USSR intervened on a large scale in Africa and was given the opportunity to do so with the fall of Emperor HAILE SELASSIE in Ethiopia and the PORTUGUESE REVOLUTION of the same year, which brought an end to PORTUGAL´S COLONIAL WARS. President SADAT had expelled Soviet advisers from Egypt in 1972, but two years later in a pact with Somalia the USSR obtained the use of the port of Berbera on the Gulf in Aden and was able to use Aden too after an agreement with South Yemen. When Somali irredentism led to an attack on Ethiopia in 1977, MENGISTU asked for Soviet help. The USSR therefore changed sides, airlifted Cuban troops to Ethiopia and was expelled from Somalia, but was able to use the Ethiopian port of Massawa. Brezhnev supported the Marxist governments of Angola and Mozambique during the ANGOLAN and MOZAMBICAN CIVIL WARS which followed independence but Soviet influence in Africa was short-lived, as all its client states turned to the US-dominated IMF and WORLD BANK for the financial help the USSR could not provide. Détente came to an end with the SOVIET INVASION OF AFGHANISTAN (1979), which provoked a hostile American reaction. Brezhnev's health had been poor from 1968, when he had a heart attack. Five years later arteriosclerosis affected his nervous system. His speech became slurred, his breathing laboured and his concentration limited. For the last six years of his life he was unable to do any serious work.

Khrushchev and Brezhnev as Leaders, G. W. Breslauer (1982)

Brezhnev Doctrine (1968)   Announced to justify Soviet troops crushing the PRAGUE SPRING. BREZHNEV said that the Soviet Union had the right to interfere in the internal affairs of its satellite states in Eastern Europe if the communist system was threatened. The doctrine was not new and had been applied by STALIN in the SHOW TRIALS in Eastern

Europe. It effectively ended political and, to a large extent, economic reform in those states. The HELSINKI FINAL ACT (1975) negated the Brezhnev Doctrine ('No one should try', Brezhnev said in Helsinki, 'to dictate to other peoples how they should manage their internal affairs') but it was not finally abandoned until GORBACHEV repudiated it in 1988.

Brown v Board of Education of Topeka (1954)   US Supreme Court judgement that segregation in public schools was unconstitutional. The decision resulted from a case brought by the NAACP (National Association for the Advancement of Colored People) on behalf of an 11-year-old girl who, by order of the Topeka School Board in Kansas, was forced to attend a negro school. The ruling reversed that of *Plessy v Ferguson* (1896), which said that segregation did not violate the fourteenth amendment of the constitution (this guaranteed equal protection of the laws to all, provided that equal facilities were provided for each race). The 'separate but equal' doctrine had provided a legal sanction for segregation in other public places. Chief Justice Earl WARREN obtained a unanimous decision by persuading his fellow judges that segregation was based on an intolerable and discredited theory of racial superiority and that segregation in public schools was unconstitutional because 'separate educational facilities are inherently inferior'. He realized that gradual change was necessary to give time for attitudes to alter, so he did not set a time table for desegregation, though in 1955 the Supreme Court called for 'all deliberate speed'.

The court ruling was warmly welcomed by liberals and moderates in the North but most Southerners indignantly denounced it as a violation of states' rights or as an attempt to change their social system. President EISENHOWER made no comment on the court's decision but opposed suggestions that he should use federal power to enforce it, until he was forced to do so at LITTLE ROCK. In the Upper South and border states a start was made in desegregating schools, particularly in the big cities like Washington, but in the Deep South there was prolonged, and often violent, resistance from White Citizens' Councils. White parents sent their children to private schools (unaffected by the court ruling) or even closed down the public schools. Most evaded the court decision by passing local 'pupil placement' laws, which made it possible to reject black pupils in white schools on grounds other than race, such as scholarly aptitude or the psychological ability to adapt to a new environment. The Supreme Court upheld Alabama's 'pupil placement' law in 1958 and so helped to maintain the segregation it had declared unlawful. The controversy was far from settled 20 years later, as the busing issue showed. In 1994 66 per cent of black children still attended black schools and 450 school districts remained under federal court supervision to ensure desegregation took place. *Brown v Topeka* became the basis for rejecting segregation in nearly all other areas of life and greatly encouraged the CIVIL RIGHTS MOVEMENT, which became more confident and active, as the MONTGOMERY BUS BOYCOTT indicated.

Bush, George Herbert Walker (1924–)

President of the United States (1989–93). From a prosperous family (his father was a partner in a Wall Street investment firm and a US Senator from 1952–63) he attended private schools and then served as a navy pilot from 1942–5 in the Second World War, winning the Distinguished Flying Cross. At the end of the war he read economics at Yale, graduating in 1948 before going to Texas to make a fortune in the oil business. President NIXON appointed him as ambassador to the UNITED NATIONS (1971–2), after which he was Chairman of the Republican National Committee (1972–4), at the time of WATERGATE, when he had the unpleasant task of presiding over Nixon's resignation. President FORD made him ambassador to China (1974–5) and then director of the CIA (1976–7). He tried to become the presidential nominee of the REPUBLICAN PARTY in 1980 but withdrew late in the primaries when it became clear that Ronald REAGAN would be nominated and instead became his running mate. After Reagan was elected as President, Bush served for eight years as Vice-President, becoming the Republican presidential candidate in 1988 when Reagan retired. He won the election comfortably carrying 38 states, though the DEMOCRATIC PARTY had a majority in both houses of Congress.

Bush devoted most of his time to foreign affairs. He soured relations with China by condemning the TIANANMEN SQUARE MASSACRE. In Central America he continued Reagan's policy of looking on the SANDINISTA government in Nicaragua as a Soviet and Cuban puppet. He would not endorse the peace plan drawn up by President Arias of Costa Rica and other Central American presidents, but continued to send aid to the CONTRAS and to maintain the blockade which crippled the Nicaraguan economy. US INTERVENTION IN PANAMA in December 1980 to get rid of the Noriega regime was successful and popular in the US, though many in Latin America disliked the revival of 'big stick' diplomacy.

The REVOLUTIONS OF 1988–91, when communism in Eastern Europe collapsed, brought an astonishing decline in the fortunes of the Soviet Union. Bush avoided triumphalism, discouraged GORBACHEV from intervening in the Baltic states when they sought their independence and persuaded him to accept GERMAN REUNIFICATION, when other Western leaders were opposed to it. He developed a close 'partnership' with Gorbachev: its greatest achievement was the signing of START (Strategic Arms Reduction Treaty) in July 1991 and other arms reduction measures.

The first great crisis in the post-COLD WAR era took place in the Persian Gulf, when Saddam HUSSEIN invaded Kuwait on

2 August 1990 and annexed it. This began a series of events which led to the GULF WAR, which, like the KOREAN WAR of 1950–3, was essentially a war waged by the US. Bush showed great diplomatic skills in assembling an international coalition, which included Arab nations, to fight Iraq, but nearly all the equipment and most of the troops were provided by the US and an American general was in command. The ground battle lasted only four days in February 1991, before Bush called a cease-fire. He has been much criticized for this, as it enabled Saddam Hussein to survive as ruler of Iraq, but Bush had no UN mandate to overthrow Saddam and any attempt to do so would have led to the collapse of his coalition, as the Arab states would have left it. The war ended on a sour note, as Bush incited the SHIIS and Kurds to rebel against Saddam and then left them to their fate. It did not create stability in the Gulf or promote democracy there, as the despotic al-Sabah regime was restored in Kuwait.

At home the economy declined in 1990 and then remained stagnant for the rest of his presidency. Unemployment rose (reaching ten million in 1992), as did corporate and personal bankruptcies. This recession was different from previous ones, which had affected mainly factory workers and farmers, as it hit the managerial élite (accountants, lawyers, bankers, stockbrokers). The giant MULTINATIONAL CORPORATIONS, such as IBM (International Business Machines), made tens of thousands redundant. The decline in Bush's popularity was enhanced by his breaking his word on taxes. In the 1988 election campaign he had foolishly pledged: 'Read my lips. No new taxes'. By the summer of 1990 he had decided that tax increases were necessary to reduce the federal deficit. In October he raised the top income tax rate from 27 per cent to 31 per cent and increased taxes on petroleum, cigarettes, alcohol and several luxury items. Riots in Los Angeles, reminiscent of the BLACK GHETTO RIOTS of the 1960s, added to his problems. In the presidential election of 1992 he was defeated by Bill CLINTON, the young and comparatively unknown Governor of Arkansas, who won in 32 states to Bush's 18. Bush's popular vote (38 per cent) was the lowest by a Republican candidate since Barry Goldwater.

George Bush and the Guardianship Presidency,
    D. Mervin (1996)

Buthelezi, Mangosuthu Gatsha (1928–)
Zulu chief and South African politician. Descended from the Zulu king Cetshwayo he became hereditary chief of the Buthelezi clan in 1953 and adviser to two Zulu kings. He was expelled from Fort Hare, a university college for Africans, in 1952 for ANC Youth League activities and, hostile to VERWOERD'S APARTHEID, he opposed the creation of KwaZulu as a BANTUSTAN (homeland) for the Zulus. Chief Minister of KwaZULU from 1972, Buthelezi formed Inkatha, a political movement to give Africans pride in their own culture and to take a stand against racism and separate development.

By the early 1980s he had moved away from the ANC, as he rejected socialism, its armed struggle to overthrow the government, and international sanctions, as they deprived blacks of jobs. These attitudes made Buthelezi very popular with the South African and many foreign governments and with liberal whites, but he was denounced by BLACK CONSCIOUSNESS leaders as a collaborator and began a bitter sruggle with the ANC, as he sought to make Inkatha the largest African political organization in the country. He rejected 'independence' for KwaZulu, offered by the South African government, as he wanted a federal state in which KwaZulu would have a major role, as the seven million Zulus were South Africa's largest ethnic group. In the Soweto riots (1976) he came down on the side of order and was accused of being a government stooge, but he campaigned against BOTHA's tricameral constitution (1983), which created representative bodies for coloureds (of mixed race) and

Indians but not for blacks. There were increasingly bloody clashes between ANC and Inkatha supporters in the BLACK TOWNSHIP REVOLTS in Natal, in which an estimated 4,000 people were killed (1985–90). When multiparty talks began in 1991 about South Africa's future Buthelezi pressed for a federation of independent states. Though Inkatha gained only 10 per cent of the vote in the 1994 elections it had a majority in KwaZulu–Natal. Buthelezi became Minister of Home Affairs in the new government of national unity headed by Nelson MANDELA.

Marginalized since 1994, when he was dismissed as Chief Minister of KwaZulu–Natal by the Zulu king, he refused to take part in making a new constitution and sought to undermine the ANC by continuing the attacks on ANC supporters in KwaZulu–Natal, which by 1997 had produced 14,000 deaths. He backed the hardliners in Inkatha who were not prepared to compromise but was increasingly opposed by moderates in the party, who included the chairman, Ben Ngubane, who wanted a dialogue with the ANC and an end to confrontation. Buthelezi's weakening power base was evident in the 1996 municipal elections, when Inkatha gained only 1 per cent of the vote outside Kwa-Zulu–Natal. Even there it lost ground to the ANC, which won control of the larger cities.

An Appetite for Power: Buthelezi's Inkatha and the Politics of Loyal Resistance, G. Mare and G. Hamilton (1987)
Gatsha Buthelezi: Chief with a Double Agenda, Mzala (1988)

Butler, Richard Austen ('Rab'), Baron (1902–82)

British politician. Born in India, where his father was a member of the Indian Civil Service, he obtained first class honours in history and French at Cambridge University before he was elected as a Conservative MP in 1929. Appointed Under Secretary of State for India in 1932, he saw the India Act (1935), which gave autonomy to the Indian provinces, through the House of Commons. In 1938 he was Under Secretary at the Foreign Office and an arch-appeaser, strongly approving the Munich agreement. Soon after Winston CHURCHILL became Prime Minister he made Butler President of the Board of Education (1941–5), where he was responsible for the Education Act of 1944, which established the framework of state education for the next generation. The Act received much praise at the time, as it provided secondary education for all based on selection at 11 for grammar, secondary modern or technical schools. As there were few technical schools, the new system simply reinforced the existing class division in education: nearly all working-class children went to the secondary modern schools, the grammar schools being filled predominantly with middle-class pupils. Butler, however, allowed local education authorities to introduce comprehensive schools for all pupils: by 1964 there were 200 and by 1974 2,000, with 60 per cent of all pupils. When the CONSERVAT-IVE PARTY was in opposition from 1945–51 Butler was head of the Conservative Research Department. Like Harold MACMILLAN, a 'one-nation' Tory, he adjusted Conservative policies to the postwar consensus in what became known as BUTSKELLISM. In 1947 a committee on which he sat produced *The Industrial Charter*, which accepted state intervention in the economy and talked of the case for leaving certain industries nationalized. 'Our first purpose', he wrote later, 'was to counter the charge...that full employment and the WELFARE STATE were not safe in our hands'.

Butler became Chancellor of the Exchequer (1951–5) in Churchill's second administration and began the 'stop-go' policies which were characteristic of the 1950s and 1960s. Faced with a balance of payments deficit he increased the bank rate (from 2 per cent to 4 per cent) for the first time since 1932 and so began the classic means of imposing a credit squeeze to reduce demand. With a balance of payments surplus by 1953 he moved to the 'go' phase and reduced income tax. He did this again in 1955 as an election was approaching, but this time with unfortunate results: inflation, a run on sterling and a fall in the balance of payments. Shortly after the Conservatives won the election he had to introduce a supplementary budget which clawed back in the autumn all that had been given away in the spring. Macmillan therefore replaced him at the Treasury with Anthony EDEN in December 1955. In the SUEZ CRISIS Butler was prepared to use force only as a last resort, when all other options had been tried. He did not condemn collusion with the Israelis, but opposed the landing of British troops on 4 November and insisted two days later that the operation should be ended. After Suez he tried to minimize the damage to the government's reputation by tact and conciliation, but when Eden resigned Macmillan was chosen to be the new premier. 'I couldn't understand', he later complained, 'when I had done a most wonderful job – picking up the pieces after Suez – that they then chose Harold'.

Macmillan made him Home Secretary (1957–62). At the Home Office he supported penal reform and built more prisons but retained capital punishment. Reluctantly he introduced the IMMIGRATION ACT (1962), which for the first time restricted COMMONWEALTH immigration. His greatest success at this time was to bring the CENTRAL AFRICAN FEDERATION to an end. Butler was one of the seven cabinet ministers sacked by Macmillan in 1962 in the 'Night of the Long Knives'. When Macmillan resigned owing to ill-health Butler had the support of several ministers for the succession, but Macmillan reported to the queen that the majority of the cabinet and of the Conservative Party favoured the Earl of Home (see DOUGLAS-HOME). Butler would not intrigue or fight for the leadership. 'We put the gun in his hands', Enoch Powell recalled, 'and he refused to fire it'. When Douglas-Home became Prime Minister, Macleod and Powell refused to serve under him. 'He [Butler] lacked the last six

inches of steel', was Macmillan's ungenerous comment. Butler agreed to serve as Foreign Secretary under Douglas-Home but took no initiatives. After the Conservative defeat in the 1964 election he refused an earldom and when it was clear that his talents would be neglected by the Conservatives in opposition, he became Master of Trinity College, Cambridge (1965–78) and accepted a life peerage from Harold WILSON.

Churchill's Indian Summer, A. Seldon (1981)
Rab: The Life of R. A. Butler, A. Howard (1987)

Butskellism   *The Economist* referred in February 1954 to 'Mr Butskell', a compound of the names of R. A. BUTLER, a prominent member of the CONSERVATIVE PARTY, and of Hugh GAITSKELL, soon to be leader of the LABOUR PARTY. It implied that their policies were indistinguishable from one another and referred to the consensus which had grown up during the Second World War. In his first speech as Leader of the Opposition in 1945 Winston CHURCHILL said 'not only are we two parties in the House agreed on the main essentials of foreign policy ... but we also have an immense programme, prepared by our joint exertions during the Coalition. .... Here and there may be differences of emphasis and view but, in the main, no parliament has ever assembled with such a mass of agreed legislation'. Both parties agreed on the WELFARE STATE, full employment, a mixed economy and consultation with the TRADE UNIONS. Foreign and defence policies were also shared by the two parties: a commitment to NATO, the nuclear deterrent, DECOLONIZATION and the COMMONWEALTH. When Churchill was in office again from 1951–5 he privatized steel and road haulage but left under state control the other industries which the Labour Party had nationalized. He made no attempt to dismantle the Welfare State and in fact increased the real value of pensions and other benefits.

By 1951 the Labour Party had moved away from nationalization to KEYNESIANISM as a way of managing the economy. Gaitskell even tried (unsucessfully) to get rid of Clause IV, which committed Labour to the state ownership of production. Harold MACMILLAN, like Butler, was a 'one-nation' Tory, who had written about 'The Middle Way' as early as 1927 and when in office as Prime Minister (1957–63) was a determined interventionist and Keynesian. Butskellism continued until the late 1970s, when it was abandoned by Margaret THATCHER, though a different form of consensus appeared as the Labour Party under Tony BLAIR adopted a largely Conservative agenda.

Consensus Politics: From Attlee to Thatcher, D. Kavanagh and P. Morris (1988)
'The Rise and Fall (and Rise Again?) of the Post-war Consensus', A. Seldon in *Politics UK*, Bill Jones et al. (eds) (1994)

C

Callaghan, James, Baron (1912–)
British Prime Minister (1976–9). He grew up
in poverty in Portsmouth with his widowed
mother, who was a strict Baptist. A chapelgoer,
teetotaller and non-smoker, he worked for the
Inland Revenue as a clerk and rose to be head
of its white-collar union. When elected as a
Labour MP in 1945 he was on the right wing
of the LABOUR PARTY. In the 1950s he was a
supporter of Hugh GAITSKELL and acerbic
critic of Aneurin BEVAN, fiercely opposing
CND and unilateralism. He was a candidate
for the Party leadership in 1963 but lost to
Harold WILSON.

When Labour won the 1964 general election, Wilson made him Chancellor of the
Exchequer. Jim Callaghan was faced with
recurrent economic crises, which he met
with massive doses of deflation. He and the
Prime Minister refused to devalue until
forced to do so in 1967, a humiliating experience which led to his resignation and transfer
to the Home Office (1967–70). Here he was a
conservative figure who disliked the permissive society, took a firm stand on law and order
and limited COMMONWEALTH immigration.
During the TROUBLES in Northern Ireland
he sent British troops there to provide security and sought to protect the rights of the
Catholic minority. The most dramatic event
while he was Home Secretary was his opposition to IN PLACE OF STRIFE. He was
openly hostile, as he did not want to harm
the alliance of the Labour Party with the
TRADE UNIONS and supported a motion of
the National Executive Committee of the
Labour Party against the government of
which he was a member. This rejection of
cabinet responsibility led to calls for his resignation, but he refused to resign. Labour was
in opposition from 1970–4 but when it
returned to power, again with Wilson as
Prime Minister, Callaghan was a vigorous if
conservative Foreign Secretary (1974–6),
whose main aim was to build up the 'special
relationship' with the US. When Wilson
unexpectedly resigned in 1976, Callaghan
defeated Michael Foot by 176 votes to 137
for leadership of the Labour Party and
became Prime Minister.

His relaxed, avuncular bonhomie was very
popular (his popularity constantly exceeded
that of his party) and earned him the name
'Sunny Jim'. He was a great communicator,
whose blunt honesty appealed to the public,
as when he told the Labour Party Conference
in 1976 that 'You cannot now, if you ever
could, spend your way out of a recession'. A
highly astute and professional politician, a
fixer, he needed all his skill to cope with yet
another economic crisis in 1976. With unemployment of over a million, inflation at 16 per
cent, a record budget deficit and sterling falling, it appeared that government spending
was out of control: it had increased by 6 per
cent of GNP in two years. The government
needed a loan from the IMF, which demanded
massive spending cuts of £5 billion. Callaghan fought tenaciously to reduce these to
£2.5 billion and to keep his cabinet intact, so
that no one resigned over the issue. He succeeded. The severe cuts, the largest since the
Second World War (the proportion of GNP
spent on the social services fell from 1974–9)
were very unpopular and soon, with by-
election losses, Labour was a minority

government. Callaghan survived, as he first made a pact with the LIBERAL PARTY and when this ended because he could not commit himself to proportional representation, he had the support of the SNP because he promised a devolution bill.

Callaghan was not a great reformer. He had promised to reform the Official Secrets Act but did nothing and so blocked moves towards freedom of information. An Education Act required local authorities to abolish selection for secondary schools and brought direct grant schools into the public system, but it left the public (independent) schools alone. His Achilles heel proved to be the area where he was considered supreme: his relations with the trade unions. Callaghan had been expected to call an election in October 1978, which he might have won, as Labour was leading in the opinion polls, but his fateful delay produced the WINTER OF DISCONTENT, which was disastrous for the Labour Party (and in the long run for the unions) as it showed that Labour was no more able to deal effectively with the trade unions than the CONSERVATIVE PARTY. Though there were massive defections from Labour, it was not strikes which brought down the government but the referendum on devolution. When this was held in March 1979 33 per cent of all Scots voted for devolution but an amendment had been added to the bill which required a 40 per cent 'yes' vote. The SNP had no longer any reason to keep Labour in office: the government lost a vote of confidence by one vote and so Callaghan resigned. A year later, after a Conservative victory in the general election, he gave up the leadership of the Labour Party, accepted a life peerage and as an elder statesman in the Lords made a dignified and authoritative contribution to its debates.

Prime Minister: The Conduct of Policy Under Wilson and Callaghan, B. Donoughue (1987)
Callaghan: A Life, K. O. Morgan (1997)

Cambodia, US attack on (1969–73)

Prince SIHANOUK had managed to keep Cambodia out of the VIETNAM WAR by turning a blind eye on VIET CONG bases in eastern Cambodia and the Ho Chi Minh trail which passed through Cambodia and along which men and supplies moved from North to South Vietnam. President NIXON decided that the trail had to be blocked and the Viet Cong headquarters (which the American military thought was in Cambodia) destroyed. He ordered secret air strikes in 1969 and after Sihanouk had been overthrown by officers friendly to the US, announced on television in April 1970 that US and South Vietnamese troops were crossing into Cambodia to destroy the communist sanctuaries. The US therefore invaded a country with which it was not at war and began to withdraw in June without driving the Viet Cong out of Cambodia. Air raids, however, continued with a devastating effect.

In the next few years half the population abandoned the countryside to escape the air raids and moved to the towns: the population of the capital Phnom Penh rose from 600,000 to two million (1970–5). The bombing caused widespread starvation and created conditions in which the Khmer Rouge prospered. In February 1973 there was a cease-fire in Vietnam and Laos but the Khmer Rouge refused one. Nixon therefore ordered an intensification of the air raids: between February and August 1973, before the US Congress ordered an end to the bombing in Cambodia, 250,000 tons of bombs were dropped, one and a half times the total dropped on Japan in the Second World War. Between 1969 and 1973 the US dropped 540,000 tons of bombs on Cambodia, killing up to 150,000 civilians. The invasion of Cambodia intensified the VIETNAM ANTI-WAR MOVEMENT in the US, as it appeared to reverse the policy of 'bringing the boys home'.

Sideshow: Kissinger, Nixon and the Destruction of Cambodia, W. Shawcross (1979)

Camp David Accords (1978)   Agreements between Israel and Egypt. In September 1978 President CARTER brought Israeli Prime Minister Menachem BEGIN and President SADAT of Egypt to his Camp David retreat in Maryland, where two agreements were made. 'A framework for peace in the Middle East' sought to deal with the WEST BANK of the Jordan and the Gaza Strip, territories which the Israelis had occupied since the SIX DAY WAR (1967). There was to be a transitional period of at most five years during which those territories would obtain self-government. Their 'final status' would be decided before the end of the transitional period. It was not clear who would represent the Palestinians in the negotiations (Israel refused to talk to the PLO) and nothing was said about the Jewish settlements in the OCCUPIED TERRITORIES, a topic certain to engender a bitter dispute. 'A framework for peace between Israel and Egypt' laid the foundations for the Treaty of Washington (March 1979), by which the state of war, which had existed between the two countries since 1948, ended. Egypt recognized the state of Israel, established diplomatic relations and promised Israel the use of the Suez Canal and the Straits of Tiran. Israel agreed to withdraw completely from Sinai by 1982.

Sadat had promised other Arab states not to make a separate peace with Israel, so the Accords isolated Egypt in the Arab world. In November 1978 Egypt was expelled from the ARAB LEAGUE, which moved its headquarters from Cairo to Tunis and after the Washington Treaty Arab states broke off trade and diplomatic relations with Egypt and the GULF STATES cut off aid. For a decade Egypt was no longer the leader of the Arab World. In 1978 Sadat and Begin were awarded the Nobel Peace Prize.

Camp David, W. B. Quandt (1986)

Carter, James Earl (Jimmy) (1924–)
President of the United States (1977–81). The son of a Georgian landowner and businessman, he served in the submarine service of the US navy from 1946–53. When his father died he returned to Georgia to manage the family firm and peanut processing business. In 1962 he was elected to the Georgian state legislature and from 1971–5 was state Governor. A deeply religious man, he was influenced by the CIVIL RIGHTS MOVEMENT and sought to end racial discrimination. When he became the Democratic presidential candidate in 1976 his commitment to civil rights and his Southern background helped him to gain 80 per cent of the black vote and he narrowly defeated President FORD with 50.1 per cent of the popular vote.

At home he faced many problems (inflation, unemployment, falling production) which he was unable to cope with. Both unemployment and inflation doubled during his presidency and the budget deficit rose to $50 billion. He turned the DEMOCRATIC PARTY away from New Deal policies to deregulation, deregulating the airline industry and interstate trucking, natural gas and crude oil prices. In favour of AFFIRMATIVE ACTION and the Equal Rights Amendment, which would have banned sexual discrimination, he was unable to persuade enough states to support the latter for it to become law. Although Democrats had a large majority in both houses, Carter did not cultivate the powerful congressional leaders whose support was vital, so much of his proposed legislation (for tax reform, government reorganization and expanded health care) was rejected.

His foreign policy was, at first, based on idealism. 'Our commitment to human rights must be absolute', he affirmed in his inaugural, in stark contrast to KISSINGER's *realpolitik*. In February 1977 he reduced aid to Argentina, Uruguay and Ethiopia because of their poor human rights record and it was in Latin America that this policy was most successfully carried out. NIXON's policy of supporting the repressive junta in Chile was abandoned and in 1978 all military aid to Anastasio SOMOZA in Nicaragua was withdrawn. When the SANDINISTAS overthrew

Somoza in 1979 the US immediately recognized the left-wing Sandinista government and provided it with aid. Carter soon had to make exceptions of allies such as the Shah of Iran and had to ignore the human rights violations of powerful enemies like the Soviet Union. He wanted to free the US from its 'inordinate fear of communism', and continue Nixon's policy of DÉTENTE. In 1979 he signed the SALT II agreement with BREZHNEV in Vienna to limit the number of missile launchers. A real change came with the SOVIET INVASION OF AFGHANISTAN in 1979, which Carter called 'a stepping-stone to their possible control over much of the world's oil supplies'. This over-reaction to what was essentially a defensive measure to prevent the spread of ISLAMIC FUNDAMENTALISTS to the Muslim parts of the Soviet Union, led Carter to suspend efforts to secure ratification of the SALT II treaty by the Senate, to put an embargo on grain sales to the Soviet Union and to organize a boycott of the Olympic Games to be held in Moscow in 1980. Having promised to cut the military budget, he now proposed to increase it and issued the Carter Doctrine, stating that the US would be justified in preventing outside domination of the Persian Gulf, if necessary by military intervention.

Carter said in his inaugural that the elimination of nuclear weapons was his ultimate goal. Once again rhetoric differed from practice. He accelerated the arms race by developing several new weapons systems: the Missile Experimental (MX), difficult to attack because it could be shuttled along ten thousand miles of rails; the cruise missile, which could fly beneath radar and reach any part of the Soviet Union; and the neutron bomb, a tactical nuclear weapon with low heat and blast but high short-range radiation, so there would be minimum damage to civilians. The President had his successes in foreign affairs. He persuaded a reluctant Senate to ratify the Panama Canal Treaty that provided for complete American withdrawal from the Canal Zone by 2000. Carter also completed Nixon's

rapprochement with China by establishing full diplomatic relations with the People's Republic in 1979, at the same time severing relations with Taiwan. His most famous achievement was the CAMP DAVID ACCORDS (1978), which brought peace between Egypt and Israel few thought was possible and deprived the Soviet Union of its most important friend in the Middle East.

This area, the scene of his greatest triumph, was also to produce his downfall. Neither Carter nor the CIA had foreseen the overthrow of MUHAMMAD REZA PAHLAVI, the Shah of Iran and great friend of the US, by the IRANIAN REVOLUTION and the establishment of the violently anti-Western ISLAMIC REPUBLIC OF IRAN, led by the Ayatollah KHOMEINI. The IRAN HOSTAGE CRISIS (1979–81), when the US embassy in Teheran was invaded and 69 Americans seized as hostages, was a humiliation for the US. It dominated US foreign policy for the next 14 months and made the President appear impotent, especially when an airborne attempt to rescue the hostages failed in May 1980. Carter's popularity plummeted and he was given only reluctant endorsement as the Democratic presidential candidate in 1980. The election marked the most overwhelming rejection of an incumbent President since Hoover's defeat in 1932. Carter won 41 per cent of the popular vote to Ronald REAGAN's 51 per cent. After his defeat Carter was active as a peacemaker in Ethiopia, Sudan and Liberia and in 1994 persuaded the military junta in Haiti to give up power and accept a peaceful US occupation. In 1986 he founded the Carter Center to promote health in developing nations. It was soon a respected champion of human rights.

Jimmy Carter, B. Glad (1980)
Jimmy Carter as President, E. C. Hargrove (1988)

Castro, Fidel (1926–) Prime Minister (1959–76) and President (1976–) of Cuba.

The illegitimate son of a Spanish-born sugar planter and his cook, he was educated at a Jesuit school and at the University of Havana, where he obtained a doctorate in law, which he practised in Havana, working mainly for the poor. At university he was greatly influenced by the ideas of the Cuban revolutionary hero Jose Martí and in 1953 tried unsuccessfully to overthrow the dictator Fulgencio BATISTA. Captured and imprisoned, he was released in 1955 and a year later led the Cuban Revolution (1956–9) which ended with the flight of Batista. Castro had succeeded with the help of established opposition parties but he soon concentrated power in his own hands. Executive and legislative power was entrusted to the Council of Ministers, which ruled by decree with Fidel as Prime Minister. Batista's officials were tried in 'people's courts' and many were executed. Democratic institutions were abolished, promised elections were not held, trade unions and professional associations lost their independence and the free press was closed down. The replacement of one dictatorship by another was strongly opposed by the middle class, many of whom began the first exodus by emigrating to Miami.

Castro wanted to redistribute wealth in favour of peasants and workers and, as a fervent nationalist, to remove control of the economy from foreigners (mainly Americans). He carried out populist measures, imposing a price freeze and granting large wage rises for workers, which made him very popular. An agrarian reform law expropriated the large estates and converted them into co-operatives. Large companies and banks were nationalized. These measures were opposed by the US, so he sought other markets, making trade agreements with the USSR, China and Poland. Relations with the US deteriorated further when American oil refineries were nationalized, as they refused to process oil from Russia. The US responded by withdrawing its quota for the import of Cuban sugar, so Castro seized all US businesses without compensation. In October 1960 President EISENHOWER put a complete embargo on US exports to Cuba. An invasion by Cuban exiles at the BAY OF PIGS, sponsored by the US, took place in April 1960 and failed disastrously. Further conflict with the US took place in October 1962, when a US spy plane showed that there were Soviet nuclear missiles on the island. The CUBAN MISSILE CRISIS brought nuclear war close but this was avoided by KHRUSHCHEV pulling back from confrontation.

Castro announced in 1961 that Cuba was a socialist country and that he was a Marxist. The Cuban Communist Party (CCP), formed in 1965 and the only legal party in Cuba, was modelled on the CPSU (Communist Party of the Soviet Union), with a Central Committee and Politburo. The Cuban state was reorganized on Soviet lines with popular assemblies like the soviets in the USSR. The first nation wide direct elections for municipalities were held in 1976 but not until 1992 for the National Assembly. This had little power and simply rubber-stamped decisions made by the Politburo. Real power was in the hands of Castro, First Secretary of the CCP and Chairman of the Council of Ministers. The first Congress of the CCP, held in 1975, produced a constitution in 1976 modelled on that of the Soviet Union. Fidel became President of Cuba.

The economy was Castro's prime concern. He wanted to end Cuba's dependence on sugar (which provided 80 per cent of exports) by diversifying agriculture and by import-substitution in industry, as in other Latin American countries. Under the direction of Che GUEVARA, head of the National Bank and later Minister of Industry, a Four Year Plan was drawn up but it failed owing to the lack of economic expertise among the planners and a shortage of capital. By 1963 Soviet advisers were recommending an abandonment of industrialization and a return to concentrating on sugar. Cuba remained dependent on the export of one crop and on the patronage of one country, the Soviet Union, which provided Cuba with all its oil (at below world prices) and bought Cuban sugar at above market prices. The economy deteriorated from the mid-1970s with the world recession brought about by the OPEC PRICE RISE of 1973. Slow growth and a rising population produced unemployment and inflation of 20–30 per cent, though this was lower than in most Latin American countries. The average economic growth of 5 per cent a year between 1960–90 was also considerably better than in most of Latin America.

The Castro regime had considerable success in eliminating social and economic inequalities. Although rationing was a permanent feature of life, the population was adequately fed, clothed and housed and rents were low. Free and excellent medical services produced a mortality rate of 11 per thousand, lower than in any other THIRD WORLD country and lower than in many parts of the US. Free education and training made higher education open to all for the first time. There was a revolution, too, in attitudes and values. Racial equality, in a society where 75 per cent of the population was black or of mixed race, was promoted and women were given the same rights as men.

The new dependence on the USSR and anti-Americanism were mirrored in Castro's foreign policy. Revolutionaries came to Cuba to be trained in guerrilla warfare and he sought to instigate revolution in other countries. This was unpopular with Latin American governments, which expelled Cuba from the OAS (Organization of American States) and, with the exception of Mexico, broke off diplomatic relations. After the fall of ALLENDE in Chile in 1973 there was less emphasis on revolution in Latin America but Cuban troops were sent abroad to help Marxist states: to take part in the ANGOLAN CIVIL WAR in 1976, where the government faced South African-backed guerrillas, and a year later to Ethiopia, which was at war with Somalia. After the SANDINISTA victory in Nicaragua in 1979 Castro sent advisers to help the new regime. The US was alarmed at this and at Cubans being sent to help the

Marxist government in Grenada. Following the US INVASION OF GRENADA in 1983 the Cubans there were expelled.

The COLLAPSE OF THE SOVIET UNION and the REVOLUTIONS OF 1989–91, which marked the end of communism in Eastern Europe, were great blows to Castro, as they deprived him of his protected markets and his cheap source of oil. A defiant Castro, who had strongly attacked GORBACHEV's perestroika and GLASNOST, said he would never abandon socialism and refused to adopt a market economy and political democracy, essential measures if the US embargo was to be lifted. Instead, he tightened the Cuban belt and extended rationing to all products. Between 1989–93 Cuban GNP declined by 34 per cent. The increased austerity led many Cubans to emigrate on unseaworthy craft to the US, large numbers being lost at sea. In 1994 Castro allowed the first large PRIVATIZATION, when a Mexican group bought 49 per cent of the state telecommunications industry. Steep price increases and a reduction in public sector employment helped to bring about a slight increase in GNP (of 0.7 per cent) in 1995, for the first time since 1989, and a new law allowed 100 per cent private ownership of enterprises in Cuba. The US, however, was tightening the blockade with the Helms–Burton Act, which sought to penalize foreign companies doing business with Cuba. The sugar harvest of 1994–5 at 3.3 million tons was the worst for 50 years. The economy, therefore, remained in a precarious position, with most export earnings being used to repay Cuba's INTERNATIONAL DEBT.

The Cuba Reader: The Making of a Revolutionary Society, P. Brenner, W. M. Leogrande, D. Rich and D. Siegel (eds) (1989)
Castro, S. Balfour (1995)
Cuba: Twenty-Five Years of Revolution 1959–84, S. Halebsky and J. M. Kirk (eds) (1995)

CDU (*Christlich Demokratische Union:* Christian Democratic Union) German political party. Formed after the Second

World War, it was affiliated with Bavaria's CSU (Christian Social Union) and won the first general election in the Federal Republic of Germany (FRG: West Germany) in 1949, its leader Konrad ADENAUER becoming the first Chancellor. Adenauer was determined that the CDU should not be like the Centre Party of the Wiemar Republic, a predominantly Catholic party, but should be a *Volkspartei* (People's Party) with a wide popular appeal. Most of the Catholic vote went to the CDU but many Protestants voted for it too, as its main rival, the SPD (Social Democratic Party), was anti-clerical. The CDU advocated the SOCIAL MARKET ECONOMY, integration of the FRG with the democracies of Western Europe and close co-operation with the US in foreign policy, as the FRG relied on the protection of the US nuclear umbrella. The success of the CDU (it has been the leading party in every election, except that of 1972) has been based on the WIRTSCHAFTSWUNDER (economic miracle), which saw the FRG become the leading industrial power in Western Europe by 1961.

Owing to the system of proportional representation in the FRG, the CDU/CSU never had a clear majority in parliament (except for the 1957 election, when it gained 50.2 per cent of the votes), so it has ruled in a coalition, usually with the FDP (Free Democratic Party). When the FDP withdrew its support in 1969 and formed a coalition with the SPD, the CDU lost power and remained in opposition until 1982, when the FDP again changed partners. A constructive vote of no confidence in the SDP's Chancellor Helmut SCHMIDT enabled Helmut KOHL to become Chancellor of a CDU–FDP coalition. With the collapse of communism in the GDR (German Democratic Republic: East Germany) in the EAST GERMAN REVOLUTION of 1989 the SPD had an opportunity of returning to power, but Kohl took the lead in bringing about GERMAN REUNIFICATION. The SPD, lukewarm about a united Germany, was comprehensively defeated by the CDU in the 1990 election for the whole of Germany: the CDU

gained 43 per cent of the vote, the SPD 33.5 per cent. Kohl also won the 1994 election by a narrower (5 per cent) margin.

Party Government and Political Culture in West Germany, H. Doring and G. Smith (eds) (1982)
Parties, Opposition and Society in West Germany, E. Kolinsky (1984)

Ceauşescu, Nicolae (1918–89) President of Romania (1974–89). One of nine children in a peasant family, he left school at 11 and became a shoemaker's apprentice and later an electrician. He joined the Communist Party in 1936 and spent most of the time from 1938–44 in prison, where he met Gheorghiu-Dej, who became his patron. On Gheorghiu-Dej's death in 1965, Ceauşescu became the leading figure in Romania. He revived the title of General Secretary of the Party and in 1967 became President of the State Council. This made him head of state, but control of the government was in the hands of the Prime Minister. Not until 1974, when Ceauşescu was 'elected' as the first President of the Socialist Republic of Romania, did he become both head of the Communist Party and of the government, as the new President had many powers formerly held by the Prime Minister. As commander-in-chief he was also in charge of the armed forces and had total control of the country. He retained this control until his death by skilfully manipulating the levers of power and by encouraging conflict between rival forces. The Securitate, the secret police, penetrated every aspect of Romanian life and was a rival of the army. The only completely trustworthy people were members of his own and his wife's families, so he placed 50 of his relations in the highest offices of state. Ceauşescu was never a popular or charismatic figure: he was too rigid and read his interminable speeches in a dull monotone and with a stutter. To give himself the authority he naturally lacked he developed a cult of personality, with the name *Conducator* (leader), the same title as that taken by the war-time Fascist leader Antonescu. This cult of personality was fostered by the adulation he received in the West (he was knighted by Queen ELIZABETH of England in 1978), where he was undeservedly regarded as a liberal, because he pursued a foreign policy at odds with that of the Soviet Union. Ceauşescu was the only leader in the communist bloc not to break off relations with Israel as a result of the SIX DAY WAR (1967) and he did not allow Romanian troops to join other WARSAW PACT forces in bringing the PRAGUE SPRING (1968) to an end. Consequently, Romania was given large loans and trading privileges by the US and Western European countries and joined GATT in 1971 and the IMF a year later, the first East European country to do so.

Ceauşescu followed a Stalinist economic policy by concentrating on heavy industry (steel and oil), but he did little to develop the infrastructure, so that the electricity supply and transport could not cope. The production of Romanian oil declined in the 1970s as the wells dried up and the USSR would not provide cheap oil (as it did for other COMECON countries) owing to Romania's foreign policy. Ceauşescu had to turn, therefore, to the Middle East, but prices there shot up with the OPEC PRICE RISE of 1973. Romania built up a huge foreign debt which, in 1982, the *Conducator* decided to repay in full by 1990. Imports were forbidden (even of machinery) and exports of food were increased to pay off the debt. This could be done only by severe cutbacks in the standard of living: rationing was introduced in 1982, by 1985 most foods were unobtainable and there was serious malnutrition. Romania became the most miserable country in Europe, a situation made worse by Ceauşescu's policy of 'rural systematization'. This involved destroying about half the villages in Romania to provide more agricultural land and to relocate the population in towns. Fortunately for the Romanian peasantry, only 70 villages had been affected by the time of the revolution of 1989.

This began in Timisoara, populated largely by Hungarians, where László Tökeś, a Hungarian pastor and critic of the regime's human rights record, was ordered to move to another part of Romania. He refused to go and between 16–20 December there were demonstrations in support and calls for an end to the dictatorship. The Securitate killed 71 people but this simply spread the discontent. On 22 December after a night of violence and bloodshed, the army sided with the people and the National Salvation Front (led by former NOMENKLATURA) smoothly took over control, as it was supported by the generals. Ceauşescu and his wife Elena fled by helicopter but were captured and after a summary trial were executed on Christmas Day.

Nationalism and Communism in Romania: The Rise and Fall of Ceauşescu's Personal Dictatorship, T. Gilberg (1990)
'*Kiss the Hand You Cannot Bite': The Rise and Fall of the Ceauşescus*, E. Behr (1992)
Nicolae and Elena Ceauşescu, M. Almond (1992)

Central African Federation (CAF) (1953–63)

Set up by the British government to join together the self-governing colony of Southern Rhodesia with the protectorates of Northern Rhodesia and Nyasaland. Africans had not been consulted and feared that a federation would entrench white domination and hold up progress to majority rule, a fear confirmed when only 6 out of 35 seats for the Federal Parliament were allocated to Africans.

Economic growth in the CAF was rapid at first and one of the world's largest dams was contructed at Kariba on the Zambezi to provide cheap electricity for the copper mines of the north and the industries of the south. The boom, which depended on the price of copper, had come to an end by 1958 as the copper price fell and there was increasing unemployment. However, it was not economic decline which brought an end to the Federation but

African nationalism, fuelled by the stubbornness of the settlers, determined to maintain white supremacy. Nationalist mass parties, wanting majority rule and the break-up of the Federation, arose under Joshua Nkomo in Southern Rhodesia, Kenneth KAUNDA in Northern Rhodesia and Hastings BANDA in Nyasaland. Demonstrations, strikes and riots in 1959 led to the declaration of states of emergency, the banning of the nationalist parties and the arrest of their leaders. The Monckton Commission, set up by the British government to look into the working of the Federation, said that for Africans 'partnership was a sham' and recommended that territories should have the right to secede. On the last day of 1963 the Federation ended, Nyasaland becoming independent as Malawi in July 1964, Northern Rhodesia as Zambia in October. The white settlers in Southern Rhodesia demanded that the British government should grant them independence. When it refused to do this without black majority rule, Ian Smith declared UDI (Unilateral Declaration of Independence) in November 1965 and so began a struggle which did not end until 1980, when Southern Rhodesia became the independent Republic of Zimbabwe.

The Politics of Partnership: The Federation of Rhodesia and Nyasaland, P. Keatley (1963)
The Rise of Nationalism in Central Africa: The Making of Malawi and Zambia, 1873–1964, R. Rotberg (1966)
An Introduction to the History of Central Africa, A. J. Wills (1985)

Charter 77   The most important dissident group in Czechoslovakia. All forms of opposition to the communist government were rigorously suppressed after the PRAGUE SPRING of 1968, but in 1975 the Czech government, in signing the HELSINKI FINAL ACT, promised to uphold human rights. Various opposition groups came together and on 1 January 1977 issued their Charter. 'Charter 77', it stated, 'is not an organization. It has no rules, permanent bodies or formal membership'. It did not call for the overthrow of the Communist Party or of the government. Its aim was 'resisting the lie' and to draw attention to the Czechoslovak government's infringements of the UNITED NATIONS Declaration of Human Rights and the Helsinki Final Act. The chartists did not intend to be an underground movement: all 243 signatories gave their names and addresses, a very courageous act, as they were likely to lose their jobs and find their families penalized too. Between 1977 and 1980 61 chartists were imprisoned. Their immediate impact on the government was small, as there were few of them and they came from a restricted social class (nearly all were highly educated from the professions, or writers, including Václav HAVEL), who had little contact with the workers. Abroad, they inspired dissidents in Poland, Hungary and elsewhere in the Soviet bloc: at home they were in the forefront of the VELVET REVOLUTION in 1989, formed Civic Forum and led the negotiations with the communist government which resulted in a multiparty democracy in Czechoslovakia. Havel became state President in December 1989, other chartists serving in the government. In 1990 they decided to continue monitoring human rights in the new democracy.

Charter 77 and Human Rights in Czechoslovakia, H. Skilling (1981)

Chechnya conflict   The Russian attempt to end Chechen independence. Chechnya is a small territory (1 per cent of the land of Russia with a population of 1.2 million) which lies at the foot of the northern range of the Caucasus mountains. It had been annexed by Russia in the nineteenth century after a prolonged resistance. In 1944 STALIN, fearing that its Muslim population would support the Germans if they reached the Caucasus, forcibly deported the Chechens to Kazakhstan and Siberia: hundreds of thousands died in transit and in exile. KHRUSHCHEV allowed them to return in 1956–7 only to find their land and homes occupied by Russian colonists.

After the failure of the AUGUST COUP in 1991 Dzhokhar Dudayev, a former Soviet airforce commander, seized power in Chechnya and in November declared Chechen independence. Boris YELTSIN wanted to send in troops but the Russian Supreme Soviet rescinded his decree. For three years the Russians did nothing, as the Chechens established links with Iran and Turkey and became major traders in opium, heroin and arms, which they bought illegally from the Russian army as it moved north from the Caucasus. Dudayev went too far in 1994 by talking of establishing an Islamic state and imposing the *Sharia* (Islamic law). Chechnya was important to the Russians as it was the nodal point of an oil pipeline network going west from the Caspian Sea. The US and Turkish governments wanted it to go through Turkey rather than Russian territory: Russia wanted it to go through Chechnya to Russian ports on the Black Sea. The only railway linking Russia to Transcaucasia runs through Chechnya, so Russia needed to control that area in order to retain her influence in Armenia, Azerbaijan and Georgia.

In December 1994 60,000 Russian troops invaded Chechnya in an operation which the Defence Minister, Pavel Grachev, said would be over in two days. The well-armed and motivated Chechens fought so well that a long siege of Grozny, the capital, resulted, in which 20,000 civilians (many of them Russians) and 2,000 Russian troops were killed. Even after the fall of Grozny the Chechens, taking refuge in the mountains, continued the struggle. Shamil Basayev, Chechen field commander, moved into Russia in July 1995, taking hundreds of hostages in the town of Budyonnovsk. Prime Minister Chernomyrdin negotiated the release of the hostages but the hostage-takers were allowed to return to Chechnya. After the Russian presidential election of 1996 President Yeltsin appointed ex-general Lebed as his special envoy to Chechnya. He arranged a peace which gave almost complete autonomy to the Chechens, though a decision as to whether Chechnya should remain a part of Russia or be independent was postponed until 2001. The Chechnya conflict has been a disaster for Russia. It has created vast numbers of refugees, been enormously expensive, destroyed the reputation of the Russian army as a well-trained and formidable fighting force and damaged the prestige of Yeltsin, who described it as 'the biggest disappointment of my presidential career'. Estimates of the number killed during the war range from 30,000 to 80,000.

Chechnya: A Small Victorious War, C. Gall and T. De Waal (1997)

Chernobyl (26 April 1986)   A place in Ukraine where the world's worst nuclear accident so far took place. A test, which should have been carried out two years earlier, led to meltdown in the case of a reactor. The power of the reactor intensified to 440 times its full power within four seconds, fuel channels were cracked, the reactor core destroyed and a two-thousand ton upper plate was displaced, breaking off a thousand steel pipes. The local release of thermal energy was 10,000 times higher than in the nuclear accident at Three Mile Island, Pennsylvania in 1979. The authorities gave little information about the accident (reports on its medical and environmental results have still not been published), which provided a further incentive for GORBACHEV to push forward with GLASNOST. Through the heroic activity of workers (many of them servicemen) the reactor, which will remain radioactive for centuries, was buried in concrete but they were all exposed to massive doses of radiation: between five and ten thousand had died from it by 1991. Others who suffered from radiation were the 116,000 people evacuated from a 30 km (19 miles) zone around the plant and the 4.3 million who lived in Ukraine and Belarus. The Supreme Soviet declared Ukraine an 'ecological disaster area'. The delayed effect of such exposure (such as the increase in cancer) may not be evident for over 20 years.

The disaster was a crushing blow to the prestige of Soviet science and ruined the nuclear programme of the USSR and Eastern Europe. There were 14 plants of the Chernobyl-type in the USSR. Several reactors were shut down and projects to build more were cancelled. This produced an acute energy shortage from 1986–90 and a fall in investment (clearing up after Chernobyl had cost 50 billion roubles by 1990), which were partly responsible for the failure of the command economy and a move to the free market. The Soviet economy was doubly hit, as more oil was needed to produce electricity and this meant fewer exports and therefore a declining revenue. The nuclear industry in other countries was also affected, as more stringent regulations issued by the International Atomic Energy Authority made nuclear energy more expensive. In 1986 430 reactors in 26 countries generated 16 per cent of the world's electricity. Another 149 nuclear power stations were planned but cancellations reduced this number to 96 by 1988. Chernobyl showed that the effects of a nuclear accident cannot be limited to one country (the radioactive fallout affected the whole of Europe, including sheep farmers in North Wales) and caused popular opposition to nuclear energy to mount.

The Chernobyl Disaster, V. Haynes and M. Bojcun (1988)
The Legacy of Chernobyl, Z. A. Medvedev (1990)

Chinese civil war (1946–9) Fought between the armies of the Guomindang (Kuomintang), led by JIANG JIESHI (Chiang Kai-shek), and MAO ZEDONG's communist forces. In August 1945 STALIN recognized Jiang as the legitimate ruler of China and in the same month Mao flew to Chongqing (Chungking) to negotiate with Jiang. President Roosevelt had at Cairo in 1943 obtained Jiang's promise to include communists in his government, but the talks soon broke down because Jiang insisted that communist troops should be put under nationalist command before he would consider Mao's demand for a coalition government.

Jiang was confident of success because his troops at first outnumbered those of the communists by three to one, he had an air force which the communists lacked, his equipment was superior and above all he had American support. He decided that Manchuria, occupied by Soviet troops in August 1945, was the key to the control of China, as the Japanese had made it the most developed industrial area. The US therefore transported some of his best troops into the main Manchurian cities, though US generals thought it was a mistake to move into Manchuria before consolidating his hold on the south. The Russians let the Chinese communists have Japanese weapons before they left in May 1946. LIN BIAO, the Chinese commander in Manchuria, soon controlled the countryside and by guerrilla warfare cut the railway lines, leaving Jiang's troops in the cities reliant on air support. By May 1948 Jiang's position was hopeless. The two main cities in Manchuria, Mukden and Changchun, were surrounded, yet Jiang rejected American advice to pull back behind the Great Wall to defend north China. Mao now decided to change from guerrilla tactics to open warfare, a brilliant campaign of Lin Biao leading to the fall of Mukden and Changchun and the loss of 400,000 of Jiang's troops. Instead of defending the line of the Yangzi, Jiang now fought a major battle further north to protect the railway junction of Xuzhou, on the line from Beijing to Nanjing. 600,000 troops on each side were involved in the battle of Huai-hai between November 1948 and January 1949. Jiang forbade his commanders to give up any position, so they were unable to manoeuvre effectively: his armies were cut off from each other and surrounded. Two-thirds of his forces surrendered, the rest were annihilated. This battle effectively destroyed Jiang's nationalist forces. Lin Biao captured Tianjin in January 1949 and then moved on to Beijing, which surrendered on 31 January. Nanjing fell without a fight on 23 April, Wuhan shortly afterwards and Shanghai in late May. The communists advanced with remarkable speed, south to Guangzhou (Canton) and north-west into Xinjiang. Guangzhou fell in October and Chongqing, Jiang's base during the Second World War, a month later. Jiang's forces fled to Taiwan but before that, on 1 October 1949, on top of the Gate of Heavenly Peace – the main entrance to the former Ming and Qing imperial palace – Mao announced the foundation of the People's Republic of China.

Why had the communists, against apparently insuperable odds, won? One reason was that Jiang's regime was corrupt and inefficient and therefore unpopular. To pay for the War Jiang printed money, which caused hyperinflation and made savings and salaries worthless. Conscription for his armies was resented, particularly as his soldiers were brutally treated and, often unpaid, were encouraged to pillage. The communists, on the other hand, had gained widespread support by taking the lead in the Sino-Japanese War (1937–45) and they gained the backing of the peasants by reducing rents and interest on loans and by confiscating the land of the rich landlords and distributing it to the peasants in the areas they controlled. As Jiang's regime disintegrated the US became increasingly reluctant to prop him up. 'To defeat the Chinese Communists', General Marshall said, 'it would be necessary for the US virtually to take over the Chinese Government'.

Civil War in China: The Political Struggle 1945–9, S. Pepper (1978)
Seeds of Destruction: Nationalist China in War and Revolution, 1937–48 L. E. Eastman (1984)
Anvil of Victory, S. Levine (1987)

Chirac, Jacques (1932–)   Prime Minister (1974–6, 1986–8) and President (1995–) of the Fifth Republic in France. The son of a bank employee who rose to be the managing director of the aircraft company Dassault, he graduated at the élitist *École nationale d'administration* and briefly attended Harvard University, where he learnt English. He was elected to the National Assembly in 1967, in the same year became a junior minister and then held a succession of ministerial posts, a tribute to his hard work and efficiency but also to the patronage of President POMPIDOU. When Pompidou died in 1974 Chirac supported GISCARD D'ESTAING in the presidential election and was rewarded with the post of Prime Minister at the age of 42, but he felt that Giscard ignored him for much of the time and twice reshuffled cabinets without consulting or informing the Prime Minister, with whom the choice of ministers constitutionally lay. He therefore resigned in 1976. Chirac then founded a new Gaullist party, the *Rassemblement pour la République* (RPR), modelled on DE GAULLE's RPF and has since then been leader of the Gaullists. In 1977 he was elected Mayor of Paris, a significant power base which he held for 18 years. He entered the presidential election in 1981 as a rival to Giscard and was eliminated in the first round with only 18 per cent of the vote, but by splitting the vote of the right he contributed to the socialist MITTERRAND's narrow victory.

The parliamentary election of 1986 brought a slim majority for the right-wing parties, so Chirac, as the leader of the largest of those parties, became Prime Minister. He pursued a conservative economic policy, deregulating prices, privatizing over a dozen major groups which Mitterrand had nationalized, repealing the wealth tax and the housing law of 1982 which had given security of tenure to those in rented accommodation, reducing public spending and taxes. To cut the ground from under Le Pen and the National Front he took a tough stance on law and order, gave the police greater powers and tightened immigration controls. Chirac stood for President a second time in 1988 but was easily defeated by Mitterrand, who had 54 per cent of the vote. In opposition once more he led the Gaullists and their allies to a crushing victory in the parliamentary elections of 1993 but decided against becoming Prime Minister again in order to prepare for the presidential election in 1995. Here the Gaullist movement seemed about to split as Edouard Balladur, the Gaullist Prime Minister, was also a candidate. Chirac waged a populist campaign, and promised job creation, economic growth and a hard line on immigration. He defeated Balladur in the first round and the socialist Lionel Jospin in the second to become President at his third attempt, making Alain Juppé his Prime Minister.

The strong franc and high interest rates had hit French exports and increased unemployment to over three million. To meet the Maastricht criteria for EMU (European Monetary Union) the public debt and budget deficit would have to be reduced, so Juppé sought to cut costs in the health service (one of the most expensive in the world), social services, pensions and the railways. The result was a series of student demonstrations and strikes by public sector workers in December 1995 which were reminiscent of the MAY 1968 events. Much of France was paralysed as there were no trains, no public transport in Paris and most state schools closed but, as in 1968, it was difficult to keep up the momentum and strikers gradually returned to work. Chirac, like his predecessors, saw the Franco-German Alliance as a key to the success of the European Union (EU) and of European integration, but in the referendum on approval for the MAAS-TRICHT TREATY nearly half the electorate voted 'no'.

Chirac made an enormous political blunder when he called a general election in June 1997, ten months before it was necessary. He asked for a mandate to move faster in preparing France for European Monetary Union but misread the public mood when unemployment at 12.8 per cent was a postwar high and taxes at 45 per cent of GNP were at a near-record level. The centre–right suffered its greatest defeat since the beginning of the Fifth Republic in 1958, losing over 200 of its 464 seats in the 577 member parliament. The SOCIALIST PARTY and its allies were the great beneficiaries, rising from 63 to 253 seats. The Gaulist RPR was in disarray with 134 seats, falling from 258. Chirac was faced with a long period of cohabitation with a socialist Prime Minister, Lionel Jospin.

Chirac's France, 1986–8, J. Tuppen (1991)
Chirac's Challenge: Liberalization, European-ization and Malaise in France, J. T. S. Keeler and M. A. Sahair (eds) (1997)

Christian Democratic Party (*Democrazia Cristiana*: DC)   Italian political party. Formed in 1942, it was the heir to the Popular Party, a largely peasant-based Catholic party created in 1919. The support of the Vatican was crucial in making it into a mass party. It founded organizations such as the *Coldiretti* (a Catholic association of peasant proprietors) and the ACLI (association of Christian workers) to extend its support. These offered insurance, social assistance and legal services. DE GASPERI, the first leader of the DC, was determined that it should not be a clerical party and widened its appeal to all classes by emphasizing democracy, family values and anti-communism. It benefited greatly from the COLD WAR, as it obtained the powerful backing of the US. The DC used its control of the state to develop a network of clients, who became dependent on the continuation of the DC in power. By expanding the civil service and the public sector it had a large number of jobs at its disposal and used these to cement its hold on the South. Agrarian reform, which split up some large estates and handed them over to small peasant proprietors, stopped the communist advance in the South while the *Cassa per il Mezzogiorno* (Fund for the South) distributed housing, credit and jobs on a large scale, often through political client-ilism. The DC also made deals with the

MAFIA, which it left largely unhindered in Sicily and the South in return for Mafia support for DC candidates in elections. The Christian Democrats gained support by promoting the WELFARE STATE in order to undermine the appeal of communism. In 1948 the DC had a million members, rising to a peak of 1.9 million in 1973 and in the 1950s controlled nearly every major city council.

Owing to the system of proportional representation the DC never had a parliamentary majority, except after the 1948 election, so it formed coalitions with other parties. This produced considerable instability, as different factions sought to strengthen their hold on power: from 1945 to 1970 there were 28 governments with an average life of 11 months. Yet there was considerable continuity in the membership of these governments, as the DC led all of them from 1945 to 1981 and was in all administrations up to the 1990s. To maintain its dominant position the DC constantly changed its tactics. It allied with communists and socialists in postwar reconstruction until the Cold War and a split in the Socialist Party enabled De Gasperi to dismiss them from his government in 1947. From then until 1962 the DC ruled in alliance with parties of the centre. When the ties between the communists and socialists weakened, the DC congress voted by a large margin for an 'Opening to the Left' and formed centre–left coalitions with the socialists, loosening its attachment to the Catholic Church. When the OPEC PRICE RISE took place in 1973 the DC decided to do a deal with the main opposition party, the PCI (Italian Communist Party) and eventually agreed with the PCI leader, Ernesto Berlinguer, on the historic compromise. This came to an end with the SOVIET INVASION OF AFGHANISTAN in 1979, so the DC reverted to the centre–left coalition with the socialists.

From this time the DC, riddled with corruption, was in disarray and decline. Other parties in 1981 refused to serve under a DC Prime Minister so Giovanni Spadolini, a Republican, became the first non-DC Prime Minister since the war, though members of the DC held over half the ministerial posts. In the 1983 election the DC lost two million votes and once again failed to choose the Prime Minister, the socialist Bettino CRAXI being appointed. The DC never recovered and suffered a further blow with the REVOLUTIONS OF 1989–91 and the COLLAPSE OF THE SOVIET UNION, as anti-communism had been a major source of its appeal. By 1992 the huge budget deficit meant that there was no money with which to reward its supporters and its vote in the election fell below 30 per cent for the first time. The party dissolved itself in 1994, the centre and left becoming the Popular Party, the right forming the Christian Democratic Centre: both performed miserably in the election of that year. The once great institution had been reduced to the ranks as a minor party.

Italian Christian Democracy, R. Leonardi and D. Wentman (1989)
A History of Contemporary Italy: Society and Politics, 1943–88, P. Ginsborg (1990)
Modern Italy, 1871–1995, M. Clark (1996)

Churchill, Sir Winston Leonard Spencer (1874–1965)   British Prime Minister (1940–5, 1951–5). The elder son of Lord Randolph Churchill and grandson of the 7th Duke of Marlborough, Winston did badly at Harrow and scraped into Sandhurst at the third attempt. He charged with the Lancers at Omdurman, left the army and became a war correspondent in the South African War (1899–1902), where he was captured and escaped. In 1900 he became a Conservative MP but was opposed to tariff reform and so joined the Liberal Party in 1904. His rise after that was rapid: he became associated with the New Liberalism and in 1908 served in Asquith's Cabinet as President of the Board of Trade. Churchill set up Labour Exchanges and, by the Trade Boards Act (1909), created machinery for fixing (and raising) wages in

the 'sweated' traders such as tailoring. A leading advocate of smashing the power of the House of Lords in the Parliament Act (1911), Churchill moved in the same year to the Admiralty. During the First World War he was blamed for the disaster of the Gallipoli Campaign, resigned from the Admiralty and commanded a battalion for a short time in France, before Lloyd George brought him back as Minister of Munitions (1917–18) in his coalition government. Remaining in the postwar coalition government (1918–22) in various posts, Churchill strongly urged intervention in the Russian Civil War (1918–21) against the Bolsheviks, but he was overruled.

Churchill rejoined the Conservatives in 1924 and was made Chancellor of the Exchequer, a post for which he was not suited. The return to the gold standard in 1925 at the prewar parity, which was far too high, adversely affected British exports and led to a miners' strike and the General Strike of 1926. By this time Churchill had lost his earlier radicalism, was obsessed by the 'red peril' and organized government action to bring the strike to an end. The Conservatives lost office in 1929, and though they were back in power from 1931 as part of the National Government, Churchill was excluded. He fell out with Baldwin, as he bitterly opposed the negotiations leading to the India Act (1935), which gave Indians control of their provincial government. The abdication crisis (1936) was another occasion on which Churchill ploughed a lone furrow, as he supported Edward VIII and tried to form a King's Party. At this time he was mistrusted by all parties and particularly by the Conservatives, who regarded him as unstable and unreliable, 'not a safe man'. Consequently, his warnings about the threat Hitler posed to European peace and security were ignored. 'Germany', he said in 1934, 'is arming secretly, illegally and rapidly', and urged British rearmament. In 1938 he called Munich 'a defeat without a war', prophesied that the destruction of Czechoslovakia would follow and called for Russia to be brought into an anti-German alliance. When the Second World War began, Neville Chamberlain recalled Churchill to the Admiralty, his first ministerial post for ten years. He bore a major share of responsibility for the disastrous Norwegian campaign, but public and parliament blamed Chamberlain, who had to resign.

Consequently, at the age of 65, Churchill was Prime Minister for the first time and immediately gained the confidence of most of the nation by facing up to the dangers ahead. 'I have nothing to offer', he told the Commons in his first speech as Prime Minister, 'but blood, toil, tears and sweat'. The LABOUR PARTY was given key posts in the coalition government which Churchill formed in 1940, with ATTLEE officially being recognized as Deputy Prime Minister in 1942. Halifax wanted to seek peace terms from Germany after the fall of France but Churchill was adamant: 'We shall go on to the end . . . we shall never surrender'. When the war ended, the coalition broke up and Labour won a huge victory at the 1945 election.

As leader of the opposition Churchill failed to give a lead to the shadow cabinet on domestic affairs and was more concerned with his role as a world statesman, making speeches like that at Fulton, Missouri in 1946, when he said that 'From Tallinn in the Baltic to Trieste in the Adriatic an iron curtain has descended across the continent'. When he returned to power in 1951 he was 77 and had already endured two strokes. According to his doctor his 'old capacity for work had gone and with it much of his self-confidence'. Yet his administration was a successful one. He created a new Ministry of Housing and put Harold MACMILLAN in charge to build over 300,000 houses a year. Butler at the Treasury showed little financial flair, but benefited from Labour's devaluation of 1949, so there were no balance of payments problems from 1952–5. Most Tories accepted the WELFARE STATE, spending on which increased under Churchill, and a mixed economy. Iron and steel were privatized in 1953 and road haulage in 1954 but other industries nationalized by Labour remained under public ownership. Food rationing ended in 1954, full employment was maintained and living standards rose. Foreign policy was in the very capable hands of Anthony EDEN, who was a highly impressive Foreign Secretary, particularly in arranging for German entry into NATO and in negotiating the GENEVA ACCORDS, which ended the INDOCHINA WAR OF INDEPENDENCE (1946–51). Churchill had another stroke in 1953 and was out of action for months. When he returned his lack of control of ordinary business embarrassed his colleagues, whose names he could not always remember. He was reluctantly persuaded to retire in 1955.

Churchill's Indian Summer: The Conservative Government 1951–5, A. Seldon (1981)
Churchill on the Home Front 1900–1955, P. Addison (1992)
Churchill's Peacetime Ministry, 1951–5, H. Pelling (1997)

CIA (Central Intelligence Agency)   The main intelligence and counter-intelligence agency of the US government. Until the Second World War intelligence-gathering was conducted by the army, navy and Federal Bureau of Investigation, with resulting duplication and lack of co-ordination. President Roosevelt therefore created, in 1942, the Office of Strategic Services to bring the collection of all intelligence under one organization. In 1945 it was reorganized as the Central Intelligence Group, which became the CIA in 1947. It was prohibited from operating in the US and placed under the control of the President through the National Security Council.

In 1949 the Central Intelligence Agency Act empowered the Director to spend Agency money 'without regard to the provisions of law and regulation'. This enabled the CIA to carry out covert operations by supporting foreign political parties and by organizing the overthrow of foreign governments. Congressional committees in 1975–6 revealed that the

CIA had plotted the assassination of foreign leaders (Patrice Lumumba in the Congo in 1960 and Fidel CASTRO in Cuba from 1961–4) and that it had violated its charter by compiling dossiers on 7,200 US citizens in the VIETNAM ANTI-WAR MOVEMENT in the late 1960s, had tapped telephones, bugged hotel rooms, opened mail and burgled offices. There were demands for tighter control of the CIA: President FORD forbade it to conduct assassinations. In 1982 Congress, with the Boland amendment, forbade the CIA to fund the CONTRAS or activities aimed at overthrowing the SANDINISTA government in Nicaragua.

The Agency had mixed fortunes in its clandestine activities. A great success was its design and operation of spy planes (and later of satellites) at the experimental edge of aviation technology. The U2 plane (1955) could fly higher and longer than any other plane and provided invaluable photographs which showed that the Soviet Union did not have a lead in missile technology. From the early 1960s spy satellites were the main means of intelligence collecting and remain so. The CIA began interfering in foreign countries in 1948, when it made secret payments to the CHRISTIAN DEMOCRATIC PARTY to prevent a communist victory in the 1948 Italian election. This was followed in 1953 by a coup in Iran which overthrew Muhammed Musaddiq and restored to power America's ally MUHAMMAD REZA PAHLAVI. A year later the CIA overthrew another foreign government, that of Jacobo ARBENZ, who had expropriated land (with compensation paid) belonging to the American-owned United Fruit Company in Guatemala. The Agency was less successful in Indonesia, when it failed in 1958 to bring down the Indonesian government. In 1961 the CIA helped to arrange the assassination of the Dominican dictator Rafael Trujillo, who had become a liability to the US. The greatest CIA fiasco occurred in the same year, when the BAY OF PIGS invasion of Cuba did not succeed in toppling Castro. The CIA was involved in the plot to overthrow the

Marxist President of Chile, Salvador ALLENDE, in 1973. In the 1980s the CIA exercised great influence in Pakistan and Afghanistan by supplying arms and money to the *Mujahidin* guerrillas based in Pakistan, who were fighting Russian troops after the SOVIET INVASION OF AFGHANISTAN. The CIA ignored the Boland amendment by organizing support for the Contras in the IRAN CONTRA AFFAIR (1985–6), one of the events that caused such disquiet that Congress appointed an inspector-general in 1990 to supervise the Agency.

The Agency, J. Ranelagh (1987)
The CIA and American Democracy, R. Jeffrys-Jones (1989)
External Vigilance: 50 Years of the CIA, R. Jeffrys-Jones and C. Andrew (eds) (1997)

CIS (Commonwealth of Independent States)

Set up in December 1991 following the COLLAPSE OF THE SOVIET UNION. It originally consisted of the three states of Russia, Ukraine and Belarus, who were joined on 21 December by Armenia, Azerbaijan, Kazakhstan, Kirgyzstan, Moldova, Tajikistan, Turkmenistan and Uzbekistan. Georgia joined in 1993. Of the former states of the Soviet Union only the Baltic states (Latvia, Lithuania, Estonia) remained outside the CIS. All members recognized each other's independence and existing boundaries and promised to respect the cultural and political rights of all nationalities. They agreed to co-operate over foreign policy, transport and immigration but no permanent joint institutions for these purposes were set up. The supreme body of the CIS was a Council of Heads of State, which met infrequently (at least twice a year) and reached decisions by consensus. Russia was to take the seat at the UNITED NATIONS formerly held by the USSR.

The CIS faced such formidable problems that it was doubtful whether it would exist for more than a few months. Inter-ethnic conflict already existed between Armenians and Azeris over NAGORNO-KARABAGH and soon erupted in Georgia, where Abkhazians sought independence and South Ossetians wanted to join North Ossetia, which was in Russia. In the Russian Federation the Tatar Republic declared its autonomy in October 1991: Chechnya went even further in November and announced its complete independence. Some 75 million CIS citizens lived outside their own republic and had little knowledge of local languages. This complicated the problem of nation-building, as only Russia, Georgia, Armenia and the three Baltic republics of the old Soviet Union were nations in any meaningful sense. There was also the problem of who should control the former Soviet military arsenal, particularly as four states (Russia, Ukraine, Belarus and Kazakhistan) had nuclear weapons. The Black Sea fleet was another source of dispute. Based in the Crimea (largely Russian-populated but part of Ukraine) it was claimed by Ukraine. Not until 1994 did Ukraine agree to give up its nuclear weapons and reach a compromise with Russia over the Black Sea fleet.

Russia, with its population of 147 million and its vast resources (particularly of oil and gas), was bound to dominate the CIS and used its position to further Russian interests. YELTSIN supported Abkhaz separatists against Georgia until Georgia joined the CIS and helped the pro-Russian side in the Tajikistan civil war, defending that country's border against incursions from Afghanistan. In 1993 Russia forced the other republics in the CIS to pay the world price for oil, thus adding to their economic burdens. Russia was determined to control three strategic areas: Belarus, guarding the western approaches to Moscow; Kazakhstan, the gateway to Central Asia; and Georgia, a buffer against the penetration of ISLAMIC FUNDAMENTALISTS into Russia's Muslim territories. Georgia needed Russian help to end its civil war and provided Russian military bases on its territory, as did Belarus, in return for cheap Russian oil and gas.

Nations and Politics in the Soviet Successor States, I. Brenner and R. Taras (eds) (1993)

Civil Rights Acts Measures which sought to end racial discrimination in the US. The first Act was passed in 1866: it granted citizenship to negroes and the same rights to freed slaves as those enjoyed by white citizens. It was incorporated in the Fourteenth Amendment, which guaranteed to all citizens 'the equal protection of the laws'. The Fifteenth Amendment in 1869 said that a citizen's right to vote 'shall not be denied . . . on account of race'. A further Civil Rights Act of 1875 forbade the exclusion of blacks from juries and from public accommodation such as theatres or trains. The benefits blacks could expect from these Acts largely disappeared as a result of the civil rights cases of 1883, when the Supreme Court ruled that the Fourteenth Amendment forbade only states from violating civil rights and did not apply to the actions of private individuals or institutions. Racial discrimination by employers, railroads and hotels was therefore within the law. This ended the attempts of the federal government to ensure that blacks could exercise their civil rights until after the Second World War.

In 1957 and 1960 Congress passed Civil Rights Acts to strengthen federal powers in enforcing black voting rights but they made little impact. Racial discrimination was not seriously tackled until the Civil Rights Act of 1964, which had the support of President JOHNSON and that of members of both the REPUBLICAN and DEMOCRATIC PARTIES. It was the successful outcome of agitation by the CIVIL RIGHTS MOVEMENT and the most wide-ranging civil rights legislation for almost a century. It banned racial discrimination in theatres, hotels, restaurants and other public places, and authorized the Attorney-General to end segregation in public schools, libraries, museums, hospitals and playgrounds. Money could be withheld from federally assisted projects which failed to desegregate. Discrimina-

tion was prohibited in workplaces with over 100 employees and in trade unions. An Equal Employment Opportunity Commission was set up to supervise desegregation. Blacks were still effectively denied the right to register as voters by local laws which imposed a poll tax or insisted on literacy tests, so this problem was tackled in the Voting Rights Act of 1965, the most effective law of its kind ever passed. It removed all obstacles Southern states had put in the way of black voter registration and allowed the Attorney-General to send federal registrars to enrol voters in states where registration was being obstructed. According to President Johnson this was 'one of the most monumental laws in the entire history of American freedom' and it was immediately effective. On 14 August 1965 federal registrars enrolled 381 blacks in Selma, Alabama, more than had been enrolled in the previous 65 years. In 1964 35 per cent of Southern blacks had been registered: by 1969 this had risen to 65 per cent. These were the most dramatic changes in the Deep South: registration of blacks in Alabama increased from 19 per cent to 61 per cent, in Mississippi from 7 per cent to 67 per cent. A Civil Rights Act of 1968 made discrimination illegal in the sale or rent of 90 per cent of the nation's housing. As blacks remained at a disadvantage when seeking work, programmes of AFFIRMATIVE ACTION were devised to help them. The Civil Rights Act of 1991 encouraged this, as it allowed suits against employers if their hiring had a 'disparate impact' on women or minorities, even if there was no proof of discriminatory intent. The Act rejected racial hiring quotas but said that if the racial composition of an employer's work force differed from that of the local labour market the employer could be sued.

Civil Rights Movement The struggle by blacks to end segregation in the US. The movement was led in the first half of the twentieth century by the NAACP (National Association for the Advancement of Colored

People), which sought legal action in the courts to end racial discrimination, but it met with little success before the Second World War. In 1942 the Congress of Racial Equality (CORE) was formed in Chicago as a more militant organization which believed in direct action, as progress was so slow in enabling blacks to register as voters and in getting rid of Jim Crow laws which imposed segregation in the South. There blacks and whites could not attend the same schools, eat in the same place or go to the same theatres. A Supreme Court decision of 1896, *Plessy v Ferguson*, said that segregation was constitutional if 'separate but equal' facilities were provided for the two races. The 1950s was a favourable time for the Civil Rights Movement (CRM) to take off as DECOLONIZATION, when African states gained their independence, inspired American blacks to seek freedom at home. The COLD WAR rivalry of the US and the Soviet Union also helped the CRM, as the US wanted to be a democratic role model for newly independent countries, who would then reject communism. The Supreme Court in BROWN v BOARD OF EDUCATION OF TOPEKA in 1954 made a landmark ruling which overturned *Plessy v Ferguson* and declared that segregation in schools was unconstitutional. A white backlash followed: federal troops were needed to enforce this decision at LITTLE ROCK, Arkansas in 1957.

The struggle of massive, non-violent civil disobedience campaigns was pioneered by Martin Luther KING, who led the successful MONTGOMERY BUS BOYCOTT in Alabama in 1955–6. This was followed in 1960 by sit-ins, which were started by black students at Greensboro, North Carolina who were refused service at a whites-only lunch counter. Sit-ins spread to seven other Southern states within a month and succeeded in ending segregation in many public facilities. They were followed by Freedom Rides, in which white students joined blacks in breaking down segregation at bus terminals. The MEREDITH INCIDENT (1962), when a black student sought admission to the University of Mississippi, the Birmingham demonstrations (1963) in Alabama, where police brutality was covered nationwide on television, and the March on Washington (1963), during which Martin Luther King made his 'I have a dream' speech to over 200,000 people, all kept the pressure on the KENNEDY and JOHNSON administrations.

Demonstrators suffered imprisonment and physical assault and some, such as Medger Evers, a leading NAACP official, were killed. Sympathy, however, had been aroused for the CRM by the media, the Protestant, Catholic and Jewish churches and President Kennedy became a late but fervent advocate of civil rights. The result was the most significant CIVIL RIGHTS ACTS since Reconstruction, the Act of 1964 and the Voting Rights Act of 1965, both passed by Congress at the request of President Johnson. The CRM owed a great deal, too, to rulings made in the Supreme Court, particularly when Earl WARREN was Chief Justice. These protected the right to demonstrate, which local laws (concerning obstruction, breach of peace) had been used to prevent. The Supreme Court repeatedly overturned convictions based on these laws.

Black civil rights were the major issue in the US for over a decade in the 1950s and 1960s, when the leadership began to split-up. Some, like MALCOLM X, rejected non-violence, while the BLACK MUSLIMS rejected integration in favour of separation of the races. The BLACK POWER movement, led by Stokely Carmichael, repudiated both non-violence and integration. As the influence of King among blacks declined, that of Carmichael increased. BLACK GHETTO RIOTS began before the Black Power Movement was formed but were influenced by it and led many white supporters of the CRM to withdraw their approval. With the assassination of Malcolm X and of King, and the infighting among blacks, the activity of the CRM declined in the 1970s, yet it had permanently affected American society. The CRM acted as a model for other groups – women,

Chicanos, gays and lesbians – but its main achievement was to end segregation and overt forms of racial discrimination. Violence against blacks in the South declined, as the South in many ways became more integrated than the North (half black children attended integrated schools in the South, a third in the North). As blacks could vote, 2,200 blacks were elected to office in the South by 1978: Atlanta and New Orleans had black mayors. Blacks attended Southern universities and colleges. Yet changes were limited – blacks were 20 per cent of the population in the South but formed only 3 per cent of elected officials. *De facto* segregation continued to exist in housing and the gap between the incomes of whites and blacks increased. AFFIRMATIVE ACTION benefited some middle-class blacks but political and legal rights made little impact on chronic black problems: poverty, unemployment, poor housing and health care.

One Nation Divisible, R. Pollenberg (1980)
In Struggle: SNCC and the Black Awakening of the 1960s, C. Carson (1981)
Bearing the Cross, D. Garrow (1986)
Freedom Summer, D. McAdam (1988)
Parting the Waters, T. Branch (1988)
Freedom Bound: History of America's Civil Rights Movement, R. Weisbrot (1990)
The Civil Rights Era: Origins and Development of National Policy, D. Graham (1990)
Running for Freedom: Civil Rights and Black Politics in America Since 1941, S. F. Lawson (1991)
The Struggle for Black Equality, 1954–92, H. Sitkoff (1993)
Making Peace with the '60s, D. Burnet (1997)

Clinton, William Jefferson ('Bill') (1946–)

President of the US (1993–). Born William J. Blythe, his father was an alcoholic who died in a car accident before he was born. His mother married Roger Clinton and Bill eventually took his stepfather's name. He grew up in genuine poverty but through scholarships studied at Georgetown University and Yale Law School and was a Rhodes Scholar at Oxford. Clinton taught at the University of Arkansas before he was elected Governor of Arkansas, the youngest person ever to hold that office, which he served for five terms (1979–81, 1983–92). As Governor he attracted investment to his impoverished state and expanded its education system, but was relatively unknown when he was selected as the DEMOCRATIC PARTY candidate in the 1992 presidential election. His presidential campaign was almost derailed when Jennifer Flowers claimed that he had been her lover and there were further allegations that he had been a draft-dodger during the VIETNAM WAR. He survived these scandals and chose a fellow Southerner, Al Gore from Tennessee, as his running mate instead of a Northern liberal, an indication that he had abandoned the high taxation and high spending of previous Democratic administrations. Clinton distanced himself from radical blacks like Jesse Jackson but appeared as the champion of minorities including women and gays, and of 'the forgotten middle class'. He captured 43 per cent of the popular vote to George BUSH's 38 per cent and was overwhelmingly supported by blacks and Jews. Democrats continued to control both houses of Congress by large margins.

Clinton had promised 'eight million new jobs', middle-class tax cuts, health-care reform, gun control, to halve the deficit and be tough on crime. He went a considerable way towards meeting these promises. The tax deficit of $255 billion in 1993 (4 per cent of GNP) was cut to $167 billion (2.4 per cent of GNP) in 1995. To reduce the deficit he raised taxes in his first year, most of the increased tax burden falling on the wealthy. The Earned Income Tax Rebate (1993), the best of his reforms, benefited 25 million Americans by guaranteeing that the working poor should pay no tax until their incomes came close to the average industrial wage, which was well above the official poverty line. His effort, and that of his wife Hilary, to produce a comprehensive health scheme foundered in the Senate. The Family Leave Act (1993) gave those in work time off to care for a sick child or dependant. The President supported the Brady Bill (1994), which compelled people wanting to buy a hand gun to wait until police confirmed their eligibility, computerized crime records and made weapons' theft a federal offence, a bill which marked the first major defeat for the powerful National Rifle Association. Clinton was certainly tough on crime: he put 100,000 extra police on the streets, began the biggest prison-building programme in the world and made a life sentence obligatory for criminals who committed a third serious offence.

His first term as President was marred by the Whitewater Scandal (1993), when there were allegations that an Arkansas thrift (savings bank) had illegally diverted funds to Whitewater Land Development Corporation, a failed real estate investment partly owned by Bill and Hilary Clinton, or to Clinton's 1984 campaign for Governor. A special federal prosecutor was appointed to investigate. The scandal undermined the President's authority and, with the tax increases, helped to bring success to the REPUBLICAN PARTY in the congressional elections of 1994: it gained control of both houses. This appeared to mark the end for Clinton but the 'Comeback Kid' turned the situation to his advantage. When the Republican Congress refused to pass the budget, it was blamed by the public for closing down government. The Oklahoma City bombing, when white extremists exploded a bomb in a federal building and killed 168 people, enabled the President to lead the national mourning and recover his popularity.

To regain the support of the middle class he accepted much of the Republican agenda on welfare and in doing so alienated many traditional Democratic supporters. He had promised in 1992 to 'end welfare as we know it' and talked of providing a hand up not a hand out, but many traditional Democrats were dismayed when he signed the Repub-

lican Welfare Reform Act in August 1996, a measure the *New York Times* described as 'odious', as it would end a 60-year tradition going back to the New Deal that in the last resort the federal government will feed children and their mothers if they face starvation. The President agreed to impose a limit of two consecutive years for anyone to receive welfare. The Act limited the food stamp programme by imposing a 90-day maximum for which workers under 50 may receive food stamps. This affected 13 million Americans – 9 million of them children – and reduced the income of the really poor (those earning under $6,300 a year) by 10 per cent. Clinton signed it because it was popular with those in work, 70 per cent of Americans in opinion polls supporting it. A Minimum Wage Act, which raised the minimum wage, and the Kennedy–Kassebaum health reform bill were also passed. The latter guaranteed that no worker would lose health insurance through changing or losing a job and prevented insurance companies from refusing to cover people with pre-existing medical conditions. This was very popular, though it did nothing for the 35 million who had no health insurance and were left to the underfunded Medicaid.

Clinton's main foreign policy objective, as the COLD WAR was over, was to promote a global free market. The NORTH AMERICAN FREE TRADE AGREEMENT (NAFTA), affecting the US, Mexico and Canada, was signed in 1993 to create the largest free trade area in the world. The President maintained that the US had the right to take economic and military measures against any state which it believes sponsors terrorism and signed legislation to punish any foreign country investing in oil or gas in Iran or Libya. The Helms – Burton Act infuriated America's NATO allies by seeking to impose penalties on foreign businesses trading with Cuba. The Vietnam War had made US Presidents reluctant to sent troops abroad. President Bush had sent troops to Somalia in 1992 to ensure the delivery of food supplies, but as 18 were killed on 3 October 1993 in clashes with a local warlord

Clinton announced their withdrawal four days later. In July 1994 the UNITED NATIONS authorized the US to restore President Aristide of Haiti by armed force but Jimmy CARTER persuaded the Haitian military to give up power peacefully, so the US was able to land a force of 20,000 in September without opposition. The President wanted to end the YUGOSLAV CIVIL WAR, so he sent Richard Holbrooke to broker a peace settlement, which he succeeded in doing at Dayton, Ohio. In the Middle East he firmly backed Israel, America's strongest ally in an area where both Iran and Iraq were hostile. The breakthrough in the Oslo Accords, when the PLO and Israel recognized each other and Israel promised limited self-government for the Palestinians in Gaza and Jericho, owed nothing to the US but Clinton managed to get credit for the reconciliation by persuading Yasser ARAFAT and Yitzhak RABIN to sign a Declaration of Principles on Palestinian self-government in Washington.

As the 1996 presidential election approached Clinton's greatest asset was the strength of the economy. The US was the world's leading exporter (the US exported over 12 per cent of GNP in 1995 compared with 9.5 per cent in Japan) and he had presided over the largest stock market rally since the early 1960s. Some 10.2 million new jobs had been created, inflation had been reduced to 3 per cent and the US had the best economic performance of the G7 countries. Clinton was the first Democratic President since Roosevelt not to face a challenge to his nomination. He won the election convincingly with 49.2 per cent of the popular vote to the Republican Bob Dole's 40.8 per cent, but both houses of Congress remained under Republican control.

The Clinton Presidency, C. Campbell and B. A. Rockman (eds) (1995)
High Hopes: The Clinton Presidency and the Politics of Ambition, S. A. Renshon (1996)
The President They Deserve: Bill Clinton, His Rise, Fall and Comeback, M. Walker (1996)

Cold War   A term first used by the financier Bernard Baruch in 1947 and popularized by the journalist Walter Lippmann. It refers to the confrontation of the superpowers (the US and the Soviet Union) and their allies, which involved rivalry (ideological, military and economic) without resort to open war. The wartime alliance soon broke down after the Second World War as the capitalist and communist worlds opposed each other. STALIN was determined to have a line of satellite buffer states in Eastern Europe as a first line of defence against any further attack from the West. With the Soviet economy in ruins and his country exhausted, he did not look for an expansion of Soviet borders beyond those occupied by the Red Army. He pulled his troops out of Iran in 1946, did not take part in the GREEK CIVIL WAR and demobilized almost as fast as the US (there were 11.3 million Soviet troops in 1946, 2.8 million in 1947), but he feared the US, which had not suffered any war damage and emerged from the war with a vibrant economy.

The Cold War was fuelled by fear. Americans saw the Russians as aggressive and aiming at world domination and with strong communist parties in Italy and France, feared that communist governments might be elected in Western Europe. George Kennan stressed the need for the 'containment of Russian expansive tendencies'. The President therefore proclaimed the TRUMAN DOCTRINE, offering aid to all countries threatened by communism. This greatly accelerated the Cold War, as it convinced the Soviet Union of American expansionist tendencies. Fear of communism spreading in the war-torn economies of Western Europe, made worse by the harsh winter of 1947, led to the MARSHAL PLAN (1948), which Stalin saw as a threat to his hold on Eastern Europe. The CZECH COUP, when communists seized power in 1948, confirmed American suspicions of the Soviet Union. It was followed by the BERLIN BLOCKADE, when both sides were careful to avoid open warfare. West European states felt very vulnerable to an attack by the vastly superior Soviet conventional forces and this disquiet increased when the US lost its monopoly of atom bombs: the USSR exploded its own in 1949. Western Europe needed an American commitment to its defence and received this with the formation of NATO in 1949, an event which made any possible Soviet attack in the West unlikely.

The Cold War moved to Asia in 1949 when the communists defeated JIANG JIESHI (Chiang Kai-shek) and won the CHINESE CIVIL WAR (1946–9). This was seen in the US as part of a world conspiracy directed by Moscow, especially when the SINO-SOVIET ALLIANCE was signed in 1950. A virulent anti-communism, which Senator Joe MCCARTHY did much to exploit, swept the US, where Truman was blamed for the 'loss' of China. The President had to show that he was not 'soft' on communism, which he promptly did when the KOREAN WAR began in 1950. American intervention saved South Korea from communist domination but when China joined in to help the North to resist the US, DULLES explained that 'The Mao Tse-tung regime is a creature of the Moscow Politburo'. This was not true but the US opposed the People's Republic of China being a member of the UNITED NATIONS and recognized Jiang in Taiwan as the legitimate government of China. The Korean War further increased tension in the Cold War as it resulted in the JAPAN–US SECURITY TREATY (1951), which allowed the US to retain military bases in Japan and to form anti-communist pacts such as ANZUS (1951) and SEATO (1954), which was intended to be a Far Eastern counterpart of NATO.

After the death of Stalin there were more cordial relations for a short time between the US and the USSR. KHRUSHCHEV talked of 'peaceful coexistence' and when both sides developed a HYDROGEN BOMB in 1953 it was clear that there could be no victor in a nuclear war but only mutually assured destruction (appropriately called MAD). Both sides abandoned the idea of fighting one another: when Soviet tanks crushed the HUNGARIAN RISING of 1956 the US did not attempt to intervene. The Soviet Union agreed to withdraw from Austria in the AUSTRIAN STATE TREATY of 1955 and established diplomatic relations with West Germany. This early period of DÉTENTE did not last. French defeat in the INDO-CHINA WAR OF INDEPENDENCE (1946–54) led Eisenhower to invoke the DOMINO THEORY and to replace French influence there. He undermined the GENEVA ACCORDS (1954) to make South Vietnam a separate state and supported the dictator DIEM to prevent the South becoming communist. Thus, what was an internal Asian conflict was turned by the Cold War into an American war, as future Presidents, particularly Lyndon JOHNSON, escalated American involvement. The SUEZ CRISIS (1956) enabled the Soviet Union to gain influence in the Middle East. Another Berlin crisis ended with the erection of the BERLIN WALL (1961), but it was on America's doorstep that the Cold War threatened to turn into a hot one. The CUBAN MISSILE CRISIS was the nearest that the superpowers came to nuclear war, but both sensibly backed off.

There was a period of *détente* in the early 1970s with the SALT I agreement (1971) and the HELSINKI ACCORDS (1975), but like the earlier period it proved temporary. The revival of hostility between the superpowers in the late 1970s has been called the Second Cold War and showed a more confident Soviet Union and an apparently weaker US. The cost of the VIETNAM WAR caused President NIXON to abandon the gold standard and fixed exchange rates in 1971, while the failure to win that war deflated American prestige. The US suffered from the OPEC PRICE RISE in 1973: the Soviet Union benefited from it, as it quadrupled the value of its recently discovered oil and gas fields in Siberia. The balance of power between the superpowers appeared to be changing, as there were revolutions in Africa, Asia and Latin America, in which some countries moved to the Soviet side. For the first time the Soviet Union intervened on a large scale in Africa, where communist regimes were set up in Ethiopia after the fall of HAILE SELAS-SIE and in Guinea-Bissau, Angola and Mozambique after the PORTUGUESE REVO-LUTION of 1974 and the collapse of the Portuguese Empire. As America's ally in Iran, MUHAMMAD REZA PAHLAVI, was overthrown in the IRANIAN REVOLUTION of 1979 there was hysteria in the US, which claimed inplausibly that the SOVIET INVA-SION OF AFGHANISTAN (1979) was the first step towards the Persian Gulf and the seizure of the world's main oil supplies. The superpowers' confrontation intensified in the early 1980s with the deployment of cruise missiles in Europe, the SDI (Strategic Defense Initiative) and US support for anti-communist guerrillas in Afghanistan, Angola and Nicaragua. Appearances were deceptive. BREZH-NEV was bankrupting the Soviet Union by increasing military spending in real terms by 4–5 per cent a year: it took up to 25 per cent of GNP, 7 per cent in the US. GORBACHEV realized this and that confrontation with the US served no purpose. He brought the Cold War to an end by convincing President REA-GAN of his sincerity by making agreements with the US for arms control and reductions, and by withdrawing support from THIRD WORLD revolutionary regimes and from the communist parties of Eastern Europe, thus allowing the REVOLUTIONS OF 1989–91 to take place. The COLLAPSE OF THE SOVIET UNION completed the process.

America, Russia and the Cold War, 1945–80,
   W. LaFeber (1980)
The Turn: How the Cold War Came to an End: The US and the Soviet Union 1983–90, D.
   Oberdorfer (1992)
We Now Know: Rethinking Cold War Victory:
   G. L. Gaddis (1997)

COMECON (Council for Mutual Economic Assistance, or CMEA) (1949–91)

An economic organization set up by the Soviet Union in response to the MARSHALL PLAN and OEEC. It originally consisted of the Soviet satellite states of Eastern Europe (Albania was expelled in 1961), but was later joined by Mongolia (1962), Cuba (1972) and Vietnam (1978). Yugoslavia had a 'special' but non-member status. COMECON was the economic equivalent of the COMINFORM and imposed economic uniformity on Soviet satellites: all had Five Year Plans, the nationalization of industry, the collectivization of agriculture and all took their orders from Moscow. Through it the USSR tried to create a self-sufficient regional economy, separate from the capitalist GLOBAL ECONOMY. The foreign trade of all its members was heavily directed towards the Soviet Union and each other: Bulgaria's trade with Russia and Eastern Europe rose from 12 per cent in 1937 to 92 per cent in 1951. Hungary's from 13 per cent to 67 per cent, Romania's from 18 per cent to 79 per cent and Czechoslovakia's from 11 per cent to 60 per cent. Trade outside COMECON was discouraged, the currencies of its members were non-convertible and they did not take part in GATT. This was not an alliance of equals: Soviet exports of raw materials and machinery to members were well above world market prices, whereas the Soviet satellites had to sell their goods to the USSR cheaply.

GORBACHEV in the late 1980s brought about the disintegration as COMECON as it no longer served Soviet purposes. The USSR, wanting more contact with the West, made the rouble convertible, applied for membership of GATT and announced that from 1991 Soviet trade with Eastern Europe would be in hard currency only. The REVO-LUTIONS OF 1989 created an economic system in which COMECON had no place, so it ceased to exist by 1991.

Cominform (Communist Information Bureau) (1947–56)

Established by STA-LIN as a response to the TRUMAN DOC-TRINE and the MARSHALL PLAN. It included representatives of the French and Italian communist parties, as well as those of Eastern Europe. The Cominform never had the importance of its predecessor, the Comintern (dissolved in 1943), but it was used to make sure that the communist states of Eastern Europe followed the same ideology and political practices (the same constitutions, educational and social systems) as the Soviet Union. It expelled Yugoslavia in 1948, after the YUGOSLAV–SOVIET SPLIT. When KHRUSHCHEV was reconciled with TITO after Stalin's death, the Cominform was dissolved in 1956.

owing to the high duties on their agricultural exports and the dumping of EEC produce in the GLOBAL ECONOMY. Yet, in spite of the protection of CAP, the EEC was by far the largest importer of agricultural produce. By 1990 under 6 per cent of employment in the EC was in agriculture, though agricultural lobbies remained powerful, especially in France. Ten out of the twelve member states were net exporters of farm produce and so benefited from CAP.

The Common Agricultural Policy: Past, Present and Future, B. E. Hill (1984)

Common Agricultural Policy (CAP)

Adopted by the EEC (European Economic Community) to protect its farmers. In 1957, when the TREATY OF ROME was signed, agriculture was a major factor in most European states, employing 20 per cent of the work force (35 per cent in Italy, 25 per cent in France). DE GAULLE, who disliked France's loss of sovereignty in the EEC, regarded the CAP as essential if France was to remain in the community. CAP provided free trade in agricultural produce within the EEC, a minimum level of prices and a guaranteed market (through storing and the dumping of surpluses). There were also high duties on competitive agricultural imports. High prices and a guaranteed market resulted in overproduction and the appearance of butter mountains and wine lakes: to cope with this, farmers were paid for not cultivating all their land. By 1977 CAP was taking 80 per cent of the EEC budget.

CAP boosted agricultural production and gave a reasonable standard of living to farmers but at the expense of the consumer, who had to pay much higher prices than those on the world market. As so much of the EEC budget was spent on the CAP (even after attempts to reduce it, over 50 per cent of the budget was spent on it in 1995) there was little left to spend on industrial regeneration and social policy. The THIRD WORLD also suffered,

Commonwealth of Nations Consisted

in 1990 of Britain and 49 other members, all of whom are independent states but were at one time part of the British Empire. They all accept the British monarch as its honorific head. In the 1920s the term 'British Commonwealth' was used to refer to the white dominions (Canada, Australia, New Zealand, Ireland), but with the independence of India and Pakistan in 1947 the title Commonwealth of Nations was adopted. A small minority of the old colonies chose not to become members on independence (Burma, 1947: Aden, 1967) or withdrew later: Ireland in 1949, South Africa in 1961 (because of the hostility to APARTHEID), Pakistan in 1972 (when Commonwealth members recognized Bangladesh as an independent country: it rejoined in 1989), Fiji in 1987. Namibia joined the Commonwealth in 1990, South Africa in 1994 and Cameroon in 1995.

The Commonwealth is a very loose-knit structure, with no treaty holding the members together. Heads of state meet at Commonwealth Conferences in different locations every two years, but no resolutions are passed and there is no attempt to formulate common policies: members are bound only by commitments into which they have entered freely. Since 1965 there has been a Secretariat, with a Secretary General at its head, which organizes meetings. On several occasions the

Commonwealth has seemed about to disintegrate but has shown remarkable resilience. During the SUEZ CRISIS (1956) Britain was severely criticized by many members, particularly by the Indian leader NEHRU. In the BIAFRAN WAR (1967–70) Britain supported the Nigerian government, KAUNDA of Zambia and NYERERE of Tanzania the breakaway state of Biafra. British IMMIGRATION ACTS restricting immigration from Commonwealth countries (mainly from the West Indies, India and Pakistan) from 1962 caused bitterness in the countries most deeply affected, but it was the British attitude to minority white regimes in southern Africa which came closest to destroying the Commonwealth. Afro-Asian members constantly attacked Britain for taking no action against Ian Smith's regime in Rhodesia after UDI. Ghana and Tanzania temporarily broke off diplomatic relations with Britain, though they remained members of the Commonwealth. British opposition to sanctions against South Africa led to a split in 1986 between Britain and the rest. This caused some members of the CONSERVATIVE PARTY, particularly Margaret THATCHER, to show some hostility towards the Commonwealth.

The Commonwealth has survived in spite of its often acrimonious disputes, because it serves the interests of its members, who could expect economic and even military aid from Britain and privileged access to British markets. Only four members (Britain, Canada, Australia, New Zealand) are developed countries: nearly all the rest belong to the THIRD WORLD and 27 have populations of less than a million. These countries have little say in the organizations which regulate the GLOBAL ECONOMY: the IMF, WORLD BANK and GATT (General Agreement on Tariffs and Trade). As Commonwealth members they can discuss their problems with industrial nations, especially Britain and Canada, who have great influence in such organizations. For 'front-line states' in central and southern Africa membership was a means of putting pressure on South Africa to abandon *apart-*

heid. Britain, too, was grateful for Commonwealth membership in critical situations. Support of Commonwealth countries in the FALKLANDS WAR ensured that there would be no bloc vote of Third World countries behind Argentina at the UNITED NATIONS.

Stitches in Time: The Commonwealth in World Politics, A. Smith (1981)
The Commonwealth Secretariat and the Contemporary Commonwealth, M. P. Doxey (1989)

Communes, People's   The basic unit of government in the Chinese countryside, created in 1958 during the GREAT LEAP FORWARD (GLF). In 1957 MAO ZEDONG called for the amalgamation of collective farms into larger units to provide the manpower to build dams and terrace the countryside. They were to be large enough to use local resources efficiently yet small enough to be democratically controlled. By the end of 1958, 740,000 collectives had become 26,000 communes, each with an average of 5,000 households (30,000 people). The communes were to be social, economic and political units, providing all the social services their inhabitants required. 'Barefoot' doctors, paramedics with training in traditional Chinese medicine, were to run part-time clinics. The distinction between mental and manual labour was to be eliminated by part-time schools, in which students spent half their time studying and half their time working on the land. People's militias were formed with the slogan 'everyone a soldier', so that money could be saved on a regular army and spent on industrialization. To encourage a more egalitarian society peasant property was confiscated, private plots were abolished and peasants had to eat in communal canteens. Peasant opposition to the break-up of family life and the disastrous results of the GLF led to some commune functions being handed back to the production brigade (the former collective) after 1959: private plots and ownership of personal goods were restored to the peasants. The communes were dismantled in the 1980s, as agricultural production was restored to the individual peasant householder.

Mao's China and After, M. Meisner (1986)
Bureaucracy, Economy and Leadership in China, D. Bachman (1991)

Communist take-over of Eastern Europe (1945–8)   The stage was set for the communists to seize control of much of Eastern Europe by the 'percentage agreement' of October 1944, when CHURCHILL agreed that STALIN should have predominance in Romania and Bulgaria, that Greece should remain in the West and that power should be shared with the communists in Yugoslavia and Hungary. 'Make no mistake', Churchill told his personal secretary at Yalta, 'all the Balkans, except Greece, are going to be Bolshevised and there is nothing I can do to prevent it. There is nothing I can do for Poland either'. The Red Army also helped greatly, as it overran most of Eastern Europe towards the end of the Second World War and was therefore in a strong position to aid local communist parties. 'This war is not as in the past', Stalin told Milovan Djilas. 'Whoever occupies a territory imposes his own social system as far as his army can reach'. Without the Red Army it would have been impossible for the small communist parties in Hungary and Romania to take power. The Red Army played a vital role in Poland too.

In 1945 communism seemed to many the ideology of the future. Capitalism was associated with the Great Depression (1929–39), Fascism and war, whereas the Soviet Union had avoided the depression (little was known of Stalin's terror and famine in the USSR). Communists enjoyed great prestige from leading the Resistance to Nazi Germany and were the best organized, disciplined and dynamic party, setting up organizations to run local administration. They were able to fill the power vacuum at the end of the war as their enemies had been destroyed or weakened, particularly the large estate owners. Stalin's priority was to establish a secure Western border, which meant having a pro-communist government in Poland to ensure Soviet access to garrisons in East Germany, the USSR's first line of defence. 'Throughout history', Stalin said, 'Poland had been the corridor for attack on Russia. . . . It was not only a question of honour for Russia but one of life and death'. It is not clear whether he intended to establish communist regimes throughout Eastern Europe: probably he simply took advantage of opportunities as they appeared. Almost everywhere the communist take-over followed the same pattern. Coalition governments were formed in which communists shared power but acquired posts which gave them control of the armed forces and police. Leaders of non-communist parties were then undermined and socialist parties were pressurized into merging with communists. Finally, opposition parties were banned or allowed only as part of a National Front dominated by communists.

Communist take-overs took place first in Albania and Yugoslavia and owed nothing to the Red Army. In Albania Enver HOXHA was leader of the Resistance and was left in control when the Germans withdrew in December 1944. There was a similar situation in Yugoslavia, where the Partisans under TITO were in charge of much of the country when the Germans left and eliminated the last of their domestic opponents when Mihajlović was captured in March 1946 and executed in July. In the elections of 1945 there was a single list of government candidates: the constitution of 1946 established the leading role of the Communist Party.

In Poland the Communist Polish Workers' Party (PWP) was small and weak, as it was regarded as pro-Russian and depended heavily on Soviet support. When the Red Army entered Poland in July 1944 the Soviet Union set up a Lublin Committee of Polish communists as a provisional government for the areas under their control. The Warsaw Rising

(July–August 1944) of the Home Army, loyal to the anti-communist government-in-exile in London, was brutally put down by the Germans, destroyed much of the opposition leadership and benefited the communists. In December 1944 the USSR recognized the Lublin Committee as the provisional government of Poland and established it in Warsaw in January 1945 after the city was liberated. The Allies, however, did not recognize the government, so a new government was formed which included various parties, particularly the Peasant Party, led by Stanislaw Mikolajczyk. From the autumn of 1945 to July 1946 there was in effect a civil war between communists and their opponents: GOMULKA later said that without the Red Army the communists would not have been able to 'fight reaction'. Mikolajczyk, who wanted the 'Finlandization' of Poland (independence from, but close ties with, the Soviet Union) formed his own Polish Peasants' Party (PPP), which in January 1946 was by far the largest party in Poland with 600,000 members. In January 1947, however, PPP candidates were disqualified, party workers arrested and in a rigged election the PPP were allowed only 10 per cent of the votes. Mikolajczjk, fearing arrest, went into exile in the autumn, thus ending effective opposition. In December 1947 Gomulka decided that the working class needed only one party to represent it, so the socialists and communists merged in the Polish United Workers' Party.

Stalin expected the West to bargain over Hungary and Czechoslovakia and was surprised when they did not do so. When the Red Army entered Hungary in December 1944 he ordered the communists not to bid for power but to form a coalition government, which they did. The election of November 1945 shocked the communists, as they gained only 17 per cent of the vote, the Smallholders' Party (SHP) winning 45 per cent. Ferenc Nagy of SHP became Prime Minister and the party leader, Zoltan Tildy, President in a coalition government, but the communists were in charge of the Ministry of the Interior

and the security forces. Matyas RÁKOSI, the communist leader, then began his 'salami tactics', destroying the opposition bit by bit. The Ministry of the Interior announced an SHP conspiracy to overthrow the republic and in 1946–7 held SHOW TRIALS (with the cooperation of, or on instructions from, the Soviet NKVD). In June 1947 Ferenc Nagy, under investigation, resigned. The communists were the largest party, with 22 per cent of the vote, in the August elections of 1947. They took control and in June 1949 fused with the socialists to become the Hungarian Workers' Party. In Bulgaria the Soviet Union was popular so, with help from the Red Army, the communists were able to dominate the National Front formed in March 1945 and, a year later, to merge with the socialists. In the election of November 1946 the Front won 80 per cent of the vote in a rigged election. The most severe critic of the communists, the peasant leader Nikola Petkov, was executed in September 1947 after a disgraceful show trial. The Red Army was confident enough to withdraw from Bulgaria in December 1947.

The Romanian Communist Party had under 1,000 members in August 1944, so relied heavily on Soviet influence in the National Democratic Front, a coalition formed in October 1944. In September 1947 parties of the left merged with the communists in the Romanian United Workers' Party, confirming communist control of the country. The communist take-over in East Germany followed directly from the DIVISION OF GERMANY into military zones at the end of the Second World War. In the Soviet zone the communist and socialist parties were fused in April 1946 in the Socialist Unity Party of Germany (SED), though in the August elections it did not win a majority in any province. The German Democratic Republic was born, under communist control, in October 1948, after the formation of West Germany from the British, French and American zones. In Czechoslovakia there was initially strong support for the communists after the Second World War and in the May 1946 elections they were by far the largest party with 38 per cent of the vote. When their popularity began to ebb the CZECH COUP of February 1948 enabled them to seize power. By the end of 1948 the whole of Eastern Europe had come under communist control.

The Anatomy of Communist Takeovers, T. Hammond (ed.) (1975)
Communist Power in Europe 1944–49, M. McCauley (ed.) (1977)
The Establishment of Communist Regimes in Eastern Europe, 1944–49, N. Naimark and L. Gibianskii (eds) (1997)

Congo crisis (1960–5)   For most of the 1950s the Belgians had no intention of granting independence to the Belgian Congo (later Zaire). Africans had no access to higher education before 1954 (in 1960 only 3 out of 4,600 of the top posts in the civil service were held by Congolese), but change came very rapidly from 1958 when DE GAULLE offered the neighbouring French Congo autonomy within the French Community or independence. Rioting and looting in Leopoldville (Kinshasa) in January 1959, the result of an economic recession and unemployment, prompted the Belgians, fearful of an Algerian situation (see ALGERIAN WAR OF INDEPENDENCE), to move rapidly towards independence for the Congo. Parties were formed, generally with regional and ethnic support, the most important of which were Abako, led by Joseph Kasavubu, based among the Bakongo in the lower Congo and Leopoldville, and Conakat, led by Moise Tshombe and based in Katanga (Shaba), the richest of the Congolese provinces owing to its mineral wealth. The party which had a more national appeal was the MNC (Congolese National Movement), which had support from the peasants of central Congo, the proletariat of the towns and the smaller ethnic groups of the south. In the May 1960 elections the MNC won the most seats but no party gained a majority, so on independence in June there

was a coalition government, with Patrice Lumumba, leader of the MNC, as Prime Minister and Kasavubu as President.

Almost immediately the Congo began to slide into anarchy. On 5 July the army (which did not have one African officer) mutinied against its Belgian officers and killed some white civilians too. Belgians fled in panic, leaving the country without a civil service. Lumumba ended the mutiny by promising rapid Africanization of the army, but on 11 July Tshombe, backed by the main mining company (the *Union Minière*) and other Belgian interests, declared the independence of Katanga. With the country in chaos, Lumumba and Kasavubu appealed to the UNITED NATIONS for help. The UN sent a peace-keeping force but its Secretary-General, Dag HAMMARSKJÖLD, on the grounds that the UN charater did not allow interference in internal political disputes, refused to allow UN troops to be used against Katanga. Lumumba therefore turned to the Soviet Union for military aid and on 5 September was dismissed by Kasavubu, with US and Belgian backing. On 14 September Colonel Joseph MOBUTU, whom Lumumbu had made Chief of Staff of the Congolese army, seized power, again with US and Belgian support. Lumumba was arrested and his assassination plotted by the CIA. In January 1981 he was handed over to Tshombe, who murdered him. In Stanleyville (Kisangani) Antoine Gizenga, Lumumba's former deputy, formed a new government, so the Congo now had three rival centres of power and seemed about to disintegrate.

In an attempt to keep the country together a new central government was formed in August 1961 with Cyrille Adoula, a moderate and respected politician, as Prime Minister, Gizenga as his Deputy and Kasavubu still President. After Hammarskjöld, flying to negotiate with Tshombe, was killed in an air crash on 17 September, UN troops were authorized to take action against Katanga and by the end of 1962 had ended Katanga's secession, Tshombe going into exile. This did not bring unity for long, as the ruling coalition broke up and in 1964 there were revolts in much of the country. In June 1964 Tshombe surprisingly replaced Adoula as Prime Minister, having persuaded Kasavubu that he could end the rebellions by negotiation. He failed to do so and turned instead to a military solution, calling on white mercenaries. Belgian paratroops were dropped on Stanleyville, where a revolutionary regime had been set up, in November and the rising was crushed. A bitter struggle between Kasavubu and Tshombe continued into 1965 until Mobutu, now a General, seized power again and made himself President. This military coup was very popular, as there was a widespread desire for unity and an end to party squabbling based on ethnic groups.

Politics in the Congo: Decolonization and Independence, C. Young (1965)
Katanga Secession, J. Gerard-Libuz (1966)
Conflict in the Congo, T. Kanza (1972)

Conservative Party   The dominant political party in Britain in the twentieth century. The name was first used in 1830 for a party which wanted to preserve existing institutions: the monarchy, the Anglican Church, the British Empire and the landed aristocracy. It believed in a minimalist state, which should maintain law and order but not interfere with market forces in the economy, and took an organic view of society, which had grown up over centuries and should be changed only gradually. Although the Conservative Party saw its purpose as maintaining the status quo it recognized the need for some reform if it was to appeal to an expanding electorate and not become a minority party. Disraeli's Reform Act of 1867 doubled the size of the electorate, made working-class voters a majority in the boroughs and enabled him to claim that the Conservative Party was 'the national party ...the really democratic party of England'. Thus, the myth of Tory Democracy was born. The Primrose League mobilized working-

class support, helped by the right-wing mass-circulation newspapers such as the *Daily Mail*. Between the two world wars (1918–39) the Conservatives were the largest group in the House of Commons, except for the period of the Labour government from 1929–31. During the Second World War Winston CHURCHILL formed a coalition government, in which members of the LABOUR PARTY held important posts, Clement ATTLEE becoming Deputy Prime Minister in 1942.

The Conservatives, held responsible for the unemployment of the Great Depression in the 1930s and for the appeasement of Hitler, were defeated in the 1945 election, in spite of the personal popularity of Churchill as a great war-time leader, but were back in power in 1951. In the 52 years since the war to 1997 the Conservative Party has been in office for 35 years. Up to 1970 its policies differed little from those of the Labour Party. The governments of Churchill, Anthony EDEN and Harold MACMILLAN accepted the WELFARE STATE, a mixed economy full employment as a goal and consultation with the TRADE UNIONS as a means. This consensus politics, known as BUTSKELLISM (an amalgam of the names of the Conservative R. A. BUTLER and the Labour leader Hugh GAITSKELL), applied to foreign policy too: both parties were committed to NATO, DECOLONIZATION, the 'special relationship' with the US and the nuclear deterrent.

Edward HEATH's premiership marked a transition stage in the Conservative Party. His most humiliating defeat was in the MINERS' STRIKE in 1972, when he gave way, and when the miners called another strike in 1974 he decided on an election (with the slogan 'Who Governs Britain?') which he was expected to win, but lost. These traumatic events brought about a sea-change in the Conservative Party. A dominant section was convinced that a search for consensus was futile, particularly after the WINTER OF DISCONTENT. Heath was replaced as Conservative leader in 1975 by Margaret THATCHER, who won the 1979 election.

Thatcher abandoned consensus and steered the Conservative Party in a new direction. She rejected KEYNESIANISM, the dominant economic philosophy since the war, at first in favour of MONETARISM as a means of controlling inflation and when this did not work she used interest rates. Control of inflation rather than full employment was the government's main economic aim. The Conservative Party no longer appealed primarily to the managerial, professional and administrative élite but also to the *petit-bourgeoisie* of small employers and the self-employed, who saw themselves as victims of overmighty TRADE UNIONS. Instead of co-operating with the unions Thatcher crushed them. Reverting to the Manchester School of the 1840s, she did not want the state to interfere in the free working of the market. Public ownership, she believed, was inefficient, so PRIVATIZATION took place of most nationalized industries except for coal and the railways (privatized by John MAJOR) and the Post Office. A sustained attack on local government saw its powers replaced by those of unelected quangos or curtailed by reductions in government grants and rate-capping. The postwar situation, when the Conservative Party responded to initiatives of the Labour Party, was reversed. New Labour, under Tony Blair, accepted the changes brought about by Conservative governments: privatization, limitations on the trade unions and low direct taxes.

John MAJOR replaced Thatcher as leader of the Conservative Party (and as Prime Minister) in 1990 and surprisingly won the 1992 general election, when Britain was in the depths of a recession. BLACK WEDNESDAY soon followed, when a run on the pound forced Britain out of the ERM, but the effective devaluation improved British competitiveness and brought about an economic recovery. Yet the government was deeply unpopular, as local government elections showed. Job insecurity was widespread, many suffered from negative equity as the housing boom collapsed and the government broke its promise not to raise taxes. In the 1997 election the Conservative Party suffered its worst defeat since 1832. With 31 per cent of the vote it lost 177 seats, winning only 165 to 419 for the Labour Party. It was left with no MPs at all in Scotland and Wales and in many of the largest English cities such as Manchester, Leeds, Liverpool and Bristol. The longest continuous period of rule by one party in Britain since the Napoleonic Wars thus came to an end.

The British Party System, S. Ingle (1987)
UK Political Parties Since 1945, A. Seldon (ed.) (1990)

Constitution of the Fifth Republic in France   This reflected the ideas of Charles DE GAULLE, which he set out as early as 1946. He disliked the weak governments of the Third Republic, which he blamed for the fall of France in 1940 and saw parliament as an obstruction to effective government, as political parties represented sectional interests, not the common good. Horse-trading was needed in forming coalition governments, which were incapable of making effective decisions. This led to immobilism, a reluctance to make any decisions, particularly unpopular ones. De Gaulle therefore wanted a strong executive and a clear division of power between the legislature and the executive. When he accepted the post of Prime Minister of the FOURTH REPUBLIC on 1 June 1958 he insisted on the right to draw up a new constitution and to submit this for public approval in a referendum. In September 1958 79 per cent of voters endorsed it.

The main institutions of the Fifth Republic – the presidency, a bicameral legislature and independent judiciary – were the same as in the Fourth but their powers were changed: those of the President were increased, those of parliament diminished. The President was elected for seven years. He had considerable powers: the right to appoint the Prime Minister, to preside over meetings of the ministerial council, to dissolve parliament after a year, and to hold a referendum on important issues. In an emergency the President could suspend the government and rule alone. He was head of the armed forces and had wide powers of appointment to high civil and military posts. Parliament was bicameral: the National Assembly was popularly elected for five years; the Senate represented the departments and was chosen by electoral colleges. The parliament met for only five months a year but the government needed its support, as it passed laws. In keeping with de Gaulle's wish for a clear separation between executive and legislature, government ministers could not be members of parliament and if elected, had to resign their seats. This meant that a Prime Minister could choose as ministers men and women who were most suitable: in Debré's government (1959–62) only 15 out of 28 ministers were ex-members of parliament. There was some ambiguity about the relationship of President and Prime Minister who, though appointed by the President, was responsible to parliament. It was not clear what rights each had if they clashed over policy. This did not arise when de Gaulle was President, as he appointed Prime Ministers (Debré, POMPIDOU, Couve de Murville) who were loyal to him, but he regarded defence and foreign policy as a *domaine réservé* in which parliament should not interfere.

The fear that the constitution was designed for de Gaulle and would not survive him has proved unfounded. It has served equally well for Presidents with different ideologies, though problems of cohabitation (of President and Prime Minister) arose when GISCARD D´ESTAING was President in the mid-1970s and again with MITTERRAND ten years later. There was no constitutional crisis on either occasion. The constitution has made possible more effective leadership and greater political stability: the average life of governments has been three years rather than six months as in the Fourth Republic.

Democracy in France Since 1870, D. Thomson (1969)

President and Parliament, R. Derfler (1983)
France in Modern Times, G. Wright (1987)

Contras Counter-revolutionaries who fought against the SANDINISTA government in Nicaragua in the 1980s. The CIA created a force of 500, drawn from remnants of the defeated National Guard of SOMOZA and provided it with bases in Honduras. This grew into a force of 15,000, trained and equipped by the US, which objected to a left-wing regime in Central America and to the aid the Sandinistas were giving to the rebels in the SALVADOREAN CIVIL WAR. By 1983 the CIA decided that the Contras could not win a military victory, so President REAGAN allowed it to take a more direct role by mining Nicaraguan harbours. Congress provided spasmodic funding, cutting off aid in 1984, resuming it in 1986 and restricting it in 1987, when the Arias Plan called for an end to external support for rebels and when the IRAN CONTRA AFFAIR showed that some funds from the sale of US arms to Iran had been diverted to the Contras. When the Sandinistas were defeated in the 1990 general election the civil war ended and the Contras were demobilized under UNITED NATIONS supervision. They were provided with land and several commanders accepted posts in the new government of Violeta Chamorro, but in 1991 some took to the hills again, demanding an end to the continuing Sandinistan domination of the army and police and held out until 1994.

The CIA and Nicaragua's Contra Rebels, S. Dillon (1991)

Council of Europe An association of European states formed in 1949 on the initiative of Ernest BEVIN, the British Foreign Secretary. It disappointed federalists, as its Parliamentary Assembly at Strasbourg is a purely consultative body of MPs, who are appointed by the Parliaments of member states. The council's institutions have no power to make laws. Its Committee of Ministers is the decision-making body but each foreign minister has a veto and each member state decides whether or not to ratify any of the conventions it produces. The council is quite separate from the EEC (European Economic Community), though all EEC countries are members. Unlike the EEC, which overshadowed the council by 1960, it does not deal with economic affairs but is concerned mainly with human rights, protection of the environment, the suppression of terrorism and the fight against the DRUG TRADE. The council has helped to standardize civil rights across Europe, particularly the rights of women. It established a European Convention on Human Rights and a European Court of Justice to administer it as early as 1950. The court's decisions are usually respected. In 1997 representatives of member states met in Strasbourg and endorsed social codes concerning gender equality, the protection of ethnic minorities, joint action against organized crime and drug abuse and banned human cloning.

Only democracies can be members: Spain and Portugal did not therefore join until the dictatorial regimes of FRANCO and SALAZAR had ended. The membership of Greece and Turkey was suspended during periods of military rule in those countries. Since the REVOLUTIONS OF 1989–91 and the collapse of communism in Eastern Europe and the Soviet Union, nine East European states have joined: Russia was invited to join in 1997 and did so, bringing the number of member states up to 40. For some countries, which want to join NATO or the European Union, the council has a probationary role. 'All of Europe is here', said the council's Secretary-General in 1997, 'except those who have excluded themselves by abandoning democratic principles – the Yugoslavs and Belorussians'.

CPSU (Communist Party of the Soviet Union) Grew out of the Bolshevik wing of the Russian Social Democratic Workers' Party founded in 1898. It was led by Lenin, who wanted a tightly organized and disciplined party that adhered to the principle of 'democratic centralism' (i.e. that decisions once reached must be carried out without question). After a brief partnership with the Left Socialist Revolutionaries the Bolsheviks ruled the Soviet Union from March 1918 as a single-party dictatorship. The party became the All-Russian Communist Party and, after other name changes, the CPSU in 1952. 'Factions' were forbidden in 1921 and so serious opposition, or even discussion, within the party ended. This situation remained for nearly 70 years until GORBACHEV became General Secretary. Under Lenin the communists formed a vanguard rather than a mass party, with a quarter of a million members in November 1917. After that party membership rose rapidly, in spite of frequent purges, to reach six million in 1945 and 19 million (7 per cent of the population) in 1990.

The Party Congress did not meet at all between 1939–52 but thereafter met every four or five years. Between Congresses the Central Committee, which met twice a year and was elected by the Congress, was in charge of party affairs. It was too unwieldy with 470 members in 1981 to act effectively, so it elected Party Committees, of which the Politburo (known from 1952–65 as the Presidium) and the Secretariat were the real centres of power. The Politburo of between 15 and 20 full and candidate (non-voting) members, was the main policy-making body, which controlled all domestic and foreign policy. The party boss in each area was the First Secretary. There was a hierarchy of district, city, regional and republican First Secretaries, culminating in the General Secretary of the CPSU. As the Secretariat controlled the appointment of party members throughout the country, the career of party officials depended on their loyalty to the First or General Secretary, who could influence who was elected to the Party Congress, Central Committee and Politburo. STALIN's role as head of the Secretariat was decisive in his rise to dominance. The party structure of the CPSU was a model for that of the communist states of Eastern Europe after the Second World War.

The CPSU had a monopoly of power in the USSR. Article 6 of the 1977 constitution referred to it as 'the leading and guiding force of Soviet society and the nucleus of its political system, of all state institutions and public organizations'. It dominated the state, made party policy into law and then carried it out. The party appointed the NOMENKLA-TURA, which ran the country. There were 213,000 salaried officials in the *apparat* (machine) in 1990, who gave orders to soviets, trade unions and mass organizations. Gorbachev found that most party officials opposed his reforms, so he introduced GLASNOST and perestroika to undermine them. They lost their control of ideology, then of the economy and in 1990 their monopoly of power was removed when authority passed from the Politburo to the State President. In March 1990 Gorbachev persuaded the Central Committee of the CPSU to remove Article 6 from the constitution. The CPSU split into factions, four million people left it (1990–1) and after the failure of the AUGUST COUP of 1991 the party was discredited as it had not initially condemned the coup. The governments of Russia and other republics banned the CPSU and confiscated its property, though former party members continued to hold office in many independent states after the COLLAPSE OF THE SOVIET UNION. The Russian Communist Party was reconstituted in 1993 and soon became the largest party in Russia.

The Soviet Communist Party, R. J. Hill and P. Frank (1988)
The Communist Party of the Soviet Union from 1934 to the Present, J. Armstrong

Craxi, Bettino (1934–)   Prime Minister of Italy (1983–7). Born in Milan, the son of a socialist who had moved from Sicily to find work, Craxi joined the PSI (Italian Socialist Party) in 1952 and entered Milan University to study law but found politics more interesting and left without a degree. He was elected to the central committee of the PSI at the age of 23, his rise in the party owing much to his friendship with Pietro Nenni, the veteran socialist leader. Elected to the Chamber of Deputies in 1976, he became General Secretary of the PSI in the same year. He worked hard to unite his faction-ridden party, committed it to moderate social and economic policies and, with US backing, moved away from a Popular Front with the much larger PCI (Italian Communist Party). Coalition governments were the norm in Italy, with its system of proportional representation, so the PSI, by skilful manoeuvring, was able to exert greater influence than its electoral support justified.

The PSI under Craxi was a member of five out of six coalition governments between 1980–3. Craxi became Italy's first socialist Prime Minister in 1983 when the PSI had only 11.4 per cent of the vote in the general election and stayed in office for four years, longer than any postwar government. His administration was successful in bringing down inflation, in improving economic growth and in increasing fourfold the capitalization of the Milan stock market. In 1987 Italy (according to OECD figures) overtook Britain in GDP and moved from sixth to fifth place among the world's economies. Corruption, however, remained. In 1993 Craxi was charged with receiving millions of dollars as bribes and had to resign as party leader. He was found guilty and sentenced to eight years in prison but fled to Tunisia before his appeal could be heard.

Cuban missile crisis (October 1962)

Took place when the Soviet Union began to set up nuclear missile sites in Cuba. After the BAY OF PIGS fiasco in 1961 Fidel CASTRO asked the USSR for military protection, as he expected a US invasion. KHRUSHCHEV responded in the spring of 1962 by deciding to build missile sites in Cuba, partly to deter a US invasion but also to counterbalance the US's massive superiority in long-range nuclear weapons. 'At the time', Robert McNamara, President KENNEDY's Secretary of Defense, wrote later, 'we had 5,000 nuclear weapons we could deliver on the Soviet Union and they had only 300 they could deliver onto the US'. Khrushchev realized that by installing SS4s (with a range of 600 to 1,000 miles, or 960–1600 km) and SS5s (with a range of 2,000 miles, or 3,200 km) in Cuba most of the US and all its Strategic Air Command bases would be within range and the US would have virtually no warning of any attack. Only 15 per cent of US strategic forces could be assured of surviving a Soviet first strike. The preparation of sites began in early September but was unknown to the US until a U-2 flight on 15 October. The next fortnight was the most dangerous period of the COLD WAR, when nuclear war seemed likely.

Kennedy discussed the possible options with only a close circle of advisers. Bombing the sites or invading Cuba was rejected, as this would provoke Soviet reprisals which might lead to a full-scale nuclear war which neither side wanted. He therefore opted for a block-ade, which would allow the USSR a way out, and on 22 October broadcast to the nation on television. The President demanded that the missiles be withdrawn and announced a 'quarantine' on the shipment of offensive weapons to Cuba. The 'quarantine' was supported unanimously by the OAS (Organiza-tion of American States) and by the US's NATO allies and began on 24 October, when eight aircraft carriers and 170 other vessels formed an arc 500 miles (800 km) from the eastern tip of Cuba. Khrushchev ordered the Soviet ships sailing to Cuba to return home, so confrontation was avoided but the crisis continued, as there was pressure on both sides to take decisive action. On 26 October Khrushchev offered to withdraw the missiles if the US promised not to invade Cuba, but a day later he delivered a stronger message on

Moscow radio by demanding that the US should withdraw its missiles (medium-range Jupiter missiles which were due to be removed, as submarine-based Polaris missiles made them obsolete) from Turkey. Kennedy decided against openly agreeing to this, as it would be seen as weakness and a betrayal of Turkey, so he accepted Khrushchev's first offer, giving a private undertaking to with-draw the missiles in Turkey, which was done in 1963. On 28 October Khrushchev agreed and the crisis was over, though Castro was furious as he had not been consulted. On 21 November the quarantine ended.

The crisis paradoxically improved US–Soviet relations, as both sides realized how easily a conflict could lead to nuclear war. A hot-line was set up between Washington and Moscow so that future crises could be pre-vented from escalating. DÉTENTE was furth-ered too by the limited NUCLEAR TEST BAN TREATY of 1963 but the crisis accelerated the SINO-SOVIET SPLIT and severely weakened Khrushchev's position at home. He had been incredibly reckless in beginning something that could not be carried out if challenged and in giving Soviet commanders in Cuba permission to fire missiles on their own authority. Above all, he had made a humiliat-ing retreat under American pressure. As the US Secretary of State Dean Rusk said: 'Eye-ball to eyeball, they blinked first'.

Reflections on the Cuban Missile Crisis, R. L. Garthoff (1989)
On the Brink: Americans and Soviets Examine the Cuban Missile Crisis, J. S. Blight and D. A. Welch (1990)
'One Hell of a Gamble': Khrushchev, Castro, Kennedy and the Cuban Missile Crisis, 1958–64, A. Fursenko and T. Naftali (1997)

Cultural Revolution (1966–76)   A mass movement in China through which MAO ZEDONG hoped to perpetuate the communist revolution and to recover control of events.

LIU SHAOQI and DENG XIAOPING had reversed the policies of the GREAT LEAP FORWARD, restoring central control of the economy, reducing the functions of the COMMUNES, allowing private plots of land and putting more emphasis on expertise than ideological correctness. These moves Mao condemned as 'revisionism' and claimed that there were 'people in positions of authority within the Party who take the capitalist road'. He was also concerned about what would happen after his death and wanted to ensure that his revolutionary legacy would be perpetuated. This could best be done, he thought, by giving students some experience of revolution by encouraging them to take part in struggles against those in authority.

His assault on the Chinese Communist Party (CCP) became known as the Great Proletarian Cultural Revolution. The mass phase (1966–9) of the Revolution was led by the Red Guards, students who persecuted and humiliated intellectuals and party officials, killing many. The peak of their power came in the 'January Revolution' of 1967, when they tried to take over party organizations throughout China. As they had no central organization they fought each other and created chaos in all Chinese cities. Liu and Deng were removed from the Party leadership but by September all the leaders – Mao, his wife JIANG QING, ZHOU ENLAI and LIN BIAO – seemed to agree that anarchy prevailed and that order would have to be restored. This task was given to the People's Liberation Army (PLA): the Red Guards were disbanded but order was not restored until the summer of 1968. Revolutionary committees, representing the mass organizations, the PLA and the CCP, were formed but the PLA was dominant. In 1970 Mao authorized the subordination of the revolutionary committees to the party and called for the rehabilitation of cadres purged in 1966–8. Meanwhile, there was a power struggle in which Lin Biao was killed after an attempted coup in 1971. This was followed by a bitter conflict between the GANG OF FOUR, radicals who wanted to continue the policies of the Cultural Revolution, and the victims of that revolution led by Deng, who wanted a return to party control. The beneficiary of this conflict was HUA GUOFENG who, on succeeding Mao, promptly arrested the Gang of Four, which marks the official end of the Cultural Revolution.

The 620 million people in rural China were hardly affected by it and the economy too suffered remarkably little. Grain production rose in 1966 and 1967 and though it fell in 1968 it increased again a year later. Industrial production fell by 13 per cent in 1967 but it revived quickly and had fully recovered by 1971. The Cultural Revolution was largely an urban movement and there, in the cities, the effects were widespread. Education suffered as the universities, closed in 1966, did not reopen until 1970 and even then they were greatly changed: students were selected according to their class background and were expected to mix physical labour with their studies. CCP organizations were deeply affected: 70–80 per cent of provincial party officials were purged, as were 60–70 per cent of those in central party institutions. There were no mass executions as in STALIN's purges, but three million cadres (20 per cent of the bureaucracy) were sent to labour in the countryside and three million, condemned as 'revisionists', were rehabilitated in the late 1970s. Some officials were killed, others died in detention or committed suicide: Liu Shaoqi, beaten by Red Guards in 1967, died in prison two years later. It is estimated that between 400,000 and half a million people died as a result of the Cultural Revolution. Its long-term effects were a divided leadership and weakened CCP, which no longer had the allegiance of the young. China's Lost Generation (17 million students were sent down to the countryside, of whom 10 million were still there in 1978) lost its faith in communism. The policies pursued in China since the late 1970s reject everything that the Cultural Revolution stood for but it still casts a long shadow over China. The TIANANMEN

SQUARE MASSACRE in June 1989 arose out of the fear of Deng and his fellow gerontocrats that if they did not crush the student demonstrations they would escalate into another Cultural Revolution. This was officially described in 1981 as having caused 'the most severe setbacks and the heaviest losses suffered by the Party, the state and the people since the foundation of the People's Republic'.

New Perspectives on the Cultural Revolution, C. P. W. Wong and D. Zweig (1991)
The Politics of China 1948–1989, R. MacFarquhar (ed.) (1993)
Radicals and Radical Ideology in China's Cultural Revolution, P. H. Chang

Czech coup (1948) The communist seizure of power in Czechoslovakia, which was part of the COMMUNIST TAKE-OVER OF EASTERN EUROPE. Communists had been prominent in the resistance to Hitler: the liberation of Czechoslovakia by the Red Army increased their popularity. Eduard Beneš, the leader of the Czech government-in-exile in London, convinced that he could 'swallow and defeat' the Czech communists in Moscow, had promised them important posts, including Minister of the Interior, in the coalition government which ruled Czechoslovakia when the war was over. A coalition was formed in 1945 with the communist GOTT-WALD as Prime Minister; half his ministers were pro-communist. The communists were in a strong position to seize power but avoided this because STALIN did not want to alarm the Western powers and because of the popularity of Beneš: they also thought that they would soon win an election. In the elections of 1946 the Communist Party (CCP), with 38 per cent of the vote, was the largest party and, with its socialist allies, had a majority in parliament. By 1947 the CCP had 1.3 million members, more than all the other parties put together, but the situation changed in July.

The government wanted to accept MARSHALL PLAN aid but Masaryk, the Foreign Minister, was summoned to Moscow and forced to reject this: he called it a second Munich. After this, support for the communists dropped away. A public opinion poll in January 1948 showed communist support of 25 per cent, with a general election due in the summer. On 12 February non-communist ministers demanded that the communists should stop packing the police with their supporters, but Gottwald ignored them. He feared a French or Italian-style expulsion (in 1947 French and Italian communists had been left out of government coalitions), so he mobilized communist support in the trade unions and set up 'action committees', who were given arms, to by-pass local government councils. On 20 February a People's Militia was formed, a communist private army of 15,000. Twelve non-communist ministers resigned, hoping that Beneš would call for new elections or form a new administration without communists. Instead, he delayed taking a decision as tension rose and on 22 February thousands of armed workers paraded through Prague, attacking non-communist organizations. The head of the army, Ludvik Svoboda, said his army would support 'the people'. On 25 February Beneš, fearing civil war or Soviet intervention, handed over power to the communists. A new government, led by Klement Gottwald, was formed, consisting only of communists and their sympathizers. The communists took power without the aid of Soviet troops and without serious resistance. In the elections of May 1948 there were no opposition parties: the only candidates were those approved by the CCP. Beneš resigned in June, to be succeeded as President by Gottwald, so communist control was complete. The coup convinced West European governments that the Soviet Union would be satisfied with nothing less than the total subjugation of Eastern Europe and so led to an intensification of the COLD WAR.

The Short March: The Communist Takeover in Czechoslovakia 1945–8, K. Kaplan (1987)

Socialism and Democracy in Czechoslovakia 1945–8, M. Myant (1981)

Czechoslovakia, division of (1993)

The separation of Czechoslovakia into two independent states, the Czech and Slovak Republics. Ever since Czechoslovakia became an independent country in 1918 the Slovaks had resented Czech dominance in the economy and the government. After the VELVET REVOLUTION of 1989 and the collapse of communism the Slovak question was the main topic of debate, as several parties campaigned for Slovak autonomy. There was a division between the moderate Public Against Violence (PAV), the strongest party in the Slovak assembly, which wanted to preserve the federation, and the radicals who wanted complete independence. In March 1991 Vladimir Meciar, the Slovak Prime Minister and a founder of PAV, formed a faction within PAV, the Movement for a Democratic Slovakia (MDS), which wanted greater Slovak self-government. Many Slovaks saw his aggressive tactics as harmful to Czech–Slovak relations and in April the Slovak National Council removed him from the post of Prime Minis-

ter. Meciar therefore left PAV and made the MDS a separate party. Representatives of all political parties in Czechoslovakia agreed in 1991 on the framework for a new federal constitution, with two 'sovereign and equal republics', but there was no agreement on how power should be divided between the Czech and Slovak parts of the federation. Opinion polls showed that both Czechs and Slovaks wanted to preserve the federation, but it was agreed to postpone a new constitution until after elections in June 1992. These elections were decisive in bringing about the division of Czechoslovakia, as the MDS became the leading party in Slovakia (with 34 per cent of the vote) and Meciar became Slovak Prime Minister again. In the Czech lands Václav KLAUS and his allies won the election, dedicated to PRIVATIZATION and a market economy. Meciar, opposed to Klaus's economic reforms, wanted independence. An agreement was reached to divide Czechoslovakia into the Czech and Slovak Republics on 1 January 1993, a change brought about peacefully.

The End of Czechoslovakia, J. Musil (ed.) (1995)

D

Dayan, Moshe (1915–81) Israeli Minister of Defence (1967–74) and Foreign Minister (1977–9). His parents emigrated from Ukraine to Palestine in 1908 and it was there at Degania, the first kibbutz in the country, that he was born. Brought up in poverty, he learnt colloquial Arabic and, as a member of Haganah (the Jewish defence force), fought in the Arab rebellion (1936–9). He lost his left eye and subsequently wore a distinctive black patch when fighting for the British against the Vichy French in Lebanon in 1941. A founder member of the Palmach (the commando unit of the Haganah), he was commanding officer in Jerusalem during the Israeli War of Independence (1948–9) (see ISRAEL, BIRTH OF).

Dayan greatly impressed BEN-GURION, who made him Chief of Staff (1953–8), so he was present at the collusion meetings with Britain and France which decided to attack Egypt during the SUEZ CRISIS. His campaign in 1956 was brilliantly successful: in five days he defeated the Egyptians and seized Sinai and the Gaza Strip, though US and UNITED NATIONS pressure forced Israel to give these up. From 1959–64 he was Minister of Agriculture and, with Ben-Gurion, founded the Rafi Party, which in 1968 joined with other left-wing parties to form the Israeli Labour Party. As tension with Egypt mounted Levi Eshkol formed a Government of National Unity and Dayan returned to the cabinet in 1967 as Minister of Defence just before the SIX DAY WAR. This was another military triumph for Dayan, as Israel captured Sinai, the Gaza Strip, the WEST BANK and the GOLAN HEIGHTS. The YOM KIPPUR WAR (1973), however, saw a precipitous decline in his reputation, as he was surprised and caught unprepared by the Egyptian attack. The Israeli army suffered some major reverses initially and though Dayan successfully counter-attacked, the early defeats probably cost him the premiership when Golda Meir retired in 1974. The new Prime Minister, Yitzhak RABIN, dismissed him in 1974 but he returned again to the cabinet, this time under Menachem BEGIN, in 1977 as Foreign Minister. As such he played a key role in securing the CAMP DAVID ACCORDS (1978) with Anwar SADAT, which brought peace between Israel and Egypt. Angered by Begin's intention to assert Israeli sovereignty over the West Bank, he resigned in 1979. He formed a new party, which advocated Israeli withdrawal from the OCCUPIED TERRITORIES, in 1981, but died in the same year.

De Gasperi, Alcide (1881–1954) Prime Minister of Italy (1945–53). Born in Trentino, which was part of the Austro-Hungarian Empire, he received his higher education at the University of Vienna. In 1911 he was elected to the Austro-Hungarian parliament and was a member until the end of the First World War. When Trentino became part of Italy in 1919 De Gasperi was active in the Popular Party and was elected to the Chamber of Deputies in 1921. He denounced Fascism and was prepared to collaborate with the socialists to prevent its rise, but Pope Pius XI forbade such collaboration. When Mussolini banned all opposition in 1926 De Gasperi lost his seat and a year later was sentenced to four years in prison, of which he served 16 months. He was then employed by the Vatican library until Rome was liberated in 1944.

De Gasperi helped to found the CHRISTIAN DEMOCRATIC PARTY (DC) and was soon its undisputed leader. A devout Catholic, stern and aloof, he saw the need to co-operate with the PCI (Italian Communist Party) as communists had dominated the Resistance, but with the advent of the COLD WAR, and under pressure from the US and the Vatican, he dismissed them from the government in 1947. In 1948 the DC won a majority of seats in parliament but De Gasperi continued his coalition government with parties of the centre. A centrist himself, he rejected Vatican pressure to make the DC into a Catholic party, though he relied heavily on the Church's backing. To provide support for the DC he took over parts of the great landed estates and redistributed them to the peasants. Although the agrarian reform laws were inadequate to meet peasant needs and did not affect the conditions and wages of landless labourers, they were the first attempt to help the rural poor. De Gasperi approved of Italy's transition from a monarchy to a republic, which a referendum in 1946 confirmed, 12.7 per cent million voting for a republic, 10.7 million against it.

In February 1947 De Gasperi had to accept a peace treaty imposed by the Allies, by which Italy lost Dalmatia, Istria and Fiume to Yugoslavia and all her colonies, though she kept the German-speaking South Tyrol. The fate of Trieste was not decided until 1954, when it was allocated to Italy. De Gasperi aligned Italy with the US, accepting MARSHALL PLAN aid and joining NATO. He was a fervent supporter of a political federation of European states and of economic union. When the ECSC (European Coal and Steel Community) was formed De Gasperi made sure that Italy joined, in spite of opposition from Italy's steel manufacturers. By the time he resigned he had made DC the dominant political party, a position it was to retain until the 1990s.

The Rebirth of Italy 1943–50, S. J. Woolf (ed.) (1972)

De Gaulle, Charles (1890–1970)   President of the Fifth Republic in France (1959–69). Born in Lille, he grew up in a Catholic and royalist household. He graduated from the military academy of St-Cyr in 1912, served in an infantry regiment in the First World War, was wounded at Verdun in 1916 and became a prisoner of war. Between the wars he was a lecturer at the *École de Guerre*, where he became a severe critic of the defensive strategy (exemplified by the building of the Maginot Line) of Pétain. De Gaulle wanted the formation of mobile, mechanized divisions that, supported by air power, could operate, independently of the infantry, behind the enemy lines and so disrupt communications and cause confusion. His recommendations were ignored in France (but not in Germany). In 1940 Reynaud brought him into his government as a junior minister at the War Office but when Pétain sued for peace, de Gaulle escaped to London, where he broadcast on 18 June asking Frenchmen to join him in continuing the war. Few responded. De Gaulle then declared himself the head of a Free French government-in-exile, which was recognized by Winston CHURCHILL, and was sentenced to death by the Vichy government. He felt slighted by the Allies (Roosevelt loathed his arrogance) when he was excluded from the Normandy landings in June 1944, though EISENHOWER, supreme Allied Commander, allowed him to liberate Paris in August. Deeply offended that France was excluded from the Yalta and Potsdam conferences that decided the post war settlement, he was able to secure for France a permanent seat on the Security Council of the UNITED NATIONS and a French zone of occupation (which included the Saar) in Germany.

The Committee of National Liberation was transformed into a provisional government, which included communists, with de Gaulle as President. He organized a referendum in October 1945 which voted for an assembly to be elected to draw up a new constitution. This assembly elected de Gaulle as head of government in November. He wanted a constitution which would give greater power to the executive and diminish the role of parliament, but when it was clear that the Constituent Assembly did not agree with him, he resigned in January 1946, expecting to be recalled to office soon. In 1947 he formed the RPF (Rally of the French People) but abandoned it in 1953 and was not able to return to power until events in the ALGERIAN WAR OF INDEPENDENCE brought about the demise of the FOURTH REPUBLIC in 1958. He had demanded the right to draw up a new CONSTITUTION OF THE FIFTH REPUBLIC and submit it to a referendum. The constitution he devised gave much greater power to the executive and particularly to the President and was approved in a referendum in September by 79 per cent of voters. In the November elections the Gaullists and their allies won an overwhelming victory, the Communist Party being reduced to ten seats. General de Gaulle was elected President of the Fifth Republic by 77 per cent of the vote in December.

His first problem was to deal with Algeria. Secret negotiations with the FLN produced the Evian agreements in 1962, which recognized the independence of Algeria. This was endorsed by referenda in both France (with 65 per cent in favour) and Algeria. By this time French colonies south of the Sahara were independent. De Gaulle in 1959 had offered them independence and a withdrawal of French aid or membership of the French Community. Only Guinea under Sékou Touré chose independence at the time, but by 1962 all the other colonies had become independent and had retained French aid.

De Gaulle showed considerable hostility towards the Anglo-Saxons. He did not think the US had been very helpful to France either in Indochina or Algeria and it had rejected his proposal that NATO should be run by the US, France and Britain, all having equal status. He therefore withdrew the French Mediterranean fleet in 1963: in 1966 he removed all French land and air forces from NATO,

expelled American military personnel from France and demanded that NATO headquarters be removed from Paris. Yet there were limits to de Gaulle's anti-Americanism. A pragmatist, he realized France needed the protection of US nuclear forces and supported the US in the CUBAN MISSILE CRISIS of 1962. He regarded Britain as an American puppet and twice vetoed its application to join the EEC (in 1963 and 1967), as he thought it would be a Trojan horse, enabling American influence to extend further into Europe. In 1967 he enraged both the Canadian and British governments by encouraging QUEBEC NATIONALISM when he shouted, at Montreal town hall, 'Vive le Québec libre!'

De Gaulle's desire for independence from the superpowers and a major role in international affairs led him to develop his own nuclear arsenal: France exploded an atom bomb in 1960 and a hydrogen bomb in 1968. He also spoke of 'détente, entente and co-operation' with the Soviet Union and talked airily of a Europe from the Atlantic to the Urals, but his failure to obtain a softening of Soviet attitudes in Eastern Europe was evident in the crushing of the PRAGUE SPRING. De Gaulle disliked supranational bodies, as they impinged on French sovereignty, and regarded the United Nations as inefficient and dangerous, as it was dominated by the superpowers. His attitude to the EEC was more equivocal. He had opposed the formation of the ECSC and the TREATY OF ROME, but saw that the COMMON AGRICULTURAL POLICY benefited France and that the EEC provided opportunities for close co-operation with Germany (he signed a treaty of friendship with ADENAUER, the West German Chancellor, in 1963) and for French leadership in a third 'bloc', independent of the two superpowers. Yet he had no time for the EEC as a supranational body and held up EEC business in 1965 until he obtained the LUXEMBOURG COMPROMISE, which allowed any member to veto decisions. His method of confrontation and threats, which was rewarded by appeasement, was a lesson that Margaret THATCHER learnt well. De Gaulle's foreign policy was very popular in France (particularly his anti-Americanism) and helped to consolidate his regime.

The popularity of de Gaulle was evident in the 1962 elections when the Gaullist UNR (Union for the New Republic) obtained 35.5 per cent of the vote, the highest proportion any party had gained since the war and only eight votes short of an absolute majority. The presidential election of 1965 showed a decline in support for his regime but he won comfortably in the second round, beating MITTERRAND by 54.5 per cent to 45.55 per cent. MAY 1968, when there were student riots and widespread strikes, seemed a threat but when he called a general election in June there was a backlash against the disorder of May and the Gaullist UDR (Union for the Defence of the Republic) won 358 out of 485 seats. De Gaulle had never seemed more secure, but in April 1969 he committed political suicide. He wanted to curb the power of the Senate and introduce regional reform and made this a matter of confidence in a referendum. When the electorate rejected his proposals with a 53 per cent 'no' vote he resigned. In the last 18 months of his life he did not appear in public and gave no interviews.

De Gaulle: vol. 1, The Rebel: 1890–1944; vol. 2, The Ruler: 1945–70, J. Lacouture (1992)
De Gaulle, A. Sherman (1993)
The Republic of de Gaulle, 1958–69, S. Berstein (1993)
De Gaulle and Twentieth Century France, H. Gough (ed.) (1996)

De Klerk, Frederik Willem (1936–)   President of South Africa (1989–94). An active member of the National Party while practising law (1961–72), he was elected to parliament in 1972 just after becoming Professor of Administrative Law at Potchefstroom University. He joined the cabinet in 1978, held a variety of ministerial posts and in 1982 became leader of the National Party in the Transvaal. De Klerk succeeded P. W. BOTHA as President of South Africa in 1989 and surprised the nation by the rapidity with which he moved to end the stalemate in South Africa. In February 1990 he said that the ANC, PAC (Pan-Africanist Congress) and Communist Party were no longer banned and in the following weeks released many political prisoners, including Nelson MANDELA. APARTHEID legislation, of which he had been an enthusiastic supporter, was repealed: the Separate Amenities Act which imposed segregation in public places, in June 1990, followed in 1991 by the Land Act, which restricted African land ownership to 14 per cent of South Africa in the BANTUSTANS; the Group Areas Act, which provided for separate areas where each race must live, and the Population Registration Act, which divided all South Africans into four racial categories. De Klerk carried out these reforms partly because of popular protest and international pressure, but mainly because there was an economic crisis, as sanctions were effective, prices were rising and real wages falling sharply. Without reform the economy was in danger of collapsing, with consequent unrest and repression. He wanted to recover the initiative and cope with the danger of the extremist Afrikaners in the Conservative Party, who increased their vote in the white election of 1989 and were determined to maintain white supremacy. De Klerk believed that an alliance of the new National Party (open to all races in 1990) with the Inkatha Freedom Party of BUTHELEZI could win the Nationalists a share of power in a democratically elected parliament. The government, therefore, entered formal negotiations with other parties, including the ANC, at the Convention for a Democratic South Africa (CODESA) and committed itself to a new democratic constitution.

De Klerk's new policy brought an end to some sanctions and South Africa took part in the Barcelona Olympic Games. In a white referendum 69 per cent supported negotiations at CODESA, but these broke down in mid-1992. The ANC withdrew because of violence in the black townships, which the security forces were accused of fomenting. As tension rose and there was a danger of South Africa slipping into anarchy, de Klerk and Mandela agreed that the first democratic elections would be held in South Africa in 1994 for a Constituent Assembly, in which the major parties would share power for a transitional period and would have seats in the cabinet proportional to their share of the vote. The National Party won 20 per cent of the vote in the elections and four cabinet posts and de Klerk became a Deputy President. He and Mandela were awarded the Nobel Peace Prize in 1993.

Parliament ratified a democratic constitution in April 1996 and a month later de Klerk withdrew the National Party from the coalition government and became leader of the opposition. In September 1997 he announced his retirement from politics because, he said, he was tired and politically stale.

F. W. de Klerk: The Man in His Time, W. de Klerk (1991)
Forty Lost Years: The Apartheid State and the National Party, 1948–94, D. O'Meara (1996)

decolonization   The gaining of independence by colonies. Decolonization long preceded the twentieth century (the USA became independent in the eighteenth century, the Spanish and Portuguese colonies in Latin America as a result of the Napoleonic Wars), but the collapse of most empires did not take place until after the Second World War. From 1945–60 40 countries with a population of 800 million, over a quarter of the world's inhabitants, became independent in an unprecedented and in many ways unexpected series of events. The European powers were weakened and humiliated in the war by the ease with which Japan overran their colonies in Southeast Asia: the British, Dutch and French empires there ceased to exist, as did the Italian empire in Africa. When the war was over the two victorious superpowers, the US and Soviet Union, were both opposed to colonialism, as was the UNITED NATIONS, whose charter stated that all peoples had the right to freedom and justice. Britain, with the largest empire, was a huge debtor nation in 1945 and wanted to concentrate on economic recovery at home: it did not want to use its scarce resources in fighting colonial wars.

In India Britain was faced with a strong nationalist movement led by NEHRU and inter-communal violence between Muslims and Hindus. A quick solution was needed, so in February 1947 ATTLEE, the British Prime Minister, announced that Britain would leave India in June 1948, a date brought forward to August 1947 owing to the escalating conflict. The INDEPENDENCE AND PARTITION OF INDIA between a mainly Hindu India and a Muslim Pakistan, therefore took place. The impact of India's independence was immediately felt in the rest of Asia. Burma and Ceylon (renamed Sri Lanka in 1972) became independent in 1948. Malaya, which had to cope with communist guerrilla warfare in the MALAYAN EMERGENCY (1948–60), gained independence under the Tunku ABDUL RAHMAN in 1957. Brunei, Britain's last possession in this area, gained independence in 1984. In Africa the pace was set by the Gold Coast, where NKRUMAH had set up a mass party, the Convention People's Party. The Gold Coast became independent as Ghana in 1957. From that time to 1964, when Northern Rhodesia acquired its freedom as Zambia, most of British Africa was decolonized. France, struggling to cope with the ALGERIAN WAR OF INDEPENDENCE (1954–62), granted independence to Tunisia and Morocco in 1956 and in 1958 gave France's other African colonies the choice of independence without French aid or membership of the French Community. Only Sékou Touré in Guinea chose independence, but by 1960 14 French colonies had become independent.

The Belgians were so anxious to avoid an Algerian situation in the Belgian Congo (Zaire) that they hastily granted independence without any adequate preparation, in 1960, thus producing the CONGO CRISIS (1960–5). In the West Indies Jamaica and Trinidad became independent in 1962 and by 1983 most of the smaller islands, except Bermuda. On the mainland, British Guiana became independent as Guyana in 1966: British Honduras (named Belize in 1973) had its independence delayed until 1981, when Guatemala gave up its claim to the territory.

All these countries gained their independence peacefully but there were other areas, particularly those with white settler populations, which had to fight to throw off control by colonial powers. The French desperately tried to cling on to Indochina but, defeated at DIEN BIEN PHU, they lost the INDOCHINA WAR OF INDEPENDENCE (1964–54), but before its end Laos (in 1949) and Cambodia had become independent. The US saw this war as a struggle against communism, especially after MAO ZEDONG's success in the CHINESE CIVIL WAR (1946–9), and after France's defeat became in effect a colonial power in South Vietnam with a puppet government, until it too was defeated in the VIETNAM WAR and Vietnam was united in 1975. The ALGERIAN WAR OF INDEPENDENCE (1954–62) was another bitter war in which France tried vainly to hang on to this part of its empire, where there were a million *colons* (European settlers). The Dutch tried to recover control of the Dutch East Indies but, denied US support, gave up the struggle in 1949, when Indonesia became independent. Portugal, a poor country, felt it needed to exploit the resources of Angola and Mozambique and so became involved in PORTUGAL′S COLONIAL WARS (1961–75). The PORTUGUESE REVOLUTION (1974–5) brought these wars to an end, with Angola, Mozambique and Guinea-Bissau becoming independent, but their difficulties were not over, as foreign powers intervened in the MOZAMBICAN and ANGOLAN CIVIL

WARS which followed. 'The Africans are not the problem in Africa', said Harold MACMILLAN, the British Prime Minister. 'It is the Europeans who are the problem'. When the CENTRAL AFRICAN FEDERATION was dissolved in 1963, the British government would not grant independence to the white minority government in Southern Rhodesia until there was black majority rule. Ian Smith's government therefore declared UDI in 1965 and so began a protracted struggle against black opposition parties. When the Portuguese Empire collapsed and South Africa withdrew its support the Smith regime had to accept majority rule and Rhodesia became independent as Zimbabwe in 1980.

By 1990 the process of decolonization was almost complete. Some small islands with few resources (the Caymans, St Helena, Tristan da Cunha) remained as colonies, as did Bermuda, which rejected independence. Gibraltar, seized from Spain in 1713, chose to remain under British rule in a referendum in 1969, though Spain claims it. HONG KONG, where the lease of the New Territories ran out in 1997, then returned to China. Spain gave up the Western Sahara in 1976 but this was taken over by Morocco, which has been fighting against POLISARIO for control ever since. In another change of colonial ownership Indonesia seized East Timor from Portugal in 1975.

European Decolonization, 1918–81, R. F. Holland (1985)
The Dissolution of the Colonial Empires, F. Ansprenger (1989)
The End of the British Empire: The Historical Debate, J. Darwin (1991)

deindustrialization A word which became popular in the 1980s to indicate the loss of well-paid factory jobs in industrial countries and the move of employment from manufacturing to the service sector. This was not a new phenomenon. Until 1910 most US workers were in agriculture. From that time services have become the dominant sector, employing over half US workers as early as 1920. From the 1970s, however, with increased competition in a GLOBAL ECONOMY and more capital-intensive and efficient industries, the pace of change has increased. Between 1974–88 nearly half the steel-making jobs in the US disappeared, falling from 460,000 to 260,000. Automobile production was affected too: in the 1980s the Auto Workers Union lost half a million members, a third of their total. Some 2.8 million manufacturing workers lost their jobs in the US in the early 1980s and many more in the early 1990s, as the COLD WAR ended and the 'peace dividend' brought a decline in the MILITARY–INDUSTRIAL COMPLEX, which had sustained the US economy for half a century. In 1992 industrial giants General Motors, General Electric, IBM, IT and T, Xerox and Du Pont announced the closure of plants with resulting unemployment. Boeing and McDonell Douglas cut back in 1993. This does not mean that manufacturing has declined – in the early 1990s it produced the same proportion of US GNP as 20 years earlier – but it employed fewer people: 30 per cent of the workforce in 1975, 23 per cent in 1990. Jobs for life became a thing of the past and were replaced by temporary jobs, often with low wages, no security and no benefits.

Manufacturing also contracted in those European countries which had been in the forefront of the industrial revolution in the nineteenth century. Coal-mining, which had employed millions in Britain, almost disappeared there, as did textile production and ship-building. Britain lost 25 per cent of its manufacturing industry in the early 1980s, where old industrial areas became 'rustbelts'. The number employed in manufacturing in the six old industrial countries of Europe fell by a quarter between 1973–90, when it was about a quarter of the total workforce. Ship-building and steel-making did not disappear but moved to the NEWLY INDUSTRIALIZING ECONOMIES (NIEs) such as Korea and Brazil.

The Deindustrialization of America, B. Bluestone and B. Harrison (1982)
The Work of Nations, R. B. Reich (1991)

Deir Yassin (Dayr Yasin) (9 April 1948)
Deir Yassin was an Arab village in Palestine which had observed a non-aggression pact with Haganah, the Jewish defence force, but was attacked by Irgun Zvai Leumi, which was under the command of Menachem BEGIN. When it resisted, the entire population of 245 men, women and children was massacred. Begin spoke of the 'heroic' acts of his men at Deir Yassin, and attributed the flight of Arabs from Israel to this incident. Haganah denounced the atrocity.

Democratic Party   Political party in the US. It goes back to 1792, when Jefferson and Madison founded the Democratic–Republican Party, which adopted its present name in the 1830s. The Democrats stood for states' rights and a weak federal government and were free-traders opposed to high tariffs. Their support came from the 'solid South' and from those who were not well off: small farmers, urban labourers and immigrants, especially Irish Catholics. The Democratic Party held the presidency for all but eight years between 1828 and 1860, but split over slavery when the North and South wings of the party put forward different candidates in the presidential election of 1860. This let in Abraham Lincoln, the REPUBLICAN PARTY's first President. As most Confederate leaders were Democrats the Republicans appeared as the party of Union.

The Democratic Party began a long period as a minority party. From 1860 to 1932 only two Democrats were elected as President, Grover Cleveland (1864–8, 1892–6) and Woodrow Wilson (1912–20). The Democratic Party was divided in the 1920s over Prohibition and civil liberties and did not return to power until the Great Depression, when many Americans became disillusioned with Herbert Hoover's handling of the economy. The Democrats won control of Congress in 1932 and did not lose it until 1946. Also in 1932 Hoover was crushingly defeated by the Democratic presidential candidate Franklin D. Roosevelt. Democrats had been the party of states' rights; now they became the party of strong federal government, as the New Deal sought to attack unemployment and get the economy moving again. FDR's policies made small farmers, organized labour, blacks and other minorities firmly Democratic.

When Roosevelt died in office Harry S. TRUMAN became President and was elected in his own right in 1948, though the Democratic Party lost control of Congress from 1947–9 and 1953–4. From then until 1995 it dominated both houses, except for the Senate from 1981–6. It did less well in the presidential elections, winning five out of twelve from 1952–96: KENNEDY (1960), JOHNSON (1964), CARTER (1976) and CLINTON (1992, 1996). During this time the party lost the support of the South's white voters and began to split under Truman, when segregationists and states' rights Southerners (called Dixiecrats) broke away and put forward their own candidate, Strom Thurmond (he later joined the Republican Party in 1964), in the presidential election of 1948. Truman triumphed, with the support of industrial workers, immigrants and minorities, but a coalition of Republicans and conservative Southern Democrats ensured that much of the President's Fair Deal legislation was rejected. The move of the South away from the Democrats was apparent in the 1964 presidential election. Barry Goldwater, the Republican candidate, won only six states but five of them were in the Deep South (Georgia, South Carolina, Alabama, Mississippi and Louisiana), four of which had never voted for a Republican presidential candidate since Reconstruction. President Johnson was well aware that support for civil rights would lose Democrats the support of Southern white voters and told an aide when he signed the CIVIL RIGHTS ACT of 1964: 'This will keep us out of power for a generation'. By 1972 most of the South voted for the Republican Richard NIXON, a process that was completed in the 1994 congressional elections when the Democrats lost control of both houses and a majority of Southern congressmen were Republicans.

The Cycles of American History, A. Schlesinger, Jr (1986)

Deng Xiaoping (1904–97)   Chinese politician. The eldest son of a wealthy landowner in Sichuan province, he went to France in 1920 as a work-study student. He met ZHOU ENLAI there and joined the French branch of the Chinese Communist Party (CCP) in 1924. In 1926 he studied in Moscow before returning to China. Deng then joined MAO ZEDONG in the Jiangxi Soviet (1928–34) and became part of his inner circle. He took part in the Long March (1934–5), when the communists were forced north to the safety of Yanan by the nationalists under JIANG JIESHI (Chiang Kai-shek) and was a political commissar in the communist armies which fought in the Sino-Japanese War (1937–45) and the CHINESE CIVIL WAR (1946–9).

After the communist victory he took control of the South-west region of China. He was transferred to Beijing in 1952 and then rose rapidly, partly owing to his long association with Mao, in the CCP and state: Vice-Premier 1952, Minister of Finance 1953, General Secretary of the CCP 1956, a member of the Politburo 1955. Deng joined LIU SHAOQI in rejecting Mao's 'cult of personality'. He opposed the HUNDRED FLOWERS MOVEMENT (1956) and was responsible for the savage Anti-Rightist campaign which followed it, when between 400,000 and 700,000 intellectuals were persecuted. After the failure of the GREAT LEAP FORWARD (1958–60) he co-operated with Liu in reversing its policies by giving to production teams rather than the COMMUNES responsibility for agricultural production and by introducing production bonuses in industry. Mao complained of being ignored by Deng and Liu and sought to recover his control by allying with radicals and calling for a renewal of the class struggle. In the ensuing CULTURAL REVOLUTION (1966–76) Deng was twice dismissed and rehabilitated. In 1969 he was disgraced and moved to Jiangxi province, where he worked as a fitter in a tractor plant. He was restored to favour in 1973 when the worst excesses of the Cultural Revolution were over and by 1975 was acting Prime Minister and Vice-Chairman of the CCP. With day to day control of both party and government it appeared that he would succeed the ailing ZHOU ENLAI as Prime Minister, but his modernization programme was strongly opposed by the GANG OF FOUR and when Zhou died in January 1976 Deng was again purged. He was restored to his previous positions in July 1977 only after the death of Mao and the arrest of the Gang of Four. His hold on power was consolidated when Mao's successor, HUA GUO-FENG, was demoted in 1980. From that time until his death Deng's was the dominant voice in China's affairs. He did not seek the highest posts, such as that of General Secretary of the CCP or Prime Minister, but used his connections with the army (as Chairman of the Military Affairs Committee) to promote people he wanted to succeed him.

Deng's prime purpose was to develop the economy and so improve the standard of living of the Chinese people. He began by dismantling the Communes and handed over production to individual farmers, though the state still formally owned the land. Higher prices paid to the peasants greatly increased production and their incomes, so that 800 million peasants benefited. 'To get rich is glorious', declared Deng, in a rebuttal of Maoism. For industrialization Deng proclaimed that 'Practice is the sole criterion of truth'. He maintained that China had been backward and impoverished for 300 years because of its self-imposed isolation from the world. Modernization was needed and this meant the import of Western technology and a more open market. China therefore joined

the IMF and the WORLD BANK in 1980 and set up SPECIAL ECONOMIC ZONES (SEZs), where foreigners were invited to invest in what was a capitalist market. This policy of 'opening up' made China more accessible to foreign ideas and influence than at any time since the Tang dynasty in the seventh century. Marxist self-reliance and autarchy were abandoned as China was integrated into the GLOBAL ECONOMY and the international financial system. There was a move from heavy to light industry and from import-substitution to production for export.

To provide trained specialists key schools creamed off the brightest pupils, and entrance examinations (abandoned during the Cultural Revolution) were reintroduced for universities. Thousands of students were sent abroad to study. The results were remarkable – GNP grew by 8.9 per cent per annum from 1980–9, manufacturing exports increased from $9 billion in 1980 to $37 billion in 1989. The downside was that this new wealth was not evenly spread, as the inland provinces benefited little from it and as the large state industries, with obsolete equipment and low levels of growth, needed huge state subsidies to provide economic security ('an iron rice bowl') for their tens of millions of workers. Token wages paid to workers in state enterprises kept unemployment officially at 5 per cent but it was generally accepted that it was over 20 per cent. Opening the state-owned enterprises (SOEs) to market forces would have meant bankruptcies and mass unemployment, so they received about 60 per cent of national investment and subsidies amounting to a third of the budget. About three-quarters of the funds the Chinese saved were tied up in the SOEs via investment by state banks. The SOEs therefore stunted growth and were a financial and political time-bomb. State-owned enterprises lost $20 billion in 1990. As prices were freed they rose and there was unrest, so some controls were reimposed in a stop–start policy. Corruption was another drain on the economy which Deng was unable to control. It spread to all levels of the bureaucracy to such an extent that the regime was paralysed.

Political freedom did not accompany moves towards a free market. Deng suppressed the Democracy Wall movement in 1978 and imprisoned its leaders because he feared instability and a return to the anarchy of the Cultural Revolution. 'Bourgeois liberalization', said Deng in 1986, 'means rejection of the Party's leadership; there would be nothing to unite our one billion people'. Like the mandarins in the Self-Strengthening Movement of the late nineteenth century, he seemed to think that economic ideas could be borrowed from the West while the political system remained unchanged, though the abandonment of socialism meant that the ideological justification for the regime disappeared. The COLLAPSE OF THE SOVIET UNION in 1991 showed that a system based on total control could collapse overnight, without defeat in a major war, but this was a lesson Deng ignored. There would be no diminution in the dominant role of the CCP. His determination to crush the democracy movement led to the TIANANMEN SQUARE MASSACRE in 1989.

In his foreign policy Deng sought conciliation with the US, which opened full diplomatic relations with China and broke off relations with Taiwan in 1979. When Vietnam invaded Cambodia to oust POL POT, the People's Liberation Army (PLA) invaded Vietnam but withdrew when it performed badly. Deng regarded the Soviet Union as the main threat to China, especially after the SOVIET INVASION OF AFGHANISTAN (1979) and the Soviet acquisition of naval bases in Vietnam. Good relations were not restored until GORBACHEV withdrew from Afghanistan and persuaded Vietnam to retire from Cambodia. Deng ardently promoted national reunification and so made the Sino-British Joint Declaration of 1984, which ensured that HONG KONG RETURNED TO CHINA. There were links too with Taiwan – Taiwanese investment in and trade with China – which the People's Republic had

always maintained was a part of China, but when it appeared that Taiwan sought complete independence the mainland Chinese adopted a more bellicose attitude. There were closer relations too with ASEAN. Friction with the US arose when the US restricted the import of Chinese textiles, when China sold arms to Arab states in the Middle East and supported the PLO and the US criticized human rights abuses in China. Yet economic ties survived these differences and the Tiananmen Square massacre.

Deng gave up his last official post in 1990 but continued to dominate both party and government from behind the scenes. He appeared rarely in public and was last seen in 1994. His attempts to find a successor were at first fruitless, as both HU YAOBANG and ZHAO ZIYANG were disgraced, but in JIANG ZEMIN he found someone to follow him when he died at the age of 92.

Deng Xiaoping, D. Shambaugh (1995)
Deng Xiaoping and the Chinese Revolution, D. Goodman (1995)
The Politics of China: The Eras of Mao and Deng, R. MacFarquhar (1997)

détente   The policy of reducing tension and the possibility of war between the US (and its NATO allies) and the communist states of the Soviet Union and China. It usually refers primarily to the improvement of US–Soviet and US–Chinese relations in the 1970s, but there was a brief period of *détente* following the death of STALIN, when the Soviet Union helped to bring about peace in the KOREAN WAR (1950–3) and in Indochina with the GENEVEA ACCORDS (1954). It also agreed to the AUSTRIAN STATE TREATY and the evacuation of Soviet troops from Austria. These moves to improve the relations of the superpowers came to an end when KHRUSHCHEV put pressure on the Western powers to leave Berlin by threatening to make a separate peace treaty with East Germany, which might then cut off Western access to

Berlin. This and the CUBAN MISSILE CRISIS (1962) ended *détente* for a decade.

President NIXON and Henry KISSINGER were mainly responsible for its revival, Nixon announcing in his inaugural address that 'After a period of confrontation we are entering an era of negotiation'. Kissinger saw 'linkage' as an essential element of *détente* – the US would offer incentives in the form of technology and finance in return for Soviet co-operation in the Middle East and in ending the VIETNAM WAR. BREZHNEV, who saw no alternative to *détente* in a nuclear age, as a nuclear war would be catastrophic for all participants, rejected linkage for an approach in which different issues (arms control, regional conflicts and economic agreements) would be considered as separate, not linked, issues. *Détente* was welcome to both sides, as it would enable them to cut their enormous defence budgets.

Nixon saw an agreement with China as beneficial to the US and stunned world leaders by visiting MAO ZEDONG in Beijing in February 1972, thus reversing the American policy of isolating China. The US withdrew its objection to the People's Republic taking China's place (previously held by the nationalist government in Taiwan) on the Security Council of the UNITED NATIONS, though full diplomatic relations did not take place until 1979. Soon after seeing Mao Nixon visited Moscow and made an agreement on arms control with Brezhnev: the SALT I accord.

Willy BRANDT'S OSTPOLITIK showed West Germany as a leading proponent of *détente*. In 1970 West Germany and the USSR signed a non-aggression pact and declared that the boundaries of Germany, Poland and the Soviet Union as decided at Yalta in 1945 were inviolable. The Soviet Union had long wanted West European recognition of the postwar boundaries and this was obtained in the HELSINKI FINAL ACT (1975), which also committed the signatories to maintain fundamental human rights. The failure of Brezhnev to observe these (he continued to persecute dissidents and Jews) led to criticism of *détente* in the US, particularly when the communists took over South Vietnam. When Jimmy CARTER became US President he intended to continue *détente* but found Brezhnev, newly confident with the huge revenues flowing from the vast Siberian oil and gas fields after the OPEC PRICE RISE of 1973, prepared to extend Soviet influence to Africa by backing the MENGISTU regime in Ethiopia and by interfering in the ANGOLAN CIVIL WAR. These actions undermined *détente*, which ended completely with the SOVIET INVASION OF AFGHANISTAN in 1979. President REAGAN returned to a more confrontational approach to 'the evil empire' until GORBACHEV's rise to power once again improved Soviet–US relations.

Détente and the Nixon Doctrine: American Foreign Policy and the Pursuit of Stability, 1969–76, R. S. Litwak (1984)

Détente and Confrontation, R. L. Garthoff (1986)

The Rise and Fall of Détente: Relaxations of Tension in US–Soviet Relations 1953–84, R. W. Stevenson (1985)

Diefenbaker, John George (1895–1979)

Prime Minister of Canada (1957–63). A lawyer from Western Canada, he entered the House of Commons as a Conservative in 1940. He was elected leader of the Progressive Conservative Party in 1956 and a year later, taking advantage of unease at increasing American domination of the economy which the Liberals had encouraged, he won a small majority in the federal election of 1957, ending 22 years of Liberal rule. A year later he took the Conservatives to their biggest electoral landslide, when they won 208 out of 265 seats. An Anglophile and strong supporter of the COMMONWEALTH, he played a leading part in the Commonwealth Conference of 1959 in obtaining condemnation of APARTHEID, which influenced South Africa's decision to leave the Commonwealth in 1961. Diefenbaker strengthened Canada's ties with the US by making the NORAD agreement that integrated US and Canadian air defences. He found new markets in China and Eastern Europe for Canadian wheat and extended federal aid to farmers, but he could not stop the decline in economic growth and the increasing unemployment. The 1962 election left the Tories as a minority government. Diefenbaker remained as Prime Minister until the resignation of several ministers over the deployment of nuclear weapons in Canada forced him to call an election in 1963, which he lost. He continued as party leader until 1967.

Renegade in Power: The Diefenbaker Years, P. C. Newman (1973)
Canada, 1957–67, J. Granatstein (1988)
Rogue Tory: The Life and Legend of John G. Diefenbaker, D. Smith (1995)

Diem, Ngo Dinh (1901–63) President of the Republic of [South] Vietnam (1955–63). A devout Catholic from a wealthy family which had provided many high officials for the Vietnamese royal court at Hue, he considered becoming a priest but took up a career in administration instead and was quickly a provincial chief. In 1933 he joined the cabinet of the young emperor Bao Dai as Minister of the Interior but soon resigned because the French (Vietnam was part of the French Empire) would not give more power to the Vietnamese government. Diem was captured by the VIET MINH in 1945 and invited to join HO CHI MINH's government in the North but, anti-communist as well as anti-French, he refused. In 1947 he went abroad. The GENEVA ACCORDS (1954) gave him an opportunity to return to Vietnam, as the French withdrew and Bao Dai, under American pressure, made Diem his Prime Minister. In 1954 South Vietnam was controlled by three religious–military sects: the Cao Dai, the Hoa Hao (each of which had private armies of 50,000) and Binh Xuyen. In the first six months of his administration Diem crushed them and rehabilitated a million refu-

gees from the North. A year later he rigged a referendum which abolished the monarchy: he then proclaimed the Republic of Vietnam with himself as President.

Aloof and aristocratic, he did not make a successful or popular ruler. He had little understanding of, or sympathy for, the peasants and did not keep his promises of land reform. Indeed, he restored property to landlords who had been dispossessed by communists before 1954 and replaced elected village councils by appointed officials. His 'strategic hamlets' programme to deprive the VIET CONG of support was based on British action during the MALAYAN EMERGENCY (1948–60) but was deeply unpopular, as hundreds of thousands of villagers were forced to leave their homes for fortified encampments, which were little better than concentration camps. The small minority of Catholics (about one million compared with the 14 million Buddhists in South Vietnam) were made a privileged ruling élite. His brother Ngo Dinh Nhu, head of the political police, ran gambling, drug-trafficking, prostitution and extortion rackets. All opponents, particularly the communists, were ruthlessly persecuted and many were executed. In May 1963 Diem's forces fired on a demonstration of Buddhists in Hue, killing several. There were protests throughout the coastal cities, some Buddhist monks burned themselves to death and the US advised conciliation. This advice was ignored as Nhu sent his security forces into the temples to arrest 1,400 Buddhist monks. In the same month the US ambassador in Saigon received a thinly disguised instruction to encourage a coup against Diem. On 1 November there was a military coup, in which Diem and Nhu were murdered.

Dien Bien Phu A district capital in north-west Vietnam, 10 miles (16 km) from Laos and the site of a major battle in the INDO CHINA WAR OF INDEPENDENCE (1946–54). In November 1953 a French airborne attack captured Dien Bien Phu, which had an airstrip and from which the French could control the communication routes between China, Laos and North Vietnam. The French proceeded to make a giant 'hedgehog', a series of eight strongpoints with interlocking fields of fire. They hoped to lure Vietnamese general Vo Nguyen GIAP into a frontal assault, when his forces would be destroyed by superior French fire-power. As Dien Bien Phu was in a wide valley surrounded by hills, with poor communications, they thought that Giap would not be able to deply more than 20,000 troops or guns larger than 75 mm, which had a short range. In fact by building supply trails Giap brought up 60,000 troops and 24 105 mm guns, which could fire on the airfield from the hills. His attack began on 13 March when, using wave attacks which gave him local superiority, he captured two strongpoints. On the 15th the airstrip came under artillery fire, so supplies and reinforcements had now to be dropped by parachute: many landed in VIET MINH territory. On 7 May the last French strongpoint was overrun and France had suffered her biggest colonial defeat. Of 15,000 French troops 3,000 were killed, the rest captured. Support in France for the war disappeared, so peace was made in the GENEVA ACCORDS in June.

Dien Bien Phu and the Crisis of Franco-American Relations, 1954–5, L. S. Kaplan, D. Artaud and M. R. Rubin (eds) (1990)

domino theory   An idea first put forward by President TRUMAN in 1946, who said that action must be taken (hence the TRUMAN DOCTRINE) to prevent communist subversion in Greece and Turkey, otherwise neighbouring states would fall like a line of dominoes. He also applied the theory to Southeast Asia when the KOREAN WAR began. 'If we let Korea down', he said, 'the Soviets will keep right on going and swallow up one piece of Asia after another . . . If we were to let Asia go, the Near East would

collapse and no telling what would happen in Europe'. President EISENHOWER took up the theme in 1954, when he also applied the doctrine to Southeast Asia and talked of 'a row of dominoes set; you knock over the first one and what will happen to the last one is the certainty that it will go over very quickly . . . the loss of Indo-China, of Burma, of Thailand, of the Peninsula [Malaysia] and Indonesia following'. The commitment of all Presidents from Eisenhower to FORD to US participation in the VIETNAM WAR was based on this theory. It was applied too to Central America in the 1980s, when President REAGAN maintained that if the SANDINISTAS were in control of Nicaragua all other states in the region would become communist and the US, 'the last domino', would be threatened by Soviet and Cuban bases.

The theory was falsified in practice. As the Vietnamese communists took control of the whole of Vietnam in 1975, Laos became communist and Cambodia fell to the Khmer Rouge, but this had most to do with the US ATTACK ON CAMBODIA, which gave the Khmer Rouge the support it had hitherto lacked. The other states of Southeast Asia did not become communist and remained on friendly terms with the US. The domino theory can be more usefully applied to the fall of communist regimes in Eastern Europe in the REVOLUTIONS OF 1989–91.

Dominoes and Bandwagons: Strategic Beliefs and Great Power Competition in the Eurasian Rimland, R. Jervis and J. Snyder (eds) (1991)

Douglas-Home, Sir Alec [Lord Dunglass, 14th Earl of Home, Baron Home of the Hirsel] (1903–95)   British Prime Minister (1963–4). He was born Alexander Frederick Douglas-Home, the eldest son of Lord Dunglass, who had extensive estates in Berwickshire and Lanarkshire in the Scottish Border country. When Dunglass succeeded his father as the 13th Earl of Home in 1918, Alec became Lord Dunglass, in turn becoming the 14th Earl when his father died in 1950. He had a traditional aristocratic education at Eton and Oxford and then decided to go into politics, was elected as a Conservative MP in 1931, held various governmental posts and entered the House of Lords in 1951. Harold MACMILLAN's appointment of him as Foreign Secretary (1960–3) was remarkable, as it had been assumed that holders of the highest offices of state should sit in the Commons.

When Macmillan resigned after a prostate operation Home surprisingly emerged as Prime Minister, a choice which produced a damaging split in the CONSERVATIVE PARTY, as Iain Macleod and Enoch Powell refused to serve under him. Macleod wrote in *The Spectator* that a 'magic circle' of Old Etonians had made the decision. R. A. BUTLER, he believed, was the choice of the majority of the cabinet and was prevented from becoming premier only by Macmillan's hostility. Unknown to the public, Home was the first peer to be Prime Minister since Salisbury at the beginning of the century, but it was out of the question that he should remain in the Lords. The Peerage Act of 1963 enabled him to renounce his title so, after winning a safe seat in Scotland, he returned to the Commons as Sir Alec Douglas-Home. Courteous, considerate and accessible, he was woefully ignorant of economics and was faced by a dynamic leader of the LABOUR PARTY, Harold WILSON, who ran rings round him in the Commons. Innately conservative, he did not introduce any major policy changes, though he did introduce a new method of choosing the party leader: Conservative MPs were to vote in a two-ballot election. He managed to revive the tired and demoralized party so that the Conservatives only narrowly lost the 1964 election, though many Conservatives (and Wilson) believed that the Conservative Party would have won with Butler as Prime Minister. His premiership was the shortest in the twentieth century except for that of Bonar Law.

Douglas-Home resigned as Conservative leader in 1965 and was replaced by Edward HEATH, who made him Foreign Secretary (1970–4) again after the Conservatives won the 1970 elections. Except for Britain's successful application (which Heath controlled) to join the EEC (European Economic Community), he had a freer hand than under Macmillan and withdrew British forces from the GULF STATES. After the Conservative electoral defeat in 1974 he retired and returned to the Lords with a life peerage as Baron Home of the Hirsel.

Sir Alec Douglas-Home, K. Young (1970)

drug trade Widely used in Asia in the nineteenth century, 80 per cent of all opium (from which morphine is derived) was produced in Iran and China in the 1930s. After the communist victory in the CHINESE CIVIL WAR (1946–9) there was a drive to wipe out drug use, so production moved to the inaccessible mountains of Burma, Thailand and Laos (the Golden Triangle), where the borders of the three countries meet, and isolated areas of North Pakistan and Afghanistan. The Burmese trade was run by Chinese syndicates in Bangkok and Hong Kong. As the Chinese market had almost disappeared Western Europe became the main target for heroin (an opium derivative first produced in 1898).

From the 1960s large quantities of cannabis and cocaine as well as heroin were consumed in the US and Western Europe. In Mexico, Bolivia, Peru and above all, Colombia, drug cartels grew up to supply drugs to North America. The Medellin cartel in Colombia was formed in 1981 with its own armed forces and waged war against the government when a massive amount of cocaine was seized in 1984. The Justice Minister was murdered and in 1989 a presidential candidate. In 1991 the government made an agreement with the cartel: extradition to the US ended, the leaders surrendered and the richest, Pablo Escobar, went to a prison of his own design. A year later he walked out and was eventually gunned down in December 1993, by which time much of his business had passed to the rival Cali cartel. The 1980 coup in Bolivia was known as 'the cocaine coup' as it ended US anti-narcotic activities in the country. In Peru the President claimed that most of SENDERO LUMINOSO's funds came from drug trafficking. Cubans were involved too: in 1989 a general was executed by CASTRO for helping the Medellin cartel to smuggle cocaine into the US. Although the drug barons gained most from the trade, peasant farmers benefited too. 400,000 of Bolivia's 6.5 million population worked directly in the drug trade, as coca was the most profitable crop. In 1990 Peruvian coca farmers earned between $1,500 and $2,000 a year: their income per acre was ten times that of a coffee farmer and 20 times that of a grower of rice.

By 1988, when 106 countries signed the UNITED NATIONS Drugs Convention, many countries saw drugs as a threat to their national security and social well-being. The US sought to destroy the crops at source and so became deeply and unpopularly involved in the internal affairs of Latin American countries. American military advisers went to Colombia and Bolivia but there were complaints that the military approach to crop destruction destroyed the livelihood of peasants without providing them with an alternative, in spite of a $2 billion Andean aid programme (begun in 1989) as part of the US National Drug Control Strategy. The problems of eradicating the drug trade were exacerbated by the COLLAPSE OF THE SOVIET UNION: in 1992 it was estimated that farmers in the former USSR were cultivating three million acres of marijuana and an increasing area of poppies. The value of the drug trade in the late 1980s was put at $300 billion, which had risen to $500 billion by 1992, when it was the most lucrative business in the world after the arms trade. The GLOBAL ECONOMY, with its financial deregulation, facilitated money-laundering, while regional integration made borders easier to cross. It was estimated that $85 billion of drug money was laundered in the US and Europe in 1988, $250 billion by 1992.

International Drug Trafficking, D. Rowe (ed.) (1988)
Mountain High, White Avalanche: Cocaine and Power in the Andes States and Panama, E. Shannon (1988)
Cross-Border Drugs Trade in the Golden Triangle, B. Lintner (1991)

Dulles, John Foster (1888–1959)   US

Secretary of State (1953–9). The deeply religious son of a Presbyterian minister, he was educated at Princeton and the Sorbonne and became a renowned international lawyer who attended the Versailles Conference in 1919. Dulles was the Republican spokesman on foreign policy during the presidencies of Franklin Roosevelt and TRUMAN, was an adviser to the US government when the UNITED NATIONS was formed and negotiated the SAN FRANCISCO TREATY (1951) with Japan to end the Allied OCCUPATION OF JAPAN. President EISENHOWER appointed him Secretary of State in 1953.

He loathed atheistic communism and condemned George Kennan's policy of containment, adopted by Truman, as 'negative, futile and immoral', as it accepted the *status quo* and was 'not designed to win victory conclusively'. He talked about the 'roll-back' of communism in Eastern Europe, the 'liberation' of captive peoples and the 'unleashing' of JIANG JIESHI (Chiang Kai-shek) against the Chinese mainland. Such rhetoric alarmed many, as it seemed to make war inevitable, but Dulles was restrained by the moderate and cautious Eisenhower, so that in practice the foreign policy of Eisenhower and Dulles was little different from that of Truman and ACHESON. As Eisenhower cut back on defence spending, Dulles based his diplomacy on 'massive retaliation', which meant responding with tactical nuclear weapons and therefore overwhelming force to any threat to US interests. Dulles wanted to end the KOREAN WAR (1950–3) 'by giving the Chinese one hell of a licking' but Eisenhower decided to accept an armistice without attacking China. He made anti-communist alliances in the Middle East (the BAGHDAD PACT, later CENTO) and Southeast Asia (SEATO), thus in effect following the policy of containment. Dulles had two successes within 18 months of taking office, when he used the CIA to topple MUSADDIQ in Iran and the democratically elected government of ARBENZ GUZMAN in Guatemala. When the French were losing the INDOCHINA WAR OF INDEPENDENCE (1946–54) Dulles wanted to intervene directly to prevent a communist victory but Eisenhower refused. To keep Egypt out of the communist camp Dulles offered to finance the building of the Aswan Dam, but when NASSER acquired arms from the Soviet bloc he withdrew the offer and so precipitated the SUEZ CRISIS, as Nasser nationalized the Suez Canal to fund the project. When the crisis was resolved he drew up the Eisenhower doctrine to keep communist influence out of the Middle East, though this was largely irrelevant as the main danger to America's friends in that area came not from the communists but from Nasser. Early in 1959 Dulles resigned, as he was suffering from cancer and died shortly afterwards.

John Foster Dulles, R. W. Prenseen (1982)
John Foster Dulles and the Diplomacy of the Cold War, R. H. Immerman (ed.) (1990)

Duvalier family   Ruled Haiti as dictators from 1957 to 1986. François Duvalier (1907–71), President of Haiti (1957–71), was black, the son of a teacher. He graduated in medicine in 1934 and in the 1930s embraced *noirisme*, a belief in the superiority of blacks to mulattos (of mixed race) in Haiti's colour-conscious society. The small urban élite of mulattos, Catholic and French-speaking, dominated government and commerce and repressed the black majority (95 per cent of the population), Creole-speakers and followers of voo-

doo, which mixed the beliefs of various African religions with some elements of Catholicism. The army, trained by the US (which occupied Haiti from 1915–34), acted as arbiter between the two groups and it was with army support that Duvalier won the rigged presidential election in 1957.

'Papa Doc', as Duvalier was known, brought the army under control by creating his own paramilitary force, the *Tontons Macoutes* (Bogeymen). They infiltrated the army to give early warning of any coup attempts and kept watch on the population. From the black and urban poor, they practised state terrorism. Executions were televised live and whole families were exterminated for the subversive acts of one of their members. Papa Doc's control extended to the Catholic Church: he appointed the first black and Haitian archbishop and expelled the Jesuits. The economic decline of the poorest country in the Western hemisphere accelerated under Duvalier, as he siphoned off hundreds of millions of dollars from the government control and sale of basic foods. In 1963 he promoted a cult of himself as a semi-divine figure and a year later declared that he was President for life. The US cut off aid in 1963 because of his corruption and violation of human rights, but he stayed in power longer than any of his predecessors.

When he died his son Jean-Claude (1951–) succeeded him as President (1971–86) for life at the age of 19, the foreign press calling him 'Baby Doc'. The US restored aid and put pressure on him to make reforms, so press censorship was eased and some political prisoners were released but there was little real change. In 1980 he married Michèle Bennett, the daughter of a rich mulatto businessman, against the wishes of his mother and leading Duvalierists, who were shocked at his symbolic reconciliation with the old ruling class his father had fought. Opposition grew, particularly from the Catholic base communities where priests, inspired by LIBERATION THEOLOGY, criticized the government, as did Radio Soleil, the Church's popular radio station. Opposition demonstrations grew in size and frequency, the US suspended aid again and as a nationwide rebellion began the US flew Baby Doc into exile in France in 1986, though this did not lead to more democracy in Haiti but to the establishment of a vicious military dictatorship.

The Comedians, Graham Greene (1961)
Papa Doc, Baby Doc: Haiti and the Duvaliers, J. Ferguson (1987)

E

East German revolution of 1989 A popular, peaceful revolution which overthrew communism in the German Democratic Republic (GDR). Opposition groups in the 1980s had been small and insignificant. This changed when the REVOLUTIONS OF 1989–91 began in Hungary and Poland. Protest centred round the Protestant churches, particularly the *Nikolaikirche* in Leipzig. In late September 1989 there were peaceful marches through the city, which became protest demonstrations against the regime. On 9 October 70,000 gathered in the largest demonstration since 1953 chanting 'we are the people'. HONECKER (who had approved of the TIANANMEN SQUARE MASSACRE in Beijing) wanted to use force against the demonstrators but was overruled by other members of the Politburo. The marches grew in size: 300,000 on 23 October, half a million on 6 November. There were half a million too in East Berlin, as similar marches took place in other East German cities. The demonstrators were not calling for unification but for free elections and 'socialism with a human face' of the kind Dubček had tried to establish in Czechoslovakia in the PRAGUE SPRING of 1968.

The communist élite tried to recover the initiative by removing Honecker as leader on 17 October and by lifting the ban on travel to Czechoslovakia, from where East Germans were allowed to enter Austria on 3 November. On 7 November the Council of Ministers (cabinet) resigned and the next day so did the Politburo. Another landmark in the revolution took place on 9 November, when the East Berlin party boss gave the impression

that anyone who wanted to go to the West could do so. Thousands flocked to checkpoints on the BERLIN WALL leading to the West. There was some confusion and then the guards let them through. In four days over four million people visited West Berlin and some began dismantling the Wall. Demonstrations continued, this time with chants of 'We are one people'. For the first time GERMAN REUNIFICATION became a popular rallying-cry. Censorship was abolished and on 1 December the leading role of the party was removed from the constitution. As press disclosures showed the corruption and privileges of the communist élite, the Politburo and Central Committee of the SED were dissolved and the SED changed its name to the Party of Democratic Socialism. The communist regime ceased to exist.

We the People: The Revolution of 1989, T. Garton Ash (1990)
The German Revolution of 1989: Causes and Consequences, G. J. Glaessner and I. Wallace (eds) (1992)
Dissolution: The Crisis of Communism and the End of East Germany, C. Maier (1997)

ECSC (European Coal and Steel Community) The first supranational organization to be formed in Europe. It was based on the Schuman Plan, put forward by the French Foreign Minister but drawn up by Jean MONNET, which proposed the 'pooling' of Western European steel production, which should be placed under a supranational authority. There were also political motives for the union. Coal and steel were essential for economic recovery but also for waging war. If they were placed under a supranational authority war between Germany and France would be impossible. For Germany the union would enable it to escape the limitations imposed by the Allies after the Second World War on its coal and steel production.

The BENELUX countries and Italy joined in to form the Six and sign the Treaty of Paris (1951), which was ratified a year later. Its object was to remove tariffs between member states, have a common policy on imports, and move towards the convergence of prices and state aid. There were four main institutions: a Council of Ministers, which controlled the executive of the ECSC, the High Authority, a Common Assembly, chosen by the individual states from their MPs, and a Court of Justice to settle disputes. Thus were established the institutions which were a model for those used by the EEC (European Economic Community) when it was founded in 1957. Supranational institutions were new and welcome to Konrad ADENAUER, the West German Chancellor, who said in the Bundestag in 1952 that the 'political meaning' of the ECSC was 'infinitely larger than its economic purpose. . . . For the first time in history, countries want to renounce part of their sovereignty, voluntarily'. This was precisely what the British government did not want to do, so it stayed aloof and would not take part. Coal and steel production rose rapidly in the ECSC in the 1950s but from 1957 it was overshadowed by the EEC, which absorbed the institutions of the ECSC in 1967.

The Reconstruction of Western Europe, 1945– 51, A. Milward (1987)

Eden, Sir (Robert) Anthony, 1st Earl of Avon (1897–1977)   British Prime Minister (1955–7) and Foreign Secretary (1935– 8, 1940–5, 1951–5). He fought bravely in the First World War and was awarded the Military Cross. After the war he gained first class

honours in oriental languages at Oxford. He entered parliament in 1923, received his first ministeral post in the National Government of 1931 and then rose rapidly to become Foreign Secretary at the age of 38, the youngest holder of that post since Lord Granville in 1851. Eden was not at first a resolute opponent of appeasement, and made no attempt to oppose Hitler's remilitarization of the Rhineland. After dithering, he opposed the decision to recognize Mussolini's annexation of Abyssinia and resigned. Out of office until CHURCHILL became Prime Minister in 1940, he then moved to the War Office. In December 1940 he was Foreign Secretary again and a member of the War Cabinet, becoming Churchill's deputy and attending most of the international conferences, including Tehran, Yalta and Potsdam, though most policy decisions were made by Churchill. When the CONSERVATIVE PARTY was in opposition from 1945–51 Eden was frustrated at Churchill's reluctance to retire and did not want to take on the Foreign Office again when the Conservatives returned to power, but Churchill insisted. His period as Foreign Secretary from 1951–5 was highly successful, in spite of three operations in 1953 which kept him away from the Foreign Office for six months. Eden followed the same policy as BEVIN on the UNITED NATIONS, the KOREAN WAR, NATO, the COMMONWEALTH and on relations with the US. He made agreements with Egypt on the independence of Sudan and on the removal of British troops from the Suez Canal and in 1955 joined the BAGHDAD PACT. This was seen as a bridge between NATO and SEATO (which Britain had joined in 1954) in a system of alliances which would provide a global defence network against the spread of communism. Eden's greatest successes, which established his reputation as an international statesman, concerned Indochina (Vietnam) and West Germany. He persuaded Molotov and DULLES to accept the GENEVA ACCORDS (1954) which brought the INDOCHINA WAR OF INDEPENDENCE (1946–54) to an end and created the new states of Laos, Cambodia and North and South Vietnam. The US had wanted a European Defence Community, which would include West Germany, and was furious when the French National Assembly rejected this in 1954. Eden then brought together the major European powers, the US and Canada and arranged for Germany and Italy to become members of NATO. The commitment of the US and Canada to Europe's defence was confirmed, as was a permanent British military force on the Continent.

Eden became Prime Minister when Churchill eventually retired in 1955. In June 1955 Britain was warmly invited to take part in negotiations which eventually led to the TREATY OF ROME (1957) and the formation of the EEC (European Economic Community) but, after some hesitation, Eden rejected the invitation. Irascible and highly strung, he was not popular with his colleagues, as he constantly interfered in their departments, but it is his handling of the SUEZ CRISIS which led to the collapse of his authority. Obsessed with NASSER as another Hitler, he believed that Nasser was being used by the Soviet Union 'first to dislodge the West from the Middle East and second to get a foothold in Africa so as to dominate that Continent in turn'. Eden urged the US to withdraw aid for the building of the Aswan Dam. When Dulles did so and Nasser nationalized the Suez Canal, Eden contemplated military force 'to bring about the downfall of the present Egyptian government'. Though warned by President EISEN-HOWER not to take any military action, Eden colluded with MOLLET and BEN-GURION to attack Egypt. Surprised at the international reaction and the run on the pound, he had to declare a cease-fire and withdraw British troops. He lied to the House when he said that he had no foreknowledge of the Israeli attack. On 9 January 1957 Eden, exhausted, resigned on medical advice, still convinced that he had been right. He became Earl of Avon in 1961.

Anthony Eden, D. Carlton (1981)

Anthony Eden, R. Rhodes James (1986)
Anthony Eden, D. Dutton (1991)

EEC (European Economic Community)

A common market in industrial goods formed by members of the ECSC (France, Germany, Italy and the BENELUX countries) at the TREATY OF ROME (1957). It changed its name to the European Community (EC) in 1986 and to the European Union (EU) in 1991. Its aim was to create a large market of 170 million people, in which there would be free movement of goods, labour and capital, though it was not till 1992 that all these aims were realized. Some founders saw the EEC as a supranational body which would lead to the fiscal, monetary and even political union of the member states. The move to Economic and Monetary Union (EMU) took even longer and is not due to be completed, according to the MAASTRICHT TREATY, until 1999. The move to political union may never come about, as there is unremitting hostility, particularly from Britain, to the loss of national sovereignty this move would entail.

Britain took no part in the discussions which led to the formation of the EEC, as 50 per cent of its trade was with the COMMONWEALTH and it did not want to jeopardize its 'special relationship' with the US, but it soon realized that it needed entry to such a large and thriving market as that of the EEC. Harold MACMIL-LAN, the British Prime Minister, therefore applied for membership but DE GAULLE vetoed Britain's application in 1963 (and again in 1967) as he saw Britain as an American 'Trojan Horse', which would enable the US to enter the EEC and he did not want a challenge to French leadership in Western Europe. After de Gaulle's retirement Georges POMPIDOU withdrew French objections to British entry. Negotiations on enlarging the Community resulted in Britain, Denmark and Ireland joining in 1973. This was of great benefit to the EEC, as Britain was a net contributor to the budget and a boon to EEC farmers, as it imported 70 per cent of its food.

Britain's entry coincided with the end of the post-Second World War boom. The Bretton Woods system of fixed exchange rates had broken down in 1971–3 when President NIXON allowed the dollar to float, thus creating volatility in the financial markets. The OPEC PRICE RISE brought about a worldwide recession, unemployment and inflation. The Werner Report's (1970) aim of creating a common currency by 1980 was wrecked. Instead, following the initiative of the EEC President Roy Jenkins, there was a move in 1978 towards a European Monetary System (EMS), with an Exchange Rate Mechanism (ERM) which allowed currencies to fluctuate within narrow limits. This tried to provide stability in the financial markets but a second oil price rise in 1979 caused further turbulence.

During the 1970s and 1980s the EEC lost its competitive edge. It had a $10 billion trade deficit with Japan in 1980 and its deficit with the Asian NEWLY INDUSTRIALIZING ECONOMIES (NIEs) doubled between 1980–7. It also lost markets in the rest of the world to the NIEs and recovered more slowly than the US and Japan from the 1979 oil price rise. The growth rate in the EEC from 1982–7 was 2.2 per cent: in the US it was 3.6 per cent and in Japan 3.7 per cent. EEC car exports fell by 23 per cent between 1970–80, a time when world car exports increased by 426 per cent. The EEC's share of world trade in manufactured goods fell from 45 per cent to 36 per cent between 1973–85: it was particularly weak in high technology, such as the production of computers, telecommunications and consumer electronics. The weakness of the EEC was due to the division of research and development on national lines (EEC companies were too small to compete effectively in the GLOBAL ECONOMY) and to the institutional weakness which resulted from the LUXEMBOURG COMPROMISE of 1966, which enables any member to veto Community proposals and so made it very difficult to secure agreement on any new measures. The EEC responded to stagflation (inflation com-

bined with stagnant production) by adopting protectionist measures. In the 1970s most members subsidized ailing industries, limited the importation of Japanese cars and protected their textile and shoe industries from THIRD WORLD competition.

From 1980–4 much of the EEC's time was taken up with two issues: Britain's 'budgetary imbalance' (it paid far more into the Community budget than its share of Community GNP) and the escalating cost of the COMMON AGRICULTURAL POLICY (CAP). When Britain's net contribution was reduced by two-thirds in 1984, the EEC could concentrate on making itself more competitive. The Single European Act (SEA) of 1986 aimed to create a single market by 1992, in which there would be the free movement of goods, people, services and capital. A major constitutional change was to introduce qualified majority voting (54 out of 77 votes were needed) for all internal market legislation. The SEA looked forward to Economic and Monetary Union (EMU), a matter taken up by the Maastright Treaty (1991). This was designed to strengthen the EU by getting rid of the costs of currency exchanges and by making large-scale speculation against a common currency much more difficult.

A further enlargement of the EEC took place in 1981, when Greece became a member, and in 1986, when Spain and Portugal joined. The accession of Spain and Portugal followed prolonged negotiations, as they would add to the EC's agricultural surpluses (in olive oil and citrus fruits) and thus to the cost of CAP and would draw heavily on regional development funds. EFTA states had access to the EU market in 1993 when the European Economic Area was created, but they wanted full membership so that they could take part in decision-making. Finland, Sweden and Austria therefore joined in 1995. As small, rich economies they would be net contributors to the EU budget. The Swiss and Norwegian electorates rejected membership, though their governments favoured it. Another enlargement of the EU was proposed in July 1997, when the European Commission invited six countries to begin negotiations for membership: Hungary, Poland, the Czech Republic, Estonia, Slovenia and Cyprus. The EU had a market of 348 million people in 1995 and accounted for 40 per cent of world trade.

The European Community, A. M. Williams (1994)
The Emerging European Union, D. M. Wood and B. A. Yesilado (1996)
The Origins and Development of the European Union, 1945–95, M. J. Dedman (1996)

EFTA (European Free Trade Association)

The establishment of a free trade area for industrial goods by several countries which had not joined the EEC (European Economic Community) when it was formed in 1957. Britain, Norway, Sweden, Denmark, Austria, Switzerland and Portugal were the original Seven who signed the Treaty of Stockholm in 1959: it came into force a year later. Finland became an associate (and later full) member in 1961 and Iceland joined in 1970. The aim was to reduce tariffs between member states in stages, as in the EEC, a process completed in 1966. Unlike the EEC, EFTA did not have a common external tariff, common policies or any supranational institutions, as Britain in particular wanted to avoid any loss of sovereignty. Small states such as Sweden and Switzerland benefited from EFTA, as they had access to the heavily protected large market of Britain, which provided 51 million of EFTA's 89 million population. The gains for Britain were much less: EFTA took only 10 per cent of British exports in 1960. EFTA could never be a substitute for the EEC, with its population of 170 million and so, only seven months after EFTA came into being in May 1960, Harold MACMILLAN, the British Prime Minister, decided that he would try to take Britain into the EEC. Rebuffed twice by DE GAULLE, Britain and Denmark finally left EFTA in 1972 in order to join the EEC

(Portugal also left in 1985 for the same purpose). EFTA states made bilateral free trade agreements for industrial goods with the EEC, but when the Single European Act was passed in 1986 to create a single market in the EC by 1992, EFTA opened negotiations with the EC, as it would have to adopt EC legislation in order to trade within it. As investment boomed in the EC in preparation for the single market, it stagnated in EFTA. This prompted Austria to apply for membership in 1989, Sweden in 1991 and Finland in 1992. Their neutral status had prevented their joining in the past (the EEC was too closely identified with NATO): this constraint disappeared with the end of the COLD WAR. All joined in 1995, leaving only Norway, Switzerland, Iceland and Liechtenstein as EFTA states.

EEC–EFTA: More Than Just Good Friends? J. Jamar and H. Wallace (eds) (1988)

Eisenhower, Dwight David (1890–1969)

American general and President of the United States (1953–61). The son of a railroad worker, he graduated at West Point and served under MACARTHUR in Washington (1930–5) and in the Philippines (1936–8). After Pearl Harbor he worked in the Planning Division of the War Department, where he greatly impressed the Chief of Staff, George Marshall. A warm, humane and friendly man, he first became widely known as Allied Commander-in-Chief for the invasion of North Africa in November 1942. He remained Supreme Commander of Allied forces in the Mediterranean during the conquest of Sicily (May 1943) and in the invasion of Italy (September 1943), until he was recalled in January 1944 to plan the invasion of France. During this time he showed a remarkable ability in co-ordinating the activities and securing the co-operation of ambitious generals of disparate views and of different nationalities. 'Ike' was a great conciliator, tactful and sensitive, reluctant to dominate but prepared to exert his authority when it was necessary, as it some-times was with Montgomery. He was an excellent administrator and planned the invasion of France on D-Day (6 June 1944) with meticulous care. At the end of the war he was in charge of US occupation forces in Germany until he replaced General Marshall as Army Chief of Staff in 1945. He was President of Columbia University from 1948–51 and took command of the newly created NATO (North Atlantic Treaty Organization) in 1951. In June 1952 he resigned to become the Republican candidate for the presidency of the USA.

He reluctantly agreed to be a candidate in order to prevent the nomination going to Robert Taft, an isolationist who had voted against NATO. He won the nomination narrowly but triumphed in the election, winning all but nine states. A cautious conservative, he believed that the functions of the executive were different from those of the legislature and that Franklin Roosevelt and Harry TRUMAN had interfered with the powers of Congress in attempting to influence legislation. He was reluctant to impose his will on Congress, the administration or the REPUBLICAN PARTY. Determined to remove the 'Left-wingish, pinkish influence in our life' he got rid of wage and price control, cut the civil service by 200,000 and federal spending by 10 per cent in his first year. Defence spending and foreign aid were reduced in an attempt to balance the budget, but he would spend to stimulate the economy in a recession. In 1956 he obtained congressional approval for a ten-year interstate highway programme that eventually cost $25 billion and gave a great boost to the automobile, engineering and building industries. Eisenhower made no attempt to repeal the social welfare legislation of the New Deal and in fact spent more on the WELFARE STATE. Unemployment benefits rose, as did the minimum wage, the age for old age pensions was reduced and four million more workers were covered by unemployment insurance. 'Ike' was much more popular than his party; the DEMOCRATIC PARTY

regained control of Congress in 1954 and retained it for the rest of his presidency. Eisenhower had a heart attack in 1955 but recovered to win the presidential election of 1956 even more convincingly than that of 1952, but failed to carry either house of Congress.

Civil rights was the President's Achilles heel. Apart from making Earl WARREN Chief Justice, he did little for blacks, women, the poor or other minorities. Ike wanted popular approval and avoided making decisions that might threaten it. He endorsed the odious Senator MCCARTHY during the 1952 election campaign, was silent when he questioned the loyalty of George Marshall and did nothing to stop his witch-hunting thereafter, though he disliked McCarthy personally and his methods. Eisenhower believed that progress in race relations would occur only when whites wanted it and that action by legislation or the courts would simply make matters worse until attitudes changed. He therefore refused to support publicly the BROWN V TOPEKA ruling of the Supreme Court, which declared segregated schools unconstitutional, though he was prepared to enforce it at LITTLE ROCK.

Eisenhower's foreign policy was normally restrained. 'I hate war' he wrote, 'as only a soldier who has lived it can, only as one who has seen its brutality, its futility, its stupidity'. He ended the KOREAN WAR with an armistice within six months of taking office, rejecting DULLES's advice to give the Chinese 'one hell of a licking'. He allowed the CIA to overthrow the radical Musaddiq regime in Iran and restore the more amenable MUHAMMAD REZA PAHLAVI and in Latin America prized security and stability over democracy and human rights, as in the CIA intervention in Guatemala in 1954 (carried out with the President's approval), which brought down the democratically elected government of ARBENZ GUZMAN. This broke a pledge to the OAS (Organization of American States) not to interfere in another nation's internal affairs and to settle disputes peacefully.

Eisenhower again rejected Dulles's advice to intervene directly in the INDOCHINA WAR OF INDEPENDENCE (1946–54) by refusing to send American troops there, but he paid for 80 per cent of the French war effort. When the French were defeated, the US replaced France as the leading foreign power in Southeast Asia. His refusal to agree to elections in South Vietnam in 1956 led to civil war there and eventual full-scale American intervention in the VIETNAM WAR. Eisenhower put forward the DOMINO THEORY to justify American involvement in Vietnam and created SEATO in a vain attempt to contain communism in the region.

Dulles's withdrawal of funding for the Aswan Dam helped to bring about the SUEZ CRISIS in 1956, during which the Soviet Union was able to gain a foothold in the Middle East. When the Soviet Union threatened to use military force there, Eisenhower said the US would send in its own troops to combat them. This was one of the most frightening episodes of the COLD WAR. The Eisenhower Doctrine offering armed assistance to any nation threatened by a communist country, was drawn up in an attempt to prevent the spread of communism in the Middle East. The HUNGARIAN RISING of 1956 exposed Dulles's bluster about rolling-back communism: the US did nothing to help the insurgents. Hungary, Ike said, was 'as inaccessible to us as Tibet'. When Fidel CASTRO overthrew the BATISTA dictatorship in Cuba, and turned to the Soviet Union for aid and arms (the US having refused assistance) Eisenhower first cut back sugar imports from Cuba and then authorized the training of 1,400 anti-Castro Cubans by the CIA, but did not decide when or whether they might be used. In January 1961 he cut off diplomatic relations with Cuba. In spite of seeing all THIRD WORLD issues as part of the Cold War and failing to distinguish between national movements for social reform and Soviet-controlled communist parties, Eisenhower wanted DÉTENTE with the Soviet Union and an end to the arms race, as he did not believe that an increase in the number of nuclear weapons brought greater security. Yet he quickly built up America's nuclear weapons from 1,500 in 1953 to 6,000 in 1959, at the same time cutting the army by 671,000 to 862,000. Critics said that his and Dulles's concept of 'massive retaliation' (the use of nuclear weapons to strike quickly at the aggressor's own territory) was too inflexible to cope with local conflicts and might encourage aggression, as opponents would feel confident that the US would not use nuclear weapons in regional wars. Ike knew, after U2 flights over the Soviet Union, that Soviet superiority in missiles was a myth. A summit meeting with KHRUSHCHEV planned for Paris in 1960 was aborted owing to the U-2 INCIDENT. Eisenhower's transparent attempts at deception when the spy plane was shot down allowed Khrushchev to exploit the incident and leave Eisenhower humiliated. Yet he had given the US eight years of peace and prosperity, which no other President had done in the twentieth century. In his farewell address he warned against an escalation of the arms race: 'We must guard against the acquisition of unwarranted influence...by the MILITARY–INDUSTRIAL COMPLEX'. He then retired to his farm in Gettysburg.

Dwight D. Eisenhower: Hero and Politician, R. Burk (1986)
Eisenhower: Soldier and President, S. E. Ambrose (1990)
Dwight D. Eisenhower and American Power, W. Pickett (1995)

Elizabeth II (1926–) Queen of the United Kingdom of Great Britain and Northern Ireland (1952–) and head of the COMMONWEALTH. The elder daughter of the Duke of York (who became King George VI when his brother, Edward VIII, abdicated in 1936), she was privately educated and in 1947 married Philip Mountbatten, formerly Prince Philip of Greece and Denmark and later

Duke of Edinburgh. They had four children: Charles (1948–), Prince of Wales; Anne (1950–), the Princess Royal; Andrew (1960–), Duke of York and Prince Edward (1964–). Elizabeth had a close relationship with her father, who prepared her for the succession by making her a State Counsellor at the age of 18. She became queen on her father's death in 1952 and, unlike Queen Victoria, was extremely conscientious in carrying out her duties, which were mainly of a ceremonial nature: opening parliament, acting as host to foreign leaders, making state visits to other countries and holding investitures to award decorations and titles. Elizabeth II was widely admired and very popular but the political influence of the crown had almost disappeared. On two occasions she made controversial decisions but only after taking the advice of leading politicians. The first was in 1963, when Harold MACMILLAN resigned as Prime Minister. There was at the time no formal procedure for appointing a leader of the CONSERVATIVE PARTY, so she sought the advice of the retiring Prime Minister and other prominent Conservatives before asking the Earl of Home (who gave up his title to become Sir Alec DOUGLAS-HOME) to be Prime Minister. The second occasion was in Australia in 1975, when the two houses of parliament were deadlocked, as the Senate, controlled by the Liberal leader Malcolm FRASER, refused to pass the budget of Gough WHITLAM's government. Elizabeth, as Queen of Australia, through her Governor-General dissolved parliament and called a general election.

The queen appeared to meet Bagehot's requirements in *The English Constitution* (1865) for a monarch who was an exemplar of family life, a moral example and also a religious figurehead (she was head of the Church of England). Yet Prince Charles, the heir to the throne, said in an interview with Jonathan Dimbleby that he grew up feeling 'emotionally estranged' from his mother, craving affection which she seemed 'unable or unwilling to offer'. The marriages of Charles, Anne and Andrew all ended in divorce, with much public acrimony in the case of Charles and Princess Diana. Criticism of the monarchy arose too as the queen did not pay tax on her considerable income. When part of Windsor Castle was gutted by fire in November 1992 it was disclosed that none of the royal palaces was insured and that the government pays for their upkeep and refurbishment. The bill for repair at Windsor was estimated at £60 million. To reduce criticism the queen announced in February 1993 that she would pay tax on her private income.

Majesty: Eliabeth II and the House of Windsor, R. Lacey (1977)
Royal Fortune: Tax, Money and the Monarchy, P. Hall (1992)
The Queen: A Biography of Elizabeth II, B. Pimlott (1996)

Enosis   The attempt to unite Cyprus with Greece. Cyprus was part of the Ottoman Empire in the nineteenth century but came under British control in 1878 and was annexed by Britain in 1914. Around 80 per cent of the population was Greek (nearly all the rest was Turkish) and demanded *enosis* (union) with Greece. The British wanted to retain Cyprus as a base in the eastern Mediterranean, particularly when they agreed in 1954 to remove their troops from the Suez Canal. Georgios Grivas, a Cypriot-born Greek army officer, therefore began a campaign of civil disobedience and attacks on British installations. Those were carried out by the National Organisation of Cypriot Fighters (EOKA), encouraged (though publicly disowned) by the Archbishop of Cyprus, Makarios III. In March 1956 he was deported to the Seychelles by the British. As the attack on Egypt in the SUEZ CRISIS was mounted from Cyprus, EOKA stepped up its attacks, this time on British troops and Turkish Cypriots.

Makarios, released from exile in 1957, took up residence in Athens and in 1958 let it be known that he would accept the independence of Cyprus as an alternative to *enosis*. A year later an agreement was reached by the British, Greek and Turkish governments and came into effect in 1960. Cyprus was to be an independent republic in the COMMONWEALTH, with Britain retaining two bases on the island. There were to be two communal chambers, one Greek and one Turkish: a separate majority in each chamber was needed to pass bills on taxation or defence. There was to be a Greek President and Turkish Vice-President and government positions were to be divided between Greeks and Turks, but in a way which benefited the Turkish minority (18 per cent of the population): they were to hold 30 per cent of government posts. Makarios, presented with this *fait accompli*, reluctantly accepted it and became the first President of Cyprus. The constitution was unworkable, as it enabled the Turkish minority to block all majority decisions, so in 1963 Makarios announced that he would revise it and reduce the rights of the Turkish Cypriots. This seemed the first step to *enosis* and resulted in fighting between the Greek and Turkish communities. The threat of a Turkish invasion was prevented by President JOHNSON leaning heavily on Turkey.

All hopes for *enosis* were ended by the GREEK COLONELS. Brigadier Ioannidis deposed Makarios in 1974 and briefly replaced him as President of Cyprus by Nicos Sampson, one of the most ruthless former members of EOKA and a supporter of *enosis*. This prompted Turkey to invade Cyprus on 20 July and occupy 40 per cent of the island. 200,000 Greeks in the north of the island fled to the south, Turks moving in the opposite direction. A 'green line', monitored by a UNITED NATIONS peace-keeping force, was established separating the two communities. Movement across it was prohibited. Since then Cyprus has remained divided.

The Cyprus Revolt: An Account of the Struggle for Union with Greece, N. Crawshaw (1978)

environmental disasters   Damage to the environment as a result of human activity first occurred on a large scale with the Industrial Revolution, when the burning of coal as a source of energy polluted the air. This form of pollution increased dramatically after the Second World War as the countries of the Soviet bloc industrialized, as did THIRD WORLD nations such as China and India. Whole areas of Poland, Czechoslavakia and East Germany were covered in smog from industrial output. Particular catastrophes have occurred in chemical works, such as the BHOPAL DISASTER (1984) in India, when methyl isocyanide escaped into the atmosphere, killing 2,250 people and injuring 200,000. Environmental disasters have also taken place as a result of oil spillage and nuclear accidents. When the *Exxon Valdez* tanker hit a reef in Alaska it spilled 240,000 barrels of oil into the sea, creating the greatest environmental disaster in the US, with the death of an estimated 580,000 seabirds. Nuclear power was at first greeted enthusiastically as a non-polluting source of energy, but after the CHERNOBYL NUCLEAR DISASTER (1986) it came to be regarded as potentially more dangerous than anything yet created. The danger is not only from explosions but from discarded nuclear waste and the decommissioning of nuclear power stations. It is almost impossible to make nuclear waste safe or dispose of it effectively.

Agriculture as well as industry is a source of environmental pollution. By the use of pesticides and fertilizers harmful nitrates enter the soil and are washed into rivers, affecting the water supply. Overcropping and overgrazing, a result of the POPULATION EXPLOSION, has led to desertification, as in the African Sahel region, where the advance of the desert affects 30 million people. Desertification has also taken place as a result of irrigation schemes. The Soviet government used water from the feeder rivers (Amu Darya and Syr Darya) of the Aral Sea for the growing of cotton and fruit. This resulted in the level of the Aral Sea falling by 14 metres in 30 years:

the Sea lost 40 per cent of its area and in the rest mineral concentrations, especially salt, trebled, killing all fish. The irrigated land is rapidly becoming salinated, yet to end the irrigation would deprive millions of their livelihood. Deforestation is another source of environmental disasters. Forests have been cut down to provide a source of income in poor countries, for fuel and to make way for crop-growing, with largely unforeseen consequences. In the Himalayas half the forests were cut down between 1950–80. The resulting soil erosion has led, according to the Indian government, to siltation and flooding in the densely populated regions of the Ganges and Brahmaputra rivers hundreds of miles away. Latin America has about 60 per cent of the world's tropical forests and here, especially in Brazil and Central America, the felling of trees has been almost uncontrolled.

The worst threat of all to the environment comes from the global warming which is taking place. The earth is a closed system: no material enters or leaves it except for the sun's radial energy. Nearly all of this is reflected back into space, otherwise the earth would keep on getting hotter. This uniquely balanced system is threatened by two effects. Large holes have appeared in the ozone layer, which protects people from harmful solar radiation, as chlorofluorocarbon (CFC) gases, used in refrigerants and aerosols, are released into the atmosphere. There were under 40 tons of CFCs in the atmosphere in the early 1950s, a figure which rose to 3.6 million tons between 1960 and 1972. Even if there are no further emissions of CFCs, it will take 100 years for the original protective level of ozone to be restored. The second harmful effect produced by human activity results from the emission of other gases – nitrous oxide, methane and carbon dioxide (CO_2) – which come particularly from the burning of fossil fuels and from car exhausts. These act like glass in a greenhouse: they let in the sun's rays but trap some of the heat that would otherwise be radiated back into space. Since 1800 the proportion of CO_2 in the air has risen

by a quarter. This has caused the average global temperature to rise by 0.6 per cent in the last century, a rate which is expected to increase. The build up of CO_2 has in the past been reduced as trees consume CO_2 and emit oxygen, but with the destruction of the forests this safety valve is being removed. One effect of global warming is that sea levels will rise as ice caps melt, thus creating serious flooding in Bangladesh, south China, some Pacific islands and the Nile delta. Another effect is climate change: diseases carried by insects, such as malaria, will spread from the tropics to temperate zones such as northern Europe as temperatures rise.

GREEN movements, such as Friends of the Earth and GREENPEACE, have arisen to draw attention to environmental damage and have formed political parties, as in Germany. They have had some effect in persuading governments to recycle waste, clean up rivers and pursue environmentally friendly policies, but generally governments have been slow to react to dangers threatening the environment. Britain produced a Clean Air Act in 1956 and most developed countries make catalysers in cars obligatory, but international agreements are needed and those are difficult to obtain and enforce. The UNITED NATIONS Conference on Environment and Development at Rio de Janeiro in 1992 was attended by 185 governments (and 131 heads of state) and made agreements to reduce CO_2 emissions and protect species but every target set there has been missed. The NEWLY INDUSTRIAL-IZING ECONOMIES (NIEs) saw Western demands for cutting down industrial emissions as hypocritical and as denying them the means which the West had earlier used to become rich. The curtailment of global warming, certainly in the short term, therefore seems unlikely, especially as the US (which is responsible for more pollution than any other nation) refuses to set specific targets.

Beyond Interdependence: The Meshing of the World's Economy and the Earth's Ecology, J. MacNeill et al. (1991)

Global Accord: Environmental Challenges and International Responses, N. Choucri (ed.) (1993)

An Introduction to Global Environment Issues, K. Pickering and L. A. Owen (1994)

Erhard, Ludwig (1897–1977) Chancellor of the Federal Republic of Germany (FRG: West Germany) (1963–6). An academic economist, he spent the last years of the Second World War in a research institute. He was not a Nazi sympathizer and in 1944 he drafted a memorandum for reviving the German economy after the war. This was based on the SOCIAL MARKET ECONOMY, a free market for maximum efficiency and a WELFARE STATE to look after the interests of the workers. He was appointed by the American occupation authorities as Economic Director of Bizonia (the British and American sectors) in 1948. Erhard abandoned Nazi controls, abolished rationing and introduced a new currency, the Deutschmark, steps which led to the WIRTSCHAFTSWUNDER (economic miracle), whereby the FRG rose from the devastation of war to become the leading European economy. After the first federal elections Chancellor ADENAUER appointed Erhard Economics Minister, a post he held from 1948–63. His economic reforms and the affluence they produced contributed greatly to the political stability of the FRG.

When Adenauer resigned in 1963 Erhard replaced him as Chancellor and head of a coalition of the CDU (Christian Democratic Union) and the FDP (Free Democratic Party). He remained popular with the electorate in the 1965 general election, but his proposals for higher taxes to balance the budget were rejected by the FDP, whose ministers resigned. Erhard was deserted too by his own party and was forced out of office in 1966.

Germany from Partition to Reunification, H. A. Turner (1992)

A History of West Germany, vol. 2, 1963–91, D. L. Bark and D. R. Gress (1993)

German Politics, 1945–95, P. Pulzer (1995)

Eritrean war of independence (1961–91) Defeated in the Second World War, Italy lost most of its colonies. Instead of independence, which the Muslim majority of Eritrea desired, the US (which wanted to keep the Red Sea outside Russian influence) engineered a decision at the UNITED NATIONS which joined Eritrea with Ethiopia in a federation, with internal self-government. When HAILE SELASSIE ended the federation, and in effect annexed Eritrea in 1962, the UN did nothing. A year earlier the Eritrean Liberation Front (ELF) began an armed struggle against Ethiopia. In 1972 the Eritrean People's Liberation Front (EPLF), a Marxist organization, was formed. When Haile Selassie fell from power in 1974, the Dergue (the ruling military committee) continued the war, but by 1978 Ethiopia was losing the conflict and held only four towns in Eritrea.

The balance of power changed when the Soviet Union backed Ethiopia, providing massive firepower and logistical superiority. MENGISTU, leader of the Dergue, at first was successful in driving the EPLF (which had supplanted ELF) out of the towns, but as Soviet support declined in the 1980s the EPLF won spectacular victories, coming within 70 miles of the Ethiopian capital, Addis Ababa, in 1989 and in 1990 capturing Eritrea's main port Massawa. In 1991 the EPLF gained control of the Eritrean capital Asmara and established a provisional government until a referendum was held in 1993 which overwhelmingly approved of independence.

The Eritrean Struggle for Independence, R. Iyob (1995)

Erlander, Tage (1901–85) Prime Minister of Sweden (1946–69). The son of a schoolteacher, he was active in the Social Democratic Party while a student at the University of Lund. He entered the Riksdag (parliament) in 1933, was a junior minister from 1938–44 and in the cabinet from 1944–6 as Education Minister, extending compulsory education to nine years and expanding higher education. In 1946 he was chosen as party leader and Prime Minister. Industrious and pragmatic, he gained the respect of nearly all Swedes and was largely responsible for Sweden's WEL-FARE STATE. Its benefits (old age pensions, medical care, child allowances, rent subsidies) were available to all, not simply the poor and were widely supported. His belief in consensus led to his style of government being called 'Harpsund democracy', after his country estate, where he consulted leaders of all sections of society. Reforms such as a unicameral legislature and generous foreign aid were carried out with the co-operation of other parties. Erlander greatly valued Sweden's neutrality and therefore joined EFTA in 1959 rather than the EEC, because of the latter's close ties with NATO. He tolerated the attacks of his protégé, Olof PALME, on American policy in the VIETNAM WAR, but in retirement sought to restore good relations with the US.

Politics and Markets: The Social Democratic Road to Power, G. Esping-Andersen (1985)

ETA (*Euzkadi Ta Askatasuna*, 'Basque Homeland and Freedom')   Basque independence organization. Founded by a group of Basque students in 1959 to seek the independence of the Basque lands, known as 'Euzkadi', in both Spain and France. The group's most spectacular armed action against the Francoist state was the assassination in 1973 of the dictator's right-hand man, Admiral Carrero Blanco, which decisively altered the course of the TRANSITION by eliminating the only person who could have guaranteed the regime's continuity.

Throughout its history ETA has been plagued by major schisms that have undermined its effectiveness: in 1974 the organization was divided by the dispute between ETA Militar,

which stressed the supremacy of the armed struggle and Basque ethnicity, and ETA Politico-Militar, which placed a greater emphasis on the class struggle and politics.

During the Transition ETA's violence, hitherto sporadic and limited, escalated dramatically in an effort to extract the greatest possible concessions from the emerging democratic state. Between 1978 and 1980 over 200 people were killed as the organization no longer targetted select individuals but anyone belonging to the police, army, Civil Guard and judiciary. By the end of the 1970s ETA had become the most violent terrorist group in Europe.

In 1981–2, following the establishment of the Basque Autonomy Statute and the consolidation of Spanish democracy, ETA Politico-Militar dissolved itself and most of its members entered democratic politics. By contrast, ETA Militar opted to continue with the armed struggle, deploying from the mid-1980s a more indiscriminate form of violence, as exemplified in the 1987 bombing of a Barcelona supermarket that killed 20 people.

During and after the Transition, ETA lost a great deal of support in the Basque country. Yet, unlike other terrorist groups in Spain, ETA possessed a genuine social base. This was reflected in the setting up in 1978 of *Herri Batasuna* (HB: United People), a coalition of radical nationalist forces which provided ETA with a political mouthpiece, which has won between 18 per cent and 11 per cent of the vote in the Basque country.

The socialist government which came to power in 1982 adopted a more aggressive armed response, which resulted in the implementation of a shoot-to-kill policy of 1983–7 in the south of France against ETA's operations' base. Overall, the socialist offensive reduced ETA from a total of 30 commando units to a mere three, and included notable coups such as the capture of ETA's ruling triumvirate in 1992, but ETA has constantly renewed itself.

By the mid-1990s the leaderships of both ETA and HB had come under the control of young, hardline militants. As the socialists declined in power, ETA began to target figures from the opposition PP (Popular Party), resulting in 1995 in the murder of the party's leader in the Basque country and a near escape for José María Aznar, the PP's national leader. There were mass, nationwide anti-ETA demonstrations. Meanwhile, ETA's political front, HB, orchestrated a massive escalation in street violence and the intimidation of political opponents. Despite widespread rejection of ETA in the Basque country, prospects for a solution to the conflict in the late 1990s were far from promising.

The Basque Insurgents: ETA, 1952–1980, R. P. Clark (1984)
ETA and Basque Nationalism, J. Sullivan (1988)

ethnic cleansing   The removal by force (by the dominant group) of all other ethnic groups from an area. The term was first used in the YUGOSLAV CIVIL WAR (1991–5) but the concept was not new. After the treaty of Lausanne (1923) a million Greeks left Turkey and 350,000 Turks were expelled from Greece. At the end of the Second World War ten million Germans fled or were expelled from Eastern Europe, particularly from the Sudetenland and Poland. GOMULKA's aim was to get rid of all Germans: 5.5 million fled and 1.7 million were killed, leaving a German minority in Poland today of 60,000.

In what became Yugoslavia, Muslims, Croats and Serbs had lived together for over 500 years. All this changed when Croatia declared its independence in July 1991. Immediately the Serbs in Knin and Krajina declared their own independent state and began driving out Croats. The women and children were allowed to go free, the men were massacred, often after being tortured. The terror encouraged many to flee before they were attacked, so whole areas were 'cleansed', as half a million Croat refugees

took to the road. When the war extended to Bosnia in 1992, ethnic cleansing became a characteristic of the conflict there. Serbs deliberately murdered the Muslim élite – lawyers, doctors, teachers – and were accused of the organized extermination of their opponents in concentration camps, in which many were executed and others were starved to death. In August 1992 the US Foreign Relations Committee reported that ethnic cleansing had largely achieved its goal: there was an exclusively Serb-inhabited region of Bosnia, contiguous to Serbia. Widespread atrocities included 'random and selective killings...and organized massacres....We believe the death toll associated with the forcible removal of the Muslim village population far exceeds the death toll from the bombardment of cities'. The killings in the camps, it said, were 'recreational and sadistic'. 'The UN did not respond in a timely manner to early reports...about atrocities in the prison camps', nor did the US. 'The failure to respond reflects systematic defects in the way the international community and the US monitor human rights crises'. By the end of 1992 two million Bosnians, nearly half the population of Bosnia, had lost their homes. When the Croats attacked Muslims in central Bosnia in April 1993 ethnic cleansing was carried out by Croats, who copied the Serbs in murdering civilians, raping women and setting fire to Muslim villages. The Serbs became the victims in August 1995, when the Croats overran Krajina.

Genocide in Bosnia: The Policy of 'Ethnic Cleansing', N. Cigar (1995)
The Bridge Betrayed: Religion and Genocide in Bosnia, M. A. Sells (1996)

Eurocommunism   A trend among Western European communist partners to free themselves from the domination of the CPSU (Communist Party of the Soviet Union). The name was first used in the mid-1970s and received wide publicity after the publication of Santiago Carrillo's *Eurocommunism and the State* in 1976. Many of the ideas associated with Eurocommunism were not new and went back to Gramsci's *Prison Notebooks* (1929–35) and to Tito's break with STALIN in 1948. KHRUSHCHEV's secret speech to the TWENTIETH CONGRESS ON THE CPSU in 1956 gave a great boost to those seeking a revision of communist doctrine, Palmiro TOGLIATTI, leader of the PCI (Italian Communist Party), expounding his ideas on polycentrism. The brutal suppression of the HUNGARIAN RISING of the same year and of the PRAGUE SPRING in 1968 alienated many Western communists and speeded up their move towards independence.

There was no formal manifesto but the leaders of the French, Spanish and Italian communist parties signed a declaration in Madrid in 1977 which said that they were committed to independence from the Soviet Union and that they valued democratic principles: freedom of the press, of religious belief, civil liberties and political pluralism. Within communist parties Eurocommunism implied a greater participation for members in making decisions and less dictation from leaders. Yet each communist party soon went its own way. Enrico Berlinguer, leader of the PCI in the 1970s, attempted a historic compromise with the CHRISTIAN DEMOCRATIC PARTY but this collaped in 1979. The French Communist Party only briefly dallied with Eurocommunism and reverted to full support of the USSR with the SOVIET INVASION OF AFGHANISTAN. The weakness of Eurocommunism was that it never went beyond asserting general principles to work out a common programme of action. With the REVOLUTIONS OF 1989–91, which saw the end of communist regimes in Eastern Europe and the COLLAPSE OF THE SOVIET UNION, it became irrelevant.

Eurocommunism and the State, S. Carrillo (1977)
The Politics of Eurocommunism, C. Boggs and D. Plotke (1980)
National Communism in Western Europe, H. Machin (ed.) (1983)

European Union   See EEC

F

Fahd, Ibn Abd al-Aziz (1921–)   King of
Saudi Arabia (1982–). A son of Ibn Saud,
founder of Saudi Arabia, he became Minister
of Education in 1953 (he established a public
system of elementary and secondary schools)
and Minister of the Interior (1962–75). During the reign of King Khalid (1975–83) he
provided the driving force for modernizing
the administration and economy, a process
begun by King FAISAL. He used Saudi Arabia's enormous oil wealth (a quarter of the
world's known oil reserves) to play a key role
in OPEC, to purchase sophisticated arms from
the US, to create a welfare state, and to invest
abroad (particularly in the US and Britain).
His hostility to Israel led him to oppose the
CAMP DAVID ACCORDS (1978) and to proclaim a *jihad* against Israel after it had annexed
East Jerusalem in 1980. This was in marked
contrast to his close relations with the US, the
main supporter of Israel, which enabled
ISLAMIC FUNDAMENTALISTS to condemn
him as a hypocrite.

Fahd funded anti-communist movements,
such as the *Mujahidin* after the SOVIET
INVASION OF AFGHANISTAN, and groups
which the US also supported: Renamo in the
MOZAMBICAN CIVIL WAR and the CON-
TRAS in Nicaragua. In the IRAN–IRAQ WAR
(1980–8) he supported Saddam HUSSEIN
against the SHII regime of Ayatollah KHO-
MEINI in Iran. In spite of high spending on
arms, Saudi Arabia remained militarily weak
and was unable to defend Kuwait when Saddam invaded in 1990. Fahd had to call on the
US, who had built major military bases in
Saudi Arabia in the 1980s, and Arab states to
join a coalition under American command to

defeat Iraq in the GULF WAR (1990–1).
Increased corruption led to Islamist opposition to the regime and severe repression. Fahd
was one of the richest men in the world, with
an estimated personal fortune in 1995 of $20
billion.

Faisal, Ibn Abd al-Aziz (1905–75)   King
of Saudi Arabia (1964–75). The second son of
Ibn Saud, the founder of Saudi Arabia, he
became governor of Hijaz province, in which
Mecca is situated, in 1927 and was renowned
for his piety and asceticism. When his brother
Saud became king in 1953 Faisal exercised
considerable power and was in effect prime
minister for much of the reign, paying off
Saudi Arabia's debts by 1962. Saud, the traditionalist, wanted Saudi Arabia to remain a
tribal confederation, whereas Faisal realized
the need for a modern state with an efficient
bureaucracy in order to cope with the vast
influx of oil wealth. The conflict between
them ended in victory for Faisal, when Saud
was forced to abdicate in 1964.

Faisal spent much of the spiralling oil revenues ($1 billion in 1964, rising after the
OPEC PRICE RISE of 1973 to a peak of $102
billion in 1981) in creating a centralized state,
controlled by the Saudi family, on welfare
schemes (hospitals, housing, education),
infrastructure (ports, airports), petrochemical
industries and arms. In his foreign policy he
was a strong opponent of communism and of
Arab nationalism and challenged NASSER's
claim to lead the Muslim world. Faisal gained
great prestige in the Arab world for using the
oil weapon against Israel in the YOM KIPPUR

WAR (1973). He also played a leading part in the Islamic Conference, which had its headquarters in Jedda and which supported Islamic organizations throughout the world. Faisal was assassinated by a nephew in 1975.

King Faisal and the Modernization of Saudi Arabia, W. Beling (ed.) (1980)
The House of Saud, D. Holden and R. Johns (1981)
The Kingdom, R. Lacey (1982)

Falklands (Malvinas) War (2 April–14 June 1982)   A war between Britain and Argentina. The Falkland Islands (Las Malvinas) are nearly 400 miles off the Argentine coast in the South Atlantic. They had been discovered by the Englishman John Davis in 1592 and had been occupied continuously since 1833 by British settlers, of whom there were about 1,700, mainly sheep farmers, in 1982. Argentine claims to the islands, based on a Spanish settlement there in the 1760s, were revived after the Second World War by Juan PERÓN. Britain gave the wrong signal to Argentina when, as part of its defence cuts, it announced in July 1981 that HMS *Endurance*, the only British ship in the South Atlantic, would be withdrawn. General Galtieri wanted to divert attention from his domestic troubles (inflation of 130 per cent, an almost bankrupt country and agitation about the 30,000 opponents of the military junta who had 'disappeared') and was assured by his Foreign Minister, Costa Mendez, that there would be no war, as Britain wanted to get rid of the islands. He therefore invaded the Falklands on 2 April 1982 and quickly overwhelmed the 70–80 marines defending it. The US regarded the recapture of the islands as militarily impossible, but the British Prime Minister, Margret THATCHER with the support of the opposition, gathered together a task force of 70 ships, 40 of which were requisitioned merchant ships, to travel over 8,000 miles (13,000 km). It was a high-risk strategy, as the force had only 40 Harrier jets on two aircraft carriers to oppose 160

Argentine planes. The troop ships *Canberra* and *Queen Elizabeth II* were vulnerable to attack. Britain had the full support of the COMMONWEALTH and the EEC, which quickly imposed economic sanctions, thus banning 30 per cent of Argentine exports. UNITED NATIONS Resolution 502 on 3 April ordered the withdrawal of Argentine forces. The OAS (Organization of American States) supported Argentina but the US prevented it giving any active help. US support for Britain was crucial, as logistically the invasion would have been impossible without use of the American base on the Ascension Islands. The US also supplied Sidewinder air-to-air missiles which were decisive in air combat and provided intelligence gathered from satellites. On 2 May the Argentine battleship *Belgrano* was sunk by a British submarine and thereafter the Argentine fleet remained in port. 5,000 British troops were landed in East Falkland on 20–21 May without adequate air cover. In a major battle from 21–27 May two British frigates, a destroyer and a container ship were sunk, but many Argentine planes were shot down and a bridgehead was established. The Argentine commander did not commit his conscript troops to destroy the bridgehead, so the British advanced to Port Stanley, the capital, fighting only one major engagement at Goose Green on 21 May. After that there was little opposition and Port Stanley fell, without a fight, on 14 June. 255 British troops and about 750 Argentinians were killed in the conflict but the financial cost to Britain was high. As Argentina would not agree to a peace until Carlos MENEM became President in 1989, considerable forces were kept in Fortress Falklands, which cost the British taxpayer £3 billion from 1982–7. The war affected domestic politics in both Argentina, where the junta collapsed and there was a return to democracy, and in Britain. There triumphalism was in the ascendant. 'We have ceased to be a nation in retreat', declared Mrs Thatcher. 'We have instead a new-found confidence'. Her popularity soared, as did that of the CONSERVATIVE PARTY, making a Conservative victory in the 1983 election likely.

The Battle for the Falklands, M. Hastings and S. Jenkins (1983)
Britain and the Falklands War, L. Freedman (1988)
The History of the South Atlantic Conflict: The War for the Malvinas, R. E. Moro (1989)

feminist movements   These arose in most advanced industrial countries in the second half of the twentieth century, condemned the subordination of women to men and wanted WOMEN'S LIBERATION. Their core belief was that women were of equal value to men but that social attitudes denied them equality even where laws demanded equal treatment for women. They were highly critical of stereotypical ideas that women were emotional, illogical and passive and that they could find fulfilment only through having children and/or looking after the home. Their resurgence in the 1960s owed much to the CIVIL RIGHTS MOVEMENT, which made people aware of inequality in the US, though only a small minority of women called themselves feminists. Many women resented being told that raising a family was boring and saw themselves as complementary to, rather than as competing with, men.

Betty Friedan's *The Feminist Mystique* (1963) expressed the frustration of well-educated, middle-class women who were full-time housewives and mothers. They wanted freedom and the right to work, so that they could find fulfilment in interesting and demanding jobs and not be dependent on their husbands for their incomes. Friedan, a wife and mother of three in a New York suburb, called home 'a comfortable concentration camp'. In 1966 Friedan and others founded the National Organization for Women (NOW), which sought legal equality for women and called for 'a different conception of marriage, an equitable sharing of the responsibilities of home and children'. It also took up other women's causes, such as the provision of child care for working mothers, legalized abortion and paid maternity leave. NOW was originally a small, white, middle-class movement which grew to a membership of 250,000 by 1991. It had few working-class members, as they could not understand the idea of work being liberating: working-class women worked because they needed the money. NOW lobbied hard and persuaded President JOHNSON to add 'sex' to 'race, creed, color or national origin' in his Executive Order against discrimination in employment. The Equal Rights Amendment (ERA), which it strongly supported, was passed by Congress in 1972 but failed to be ratified by enough states to become law.

Other feminist movements were concerned with particular issues. The Committee for Abortion Rights and Against Sterilization was founded in New York in 1977 and Women's Global Network on Reproductive Rights in Amsterdam in 1978 to protect women's control of their own bodies. The Western Women's Liberation Movement in the 1970s and 1980s defended lesbian and gay rights. In Britain the Organization of Women of Asian and African Descent (1978) was formed to protest against the IMMIGRATION LAWS. Some women's groups aimed specifically to protest against state terrorism and violence. The *Madres de la Plaza de Mayo* in Argentina were drawn from the female relations (especially mothers) of those who had 'disappeared' in the dirty war waged by the military against its opponents.

Feminist movements in the THIRD WORLD were not middle class but were concerned with poverty, low pay, rent, prices and welfare services such as schools and hospitals. The Self-Employed Women's Association (SEWA) began organizing women in Ahmedabad, India in the 1970s and grew to have over 200,000 members (streetsellers and rural workers) who set up co-operatives. Home Net, an international network for home-based workers, was set up in 1994. Its members included embroiderers in Madeira, who had been unionized for 20 years, and the Self-Employed Women's Union in South Africa, which started to recruit poor, non-unionized women. Home-based women's organizations were recognized by the International Labour Organization of the UNITED NATIONS in 1996.

Feminists were divided between those who wanted equality, which implied that women were basically the same as men, and those who maintained that women were essentially different from men and therefore needed special rights, as in AFFIRMATIVE ACTION. In the 1980s the women's liberation movement appeared to break up and re-form as a rainbow alliance of groups with different concerns and approaches. The idea of 'sisterhood' – that all women shared the same experiences and values – was abandoned. Black lesbian and working-class feminists argued that all women were not oppressed in the same way. There were class and racial divisions *within* the feminist movement and these were largely responsible for its disintegration. Black women set up their own organizations, like the Southall Black Sisters, to fight sexism within black movements as well as the oppression of women by fundamentalist religions throughout the world.

Faces of Feminism: A Study of Feminism as a Social Movement, O. Banks (1986)
Feminism and Nationalism in the Third World, K. Jayawardena (1986)
Mapping the Women's Movement: Feminist Politics and Social Transformation in the North, M. Threlfall (1996)

Fifth Republic in France   See CONSTITUTION OF THE FIFTH REPUBLIC, DE GAULLE, POMPIDOU, GISCARD D'ESTAING, MITTERRAND, CHIRAC.

Figueres Ferrer, José (Don Pepe) (1906–90)   President of Costa Rica (1953–8, 1970–4). The son of Catalan immigrants, he was a dominant figure in Costa Rican politics

for 30 years. Educated at the universities of Costa Rica and Mexico and at MIT, he became a prosperous farmer. An outspoken critic of the government, he was exiled to Mexico, where he founded a band of exiles, the Caribbean Legion, which plotted to overthrow the government and then remove dictators, including SOMOZA, in Central America. He turned for help to President Arévalo of Guatemala, who also wanted to establish democracies in Central America. Don Pepe's opportunity came in 1948, when the opposition candidate won the presidential election in Costa Rica, which the pro-government legislature annulled. The population was enraged, so Figueres led a popular rising in a short but violent civil war, in which 2,000 were killed. It ended with the victory of Don Pepe, who received indispensable help from Guatemala. For the next 18 months he was head of the ruling junta, which abolished the army, introduced universal suffrage and a progressive tax system, nationalized the banks and banned the Communist Party. Most of these reforms were embodied in the 1949 constitution, which has been the basis for Costa Rica's democracy and stability ever since. In 1949 Figueres voluntarily gave up power.

In 1952 he formed the *Partido de Liberación National* (PLN), which became the country's best organized and most successful party. As its candidate he won the presidential election in 1953 and negotiated a new contract with the United Fruit Company of the US, which trebled the share of the company's profits received by the government and guaranteed a minimum wage for its workers. It was never under threat of expropriation, so Figueres did not suffer from American subversion as ARBENZ GUZMÁN did in Guatemala. When he was President for a second time in 1970 the end of the ALLIANCE FOR PROGRESS funds and the collapse of the Central American Common Market threatened to cripple the economy until Don Pepe found a new market for Costa Rican coffee in the Soviet Union. Costa Rica was the only country in Central

America to establish diplomatic relations with Moscow.

Don Pepe: A Political Biography of José Figueres of Costa Rica, C. D. Ameriger (1979)

financial revolution   The globalization of money markets. Most European foreign exchange controls ended in 1958, while in the US the Federal Reserve Bank set a ceiling to the interest that could be charged by banks. American investors therefore deposited their money abroad, where there was no limit to the amount of interest they could receive and so helped to found an uncontrolled global market, mainly in short-term loans. Funds were transferred to 'offshore' banks, at first mainly in London, and so the Eurodollar was created. International banks found that by setting up in the Cayman Islands or the Bahamas they could pay few or no taxes and avoid restrictions on their activities. Much international finance was therefore detached from any industrial base, though new financial centres (Tokyo, Hong Kong, Singapore, Sydney) in countries with a healthy economy also arose. The Eurocurrency market grew rapidly from $5 billion in 1960 to $110 billion in 1970, $1,120 billion in 1979 and $2,062 billion in 1995. Most of the funds came from the US or economies in surplus, such as Germany and Japan and GULF STATES after the OPEC PRICE RICE in 1973. The global money market was used to recycle the huge surpluses which OPEC countries did not know how to spend or invest.

These enormous sums, looking for quick profits, were outside the control of governments and of the original depositors. There was no central bank, such as each country possessed, and no supervision to prevent or detect fraud. The system was therefore highly volatile, moving money rapidly into and out of markets. Foreign currency transactions took place not to pay for goods or investment but for currency speculation. This was made possible by the INFORMATION REVOLUTION, which used computers, satellites and fibre-optic cables to make high-speed electronic transfers, based on political and economic information which could be known at the same time to the 200,000 monitors connected to this communications network. Electronic transfers replaced the flow of paper money and took place 24 hours a day. Daily exchange flows in the mid-1990s exceeded $1 trillion dollars a day, 90 per cent of which was unconnected with trade or investment. Millions of investors, companies and banks speculated in currencies and made it impossible for central banks to take fiscal measures, such as a reduction in interest rates, of which the markets disapproved. Governments lost control of their exchange rates and money supply, as President MITTERRAND found in France in 1980–2. By the early 1990s even joint action by the leading central banks was unable to counter the influence of the market. On BLACK WEDNESDAY, 16 September 1992, speculation forced the British government out of the European Exchange Rate Mechanism, in spite of the Treasury spending billions of pounds to prevent this.

In the 1970s and 1980s the money markets lent on a large scale to countries, mainly in the THIRD WORLD, which were hit hard by the oil price rise. This lending helped to create an INTERNATIONAL DEBT crisis in 1982, when Mexico decided that it could no longer service its debt.

As funds were deposited all over the world it was difficult to find out where fraud was committed and who was responsible. The most far-reaching chicanery was associated with the $10 billion collapse of BCCI (Bank of Credit and Commerce International) in 1991. The bank had been laundering money and swindling customers for 19 years in 69 countries before US officials exposed the fraud. Barings, the oldest merchant bank in Britain, also collapsed (in 1995) after $800 million of losses incurred by trader Nick Leeson in Singapore.

In 1997 the speculators turned on the Asian NEWLY INDUSTRIALIZING ECONOMIES

(NIEs). The capital markets believed their currencies were overvalued, as there had been risky lending to the private sector and an accumulation of bad debts. Balance of payments deficits had been covered by short-term capital inflows ('hot' money). In July 1997 speculation against the Thai currency, the baht, forced the government to abandon the baht's links to the dollar. As the Thai banking system collapsed speculators moved against the currencies of the Philippines, Indonesia and Malaysia. All had to devalue, the IMF mounting a huge rescue package for Thailand and Indonesia. The contagion spread to South Korea, the world's eleventh largest economy.

The Evolution of the International Monetary System, 1945–85, J. H. B. Tew (1985)
States and the Re-emergence of Global Finance: From Bretton Woods to the 1990s, E. Helleiner (1994)

Ford, Gerald Rudolph (1912–)   President of the US (1974–7). He attended the University of Michigan and Yale Law School, where he graduated in 1944 before serving in the navy (as a lieutenant-commander) during the Second World War. Elected to the House of Representatives in 1948, he remained there until 1973 and was Republican minority leader from 1965, gaining a reputation for integrity. When Vice-President Spiro Agnew was forced to resign in October 1973, after the disclosure of income tax evasion and bribery when he was Governor of Maryland, Ford became Vice-President. President NIXON had to resign too as a result of WATERGATE, so Ford automatically replaced him, the first President to take office without being elected either as President or Vice-President. A month later he pardoned Nixon for any federal crimes he had committed, an act which lost him much of his popularity.

He was traditionally conservative in economic policy, aiming to balance the budget and reduce government intervention. The President tried to stimulate a sluggish economy by huge tax cuts in 1975 with only partial success. As he thought control of inflation was more important than reducing unemployment, he opposed increasing government expenditure and vetoed many social welfare measures and bills to increase farm prices and create new jobs. In two and a half years he vetoed 66 bills, more than any previous President, except Grover Cleveland. When the Justice Department found that the CIA and FBI were involved in Watergate, the President dismissed William Colby, the CIA director and replaced him with George BUSH.

Henry KISSINGER, as Secretary of State, dominated Ford's foreign policy. The President, continuing DÉTENTE, met Leonid BREZHNEV, agreed to a second round of SALT talks and in 1975 signed the HELSINKI FINAL ACT. These measures met with general approval but when he asked Congress for further military aid for South Vietnam it refused, as it did when Kissinger proposed to send arms to anti-communist forces in the ANGOLAN CIVIL WAR. Ford only just defeated Ronald REAGAN for the Republican presidential nomination in 1976 but was narrowly defeated in the election by Jimmy CARTER, who won 50.1 per cent of the popular vote to Ford's 48 per cent.

Gerald R. Ford's Date with Destiny, E. I. Schapsmeier and F. H. Schapsmeier (1989)

Fourth Republic (1946–58)   At the end of the Second World War in France a provisional government under Charles DE GAULLE was formed. When a referendum in October 1945 showed that French people did not want a revival of the Third Republic, a Constituent Assembly was elected to draft a new constitution. It did not favour a strong executive, as he wanted, so de Gaulle resigned in January 1946. A new constitution was finally approved by a referendum in October 1946.

The instability of governments (there were 23 under the new constitution) seemed as bad as in the Third Republic but there was in fact considerable ministerial continuity, as Prime Ministers needed to keep the support of parties which had backed the previous government: now governments retained on average three-quarters of the members of their predecessors. Communists, as leading members of the Resistance, were members of the government until 1947, when they were dismissed for supporting a strike at the nationalized Renault car factory. In opposition the PCF (Communist Party) remained one of the largest parties but became increasingly hostile to the Fourth Republic as the COLD WAR developed and it followed a pro-Soviet line at odds with that of successive French governments. As the Gaullist RPF (Rally of the French People) was also unremittingly opposed to the Republic, the SFIO (Socialist Party), MRP (a Christian Democratic party) and the Radicals formed a third force against both Gaullists and communists. This alliance ruled France from 1947–52 and under BIDAULT helped to set up the OEEC (Organization for European Economic Cooperation) and made a military alliance, the Brussels Treaty, with Britain and the BENELUX countries. France also joined NATO and, under the guidance of Robert Schuman and Jean MONNET, formed the ECSC (European Coal and Steel Community) with West Germany, the Benelux countries and Italy.

A move to the right took place in 1952, when the RPF was the largest party after the election. The SFIO would not serve in a right-wing government and so for the first time since the war was excluded from office. A centre–right government, containing several former Vichy supporters, ruled for the next two years and was brought down by the defeat of DIEN BIEN PHU in the INDO-CHINA WAR OF INDEPENDENCE (1946–54). The Radical Pierre MENDÈS FRANCE seemed the politician most likely to bring it to an end, which he did with the GENEVA ACCORDS, shortly after becoming Prime

Minister. When he fell a Republican Front of socialists and left-wing Radicals, led by the socialist Guy MOLLET, ruled France from 1956–7, suffering humiliation in the SUEZ CRISIS but signing the TREATY OF ROME, which established the EEC.

It was during the Fourth Republic that France recovered from the devastation of war and began a dramatic economic recovery. In 1945 the economy was in ruins, with industrial production only a third of pre war levels. In 1947 production reached the 1938 level and Monnet began his Five Year Plan, which successfully renewed the infrastructure and key industries of France. Coal-mines, gas, electricity, Air France, the Bank of France and some of the big clearing banks and insurance companies were nationalized, as was the Renault car factory. The *École nationale d'administration* was founded in 1946 to provide France with highly trained and motivated administrators. Financial aid from the US, particularly that resulting from the MARSHALL PLAN, speeded up the recovery. Chemicals and engineering were the most dynamic sectors of the economy, in which industrial production increased by 85 per cent between 1950–8.

The end of the Fourth Republic came as a result of events in Algeria. By 1958 the French public was alarmed at the cost and conduct of the ALGERIAN WAR OF INDEPENDENCE (1954–62). President Coty asked de Gaulle to form a new government. On 1 June he asked the Assembly for full powers to restore order and unity, draft a new constitution and submit it to the people in a referendum. This was granted, a new CONSTITUTION OF THE FIFTH REPUBLIC was drawn up and endorsed by the electorate on 28 September 1958.

Crisis and Compromise: Politics in the Fourth Republic, P. Williams (1972)
The Fourth Republic, 1944–58, J. P. Rioux (1987)

Franco, Francisco (1892–1975)   Military dictator of Spain (1939–75). Born in the port town of El Ferrol in Galicia, Franco was the son of a naval paymaster. He had a meteoric rise in the army from 1912–26 in the Moroccan colonial wars. Undoubtedly his often reckless courage was a means of compensating for his small stature (5 ft 3 ins), unprepossessing appearance and shrill voice. He was also reserved and serious, a loner who stood out as a soldier '*sin misa, sin mujeres y sin miedo*' ('without Mass, women, or fear'). In 1926 Franco became, at 33, the youngest general in Europe.

As a monarchist and conservative, Franco was ill-disposed to the Second Republic established in 1931. With typical caution, he joined the military rebellion of 17–18 July 1936 that led to the Spanish Civil War only days beforehand. By gaining the support of the Germans and Italians, he was able to transport the Army of Africa, the most redoubtable section of the Spanish army, across the blockaded Straits to the south of Spain – the first major airlift in military history. This avoided defeat for the Nationalists and established Franco as the leading military figure in the Nationalist camp. On 1 October 1936 he was proclaimed not merely the military commander of the Nationalists but also the head of state. He rejected all offers of mediation or compromise, victory finally being achieved unconditionally on 1 April 1939.

During the Second World War Franco, although officially neutral, provided the Axis powers with important strategic and material support, such as observation posts and exports of wolfram. At the Hendaye meeting with Hitler in October 1940 Franco was prepared to enter the war on Hitler's side in exchange for French territories in North Africa, but Hitler was not prepared to pay Franco's price, preferring instead to placate Vichy France. Yet Franco continued to support the Axis – a total of 47,000 soldiers were sent to the Russian front – believing in a German victory till late 1944. Politically, his regime was based on a coalition of competing if conservative 'families': the army, the Fascist Falange party, the monarchists, the Church (also the dictatorship's chief source

of legitimation) and, later, OPUS DEI and the state bureaucracy. In the Law of Succession of 1947 Franco declared himself head of state until such time as he chose a royal successor. In the meantime, Spain was a kingdom without a king. The *Caudillo* (or leader), as he liked to be known, was to remain in power until his death nearly 40 years later, a feat achieved by skilfully playing off one 'family' against another and by a vigilant pragmatism and guile. Not being subordinate to a rigid ideology, Franco's rule, within its authoritarian limits, was therefore able to evolve. The Potsdam Conference of July 1945 ostracized the Franco dictatorship, the UNITED NATIONS declaring the regime an international pariah. The fact that the execution of significant numbers of political prisoners continued unabated until 1948 did not help Franco's cause. The isolation of the dictatorship was brought to an end by the COLD WAR. The onset of the KOREAN WAR in 1950 prompted the US to incorporate Spain into its defence system. The Pact of Madrid, or Bases Agreement, of 1953, together with the Concordat signed that same year with the Vatican, was a resounding success for Franco both at home and abroad. The US deal not only ended the regime's international ostracism, culminating with Spain's entry into the UN in 1955, but also proved a major boost for the Spanish economy through US aid and investment. Thus, the Bases Agreement played an important role in consolidating Franco's rule.

In the late 1950s Franco carried out a further major readjustment to the regime. The 1957 Cabinet reshuffle saw the downgrading of the Falange in favour of the 'technocrats' of Opus Dei, who occupied the economic portfolios, and proposed a liberalization of the economy. Naturally reluctant to open up Spain's autarkic economy for fear of losing control, Franco was eventually won over, as the economy was on the point of collapse. Economic liberalization under the Stabilization Plan of 1959 was to make possible the boom of the 1960s.

Spain was transformed as the Catholic culture and predominantly rural society of the 1940s gave way to a more urban and secular one that was increasingly susceptible to 'Western' values. The regime therefore focused more and more on economic development, in the hope that prosperity would divert the populace from politics. This proved misplaced, as from the mid-1960s the protest of students, workers, regional nationalists, as well as radicalized sections of the clergy, grew ever stronger, while the communist-linked trade unions, the *Comisones Obreras* (Workers' Commissions), did much to undermine the official *sindicatos verticales* (vertical syndicates).

Franco aimed to thwart the opposition and ensure the continuity of the regime by designating 31-year-old Prince JUAN CARLOS as his successor in 1969. He had been suffering from Parkinson's disease from the early 1960s and, at the age of 80, he finally relinquished the premiership by naming his closest collaborator and right-hand man since the early 1940s, Admiral Carrero Blanco, as head of the government. The assassination of Carrero at the hands of the Basque separatist group, ETA, in 1973 was therefore not only a devastating personal blow for the ailing Franco, but also for the regime. Indeed, Carrero's death removed the main individual obstacle to the opening up of the dictatorship after Franco's death in November 1975.

The Franco Regime, 1936–1975, S. Payne (1987)
Franco, P. Preston (1993)
Franco, S. Ellwood (1994)

Fraser, John Malcolm (1930–) Prime Minister of Australia (1975–83). A wealthy grazier, educated at Melbourne and Oxford universities, he became a Liberal member of parliament in 1955 and held various cabinet posts from 1966–72 in the Liberal and Country Party coalition government. He was regarded as an extreme right-winger when he became leader of the Liberal Party in 1975. His ruthlessness was evident in the tactics he used to topple the Labor government of Gough WHITLAM by refusing to pass the budget (the Liberal Party and its allies had a majority in the upper house, the Senate). He was aided by the unprecedented actions of the Governor-General Sir John Kerr, who dismissed Whitlam and called a general election, in which the Liberal and Country parties won the largest majority of seats of any government since federation. Accusations that he had obtained office by underhand means did not prevent him winning the elections of 1977 and 1980.

He soon established a reputation for breaking promises, such as that he would maintain Medibank and wage indexation. Both were abolished in 1981: a free health service was then restricted to the poor, who qualified by a means test or as old-age pensioners. He claimed that the state of the economy required cuts in public spending but it was the poor and unemployed who had to bear the main burden, while farmers benefited by a restoration of the fertilizer subsidy removed by Whitlam and by new subsidies for dairy farmers. These ensured that government spending was not cut substantially. There was little attempt to privatize nationalized industries. Many of Whitlam's reforms – the indexation of pensions, the abolition of university fees – remained, while several of Fraser's measures were surprisingly liberal. He passed a Federal Freedom of Information Act, created an Ombudsman and showed an abhorrence of racism. The first Aboriginal Land Right Act granted Aborigines 20 per cent of the Northern Territory. In South Australia 100,000 square kilometres of land were given to Aborigines and an Aborigine was appointed State Governor. Anti-discrimination laws on race and gender were also passed.

Fraser's anti-racism was forcibly expressed in his foreign policy. He continued the friendly relations with China established by Whitlam and was a champion of black Africa, pressing the government of South Africa to moderate APARTHEID and playing a key role at the COMMONWEALTH heads of government meeting in 1979 in ensuring black majority rule in Zimbabwe. He also accepted refugees from Vietnam as immigrants, 100,000 of whom settled in Australia. The recession, however, continued. There was a record devaluation of the Australian dollar in 1976, even higher interest rates and a credit squeeze to counter inflation, while unemployment at 10 per cent was at the highest level since the Great Depression of the 1930s. Fraser called a snap election in 1983, as he had done before, but this time he miscalculated. Bob HAWKE and the Australian Labor Party (ALP) won the ALP's greatest election victory since 1929.

Oxford History of Australia, vol. 5, 1942–88,
  G. Bolton (1990)

Frei Montalva, Eduardo (1911–82) President of Chile (1964–70). The son of a Swiss immigrant, he studied law in Santiago. Extremely active in student politics, Frei was elected President of the National Association of Catholic Students. In 1948 he was elected a senator. The political centre had lost a great deal of credibility as a result of the administration of 1946–52 (when it outlawed and persecuted its former allies, the communists), but in 1957 a process of recovery began with the formation of the Christian Democratic Party (*Partido Democrático Cristiano*, PDC) through the fusion of the National Falange with the Social Democratic, Radical, and Conservative parties. The following year, 1958, Frei stood as the PDC's presidential candidate, finishing third.

Frei was finally elected President in 1964 due to the tactical decision of the right, alarmed at the prospect of a left-wing victory under Salvador ALLENDE, not to present its own candidate, as well as through the financial backing of European Christian Democrats and the US (including the CIA). None the less Frei's programme, embodied in the campaign slogan of 'Revolution in Liberty' (that is to say, radical change within the existing constitutional framework), overlapped strongly with that of the left. Indeed, the Christian Democrats had already done much to promote 'popular power' through the establishment of grassroots organizations such as neighbourhood committees, peasants' associations, and women's and youth groups. However, the intense rivalry that had developed between the left and centre during the 1950s and early 1960s gravely undermined Frei's efforts at reform.

Although meaningful reform was achieved under Frei in health, education and taxation, the lack of support from the left, which often allied with the right to block or discredit the government's proposals, greatly hampered the administration's two main projects: the partial PRIVATIZATION of Chile's principal industry, the copper business, and agrarian reform.

Mounting economic problems from 1966 onwards enveloped Frei's later years in a climate of crisis. Prevented from standing as presidential candidate in the 1970 election by his own party, which preferred the more left-wing Radomiro Tomic, Frei became a senator again following Allende's victory. Having been undermined by the left during Frei's presidency, the Christian Democrats now thwarted many of the left's plans for reform. Indeed, the experience of 1964–73 revealed that neither the left nor the centre could achieve major reform alone. Although Frei supported the coup which overthrew Allende in September 1973, he soon became disillusioned by the military dictatorship. Frei's political legacy was assumed by his son, Eduardo Frei Ruiz-Tagle, who was elected President in December 1993.

*Bureaucratic Politics and Administration in
  Chile,* P. Cleaves (1974)
The Penguin History of Latin America, E. Williamson (1992)

Fujimori, Alberto (1938–) President of Peru (1990–). Born in Lima, the son of

Japanese immigrants, he studied agriculture and mathematics at university. In the 1990 presidential election he stood as a candidate of his Cambio 90 Party, formed only six months before, and seemed a certain loser to the right-wing Democratic Front, led by the novelist Mario Vargas Llosa. A public opinion poll at the beginning of March showed that he had 1 per cent support, though this had risen to 24 per cent by the time of the first round of the election in May. In the June run-off against Vargas Llosa he surprisingly won 57 per cent of the vote, with the support of the radical APRA and some left-wing parties.

A further surprise was the adoption of the austerity measures proposed by his opponents to deal with the economic chaos he inherited. There was high unemployment, inflation of 2,700 per cent and an INTERNATIONAL DEBT of $20 billion. Without the 'informal' and illegal sectors (Peru produced 60 per cent of the coca leaf used in the production of cocaine, an industry which employed 300,000 and generated a billion dollars in foreign exchange) the economy would have collapsed. Fujimori abolished subsidies for consumers, so the price of petrol rose by 3,000 per cent and that of basic foods by between 300–600 per cent. This plunged Peru into recession but impressed the financial markets. García's bank nationalization was repealed and the economy liberalized by deregulating docks and transport, ending state monopolies in telecommunications, the postal service and railways and there was some PRIVATIZATION. Widespread industrial unrest followed but Fujimori succeeded in turning the economy around: there was

renewed growth of 7 per cent in 1993 and inflation was reduced to 22 per cent in 1994.

In yet another of his surprises, Fujimori carried out an *auto-golpe* (self-coup) in 1992, when he suspended the constitution and the Congress, with army support, and ruled by decree. This destruction of democracy led to the suspension of foreign loans, which threatened to end the economic recovery, so he proposed a return to democracy in 1993 with the election of a Congress to draft a new constitution, which increased the powers of the President, who could be elected for a second consecutive term, and provided for a unicameral legislature. This was approved by a small majority in a plebiscite and Fujimori was duly re-elected as President in 1995 with 65 per cent of the vote. Foreign loans and investment then returned to Peru, though Fujimori continued to face criticism over his autocratic style of government.

Fujimori had considerable success in dealing with the terrorism of SENDERO LUMINOSO and of MRTA (*Movimiento Revolucionario Tupac Amaru*). The leaders of both groups were captured in 1992 and sentenced to life imprisonment and though these movements continued their activities they were near to collapse by 1994. MRTA, with its one remaining leader Nestor Cerpa, staged a last dramatic act in 1996 when it seized hostages at the Japanese embassy in Lima. A long siege followed until 1997, when Fujimori recovered his popularity by a commando raid which killed the guerrillas and freed the hostages.

Politics in Peru: The Evolution of a Crisis, J. D. Rudolph (1992)

G

Gaddafi, Muammar   See QADDAFI

Gaitskell, Hugh (1906–63)   British politician and leader of the LABOUR PARTY (1955–63). The son of a civil servant, he was educated at Winchester and Oxford, where he obtained a first in politics, philosophy and economics and then became a lecturer in economics at London University, where he remained for 11 years. When the Second World War began he took up a civil service post as a German-speaking economist in the Ministry of Economic Warfare. The General Strike of 1926 had convinced him that his future lay 'with the working classes', but he did not decide to become a politician until 1945, when he was elected as a Labour MP. Almost immediately he became a junior minister in Clement ATTLEE's government and in 1949, when Sir Stafford Cripps, the Chancellor of the Exchequer, was ill, persuaded the government that devaluation was necessary. He succeeded Cripps at the Treasury in October 1950. Fervently believing that Britain still had a global role through the COMMONWEALTH and its special relationship with the US, he intended to support the US in the KOREAN WAR by introducing a vast rearmament programme of £4,700 million over three years. His budget of 1951 was a political decision and made little economic sense, as Britain could not afford the expenditure proposed. Income tax was raised and defence spending doubled to 14 per cent of GNP. The health charges imposed on patients were minor (£13 million in a budget of £4 billion) but the principle of a free health service was at stake,

so Aneurin BEVAN resigned and was joined by Harold WILSON, who opposed the defence expenditure. Gaitskell was therefore largely responsible for the split in the Labour Party which was to keep it weak and divided for over a decade. The inflation which resulted from the budget and the balance of payments deficit did much to bring about the defeat of the Labour Party in the 1951 election.

When Attlee retired as leader of the Labour Party in 1955 Gaitskell was elected to succeed him, easily defeating Bevan and Herbert Morrison. In some ways he was a strange choice, as he seemed to epitomize the permissive society. An adulterer who began an affair with his wife Dora when she was already married, he later had a long relationship with Ian Fleming's wife Ann, who was a wealthy Tory. A passionate jazz fan and lover of late-night parties, he preferred the company of fellow Wykehamists to that of the trade unionists on whose block vote he relied at party conferences. During the SUEZ CRISIS he condemned NASSER's nationalization of the Suez Canal and was not opposed to the use of force, provided this was done through the UNITED NATIONS with US and Commonwealth approval. When Anthony EDEN invaded Egypt in collusion with France and Israel, Gaitskell bitterly attacked him, a courageous thing to do as most people in Britain supported the government. After the Labour Party was defeated in the 1959 election for the third successive time, Gaitskell decided that it must be modernized. The German SPD (Social Democratic Party) was abandoning Marxism and he wanted the Labour Party to do the same, so he divided it again by proposing that Clause IV, which committed it to the common ownership of the means of production, should be abolished. Many Labour supporters saw Gaitskell as abandoning socialism, so he had to give up his quest. His rejection of the class war and further nationalization, as well as his pro-US and anti-communist foreign policy, gave rise to the term BUTSKELLISM. There was a further clash in the Labour Party over unilateral nuclear disarmament, which Gaitskell opposed. When the Party Conference approved it in 1960 he promised 'to fight, fight and fight again' and had the decision reversed a year later. Pugnacious and passionate, he led from the front but exhausted the party until he died unexpectedly from a rare disease.

Hugh Gaitskell, P. M. Williams (1979)
Labour People, K. D. Morgan (1987)
Hugh Gaitskell, B. Brivati (1996)

Gandhi, Indira (1917–84)   Prime Minister of India (1966–77, 1980–4). The only child of Jawaharlal NEHRU, she was educated at schools in England and Switzerland and at the universities of Bengal and Oxford. She joined the CONGRESS PARTY in 1938 and in 1942 married Feroze Gandhi (he died in 1960). When Nehru died she was appointed Minister of Information in Lal Bahadur Shastri's government, succeeding him as leader of the Congress Party and Prime Minister in 1966.

She was beset by many problems, as there was famine after the failure of the monsoon in 1965, strikes and food riots and Sikhs in the Punjab were demanding a separate state. She sought to defuse Sikh agitation by creating the states of Punjab and Haryana out of the former Punjab, but the elections of 1967 were disastrous for her. The Congress majority in the Lok Sabha (the lower house of parliament) fell from 200 to 20. The President therefore persuaded her to accept Morarji Desai as her Deputy and Minister of Finance. The arrangement did not last long, as Indira Gandhi moved to the left, nationalized 14 banks and took personal control of the Min-

istry of Finance, causing Desai to resign as Deputy Prime Minister. She was expelled from Congress for 'indiscipline' but retained the support of most Congress members in parliament (200 supported her, 65 Desai). As she did not have a majority in the Lok Sabha, she formed a left-wing coalition, which included communists. The 1971 election was a triumph for her as her branch of Congress won 350 out of 515 Lok Sabha seats.

Another victory for her in the same year came in the INDEPENDENCE OF BANGLA-DESH, when her intervention ensured that East Pakistan was able to become an independent state. She continued the economic policies of her father, the state playing a leading role in heavy industries, but economic growth continued to be sluggish, in spite of India becoming a nuclear power in 1974 and spectacular agriculture yields because of the GREEN REVOLUTION, which saw the introduction of new wheat and rice varieties. Politically she became more autocratic, making loyalty to herself the main qualification for holding office. She established a highly centralized system of government and strengthened control over the party by replacing local Congress bosses who had an independent power base. Her son Sanjay was made the head of India's new car manufacturing unit. Indira Gandhi's political career almost came to an end in 1975 when the Allahabad High Court found her guilty of malpractice in the 1971 election. This judgement would have made her ineligible for holding any elective office for six years, a penalty she avoided by declaring a state of 'emergency' and ruling as a virtual dictator for two years. Her sudden decision to end the Emergency in 1977 and hold elections was a gamble that failed, as she was defeated and 30 years of Congress rule came (temporarily) to an end.

She lost her Lok Sabha seat in 1977 but was returned in a by-election a year later and in 1980 her Congress (I) ('I' for Indira) won two-thirds of the seats and she returned as Prime Minister. Sanjay was elected for the first time and was clearly his mother's closest confidant and heir-apparent, but was killed when his private plane crashed in 1980. Rajiv GANDHI, his elder brother, was elected to Sanjay's vacant seat in 1981. Indira Gandhi's second term of office was dominated by regional and religious separatism. In Assam and Tripura there were attacks on Bengalis in which up to 3,000 were killed. The most serious disturbances, however, took place in the Punjab, where militant Sikhs wanting a separate Sikh state, Khalistan, murdered hundreds of Hindus. The followers of Bhindranwale made the Sikhs' holiest shrine, the Golden Temple at Amritsar, into a terrorist stronghold. On Indira Gandhi's orders the Indian army stormed it in 1984, killing Bhindranwale and 450 of his supporters. In revenge, Indira Gandhi was assassinated in October 1994 by Sikh members of her bodyguard. She left a legacy of centralized and personal power, with a weakened judiciary, parliament and Congress Party.

Indira Gandhi, I. Malhotra (1989)
Dominance and State Power in Modern India, 2 vols, F. Frankel and N. S. Arao (1990)
India: A Million Mutinies Now, V. S. Naipaul (1990)

Gandhi, Rajiv (1944–91)   Prime Minister of India (1984–9). The eldest son of Indira GANDHI and grandson of Jawaharlal NEHRU, he failed to complete an engineering course at Cambridge University before becoming an Indian Airlines pilot in 1968. Unlike his younger brother Sanjay he showed little interest in politics and did not take part in political life until Sanjay was killed in an air crash in 1980. He was then persuaded to contest and win his brother's vacant seat in parliament in 1981, becoming President of Congress (I) in 1983. When his mother was assassinated in 1984 he followed family tradition by becoming Prime Minister and, taking advantage of the outrage at his mother's death, won a convincing victory for Congress in the elections of December 1984.

Conciliatory and progressive, he brought in young technocrats to increase the efficiency of the government. The budget of 1985 was drawn up by the Finance Minister V. P. Singh and began the economic liberalization which continued after him and marked a rejection of Nehru's economic planning. He reversed too his mother's centralization and consulted the leaders of various regional movements, in order to combat the religious, regional and ethnic conflicts which bedevilled his period of office, as they had that of Indira Gandhi's second term. His success was patchy, as concessions to one group angered others and led him to impose presidential rule in Punjab in 1987, where thousands died in the struggle between government and terrorists. Also in 1987 he sent Indian troops to Sri Lanka to help bring hostilities to an end between the TAMIL TIGERS in the Jaffna peninsula and the Sri Lankan government. They soon became involved in trying to disarm the Tamil Tigers and, when they resisted, launched a major attack against their guerrilla strongholds. The number of Indian troops in Sri Lanka rose to nearly 100,000 and in 1989, when Rajiv Gandhi called an election, there were still 45,000.

His government was beset by allegations of massive corruption in the Bofors affair, when the Swedish arms manufacturing firm was accused of paying large bribes in order to obtain munitions sales in India, and in the parliamentary elections of 1989 Congress was defeated. Rajiv Gandhi was replaced as Prime Minister by V. P. Singh, who had resigned from the government in 1987, but factional rivalry within his coalition led to its collapse and new elections took place in 1991. In the first days of polling Rajiv Gandhi was assassinated while campaigning in Tamil Nadu by members of the Tamil Tigers who had suffered from India's intervention in Sri Lanka.

Nehru to the 1990s, J. Manor (ed.) (1994)
Contemporary Indian Politics, M. Limaye (1990)
Power, Protest, Participation: Local Elites and the Politics of Federalism, S. Mitra (1993)

Gang of Four   Leaders of the radicals during the CULTURAL REVOLUTION (1966–76) in China. MAO ZEDONG gave this name in 1974 to his wife JIANG QING and her allies Wang Hongwen, Zhang Chunqiao and Yao Wenyuan. Zhang and Yao had worked for years in Chinese Communist Party organizations in Shanghai, Zhang taking control of Shanghai in January 1967 on behalf of the Cultural Revolution Group. Wang had risen to be the workers' leader there. After the most turbulent phase of the Cultural Revolution the Gang took part in a fierce power struggle from 1971–6 between the pragmatists, such as ZHOU ENLAI and DENG XIAOPING, the radicals and HUA GUOFENG, a Mao protégé. All members of the Gang were elected to the Politburo in 1973. They wanted to maintain the ideals of the Cultural Revolution and bitterly criticized the emphasis of Zhou and Deng on economic development at the expense of ideology and on the importation of Western technology. After the death of Zhou early in 1976 they had a minor victory when they prevented Deng becoming Prime Minister (a post taken by Hua Guofeng) but were furious when Hua became Chairman of the People's Republic on Mao's death. Refusing to accept his promotion they planned a military coup and were arrested. At their trial in 1980–1 Wang and Yao admitted their guilt and were sentenced to life imprisonment and 18 years respectively. Zhang, who refused to answer any questions, and Jiang Qing, truculent to the end, were sentenced to death but the sentences were commuted to life imprisonment.

Gastarbeiter (guest workers)   Foreigners who came to work in the Federal Republic of Germany (FRG) during the WIRTSCHAFTSWUNDER. When industry boomed in the FRG during the 1950s the acute labour shortage was met by immigrants from the poorer Mediterranean countries (Italy, Yugoslavia, Greece) and by Germans who fled from the communist GDR (German

Democratic Republic: East Germany). This source was cut off by the building of the BERLIN WALL in 1961, so the FRG turned to Turkish workers, who grew from 13,000 in 1962 to 800,000 in 1974. Most were single, stayed in hostels and sent money back home and were employed in low-paid, unskilled jobs which German workers did not want. They were entitled to the same pay and welfare as Germans. The recruitment of *Gastarbeiter* outside the EEC stopped after the OPEC PRICE RISE of 1973, but the number of Turkish immigrants continued to rise, as wives and children joined their husbands. Few acquired, or applied for, German citizenship, as the FRG was opposed to dual nationality and applicants had to fulfil stringent conditions, including a stiff language test. When there was a recession in 1973 the *Gastarbeiter* (10 per cent of the work force) were no longer welcome, as they were accused of depriving Germans of jobs.

Asylanten (asylum-seekers) became an issue in the 1970s when Vietnamese BOAT PEOPLE arrived in West Germany to take advantage of Germany's liberal asylum laws. In the mid-1980s thousands fleeing from the civil war in Sri Lanka (see TAMIL TIGERS) sought residence in the FRG, but the greatest influx of all came after the fall of the Berlin Wall and the REVOLUTIONS OF 1989–91, when Poles, Iranians, Russians and Yugoslavs all flooded in. The number of foreigners living in Germany doubled to 7.2 million (9 per cent of the population) in the decade to 1997. Hostility to *Gastarbeiter* and *Asylanten* became violent from 1990.

GATT (General Agreement on Tariffs and Trade)   Based in Geneva it was an agency of the UNITED NATIONS, which aimed to boost world trade by reducing commercial barriers and so avoid the protectionism of the 1930s. Originally it was seen as a temporary treaty and was signed in 1947 by 23 countries. Although it was supposed to oversee the rules for world trade it could not impose punitive sanctions like the IMF and WORLD BANK on members who broke its rules. It was limited to one trade issue (tariffs on industrial products) and so had little relevance to the THIRD WORLD. It was a rich man's club run by and for the world's largest trading nations (the US, the EEC and Japan) and was based on non-discrimination: any concession granted by one member to another is automatically extended to all the rest. The Kennedy round (1962–7) of trade negotiations led to a decline in tariff barriers and a remarkable increase in world trade and prosperity, as the US, Europe and Japan were absorbed into the emerging GLOBAL ECONOMY. The US was the driving force behind all negotiations.

The OPEC PRICE RISE of 1973 produced a worldwide recession, inflation, unemployment and balance of payments deficits. The US and Europe were also affected by the rise in international competitiveness from Japan and the Asian NEWLY INDUSTRIALIZING ECONOMIES (NIEs) and the loss of so much traditional manufacturing to these countries. GATT was almost abandoned by its founders as the West resorted to protectionism in response to these pressures. Voluntary export restraints became common in many industries – steel, cars, textiles, machine tools and electronic products – and covered half of world trade. Most of these restrictions, which violated the spirit of GATT, were imposed by the US and EEC and were directed at Japan and the NIEs. Agriculture had been deliberately left outside GATT, as most industrial countries heavily subsidized their farmers (by $180 billion in 1990). The EEC's COMMON AGRICULTURAL POLICY (CAP), with its import levies and subsidies, reduced foreign competition and produced surpluses which were dumped on the world market through export subsidies. The US raised its export subsidies for farmers sharply in the 1980s in response to CAP.

GATT has been remarkably successful in removing tariffs on industrial goods almost completely: the average tariff in industrial countries was over 40 per cent in 1947, 5 per cent in 1990. It therefore addressed other issues, particularly in the Uruguay round (1986–94) of talks. Developing countries resented the restrictions placed on their clothing exports to industrial countries, which for 30 years were limited by the Multi-Fibre Agreement, which imposed quotas. Services were the most important new issue: banking, insurance, telecommunications, which were the fastest-growing areas of world trade. During the Uruguay round ex-communist countries sought to join GATT as did developing countries, which wanted freer agricultural trade in order to reduce the NORTH – SOUTH DIVIDE. Eventually agreement was reached in 1994, the most significant in GATT's history. Tariffs on industrial goods were reduced further, GATT rules were extended to agriculture (agricultural tariffs were lowered in the European Union by 36 per cent) and services, and there were stricter safeguards against pirated goods and the infringement of copyright. The World Trade Organization replaced GATT in 1995 as an organization to regulate international trade and adopted the trade deals GATT had made. Its 125 members signed agreements which covered 90 per cent of world trade.

Trade Policy in the 1980s, W. R. Clive (ed.) (1983)
Restructuring the GATT System, J. H. Jackson (1990)
The World Trading System at Risk, J. Bhagwati (1991)

Gaullism   A political movement in France based on the ideas of Charles DE GAULLE. Its followers believed that national unity should override personal and class interests and greatly disliked the political parties of the FOURTH REPUBLIC, which they blamed for putting sectional interests first, thus creating political instability. National unity required a strong head of government, who derived authority directly from the people and not from the squabbling parties in the legislature. Gaullism favoured referenda, in which people were directly consulted over the head of parliament. A united France necessitated a strong economy and a stable society, hence Gaullism supported economic modernization and social justice, which would protect the interests of the poorer sections of society. NATIONALISM was also a driving force of Gaullism. De Gaulle saw France as a world power, which should be independent of the two superpowers and have its own nuclear deterrent. To counterbalance the superpowers de Gaulle turned to the EEC (European Economic Community), which he saw not as a supranational body but as a confederation of independent states led by France.

Gaullism found political expression through Gaullist parties. De Gaulle founded the RPF (Rally of the French People) in 1947. When some Gaullist deputies joined government coalitions de Gaulle was disgusted, withdrew his support and in 1955 announced his retirement from public life. In the 1956 parliament elections the RPF won only 22 seats. The movement revived in 1958, when de Gaulle was recalled to power to deal with the ALGERIAN WAR OF INDEPENDENCE (1954–62), as the UNR (Union for the New Republic), which won 198 seats in the general election. For the next ten years Gaullists held most key ministries. After the MAY 1968 events the party changed its name to UDR (Union for the Defence of the Republic) and won an absolute majority in the National Assembly in the elections of that year. It suffered its first defeat in 1974 when GISCARD D´ESTAING became the first non-Gaullist President, though this was partly brought about by the UDR leader, Jacques CHIRAC, who became Prime Minister. He soon clashed with Giscard, resigned in 1976 and called for a reform of the party which took the name RPR (Rally for the Republic) and was soon one of the best organized parties in Europe. After the socialist victory in 1981, when François MITTERRAND became President, it embraced free enterprise more firmly and while maintaining support for the nuclear deterrent and France's role as a world power, rejected de Gaulle's attitude to the EEC and supported European integration. Chirac took the Gaullists and their allies to a crushing defeat of the socialists in the 1993 election and in 1995 became President.

The CONSTITUTION OF THE FIFTH REPUBLIC, drawn up by de Gaulle, is no longer the subject of controversy. The President's powers have been reinforced by all de Gaulle's successors, including Mitterrand, who showed that a socialist President could cohabit with a conservative Assembly. Gaullist foreign policy – the nuclear deterrent, an independent world role for France and the Franco-German Alliance – has shaped French foreign policy since the war. Gaullism has therefore moulded postwar France.

Contemporary French Political Parties, D. Bell (ed.) (1982)
French Political Parties in Transition, A. Cole (1990)
Parties and Voters in France, J. Frears (1991)

Geneva Accords (July 1954)   The agreement which ended the INDOCHINA WAR OF INDEPENDENCE (1946–54). The conference met at Geneva, chaired by the Soviet Union and Britain, with representatives from France, the US, China, the VIET MINH, South Vietnam, Laos, Cambodia, India, Canada and Australia attending. Talks on Indochina began on 8 May, the day after the French defeat at DIEN BIEN PHU. In June MENDÈS-FRANCE, the new Prime Minister of France, pledged to arrange a cease-fire within a month and worked out a settlement with Molotov and ZHOU ENLAI.

The Geneva Accords ended the war. Vietnam was to be temporarily partitioned on the 17th Parallel: the Viet Minh would administer the North, Ngo Dinh DIEM, an American-educated Catholic, the South. French troops would withdraw from the North, the Viet Minh from the South. Neither side would allow foreign bases on its territory or receive foreign military assistance. The country was to be reunited in two years after general elections. The independence of Laos and Cambodia was also recognized. HO CHI MINH, the Viet Minh leader, had to give up 20 per cent of the territory he had seized but was prepared to accept the Accords because he knew that he was likely to win in an election. Diem and the US knew this too and so did not sign the Accords. The US soon showed that it would prevent the unification of Vietnam, when in September John Foster DULLES organized SEATO, which committed the US to defend South Vietnam against the communist North and Laos and Cambodia against communist aggression. By the end of 1954 the US had replaced France as the main Western power in the region and sent military advisers to train the South Vietnam army. When Diem, supported by the US, refused to hold elections in the South, Ho resumed guerrilla warfare in what became the VIETNAM WAR (1960–75).

The Geneva Conference of 1954 on Indochina, J. Cable (1986)

Genscher, Hans-Dietrich (1927–)   Foreign Minister (1974–92) of the Federal Republic of Germany (FRG: West Germany). From East Germany, he studied law and economics at Halle and Leipzig and became a barrister before fleeing to the FRG in 1952. There he joined the FDP (Free Democratic Party), was elected to the Bundestag in 1965 and masterminded in 1969 the move of the FDP from a coalition with the CDU (Christian Democratic Party) to one with the SPD (Social Democratic Party), led by Willy BRANDT. This ended 20 years of CDU dominance and brought the socialists to power. Genscher was appointed Minister of the Interior (1969–74) and when Helmut SCHMIDT became Chancellor in 1974 he was his Foreign Minister. He remained in this post until 1992, becoming the longest-serving European foreign minister in the twentieth century. During this time he became Chairman of the FDP and changed sides in 1982 to oust Schmidt as Chancellor and bring in Helmut KOHL of the CDU.

Genscher was a firm supporter of DÉTENTE and of OSTPOLITIK and believed in negotiation rather than confrontation with the communist bloc. He approved of the deployment of Pershing and cruise missiles in the FRG as a response to the installation of SS-20s in the GDR (German Democratic Republic: East Germany) but supported the double zero option (the removal of ICBMs from the FRG and GDR) proposed by GORBACHEV in 1986 and overcame Kohl's resistance to it. West German public opinion, which wanted nuclear weapons removed from Germany, was behind Genscher in this and shared his view that the Soviet Union was not a threat to peace. Genscher rejected neutralism and was firmly tied to the US alliance but believed that Gorbachev should be supported, as he wanted peace and arms control, so that he could modernize the Soviet economy. It was in the West's interest to help him, as he would bring the Soviet system closer to that of the Western democracies. Genscher wanted to build on the HELSINKI FINAL ACT (1975) to bring about change in Eastern Europe and thought that the INFORMATION REVOLUTION was tying different societies together. 'The information society', he said in 1988, 'calls for more openness, necessitates global co-operation and exchange, fosters even more interdependence'. Genscher was in favour of interdependence, which he believed would further peace and prevent war, and saw European integration as part of this process. He had proposed greater political, as well as financial and economic, integration in 1981, with greater powers for the European Parliament and increased reliance on majority voting. With Kohl, he played a decisive role in bringing about GERMAN REUNIFICATION, though he was anxious to persuade Germany's allies that this would advance and not obstruct European unity. His desire for co-operation enabled him to keep on good terms with Iran during the IRAN–IRAQ WAR and with both Arabs and Israelis. He would not get directly involved in the GULF WAR but made cash payments to the US. Genscher's was the lone voice in the cabinet which opposed the recognition of Slovenia and Croatia in 1991.

West Germany's Foreign Policy in the Era of Brandt and Schmidt, 1969–82, M. Wolff-sohn (1986)
Germany, America, Europe: Forty Years of German Foreign Policy, W. F. Hanrieder (1989)

German reunification (1990) The uniting of the German Democratic Republic (East German: GDR) with the Federal Republic of Germany (West Germany: FRG). Communist power in the GDR had collapsed with the EAST GERMAN REVOLUTION of 1989 and the opening of the BERLIN WALL. There was an urgent need for new elections as the authority of the government disintegrated. Half a million people had fled to the West by March 1990, which depressed the East German economy and placed a great strain on the housing and welfare systems of the FRG. The first free elections in the GDR were held in March and showed a clear desire for unification. Parties with Western links, the Christian Democratic Union (CDU) and the Socialist Party (SPD), dominated the election, the CDU with its partners in the Alliance for Germany gaining 48 per cent of the vote, the SPD doing badly with 22 per cent, as it wanted a confederation rather than unity. The Party of Democratic Socialism (PDS – former communists) had 16 per cent of the vote. To stop the flow of East Germans to the West KOHL proposed on 20 March an economic union of the two Germanies by 1 July. This was accepted by the GDR, so the East German economy was absorbed by that of the FRG, with the Western Deutschmark as the currency of both countries. To persuade the East Germans to accept the merger Kohl overruled the Bundesbank in agreeing to an overgenerous exchange rate of one East Ger-

man to one West German mark for the first 2,000 marks and 1:2 thereafter. Agreement was reached that the five East German states, into which the GDR was now divided, should be absorbed into the FRG on 3 October, a decision ratified by large majorities in both parliaments.

The USSR was the only remaining obstacle. GORBACHEV had 400,000 troops in the GDR and could prevent union if he chose. When he met Kohl in the Caucasus in July 1990 he agreed to unification, in return for DM 5 billion paid by the FRG to the Soviet Union. 'Two Plus Four' talks between the two Germanies and the postwar occupying powers of the US, USSR, Britain and France ended when they signed a treaty on 12 September. This said that a united Germany would have full sovereignty over its internal and external affairs and could join the alliance of its choice, which in practice meant NATO. The FRG would not permit foreign troops in the former GDR, renounced chemical, biological and nuclear weapons and would reduce its army to 370,000 troops. The USSR agreed to withdraw its troops from East Germany by the end of 1994. The Soviet Union was to receive a further DM 12 billion in credits and a further DM3 billion to cover the cost of Soviet troops in the GDR and their withdrawal. The way was now clear for the reunification of Germany, which took place on 3 October 1990, the laws of the FRG replacing those of the GDR.

Beyond the Wall: Germany's Road to Unification, E. Pond (1993)
From Bundesrepublik to Deutschland, M. G. Huelshoff et al. (eds) (1993)
Dissolution: The Crisis of Communism and the End of East Germany, C. Maier (1997)

Germany divided The events which led to the division of Germany into the Federal Republic of Germany (West Germany) and the German Democratic Republic (East Germany) in 1949. When Germany surrendered unconditionally in 1945 the Allies divided the country into zones of military occupation: American, Soviet, British and later French. The capital of Berlin was also divided into four sectors for each of the victors. The first question for the Allies to decide was the frontiers of Germany. Hitler's annexations (Austria and the Sudetenland in Czechoslovakia) were given up and at the Potsdam Conference (July–August 1945) it was decided that the area round Konigsberg in East Prussia should be annexed by the Soviet Union and that Germany east of the rivers Oder and Western Neisse should be given to Poland, as compensation for the eastern part of Poland annexed by the Soviet Union following the Nazi–Soviet Pact. The German population there and in the Sudetenland was to be expelled, thus creating nearly ten million refugees who had to be absorbed in Germany.

All the Allies at first wanted to punish and demilitarize Germany, so that it would never again be a threat to its neighbours, and decided that reparations should be taken in kind from each of the zones. The Soviet military administration was the first to introduce far-reaching changes in its zone. In 1945 banks were taken over and there was land reform, with large *Junker* estates (about 30 per cent of the land) redistributed to poor peasants. The assets of the German state were confiscated and private enterprises nationalized. All these measures created an economy in eastern Germany very different from that in the west. The Americans and British decided that they needed to revive the German economy, so that their occupation costs would decline and because the recovery of Western Europe was not possible without a strong German economy. They feared too that an impoverished Germany would find communism attractive.

In December 1946 the American and British zones were merged, creating a West German state in embryo. The harsh winter of 1946–7, when many Germans were near to starvation, made economic revival more necessary than ever, so in 1948 the MAR-SHALL PLAN was extended to the western

zones of Germany. The biggest step yet to the formation of a West German state came with the currency reform of June 1948. The Reichsmark was replaced in the three western zones by the Deutschmark at a conversion rate of 10 : 1. The new currency and the freeing of prices killed the black market and stimulated the economy. When the Western powers introduced the Deutschmark into their sectors of Berlin, the Soviet Union closed land access routes to West Berlin and so began the BERLIN BLOCKADE. This convinced the US and Britain that they should create a West German state. The task of drawing up a constitution was given to a Parliamentary Council representing the *Länder* (regions). Its BASIC LAW was approved by the occupying powers and in May 1949 the Federal Republic of Germany was formed. The Soviet Union, as usual reacting to events in the West, proclaimed its own zone an independent state as the German Democratic Republic in October 1949. The division persisted until GERMAN REUNIFICATION in 1990.

From the Ruins of the Reich: Germany 1945–9, D. Botting (1985)
The Impossible Peace: Britain, the Division of Germany, the Origins of the Cold War, A. Deighton (1990)
From Reich to Republic, H.-P. Schwarz (1995)

Giap Vo Nguyen (1911–)   Vietnamese general. The son of a peasant, he began to work as a youth for Vietnamese independence, read law at Hanoi University and joined the Indochinese Communist Party in 1933. When the party was prohibited in 1939 he escaped to China, but his wife and sister-in-law were arrested by the French: his sister-in-law was guillotined, his wife, sentenced to life imprisonment, died three years later in prison. In 1941 Giap formed a guerrilla movement which, with HO CHI MINH, fought against the Japanese, who had overrun Vietnam. After the Japanese surrender in 1945 they entered Hanoi together. When Ho proclaimed the independence of the Democratic

Republic of Vietnam in September 1945, Giap was made Commander-in-Chief of the VIET MINH army, and executed many non-communist nationalists. During the INDO-CHINA WAR OF INDEPENDENCE (1946–54) he advocated the use of terror to coerce the masses and reduce the morale of his opponents: he regarded psychological victory as essential for success on the battlefield. He admitted in 1956 that 'We have executed too many honest people.... Worse still, torture came to be regarded as a normal practice'. His brilliant planning at the battle of DIEN BIEN PHU ensured the defeat of the French and their withdrawal from Vietnam in the GENEVA ACCORDS (1954). Vietnam was now divided and Giap became Minister of Defence (1954–80) in the North.

During the VIETNAM WAR (1960–75) Giap commanded the Viet Minh and personally took charge of the TET OFFENSIVE (1968). Though this shocked the Americans into looking for a way out of the war, it was a disastrous military defeat, which almost destroyed the VIET CONG and so weakened the Viet Minh that they were unable to mount another major offensive until 1972. Giap then, pursuing the same strategy which had failed in 1968, tried an ambitious three-pronged attack on the north, centre and south of Vietnam. This was another catastrophe, as US air power played havoc with Giap's forces. When the war was over and Vietnam united, Giap gave up his post as Commander-in-Chief in 1976 and was dismissed as Minister of Defence in 1980 and from the Politburo in 1982, possibly for opposing the VIETNAMESE OCCUPATION OF KAMPUCHEA. Giap is the author of *People's War, People's Army* (1961), a manual of guerrilla warfare based on his own experiences.

Victory At Any Cost: The Genius of Viet Nam's General Vo Nguyen Giap, C. B. Currey (1997)

Giscard d'Estaing, Valéry (1926–) President (1974–81) of the Fifth Republic in France. Giscard came from a wealthy Catholic, conservative family: his mother was distantly related to French royalty, his father, a member of the *Action Française* in the 1930s and a Pétainist in the 1940s, was a high official in the civil service. A brilliant student, he graduated from two of the most prestigious *Grandes écoles*, the *École polytechnique* and the *École nationale d'administration*, and married into the wealthy Schneider family. Like his father, he entered the inspectorate of finance. He succeeded his grandfather as deputy for Puy-de-Dôme in 1956 and called himself an Independent Republican, but he voted with the Gaullists and supported DE GAULLE on independence for Algeria. In 1962 de Gaulle made him Minister of Finance at the age of 35, but dismissed him four years later for pursuing policies the President regarded as too deflationary. After de Gaulle's resignation Georges POMPIDOU made him Minister of Finance again (1969–74). He devalued the franc by 12.5 per cent, which was a great boost to French exports, and cut the deficit in the balance of payments. When Pompidou died in office, Giscard decided to stand in the presidential election. Though the Gaullist party adopted Chaban-Delmas as its candidate it soon became clear that Giscard had the best chance of defeating the socialist MITTERRAND, so the Gaullist Jacques CHIRAC threw his weight behind Giscard, who narrowly defeated Mitterrand with 50.8 per cent of the vote.

Articulate, self-confident and highly intelligent, Giscard had a narrow powerbase in the Independent Republicans (in 1978 he formed a new coalition of centrists, the UDF – Union for French Democracy), so he had to make Chirac Prime Minister to keep Gaullist support. Giscard favoured 'an advanced liberal society' and, appearing both relaxed and dynamic, pushed through several reforms in his early years as President. The voting age was reduced from 21 to 18, contraceptives were made available to teenagers without parental consent, divorce by mutual agreement was allowed, as was abortion in the first ten weeks of pregnancy, in spite of considerable opposition from the Catholic Church. Legislation to provide equal pay and equal employment opportunities for women was introduced. The retirement age was to be gradually reduced to 60 and Paris was given the right to elect its own mayor.

Giscard's main preoccupation was with the economy, but here he suffered from events outside his control. President NIXON had thrown the money markets into confusion by suspending the conversion of the dollar into gold in 1971. Two years later the OPEC PRICE RISE created a worldwide recession. In 1976 Chirac, at odds with the President, who had imposed cabinet changes on him, resigned and was replaced as Prime Minister by Raymond Barre. The economy grew by 3 per cent a year, and the balance of payments (in deficit 1973–7) showed a surplus in 1978. These were notable achievements but inflation remained high and unemployment continued to rise from 2.8 per cent to 7.5 per cent of the working population, creating a feeling of insecurity. The second oil shock of 1979–80 (a result of the IRAN–IRAQ WAR) required tough measures – a devaluation of the franc and the cutting of social services which were a great tax burden on employers – which Barre and Giscard were unwilling to implement, as they were so electorally unpopular. He left a 60 billion franc deficit in the balance of payments and inflation of 13 per cent.

There was considerable continuity in Giscard's foreign and defence policies. He cultivated the NON-ALIGNED MOVEMENT and maintained the pro-Arab policies of his predecessors. The embargo on arms to Israel, imposed by de Gaulle after the SIX DAY WAR in 1967, was lifted but Giscard supported a place at the UNITED NATIONS for the PLO and proposed the setting up of a Palestinian state, which would involve Israel giving up the OCCUPIED TERRITORIES. He also gave asylum to the Ayatollah KHOMEINI in 1978 and when the IRAN HOSTAGE CRISIS erupted in 1979 did little to help the US. Giscard further irritated President CARTER

after the SOVIET INVASION OF AFGHANISTAN, as he refused to impose sanctions on the USSR or to boycott the Olympic Games in Moscow in 1980. In Africa he maintained close ties with Francophone leaders, providing financial and military aid in a form of neo-colonialism: 14,000 French troops were kept ready for deployment in Africa and were used to prop up pro-French regimes, as in Chad. French paratroops were also used in Zaire in 1978–9 to crush rebels against MOBUTU. In Europe Giscard formed a close friendship with the German Chancellor Helmut SCHMIDT. They conversed in English without interpreters and met informally before European summits to establish a common position. Together they secured agreement for the EMS (European Monetary System), which limited fluctuations in the value of European currencies, introduced a six-month rotating chairmanship for the Council of Ministers in the EEC and established direct elections for the European Parliament. Yet Giscard was quite prepared to ignore EEC rules if they adversely affected France: in 1975 he illegally stopped the import into France of Italian wine and in 1979 of British lamb. In the 1981 presidential election he was blamed for the economic downturn and lost to Mitterrand, who obtained 51.7 per cent of the vote.

France in the Giscard Presidency, J. R. Frears (1981)
President and Parliament, L. Derfler (1983)
Policy-making in France from de Gaulle to Mitterrand, P. Godt (ed.) (1989)

glasnost (openness)   A concept of Mikhail GORBACHEV which gave greater freedom to Soviet citizens than they had ever enjoyed. He saw it as a precondition of perestroika (restructuring), as people would not be prepared for political and economic change unless they were aware of the true state of affairs in the USSR. Glasnost would also allow alternative policies to be discussed and would involve people more actively in public life. From 1988 there was an information explosion, as new books, journals and films appeared which criticized and often condemned the official version of Soviet history. KHRUSHCHEV's secret speech to the TWENTIETH CONGRESS OF THE CPSU in 1956 was published, as was SOLZHENITSYN's *The Gulag Archipelago* which exposed STALIN's labour camps and showed how they had arisen out of Lenin's drive for total power. George Orwell's *Animal Farm* and *1984* were other books which undermined the ideological foundations of the Soviet system. Archival material on the Nazi–Soviet Pact of 1939 and on Stalin's purges also became available for the first time, the KGB reporting that there had been 3.8 million victims of the Terror between 1930–53, of whom 786,000 had been shot.

Glasnost revealed the Soviet present as well as its past. Newspapers discussed for the first time the deplorable state of the health service, whose share of national income was one of the lowest in the world, and social problems such as drugs, crime, prostitution and alcoholism (there were 4.5 million registered alcoholics in the USSR). Opinion polls were organized from 1987 and censorship abolished in 1990. There were some failures of glasnost (the extent of the CHERNOBYL disaster was concealed) but it did create a much more open society. One unexpected effect was on the nationalities in the USSR, who used their new-found freedom of expression to demand independence, thus beginning a movement which ended with the COLLAPSE OF THE SOVIET UNION.

Glasnost in Action, A. Nove (1989)

global economy   The bringing together of different parts of the world into one economic system, in which the separate areas are interdependent. Towards the end of the Second World War the great powers were planning for the future and were determined that there should not be another Great Depression like that in the 1930s, when the international trading and financial system broke down. The US was the dominant voice and at Bretton Woods (1944) set up the IMF (International Monetary Fund) and WORLD BANK, both under US control, to promote international investment and exchange rate stability and to deal with balance of payments problems. GATT (General Agreement on Tariffs and Trade), established in 1947, reduced tariffs and began an era of free trade.

The US was economically supreme: in 1959 it produced 60 per cent of the world's industrial output (and 50 per cent as late as 1970). Its attitude was therefore vital for the creation of a global economy, which was given a great boost by the COLD WAR. The US decided that the free world must be made safe from communism and so contributed to the recovery of Western Europe through the MARSHALL PLAN. America's war-time enemies benefited, as Germany received aid to begin the WIRTSCHAFTSWUNDER. After the KOREAN WAR (1950–3) began the US needed Japan as a bulwark against communism in the Far East and so helped it to revive economically and produce the JAPANESE ECONOMIC MIRACLE. The Soviet bloc, whose member states traded with each other through COMECON, was largely outside the global economy, which grew enormously: world trade in manufactured goods increased ten-fold between 1953 and 1973, though much of this was in old industries (steel, textiles).

From the 1970s there was a major change as scientific research generated the INFORMATION REVOLUTION, the TECHNOLOGICAL REVOLUTION and new biotechnological industries arose. MULTINATIONAL CORPORATIONS, taking advantage of the international division of labour, spread their tentacles worldwide, so products could no longer be ascribed to one nation. A jet could be designed in the US and Japan and assembled in Seattle, with tail cones from Canada, other sections from China and Italy and engines from Britain. The FINANCIAL REVOLUTION followed from deregulation of the markets: international bank lending, which was $3,246 billion by 1980, was $7.5 trillion by 1991, a 20-fold increase, though it contributed to the mounting INTERNATIONAL DEBT of countries such as Mexico, which was a threat to the stability of the system. National governments lost control of their exchange rates which were decided by the international money markets. The global economy made NATIONALISM an economically redundant doctrine.

Industrial production began to move out of Europe and North America in the 1970s, as the NEWLY INDUSTRIALIZING ECONOMIES (NIEs) of the Pacific rim (Korea, Taiwan, Singapore, Hong Kong) began exporting on a large scale to the developed countries and in the process changed the nature of their own economies. South Korea in 1960 derived 75 per cent of its national income from agriculture. It began its first Five Year Development Plan in 1962 and by 1990 was the eighth largest industrial country in the non-communist world, with only 10 per cent of its GNP from agriculture.

The global economy has grown more since 1945 than in the whole of world history up to that time, yet its volatility was demonstrated in 1997 when speculation against the currencies of some NIEs (Thailand, Indonesia, Malaysia) produced a series of devaluations, stock market crashes, bank collapses and IMF rescue packages, which formed the most serious shock to the global economy since the OPEC PRICE RISE of 1973.

Prosperity and Upheaval: The World Economy, 1945–80, H. van der Wee (1986)
The World Economy: Patterns of Growth and Change, B. J. McCormick (1988)
The Asian Pacific Rim and Globalization, R. Le Heron and S. O. Park (1995)

Golan Heights A mountainous area on the Israeli–Syrian border of great strategic importance, as it overlooks northern Israel and southern Syria. It was part of Syria until seized by Israel in the SIX DAY WAR (1967).

Israel built Jewish settlements there and annexed the area in 1981: ten years later about half the population was Jewish. The Middle East PEACE PROCESS will never be complete until Syria recovers Golan. Negotiations to this end and to Syria's acceptance of Israel began in 1994 but came to a halt with a Likud victory in the 1996 Israeli general election and the appointment of Binyamin NETANYAHU as Prime Minister.

Gomulka, Wladyslaw (1905–82) General Secretary of the Polish United Workers' Party (PUWP) (1943–8, 1956–70). He joined the Polish Communist Party (PCP) in 1926 and spent much time in prison before the Second World War for his trade union and political activities. During the war he fought in the resistance and joined the PUWP, the successor to the PCP, becoming its General Secretary in 1943 and retaining this post when the party merged with the Lublin Committee, established by Moscow-based Polish communists. He opposed the collectivization of agriculture and persecution of the Catholic Church and did not want the Soviet Union to dictate what happened in Poland, so, after STALIN's break with TITO in 1948, he was accused of 'bourgeois nationalism', 'right-wing deviationism' and Titoism and relieved of all his party posts. Arrested in 1951, he was imprisoned without trial until 1955 and was fortunate not to be executed like other leading communists in the SHOW TRIALS which took place in Eastern Europe.

In 1956 there were serious riots at Poznan, when work norms were increased by 25 per cent without extra pay. The army restored order but killed 53 workers and wounded over 300. Fearing a general rising, party leaders readmitted Gomulka to the party and elected him First Secretary. Immediately he began to relax the stranglehold the Soviet Union had on Poland: he removed the Soviet Marshal Rokossowski as Defence Minister and Soviet officers from their posts in the Polish army. There was a danger of Soviet intervention but Gomulka made it clear Poland would fight if attacked and, as the leading role of the Communist Party in Poland was not threatened, KHRUSHCHEV took no action. Gomulka dismissed Stalinists from leading posts in the government, ended the secret police terror and came to an accommodation with the Roman Catholic Church, which enjoyed greater freedom than anywhere else in Eastern Europe. Yet he was basically authoritarian and anti-Semitic and dismissed most Jews who held leading posts. Then, from 1957, he stopped further reform. There was no collectivization of agriculture, so that Polish farming remained small-scale and inefficient. The economy declined, as did Gomulka's popularity, and when food prices increased by 30 per cent in 1970 there were demonstrations in Gdansk shipyard which spread to other Baltic cities and Warsaw. Gomulka bullied the Politburo into using force: 75 workers were killed and over 1,000 wounded by troops. Party leaders, fearing a revolution, therefore forced Gomulka, bitter and humiliated, to retire.

Gomulka, his Poland and his Communism, N. Bethel (1969)

González, Felipe (1942–)

Spanish Prime Minister (1982–96). Born in the Andalusian city of Seville to a livestock handler, he studied law at university before opening a legal practice dedicated to labour affaris. He entered the PSOE *Partido Socialista Obrero Español* – Spanish Socialist Workers' Party), an illegal organization under the Franco dictatorship, in 1962. In collaboration with his close friend Alfonso Guerra, he rapidly assumed a dominant position within the party inside Spain. At the PSOE Congress of 1974 in Suresnes (France), González successfully led the internal party's revolt against the exiled leadership, becoming leader of the PSOE at the age of 32.

At the time of Franco's death in 1975, the Spanish socialists were not only split into numerous parties but were also bereft of sup-

port, having been completely overshadowed in the opposition to the Franco regime by the PCE (Spanish Communist Party). González, with the indispensable aid of Alfonso Guerra, set about revitalizing the PSOE by winning the crucial backing of the Socialist International (thereby seeing off the other socialist parties) and by greatly moderating the party's image through a major organizational and ideological overhaul. González's enormous popularity was reflected in the fact that he was the only national politician popularly referred to by his first name, Felipe.

Along with the party's social democratic programme, the appeal of González was central to the PSOE establishing itself as the second largest national party in the June 1977 general election. However, the failure of the party to improve on this performance in the March 1979 election led González to call for the rejection of the PSOE's Marxism, which the party renounced in September 1979. The PSOE won the 1982 general election with a handsome overall majority.

Over the next four years, the socialists further consolidated democracy in Spain by negotiating its entry into the European Union, extending the process of regional autonomy, and pacifying the armed forces. It was partly in order to bring the army under greater control that the socialists reversed their position on NATO and successfully backed Spain's continued membership of the military alliance in the 1986 referendum. They also greatly extended the higher educational system, boosted the state pensions scheme, improved the social security system, and passed a limited abortion law, though housing and health reforms left much to be desired, while their long-promised overhaul of the state bureaucracy was a major failure. Following the disastrous results in France of MITTERRAND's state-led economic policy of 1981–2, the PSOE government adopted a largely neoliberal approach that saw the economy boom, especially in finance and property, but at the cost of many jobs and by leaving social and regional inequalities intact.

In the 1986 general election González won a resounding victory. Although the PSOE retained its majority in the 1989 election, his government was now in decline (the party polled two million less votes in 1989 than in 1982), as a result of the internal split between *guerristas* (followers of Alfonso Guerra) and *reformistas* (reformists), the steady deterioration in relations between the party and the unions (manifested in the 1988 general strike), a series of corruption scandals (one of which forced Alfonso Guerra to resign as Vice-President in 1991, though he continued to work closely with González), and revelations concerning the Ministry of the Interior's involvement in a 'dirty war' against the Basque terrorist group, ETA, in the mid-1980s. González became increasingly aloof and disdainful, avoiding parliament and rarely being seen in public. By contrast, his international reputation continued to grow, as a result of his presidency of the European Union (1989 and 1995). After losing his overall majority in the 1993 general election, González continued in power with the support of the Basque and above all the Catalan nationalists, though this arrangement further eroded his domestic standing.

By the time of the 1996 general election, González's reputation abroad remained high but his image at home had been badly tarnished by a wave of corruption scandals that involved numerous high-ranking socialist officials and the funding of his own party and by the emergence of further damaging evidence concerning the shoot-to-kill policy of 1983–7. Yet he only narrowly lost the general election to the Partido Popular under the uninspiring José María Aznar.

Since the early 1980s Felipe González, winner of four consecutive general elections, has been the overwhelmingly dominant figure in Spanish politics and one of the most successful and respected politicians in Europe. He has overseen not only the integration of Spain into the European Union and a greater international role for his country, but also impressive economic growth and massive modernization, as well as the definitive consolidation of Spanish democracy.

The Spanish Socialist Party, R. Gillespie (1990)
The New Spaniards, J. Hooper (1995)

Gorbachev, Mikhail Sergeevich (1931–)

General Secretary of the CPSU (1985–91). The originator of the most extensive reforms in Soviet history. The son of a tractor driver in the Stavropol region of the northern Caucasus, he worked as a mechanic at a machine-tractor station until in 1950, with the help of the local Communist Party (CP), he went to the prestigious Moscow State University to study law. After graduating in 1955 he returned to Stavropol and began a political career, first in the Komsomol (Communist Youth League) and then in the CP and so entered the NOMENKLATURA. He obtained another degree, in agriculture, before becoming First Secretary of the CP in the Stavropol region in 1970. In 1978 he was called to Moscow to take control of agriculture in the USSR and in 1980 became a full member of the Politburo. ANDROPOV furthered his rapid rise but he had to wait until Chernenko died before becoming First Secretary of the CPSU.

Gorbachev had spoken in 1984 of GLASNOST (openness) and perestroika (restructuring) and had impressed Margaret THATCHER with his intelligence, charm and dynamism as 'a man one could do business with'. His wish for radical political and economic reform was apparent by his ending BREZHNEV's 'stablity of cadres' and by wholesale changes in personnel at the top levels of the government and of the CPSU: reformers such as Yakovlev and SHEVARDNADZE were brought into the Politburo. Aware of the declining growth-rate of the Soviet economy, he wanted 'acceleration' by introducing new technologies such as computerization and by decentralizing decision-making. These measures were designed to make the existing system work better, not to replace it, but they met with opposition in the *nomenklatura* as the economic situation continued to deteriorate. Money was printed to cover state deficits, so inflation rose, goods became even scarcer and by 1990, when GNP fell by 2 per cent for the first time since the Second World War, a quarter of the population was living in poverty. Only then did Gorbachev blame state ownership as 'the chief cause of the present crisis', call free enterprise the 'motor' of economic growth and approve of PRIVATIZATION. Even so, he pulled back when a working group, set up by Gorbachev and YELTSIN, proposed shock therapy in a rapid move to a market economy, as the Prime Minister Ryzhkov said it would lead to a fall in living standards, unemployment and political instability. Gorbachev's economic policy was therefore disastrous and was compounded by his insistence that the East European communist bloc should pay for Soviet exports in hard currency, which they did not have. The market was disrupted and COMECON fell apart.

Many party officials obstructed his reforms, so Gorbachev decided that political change was essential if perestroika was to be successful. He wanted to create an executive presidency, so that reforms could be pushed through. The leading role of the party was dropped from the constitution in 1990, making possible multiparty elections, which in several republics produced non-communist majorities. Gorbachev became the new President with extensive powers: he commanded the armed forces, could appoint and dismiss ministers, declare a state of emergency and issue decrees which had 'binding force'. Yet he made the mistake of not being popularly elected to this post (he was elected by the USSR Congress of People's Deputies) and so his legitimacy was undermined. The executive presidency came too late to have much effect: his decrees were ignored.

Gorbachev's foreign policy made an enormous impact in bringing the COLD WAR to an end. He abandoned the idea that the Soviet Union should have a global role, withdrew Soviet troops from Afghanistan, cut aid to Cuba and persuaded his ally Vietnam to pull out of Cambodia. In Africa Soviet clients were left to look after themselves. Much better relations with China ended the SINO-SOVIET DISPUTE and followed the removal of three 'obstacles': the withdrawal of Soviet troops from Afghanistan and of Vietnam from Cambodia and the conceding of Chinese border claims. Relations with Japan remained tense as the USSR refused to hand back the Kurile Islands, seized at the end of the Second World War.

Among the most remarkable changes, which Gorbachev allowed and even encouraged, were the REVOLUTIONS OF 1989–91, which saw an end to communist regimes in Eastern Europe. Gorbachev's intention was to invigorate the communist parties there but he told their leaders as early as 1986 that he would not interfere in their domestic crises and so rejected the BREZHNEV DOCTRINE. He tried to slow down GERMAN REUNIFICATION and prevent a united Germany joining NATO, but to do this he would have had to use force, which would have negated much of what he was trying to do and would have given power to the conservatives, who blamed Gorbachev for losing all that the USSR had gained from the Second World War. Soviet–US relations improved enormously with the INF TREATY of 1987, which removed SS-20s and US Cruise and Pershing missiles from Europe, and the START agreement to reduce strategic nuclear arms. In the GULF WAR Gorbachev supported UNITED NATIONS action. By changing the image of the Soviet Union as an aggressive, confrontational state into a co-operative peace-loving one, he earned the Nobel Peace Prize, became Man of the Year for *Time* magazine in 1987 and for *Der Spiegel* a year later. His popularity in West Germany was known as 'Gorbymania' but this was not mirrored in the USSR, where many saw his foreign policy as being as calamitous as his economic programme. Soviet influence throughout the world had declined precipitously and where it remained it was among the poorest nations, who were a liability. All the world's major industrial and military powers were allied, or friendly, to the US, whereas the USSR had no allies when the WARSAW PACT ceased to exist and was increasingly dependent on the West.

An unintended effect of *glasnost* was the rise of independence movements in the republics of the USSR. These began in the Baltic states of Latvia, Lithuania and Estonia but spread to almost half the Union's 15 republics and were sometimes accompanied by ethnic violence, as in NAGORNO-KARA-BAGH. In an effort to prevent the COLLAPSE OF THE SOVIET UNION Gorbachev agreed to free the republics from much central control. An agreement to do this was due to be signed on 20 August 1991. This was too much for the hard-liners in the CPSU, the KGB and the army, who staged the AUGUST COUP to prevent it happening. The failure of the coup destroyed Gorbachev's credibility (the coup leaders were all people he had appointed to high government posts), made Yeltsin a much more powerful figure and brought about what it had tried to avoid, the disintegration of the USSR. On 25 December 1991 Gorbachev announced his resignation as the President of the Soviet Union and handed over his role as commander of the armed forces to his rival Yeltsin. He remained popular in the West but his deep unpopularity in Russia was evident in the 1996 presidential election, when he gained only 0.5 per cent of the vote.

Gorbachev and After, S. White (1993)
The Gorbachev Factor, A. Brown (1997)
Gorbachev and His Revolution, M. Galeotti (1997)

Gottwald, Klement (1896–1953)   President of Czechoslovakia (1948–53). He was a founder-member of the Czechoslovak Communist Party (CCP) in 1921 and its General Secretary from 1927. After the Munich agreement (1938), when Czechoslovakia was forced to hand over the Sudetenland to Germany, he went to live in the Soviet Union, where he made an agreement with Beneš in 1945 that communists would hold leading posts in the postwar government of Czechoslovakia. He followed STALIN's orders in 1945 and did not attempt to seize power until the CZECH COUP of 1948, which gave the CCP total control of the country.

When Beneš resigned, Gottwald succeeded him as President. He quickly removed all vestiges of opposition. All political parties were emasculated (the Social Democratic Party was forced to merge with the CCP) or disbanded. Religious schools and seminaries were closed and Church property confiscated. In the 1948 election no opposition parties were allowed. Non-communist trade unions and other organizations were dissolved, the universities and civil service purged and forced labour camps opened. A devoted Stalinist, Gottwald used terror to consolidate his position and, after TITO's break with Stalin, staged a series of SHOW TRIALS in 1951 in which leading communists, such as Rudolf Slánský, the Vice-Premier, and Vladimir Clementis, a former Foreign Minister, were found guilty and hanged.

Gottwald also followed the Stalinist model of running the economy. There was rapid industrialization, a Five Year Plan, the collectivization of agriculture and submission to COMECON directives, which meant that Czech foreign trade, mainly with the West before the war, was now primarily with the USSR and the Soviet bloc. Gottwald died from pneumonia, which he caught while attending Stalin's funeral.

A History of Czechoslovakia Since 1945, A. Renner (1989)

Great Leap Forward (1958–60)   A Chinese attempt to overtake the capitalist West by rapid economic development. MAO ZEDONG was dissatisfied with the Soviet model for China's first Five Year Plan (1953–7), as most resources were invested in heavy industry and as it relied on central control and planning, which gave considerable power to experts such as statisticians. As early as 1956 Mao called for an emphasis on light industry and agriculture, the industrialization of the countryside and the decentralization of planning. China had an abundance of human resources and a shortage of capital, so labour-intensive projects should be fostered. Decentralization would encourage local initiative and would reduce the distinction between town and country, industry and agriculture, by developing light industry in rural areas. Ideology was to be more important than expertise: cadres were to be both 'red' and 'expert'. The key unit in carrying out the Great Leap Forward (GLF) was to be the COMMUNE. Mao had the enthusiastic support of LIU SHAOQI and DENG XIAOPING: the main dissenters in the Politburo were the economist Chen Yun and Peng Dehuai. Peng was dismissed as Defence Minister and replaced by LIN BIAO.

There was frenzied activity as giant dams and terracing projects changed the face of China and brought prosperity to previously infertile regions. A million 'backyard' furnaces were set up to provide iron for local industries. However, by the end of 1958 it was clear that there were serious problems. Agriculture was neglected as peasants were used on building projects and the 'backyard' furnaces produced iron of such poor quality that it could not be used. To make matters worse the SINO-SOVIET DISPUTE erupted in 1960, when KHRUSHCHEV suddenly withdrew all the Soviet experts who were helping with China's industrialization. The GLF formally ended in 1960, as Liu Shaoqi and Deng Xiaoping began to restore central control. It had been a spectacular failure. Agricultural production in 1960 was 75 per cent of what it had been in 1958 and it dropped further in 1961: heavy industry's output fell by 46 per cent in 1961 and a further 22 per cent in 1962. The major result of the GLF was the most devastating famine in twentieth-century China, a man-made famine in which over 20 million people died between 1959–61: some estimates put the figure as high as 43

million. Agricultural production did not return to the level of 1957 until 1965. Mao lost prestige with the failure of the GLF. He stepped down as Chairman of the Republic in April 1959 and was replaced by Lui Shaoqi. Though he retained his other posts, he complained that he was ignored when important decisions were taken and was treated 'like a dead ancestor'. Another result of the GLF was that the consensus which had existed among China's leaders since their days in Yanan (1937–47) came to an end with the dismissal of Peng Dehuai.

The Origins of the Cultural Revolution, vol. 2: The Great Leap Forward 1958–60, R. MacFarquhar (1983)
The Cambridge History of China, vol. 14, part I, R. MacFarquhar and J. K. Fairbank (eds) (1987)
The Origins of the Great Leap Forward, J. L. Domenach (1995)

Great Society   The domestic reforms of US President Lyndon JOHNSON, who said that the Great Society 'rests on abundance and liberty for all. It demands an end to poverty and racial injustice'. The 1960s was an opportune time for reform, as it was a period of unprecedented prosperity, which enabled the federal government to spend more on social reforms without increasing taxes. It was also a time when the CIVIL RIGHTS MOVEMENT had drawn national attention to the deprivation of blacks and when remorse following the assassination of President KENNEDY spurred Congress into action. The 1964 elections produced the most liberal Congress since 1936. Within a year of Kennedy's death Johnson obtained congressional approval for several of his predecessor's reforms which had hitherto been blocked: above all the CIVIL RIGHTS ACT of 1964, the most extensive measure of its kind ever passed. The Voting Rights Act (1965) also helped blacks by preventing white Southerners from using various devices to keep them off the electoral rolls. This, with the 24th

Amendment to the Constitution, which declared poll taxes as a requirement for voting illegal, greatly increased black voting and office-holding in the South.

An 'all-out war on poverty' was a central feature of Great Society legislation. LBJ thought that federal aid could break down the isolation and destitution of the South, the nation's most poverty-stricken area, so he directed as much federal aid as he could to the South and West, thereby helping to make the Sun Belt a part of the main American economy. Yet he did not consider redistributing wealth (which in any case was politically unrealistic). He saw his task as creating greater opportunities for the poor and refused to raise taxes to pay for any programmes.

The Equal Opportunity Act (1964) provided work experience and retraining for the unemployed, gave better educational opportunities for poor children and established a peace corps, Volunteers in Service to America, to work in deprived neighbourhoods. An Equal Opportunities Commission was set up to end job discrimination based on sex, religion or race. It sponsored communal action programmes to increase employment and improve health care, housing and education in poor neighbourhoods. $750 million were spent on these schemes in 1965, $1.6 billion in 1966: those living in poverty, according to government statistics, fell from 22.1 per cent of the population in 1959 to 15.4 per cent in 1966. The Housing Act (1965) provided $8 billion to build houses for the poor and give rent supplements to low-income families. This was extended in 1968 for the building of a further 1.7 million new or rehabilitated houses. In 1965 over half the Americans over 65 had no health insurance. Medicare provided some medical insurance for those over 65 (something President TRUMAN had proposed 20 years earlier) and helped 19 million people in its first year. Medicaid did the same for the blind, disabled and needy poor. Medicare and Medicaid affected 15 per cent of the population by 1976 but they did not provide

comprehensive medical insurance. Most Americans, including the working poor, had to provide their own insurance, which millions (15 per cent of the population) failed to do. In spite of their limitations, these programmes marked a great advance in the next 30 years. The Elementary and Secondary Education Act (1965) made education a major federal responsibility in giving money to local school districts and extended aid to Church schools. Federal expenditure for schools rose to $4.2 billion by 1968, over ten times the amount spent ten years earlier. A Higher Education Act gave federal assistance to colleges and universities and funded undergraduate scholarships.

All these reforms were backed up by rulings in the Supreme Court, where Earl WARREN was Chief Justice, but in the late 1960s the momentum was lost. The VIETNAM WAR reduced the money available for social change, while the BLACK GHETTO RIOTS turned many against reform. Conservative administrations under NIXON and REAGAN dismantled parts of the Great Society (job training and the provision of employment). Other parts remained: the federal government continues to finance health care for the poor and elderly and some aid to education. Many community organizations still provide social services in poor neighbourhoods but the programmes that survive are poorly funded. Yet the Great Society was a considerable achievement and produced the most extensive social reforms since the New Deal.

Politics and the Professors: The Great Society in Perspective, H. J. Aaron (1978)
The Unravelling of America: A History of Liberation in the 1960s, A. J. Matusow (1984)
Lyndon Johnson and American Liberalism, B. Schulman (1995)

Greek civil war (1943–9)   After Germany invaded the Soviet Union in 1941 the communists in Greece formed the National Liberation Front (EAM) to organize resistance and raised the National People's

Liberation Army (ELAS). Soon EAM was the largest of the resistance movements with over 500,000 members, with 60,000 in ELAS. The most important of the other resistance movements was the National Republican Greek League (EDES) in the north-west. The communists' aim was to be the only organized armed force at the liberation, so that they could seize power. They therefore attacked EDES in October 1943 and continued fighting until a truce was made in February 1944. In May CHURCHILL made an agreement with STALIN that the Soviet Union should be dominant in Romania and Britain in Greece. Consequently, perhaps on instructions from Stalin, the communists surprisingly accepted a subordinate position in the Greek government-in-exile, led by Georgios Papandreou, and so lost their best chance of seizing control when the Germans withdrew in October 1944. A month later the British ordered the guerrilla forces to disband. EDES agreed but EAM refused and resigned from the government. Fighting began on 3 December and went on for six weeks between the British and ELAS, who almost succeeded in taking control of Athens. The communists were supplied with arms by Yugoslavia, Bulgaria and Albania.

In February 1947 the British government told the US that it could no longer afford to keep 40,000 British troops in Greece and that they would be withdrawn. The US response was the TRUMAN DOCTRINE, which promised support for free peoples endangered by internal subversion. The US now replaced Britain as Greece's chief benefactor, so the communists stepped up the fighting to seize control of Greece before American aid became decisive. They succeeded in taking most of the north and as late as October 1948 held much of the Peloponnese as well. The Greek government was saved from total collapse by US aid – command of the air was vital – and by TITO ceasing to support ELAS. The Greek communists had supported the Soviet Union when Yugoslavia was expelled from the COMINFORM in 1948, so Tito closed the Yugoslav border to the guerrillas in 1949. ELAS was defeated in pitched battles by the Greek army, trained and equipped by the US, and was forced into Albania. In October 1949 the Greek communists announced that they had stopped fighting. They left behind an economy in ruins and a devastated country.

The Greek Civil War 1944–1949, E. O'Ballance (1966)
The Struggle for Greece, 1941–1949, C. M. Woodhouse (1976)

Greek Colonels (1967–74)   A military dictatorship established in Greece by Colonel Papadopoulos, Colonel Makarezos and Brigadier Pattakos. On 21 April 1967 tanks commanded by Brigadier Pattakos moved into Athens, took over the telephone exchange, radio station and airport and surrounded the parliament and royal palace. The Colonels claimed they were forestalling a communist coup. The king, all the political parties and the high ranks in the army were caught by surprise: there was no resistance to the coup. The junta had no allies among leading politicians, whom they despised, and were loathed as much by the right as by the left. The Colonels had no political programme, apart from a violent hatred of communism and a vague desire to defend the traditional values of 'Helleno-Christian civilization'. This involved banning mini-skirts for women and long hair for men. Thousands of left-wingers were imprisoned. Martial law was proclaimed, parliament suspended, political parties and trade unions banned, censorship imposed and military officers were put in charge of the state bureaucracy.

The main support for the coup came from the army, whose pay was increased. Officers senior to the Colonels were purged, thus making possible rapid promotion for junior officers. The secret police (ESA), who made extensive use of torture, ensured there was little overt opposition. The public was apathetic, even contented, as the economy continued to grow and living standards rose, largely because of steps taken by earlier governments. High borrowing, however, led to inflation of over 30 per cent in 1973. The junta was greatly disliked in Western Europe but the US showed little desire to get rid of it, and gave it active support from 1970, as it was anti-communist and the US needed Greek bases to protect Israel after the SIX DAY WAR (1967).

In December 1967 King Constantine attempted a counter-coup. He flew to the north to rally support but the army was loyal to the dictatorship, so he fled to Rome. It was events in Cyprus which brought about the downfall of the military regime. Turkey, determined to prevent ENOSIS, invaded northern Cyprus on 20 July 1974 and seized 40 per cent of the island. Greece and Turkey mobilized and war appeared likely, but the Greek mobilization was chaotic and military commanders refused to obey orders to attack Turkey. With no support at home or abroad the junta collapsed. Senior army officers called for a return to civilian government and asked KARAMANLIS to oversee this. When brought to trial in 1975 Papadopoulos, Makarezos and Pattakos were condemned to death but this was commuted to life imprisonment.

Greece Under Military Rule, R. Clogg and G. Yannopoulos (1972)
The Rise and Fall of the Greek Colonels, C. M. Woodhouse (1985)

green revolution The introduction of new, high-yield varieties of rice and wheat. The first success was in 1946 at the International Maize and Wheat Center in Mexico, where new high-yielding varieties of wheat were developed which doubled Mexican yields in the 1950s and again in the 1960s. From 1956 they were introduced into other countries, especially Pakistan and India. Their success was so great that the International Rice Research Institute was set up in the Philippines in 1959. Research sponsored by the UNITED NATIONS' Food and Agriculture Organization and other institutions produced high-yielding varieties which have resistance to diseases and pests, yields two to three times higher than those of traditional varieties and which have shorter growing seasons, as they are not sensitive to the length of day. World rice production rose from 257 million tons in 1965 to 468 million tons in 1985, benefiting mainly the well-watered regions of Southeast Asia and China. 'Miracle rice' spread more quickly than any other innovation in the history of agriculture, but it did not eliminate rural poverty as it required the use of fertilizers, pesticides and special irrigation systems which only large landowners could afford. The Green Revolution therefore increased income inequalities as big landowners bought land from peasants (in Central America, Pakistan and India), who became wage labourers. From 1984 rice yields have levelled off.

The biotechnological revolution has not been an unmixed blessing to the THIRD WORLD. Companies can produce laboratory substitutes for tropical foodstuffs such as palm oil and sugar. Isoglucose can replace sugar and barbasco (a plant grown in Mexico which produces steroids) can now be manufactured chemically. The export of coconut oil, on which a quarter of Filipino families depend, is threatened by genetically engineered soyabeans and rapeseed as well as by the realization that it produced cholesterol. The biotechnological revolution can therefore reduce the exports of the underdeveloped world, adding to its unemployment and indebtedness.

New Seeds and Poor People, M. Lipton with R. Longhurst (1989)
The Gene Hunters, C. Huma (1989)
Modern Rice Technology and Income Distribution in Asia, C. R. David and K. Otsuka (eds) (1994)

Greenpeace Founded in 1971 in Canada to oppose US nuclear testing in Alaska, it rapidly became a worldwide organization to preserve endangered species and prevent ENVIRONMENTAL DISASTERS. It uses the media skilfully to draw attention to its activities and to raise substantial funds. It campaigns to protect whales and seals, to prevent the dumping of toxic chemicals and radioactive waste at sea and to end nuclear tests and seeks rulings, often successfully, from national and international regulatory institutions. Although Greenpeace is non-violent its ships have been rammed (in 1992) while trailing a Japanese ship loaded with plutonium, shot at (1992) by Russian coast-guards while looking for nuclear waste dumps in the Arctic Circle and in 1985 the *Rainbow Warrior* was sunk by French secret service agents in Auckland harbour, New Zealand, while it was demonstrating against French nuclear tests in the Pacific.

Greens   A European movement, formed in the late 1970s, of disparate groups who were concerned about the destruction of the environment by industrial effluents and the dangers of a nuclear war arising from the deployment of cruise and Pershing missiles in Western Europe and of SS-20s in Eastern Europe. Most Greens were young, middle class and well educated, many coming from the liberal professions: social workers, doctors, teachers. Greens believed in direct rather than representative democracy and split into Fundamentalists and Realists. Fundamentalists wanted a utopian return to a non-industrial society and opposed forming coalitions with other political parties, as this would corrupt the movement. The Realists accepted that there was no alternative to an industrial economy but wanted it to be controlled, so as to protect the environment. They also believed that the movement would be impotent unless it shared power with other parties.

In the Federal Republic of Germany (FRG: West Germany) the Realists emerged as a political party in 1980 to fight in state and federal elections. In 1983 the Greens won 5.6 per cent of the vote and 27 seats in the Bundestag, the first new party to enter the lower house of parliament since 1953. They repeated their success in 1987 and 1994, though not in 1990. After the end of the COLD WAR, and particularly as a reaction to the ETHNIC CLEANSING in the YUGOSLAV CIVIL WAR, the German Greens changed their foreign policy. They ceased to be anti-American and anti-NATO, regarding NATO as the foundation of a pan-European security system. At the state level they took part in coalition governments with the SPD in Hesse (1981–7), Berlin (1989–90) and Lower Saxony (1990–). In other European countries Greens have been elected to national parliaments only where there is proportional representation: in Austria, Belgium, Finland, Italy, Luxemburg, Sweden and Switzerland. In the European Parliament there are Greens from Belgium, Denmark, the FRG, Italy, the Netherlands and Spain, all of whom joined together in the Rainbow Faction. Although the Greens have under 10 per cent electoral support, poor party organizations and few members, they have made a major impact by persuading governing parties to adopt parts of the Green programme to protect the environment. Largely owing to Green lobbying German industry has been a leader in environmental technology.

The Greens in West Germany, E. Kolinsky (ed.) (1989)
New Politics in Western Europe: The Rise and Success of Green Parties and Alternative Lists, F. Muller-Rommel (ed.) (1989)

Grenada, US intervention in (1983)

Grenada, a small Caribbean island, was granted independence by Britain in 1974. Five years later Maurice Bishop's New Jewel Movement overthrew the government, proclaimed 'a people's revolutionary government' and established a strongly anti-American regime, forming close ties with China and Cuba and fomenting unrest in nearby islands.

On 19 October 1983 a rival Marxist group killed Bishop and some of his ministers and seized power. President REAGAN saw this as a communist threat to the region and so sent in 7,000 American troops, followed by 400 from English-speaking Caribbean states. Resistance ended in five days: 18 US troops, 45 Grenadians and 24 Cubans were killed. The UNITED NATIONS General Assembly 'deeply deplored' the US action, which was seen by many Latin Americans as a resurgence of Teddy Roosevelt's 'big stick' diplomacy. The British Prime Minister, Margaret THATCHER, was outraged that she had not been consulted or even informed by Reagan of the invasion of a COMMONWEALTH country. Most American troops were withdrawn in December, the rest in 1985. Fourteen people were sentenced to death in 1986 for Bishop's murder.

Grenada: Revolution and Invasion, A. Payne, P. Sutton ad T. Thorndike (1984)

Gromyko, Andrei Andreivich (1909–89)

Soviet Foreign Minister (1957–85) and President (1985–8). Born in Belorussia, he was the son of a peasant family which took its name from that of its village, Gromyki. He studied agricultural economics and was a university lecturer (1936–9) before joining the diplomatic service as one of the new entrants replacing those killed in STALIN's Great Purges (1936–8). Soon he came to the attention of the Foreign Minister Molotov and was appointed ambassador to the USA from 1943–6, during which time he led the Soviet delegation in setting up the UNITED NATIONS. He was Soviet representative in the Security Council in 1946, freely exercising the veto, ambassador to Britain 1952–3 and, after Stalin's death, deputy to Molotov in the Foreign Ministry. He succeeded his mentor in 1957 and held the post for nearly 30 years, becoming the USSR's longest serving Foreign Minister. As such he showed great negotiating skills and built up a formidable knowledge of international affairs, meeting

every American President from Roosevelt to REAGAN. Until 1964 KHRUSHCHEV took the lead in foreign affairs but Gromyko became increasingly powerful under BREZHNEV, especially after he was made a full member of the Politburo in 1973. His influence was at its peak in the early 1980s, when there was a succession of sick or dying General Secretaries (Brezhnev, ANDROPOV, Chernenko). Gromyko gave crucial support to enable GORBACHEV to become General Secretary after Chernenko's death in 1985 but he was not in tune with the new thinking and was replaced as Foreign Minister by SHEVARDNADZE in June of that year. He was then made head of the Soviet state, an honorary position which he held until he retired three years later.

Guatemalan civil war (1962–96)

The longest and bloodiest in Latin America. After the US-backed coup which got rid of the democratically elected President ARBENZ GUZMÁN in 1954, Guatemala was ruled by a series of brutal military dictatorships. The democratic reforms of Arbenz Guzman and of his predecessor Arévalo were repealed. Guerrilla warfare began in 1962 by young soldiers inspired by Fidel CASTRO, but the US was determined that there should not be another Cuba in the area, so it organized and financed counter-insurgency. The first of the 'dirty wars' in Latin America began with the death squads of the security forces murdering leading opponents, many of whom simply 'disappeared'. This rebellion was small and, not supported by the peasants, was over by 1968.

In the 1970s more land was expropriated from the peasants, often by army generals. The depression in the GLOBAL ECONOMY in the early 1980s led to unprecedented inflation and unemployment, so that in the late 1980s 87 per cent of the population lived in poverty, many unable to afford even a basic diet. Peasant discontent produced a renewal of rebellion – half a million became involved in the western highlands – and threatened the army's century-old control. This second rising saw different rebel factions unite in 1982 in the Guatemalan National Revolutionary Unity (URNG), with its mixture of LIBERA-TION THEOLOGY, social democracy and Marxism. The army reacted with typical barbarity and used scorched earth methods which completely destroyed 440 villages, killed between 100,000 and 150,000 Indian peasants and displaced over a million. By 1985 the army saw the need to return to formal civilian rule to win Western support and attract aid but it had no intention of giving up power, so civilian Presidents were largely figure-heads. The US, which had turned a blind eye to atrocities in Guatemala in the 1970s and 1980s, felt by 1991 that it could afford to support human rights again, as communism was no longer a threat with the COL-LAPSE OF THE SOVIET UNION. The SANDINISTAS had been defeated in the 1990 Nicaraguan elections, so the US pushed for a negotiated settlement. The Guatemalan government began negotiations with the URNG rebels but the army was in no hurry for a settlement which would undermine its position. Not until 1996 did a civilian President gain control of the army for the first time in 42 years, when President Arzú dismissed 13 of the army's 23 generals and took steps to end Central America's longest civil war.

Guatemala: False Hope, False Freedom, J. Painter (1989)
The Battle for Guatemala: Rebels, Death Squads and US Power, S. Jones (1991)
Guatemala: Burden of Paradise, D. Green (1992)

Guevara de la Serna, Ernesto 'Che' (1928–67) South American revolutionary. Born into a well-to-do though progressive family in Argentina, Guevara had an erratic education on account of grave asthma. However, as an outstanding student he managed to graduate in 1953 in medicine. He was radicalized by the poverty and suffering which he encountered on his travels through Latin America while still a student. On graduation, Guevara took part in an abortive rising against the regime of General Juan PERÓN.

Further travels took Guevara to Guatemala where, in 1954, he joined in the defence of Jacobo ARBENZ's progressive government against US-backed forces. Arbenz's violent overthrow reinforced Guevara's belief that meaningful change could only be achieved by revolutionary means. He then fled to Mexico where, in 1955, he met the Cuban revolutionary Fidel CASTRO. Nicknamed 'Che' by the Cubans after the colloquial Argentine form of address (equivalent to 'mate'), he decided to join Castro's expedition of November 1956 against the unpopular regime of Fulgencio BATISTA in Cuba. Assigned to the expedition as doctor, Guevara soon became a guerrilla fighter himself. By the end of the Sierra Maestra campaign of 1956–8, he had proved himself an outstanding leader in guerrilla warfare. His writings based on the Cuban campaign, *Guerrilla Warfare* and *Reminiscences of the Cuban Revolutionary War*, were overnight classics on the subject while defying Marxist–Leninist orthodoxy by emphasizing the revolutionary potential of the peasantry.

Following the overthrow of Batista in January 1959, Guevara participated in the repression of alleged Batista supporters and was involved too in the creation of the G2 secret police service. Thereafter, he was a key figure in the Revolution's economic policy, being director of the agrarian reform agency, president of the National Bank, and finally Minister of Industry. Guevara aimed to accomplish the Revolution's overriding economic goal of liberating Cuba from its dependency on sugar through industrialization and the creation of a more diverse agriculture. This was to be done through rigid central planning, as manifested in the 'Four Year Plan', while workers, embodying the values of the New Man and Woman, would be motivated by 'moral incentives' rather than material gain. Guevara's inflexible centralist approach highlights the contradiction between organization and liberty that characterizes all his thought. A lack of capital, the US embargo, general inefficiency, poor productivity, and the sudden shifts in policy that reflected the guerrilla mentality of the economically inexperienced leaders militated against success. In 1964, Castro, in line with Soviet advice, overturned Guevara's policy and switched back to sugar. Still, Guevara's charm, good looks, and unusual capacity for self-criticism made him a hugely popular leader in Cuba.

Having resigned as minister in Cuba in 1963, Guevara dedicated himself to spreading the practice, and gospel, of revolution abroad. After fighting in the CONGO CRISIS he set about organizing a guerrilla offensive in South America that would create 'two, three, many Vietnams' in order to take on the US and other imperial powers. He eventually settled on Bolivia, arriving in November 1966 with two dozen fighters. Bereft of support from both the local Communist Party and the tightly knit Indian communities of the Andes, Guevara's efforts to incite a popular, rural-based revolution in Bolivia failed completely.

Through CIA assistance Guevara was eventually hunted down in Bolivia on 8 October 1967, and, following his identification by CIA Cuban agents, shot. Guevara was the inspiration for numerous guerrilla movements in Latin America in the 1960s and 1970s, as well as being a cult figure for rebellious youth throughout the world.

Che Guevara: A Revolutionary Life, J. L. Anderson (1997)
Compañero: The Life and Death of Che Guevara, J. Castañeda (1997)

Gulf states   The six monarchies that border the Gulf: Bahrain, Kuwait, Oman, Qatar, Saudi Arabia and the United Arab Emirates. Iran and Iraq also have boundaries on the Gulf.

Gulf War (January–February 1991)
Resulted from the invasion (2 August 1990) and annexation (8 August) of Kuwait by Iraq

and Saddam HUSSEIN's refusal to accept resolutions of the UNITED NATIONS ordering him to withdraw. Iraq had first called for the incorporation of Kuwait in 1935, as it had been part of the Ottoman province of Basra. Saddam Hussein revived this claim as Iraq had ended the IRAN–IRAQ WAR (1980–8) with a debt of $60 billion, $10 billion of which was owed to Kuwait. He accused Kuwait of exceeding its OPEC production quota and so of being responsible for falling oil prices, which caused Iraq to lose substantial oil revenues. Saddam Hussein was misled by the US ambassador to Iraq, April Glaspie, into thinking that the US would not object if he moved on Kuwait. On 15 July 1990 she told him: 'We have no opinion on Arab–Arab conflicts like your border disagreement with Kuwait'.

Saddam Hussein's invasion and occupation of Kuwait surprised other Arab states and caused consternation as his troops advanced to the Saudi Arabian border. If he seized the oil fields there he would control over half the world's known oil reserves. King FAHD urgently asked President BUSH of the US to send troops to defend his kingdom, so on 7 August Bush sent naval and ground forces to the Gulf, for which he obtained the backing of the UN. The UN Security Council demanded Iraq's withdrawal and imposed sanctions on Iraq. Britain and France, the NATO allies of the US, contributed to the multinational force, as did Egypt, Syria, Morocco, Bangladesh and Pakistan, though a price had to be paid. $7 billion of Egypt's debt to the US and $6.7 billion owed to the GULF STATES were written off, and Syria received $2 billion from Saudi Arabia. The ARAB LEAGUE condemned the invasion but only 12 out of 21 members approved of the international force. Three-quarters of the armed forces and an even higher proportion of heavy weapons, aircraft and ships were provided by the US, whose troops were under US and not UN command. 750,000 troops of the international force, 1,200 aircraft, 1,800 tanks and 300 ships, including eight aircraft carriers, were assembled, an enormous number made possible by the ending of the COLD WAR. Iraq was supported by the PLO, Jordan and Libya but had much popular sympathy among Muslims, as Saddam Hussein linked the Gulf crisis with the Palestine question, called for the withdrawal of Israel from the OCCUPIED TERRITORIES and declared a *jihad* against foreign intervention. There were demonstrations in support of Saddam in many parts of the Muslim world: when his Scud missiles landed on Tel Aviv he appeared to be the only Arab leader prepared to strike directly at Israel. On 3 February 1991 300,000 people took to the streets of Rabat demanding that Morocco should withdraw its troops from the coalition. The UN had on 29 November 1990 authorized the use of force if Iraq did not withdraw from Kuwait by 15 January 1991. When Saddam Hussein did not comply Bush decided to go to war rather than wait to see if the blockade of Iraq was effective.

The war began on 16 January with air attacks on military targets and on Iraq's infrastructure (power plants, bridges, factories) during which civilians were killed. The coalition rapidly seized command of the air (120 Iraqi planes took refuge in Iran), deprived the Iraqis of aerial intelligence and destroyed their command centres before beginning the ground attack on 24 February. Iraqi morale had been destroyed by the constant air bombardment and there was little resistance. Iraqi troops surrendered in droves, the rest beating a hasty retreat in which they suffered terrible losses from air attack. According to General Schwarzkopf, the US Commander, 'there was nobody between us and Baghdad' on the afternoon of the 24th but no attempt was made to capture the Iraqi capital. The ground campaign was over in four days. Iraq had to accept all Security Council resolutions, give up all claims to Kuwait, agree to pay heavy reparations for the damage done there (as Iraqi troops retreated they had set on fire most of Kuwait's oil wells, thus creating a monumental ENVIRONMENTAL DISASTER). Iraq also authorized the UN to search for and destroy all its chemical and nuclear weapons facilities. The UN imposed strict conditions before sanctions would be lifted: as Iraq did not observe them, the 18 million population suffered severely from the shortages which resulted.

Between 50,000 and 100,000 Iraqi troops were killed in the war and 10,000 civilians: casualties in the coalition were under 500. The cost of the war was estimated at $150 billion, Saudi Arabia ($54 billion) and Kuwait ($25 billion) paid the most, followed by Japan and Germany ($10–20 billion each): the US, Britain, France and the smaller Gulf States paid the rest. A few days after the war ended there were risings in the Kurdish north of Iraq and the SHII south of the country, but they were quickly put down by the Republican Guard with great loss of life. The Kurds and Shii had been encouraged to rise by the US and its allies (Bush had said that the removal of Saddam Hussein was necessary for a real peace) but were then abandoned, in case Iraq's unity as a state was destroyed. The war and these risings produced a huge displacement of people: half a million fled from Kuwait; Iraq expelled between one and two million Egyptian and foreign workers; Saudi Arabia evicted a million Yemenis because Yemen did not support the coalition; there were two million refugees from the risings, Kurds fleeing to Turkey and Iran, Shii to Iran and Saudi Arabia. Altogether between four and five million people migrated in eight months in one of the largest population movements in the twentieth century. The Gulf War left the US as the undisputed world leader, politically and militarily.

Desert Victory, N. Friedman (1991)
Saddam's War, J. Bullock and H. Morris (1991)
The Gulf Conflict, 1990–1: Diplomacy and War in the New World Order, L. Freedman and E. Karsh (1993)

H

Haile Selassie (1892–1976) Emperor of Ethiopia (1930–6, 1941–74). Baptized Tafari Makonnen, a Coptic Christian, he was related to the Emperor Menelik II and was appointed governor of Harar province shortly before Menelik's death in 1913. As Ras (Prince) Tafari he was Regent and effective ruler of Ethiopia when Zawditu, Menelik's daughter, was Empress (1916–30), making Ethiopia a member of the League of Nations in 1923. When Zawditu died he became Emperor, taking the new name Haile Selassie (Power of the Trinity). In 1935 Italy invaded Ethiopia. The Emperor unsuccessfully appealed to the League of Nations for help and after Ethiopia's defeat lived in exile in England. When Italy entered the Second World War on Hitler's side British-led troops enabled him to recover control of his country in 1941.

The former Italian colony of Eritrea was joined in 1952 to Ethiopia in a federation with internal self-government, but in 1962 Haile Selassie annexed Eritrea and became involved in the ERITREAN WAR OF INDEPENDENCE (1961–91). He played an active role in 1963 in the formation of the OAU (Organization of African Unity), which made its headquarters in Addis Ababa. The dominant northern groups in Ethiopia imposed Christianity and the Amharic language on all others, including the Muslim majority in the south, and this caused discontent, as did the southern system of landholding, in which most peasants were tenants who had to give up to half their crops as rent to absentee landlords. Ethiopia was the largest recipient in Africa of US military and civil aid in the 1950s and 1960s. Some of this was spent on a modern education system but

intellectuals were alienated by their exclusion from political power and gave up hope of meaningful political reform and social change as long as the Emperor was alive. Favouritism, nepotism and corruption prevailed in the royal autocracy, as students turned to Marxism for their ideology. The revolution to overthrow Haile Selassie began in February 1974, with army mutinies, followed by strikes and demonstrations and peasants in the south rose against landlords. These were followed by revelations of famine (200,000 had died), which the government had ignored and then tried to conceal and had rejected offers of foreign help. In September the Dergue, a group of junior officers, NCOs and ordinary soldiers, deposed the Emperor. He died a year later in mysterious circumstances, while under house arrest.

Haile Selassie's Government, C. Clapham (1969)
Ethiopia: Anatomy of a Traditional Polity, J. Markakis (1974)
Ethiopia: Power and Protest, Peasant Revolts in the Twentieth Century, G. Tareka (1991)

Hamas   Arabic 'zeal'; acronym of *Harakat al Muqawama al Islami*, Movement of Islamic Resistance. Islamic organization in the OCCUPIED TERRITORIES. Founded by Sheikh Ahmad Yasin and six other leaders of the MUSLIM BROTHERHOOD soon after the INTIFADA began in December 1987, it aimed to end the Israeli occupation of Gaza, the WEST BANK and East Jerusalem and to form an Islamic state there. Its long-term aim was the creation of an Islamic state in the whole of Palestine (including Israel) which had been British mandated territory. Hamas was a popular movement which founded clinics and mosques and, with HIZ-BULLAH, took the leading part in the Intifada. As it was a decentralized organization, it was little affected by the seizure and imprisonment of Yasin by the Israelis in 1989.

Hamas received grants from Iran and also from the GULF STATES, after they stopped funding the PLO for supporting Saddam HUSSEIN in the GULF WAR. It opposed the PLO's decision to take part in the Middle East PEACE PROCESS which began in 1991 and rejected the Oslo Accords of 1993. When the PLO set up the Palestinian Authority in the Gaza Strip in May 1994, with several Jewish settlements still existing there, Hamas intensified its opposition. It used suicide bombers on Israeli buses and in markets to disrupt the peace process and helped to bring about the fall of the Labour government under Shimon PERES in 1996 by creating more support in Israel for the hard-line Likud Party under Binyamin NETANYAHU. Hamas's popularity was shown when its master bomber was assassinated by the Israelis: 300,000 people, almost half the population of Gaza, turned out at his funeral in January 1996. Opinion polls put the support for Hamas in Gaza at about 40 per cent, a threat to Arafat's authority there.

Hammarskjöld, Dag (1905–61) Secretary-General (1953–61) of the UNITED NATIONS. The son of a former Conservative Prime Minister of Sweden, he read law at Uppsala and Stockholm universities and lectured in political economy before entering the civil service. From 1941–8 he was chairman of the Bank of Sweden, head of the Swedish Foreign Office in 1949 and a cabinet minister from 1951 to 1953, when he became Secretary-General of the UN. An intellectual, who showed considerable ability as an economist, lawyer, diplomat and administrator, he was passionately interested in art and literature.

He took over a UN demoralized by the COLD WAR and frequent use of the veto by the Soviet Union and restored its confidence, at the same time making the role of the Secretary-General more important by his personal diplomacy. Hammarskjöld obtained the release of US prisoners in China in 1955, assembled a UN expeditionary force (UNEF) to cover the Anglo-French withdrawal in the SUEZ CRISIS and persuaded NASSER to accept it. UNEF stayed after the war was over and stopped guerrilla raids and Israeli reprisals in 'preventive diplomacy' which set an example for other peace-keeping exercises. Yet there were limits to UN influence. Hammarskjöld's attempt to mediate during the HUNGARIAN RISING of 1956 failed and the UN played no part in the Berlin crisis of 1958–62.

His most difficult problem was the CONGO CRISIS (1960–5). Lumumba appealed to the UN when Tshombe declared Katanga independent. Hammarskjöld quickly gathered together a force of 10,000 UN troops but would not place it at Lumumba's disposal and laid down the principles for UN peace-keeping which still apply in civil wars. He declared that the UN should not 'in any way intervene or be used to influence the outcome of any internal conflict' and would use force only in self-defence. Lumumba then turned to the Soviet Union for arms and was dismissed by President Kasavubu. Hammarskjöld approved and told the US that 'what he was trying to do was get rid of Lumumba' without 'compromising' the UN. KHRUSHCHEV certainly regarded Hammarskjöld as anti-Soviet. When Lumumba was murdered the Soviet Union condemned Hammarskjöld as an accomplice and demanded his dismissal. The Security Council decided that measures 'including the use of force' should be taken to 'prevent the occurrence of civil war' in the Congo: Tshombe then moved into Northern Rhodesia (Zimbabwe). Hammarskjöld was flying there to meet him when his plane crashed and he was killed. Foul play was suspected. He was awarded the Nobel Peace Prize in 1961 after his death.

From Cold War to Hot Peace: UN Interventions 1947–94, A. Parsons (1995)

Hassan II (1929–)   King of Morocco (1961–). The elder son of Muhammad V, he was exiled with his father (1953–5) when the king demanded independence from France. As unrest increased they were allowed to return and on Morocco's independence in 1956 Muhammad made Hassan Commander-in-Chief of the army. In 1960 he was appointed Prime Minister and Minister of Defence: a year later, on the death of his father, he succeeded to the throne. His regime was the most conservative in North Africa. The large estates held by rich landowners have not been broken up, 75 per cent of the population is illiterate and almost half live in poverty, while the King enjoys fabulous luxury in his ten palaces and his courtiers enrich themselves by unchecked corruption. In 1965, following riots in the major cities, the king dissolved parliament and for the next five years ruled by emergency powers. Senior army officers almost succeeded in a coup attempt in 1971. A year later air force jets tried unsuccessfully to shoot down the royal plane. General Oufkir, the Minister of the Interior, was the leader of this second coup. Hassan had him, and many of the rebels, shot.

Hassan, French-educated, was a strong supporter of the West in his foreign policy and was therefore given considerable military and security assistance by France and the US, who helped him to defeat his domestic opponents. To rouse national support for the monarchy he led the Green March (green being the colour of Islam) of 350,000 Moroccans into the Western Sahara in November 1975 to claim that territory. When Spain handed over two-thirds of it to Morocco in 1976 (Morocco seized the rest in 1979 when Mauritania gave up its share), a war began against POLISARIO for control of the territory. This was prolonged and costly, eating up almost 40 per cent of the budget and doubling the size of the Moroccan army. Morocco's economic problems increased when the price of phosphates (Morocco has two-thirds of the world's supply) fell in the late 1970s. Real wages fell sharply and when, in response to IMF pressure, the prices of necessities were raised, trade unions called a general strike and in June 1981 the poor of Casablanca (one of Africa's largest cities) rose, burning banks and night clubs and taking control of the city. There were many casualties as the security forces took four days to recover control. There was a further wave of riots in 1984. In the 1980s ISLAMIC FUNDAMENTALISTS became a serious threat to the government, as they did in other Arab countries, flourishing in the urban slums, where their followers sought to succour the poor, and finding supporters in the universities and even in the army.

The Political Economy of Morocco, I. W. Zartman (1987)

Haughey, Charles James (1925–)   Taoiseach (Prime Minister) of Ireland (1979–81, 1982, 1987–92). Born in Northern Ireland, Charles Haughey grew up in Dublin, where he studied law and accountancy at University College. He made a fortune in property development, joined Fianna Fail and in 1951 married the daughter of Sean LEMASS. Elected to the Dail (parliament) in 1957, his opportunity for advancement came when his father-in-law became Taoiseach in 1959. Exceptionally industrious, he held various ministerial posts: justice, agriculture and then (under Jack Lynch) finance. In 1970 he was dismissed and indicted by the government of which he had been a member for conspiring to use government funds to smuggle arms into Ireland for use by the outlawed IRA in the North. This seemed the end of his public career but he was acquitted and slowly worked his way back when his party was in opposition. Fianna Fail returned to office in 1977, Haughey becoming Minister for Health and, when Lynch retired, party leader and Taoiseach in 1979.

He faced a declining economy and the need to cut the country's deficit and government spending. In the 1981 election Fianna Fail lost its majority, though it was still the largest party and Garret Fitzgerald of Fine Gael became Taoiseach of a minority government. This did not last long. After another election in February 1982 Haughey was Taoiseach again, though his party did not have an overall majority. His second brief administration was marked by party divisions and scandals: the government was accused of illegal phone-tapping and lost a vote of confidence over proposals to cut back the health service. A second election in 1982 brought Fitzgerald back as Taoiseach. Haughey was a formidable leader of the opposition (1982–7) but his attack on the ANGLO-IRISH AGREEMENT (1985) split his Party, Desmond O'Malley and Mary Harney forming a new party, the Progressive Democrats, which prevented Haughey having a majority when he was Taoiseach again in 1987. By this time Fianna Fail had agreed to honour the Anglo-Irish Agreement, though Haughey's anti-British stance (he saw Britain as an imperial power in the North) made it difficult for him to co-operate in the war against the IRA in Northern Ireland. Yet Margaret THATCHER, the British Prime Minister, according to her memoirs, 'found him easy to get on with . . . Charles Haughey was tough, able and politically astute with few illusions'. With the budget deficit halved and growth of 4 per cent a year, largely owing to membership of the EC, he felt confident of winning a majority and in 1989, against the advice of his senior ministers, called an unnecessary election. The outcome was a disaster: he remained Taoiseach but was forced into a coalition with his old enemies, the Progressive Democrats. Revelations in 1992 of Sean Doherty, a former Minister of Justice, that Haughey had been fully informed of the illegal phone-tapping ten years earlier, made his position untenable. The Progressive Democrats threatened to withdraw from the coalition, forcing him to resign. Accusations of corruption continued to

plague him and in July 1997 he admitted that he had 'mistakenly instructed his legal team' and had earlier accepted $2 million from the former head of Ireland's largest stores chain.

The Haughey File, S. Collins (1992)
Haughey's Thirty Years of Controversy, T. R. Dwyer (1992)

Havel, Václav (1936–) Czech playwright, President of the Czech and Slovak Federative Republic (1989–92) and of the Czech Republic (1993–). Born in Prague of affluent parents (his father was a businessman whose property was confiscated by the communist government in 1948), he was denied a university education because of his bourgeois background and so worked as a stagehand in a Prague theatre, before becoming a playwright. His early plays, critical of the way dictatorships corrupted people, were produced in the 1960s, but after the failure of the PRAGUE SPRING the government banned the publication or performance of his plays in Czechoslovakia. He nevertheless continued to write plays and other books, which were published and received enthusiastically abroad. In 1965 he was awarded the Austrian State Prize for European Literature. Havel's defence of human rights and the part he played in drawing up CHARTER 77 resulted in further foreign awards. He paid a high personal price for his defiance of the communist regime: imprisoned from January to May 1977, under house arrest 1977–9 and sentenced to four and a half years hard labour in 1979. After his release in 1983 he continued 'living in truth' (the title of a book he published in 1987) and was imprisoned again from January–May 1989. Largely responsible for bringing opposition groups together in Civic Forum during the VELVET REVOLUTION, which brought an end to communist rule in Czechoslovakia, he was elected state President by the federal parliament in December 1989, and re-elected after the 1990 elections.

Havel's refusal to compromise with the communist regime gave him a moral authority which no one else in Czechoslovakia possessed. He negotiated the withdrawal of Soviet troops, formed close relations with the US, became a member of the COUNCIL OF EUROPE and made an agreement of association with the EC (European Community). At home he was unable to prevent the grievances of the Slovaks leading to the DIVISION OF CZECHOSLOVAKIA into two separate states, a move he opposed. He resigned in 1992 but was elected President of the new Czech Republic a year later.

Vacláv Havel on Living in Truth, J. Vladislav (ed.) (1986)
Disturbing the Peace, V. Havel (1990)
Resistance and Revolution: Václav Havel's Czechoslovakia, R. McRae (1997)

Hawke, Robert James (1929–)   Prime Minister of Australia (1983–91). The son of a Congregational minister, he was a Rhodes Scholar at Oxford University but gave up an academic career for one in the labour movement. His intelligence and hard work ensured that he became President of the Australian Council of Trade Unions in 1970, a position he held for ten years until he was elected to the federal parliament. He had joined the Labor Party as a student and was its national President from 1973–8. His biography, written before he was chosen as leader of the Labor Party in 1983, showed that he had been a womanizer and heavy drinker, but these revelations did not appear to harm his reputation, as he won the 1983 general election and three subsequent elections to become the most successful Labor Prime Minister in Australian history.

In office he did not pursue socialist policies, though Medicare, financed by a 1 per cent levy on incomes, provided basic health and hospital care for all Australians. He also introduced a scheme in 1992 to improve the education, housing and health care of the Aborigines, the most deprived section of the Australian population. Hawke sought consensus in industrial relations and to persuade all

sides to work together. As the economy dominated political life, Paul KEATING, the Treasurer, was his most influential minister, who persuaded Hawke to abandon many traditional Labor policies. The currency was floated, financial markets deregulated and the economy opened up to foreign competition. Business approved but Labor lost support in its traditional working-class strongholds. The recession (and the drought of 1980–3) ended, inflation and unemployment fell and the economy grew from 1983–6, but as imports were sucked in the balance of payments moved further into deficit. Hawke and Keating responded with high interest rates to curb imports but the foreign debt grew and in 1986 Keating warned that Australia was becoming 'a banana republic'. Deregulation of the financial markets encouraged speculation and in October 1987 there was a world stock-market crash. Many Australian business empires collapsed and state-owned banks in Victoria and South Australia suffered heavy losses. In 1990 Australia moved into recession again and unemployment rose.

Ill-feeling between Keating and Hawke was apparent in 1991, when Keating accused the Prime Minister of ignoring a promise to step down before the next election to let Keating take over. He challenged Hawke for the leadership and lost, so he retired to the back benches. There was political instability for six months before Keating challenged the Prime Minister again in December 1991 and was successful. Hawke, the first Labor Prime Minister to be defeated in a leadership challenge, gave up the premiership and resigned from parliament in 1992.

Oxford History of Australia, vol. 5, 1942–88, G. Bolton (1990)

Haya de la Torre, Victor Raúl (1895–1979) Peruvian politician and founder of the first mass party in Peru, the American Popular Revolutionary Alliance (APRA). His influence extended far beyond Peru, as several

Latin American parties, such as Democratic Action in Venezuela, the National Revolutionary Movement in Bolivia and the National Liberation Party in Costa Rica, were founded on *aprista* principles. They aimed to get rid of the political domination of the large landowners and of economic dependence on foreign countries and to carry out social reforms to benefit the mass of the people.

Haya was President of the Peruvian Student Federation in 1920 and built up a student–worker coalition, but he was deported in 1923 for opposing the dictator Leguía and spent the next eight years in exile. He founded APRA in Mexico in 1924 as a continental anti-imperialist movement. Haya called himself a Marxist but a visit to the Soviet Union convinced him that the Soviet system was unsuitable for Latin America: he wanted an alliance of workers, peasants and the middle class, with the latter taking the leading role. Through APRA it would control the necessary evil of foreign investment. The military were strongly opposed to Haya and APRA, which was often banned, though Haya became less radical after the Second World War and sought a *modus vivendi* with the other parties. When General Odría seized power in a military coup in 1948 Haya had to spend five years in the Colombian embassy and a further three in exile. He returned to Peru in 1957 and won the highest number of votes in the presidential election in 1962, but the military would not allow him to take office and in 1963 Belaúnde became President. Haya then did a remarkable U-turn and joined forces in Congress with his old enemy Odría to block Belaúnde's legislative programme and so helped to bring about Peruvian millitary rule in 1968. As the military were preparing to return to democracy in 1979 Haya presided over the Constituent Assembly, which drafted Peru's present constitution. He died later that year, six years before APRA gained power with his disciple and chosen successor Alan García as President.

The Ideology and Program of the Peruvian Aprista Movement, H. Cantor (1966)

Aprismo: The Ideas and Doctrines of Victor Raúl Haya de la Torre, R. J. Alexander (ed.) (1973)

Heath, Edward (Richard George) (1916–)

British Prime Minister (1970–4). Born in Kent, the son of a carpenter and a lady's maid, he was educated at a local grammar school and Oxford University. Elected as a Conservative MP in 1950, he was soon a junior whip and as Chief Whip (1955–9) helped to keep the CONSERVATIVE PARTY together during the SUEZ CRISIS. He was very close to Harold MACMILLAN, who succeeded Anthony EDEN as Prime Minister in 1957 and was promoted by him to be Minister of Labour (1959–60) and Lord Privy Seal (1960–3), in which capacity he handled the negotiations for British entry to the EEC which DE GAULLE vetoed in 1963. President of the Board of Trade (1963–4) under Sir Alec DOUGLAS-HOME, he encouraged competition by making resale price maintenance (which compelled shops to sell goods at prices fixed by suppliers) illegal. When Douglas-Home resigned Ted Heath was the first Conservative leader to be elected under the new system of voting by Conservative MPs and at 49 was the youngest head of the Conservatives for over a century.

A highly cultured and humane man, with a deep love and knowledge of music, he was a 'one nation' Tory, who took a liberal view of race relations and removed Enoch Powell from the shadow cabinet in 1968 for making a racist speech. The Conservatives unexpectedly won the 1970 election, so Heath became Prime Minister, committed to reducing public expenditure and state intervention in the economy; there was to be no help for 'lame ducks' (inefficient firms). 'We utterly reject the philosophy of compulsory wage control', declared the Conservative manifesto. He was in a strong position with a majority of 70.

Heath carried out a varied programme of reform, raising the school leaving age to 16, decimalizing the currency, beginning the process of metrication and reorganizing local government by removing historic counties such as Rutland and creating new ones (Avon, Humberside, Cleveland). His most lasting reform was to take Britain into the EEC in 1973 as 'Europe's economic invalid' (according to *The Economist*), though this meant accepting the COMMON AGRICUL-TURAL POLICY, which pushed up the price of food in Britain. The TROUBLES in North-ern Ireland caused concern, as internment led to more violence and Bloody Sunday (30 Jan-uary 1972), which completed the alienation of Catholics. In 1972 Heath abolished the Stor-mont Parliament and imposed direct rule from England: a settlement seemed as far away as ever.

The most intractable problem he was to face was that of the British economy, in spite of inheriting a large balance of payments sur-plus. Income tax was reduced and govern-ment expenditure cut: subsidies on council houses were lowered, free school milk ended and the Prices and Incomes Board abolished. Yet as unemployment crept up to a million and high wage settlements pushed up infla-tion, there was a U-turn in 1971. Anthony Barber, the Chancellor of the Exchequer, tried to create a boom by tax cuts and increased government spending. More was spent on housing, education and the National Health Service than under Labour. There was a consumer spending spree as purchase tax was cut, higher purchase controls abolished and the money supply expanded by 25 per cent in 1972 and again in 1973. There was an explosion in house prices, which in some cases doubled in two years. In 1971 Rolls Royce, facing bankruptcy, was nationalized to keep it afloat and Upper Clyde Ship-builders received subsidies to protect 3,000 jobs. To check the escalating wage increases and unofficial strikes Heath passed the Indus-trial Relations Act (1971), which required pre-strike ballots and a 60-day cooling-off period. TRADE UNIONS had to register, their legal immunities were reduced and there was to be no closed shop. The TUC

threatened to expel any union which regis-tered under the new Act, which was rarely invoked and quietly abandoned. In 1972 23 million working days were lost in strikes, the highest number since 1926. Most damaging was the MINERS' STRIKE of 1972. The Heath government simply caved in and allowed the miners to win increases of 17–24 per cent. By the winter of 1972–3 Heath, after long talks with the TUC and CBI, had failed to produce a policy of voluntary restraint, and had reverted to a prices and incomes policy. This coincided with the OPEC PRICE RISE of 1973, which increased Britain's already high inflation and produced a balance of payments deficit of £1.5 billion, the highest ever recorded. The dash for growth ended, the fight against inflation took priority and there were large cuts in expenditure. Once again the miners came to the fore. The NUM (National Union of Mineworkers) imposed an overtime ban in November and in February 1974 called for a strike. Heath put industry on a three-day week in December 1973 and in February 1974 held a general election on 'Who Governs Brit-ain?' This was unprecedented, as it did not follow a defeat in the Commons. Labour ended up with more seats (301) than the Con-servatives (297), though they received fewer votes: for the first time since 1929 no party had an overall majority. Heath tried and failed to do a deal with the Liberals, so the LABOUR PARTY came to power as a minority govern-ment.

This was an election the Conservatives had expected to win. They were defeated once more when Prime Minister Harold WILSON called another election in October, which left Labour with an overall majority of three. Heath had now lost three elections out of four and, a lonely and isolated figure, was defeated by Margaret THATCHER in Febru-ary 1975 in an election for the leader of the Conservative Party. Thereafter he saw much of his legislation rejected (Labour repealed the Industrial Relations Act and statutory controls on income) and his policies were abandoned by Thatcher. Almost alone among leading Conservatives he did not move sharply to the right in the next two decades and was a consistent critic of Thatcherism. He attacked the 'ruinous MONETARISM' of Milton Friedman and the partial destruction of the country's industry, described the abolition of the Greater London Council as 'bile against an authority ... that did not happen to be Conservative', used a golfing metaphor to say that Nigel LAWSON was 'a one-club man and that club is interest rates' and saw the folly of the POLL TAX. Ted Heath remained staunchly pro-EEC, supporting the European Social Chapter and the minimum wage. To Thatcherites he was stubborn, resentful and the worst of losers. He was, remarkably for an ex-Prime Minister, still a backbencher 20 years after he ceased to be Prime Minister.

Political Pressures and Economic Policies: British Government, 1970–4, M. Holmes (1982)
Edward Heath, J. Campbell (1993)
The Heath Government 1970–4, S. Ball and A. Seldon (eds) (1996)

Helsinki Final Act (1975) of the Conference on Security and Cooperation in Europe (CSCE)   It was signed by all American and European states, except Albania, and concluded negotiations concerning peace and security which began formally in 1973. Ever since the Second World War the USSR had wanted an international conference which would recognize the postwar political status quo in Europe, including the sovereignty of East Germany and the western borders of Poland. Chancellor ADENAUER of West Germany had refused to recognize East Germany as an independent state and it was not until Willy BRANDT became Chancellor and sought reconciliation with East Germany in his policy of OSTPOLITIK that such a conference became possible.

The Act recognized East Germany as an independent state and all existing European frontiers: all signatories agreed to refrain from the threat or use of force. This gave the Soviet Union the political security it wanted but in

return, at the insistence of West European states, it had reluctantly to agree to respect 'civil, economic, social, cultural and other rights and freedoms'. These rights – 'freedom of thought, conscience, religion and belief' – were spelt out in some detail and so gave dissidents in the USSR and Eastern Europe a legal basis for insisting that their governments should uphold such rights. Helsinki Watch Committees were formed – the most important was CHARTER 77 in Czechoslovakia – to monitor the human rights record of the communist regimes. After the REVOLUTIONS OF 1989–91 the Act provided standards of behaviour for ex-communist states and helped to transform communist dictatorships into democracies.

The Helsinki Agreement: Dialogue or Delusion?
J. Luxmoore (1986)
Helsinki, Human Rights and European Security, V. Mastny (1986)

Hirohito (1901–89)   Emperor of Japan (1926–89), who took the reign name Showa (Enlightened Peace). The son of Crown Prince Yoshihito (1874–1926), who became the Taisho Emperor (1912–26), Hirohito was the first member of the Japanese imperial family who was allowed to travel abroad. In 1921 he visited the USA and Europe and shortly after his return he became regent, as his father was declared insane. Austere, hardworking and frugal, he ended the long tradition by which the empress's ladies-in-waiting served as the emperor's concubines. Although he was the key figure in the emperor system, his divinity placed him above party politics. He was a silent presence at all cabinet meetings but followed the convention by which it was the emperor's duty to accept his ministers' advice when that was unanimous, so that he could be a focus of national unity. As he played a passive role, it is difficult to assess what his opinions and influence were. There were at least two occasions when he effectively expressed his personal views, as his ministers were not agreed on what action to take. He insisted on the suppression of the February Rising (1936) and he took the decision to surrender in 1945. When the atomic bomb was dropped on Nagasaki an imperial conference was called. Civilian ministers wanted to end the war at any price but three out of four military advisers wished to continue fighting, if the Allies would not guarantee to preserve the imperial throne. The Prime Minister, therefore, asked the emperor to decide what should be done. Hirohito said that 'we must bear the unbearable' and on 15 August 1945 addressed his people for the first time, on radio, to announce Japan's surrender.

Many Chinese and Allied soldiers wanted him tried as a war criminal but General MACARTHUR, the Supreme Commander of the Allied Powers (SCAP) in Japan, refused, as he wanted the emperor to provide stability and legitimize the reforms of SCAP. There has been considerable dispute about Hirohito's role in preparing for, and in the conduct of, the Pacific War (1941–5). Most Japanese believed that he was a gentle, peace-loving emperor manipulated by his military advisers. His own testimony, recorded before the war crimes trials of 1946 and published in 1990–1, shows that the emperor was fully imformed about all aspects of the Sino-Japanese (1937–45) and Pacific Wars. He intervened constantly in making decisions, not only on broad policy but on detailed operations too, and supported the continuation of the war until June 1945. His decision to accept unconditional surrender was based almost entirely on his desire to preserve the throne rather than a concern to save the Japanese people from mass destruction.

In 1946 Hirohito publicly renounced his claim to divinity and in the JAPANESE CONSTITUTION was given a purely symbolic role, sovereignty residing with the people. He visited Europe in 1972, the US in 1975 and appeared occasionally at ceremonial functions but for most of the time he lived in seclusion, devoting much of his time to his favourite hobby of marine biology. Opinion polls showed that 30 per cent of Japanese were indifferent to the emperor in 1961, rising to 47 per cent in 1988, though he retained the loyalty and devotion of most of his people until his death.

Hirohito: Behind the Myth, E. Behr (1990)
Emperor Hirohito and Showa Japan, S. Large (1992)

Hizbullah (the party of God)   Founded in 1978 it became the most prominent of the ISLAMIC FUNDAMENTALIST groups which arose during the LEBANESE CIVIL WAR. It was a coalition of factions rather than an organized party, whose leaders sometimes co-operated with one another but often acted on their own. Mosque based, its followers grew beards and women wore the *hijab* (headscarf), as in Iran, which provided the inspiration for Hizbullah after the IRANIAN REVOLUTION of 1979. The Ayatollah KHOMEINI sent 1,500 Revolutionary Guards shortly after the Israeli invasion of Lebanon in 1982 to provide training for Hizbullah. Iran also provided money for the social services (housing, schools, hospitals) Hizbullah provided for the SHII community. In the mid-1980s Hizbullah consisted of a number of revolutionary groups with different names, all of which wanted an Islamic state, accepted Khomeini as a model and regarded the US, European and pro-Western Arab governments (such as that of Saudi Arabia) as 'enemies of God', which should be destroyed through jihad.

A violent campaign of kidnapping, car bomb and suicide attacks against Israeli and Western targets culminated in the destruction of the French and US headquarters of the multinational peace-keeping force on the outskirts of Beirut in October 1983, when 265 US marines and 56 French soldiers were killed. This had much to do with the withdrawal of the international force from Lebanon and the retreat of Israeli forces to their security zone in the south. Towards the end of the civil war Hizbullah rejected the Taif Accords, which gave more power to Muslims in the Lebanese government, but after Khomeini's death the new Iranian President, Hassemi RAFSAN-JANI, pursued a less militant foreign policy and cut aid to Hizbullah dramatically. Syria too put pressure on Hizbullah to release their hostages, which eventually they did. Israel abducted Sheikh Abd al-Karim Obeid, a Shii Muslim leader, in 1989 and killed Hizbullah's Secretary-General, Sheikh Abbas Moussari, in February 1992, the year in which Hizbullah won eight of the 27 seats reserved for Shii in the Lebanese parliamentary elections. Hizbullah's determination to drive Israel out of its security zone in southern Lebanon remained, with ambushes of Israeli troops and their Lebanese allies there and rocket attacks on Israeli settlements in Galilee.

Hezbollah: Born With a Vengeance, H. Jaber (1997)

Ho Chi Minh (1890–1969)   President of the Democratic Republic of Vietnam (1945–69). Born Nguyen Tat Tanh, the son of a notable Chinese scholar who was a minor official dismissed by the French, he worked as a teacher, then as a sailor, before taking up various menial jobs in London and Paris, where he took the name Nguyen Ai Quoc (Nguyen the Patriot), became involved in revolutionary politics and was a founding member of the French Communist Party in 1920. In 1923 he was called to Moscow and trained as an agent of the Comintern (Communist International). He formed the Indochinese Communist Party in 1930, which wanted to get rid of French rule in Indochina (Vietnam, Laos and Cambodia). From 1933–6 he was in Moscow and from 1936–41 in China, where he took the lead in the anti-French movement, assumed yet another name, Ho Chi Minh (He Who Enlightens), and formed the VIET MINH (League for the Independence of Vietnam) in 1941. Though this was a coalition of disparate groups, the communists under Ho and Vo Nguyen GIAP took control. They waged some guerrilla warfare against the Japanese, who had taken control of Indochina, and by the time of the Japanese surrender controlled large areas of North Vietnam.

In September 1945 Ho proclaimed the independence of the Democratic Republic of Vietnam with himself as President, and began a campaign of terror to eliminate moderate or pro-French opponents. Ho was prepared to negotiate with the French for an independent Indochina within the French Union but the French did not want to give up their empire. When they bombarded the port of Haiphong the INDOCHINA WAR OF INDEPENDENCE (1946–54) began. The French defeat at DIEN BIEN PHU brought an end to the war and left Ho in control of North Vietnam. The GENEVA ACCORDS (1954) divided Vietnam along the 17th Parallel. Ho accepted this as it was intended to be a temporary measure until elections were held for the whole of Vietnam in 1956. He was confident that he would win these elections and so unite Vietnam. Ngo Dinh DIEM in the South and the US also believed this and refused to hold elections, thus seeking a permanent division of Vietnam. Ho rejected this and so the VIETNAM WAR began in 1960. He skilfully maintained good relations with both China and the Soviet Union during the SINO-SOVIET DISPUTE and so received aid from both. In the North Ho followed the model of MAO ZEDONG in ruthlessly eliminating the landlord class, in collectivizing agriculture and in nationalizing industry. He played a less direct part in running the war as he grew older but lived long enough to see the US begin negotiations to end the war after the TET OFFENSIVE. His mild, benevolent manner, charm and humour earned him the affectionate name of 'Uncle Ho'.

Ho Chi Minh, C. Fenn (1973)
Ho, D. Halberstam (1987)

Honecker, Erich (1912–94)   Head of state in the German Democratic Republic (GDR: East Germany) (1976–89). The son of a coalminer in the Saarland, he joined the Communist Party at the age of 17 and became an official of its youth organization two years later. He attended the Comintern School in Moscow and, after Hitler came to power in 1933, went underground. Arrested in 1935 he spent the next ten years in prison, much of it in solitary confinement. Freed by the Red Army he was put in charge of the communist youth wing (1946–55), was sent to the KGB school for security police in the USSR, and on his return rose rapidly up the communist hierarchy, becoming a member of the Politburo and Central Committee in 1958, in charge of internal security. As such, he had the task of building the BERLIN WALL in 1961. He came to be regarded as ULBRICHT's heir and in 1971 replaced him as head of the Socialist Unity (communist) Party of Germany (SED). Succeeding Ulbricht too as Chairman of the National Defence Committee put him in charge of the armed forces. In 1976 he added Chairman of the Council of State to his other offices.

Honecker was seen as a liberal in social and cultural affairs. He built more houses, made consumer goods more available, increased holidays for the workers and benefits for the elderly and handicapped. He proclaimed 'No taboos in the field of art and literature' and allowed the churches more freedom, but no one was allowed to criticize the system openly. His regime was based on repression, on rule by a single party with a monopoly of appointments in the huge public sector and on the Stasi, the secret police, whose numbers increased from 53,000 in 1973 to 85,000 in 1989, with between 100,000 and 200,000 paid informers and from one to two million unpaid. Soviet outnumbered German troops in the GDR. Honecker closely followed the Soviet model of economic development and abandoned Ulbricht's experiments with decentralization. On the contrary, he tried to make the command economy more effective by increased centralization. The remaining private businesses were nationalized, huge conglomerates were set up and in agriculture collective farms grew larger. Farming was

highly mechanized and the GDR became almost self-sufficient in food. Industry too was successful in comparison with that of other East European states: in the 1980s Honecker concentrated on developing high technology industries such as micro-electronics, computers and electrical engineering. He benefited greatly from his close economic links with the Federal Republic of Germany (FRG: West Germany), which insisted that there should be no trade barriers between East and West, so the GDR gained many of the benefits membership of the EEC would have brought. By the end of the 1980s West German subsidies amounted to 15 per cent of the GDR's national income. The OPEC PRICE RISE of 1973 helped the GDR, which obtained its oil cheaply from the USSR in non-dollar trade and sold refined oil products on the world market for dollars. It was the oil price fall in 1986 which hit the GDR badly, as its income from this strategy was much reduced. In the West the GDR under Honecker was regarded as stable and successful; the WORLD BANK at the end of the 1970s announced that it had overtaken Britain in production per head. Yet its apparent prosperity was based on the closed barter system of COMECON and oil supplied by the Soviet Union at well below market prices. In fact the GDR was uncompetitive: in 1989 it produced only 2 per cent of the computer output of Austria and what it did produce was obsolete and poorly made. Its INTERNATIONAL DEBT was then $26.5 billion, servicing which took up 60 per cent of its export earnings.

Honecker profited from Willy BRANDT's OSTPOLITIK, which aimed at closer contacts with the GDR to improve the quality of life there. In 1972 both Germanies recognized one another and entered the UNITED NATIONS together. GORBACHEV's ideas of GLASNOST and perestroika made no impact on Honecker, who continued to crush what little dissent there was and congratulated the Chinese authorities on the TIANANMEN SQUARE MASSACRE in June 1989. The EAST GERMAN REVOLUTION of 1989 sealed his fate. He wanted to use the army to suppress the demonstrations against the regime, as the Chinese had done, but was overruled by the Politburo and resigned as leader of the SED on 17 October and a week later as Chairman of the State Council. Honecker was later charged with manslaughter for ordering his security guards to 'shoot to kill' those trying to escape from the GDR, but the charges were dropped in 1993 because he was suffering from terminal cancer. He was allowed to go to Chile, where he died.

Honecker's Germany, D. Childs (ed.) (1985)
Dissolution: The Crisis of Communism and the End of East Germany, C. Maier (1997)

Hong Kong returned to China (1997)

Hong Kong island was given to Britain 'in perpetuity' in 1842 after the first Opium War. Kowloon, on the mainland, was ceded in 1860 after the second Opium War, the New Territories (92 per cent of Hong Kong) coming under British control on a 99-year lease in 1898. In the early 1980s China indicated that she intended to recover the whole of Hong Kong, so protracted negotiations took place between the British and Chinese governments, which produced the Sino-British Joint Declaration of 1984. Britain agreed to hand over Hong Kong in 1997. China conceded that for 50 years after that Hong Kong would be a 'special administrative region' with a capitalist economy ('one country, two systems'). Beijing would control Hong Kong's foreign and defence policy but other matters would be 'run by the local inhabitants', Hong Kong continuing as a free port and world financial centre. Residents would not pay taxes to the People's Republic of China and English would remain the official language for 50 years. Two clauses sought to protect the rights of Hong Kong citizens. Clause 3 said 'the laws currently in force in Hong Kong will remain basically unchanged', while clause 5 stated that 'Rights and freedoms including those of the person, of speech, of the press, of assembly, of association, of

travel... and of religious belief will be ensured by law in the Hong Kong Special Administrative Region'.

After a century of colonial rule in which the Hong Kong Chinese had been denied the right of self-determination or to elect their own representatives, the British government belatedly decided to make Hong Kong's political system more democratic. The British government proceeded, for the first time in the colony's history, to introduce in 1991 direct elections by universal suffrage for 18 of the 61 seats on the Legislative Council. A year later Chris Patten, the Governor of Hong Kong, announced his intention of allowing the people of Hong Kong to elect a majority of the members of the Legislative Council, without securing the agreement of the Chinese government. The Chinese protested vehemently and relations with Britain became very strained. As a result the elected legislature did not survive the handover but was replaced by one appointed by the Chinese government.

Hong Kong residents were refused British nationality, so they had no right to emigrate to Britain, but a mass exodus began to other countries. It is estimated that from 1984–97 between 500,000 and 700,000 left Hong Kong.

Hong Kong's Transition 1842–1997, J. M. Brown and R. Foot (eds) (1997)
Hong Kong: The Road to 1997, R. Buckley (1997)

Hoover, John Edgar (1985–1972)   Director of the Federal Bureau of Investigation (FBI) (1924–72). After studying law he entered the Justice Department in 1917 and made his reputation during the Red Scare (1919–20), when there was considerable labour unrest. Federal marshals under Hoover, who assembled a card index of 450,000 radicals and developed the first informer network, arrested 2,700 suspected communists. In 1924, when the FBI was set up, he became its first Director. He removed

corrupt officials, employed rigorous methods of selection and training and made the FBI an efficient agency of federal law enforcement. A vain hypochondriac, obsessed with order and routine, he expected complete loyalty from his subordinates. He ruled the FBI as a dictator under eight Presidents and made major innovations in crime detection and prevention. Hoover established a central fingerprint file (1925), a crime detection laboratory (1932) and an FBI Academy (1935) to train FBI agents. He also set up the National Crime Information Center, a computer network used by 4,000 local law-enforcement agencies. In the 1930s he waged a well-publicized war against gangsters, his G-men shooting John Dillinger, 'Pretty Boy' Floyd and 'Baby Face' Nelson.

President Roosevelt in the late 1930s gave him the task of investigating foreign espionage in the US and the activities of communists and Fascists. He continued this work after the Second World War, when he began an intensive surveillance of all radicals, not only communists but members of the Ku Klux Klan and black activists (he harassed Martin Luther KING) in the CIVIL RIGHTS MOVEMENT. He used a vast array of informers, including some public figures like Cardinal Spellman, in his anti-communist crusade. At the same time he neglected to target the MAFIA, which was able to conduct its nationwide operations almost with impunity. Hoover used the FBI to collect damaging information on politicians, which he used to keep himself in office. 'We want no Gestapo or Secret Police', President TRUMAN complained privately. 'FBI is tending in that direction. They are dabbling in sex life scandals and plain blackmail... This must stop'. It did not stop. Truman did not dismiss or censure Hoover. He was apparently able to intimidate Presidents by threatening to leak damaging disclosures about them. By 1970 he was publicly criticized for his authoritarian methods, abuse of civil liberties and for his hostility to civil rights, but he remained in office until he died at the age of 77.

Houphouët-Boigny, Félix (1905–93)

President of the Ivory Coast (1960–94). The son of a tribal chief, he studied medicine at Dakar, Senegal and was a successful doctor, coffee planter and chief in the Ivory Coast. He became important politically in 1944, when he organized a union of African coffee planters, which in 1945 changed into the *Parti Démocratique de la Côte d'Ivoire* (PDCI), one of the earliest mass parties in Africa. Elected to the French National Assembly in 1946, where he successfully introduced a law to abolish forced labour in all French colonies, he held cabinet posts in several French governments from 1956–9.

Houphouët became Prime Minister of the Ivory Coast in 1959 and President in 1960, on its independence. From that time the PDCI ruled the Ivory Coast as a one-party state, with a strictly controlled press. The remarkable stability of the country was due to French technical and financial aid, the presence of a French garrison and economic prosperity, though there was resentment among the educated at the slow pace of Africanization, with Frenchmen occupying many prominent positions in the civil service and the professions. Ivorians had an average income higher than anywhere else in Africa, except South Africa, but also the biggest per capita debt. The danger of exports relying so heavily on cocoa and coffee became apparent when the market collapsed in the 1980s. In 1990 he won a landslide victory in the country's first contested presidential election. He died in office.

Ivory Coast: The Challenge of Success, B. A. Tuinder (1979)
The Political Economy of the Ivory Coast, I. W. Zartman (1984)

Howe, Sir (Richard Edward) Geoffrey, Baron (1926–)

British Chancellor of the Exchequer (1979–83) and Foreign Secretary (1983–9). The son of a Welsh solicitor, he was educated at Winchester and Cambridge University, where he took a degree in law and was called to the Bar in 1952. He was elected as a

Conservative Member of Parliament in 1964 and in the HEATH government (1970–4) was Solicitor-General and then in charge of Consumer Affairs with a seat in the cabinet. A supporter of Heath's incomes policy, he was on the liberal wing of the party, favouring reform of race relations and equal opportunities for women. He was a candidate in the 1975 CONSERVATIVE PARTY leadership election but was defeated by Margaret THATCHER. When the Conservatives won the 1979 election Thatcher made him Chancellor of the Exchequer.

Reliable and industrious, he rejected KEYNESIANISM, the dominant economic philosophy since the Second World War, and was a convert to MONETARISM, the belief that inflation could be controlled by restricting the money supply. If that was done, neither changes in taxes nor wages would increase inflation; high wage settlements would simply mean that workers priced themselves out of a job. In his first budget in 1979 Howe cut the basic rate of tax from 33 per cent to 30 per cent and the top rate from 83 per cent to 60 per cent. To pay for this VAT was raised from 8 per cent to 15 per cent in a move from direct to indirect taxation, a regressive system which favoured the better-off. To restrict the money supply (M3 – the amount of money in circulation and sterling deposits) the bank rate was raised from 12 per cent to 14 per cent (and to 17 per cent in November). The right-wing American economist Arthur Laffer predicted that the budget would bring about a disastrous recession, which it did. The exchange rate of sterling rose sharply because of the high interest rates and oil prices trebled owing to the IRANIAN REVOLUTION, which brought the Ayatollah KHOMEINI to power. Industry had to cope with high exchange and interest rates, high oil prices, wage inflation and a fall in demand. The result was the worst recession for 50 years, with factories closing all over the country and a rise in unemployment from 1.3 to 2 million. Production declined more rapidly than at any time since the Industrial Revolution. DEIN-

DUSTRIALIZATION was accompanied by inflation of over 20 per cent in 1980 and a rise in public spending owing to unemployment. Instead of changing its policy the Treasury announced in 1980 the Medium-Term Financial Strategy (MTFS) to 'reduce the growth of the money stock'. Declining targets were set for M3 and the PSBR (Public Sector Borrowing Requirement) for the next four years. This assumed that the government could control M3 but it was unable to do this because it had abolished exchange controls. The result was that M3 grew well above the set targets, which were then changed and finally abandoned. In his 1981 Budget Howe surprised everyone by aiming to reduce the PSBR by £3 billion by a massive increase in indirect taxation and further cuts in spending. Raising taxes and tightening fiscal policy in a depression outraged many economists, 364 of whom protested in a letter to *The Times*, as it was bound to lead to even higher unemployment. Inflation fell to 4.5 per cent in 1983, but unemployment climbed to 3.3 million. Between 20–25 per cent of Britain's industrial capacity had been destroyed since 1979.

Howe moved in 1983 to the Foreign Office, where his patience and persistence in negotiations with China produced a year later an agreement that HONG KONG would revert to China in 1997. Thatcher herself took charge of relations with President REAGAN and fought hard to reduce Britain's contribution to the EEC budget, but it was her Foreign Secretary who persuaded her to agree in 1986 to the Single European Act, which gave new powers to the European Parliament and abolished a member's right of veto over much Community legislation, an infringement of British sovereignty she had long resisted. In June 1989 Howe and the Chancellor of the Exchequer, Nigel LAWSON, forced the Prime Minister to accept in principle that Britain should join the Exchange Rate Mechanism (ERM) but she had her revenge a month later when she replaced Howe as Foreign Secretary with John MAJOR. In compensation he was made Deputy Prime Minister, a meaningless title as he was ignored. His own turn for retaliation came in November 1990, when he resigned from the government. Previously regarded as docile and submissive, he made a devastating attack on Thatcher and her attitude to the EC which led Michael Heseltine to challenge her for the leadership of the Conservative Party. The Prime Minister failed to win outright on the first ballot and was advised by her colleagues that she would not win the second ballot, so she withdrew. Howe was therefore instrumental in bringing about the fall of Margaret Thatcher.

Geoffrey Howe: A Quiet Revolutionary, J. Hillman, P. Clarke (1988)

Hoxha, Enver (1908–85)   Communist dictator of Albania (1945–85). From a middle-class Muslim family in the only predominantly Muslim country in Europe (70 per cent of Albanians were Muslim in 1940), Hoxha studied in France (1930–6), where he became a Marxist. On returning to Albania he was a teacher of French. When the Albanian communist party was formed in 1941 Hoxha became the General Secretary and played a dominant role in the wartime resistance. Communism was firmly established in Albania before the Second World War ended. Hoxha then consolidated his power by eliminating all his opponents and continued to rule Albania for the next 40 years by a vicious reign of terror. There were frequent purges of the army, security police and civil service, which reached to the highest posts in the NOMENKLATURA. Some were summarily executed, others disappeared, many were sentenced without trial, thousands were imprisoned. Internal exile usually followed imprisonment and applied also to the families of those imprisoned: not only wives and children but also parents, aunts, uncles, and this continued from generation to generation.

From 1944–8 Albania was a Yugoslav dependency. Hoxha had to accept the restoration of Kosovo (joined to Albania by Mussolini) to Yugoslavia. The economics of Albania and Yugoslavia were integrated and only the break between TITO and STALIN in 1948 prevented Yugoslavia annexing Albania. From 1948 to 1960 Albania was a Soviet satellite, joining COMECON in 1949 and the WARSAW PACT in 1955. Hoxha opposed KHRUSHCHEV's de-Stalinization and his reconciliation with Tito and moved closer to China. This was unpopular in the Soviet Union, owing to the SINO-SOVIET DISPUTE, so in 1961 Khrushchev ended aid to Albania and broke off diplomatic relations. Albania was now dependent on Chinese aid. Hoxha adopted Stalinist methods in trying to make Albania into a modern industrial state. There was centralized economic planning, the collectivization of agriculture and the exploitation of the country's natural resources (oil, chrome, copper, iron and nickel). The five year plans at first produced impressive growth rates (20 per cent per annum from 1951–60, 10 per cent 1961–75) but from a very low base, while the goods produced were of such poor quality that they could not compete in foreign markets. After the downfall of the GANG OF FOUR and the rehabilitation of DENG XIAOPING Chinese aid came to an end in 1978, leaving Albania for the first time without an economic patron. Reliant on its own resources alone, the economic growth rate dropped to 0.5 per cent per annum from 1976–80 and −0.1 per cent from 1981–5.

Hoxha, who had a heart attack in 1973, introduced a new constitution in 1976 to cement his control. The leading role of the party was affirmed and the armed forces were placed under the control of the party, whose First Secretary (Hoxha) was commander-in-chief. The practice of religion was forbidden (Hoxha had declared Albania to be an atheist state in 1967). There were some positive achievements to Hoxha's rule. Illiteracy (85 per cent in 1944) was almost wiped out, there was a free health service, infant mortality fell sharply and life expectancy rose to over 70. Yet at the time of Hoxha's death, isolated Albania remained the poorest country in Europe.

Albania a Socialist Maverick, E. Biberaj (1990)

Burying Mao, R. Baum (1994)

Hu Yaobang (1915–89)   General Secretary of the Chinese Communist Party (CCP) (1981–7). From a poor peasant family he had little education before he was recruited as a boy to fight in MAO ZEDONG's unsuccessful Autumn Harvest Uprising in 1927. He joined Mao in the Jiangxi Soviet and when the Nationalists under JIANG JIESHI (Chiang Kai-shek) drove the communists out, Hu fought on the Long March (1934–5) to Yanan in the north. He worked as a political commissar under LIN BIAO during the Sino-Japanese War (1937–45) and the CHINESE CIVIL WAR (1946–9). Hu was then a party official in Sichuan with DENG XIAOPING until 1952, when he followed Deng to Beijing and was head of the Young Communist League (1952–66), an organization with 30 million members. During the CULTURAL REVOLUTION Hu and Deng were twice purged and twice rehabilitated. After his second recall in 1977, following the arrest of the radical GANG OF FOUR, he had a rapid rise in the CCP hierarchy owing to Deng's backing: a member of the Politburo (1978), of its inner circle, the Standing Committee (1980) and General Secretary of the CCP (1981), replacing Mao's chosen successor, HUA GUO-FENG. Articulate and industrious, Hu believed that ideology should not stand in the way of economic modernization and was officially corrected for saying that Marx, a nineteenth-century thinker, could not solve China's problems in the late twentieth century. Hu purged Maoists and corrupt members of the party and replaced them with younger, better-educated cadres. In 1987, after weeks of student demonstrations demanding greater democracy, conservatives in the party forced him to resign as General Secretary but he retained his position in the Standing Committee of the Politburo. His death in April 1989 from a heart attack began a series of events which ended with the TIANANMEN SQUARE MASSACRE.

Hua Guofeng (1920–)   Prime Minister of the People's Republic of China (1976–80). Little is known about his life before the CHINESE CIVIL WAR (1946–9) ended, when he was a local Chinese Communist Party (CCP) Secretary in Hunan, MAO ZEDONG's home province. Vice-Governor of the province in 1958, he was an enthusiastic supporter of the GREAT LEAP FORWARD (1958–60). He did not play a large part in the CULTURAL REVOLUTION (1966–76) but benefited from it, as many leading officials were dismissed and he was able to obtain promotion. He was head of the CCP in Hunan by 1972, a member of the Politburo a year later and Vice-Premier and Minister of Public Security in 1975. He was surprisingly chosen by Mao for the highest offices as the only person who could be relied on to carry on Mao's policies after his death: the GANG OF FOUR was too unpopular to survive long, while the moderates led by DENG XIAOPING were likely to reverse his policies. On ZHOU ENLAI's death in 1976 Hua therefore became Prime Minister and when Mao died later the same year he succeeded him as Chairman of the Central Committee of the CCP and of the Military Affairs Committee (MAC), while retaining the post of Prime Minister. He thus combined the leading positions in both state and party and seemed in an impregnable position, particularly after the arrest of the Gang of Four, who were plotting against him. However, he was not able to dominate the Politburo when Deng (disgraced in 1976) returned in 1977. His plan to revive the economy was to revert to the Stalinist model of investing in centrally controlled heavy industry, while seeking loans from capitalist powers, especially Japan. This policy failed and when food had to be imported because of widespread famine there was pressure from Deng to change the economic strategy. In 1980 Deng's allies, HU YAOBANG and ZHAO ZIYANG joined the Politburo Standing Committee and Hua was eased out of power. Zhao replaced him as Prime Minister, Hu as General Secretary of the CCP and Deng took over as Chairman of the MAC.

Chairman Hua, T. Wang (1980)
China Without Mao, I. Hsu (1990)

Hundred Flowers Campaign (1956-7)

An occasion when MAO ZEDONG invited non-party intellectuals to criticize the Chinese Communist Party. Mao was worried that the CCP bureaucracy, which had vastly expanded since victory in the CHINESE CIVIL WAR (1946-9), was alienating the masses by becoming a privileged élite. The HUNGARIAN RISING of 1956 showed Mao that problems should be dealt with before they got out of hand, but others pointed out that the rising took place because political controls had been relaxed and that party rule must not be endangered. At the CCP Congress in September 1956 most delegates were against 'letting a hundred flowers bloom and a hundred schools of thought contend'. Mao nevertheless went ahead and encouraged intellectuals to criticize abuses in the party, so that they could be rectified. After a cautious start, the vehemence of the criticisms seemed to take him by surprise. Most did not reject the system of public ownership but they condemned the corruption and incompetence of many party officials, who were arrogant and insensitive to people's needs. Students at Beijing University covered a Democracy Wall with posters criticizing the CCP.

Mao took the lead in reversing the policy he had initiated by attacking the critics as 'poisonous weeds' in an Anti-Rightist Campaign. 'Correct criticism', he said, 'must strengthen Party leadership and support the socialist system'. 550,000 were named as 'rightists', which ruined their careers. Many were imprisoned or sent to labour camps: others were exiled to the countryside, possibly for life.

The Origins of the Cultural Revolution, vol. I: Contradictions Among the People, R. MacFarquhar (1974)

Hungarian rising (1956)

Events both inside and outside Hungary helped to bring about this anti-Soviet rising against the communist dictatorship. There was economic discontent owing to the lack of food and consumer goods, while collectivization had driven many peasants off the land. Reformers had been encouraged by KHRUSHCHEV's reconciliation with TITO, which appeared to admit that there were different national roads to communism. His speech to the TWENTIETH CONGRESS OF THE CPSU, attacking the evils of STALIN's rule, implied that greater freedom of opinion should be permitted. Events in Poland, where GOMULKA had just been elected First Secretary against Soviet wishes, also encouraged the Hungarian students who demonstrated in Budapest on 22 October to demand the withdrawal of Soviet troops and the formation of a Nagy government. That marked the beginning of the revolution. As workers joined in there were 200,000 demonstrators. The first shots were fired by the hated AVH (the secret security police) as the crowd marched on the radio station to broadcast their demands. The army, refusing to fire on the demonstrators, gave them weapons: many soldiers and regular police joined the insurgents. As Soviet tanks poured into Budapest, four days of bitter fighting began on the 24 October. A day later Mikoyan and Suslov, the CPSU's chief ideologist, arrived from Moscow and insisted on the replacement of Gerö by KÁDÁR as First Secretary. They were working for a 'Polish' solution as a lesser evil to military conflict, though China, Bulgaria, Romania and Czechoslovakia were all urging the USSR to intervene militarily. Nagy had been made Prime Minister again, in the hope that he would be able to control the situation and on 28 October announced the withdrawal of the Soviet army from Budapest and the dissolution of the AVH.

The rising seemed over but the victory was not Nagy's. Revolutionary councils had sprung up which, by 30 October, controlled all of Hungary and demanded a multiparty system and Hungary's withdrawal from the WARSAW PACT. Nagy had refused to order the Hungarian army to fight the Russians and had left the decision to local commanders. They, and especially General Pal Maleter in Budapest, were the heroes of the revolution. On 30 October Nagy's government was rejected by the national revolutionary committee, which represented the freedom fighters. Nagy therefore agreed to form a coalition government and allow a multiparty system. Cardinal Mindszenty was freed by the army and new parties were formed as the Hungarian Workers' Party (communist party) broke up.

On the same day rebels seized the headquarters of the Communist Party and killed hundreds of communists, mainly AVH, lynching some in public. The Soviet politburo decided to intervene in Hungary on 31 October, as the Hungarian rising, if it was allowed to succeed, would destabilize the whole communist bloc. The SUEZ CRISIS ended Khrushchev's doubts as, with Britain and France preoccupied, it was clear that NATO would take no action. Nagy announced on 1 November that Hungary would leave the Warsaw Pact and become a neutral state and appealed to the UNITED NATIONS for help. The Russians used this to justify their invasion, but the decision to invade had already been taken. When 6,000 Soviet tanks invaded Hungary on 4 November Nagy and some colleagues took refuge in the Yugoslav embassy. Kádár, who had disappeared, returned on 7 November with Soviet support to begin restoring communist rule. Fighting continued until 14 November when the insurgents' ammunition ran out. On 23 November Nagy, who had been promised a free passage outside Hungary, left the Yugoslav embassy and was immediately arrested by Soviet troops and was later executed.

The Hungarian government announced that 3,000 people had been killed and 13,000 injured in the rising, though this is almost certainly an underestimate. 2,000 were later executed for having taken part in the rising and 200,000 fled from Hungary. The rising,

unplanned and spontaneous, had not shown any desire to return to capitalism, except perhaps in the countryside, where 2,000 of the 3,950 collective farms dissolved themselves. The workers wanted elected workers' councils to run factories on the Yugoslav model. Most worrying for Soviet leaders was the revelation of the slender foundations of the communist regime: it was the youth and the working class who were the most dedicated revolutionaries. The rising showed clearly that no significant changes could be implemented in communist states without Soviet approval and that the West would not interfere to support communist regimes which defied the USSR. Reform would have to come from the Soviet Union itself.

Hungary 1956, B. Lomax (1976)
Hungary 1956 Revisited, F. Feher and A. Heller (1983)

Husák, Gustáv (1913–91) President of Czechoslovakia (1975–89). Born in Slovakia, he was trained as a lawyer, joined the Czechoslovak Communist Party (CCP) in 1939 and was an organizer of the Slovak rising of 1944. After the war Husák was Minister of Agriculture (1948–9) before becoming a victim of GOTTWALD's purges: he was imprisoned as a 'bourgeois nationalist' for supporting Slovak rights within the Czechoslovak Republic. Released in 1960, he worked at the Academy of Sciences (1963–8) but did not hold high office until he became First Secretary of the Slovak CP and Deputy Premier during the PRAGUE SPRING.

He appeared to be a moderate reformer but was in fact a pragmatic politician, who quickly accepted the dominant position of the Soviet Union and replaced Dubček as First Secretary of the CCP in April 1969. The reforms of 1968 were abandoned, the ministers responsible for them dismissed and there was a massive purge of the party and civil service in which half a million people lost their jobs, but there was no torture, false confessions or executions, as in Gottwald's purges. Control of the media was re-established, as was the leading role of the CCP. Husák realized that, to gain acceptance by the people, he had to improve the standard of living. Social welfare benefits were therefore increased and extended to groups previously excluded, such as collective farmers. The Slovaks were pacified, as large numbers were given jobs for the first time in the federal civil service (positions made available by the purges) and resources were transferred from Czech lands to Slovakia. Military expenditure, investment and foreign aid to Cuba and Vietnam were all cut, so that private consumption increased by 38 per cent between 1970–8. All this was done without any radical reform; energy was used inefficiently, the infrastructure was run down, and industry's obsolete machinery produced poor quality goods. Husák isolated Czechoslovakia from the GLOBAL ECONOMY by increasing trade with the communist bloc to 80 per cent of foreign trade. He therefore did not need to borrow much from the West: Czechoslovakia's foreign debt was the lowest in Eastern Europe. Like other countries it was badly affected by the OPEC PRICE RISE of 1973 and by 1980 there were trade deficits. Husák became state President in 1975 but, an austere figure who loathed the personality cult of TITO and CEAUSESCU, he continued on his inflexible way, rejecting GORBACHEV'S GLASNOST and perestroika until, with the economic situation deteriorating further, he was forced to retire as First Secretary of the CCP in 1987. Two years later he was replaced as President by Václav HAVEL during the VELVET REVOLUTION.

From Dubček to Charter 77: A Study of Normalisation in Czechoslovakia, 1968–78, V. V. Kusin (1978)
A History of Czechoslovakia Since 1945, A. Renner (1989)

Hussein (Husayn) Ibn Talal (1935–)

King of Jordan (1953–). His father Talal came to the throne in 1951 but had a complete mental breakdown a year later and was replaced by Hussein, who came of age in 1953. A Hashimite descended from the Prophet Muhammad, he had strong tribal support but also many opponents, because of his pro-English stance (he was educated at Harrow and Sandhurst Military Academy) and because his grandfather ABDULLAH had tried to seize all of Arab Palestine for his own kingdom in the Arab–Israeli war of 1948–9. With the acquisition of the West Bank in that war and the flight of many Palestinians from Israeli-occupied territory, there was a large number of Palestinians in Jordan who were given Jordanian citizenship and had to be assimilated. This could be done successfully only if the economy grew rapidly, which it did until the 1980s, benefiting by aid from Britain (until 1956) and then from the US and Arab countries. During the LEBANESE CIVIL WAR (1975–90) banking and other services moved from Lebanon to Jordan.

Hussein strictly controlled political activity: few political parties were legalized, all were banned from time to time and from 1974–84 parliament was suspended. Hussein faced several serious crises in his reign. Attempts to make Jordan a member of the BAGHDAD PACT were opposed by NASSER and by many Jordanians and were abandoned. Responding to public pressure Hussein dismissed Sir John Glubb, the British commander of the Arab Legion, in 1956 and ended the Anglo-Jordanian Treaty, which allowed Britain to have military bases in Jordan, a year later. There was a crisis in 1957 when Hussein dismissed his pro-Egyptian Prime Minister and army commander, suspended the constitution, banned political parties and trade unions, declared martial law and arrested opposition leaders. He was able to survive as the strong bedouin element in the army remained loyal. There were several attempts, backed by Syria or Egypt, to overthrow him but he survived, partly because he allowed US intelligence services to operate in Jordan.

The army saved Hussein for a second time in the crisis of 1967–71. Israel had told him that he would be left alone if he kept out of the

SIX DAY WAR (1967) but he joined in and as a result lost old Jerusalem and the WEST BANK. The PLO then tried to set up a state within a state in Jordan but was defeated by the Jordanian army by July 1971 and was forced to leave Jordan. He kept out of the YOM KIPPUR WAR (1973). Hussein still claimed the West Bank but in 1974 the ARAB LEAGUE recognized the PLO as the sole representative of the Palestinian people with the right to establish a state in the West Bank and Gaza: in 1988 he gave up his claim to it. By this time there were still 750,000 PALESTINIAN REFUGEES in Jordan but only 200,000 were in camps: most Palestinians had been integrated into Jordanian society. In the IRAN–IRAQ WAR (1980–8) he supported Iraq and so tied Jordan economically even more firmly to Iraq.

At the end of the 1980s the Jordanian economy deteriorated: price increases started anti-government riots in 1989. Hussein sought popularity by political liberalization, restoring parliament and calling a general election for the first time in over 20 years. The elections of 1989 were a triumph for the MUSLIM BROTHERHOOD, so the king included Islamist representatives in his government. The GULF WAR again showed how vulnerable Hussein was: he refused to join the coalition against Saddam HUSSEIN and so lost the financial support he had been receiving from the Gulf oil states and the US. At the same time there was an extra burden on the Jordanian economy in the 300,000 refugees – mainly Jordanians and Palestinians – who were deported from the GULF STATES. By 1992 much aid had been restored (mainly from Germany and Japan) but Hussein still had to face the challenge from ISLAMIC FUNDAMENTALISTS. He responded by promising more democracy and published a National Charter, which legalized a multi-party system and repealed martial law, which had been in place since 1967. In 1993 he held the first multiparty elections since 1956. The Oslo Accords between Israel and the PLO in the same year prompted him to join in the PEACE PROCESS and sign a peace treaty with Israel in 1994. This led to a steady decline in his popularity.

History of Jordan, J. Lunt (1989)

Hussein, Saddam (1937–)   President of Iraq (1979–). He was born in a poor peasant family near Tikrit, a small town on the Tigris 100 miles (160 km) north of Baghdad. He joined the Ba'th Party in 1955, was involved in an attempted assassination of Qasim in 1959 and escaped to Egypt. Saddam Hussein returned to Baghdad after Qasim was killed in a coup in 1963 and gained the attention of the Ba'th Party's Syrian founder, Michel Aflaq, who put him in charge of organizing the civil wing of the party in 1964. Though not in the army himself (the uniform he habitually wore was that of the Ba'th militia) he had family connections with army officers, especially to General Hasan al-Bakr. A military coup in 1968 brought the Ba'th back to power with al-Bakr as President of Iraq and Saddam Hussein as assistant Secretary-General of the Ba'th and a year later Vice-Chairman of the Revolutionary Command Council (RCC), the country's ruling body.

Cautious, suspicious, ruthless and an admirer of STALIN, he took control of the security services and the military wing of the Ba'th and became the strong-man of the regime. In the 1970s he won even more power by his close alliance with al-Bakr and by controlling the Republican Guard, an élite army unit. In 1972 Saddam Hussein nationalized the Iraq Petroleum Company. To deal effectively with the opposition of the Kurds, his constant opponents who were supported by Iran, he made the Algiers Agreement in 1975 with MUHAMMAD RIZA PAHLAVI, whereby the boundary between Iran and Iraq was adjusted to Iran's advantage and in return the Shah ended his aid to the Iraqi Kurds. In July 1979 Saddam Hussein took over from al-Bakr as Chairman of the RCC and as President of Iraq. A few days later he turned against some of his closest allies in the

Ba'th: he discovered a 'plot' in which, he said, five members of the Revolutionary Command Council were involved. They were executed in person by Saddam Hussein and the surviving members of the RCC, thus establishing among them a ghastly tie of blood brotherhood.

Saddam Hussein aimed to make Iraq the dominant power in the Gulf region and in 1980 saw an opportunity to strike at his most powerful rival Iran after the IRANIAN REVOLUTION (1979) had created confusion in the country. Following initial successes in the IRAN–IRAQ WAR (1980–8) the Iraqis were pushed back and were able to survive only because of massive aid from other Arab states and from the US. The war ended with neither side gaining any territory but Saddam claimed it as a victory. His cult of personality became ever more extravagant: huge pictures of the 'Great Leader' adorned buildings and enormous 'victory' monuments were erected. During the war Saddam had increased his army from 250,000 to 1,250,000 and was producing or developing chemical, biological and nuclear weapons. At the end of the war Saddam Hussein turned on the Kurds, who had made parts of the north into self-governing areas, and used his vast army to recover control and kill 100,000 Kurds. Then, in 1990, he made another bid for regional hegemony by invading Kuwait, which led to the GULF WAR (1991). In the Gulf War he became a Muslim hero, attacking the Israeli towns of Haifa and Tel Aviv with Soviet Scud missiles.

He survived his crushing defeat in that war with part of his army intact, so he was able to deal brutally and effectively with the risings which took place against him in Kurdistan and in the SHII areas in the south: over two million refugees fled to Turkey and Iran. Saddam Hussein would not accept the conditions the UNITED NATIONS insisted on before sanctions could be lifted, so the population of Iraq suffered severe hardship. In August 1991 the UN said it would allow Iraq to sell a certain amount of oil: the money from its sale would be paid into a UN account, part of which could be used to buy food, medicine and essential goods for the population. Saddam Hussein rejected this. A year later, because of attacks by the Iraqi army on Shii in the south, the US, British, French and Russian governments fixed a 'no-fly' zone for Iraqi planes in the south, but ground attacks on the civilian population continued. The US navy hit the Iraqi intelligence headquarters in Baghdad with missiles in June 1993 because the US alleged that Hussein had planned to assassinate President BUSH on his trip to Kuwait in April. The defection to Jordan in August 1995 of two of Saddam Hussein's sons-in-law, with their wives and children, seemed to indicate that his regime was falling apart, but this proved premature. When King HUSSEIN made it clear that they were no longer welcome in Jordan, Iraq announced a pardon for them. They returned in February 1996 but were promptly executed. Their father and a third brother were also murdered. Saddam at last agreed to the UN plan for a relaxation of the oil embargo in May 1996. Iraq would be allowed to sell oil for $2 billion every six months (about half the prewar amount): just over half would be spent on food and medicines, nearly a third on war reparations and $300 million would go to the Kurds. The Kurdish problem arose again, this time to Saddam's advantage. Factional fighting among the Kurds led to Massoud Barzani's Kurdish Democratic Party inviting Iraqi troops into Kurdistan in September 1996, where they took control of 80 per cent of the area and so ended the US–British 'safe haven' for the Kurds set up after the Gulf War.

Iraq Since 1958, M. Farouk-Sluglett and P. Sluglett (1990)
Saddam Hussein, J. Rautsi (1991)

hydrogen bomb   A fission or thermonuclear weapon, one of whose ingredients is tritium, an isotope of hydrogen, hence the name of the bomb. The idea for such a bomb was first put forward in 1942 and in January 1950 President TRUMAN, aware that the Soviet Union might develop its own H-bomb, decided to go ahead with it. The first thermonuclear explosion took place on Eni-wetok Atoll in the Marshall Islands on 1 November 1952, confounding expectations by throwing a fireball five miles high and four miles wide and leaving a hole on the Pacific floor a mile wide. The USSR exploded its own H-bomb in Siberia in August 1953. A US explosion in March 1954 on Bikini Atoll was 750 times more powerful than the atomic bomb dropped on Hiroshima in 1945 and spread radioactive fall-out from the blast 7,000 square miles across the Pacific. Britain exploded its own H-bomb in 1957, China in 1967 and France in 1968.

I

IMF (International Monetary Fund)
Established at Bretton Woods (1944) it was
designed to create stable currency relationships among the industrial nations. It is a
credit union of the most affluent states (the
US, Germany, Japan, Britain, France), which
the US dominates. Saudi Arabia was co-opted
as it was the chief supplier of borrowed money
after the OPEC PRICE RISE of 1973. Each
member contributes to IMF funds and can
draw on them, according to a quota system,
when necessary. Originally it was formed as a
reaction to the policies of the 1930s, when
world trade was disrupted as countries left
the gold standard and adopted exchange controls and devaluation. The IMF wanted to
make these unnecessary by creating a pool
on which members could draw to correct
their balance of payments difficulties. It
aimed to avoid the turbulence of floating
exchange rates and the rigidity of the gold
standard by having a modified system of
fixed exchange rates. The dollar, the world's
main reserve currency, could be freely converted into gold at a fixed price. Other members had to adopt convertibility for current
account transactions, though this was not
completed by the main European countries
until 1958 and by Japan until 1964. In the
early years of postwar reconstruction the
IMF was of little importance, as the US not
the IMF provided the money for the reconstruction of Western Europe in the MAR-
SHALL PLAN. The quarter century of
relative exchange-rate stability ended in 1971
when President NIXON, with a large US
external deficit, suspended the convertibility
of the dollar into gold.

In the 1970s the role of the IMF was undermined as international capital markets
recycled the huge OPEC surpluses after the
oil price rise and became the main source of
lending. Both developed and developing
countries, seeking to avoid the limitations
imposed by the IMF, turned to private
banks. Industrial countries, previously the
main borrowers from the IMF, stopped borrowing from it. The INTERNATIONAL DEBT
crisis, when Mexico in 1982 declared that it
could not service its debt, revived the importance of the IMF, which had to mount a
rescue operation repeated in many other
developing countries as they too went bankrupt. The rescheduling of the debt by the
IMF defused a severe threat to the international financial system and helped to avoid a
plethora of defaults or the collapse of any
major banks. However, the debt crisis showed
the limits of IMF influence: it could not persuade banks to continue their lending and did
not enable debtors to resume growth. It also
had a deleterious effect on poor countries by
making the rescheduling of their debt condi-
tional on their adopting an adjustment programme: they had to cut imports, reduce
spending, increase taxes, devalue their currencies and liberalize their trade. Where
exports could not be increased quickly, devaluation simply produced inflation without any
benefits. IMF shock treatment destabilized
countries both economically and politically,
adversely affecting the poor by higher prices
and cut-backs in social services. Compliance
with IMF adjustment programmes has been
weak, while the economic performance of
countries that do keep them has been little

different from those that do not. In the 1980s the IMF took more out of the THIRD WORLD in interest charges than it put in.

After 50 years the IMF is a very different organization from what it was originally. The Group of Seven leading industrial powers (the US, Japan, Germany, France, Britain, Italy and Canada) ignore it as they make deals among themselves about fiscal and monetary policies. They do not need the IMF as a source of lending: countries which do (the IMF had reform programmes in 50 countries in 1990) have turned to the IMF in desperation, as a lender of last resort. Although many countries were dissatisfied with the IMF, yet others sought to join with the COLLAPSE OF THE SOVIET UNION. The USSR had stayed outside the WORLD BANK and IMF during the COLD WAR but after the REVOLUTIONS OF 1989–91 the IMF took the lead in the economic liberalization of Russia and the countries of Eastern Europe, guiding them from central planning to a market-based economy.

The Quest for Stability: The IMF and the Third World, T. Killick (ed.) (1984)
The Political Morality of the International Monetary Fund, R. J. Myers (1987)
The International Monetary Fund in a Multipolar World, G. Gwin et al. (1990)

immigration (into the US)   Up to the end of the Second World War most immigrants in the US came from Europe, owing to national-origins quotas which favoured them. This policy continued until 1965. Refugees, mainly from Central and Eastern Europe, were allowed in by the Displaced Persons Act (1948–50) and the Refugee Relief Act (1952). The McCarran–Walter Act (1952) maintained the quota system of the 1920s and aimed to ensure that the vast majority of immigrants would come from Northern and Western Europe. A large number of immigrants came from Mexico under a scheme begun during the war to provide agricultural labourers (*braceros*) for farmers in the South-

west, though legal immigrants were soon outnumbered by 'wetbacks' who crossed the 2,000 mile Mexican–US frontier illegally.

There was no significant change in the laws affecting immigration until the Immigration Reform Act of 1965 (effective from 1968), which abandoned the quota system in favour of special categories of immigrants: relations of US residents and those with special skills could now enter the US. The number of immigrants from the Western hemisphere was limited to 120,000 annually for the first time, with 170,000 from the rest of the world: no more than 20,000 could come from any one country. Congress expected that most immigrants would continue to come from Europe but this was not so, the proportion of Europeans dropping from 53 per cent (1951–65) to 24 per cent (1966–78) and to 10 per cent in the 1980s. Asia and Latin America were now the main source of immigrants, the leading countries from 1976–86 being Mexico, Vietnam, the Philippines, Korea, China–Taiwan, Cuba, the Dominican Republic and Jamaica, with Britain in tenth place. Many of these immigrants were refugees: Cubans fleeing from CASTRO's communism, Vietnamese when Saigon fell to HO CHI MINH in 1975 in the VIETNAM WAR. Cambodians and Laotians joined the exodus as communism spread there: 700,000, many of them peasants, had come from Indochina by 1985.

There was also a large number of illegal immigrants, particularly from Mexico, which led President REAGAN to declare in 1984: 'We have lost control of our borders'. In the 1970s and 1980s many fleeing from the civil wars of Central America followed the Mexican route into the US. It is estimated that in the late 1980s there were a million illegal immigrants from El Salvador (20 per cent of that country's population) alone. In the 1990s many from Ireland and the Soviet Union entered on temporary visas and then disappeared.

Immigrants had an enormous impact in certain areas: 70 per cent of them settled in six states: California, New York, Florida,

Texas, Illinois and New Jersey. In the two largest US cities (New York and Los Angeles) over half the residents were immigrants and their children. Most Asian immigrants were English-speaking and well-educated: over half had professional or technical qualifications. They had little difficulty settling in their new country and by 1990 had higher average family incomes than whites. This was not true of other immigrants. Most Mexicans and Haitians were poor and illiterate and increased ethnic tension. Blacks in Miami, accusing Cubans of taking their jobs, rioted in 1980, killing 18. Hispanics and blacks attacked Korean businesses in the Los Angeles riots of 1992. Immigration had brought a change in the ethnic balance of the population: demographers calculate that the US may no longer have a white majority by 2050.

US Immigration and Reform Policy, M. M. Kritz (ed.) (1983)
Postwar Immigrant America: A Social History, R. Cheda (1994)
Immigrant America, A. Portes and R. G. Rumbaut (1996)

Immigration Acts (Britain)   After the Second World War there was a labour shortage in Britain, so immigrants were welcomed. They came mainly from the COMMONWEALTH (especially the West Indies, India and Pakistan) and took mainly unskilled jobs. As Commonwealth citizens they were 'British subjects' who had a right of entry under the Nationality Act of 1948. Tensions arose as there were problems of assimilation for people of a different culture and in 1958 there were race riots against Afro-Caribbeans in Nottingham and in Notting Hill, London. As the number of immigrants shot up to 230,000 in 1960–1 (doubling the immigrant population) the Conservative government of Harold MACMILLAN passed the Commonwealth Immigrants Act in 1962, which severely restricted immigration. Commonwealth citizens could enter Britain only if they had a job to come to or had educational qualifications or

skills. Otherwise they could enter as part of a quota decided by the government. The LABOUR PARTY condemned the Act as racist because white immigrants were hardly affected (unskilled labour from Ireland lay outside the Act), but the British working class was enthusiastic, so when Labour was in power from 1964–70 it did not repeal the Act.

Harold WILSON's government reduced the immigrant quota to 8,500 a year in 1965 but passed the Race Relations Act to give coloured people redress from discrimination in housing and employment. Racial conflict, however, continued to grow. Enoch Powell, a leading Conservative, stoked the fires of racial unrest by a speech in Birmingham, in which he said, 'Like the Roman [Virgil] I seem to see the "River [Tiber] foaming with blood"'. Edward HEATH sacked Powell from his shadow cabinet but the tabloid press applauded the speech, which appealed to the large part of the British public which was deeply racist. Workers from the East End of London, dockers and porters from the Smithfield meat market, staged strikes and marched to Downing Street in support of Powell. The Labour government of Harold Wilson, frightened of losing votes, further tightened immigration controls in 1968 by restricting the entry of Kenyan Asians to those who had a 'patrial tie' to a British resident. More restrictions were placed on immigration in 1981 and in 1990 the British Nationality (Hong Kong) Act limited the number of Hong Kong residents who could become British citizens when HONG KONG RETURNED TO CHINA in 1997 to 225,000. The 1991 census, the first to ask about colour, showed a non-white population of under three million in Britain. A large part had been born there, so talk of repatriation, as the National Front demanded, was nonsensical. The younger generation speak with local accents and are better integrated than their parents because of their education, but racism persists.

Immigration and Social Policy in Britain, C. Jones (1977)

John Bull's Island: Immigration and British Society, 1871–1971, C. Holmes (1988)

'In Place of Strife' (1969)   A White Paper produced by Barbara Castle, the Employment Secretary in Harold WILSON's Labour government. There was growing concern in Britain at what appeared to be industrial anarchy as inter-union and unofficial strikes spread, a stark contrast to the codetermination (co-operation of unions and employers) which prevailed in the SOCIAL MARKET ECONOMY of West Germany and in Scandinavia. There was growing concern too about 'over-manning', restrictive practices and resistance to new technology by the unions. Between two and three million days were lost each year in strikes from 1963–7, a number which shot up to 4.7 million in 1968. 'Both the Government and the employers were in despair', Castle wrote. The CONSERVATIVE PARTY had proposed tough action against the unions, so Wilson wanted to pre-empt it. Castle courageously proposed to bring the law into labour relations for the first time since the General Strike of 1926 and was stepping in where Tory Ministers of Labour from 1951–64 had feared to tread. She proposed that TRADE UNIONS should hold pre-strike ballots, that the Secretary should be able to order a cooling-off period of 28 days before a strike and impose a settlement where an inter-union dispute led to an unofficial strike. An Industrial Relations Board would be set up to fine those who broke the law.

The proposals were popular with the public but unions were outraged at any legal interference in industrial relations and were supported by many Labour MPs, some of whom were sponsored by trade unions. The most disturbing feature for the Prime Minister was a divided cabinet. Jim CALLAGHAN, the Home Secretary, made himself the champion of the unions, the LABOUR PARTY's National Executive rejected the proposals by 16 votes to 5 and the Chief Whip said that he could not guarantee a majority for the Industrial Relations Bill in the Commons. Wilson and Castle were therefore forced to drop the bill. The failure of *In Place of Strife* was a humiliation for Wilson. He had admitted the need for reform and then shown that he could not implement it. His climb-down was seen as a complete surrender to the TUC (*The Economist* called it 'In Place of Government') and contributed to the defeat of the Labour Party in the 1970 election.

India, independence and partition of (1947)   The independence of India after the Second World War became certain with the Cripps mission of 1942. Singapore and Rangoon had fallen to the Japanese, who were approaching India's border. Sir Stafford Cripps was sent to obtain Indian collaboration in prosecuting the war and offered dominion status for India or independence at the end of the war. To gain Muslim support he said that any Indian states that did not want to join the union would have the right to opt out. The offer was rejected by Mohandas Gandhi as 'a post-dated cheque on a bank that was failing' and by the INDIAN NATIONAL CONGRESS because of the opt-out offer: it wanted a united India. Yet it was clear that the offer of independence could not be withdrawn and by the end of the war Britain had no intention of trying to maintain her position in India by force. 'Our time in India is limited', Lord Wavell, the Viceroy, wrote in his diary in October 1946, 'and our power to control events almost gone'.

The Muslim League had won all 30 of the seats reserved for Muslims, Congress winning 90 per cent of the other seats, in the elections of 1945–6. Discussions therefore took place between Jinnah, the League President, and Jawaharlal NEHRU about the form an independent India was to take. Although the League at its Lahore Conference in 1940 had called for a separate Muslim nation not subject to a permanent Hindu majority and Jinnah had said that Hindus and Muslims could never have 'a common nationality', partition was not inevitable. Jinnah put forward his 'minimum demand' in May 1946 for six Muslim provinces, which would be self-governing within a loose federation, except for defence and foreign affairs. This was unacceptable to Congress, which wanted a strong central government.

While the politicians disputed, INDIAN COMMUNAL MASSACRES began in August 1946 and threatened to make India ungovernable and turn into civil war. The British government, the Congress and the League all therefore hastened to break the deadlock. The British Prime Minister, Clement ATTLEE, replaced Wavell with Mountbatten, who insisted on a precise timetable for Britain's withdrawal in order to force the League and Congress to reach an agreement. Attlee announced that June 1948 was the last possible date. Mountbatten brought this forward to August 1947 and negotiated with Nehru and Jinnah to reach a final agreement. India would be divided, with a 'two-winged' Pakistan in the north-west and the north-east of the continent, separated by a thousand miles. Bengal and Punjab would themselves be divided between India and Pakistan. The princely states were advised to join India or Pakistan, Nehru making it clear that independent princely states within India would not be tolerated. The partition of India was a compromise which satisfied neither side. Jinnah had a 'moth-eaten' Pakistan; Congress did not have a united country. The communal massacres reached their peak with independence, as Hindus fled from Pakistan and Muslims from India, leaving a legacy of bitterness which still persists.

Myth and Reality: The Struggle for Freedom in India, 1945–47, A. K. Gupta (1987)
India's Struggle for Independence, B. Chandra et al. (1989)
Liberty or Death: India's Journey to Independence and Division, P. French (1997)

and rallies. The disturbances related to it became known in Calcutta as the 'Great Killing', as 5,000 people were killed in the next three days, 20,000 were injured and 100,000 were made homeless. Muslims began the action but, a minority in the city, they became in the end its main victims. The orgy of violence and terror spread to Dhaka in East Bengal and reprisals followed in Bihar. In East Bengal Muslims were the aggressors and Hindus their victims, a situation reversed in Bihar, where 7,000 Muslims were slaughtered. Communal riots spread to Bombay, the Malabar and Uttar Pradesh, but elsewhere there was little trouble.

Early in 1947 disturbances continued in Calcutta, Bengal and Bihar but the worst atrocities took place in the Punjab, where there was murder, arson and looting in all the major provincial cities for four months. Sikhs, faced with the prospect of Punjab being divided between India and Pakistan at independence, tried to drive Muslims out of East Punjab. The worst violence occurred after the INDEPENDENCE AND PARTITION OF INDIA in August 1947, when trainloads of refugees crossed the Indo-Pakistan border, Hindus fleeing from Pakistan, Muslims from India. The trains were attacked and their occupants murdered. The scale of the massacres caught the authorities by surprise: order was not restored until October. It is estimated that possibly a million people were massacred as five and a half million people moved each way across the border of West Pakistan and India. About one and a quarter million Hindus moved from East Pakistan to the safety of West Bengal. Thirty million Muslims (10 per cent of the population) remained in India.

Modern India 1885–1947, S. Sarkar (1983)
The Last Days of the Raj, T. Royle (1989)
Communal Riots in Bengal, 1905–1947, S. Das (1993)

Indian communal massacres (1946–7)
On 16 October 1946 the Muslim League called for a 'Direct Action Day' of strikes

Indian National Congress (INC)   The
main political party in India. It was formed in 1885 by a group of educated, high-caste

Indians, who wanted more Indian participation in the governing of their country. They were loyal to the British Raj and did not, at this stage, seek independence for India. Congress was more a debating society, which met annually, than a political party, had no mass support and had little appeal for Muslims. The INC adopted a more aggressive attitude when Gandhi became a dominant figure in 1919. Congress ceased to be an élite club and became a mass party with a constitution (1930), largely drawn up by Gandhi, which gave it the clear aim of *swaraj* (self-rule) and an effective organization, with a hierarchy of committees (district, provincial, All-India). It supported Gandhi's civil disobedience campaign, but when the government of India Act (1935) was passed it took part in the elections under the Act and won control of six out of the eleven British-ruled provinces. Congress, therefore, had considerable power at the provincial level in 1937, but at the beginning of the Second World War the government declared war on Germany without consulting Indian opinion. Congress was outraged, ordered all its provincial ministries to resign and demanded complete independence. In 1942 Congress's call for a 'Quit India' campaign led to the arrest of its prominent leaders and the banning of the Congress Party. The ban was lifted in 1944. Congress (and the Muslim League) negotiated with Britain from 1945–7 for the INDEPENDENCE OF INDIA and became by far the largest party in the new state.

The Congress ruled India without interruption from 1947 to 1977, in spite of a split in the party in 1969 between Indira GANDHI and the old guard led by Morarji Desai. In 1977 Congress was defeated for the first time in a general election but came back to power in 1980. It lost the 1989 election, won that of 1991 but suffered its worst electoral defeat in 1996, when it lost half its seats in parliament and came second to the right-wing Bharatiya Janata Party.

Congress has been in control for 44 of 49 years since independence (up to 1996). Since independence it has been an umbrella party, encompassing a wide range of opinions and interests. Internal conflicts were resolved (until 1969) by compromises until a consensus was reached. At the provincial level Congress sought to enlist the support of local notables and so was run by landlords, but it also appealed to people outside the political élite. As the party in power for so long it controlled a great deal of patronage and so attracted able careerists, who saw membership of Congress as a means of upward mobility. Congress was also helped by the divisions among its opponents. On the two occasions it was forced out of office it was replaced by coalitions which soon broke up because of their internal rivalries.

India's Struggle for Independence, B. Chandra et al. (1989)
The Politics of India Since Independence, P. R. Brass (1990)

Indochina war of independence (1946–54)

A war fought between the VIET MINH and the French. During the Second World War, when the Japanese occupied Indochina, HO CHI MINH formed the Viet Minh, a coalition of nationalist groups which waged guerrilla warfare against the Japanese in preparation for an independent Vietnam. When the war ended in 1945 the Viet Minh controlled much of the north: in September Ho proclaimed in Hanoi an independent Democratic Republic of Vietnam. DE GAULLE, however, was determined that the French Empire in Indochina should be restored. The war began in November 1946, when the French bombarded Hanoi and its port of Haiphong (causing 6,000 casualties), after the Viet Minh had rejected a French order to evacuate Hanoi.

The Viet Minh retired to the countryside, which they soon controlled, and the French were faced with a guerrilla war. As early as December 1946 General Leclerc realized that this was a war the French could not win. The Viet Minh received a great boost with the communist victory in the CHINESE CIVIL WAR (1946–9), as they now received artillery and anti-aircraft guns from across the border. When the KOREAN WAR (1950–3) began the US also became indirectly involved in the Indochina War, which they now saw not as a colonial war but as part of a worldwide struggle against communism. The US was soon paying 75 per cent of the French cost of the war. General GIAP, who had built up a force of 170,000, made a mass attack on the French in the Red River delta in 1951 but was heavily defeated. The French too were unsuccessful in their offensives, so sought to lure the Viet Minh into a frontal attack at DIEN BIEN PHU in 1954. This produced a French defeat and an end to the war, finally agreed at the GENEVA ACCORDS. 11,000 French troops and 77,000 Vietnamese serving with the French army were killed. Viet Minh losses are unknown but were possibly 200,000 dead. The end of French involvement in Indochina (Vietnam, Laos, Cambodia), had disastrous consequences, as French generals and politicians were determined that such a humiliation must not be allowed to happen again and so fought another prolonged and unsuccessful conflict in the ALGERIAN WAR OF INDEPENDENCE (1954–62).

The First Vietnam War, P. M. Dunn (1985)
The War in Indochina 1945–54, J. Dalloz (1990)

Indo-Pakistani wars (1947–9, 1965, 1971)
The INDEPENDENCE AND PARTITION OF INDIA left many problems unsolved, particularly that of Kashmir, which had a Hindu Maharajah, Hari Singh, but a mainly Muslim (77 per cent) population. Kashmir was vital to both India and Pakistan, as it controlled the headwaters of the Indus and its tributaries, which provided irrigation for the Punjab. India was anxious to prevent it falling into hostile hands also because its southern border was close to the Ganges plain, India's heartland, and NEHRU feared that the secession of Kashmir would encourage independence

movements in other parts of India: in the Punjab, Assam and Tamil Nadu. Hari Singh would probably have preferred independence but a Muslim revolt in southwest Kashmir in September 1947 was supported by Pakistan. The Maharajah saw this as a Muslim plot to depose him and so in October asked to join India. Indian troops pushed back a tribal invasion of Pathans and cleared the Vale of Kashmir before a cease-fire was established on the line of battle, leaving Azad Kashmir with 700,000 inhabitants under Pakistani control and 3.5 million in Indian-controlled Kashmir. Both sides agreed to a plebiscite in Kashmir to decide its future but Nehru always found an excuse not to hold one, as he feared that the Muslim majority would vote to join Pakistan.

The poor performance of India in the SINO-INDIAN DISPUTE (1962) and the death of Nehru in 1964 convinced AYUB KHAN of Pakistan that this was an opportune time to seize Kashmir. Fighting broke out in the desolate Rann of Kutch in 1965 and spread to Kashmir, so India widened the conflict by invading Pakistan and coming within a few miles of Lahore before the UNITED NATIONS organized a cease-fire sponsored by the US and Soviet Union. The Soviet Prime Minister, Alexei Kosygin, brought Ayub Khan and Lal Bahadur Shastri, the Indian Prime Minister, to Tashkent in January 1966 to sign a peace agreement. Both sides agreed to withdraw their forces behind the frontier that existed before the war.

The third Indo-Pakistani war took place in 1971 and resulted in the INDEPENDENCE OF BANGLADESH. The Indian victory was a grievous blow to Pakistan, which lost over half its population to the new nation. India has not fought any wars with Pakistan since then, but relations have remained tense.

The Origins of War in South Asia: Pakistan Conflicts Since 1947, S. Ganguly (1986)

INF (Intermediate Nuclear Force) Treaty (1987) Signed by President REAGAN and GORBACHEV. Unlike previous treaties, which simply imposed a limit on the number of nuclear weapons each side could have, the INF Treaty provided for the destruction of all intermediate range (from 500 to 5,500 km – 310 to 3,400 miles) land-based missiles and for on-site verification, which the Soviet Union had always opposed. As the USSR had more missiles in this category than the US, it had to destroy 1,752 SS-20s, the US 859 cruise missiles. This was the first agreement to eliminate a whole class of nuclear weapons, though it left the two powers with most of their nuclear arsenals intact: there was no agreement on reducing long-range missiles. British and French nuclear arsenals were not covered by the treaty.

information revolution   In 1946 the world's first digital computer filled a large room and could do little more than simple arithmetic. In the 1990s cheap toys are widely available which contain microchips with more computing power than the total of all the world's computers in the 1950s. The first microchip was developed in 1971. It had 2,300 transistors on it, and the pentium chip (common in late 1990s computers) has 5.5 million transistors. Silicon chips have been made with more than 20 million transistors in an area of less than 2 centimetres square, and new technologies being continually developed promise further miniaturizations.

With the increase in efficiency, miniaturization and fall in price has come a vast increase in use. In 1970 about 10,000 computers per year were sold worldwide: mostly mainframes produced by large companies in a market dominated by IBM. In 1994, 60 million were made and it is estimated that there will be a billion users worldwide by 2000, with the IT (information technology) industry accounting for 10 per cent of the world's GDP.

In offices and homes, computers and microchips have made considerable differences to people's lives. Electronic calculators appeared in the mid 1970s, and have rendered slide rules, log tables and complex calcula-

tions by hand obsolete. The first PC (personal computer) was launched by IBM in 1981. As well as computers, offices have seen the introduction of fax machines for instant communication of documents, the opportunity for holding audio and videoconferences instead of travelling to meetings, and the virtual disappearance of typewriters. Word processing software makes the drafting and redrafting of any document possible without retyping, and simple production of a final version with a wide choice of designs. Spreadsheets allow complex numerical calculations and financial projections to be done and updated instantly, and databases allow storage and easy retrieval of large volumes of structured information.

In banking and finance, instant communication between computers anywhere in the world has far-reaching consequences. In the FINANCIAL REVOLUTION, actions and information in one part of the world can now trigger immediate responses many thousands of miles away. Money moves between individuals, companies, countries and continents electronically. Most individuals' bank balances are only numbers in a computer, and many transactions from these accounts are done automatically without any human intervention. This includes obtaining cash from machines, and the widespread payment of salaries directly into employees' accounts. The number of staff employed by banks is therefore diminishing.

In the 1940s a radio (or 'wireless') was a large mains- powered item of furniture and apart from the telephone was the only way live information and entertainment came into people's homes. Television broadcasting started in the late 1930s, but was still a rarity in the UK in 1950; by 1961, 75 per cent of families had a television. In the USA there were 70 million TV sets in 1965 and 195 million in 1986. Colour was introduced in the 1960s, and the number of channels available to most viewers continues to increase. Widely available video recording has been possible since the early 1980s. TV has become the major way in which people receive entertainment, and an important one for receiving information and education. Three ways of delivering TV have been available since the early 1990s: the long-established terrestrial broadcast via transmitters and aerials; by bouncing signals off orbiting satellites which are received with special dish aerials; and through optical fibre cables connected directly to households. In a growing convergence with computer technology, international standards for digital transmission were approved in 1996 and it is scheduled to start before the end of the 1990s. This will afford the opportunity to receive many more channels, and allow 'interactive TV' where two way transfer of information becomes possible.

In 1969 the US Department of Defense started to link certain computers together in a way which would still function in the event of a nuclear strike to any one part of the network. This system grew in an uncoordinated way, and computer experts and academic centres started to join the network. The overall structure became commonly known as the 'internet' in the 1980s, and is also called the 'information superhighway' and 'cyberspace'. By 1994 it was readily accessible to anybody with a PC and telephone line, and an estimated 350 million computers were linked to it in 1995. Its main use is transmission of e-mail, which is electronic text and computer files. This is normally done in a much shorter time than postal mail, and for home or small business users the cost is normally that of a local phone call to send e-mail to any computer in the world that is also connected to the internet.

Another widespread use is the 'World Wide Web', which has developed since 1994. This is a way of gaining access to the information on many millions of 'Websites'. In 1997 the number of web pages was estimated at 700 million. They are used by commercial companies to demonstrate and explain their products, by government departments to give information, by academic institutions to publicize and disseminate their work, by pressure groups and charitable causes to campaign on a variety of issues and by individuals.

SPACE EXPLORATION laid the basis for a global system of telecommunications by using satellites. The first purpose-built communications satellite was launched in 1962. In the 1990s plans were well advanced for a series of up to 800 Low Earth Orbiting satellites, which will make possible a single worldwide net for radio telephony, video transmission and multimedia communication.

High-Tech Society: The Story of the IT Revolution, T. Forester (1987)
The Telecommunications Revolution, H. M. Sapolsky et al. (eds) (1992)
Road Warriors: Dreams and Nightmares Along the Information Highway, D. Burstein and D. Kline (1995)

international debt   A problem on a massive scale as a result of the OPEC PRICE RISE of 1973, which quadrupled oil prices and led to a worldwide recession with high inflation, falling production and rising unemployment. All countries, rich and poor, were affected by it but it was the countries of the THIRD WORLD which suffered most, as commodity prices fell on world markets just when they needed exports to pay for the escalating costs of their imports. The OPEC price rise produced enormous surpluses for the Middle Eastern oil states which were deposited in European and North American banks, so money was available to finance the deficits of debtor countries. In 1970 only 12 countries had debts of over $1 billion and none owed over $10 billion. By 1990 the three giants of international debt in Latin America – Brazil, Mexico and Argentina – all had debts of between $60 billion and $100 billion: 28 countries owed $10 billion dollars each. The WORLD BANK counted only 7 out of 96 'low' and 'middle economies' which had foreign debts of less than $1 billion. The relatively most indebted countries were in Sub-Saharan Africa, but the greatest volume of debt (60 per cent of the whole in 1980) was in Latin America, where debt had risen from $2–3 billion in 1970 to $340 billion in 1983, when foreign debt was 47 per cent of the region's GNP: annual interest payments were over a third of the value of its exports.

Following a further rise in oil prices in 1979 the US and Britain decided to restrict the money supply and credit in order to bring inflation under control. This produced another world wide recession, as interest rates moved upwards until developing countries could not meet their interest payments. In August 1982 the Mexican government announced that it could not pay the interest on its foreign debt. It was shortly followed by nearly all Latin American countries and by others in Africa and Asia. The capitalist system faced its worst crisis since 1929, as its banking system was on the verge of collapse. To avoid this debtor countries needed more loans for investment and to service their debt, but the IMF insisted on austerity programmes (which further depressed their economies) to cut inflation and made these a precondition of new loans. As debts were rescheduled (i.e. unpaid interest was added to the capital already loaned) and new loans made, debt continued to rise at the rate of 9 per cent a year. By 1987 Latin America was a net exporter of capital to the industrial nations, having already paid to banks $121.1 billion, more than the total amount it had borrowed from 1974–81 ($100.7 billion). This helped to finance the enormous budget deficit in the US, caused by President REAGAN's arms expenditure and his unwillingness to raise taxes. When some countries tried to limit the payment of interest, as President García did in Peru in 1985, so that social welfare would not have to be cut catastrophically, the US suspended aid and the IMF declared Peru 'ineligible' for futher funds. By the end of his term of office the country was near to collapse with inflation at 2,700 per cent a year. Peru then had to accept IMF austerity measures. Brazil declared a moratorium on interest payments in 1987 but had to abandon it a year later. Debt was a great burden too in Africa and South Asia. In 1990 30.9 per cent

of Indonesian exports went to service its foreign debt, 26.8 per cent in India, 24.5 per cent in Bangladesh. Africa, which owed less than 10 per cent of total foreign debt, accounted for 40 per cent of unpaid arrears.

There appeared to be no way out of the debt crisis except to write off all or part of the debt and to provide capital for investment rather than for paying the interest on the old debt, but banks were reluctant to do this. One result of the debt crisis was to widen the NORTH–SOUTH DIVIDE.

The International Debt Crisis in Historical Perspective, B. Eichengreen and P. Lindert (eds) (1989)

Debt and Democracy in Latin America, B. Stallings and R. Kaufmann (eds) (1989)

Developing Country Debt and Economic Performance, J. Sachs (ed.) (1989)

Intifada (Arabic: uprising) (1987–93)

Violent demonstrations against the Israeli occupation of the WEST BANK and Gaza. There were 1.8 million Palestinians in these areas, where spontaneous, popular disturbances began in 1987. There was peaceful disobedience of the Israeli authorities and some stone-throwing by youths at security forces. Both the Israelis and the PLO were caught by surprise. To control the situation the Israelis had to commit a large number of troops, whose harsh treatment of protesters was shown on television and was condemned internationally. The PLO, then based in Tunis, and the MUSLIM BROTHERHOOD in the OCCUPIED TERRITORIES gave support and in early 1988 the secular PLO and Islamist factions such as HAMAS and Islamic Jihad co-operated to form co-ordinating committees to direct the movement. Israel's response – curfews, arrests, house searches and demolitions – further alienated the population and provided increased support for the Intifada. In the first four years over 1,000 Palestinians were killed (250 of them children), 120,000 wounded, 16,000 were imprisoned without trial and tens of thousands were jailed by military courts. Over 200 Israelis were also killed.

The Intifada brought about important changes in the Middle East. King HUSSEIN of Jordan gave up his claim to the West Bank in 1988 and the PLO called for the establishment of a Palestinian state in the West Bank and Gaza based on Resolution 242 of the UNITED NATIONS. Public opinion in the US for the first time became sympathetic to the Palestinians and supported such a move, as did many Israelis. The inability of the Israelis to stop the violence persuaded them to seek a negotiated settlement with the PLO about Gaza and the West Bank. An agreement was reached in 1993 in the Oslo Accords, since when the violence has been much reduced. Hamas, which opposed a negotiated settlement, simply transferred its murderous activities to Israel itself.

Intifada: Palestine at a Crossroads, R. Heacock and J. Nassar (1990)
Intifada: The Palestinian Uprising, D. Peretz (1990)

IRA (Irish Republican Army)   A terrorist organization fighting for a united, republican Ireland. Originally created by Fenians in the USA, it was revived in 1919 as a successor to the paramilitary Irish Volunteers. Its object was to use armed force to end British rule in Ireland and establish a republic. The same aim was followed politically by Sinn Fein. After the Anglo-Irish Treaty (1921) which set up an Irish Free State and a separate Northern Ireland, the IRA split between those who accepted the Treaty and those who did not. They fought each other in the Irish Civil War (1922–3) and thereafter the IRA sought to force Northern Ireland into a union with the South. In 1956 the IRA began an abortive campaign in the North waged by guerrilla units from the South but they were driven out by the RUC (Royal Ulster Constabulary) and a mainly hostile population and in 1962 it called off its campaign. It then tried political rather than military means to bring

about unification and had nothing to do with the riots and demonstrations of 1968 which began the TROUBLES. Like the Northern Irish government it was taken by surprise. It waged a violent campaign against the British army and RUC from 1968, but in May 1972 unilaterally declared a cease-fire, as violence impeded working-class solidarity. Since then the Official IRA has played little part in the Troubles and has not been a security threat.

Some members of the Official IRA who opposed the cease-fire broke away to form the INLA (Irish National Liberation Army) in December 1974. They formed a small group (police estimates put them at under 100) but they were the most uncompromising and ruthless of all terrorist groups. They suffered seriously from informers in the early 1980s and from internecine feuds from 1986.

The most important splinter-group from the IRA was the Provisional IRA, formed in December 1969, as it did not believe that the Official IRA was doing enough to protect the Catholic community in the North (40 per cent of the population there). Its name was derived from the provisional government of the Republic proclaimed at the start of the Easter Rising in 1916: any government, it maintained, would be provisional until Ireland was united. At first its main object was to protect the Catholic ghettos of West Belfast attacked by Protestant mobs and its members were from the ghettos, organized on a neighbourhood basis. This was open to infiltration by informers, so from the mid-1970s a cellular system was introduced. The Provisionals organized Catholics in mass demonstrations in the early years but later concentrated on bomb attacks on the government and security forces to destabilize the North and secure a British withdrawal. After Bloody Sunday (30 January 1972), when British paratroops shot and killed 13 unarmed demonstrators in Londonderry, car bombs were their main weapon. There were 1,400 explosions in 1972 and 500 bombs were defused. Much of the explosive used was home-made from agricultural fertilizers: this had a low explosive power so large bombs (of 1,000 pounds), which could be delivered only by vehicles, were often used. 'Spectaculars' were their aim – explosions which caused widespread devastation and/or loss of life which would draw international attention to the IRA. One such attack was in October 1984 at the CONSERVATIVE PARTY conference at Brighton, where an IRA bomb in the hotel where Margaret THATCHER and most of her cabinet were staying almost succeeded in killing the Prime Minister: five people were killed and thirty injured. By this time the Provisional IRA had become the most sophisticated and experienced terrorist group in Western Europe. The connection between the Provisional IRA and its political wing, Sinn Fein, was made clear in 1981 when Sinn Fein's publicity director, Danny Morrison, asked at the Party Conference: 'Will anyone here object if, with a ballot paper in this hand and an Armalite in this hand, we take power in Ireland?' Sinn Fein raised funds for the IRA, in the US through Noraid.

In the 1980s there was stalemate in Northern Ireland: neither the IRA nor the British could win a military victory. A breakthrough seemed possible with the Downing Street Declaration signed by John MAJOR, the British Prime Minister, and Albert Reynolds, the Irish Taoiseach, in December 1993, which offered to include Sinn Fein in talks about Northern Ireland's future if IRA violence ended. The IRA declared a cease-fire in August 1994 but progress thereafter was painfully slow. The British government claimed that the IRA had not renounced violence permanently, then in 1995 it demanded that the IRA should hand in some of its weapons as a precondition of all-party talks. This was seen by many as a delaying tactic (Major, with a wafer-thin majority, needed the votes of the Ulster Unionist Party in the House of Commons). The IRA cease-fire ended early in 1996 with another 'spectacular', a massive bomb which caused extensive damage in London's dockland. It was an act of frustration which threatened to derail the peace process, popular throughout the North, and alienated

those who supported it – the Irish government, President CLINTON and the SDLP. Tony BLAIR was determined to revive negotiations for a peace settlement in Northern Ireland when he became Prime Minister in 1997. The IRA responded by announcing another cease-fire in July.

The Provisional IRA, P. Bishop and E. Mallie (1987)
The Politics of Illusion: A Political History of the IRA, H. Patterson (1989)
Provos: The IRA and Sinn Fein, P. Taylor (1997)

Iran–Contra affair (1985–6)   The secret sale of arms to Iran in the hope of securing the release of American hostages in Lebanon: part of the profits was used to provide military aid to the CONTRAS in Nicaragua. Between August 1985 and October 1986 National Security Council Aide Lt.-Col. Oliver North, with the approval of his superior Vice-Admiral John H. Poindexter and the director of the CIA, William Casey, arranged to sell to Iran via Israel $48 million worth of arms and to transfer some of the profits to the Contras, though the Boland Amendment of October 1984, passed by Congress, made this illegal. When an Arab journalist gave some details of the arms sales in 1986 President REAGAN denied a third country had been involved and said 'no US law has been or will be violated' and that 'our policy of not making concessions to terrorists remains intact'. He denied any knowledge of the profits from the arms sales being used to fund the Contras. On 25 November 1986 the President dismissed Poindexter and North because of 'serious questions of propriety,' though he hailed North as 'an American hero'. A congressional committee conducted hearings in 1987 which were broadcast on television and aroused as much interest as WATERGATE. It concluded that the administration had produced 'confusion and disarray at the highest levels of government' and that the President had abdicated his 'moral and legal responsibility to take care that the laws be faithfully executed'. In 1989 Poindexter and North were found guilty of misleading Congress but their convictions were overturned on appeal in 1990. For the President the affair was disastrous, as his reputation was badly damaged and his relations with Congress and with his NATO allies were soured.

Firewall: The Iran – Counter Conspiracy and Cover-up, L. E. Walsh (1997)

Iran hostage crisis (4 November 1979–20 January 1981)

When President CARTER allowed MUHAMMAD RIZA PAHLAVI to enter the US for treatment for cancer, student militants stormed the US embassy in Tehran, seizing 69 hostages and embassy documents. When Ayatollah KHOMEINI endorsed their action the government of Mehdi Bazargan resigned. Iran demanded that the Shah should be handed over for trial and that his wealth should be returned: Carter imposed economic sanctions on Iran and froze Iranian assests. 16 female and black hostages were released in December 1979. An attempt to rescue the rest was abandoned, to the acute embarrassment of the Carter administration, when three helicopters broke down. In September 1980 Iran sought talks because of the deteriorating relations with Iraq which resulted in the Iran–Iraq war (1980–8) but they dragged on: failure to secure the release of the hostages by November may have lost Carter the presidential election. Helped by Algerian mediation, Iran's assets were unblocked and the hostages released on the day of President REAGAN's inauguration.

Iran–Iraq war (1980–8)

The origins of the war lay in a border dispute. SADDAM HUSSEIN rejected the Algiers agreement which he had made with MUHAMMAD RIZA PAHLAVI and which fixed the boundary between Iran and Iraq as he felt it was too favourable to Iran, but a wider issue was that of regional hegemony. Iraq wanted to be the dominant power in the Gulf and saw its opportunity in the IRANIAN REVOLUTION (1979) which brought the Ayatollah KHOMEINI to power, as the Iranian army was purged of the former Shah's supporters. Border incidents and Iranian appeals to Iraq's SHII majority (55 per cent of the population) to rise up and overthrow the secular dictatorship of Saddam Hussein were followed by Iraq's invasion of Iran.

At first Iraq did well, capturing 8,000 square miles (21,000 sq km) of Iran's oil-rich province of Khuzestan, but the predominatly Arab population there did not rise up to support Iraq. By March 1981 Iran had halted the Iraqi advance and in 1982 the war could have ended, as Iraq proposed a truce in June and offered to withdraw all Iraqi troops from Iran. The Ayatollah Khomeini rejected this and demanded that Saddam Hussein be removed from power, so the war continued. An Iranian offensive in 1982 pushed Iraqi troops out of Iran and in 1983 Iraq was invaded. A stalemate then developed, which resembled the trench warfare of the First World War. Each year Iran launched a 'final offensive' using human wave assaults of teenagers but did not break through Iraq's defences. Iraq, with fewer resources and a smaller population than Iran, survived because Kuwait and other GULF STATES gave it financial support: Egypt and Jordan provided limited military help. Syria and Libya, Algeria and South Yemen were Arab states which supported Iran. The major powers too were on Iraq's side: the Soviet Union, which had cut off military supplies to Iraq at the beginning of the war, resumed them in 1982; France supplied warplanes and missiles, the US naval support. Each side attacked the other's oil fields. Iraq's, near the war front, suffered a marked drop in production, a situation made worse in 1982 when Syria closed Iraq's oil pipeline across Syria to the Mediterranean. The last phase of the war began in 1987. Following another failed Iranian offensive, Iraq recovered lost territory, made Scud missile attacks on Iranian cities and used chemical warfare. Khomeini realized that the Iranian people were war-weary and that the mass support for his regime would be eroded if the war continued. In July 1988 Iran accepted a UNITED NATIONS resolution for a cease-fire: 'accepting this', said the Ayatollah Khomeini, 'was more deadly for me than taking poison'. There was no final settlement until 1990 when Iraq, after its invasion of Kuwait which began the GULF WAR, accepted Iran's terms for peace based on the position before the war (i.e. acceptance of the Algiers agreement).

Neither side had gained from the war in which, according to conservative Western estimates, 367,000 had been killed and over 700,000 wounded. The Stockholm International Peace Research Institute said that the war had cost Iran up to $100 billion and Iraq $150 billion and had devastated the economies of both countries. The oil production of Iran and Iraq was greatly reduced but this did not affect the world price of oil, which fell for most of the war. One beneficiary of the war was Egypt. Isolated in the Arab world after SADAT made peace with Israel in 1979, its support for Iraq helped it to recover prestige: in 1987 most Arab states agreed to restore diplomatic relations with Egypt.

Iran and Iraq at War, S. Chubin and C. Tripp (1988)

The Iran–Iraq War: Impact and Implications, E. Karsh (ed.) (1989)

The Longest War: The Iran–Iraq Military Conflict, D. Hiro (1991)

Iran, Islamic Republic of (1979–)   The first time in the modern world that religious leaders have overthrown a secular regime and established a theocracy. After the fall of MUHAMMAD RIZA PAHLAVI in the IRANIAN REVOLUTION (1978–9) a referendum in March 1979 gave overwhelming support for the establishment of an Islamic Republic. At first laymen held important posts, but after the dismissal of President Bani-Sadr in 1981 clerics held all the highest positions. The first

Prime Minister appointed by Ayatollah KHOMEINI was a devout layman, Mehdi Bazargan, but new revolutionary organizations sprang up spontaneously and, supported by Khomeini, took over the work of government institutions. Armed revolutionary committees gained control of the towns, arrested members of the former regime and confiscated their property. Revolutionary courts replaced ordinary courts and executed members of the hated Savak (security police) and army officers, creating, according to Bazargan, 'instability, terror, uneasiness and fear' in 'shameful' trials. Revolutionary Guards, the most important of the new institutions, provided a military force parallel to that of the army but under clerical control. The Islamic Republican Party (IRP), directed by radical *ulama* (religious leaders), was the most influential party in shaping the Islamic Republic (most other parties were closed down). A Revolutionary Council, appointed by Khomeini, duplicated the work of the cabinet and challenged its authority. Bazargan could give orders but they were ignored, so that he likened his government to 'a knife without a blade'. It fell in November 1979, weakened by the IRAN HOSTAGE CRISIS.

A new constitution in November 1979 consolidated the control of the SHII clergy over the country. All laws were to be based on Islam and a Council of Guardians was set up to veto any which were not. A supreme guide, *vali faqih*, was leader of the nation and controlled all important civil, military, judicial and religious appointments. Khomeini was named *vali faqih* for life. The constitution also contained an injunction to 'extend the sovereignty of God's law throughout the world', an indication that the religious radicals saw their revolution as a model for other countries. All institutions – army, civil service, universities – were purged and Islamized, religious commissars being appointed to the army to maintain ideological purity. Alcohol, gambling and contraceptives were banned, women judges and lawyers dismissed. From 1983 an Islamic code was enforced, with the amputation of a hand for theft, flogging for fornication and drinking alcohol, stoning to death for adultery. There was strong opposition to the creation of a theocracy, even from within the religious establishment. The most serious opposition, however, came from the left, which had united with religious radicals in 1978 in opposition to the Shah. From 1981 the *Mujahidin e-Khalq* fought on the streets with Revolutionary Guards, killed leaders of the IRP when their headquarters was bombed and assassinated President Rajai with another bomb. A ruthless reign of terror, in which at least 13,000 were killed and which lasted for 18 months, enabled the government to eliminate its critics.

The formation of the Islamic Republic of Iran was a momentous event which sent shock waves throughout the world. By freeing Iran from superpower dominance and providing a Third Way of Islam, as an alternative to capitalism and communism, it enjoyed great prestige in the THIRD WORLD. The fear of Iran exporting its revolution affected Middle Eastern politics for over a decade, as it posed a threat to conservative monarchies such as Saudi Arabia and to secular regimes in Egypt, Syria and Iraq. Iran's association with the hostage-taking of HIZBULLAH in the LEBANESE CIVIL WAR made President REAGAN identify Iran with worldwide terrorism and revolution, a reputation it has not yet discarded.

The Reign of the Ayatollahs, S. Bakhash (1985)
The Iranian Revolution and the Islamic Republic, N. R. Keddie and E. Hooglund (eds) (1986)
The Turban for the Crown: The Islamic Revolution in Iran, S. A. Arjomand (1988)

Iranian revolution (1978–9) Brought about the fall of MUHAMMAD RIZA PAHLAVI and the Pahlavi dynasty and the establishment of the ISLAMIC REPUBLIC OF IRAN. In 1977 the Shah seemed secure. He had an army of 400,000, a feared and efficient

secret police, Savak, controlled the mass media and had the suport of the superpowers. Yet below the surface there was considerable discontent. Religious leaders disapproved of his secular regime, the bazaar merchants felt threatened by the rise of modern industry and Iranians generally disliked the 150,000 expensive foreigners brought in to run high-technology industries, and the Shah's subservience to the US. Conditions for a revolution were created by the rapid expansion of towns (the population of Tehran rose from two million in 1960 to four and a half million in 1979), whose services broke down as immigrants, unskilled and often unemployed, poured in from the countryside to live in overcrowded and insanitary slums.

Protests against the Shah's dictatorship and the extravagance of the court began in 1977 among the middle class and university students, but the nature of the protest changed in January 1978, when there were riots in Qum after an attack on the Ayatollah KHOMEINI in a government newspaper. These were led by clerics, spread throughout the country and demanded not reform but revolution: the overthrow of the Shah and the establishment of an Islamic state. Troops fired on demonstrators and a cycle of rioting began. On 7 September half a million people marched in Tehran chanting 'Death to the Shah' and 'Khomeini is our leader'. Martial law was declared and a day later 4,000 were killed by troops who fired from tanks and helicopter gunships on a crowd of 75,000. In October a wave of strikes by workers in the oil industry, government factories, banks and newspapers paralysed the economy. The Shah abandoned repression after the greatest protest march of all, when in December up to two million people in Tehran converged on the Shahyad monument, which the Shah had built to commemorate 2,500 years of the Persian monarchy, to demand the end of that monarchy. On 16 January 1979 the Shah left Iran. Khomeini returned from exile on 1 February to an ecstatic welcome and announced the foundation of an Islamic state.

The revolution was an urban phenomenon: riots and demonstrations took place in every town, though the villages were scarcely affected. A key role was played by the mosques and Muslim associations: it was these which relayed tapes of Khomeini's speeches and organized the demonstrations, but it was Khomeini's leadership which was decisive. He had been the most persistent and virulent critic of the Shah for over 20 years and dominated the revolution from his exile in Iraq and later Paris.

Roots of Revolution: An Interpretive History of Modern Iran, N. R. Keddie (1981)
The Pride and the Fall, A. Parsons (1984)
The Turban for the Crown: The Islamic Revolution in Iran, S. A. Arjomand (1988)

Islamic fundamentalists   Muslims who seek to apply strictly the articles of their faith as expressed in the Quran, the *hadith* (traditions of the Prophet Muhammad) and the *Sharia* (Islamic law). The movements they formed are not a new phenomenon. In the nineteenth century Islamic fundamentalists created new states: Samori in West Africa, the Fulani in Nigeria, the Wahabis in Arabia and the Mahdi in the Sudan. In the twentieth century, especially after 1923, when Kemal Atatürk made Turkey a republic and abolished the caliphate a year later, secular regimes took over in many Muslim countries and established legal and educational systems based on Western models. After the Second World War secular regimes proliferated in the Islamic world: NASSER in Egypt, ASAD in Syria, Saddam HUSSEIN in Iraq, MUHAMMAD RIZA PAHLAVI in Iran, Boumédienne in Algeria and BOURGUIBA in Tunisia. Islamic fundamentalists appeared to have been marginalized, in spite of the influence of the MUSLIM BROTHERHOOD in Egypt and its spread to other countries.

A turning-point came in the SIX DAY WAR (1967). The comprehensive and humiliating defeat of the Arabs, with the loss of Jerusalem (Islam's second holiest city), Sinai, the Gaza Strip, the WEST BANK and GOLAN HEIGHTS was a devastating blow to Islamic pride. The nationalist and secular regimes were blamed for neglecting their Islamic heritage and were discredited. The belief became more widespread that Western values should be rejected and that Islam provided a self-sufficient ideology, an alternative to nationalism, capitalism and atheistic communism. A second momentous event, which did more than anything else to promote the revival of Islamic fundamentalism, was the IRANIAN REVOLUTION (1979) and the foundation of the ISLAMIC REPUBLIC OF IRAN. For the first time in the modern world a theocratic state existed. Although Iran is a SHII country, the shock waves affected SUNNI Islam, threatening all secular regimes and even traditionalist monarchies (often regarded as fundamentalist) such as that in Saudi Arabia, which was allied to the 'Great Satan' (US).

Islamic fundamentalism was seen in the West as aggressive and expansionist when, in the early 1980s, President Khamenei in Iran called on prayer leaders in 40 countries to turn their mosques into military bases and 'prepare the ground for the creation of Islamic governments in all countries'. Ayatollah KHOMEINI's *fatwa* (decree) in the RUSHDIE AFFAIR, when he sentenced the British author to death for his book *Satanic Verses*, confirmed this perception. Islamic fundamentalists were identified in the West with terrorism. The taking of hostages by HIZBULLAH during the LEBANESE CIVIL WAR, the bombing of the World Trade Centre in New York in March 1993, the attacks on European tourists in Egypt and the murder of opponents of Islamists in Algeria all caused widespread revulsion and condemnation in the West. Islamists responded by accusing the West of hypocrisy and moral bankruptcy. Why, they asked, did the US and European countries, all democracies, refuse to support the democratic elections in Algeria in 1992 which would have brought the ISLAMIC SALVATION FRONT (FIS) to power but which were overturned by the military. They accused the West of supporting autocratic, unrepresentative regimes, such as those in Saudi Arabia and the GULF STATES, in order to guarantee their supplies of oil. Western hypocrisy was never more clearly exposed than in the AFGHAN CIVIL WAR, when the US, hostile to Islamic fundamentalism, supplied fundamentalist groups with money and arms after the SOVIET INVASION OF AFGHANISTAN, as a short-term expedient in the COLD WAR against the Soviet Union.

Terrorist acts always hit the headlines in Western newspapers, as did attempts to remove features of modern life associated with the West: cinemas, night clubs, dancing, alcohol, drugs. Much more important was the way that Islamic fundamentalism was, without violence, becoming part of the mainstream of Islamic society in nearly every Muslim country. *Dawa* (call) societies worked in the social services (setting up hospitals and legal-aid societies), in the economy (establishing Islamic banks, investment houses and insurance companies), in education (founding schools and child care centres) and in broadcasting. In Egypt under MUBARAK the Muslim Brotherhood controlled professional organizations and provided social services for the poor.

The Islamic Threat: Myth or Reality?, J. L. Esposito (1992)
Islamic Fundamentalism, A. S. Sidahmed and A. Ehteshami (eds) (1997)
Spokesmen for the Despised: Fundamentalist Leaders of the Middle East, R. S. Appleby (ed.) (1997)

Islamic Salvation Front (FIS: *Front Islamique du Salut*) Algerian political party, formed in 1989, which became the biggest challenge to the FLN (National Liberation Front), which had ruled Algeria since independence in 1962. The FIS demanded a return to strict Islamic values and had its greatest support among the urban poor in the inner-city slums, as it provided social services which the government did not pro-

vide. Rioting in October 1988, caused by the high prices and shortages which the government's austerity programme brought about, began in Algiers and spread along the Mediterranean coast, where most of the population lived. As a result, the government conceded multiparty local government elections in June 1990, in which the FIS (with 54 per cent of the vote) did much better than the FLN (with 28 per cent) and took control of many towns.

There was a massive military crackdown in June 1991 against FIS leaders, several of whom were imprisoned, but this did not diminish their appeal. In the first national elections in December 1991 the FIS (with 47 per cent of the vote) won 188 of the 198 seats contested for a 430-seat parliament. A second round of voting, where there had been no overall majority, was to take place in January 1992 but the army cancelled it, annulled the elections to prevent the FIS gaining control and banned the FIS. The 1992 military repression radicalized the Islamic movement further. A spate of terrorist attacks began on the security forces, government officials and judges and spread to civilians, particularly journalists, and foreigners, so that many countries (including France and Britain) advised their nationals to leave Algeria. Many of these attacks were carried out by an ISLAMIC FUNDAMENTALIST group named the GIA (*Groupe Islamique Armée*): it is not clear whether the FIS supported the GIA. Thousands of militants were killed by the security forces, accused by AMNESTY INTERNATIONAL of using torture and of systematically killing suspects, but this did not prevent Islamists from controlling some towns. It was estimated in 1997 that 50,000 had been killed in the civil war since 1992. Secular opposition parties insist that the FIS should be part of a political solution to end the civil war.

The Islamic Threat: Myth or Reality?, J. L. Esposito (1992)
Modern Algeria, J. Ruedy (1992)

Israel, birth of   The Jews had settled in their promised land about 1200 BC but in 70 AD, after a revolt against the Romans, their temple in Jerusalem was burnt down and after a second revolt in 135 AD they were scattered throughout the world in the Diaspora, without a homeland but retaining their identity as Jews and hoping to return one day to Palestine and to their holy city of Jerusalem. There was considerable anti-Semitism and persecution of the Jews in the nineteenth century, particularly in Russia and Eastern Europe, and this prompted Theodor Herzl to call a World Zionist Congress in 1897 which declared that 'ZIONISM aspires to create a publicly guaranteed homeland for the Jewish people in the land of Israel'. This hope was encouraged by the Balfour Declaration (1917), which said that the British government favoured the establishment of a national home for the Jews in Palestine. When Britain was granted Palestine, territory west of the river Jordan, as a mandate by the League of Nations in 1920, the Balfour Declaration was included in the mandate.

The Arabs did not accept the mandate and immediately began attacks on Jews, who responded by forming their own defence force, the Haganah. The increase in Jewish immigration after Hitler came to power in Germany in 1933 led to an Arab revolution in 1936. The Arabs regarded the Jewish problem as a European one, caused by persecution of the Jews in Europe, and bitterly rejected the use of their land to solve the problem. In 1937 the British government set up a commission of inquiry under Lord Peel, which concluded that the interests of the two sides could not be reconciled and that the mandate was unworkable. He recommended the formation of both an Arab and a Jewish state in Palestine, with a small area around Jerusalem remaining under British control. Both Arabs and Jews rejected this idea. As war in Europe drew nearer the British government came down on the side of the Arabs in its White Paper of May 1939. This proposed the creation of an independent state of Pales-

tine within ten years and the limitation of Jewish immigration to 15,000 each year for the next five years, after which there was to be no immigration at all 'unless the Arabs of Palestine are prepared to acquiesce in it'. As Arabs were two-thirds of the population, the Jews did not want an independent state in which they would be a minority and so rejected the White Paper. When the Second World War began the Jews were in a dilemma. Most felt that they should support Britain against their common enemy Germany but the Stern Gang, a Jewish terrorist organization, did not take this view and attacked both Arab and British targets.

When the war ended BEN-GURION and Haganah began to strike at British communications and to bring in illegal Jewish immigrants. Irgun Zvai Leumi went further and attacked British personnel, blowing up the British headquarters at the King David Hotel in Jerusalem and killing over 90 people in July 1946. Ernest BEVIN, British Foreign Secretary, decided to withdraw from Palestine because of terrorist attacks and the cost of military operations there. In February 1947 he referred the matter to the UNITED NATIONS, which in November approved of partition into three areas: a Jewish state, an Arab state and an international zone around Jerusalem. Both the USSR and US supported this and the Jews welcomed it, but the Arabs regarded it as a grossly unfair settlement, as the 600,000 Jews in Palestine, who held 10.6 per cent of the land, were allotted 56.5 per cent of Palestine as their new state. The 1.3 million Arabs, holding 89.4 per cent of the land, were granted 43.5 per cent. Britain declared that its mandate would end on 15 May 1948. On 14 May Ben-Gurion proclaimed the state of Israel.

The first of the ARAB–ISRAELI WARS began in November 1947 with Arab attacks on Jewish settlements. Haganah defended them and did not move onto the offensive until March 1948. In April Irgun massacred all the inhabitants of an Arab village at DEIR YASSIN, which led to vast numbers of Arabs fleeing from Palestine. The Arab states of Egypt, Syria, Iraq and Lebanon rejected partition and joined in the war in May 1948 but they disagreed among themselves. ABDULLAH, King of Transjordan, wanted to incorporate Arab Palestine into his own kingdom, a move opposed by other Arab states. They had no agreed plan and fought as separate armies, though the numbers involved were small. The Arab states together provided only 21,500 troops; the Israelis had about 50,000. Both sides were poorly equipped, at first lacking armour, artillery and aircraft, so the war was basically an infantry conflict. The balance tipped in Israel's favour in 1948 as it received clandestine arms, including tanks and aircraft, from Czechoslovakia. In July Israel seized control of Galilee and in October the Negev and the port of Eilat: Israel finally defeated Egypt in January 1949. Meanwhile, Abdullah's Arab Legion had seized much of Arab Palestine and the old city of Jerusalem (the new city was held by the Israelis). The war did not end with a peace treaty but with armistices (between February and July 1949) which drastically changed the UN partition plan. There was no new Arab state for the Palestinians: most of Arab Palestine was divided between Transjordan and Israel (Egypt controlled the Gaza Strip). Israel held 75 per cent of Palestine, nearly a third more than the territory allocated by the UN. 700,000 Arabs had fled from territories under Israeli control, thus creating an enormous PALESTINIAN REFUGEE problem. Israel was admitted to the UN in May 1949 but not recognized by any Arab state until 1979.

Origins of the Israeli Polity, D. Horowitz and M. Lissa (1978)

Palestine and the Great Powers, 1945–8, M. J. Cohen (1982)

Palestine to Israel: From Mandate to Independence, M. J. Cohen (1988)

J

Japan, occupation of (1945–52)   After its surrender at the end of the Second World War Japan was ruled by foreigners for the first time in its history. SCAP (Supreme Commander Allied Powers) lacked trained personnel to govern Japan, so General MACARTHUR (General Ridgway from April 1951) used Japanese governments and the existing civil service to carry out his decisions. He was ordered to break up the armed forces (five million troops were demobilized) and carry out punitive measures: hold war crimes trials, purge (force into retirement) civilians who had worked with the military regime and dissolve the *zaibatsu* (industrial combines). A total of 28 people (including 14 generals and 3 admirals) were indicted as Class A war criminals in Tokyo trials (1946–8). Seven (including Tojo Hideki, a wartime Prime Minister and general) were executed, others being imprisoned. Several Allied leaders had wanted Emperor HIROHITO to be tried as a war criminal but MacArthur decided against this. Trials took place elsewhere in Japan and Southeast Asia, as a result of which 4,000 were convicted and 920 executed. Some 200,000 civilians were purged and a further 200,000 banned from holding positions in the public sector. The *zaibatsu* were targeted for dissolution, as an alliance of big business and the military was held to be responsible for Japanese aggression in the 1930s and 1940s. An Anti-Monopoly Law was passed in 1947.

SCAP wanted to establish democratic rights and institutions in Japan as a means of making the revival of militarism impossible. Prewar parties – the Japan Socialist Party, the Liberal Party and Progressive Party (the Democratic Party from 1947) – revived and the Japanese Communist Party was legalized. In the 1946 election the Liberal Party gained the largest number of seats and formed a coalition government, but from April 1947 to October 1948 there was, after another election, a socialist-led coalition government, the only time since the war that the conservatives did not hold power until 1993. A truly democratic system of government was established by the JAPANESE CONSTITUTION (1947). A Trade Union Law (1945) gave workers the right to form unions, to strike and to take part in collective bargaining. The Labour Standards Law (1947) provided an eight-hour working day, a 48-hour week, paid annual holidays, accident insurance and equal pay for equal work for men and women. By February 1947 there were five million trade union members (41 per cent of the work force).

Two of the most important reforms concerned the land and education. MacArthur thought that government plans for land reform were not radical enough, so SCAP imposed its own proposals in 1946. All land held by absentee landlords was transferred to tenants and a limit was fixed on the amount of land any individual could own. By 1950 2.8 million acres of riceland and 1.95 million acres of upland had been bought by 4.75 million tenants: only 5 per cent of farmers remained tenants. Prewar education in Japan was élitist, with only a small proportion of pupils going beyond primary schools. SCAP introduced a US model of education: six years in elementary school followed by three years in middle school, then three years in high school and four years in university. The first nine years of education were compulsory and there was also greater access to higher education, as many universities were created. This system, which remains largely unaltered, had an enormous impact: in 1940 only 7 per cent of pupils went to high school, in 1955 50 per cent and in 1986 95 per cent. The quality of education has contributed greatly to the JAPANESE ECONOMIC MIRACLE.

From 1947–8 SCAP policy changed and there was a 'reverse course', as earlier reforms were modified or rejected and emphasis was placed on the economic revival of Japan. As the COLD WAR intensified and a communist victory in the CHINESE CIVIL WAR (1946–9) seemed likely, the US wanted to make sure that Japan did not become a prey to communism because of economic collapse or internal subversion. The economy was run-down (production in 1945 was 16 per cent of 1940 and fell further in 1946), inflation was 365 per cent in 1945 and still 166 per cent in 1948. Japan had no foreign currency with which to buy machinery or raw materials. Mass starvation was prevented only by massive food imports by SCAP. The dissolution of the *zaibatsu* therefore ended, the Ministry of International Trade and Industry (MITI) was established to plan for economic recovery and SCAP fixed a generous exchange rate of 360 yen to the dollar (it had never before exceeded 231 yen). The undervalued yen was of long-term significance, as it enabled Japan to build up a trade surplus with the US by the late 1960s. In the short term it was the KOREAN WAR (1950–3) which ended the economic depression. A Red Purge of left-wingers in the public services in 1950 was accompanied by the rehabilitation of those purged for associating with the prewar military regime. The US also wanted Japan to rearm, in spite of the constitution forbidding armed forces, so that it could play a part in combatting the spread of communism and so that the spiralling costs of the Occupation could be reduced. A Maritime Safety Force (in fact a navy) was created in 1948 and a National Police Reserve of 75,000 two years

later. This became, in 1952, a Self-Defence Force, which by 1954 had 180,000 men.

The Occupation came to an end with the SAN FRANCISCO PEACE TREATY (1951–2), though American troops remained in Japan in accordance with the JAPAN – US SECURITY TREATY, signed on the same day.

Democratizing Japan: The Allied Occupation,
  R. E. Ward (1987)
Remaking Japan: The Occupation as New Deal,
  T. Cohen (1987)
Aftermath of War: Americans and the Remaking of Japan 1945–52, H. Schonberger (1989)

Japan–US SecurityTreaty (1951)   Associated with, and signed on the same day as, the SAN FRANCISCO PEACE TREATY, which ended the OCCUPATION OF JAPAN. The US was allowed to maintain military bases in Japan and Okinawa was to remain under American control until 1972. The 260,000 US troops in Japan could use the bases for action in Asia without consulting the Japanese government. The US had jurisdiction over American personnel who committed crimes in Japan. The treaty could be ended only by mutual consent.

Both right and left bitterly attacked the treaty, as it subordinated Japanese foreign policy to that of the US and it seemed like a return to the unequal treaties imposed on Japan in the nineteenth century. YOSHIDA SHIGERU managed to secure its passage through the Diet (parliament) but there was a major crisis when it was revised and renewed in 1960, in spite of US service personal being subject to Japanese law. Opposition members of the Diet staged a sit-in to delay ratification and there was unprecedented popular opposition, with a series of huge strikes and violent demonstrations by workers and students. On 15 June hundreds were injured when police attacked students who had invaded the Diet. When the bill was passed the Prime Minister, Kishi Nobusuke, resigned and the opposition lost its impetus, yet this had been the most severe upheaval in postwar Japan. To prevent such scenes in the future the treaty has been automatically renewed.

Protest in Tokyo: The Security Crisis of 1960,
  G. R. Packard (1960)

Japanese constitution (1947) Replaced the Meiji constitution of 1889. It was imposed on Japan by SCAP (Supreme Commander Allied Powers – General MACARTHUR). Article 1 described the emperor as 'the symbol of the state and the unity of the people deriving his position from the will of the people in whom resides sovereign power'. There was a bicameral Diet (parliament) elected by universal suffrage, which was the only law-making body and the highest state institution. The House of Representatives was the more important of the two houses, as it could force the cabinet to resign by a no-confidence vote and as bills rejected by the House of Councillors would become law if passed for a second time by a two-thirds majority in the House of Representatives. Prewar institutions, responsible to the emperor rather than the Diet (the Privy Council, the War and Naval ministries) were abolished. To prevent the military seizing control of the state, as they had done in the 1930s, the Prime Minister and most of the members of the cabinet (which was responsible to the Diet) had to be civilians and members of the Diet. A Supreme Court (on the American model) was to decide whether any law infringed the constitution. Courts at all levels were independent of the Ministry of Justice. Human rights, freedom of speech, religion and association were guaranteed, the position of women being greatly improved: they had the vote, equal rights within marriage (concerning property, inheritance and divorce) and discrimination on grounds of sex was prohibited. Article 9 renounced war and the threat of force to settle international disputes and prohibited land, sea and air forces. This was later interpreted as not to apply to defence, so an army, navy and air force were formed as Self-Defence Forces. The Constitution could be amended only by a two-thirds vote in each house of the Diet, followed by a majority in a referendum. It has never been changed.

Japan: Divided Politics in a Growth Economy,
  J. Stockwin (1982)

Japanese economic miracle The rise of Japan to become the dominant financial and industrial power in the GLOBAL ECONOMY. In 1945 the Japanese economy was in ruins: a third of its industry and three-quarters of its shipping had been destroyed in the Second World War, there was a shortage of capital and high inflation. The Allied OCCUPATION OF JAPAN under General MACARTHUR had at first little interest in making Japan more prosperous but as the COLD WAR got under way and the CHINESE CIVIL WAR (1946–9) ended in a communist victory, Japan was needed as a bulwark against the spread of communism in Asia. The US, therefore, helped to equip Japanese industry but it was not until the KOREAN WAR (1950–3) that the economy began to take off, as large orders were placed by the US in Japan for war supplies. 'Special procurements' ($930 million in 1950–3) paid for American troops in Japan, whose industry sheltered behind protectionist barriers (tariffs and exchange controls). Foreign exchange reserves were built up and used to import the latest technology, essential for the high growth of the 1950s and 1960s. Japan also benefited from the low value of the yen, fixed in 1947 at 360 to the dollar, a rate maintained until 1971, thus making Japanese goods cheap on world markets. The pool of cheap labour was used in labour-intensive industries such as textiles, but from 1960 these were phased out and priority was given to the heavy and chemical industries (steel, shipbuilding, oil-refining, petrochemicals) and to the production of cars, electrical goods and synthetic fibres. By 1960 Japan, taking advantage of the demand for supertankers which followed the SUEZ CRISIS (1956), was the largest shipbuilding nation. From 1959–73 the average annual growth rate was 10.5 per cent, which led *The Economist* in London to refer to an 'economic miracle' as early as 1962. By 1970 Japan's GNP (Gross National Product) was the second largest in the world.

How has such a remarkable transformation been achieved? US aid, in providing technology and orders, was essential, as was the international monetary stability established at Bretton Woods (1944) and the free trade system of GATT: Japan joined the IMF in 1952 and GATT in 1955. Japan spends only 1 per cent of her budget on defence (compared with the US's 5–10 per cent), thus freeing money for industrial investment. Most of the capital comes from savings: there is a higher rate of saving in Japan than in other industrial countries, as people have to save more for their old age (pension schemes are inadequate). In Britain and the US most capital is raised by selling shares, which means that the interests of the shareholders, looking for immediate and high returns, is dominant. Japanese industry relies mainly on the banks for the money it needs. As a bank is at the centre of the larger groups of Japanese companies (*keiretsu*), long-term growth and investment rather than short-term gain are paramount. Profits are reinvested rather than given to shareholders. The state played an important role too, particularly the Ministry of International Trade and Industry (MITI), in directing investment to growth industries. Japanese industry has also been aided by the attitude of its workforce, which is highly skilled, hardworking and loyal. In the larger companies salary rises the longer a person stays with the firm, as do pensions, so few change their jobs: firms are consequently prepared to invest heavily in training. Firms also provide a whole range of welfare for workers and their families. TRADE UNIONS in the private sector are organized on a company basis and there are few strikes. The Japanese education system is another boon to industry: though based on rote learning, it produces a literate and numerate work-force and more engineers, scientists and research workers than other countries. Japanese industry has also benefited from its quality control and 'just-in-time' production of components, which reduces stocks of spares, cuts the cost of warehousing and minimizes the amount of money tied up in components.

The 'Nixon Shocks', when President NIXON abandoned the fixed exchange rate for the dollar and forced an upward revaluation of the yen, and the OPEC PRICE RISE of 1973, when oil prices quadrupled, badly affected Japan, dependent on oil for energy. Average annual growth fell to 4 per cent from 1974–87, though this was much higher than that of Japan's competitors. Japan moved away from energy-intensive industries such as steel and shipbuilding, where the cheaper labour of the NEWLY INDUSTRIALIZING ECONOMIES (NIEs) of Southeast Asia provided severe competition, to electronics and became the leading producer of transistor radios, televisions, cassette recorders and household electrical goods. When these were produced by the NIEs Japan turned to knowledge-intensive industries, such as computers, robots and biotechnology. Japan has gained a quasi-monopoly in several key global industries, such as carbon fibre for the aircraft industry and laser devices. It was dominant too in production machinery, such as semiconductor 'steppers', which make microchips.

Japan has a captive market at home and is less dependent on exports than other industrialized countries. In 1965 it exported 11.1 per cent of GNP, compared with Germany's 19 per cent and Britain's 23.3 per cent, but with the slower growth after 1973 it has exported more (15 per cent of GNP in 1983). To gain access to foreign markets Japan has invested heavily in establishing subsidiaries abroad: in Britain to gain entry to the EEC, in Mexico and the US to tap the US and Canadian markets. In the fastest growing region of the Pacific rim, Japan dominated the trading bloc of the NIEs. Japan's huge balance of payments surplus has also enabled it to buy foreign property, companies, shares and government bonds, especially in the US, where President REAGAN's reduction of income tax (and hence less tax revenues) without a reduction of spending (owing to the cost of the SDI ('Star Wars') programme) produced enormous budget deficits. By buying US treasury bonds Japan helped to prop up the dollar but caused alarm in the US when in 1989 Mitsubishi bought the Rockefeller Centre and Sony purchased the Columbia Picture Corporation. All this activity has made Japan an economic superpower: in 1988 seven out of ten of the world's largest banks were Japanese, four out of five of the largest insurance companies and 37 per cent of the world's largest MULTINATIONAL CORPORATIONS. There was a recession in 1989 when land values collapsed and the high value of the yen enabled cheaper foreign imports from South Korea and Malaysia to compete successfully for the first time with Japanse goods, but in 1994 a recovery put Japan once again in a very strong position. In 1994 exports were 45 per cent up on 1989 and increased a further 10 per cent in 1995. Investment abroad continued and in 1994 Japan produced more cars abroad than it exported from Japan. At home unemployment was 3.4 per cent in 1996, one of the lowest rates in the world. Yet the failure to deal with bad debts led to the collapse of Yamaichi Securities in 1997, the biggest bankruptcy since the Second World War, which left the Japanese economy in a depressed state.

The Japanese Economy, T. Ito (1992)
Japan's Capitalism, S. Tsuru (1997)
Postwar Japan 1945–95, P. J. Bailey (1996)

Jaruzelski, Wojciech Witold (1923–)

Polish general and politician. He invaded his native Poland with Soviet forces in 1944 as German troops were being pushed back in the Second World War. Eventually he became Chief of Staff of the Polish army in 1965, Minister of Defence in 1968 and a member of the Politburo in 1971. When there was serious unrest and strikes in Poland in 1981,

and SOLIDARITY was established as an independent trade union, Jaruzelski became Prime Minister in February and First Secretary of the Communist party in October. In declaring martial law in December he believed that he was saving Poland from civil war or from a Soviet invasion, like that of 1968 in Czechoslovakia which ended the PRAGUE SPRING. He arrested the leaders of Solidarity, suppressed the union, imposed censorship and put the coal mines under military control, but he did not attempt to establish a Stalinist regime. Jaruzelski knew that Solidarity had much more support than the communist party, so he sought legitimacy by a gradual relaxation of controls and by allowing the Roman Catholic Church considerable freedom. Martial law was lifted in 1983 and some detainees released. In 1986 there was a complete amnesty for all detained under martial law and the censorship was relaxed. President REAGAN, who had imposed sanctions on Poland, restored its most-favoured-nation trade status and Poland was readmitted to the IMF. At the end of 1987 Helsinki Watch, which monitored the observance of human rights, reported that Poland was 'the freest country in the Eastern bloc'.

There were better relations too with the Soviet Union, as Jaruzelski was a firm supporter of GORBACHEV'S GLASNOST. He retained the initiative until 1988, when an increase in food prices of 40 per cent produced considerable and widespread unrest. Instead of using force, Jaruzelski began round-table talks in 1989 with Solidarity, which was legalized again, and agreed to elections in which 35 per cent of the seats in the Sejm (parliament) and all those in the Senate were open to non-communist candidates. After the overwhelming success of Solidarity in the elections, Jaruzelski made an enormous contribution to the emergence of a democratic society by agreeing to a coalition government in which the Prime Minister, Tadeusz Mazowiecki, was a non-communist and Solidarity supporter. Jaruzelski himself became President, but a year later gave way to Lech

WALESA, the first freely elected President in Poland since 1922. Jaruzelski was largely responsible, therefore, for the peaceful transfer of power from a communist to a democratically elected government, the first time this had happened in the Soviet bloc.

Jiang Jieshi (Chiang Kai-shek) (1887–1975)
Chinese general, head of the Guomindang (GMD) and President of the Republic of China (Taiwan) (1949–75). The son of a merchant, Jiang went to Tokyo (1908–10) for military training and there became closely associated with Sun Yatsen.

He joined Sun's revolutionary government in 1918 and became his Chief of Staff. After Sun's death in 1925 Jiang was the leading figure in the GMD. Jiang fought a successful campaign against warlords in the north and tried to eliminate the communists, forcing them to flee to Yanan in the Long March. Yet he lost support to the communists because he failed to resist effectively the Japanese invasion of 1937 and because of the endemic corruption in the GMD.

When the Second World War ended in 1945 Jiang was universally recognized as leader of the Republic of China but, overconfident, he would not agree to a coalition with Mao Zedong and the CCP. The result was the CHINESE CIVIL WAR (1946–9), which ended with Jiang's defeat and his withdrawal to Taiwan, 100 miles (160 km) from the Chinese mainland. Both the communist government of the People's Republic of China (PRC) in Beijing and the GMD government of the Republic of China (ROC) in Taipei, the capital of Taiwan, maintain that Taiwan is a province of China and not an independent country.

Jiang suspended the constitution, ruled by martial law and declared that no elections were to be held for the National Assembly until the government had returned to the mainland. Seats in that assembly were held by those elected on the mainland in 1947. He held local elections from 1950 but forbade the organization of new political parties. All power on the island (in the GMD, the state and the army) was held by mainlanders (the 1.5 to 2 million Chinese who came to Taiwan in 1949) to the exclusion of the native Taiwanese. The US, which had abandoned Jiang when he lost the Civil War, resumed its support when the KOREAN WAR (1950–3) began and used its fleet to prevent any possible invasion of Taiwan by the PRC. Both the US and Jiang saw that he had lost peasant support on the mainland because he had not carried out land reform. He therefore implemented a comprehensive land reform in Taiwan from 1949–53. Rents were restricted and the maximum amount of land anyone could hold was fixed: land held above that level was bought by the government and sold cheaply to peasants. Landlords were given shares in government enterprises as compensation. Peasants were also helped by cheap credit and technical advice. The result was a contented peasantry and agricultural production which grew faster than the population.

The economic development which was to make Taiwan one of the NEWLY INDUSTRIALIZING ECONOMIES began under Jiang. For this, control of inflation (3,400 per cent in 1949) was essential: a new currency in 1949 reduced inflation gradually to 3 per cent by 1961. In the 1950s labour-intensive industries, such as textiles, were developed. Under US guidance Jiang gave up some protectionist policies (high tariffs) and concentrated more on exports from 1960. The government encouraged foreign investment by providing tax incentives in export zones, where imported parts could be assembled for export. MULTINATIONAL CORPORATIONS from the US and Japan took advantage of the opportunity and made Taiwan into a centre for consumer electronics. The trade deficit became a surplus from 1970 (apart from a down-turn in 1973–4 caused by the OPEC PRICE RISE): from 1963–72 the economy grew annually at 10.8 per cent. Political change did not accompany economic growth, though Jiang allowed supplementary elections for the National Assembly in 1969. He suffered a setback in 1971 when the ROC lost its seat at the UNITED NATIONS to the PRC and most nations moved their diplomats to Beijing (neither government would allow dual recognition). A further blow was President NIXON's visit to Beijing in 1972, though this did not affect the economy, which was still growing when Jiang died.

Island China, R. N. Clough (1978)
State and Society in the Taiwan Miracle, T. B. Gold (1986)

Jiang Qing (1914–91)   The third wife of MAO ZEDONG and the most influential woman in the People's Republic of China. She was an actress in Shandong when she was imprisoned for communist activity in 1933. On her release she went to Shanghai, where she played minor roles in films. In 1937 she was in Yanan, where she soon became Mao's companion and his wife two years later. There was great opposition among Chinese Communist Party (CCP) veterans, as Mao's second wife, He Zizhen, was very popular and had suffered severely on the Long March (1934–5), which she was one of the few women to survive. Mao had to agree to keep Jiang out of politics, which he did until 1963, when she tried to make the Beijing opera and ballet more politically motivated and deal with the achievements of the working class and of the CCP.

The height of her power came in the CULTURAL REVOLUTION, when she was a leading influence on the Red Cuards and a member of the Politburo (1969). As one of the few people Mao trusted she acquired great influence over Chinese cultural life. After the waning of the Cultural Revolution she was involved, with her acolytes in the GANG OF FOUR, in a power struggle from 1971–6, which she lost when HUA GUOFENG became Chairman of the People's Republic on Mao's death. Unwilling to accept defeat she planned a coup but was arrested. At her trial, which began in 1980, she was accused of persecuting millions during the Cultural Revolution. She remained defiant and maintained that all her actions had been approved by Mao. She was sentenced to death but given two years to repent and so avoid execution. Though there was little sign of repentance she was not executed but committed suicide in prison.

The White-boned Demon: A Biography of Madame Mao Zedong, R. Terrill (1984)

Jiang Zemin (1926–)   General Secretary of the Chinese Communist Party (CCP) (1989–) and President of the People's Republic of China (1993–). The son of intellectuals who lived near Shanghai, he went to an American missionary school, where he learnt to speak English well. He joined the CCP in 1946 before taking a degree in electrical engineering in Shanghai. In the 1950s he worked in Romania and the Soviet Union and became fluent in Russian. He was then head of various technical research institutions in China before becoming a member of the CCP's Central Committee in 1982 and minister in charge of the electronics industry (1983–5). In 1985 he was appointed Mayor of Shanghai, where he did little to solve the traffic, pollution and housing problems and was known as 'the Flower Pot' because he looked good without doing anything. He joined the Politburo in 1987 and supported the suppression of the democratic movement in Beijing in the TIANANMEN SQUARE MASSACRE (1989), though he was able to maintain order in Shanghai without declaring martial law or calling in the army. Jiang won the favour of DENG XIAOPING, whom he succeeded as Chairman of the CCP's Military Affairs Commission (MAC) in 1989, the first person without military experience to be put in charge of the army. He kept the military happy by large budget increases and by letting them buy sophisticated weapons abroad and kept control of them by replacing or rotating every regional commander and by placing his own nominees on the MAC. Also in 1989 he replaced the disgraced ZHAO ZIYANG as General Secretary of the CCP, a post he has held longer than anyone except MAO ZEDONG. When he was elected President of China in 1993 he held all three of the most important offices of state.

Stout and affable (he loves to burst into song) he was unusual among Chinese communist leaders in having experience of and not distrusting the outside world: he sent his two sons to college in the US and had a taste for foreign music and films. His main concern was to continue Deng's policy of making China an economically prosperous country, a task made easier when HONG KONG RETURNED TO CHINA in 1997. He made the rebuilding of Shanghai a national priority and turned it into a vast construction site. The biggest car factory in China, run by Volkswagen, was built there. In spite of China's record economic growth, the vast state enterprises, which employed two-thirds of China's 170 million urban workers, were close to collapse. They were one trillion yuan in debt in 1997 and had unsold goods worth 450 billion yuan, including 500 million shirts and one million motorcycles. Jiang tackled this problem by PRIVATIZATION, proposing that 10,000 out of 13,000 sizeable state firms should be sold off, though this is bound to increase unemployment, which the government admits is 25 million. Another problem facing Jiang is corruption. Some party cadres became extremely wealthy by selling state assets and using state loans to finance their own businesses. As the country was getting richer the state was becoming poorer and every year spending less per capita on education. Although Jiang embraced the free market economy, he is determined that the dominant role of the CCP shall not be weakened. He therefore imprisoned all dissenters and maintained an authoritarian state.

John XXIII (1881–1963)   Pope (1958–63)

Angelo Roncalli was one of 13 children of a poor tenant farmer in Lombardy. He joined the priesthood and spent many years as a diplomat in Bulgaria, Greece and Turkey, where Catholics were a tiny minority. In 1944 he was appointed papal nuncio to France but it was not till 1953, when he was 71, that he became a cardinal and patriarch of Venice. He was elected pope in 1958 on the twelfth ballot, as a compromise candidate who was not expected to live long. Short and corpulent, his simplicity, humility and warm personality made him a much-loved figure. A traditionalist in most ways, he surprised the conservative Curia by his awareness that the world was changing and that the Church must adapt to it. He looked favourably on the 'opening to the left' (the alliance of the Italian Socialist Party with the CHRISTIAN DEMOCRATIC PARTY) and promoted the social role of the Church. In the encyclical *Mater et magistra* (1961) he rejected the free play of market forces and called for more social justice.

Pope John called the second ecumenical council of the Catholic Church (Vatican II – the first had met in 1879) 'to bring the Church up to date' and was the first pope since the Reformation who admitted that the Church needed reform. He told the 2,500 prelates who came from all over the world that the Church 'rather than merely reiterating the vetoes of the past, sees the necessity of meeting the needs of the world today, and thus demonstrates the continuing validity of its doctrine'. In July 1963 he issued the last and most famous of his encyclicals, *Pacem in terris* (Peace on Earth), which argued for co-operation between people of different ideologies, the economic and social betterment of the working classes, the entry of women into public life and the justice of the anti-colonial struggles in the THIRD WORLD. It had a profound effect on the later Church. The pope distinguished between 'false ideologies', such as Marxism, and the political movements they inspire, which may produce just and worthy demands. Discourse between believers and non-believers, he said, can produce the truth: non-believers must be allowed to keep their dignity as human beings. Vatican

II allowed the use of the vernacular in Church services, stated that each person had the right to behave according to his conscience and brought a new understanding with other churches, particularly with the Jews, who were acquitted of the murder of Christ. Pope John cordially received Orthodox and Protestant leaders, including the Archbishop of Canterbury, the first such meeting since the fourteenth century. He died during Vatican II, which was brought to a conclusion by his successor Paul VI.

Pope John and His Revolution, E. E. Y. Hales (1965)
Pope John XXIII, P. Johnson (1974)
John XXIII, P. Hebblethwaite (1984)

John Paul II (Karol Jozef Wojtyla) (1920–)

Pope (1978–). The son of a Polish army officer, he was ordained a priest in 1946 and studied philosophy and moral theology at Rome before returning to Poland in 1948, when the Roman Catholic Church was being persecuted by the communist state. A brilliant student, he became professor of moral theology at the Catholic University Lublin, a bishop in 1958 and Archbishop of Krakow in 1964. Three years later he was made a cardinal and in 1978 was elected pope, the first non-Italian to hold this office for 456 years and the first Slav to be pope.

He saw his mission as that of restoring the moral authority of the Church in a chaotic and increasingly secular world and in re-establishing a common Christian heritage across the political boundaries of Europe. An indefatigable worker and traveller, he visited 74 countries in the first ten years of his papacy and travelled 375,000 miles (600,000 km). His emotional return to Poland, when a million people gathered in Warsaw for his first pontifical mass in 1979, was followed by a further visit in 1987, when his strong anti-communism and support for reform were manifest. John Paul II is an uncompromising upholder of the Church's traditional doctrines: he condemned divorce, abortion, sexual relations outside marriage, in-vitro fertilization and artificial contraception. His attitude to other social issues is conservative: he condemns homosexuality, opposes the ordination of women and relaxation of the rules of celibacy for priests.

One major issue he faced was the politicization of the priesthood, particularly in the THIRD WORLD. Here his deep-seated conservatism gave conflicting messages. He claimed to be committed to human rights and to the 'preferential option of the poor' but he greatly disliked the attempts of Latin American priests to help the poor in a practical way. The priests who established *Comunidades de Base* – grassroots communities designed to improve the living conditions of the poor – were silenced by papal order and their LIBERATION THEOLOGY censured. John Paul II cautioned the popular Archbishop Romero of San Salvador not to make 'concrete denunciations' of right-wing death squads that had murdered a priest. When Romero was assassinated in his own cathedral, the pope declined to call him a martyr. He appeared to look more benevolently on Jose Maria Escriva, the founder of the fiercely right-wing OPUS DEI, whom he beatified in 1992, only 17 years after his death. John Paul II has had to cope with the widespread disregard by Catholics of the Church's doctrines, particularly with regard to contraception and abortion, and to the decline in recruitment to the religious life: it is estimated that 100,000 priests have left the Church and not been replaced, the largest exodus since the Reformation.

John Paul II, M. Walsh (1995)
Pope John Paul II, T. Szulc (1995)
Saints and Sinners: A History of the Popes, E. Duffy (1997)

Johnson, Lyndon Baines (1908–73)

President of the United States (1963–9). After an impoverished childhood in Texas he became an elementary school teacher for a year before entering politics. In 1934 he married Claudia Alta ('Lady Bird') Taylor, the daughter of a prosperous Texan planter. Her business acumen made the Johnsons wealthy from the radio and television stations they bought in the 1940s and 1950s. Johnson's first important political post was as an ardent New Dealer, when he became director (1935–7) of the National Youth Administration in Texas. From 1937–48 he was a member of the House of Representatives, joining the Senate in 1948. There his enormous capacity for hard work saw him become minority leader in 1953, the youngest such leader. When the DEMOCRATIC PARTY regained control of the Senate in 1954 he became majority leader. Wheeling and dealing, flattering and intimidating, he became the most effective majority leader in the history of the Senate and organized the bipartisan vote which brought about the fall of Senator MCCARTHY. Overwork resulted in a severe heart attack in 1955 but he was soon back at work, co-operating with the EISENHOWER administration to pass the CIVIL RIGHTS ACTS of 1957 and 1960, the first in over 80 years. He also played a large part in establishing NASA (the National Aeronautics and Space Administration).

When his attempt to become the Democratic candidate in the 1960 presidential election failed, he surprisingly became John F. KENNEDY's running mate. They had little in common but Kennedy needed Johnson to bring in southern votes. He campaigned hard in the South and so contributed to Kennedy's narrow victory. Johnson found his position as Vice-President frustrating, as he lacked any real power but suddenly he found himself catapulted into the position he had long desired when Kennedy was assassinated.

Personally insecure when he became President, as he lacked Kennedy's youth, glamour and sophistication, he was determined to make his mark by carrying out the greatest programme of social reform since the New Deal. This he called the GREAT SOCIETY, which showed his compassion for the poor and the deprived, particularly blacks. Some of the reforms (such as the CIVIL RIGHTS

ACT of 1964) had been initiated by Kennedy but the war on poverty was very much his own. He won the 1964 election by the largest margin in American history, with 61 per cent of the popular vote. His Republican opponent, Barry Goldwater, won only six states but five of them were in the South (the Democrats had held four of them for 84 years), where the President's reforms in favour of blacks were not appreciated by the majority of whites. 'I think' he said to an aide when he signed the Civil Rights Act of 1964, 'we delivered the South to the REPUBLICAN PARTY'. The elections also produced the most liberal Congress since the New Deal, the Democrats winning 294 seats (out of 434) in the House of Representatives and 68 (out of 100) in the Senate. Though the Civil Rights and Voting Rights Acts did much to reduce discrimination against blacks, some were dissatisfied with what they regarded as the slow pace of change. More militant organizations arose – the BLACK MUSLIMS, the BLACK POWER Movement – and there were BLACK GHETTO RIOTS in many cities from 1964–8, which alarmed many whites and eroded support for the Great Society. This suffered too from the President's foreign policy, particularly the VIETNAM WAR.

Johnson believed in the containment policy first put forward by George Kennan and used this to justify his intervention in the Dominican Republic in 1965. Determined to prevent another CASTRO appearing in the Caribbean, he sent 30,000 American troops to prop up a right-wing military *junta* against rebels who wanted a more liberal regime. His claim that he had prevented communists taking over was untrue. He announced the Johnson Doctrine: that the US would use force if necessary anywhere in the hemisphere to prevent a communist seizure of power, though this was contrary to a pledge given by the US as a member of the OAS (Organization of American States) that it would not interfere in the internal affairs of other states. To many Latin Americans Johnson's intervention was simply a repetition of the gunboat diplomacy of Teddy Roosevelt and of Woodrow Wilson.

At first he was reluctant to increase American involvement in Vietnam, as he was more concerned with domestic reform, but when it was clear that American aid to South Vietnam could not alone prevent a communist take-over of the South he decided to commit American troops, feeling that America's credibility was at stake: no country could rely on US promises of protection if he withdrew. The TONKIN GULF RESOLUTION (1964) freed him from all congressional constraints in fighting the war and led to massive air attacks on North Vietnam and eventually the deployment of half a million American troops in Vietnam. The President rejected the unpopular option of raising taxes to pay for the war and borrowed instead. This caused inflation and turned the US from a creditor into a debtor nation. As the VIETNAM ANTI-WAR MOVEMENT gained support Johnson, exceptionally sensitive to criticism, refused to admit any errors and constantly gave over-optimistic accounts of success in the war. The TET OFFENSIVE seemed to indicate that the war could never be won. On 31 March 1968 Johnson, drained physically and emotionally, dramatically announced: 'I shall not seek and I will not accept the nomination of my Party for another term as your President'. He retired more ferociously criticized than almost any of his predecessors, yet his achievements in his Great Society reforms make him an outstanding President. He died after a heart attack on his ranch in Texas.

Big Daddy from the Pedernales: Lyndon Baines Johnson, P. Conkin (1986)
The Presidency of Lyndon B. Johnson, V. D. Bornet (1988)
Lone Star Rising: Lyndon Johnson and His Times, 1908–1960, R. Dallek (1991)

Juan Carlos I (1938–)   King of Spain (1975–). Born during the Spanish Civil War (1936–9) in Rome, as a result of the royal family's exile from 1931, Juan Carlos spent the first ten years of his life in Italy, Switzerland and Portugal. The subsequent course of his life was to be shaped by the dispute between his father, Don Juan, and the ruler of Spain, the dictator General FRANCO. Although Don Juan had became head of the Spanish royal house on the death of Alfonso XIII in 1941, Franco refused to name Don Juan as his successor. This was not only due to Franco's political differences with Don Juan, who was more concerned to reconcile the Spaniards in the wake of the Civil War than to perpetuate the division between the victors and the vanquished, but also to his own desire to hold onto power at all costs. Under the Succession Law of 1947 Spain was characterized as a kingdom, but it was not specified who would accede to the throne once Franco had died.

A meeting the following year between Don Juan and Franco resulted in Juan Carlos being sent to Spain to complete his studies, both academic and military, under Franco's guidance. Tall and athletic, and bereft of any intellectual pretensions, he promptly revealed, much to Franco's satisfaction, a strong affinity for the army. In 1961 Juan Carlos married Sophia, daughter of King Paul I of Greece, a talented linguist and arts enthusiast. Eight years later, Franco finally designated Juan Carlos as his chosen successor.

Far from perpetuating an authoritarian regime upon Franco's death in 1975, the new king, advised by his former teacher and now president of the Cortes, Torcuato Fernández Miranda, and bowing to overwhelming social and political pressure, set about dismantling the Francoist state in order to replace it with a democratic one. Throughout the difficult TRANSITION period of 1976–8 he was to work closely with Prime Minister Adolfo Suarez.

The king is generally credited with playing the decisive role in quashing the attempted coup d'état of 23 February 1981, when Civil Guards stormed the Cortes and tanks under the command of the Captain-General rolled ominously onto the streets of Valencia, though his considerable delay in addressing the Spanish people has sometimes led to his motives being questioned (not least because the conspirators always claimed to be awaiting his orders).

The consolidation of democracy under socialist rule (1982–96) enhanced the king's own prestige and popularity, as well as Spain's growing international reputation, reflected not only by Spain's integration into the European Union but also by the holding of the Barcelona Olympics and the Expo in Seville in 1996. Undoubtedly, Juan Carlos's achievements along with his approachable style have made him a genuinely popular monarch, though little criticism of the royal family is permitted in Spain.

The Transformation of Spain, D. Gilmour (1985)

The Triumph of Democracy in Spain, P. Preston (1986)

The New Spaniards, J. Hooper (1995)

K

Kádár, János (1912–89)   First Secretary of the Hungarian Socialist Workers' Party (communist party) (1956–88). The son of a peasant, he was trained as a mechanic, joined the Communist Youth League and was imprisoned from 1935–7. During the Second World War he took part in the Resistance and in rebuilding the Communist Party. In 1945 he was promoted to the Politburo, became Deputy General Secretary of the Communist Party in 1946 and Minister of the Interior two years later. He began a series of SHOW TRIALS, including that of Laszlo Rajk, but was himself a victim of RÁKOSI's purges. Arrested in 1951 and charged with Titoism and treason, he was tortured and imprisoned (1951–4). During the HUNGARIAN RISING of 1956 he took over the leadership of the party and joined Nagy's government, but on 1 November he disappeared, only to return with a Soviet escort on 7 November as the head of a new government. He restored the authority of the party, which had almost disintegrated, by a reign of terror, in which the concentration camps were reopened and many people were executed, including Nagy.

The terror was accompanied by a foreign policy which devotedly followed Moscow's lead. He supported the USSR in the SINO-SOVIET DISPUTE and in its rift with Albania and provided troops to join other WARSAW PACT forces in crushing the PRAGUE SPRING in 1968. Yet Kádár realized that to legitimize his rule he would have to make life more comfortable for the mass of the people. He allowed peasants to cultivate their private plots and sell produce on the open market,

controlled and subsidized the price of essential foodstuffs and imported more consumer goods from the Soviet bloc. There was almost free social and health insurance. Kádár adopted Nagy's slogan 'those who are not against us are with us', granted a general amnesty in 1962 to all those who had been involved in the 1956 rising and relaxed the censorship. By 1978 he had moved to a position close to that of EUROCOMMUNISM: that there are several paths to socialism. 'Marxism–Leninism is not a dogma but a guide to action', he wrote, though he still accepted the party's leading role. Although there was no democracy there was more prosperity, so that, according to a popular saying, Hungary was 'the happiest barrack in the Socialist camp'. Real wages, which had fallen by 22 per cent between 1949 and 1953, trebled between 1956 and 1978.

This increase in living standards was due to the economic reforms Kádár introduced. At first he returned to Stalinist policies – the collectivization of agriculture, investment in heavy industry – but collectives elected their own leaders and were self-managing. Hungarian agriculture became third in the world in per capita grain and meat production. Industry benefited from the New Economic Mechanism (introduced in 1968, abandoned in 1972 but re-established in 1979), one of the most important economic reforms in the communist bloc and a new model to follow. The power of central planning agencies was greatly reduced, private enterprise was encouraged, especially in service industries, and private producers could employ a small number of workers. Plants had to sell their products in the market and make profits. Most prices (food excepted) were no longer fixed by the state but fluctuated according to supply and demand. The OPEC PRICE RISE of 1973, when prices quadrupled, hit Hungary hard. Exports declined and production costs increased, so Kádár borrowed heavily from Western banks, giving Hungary the highest per capita debt in Eastern Europe. Meanwhile, the second economy (private enterprise outside the state sector) was growing and by 1988 produced a third of the national income: 75 per cent of Hungarians received some income from it. However, the second economy could not make up for the obsolete state sector and from 1985 living standards declined. Kádár by this time was old and frail and refused to admit that urgent changes were needed. He was therefore pushed aside by his colleagues and relieved of his post of General Secretary in 1988. He lived just long enough to see Imre Nagy, his victim, reburied amidst general acclamation.

Hungary's Negotiated Revolution: Economic Reform, Social Change and Political Succession, 1957–90, R. L. Tokes (1996)

Kampuchea, Vietnamese occupation of (1979–89) When the Khmer Rouge seized control of Cambodia (which they renamed Kampuchea) in 1975 they expelled all Vietnamese. As relations with Vietnam deteriorated POL POT made attacks across the Vietnamese border and ordered the elimination of all Khmer Rouge cadres in the east of the country, who were in contact with Vietnam and therefore considered to be disloyal. They appealed to Vietnam for help, so on Christmas Day 1978 the Vietnamese invaded Kampuchea. By 10 January 1979 they had captured the capital Phnom Penh and proclaimed the People's Republic of Kampuchea (PRK) under Heng Samrin, a dissident Khmer Rouge official. Pol Pot and the Khmer Rouge fled to the Thai border. In February 1979 China, hostile to Vietnam for joining COMECON and the Soviet camp,

invaded Vietnam but had little success and pulled back a month later, without producing a Vietnamese withdrawal from Kampuchea.

The new government restored markets, a money economy, personal freedom and Buddhism, but relied on Vietnam and the Soviet Union for the enormous task of reconstruction. Famine was avoided largely by Soviet aid. For defence the new administration relied on the 160,000 Vietnamese troops in Kampuchea.

The invasion changed the strategic balance in Southeast Asia and roused fears among its neighbours of Vietnamese expansionism. Vietnam was condemned in the UNITED NATIONS, most of whose members (except India) refused to recognize the PRK. The Thais assisted organizations which opposed the PRK, including the Khmer Rouge and two non-communist groups, one of them led by SIHANOUK. They all joined in 1982 to form a Coalition Government of Democratic Kampuchea (CGDK), which held Kampuchea's seat at the UN. The US prevented the WORLD BANK and Asian Development Bank from granting loans to the PRK. The effect on Vietnam of its invasion was devastating. Its second Five Year Plan (1976–81) was abandoned, it was isolated in the THIRD WORLD and it became completely dependent on the Soviet Union and Eastern Europe, which provided economic assistance and enabled Vietnam to increase its army from 600,000 to 1.1 million, the fourth largest in the world. In return the Soviet Union obtained a base for its Pacific Fleet at Cam Ranh Bay in Vietnam, the only Soviet base between Vladivostok and East Africa. The COLD WAR was thus intensified.

Some 300,000 refugees on the Thai border were a recruiting ground for the Khmer Rouge, the largest faction in the CGDK with 40,000 guerillas. To crush them Vietnam launched a military offensive (1984–5), which simply drove the guerrillas into Thailand. A new approach was needed, particularly as GORBACHEV came to power in the Soviet Union in 1985. He wanted to end the

SINO-SOVIET DISPUTE, for which China demanded the withdrawal of Vietnam from Kampuchea. Gorbachev put pressure on Vietnam to do this and as it became clear that the previous level of Soviet support would not be maintained, Vietnam announced in 1985 that its troops would be withdrawn by 1990 and called for negotiations between the PRK and CGDK to form a popular government. These dragged on long after Vietnamese troops had left Kampuchea in 1989. The Vietnamese invasion had ended the barbarous Pol Pot regime in Kampuchea but it had failed to establish a stable administration in its place, largely owing to Great Power rivalry.

Karamanlis, Konstantinos (1907–98)

Greek Prime Minister (1955–63, 1974–80) and President (1980–5, 1990–5). Born in Macedonia when this was part of the Ottoman Empire, he was the son of a village schoolteacher. He first entered parliament in 1935 but his political career was cut short by the Metaxas dictatorship and the German occupation during the Second World War. Karamanlis was elected to parliament in 1946 and held minor ministerial posts but first came to public notice as an efficient Minister of Public Works (1952–5) in the government of Marshal Papagos. When Papagos died King Paul chose Karamanlis as Prime Minister. He was to hold that office continuously for eight years, a feat equalled in Greece only by Andreas PAPANDREOU.

His first years as Prime Minister were preoccupied with Cyprus and ENOSIS and he was much criticized for accepting the terms by which Cyprus became independent in 1960, as they appeared to put the interests of NATO and the US above those of Greece. In 1961 he negotiated an association, the first of its kind, with the EEC. His motives were as much political as economic – to tie Greece to Western Europe. The monetary stability and economic growth which began under Papagos continued. There was a little industrial investment – in shipyards, oil refineries – but the Greek economy was heavily dependent on US aid, on money sent home by GASTARBEITER, on shipping (the Greek merchant fleet was the biggest in the world) and increasingly on tourism. The standard of living rose slowly but steadily. Outspoken and aggressive, Karamanlis clashed with the strong-willed Queen Frederica and after a disagreement with the court he resigned in 1963. When Georgios Papandreou narrowly won the 1963 election, Karamanlis went into voluntary exile in France, where he remained for 11 years.

He was recalled in 1974 when the regime of the GREEK COLONELS collapsed and was responsible for the smooth change from military to civilian rule. For the next seven years the Greek political system worked more effectively than at any time before or since. Karamanlis pursued more liberal policies than he had done before the military coup: political prisoners were released and the Communist Party legalized for the first time since 1947. After the 1974 election, which his New Democracy Party won, he held a referendum on the monarchy, which was abolished when only 30 per cent voted for it. A series of reforms modernized the education system, nationalized much Church land, some banks and businesses and the national airline, and reduced the voting age and the length of national service. Karamanlis wanted to join the EC early so as to reduce Greece's dependence on the US, unpopular after its tacit support for the Colonels, and in order to protect its democratic institutions. He succeeded in making Greece a full member in January 1981. Relations with Turkey remained dire and led to as much as one third of the budget being spent on the armed forces. In 1980 Karamanlis stood for President and was narrowly elected. He did not stand in 1985 but was re-elected in 1990 at the age of 83.

Karamanlis: The Restorer of Greek Democracy,
C. M. Woodhouse (1982)

Kaunda, Kenneth David (1924–) President of Zambia (1964–91). The son of a missionary, he was a devout Christian who did not drink or smoke and lived austerely. Like Gandhi, whom he greatly admired, he believed in non-violence. He was a primary school teacher before he became Secretary-General in 1953 of the African National Congress–Zambia, which campaigned against racial discrimination and the CENTRAL AFRICAN FEDERATION. Kaunda broke away from this party in 1958 and formed his own party, which in 1960 became the United National Independence Party (UNIP), to press for independence. In 1959 his party was banned and Kaunda was imprisoned. After his release he led a massive campaign of civil disobedience, which resulted in the British government giving Africans a majority in the legislature (1962). He served as a minister in the coalition government from 1962–4, when UNIP won the elections and Kaunda became Prime Minister and then President of independent Zambia.

Internationally renowned as a THIRD WORLD spokesman and savage critic of APARTHEID and of Smith's UDI in Rhodesia (1965) at COMMONWEALTH conferences, Kaunda supported black liberation movements – Nkomo's ZAPU in Rhodesia, the ANC in South Africa – and international sanctions against the white minority regimes. They retaliated by attacking guerrilla bases in Zambia. At home he faced severe problems, as Zambia consisted of 73 ethnic groups with no sense of being a nation and as there were only 100 graduates and few people with technical skills. In 1972 Kaunda made Zambia a one-party state, maintaining that it was necessary to prevent the country breaking up on ethnic lines and to counter subversion. Zambia was a land-locked country, tied economically to white-dominated Rhodesia and South Africa by the railways which carried its main export of copper. Smith closed the frontier with Zambia in 1973, thus cutting off its routes to South Africa and the Mozambican port of Beira. Zambia was now dependent on

the Benguela railway to the Angolan port of Lobito, but this too was closed in 1975 because of the ANGOLAN CIVIL WAR. Zambia's exports would have been completely cut off but for the opening in the same year of the TanZam (Tazara) railway, though port facilities at Dar es Salaam were unable to cope with the volume of trade. Transport problems eased when Zimbabwe became independent in 1980 and the frontier was reopened. Dependence on Rhodesian power was reduced by building a hydro-electric dam on the Kafue River and a power station on the northern side of the Kariba Dam. Zambia also developed its own coal mines to replace coal from Rhodesia. The shortage of trained manpower was tackled by a massive expansion of secondary and technical education and by opening the University of Zambia in 1966.

The state played a leading economic role by taking a majority holding in the most important industries. The economy thrived in spite of transport difficulties for the first decade of independence, as copper prices were high (copper produced 90 per cent of exports and 50 per cent of government revenue), but the OPEC PRICE RISE of 1973 led to a recession in the industrial countries, a fall in the demand for copper and a sharp drop in its price. Owing to the needs of education and transport, there had been little investment in rural areas, so people flocked from there into the towns, where unemployment was high and crime almost out of control, a situation made worse by refugees from Rhodesia, Angola and Mozambique. As the standard of living fell there were strikes and demands for multiparty elections: in these, held in October 1991, the UNIP was crushingly defeated by the Movement for Multiparty Democracy (MMD) whose leader, Frederick Chiluba, became Zambia's second President. Kaunda accepted the will of the people and retired.

'Zambia, Kaunda and Chiluba – Enduring Patterns of Political Culture', J. K. van

Druge in *Democracy and Political Change in Subsaharan Africa*, J. Wiseman (ed.) (1995)

Keating, Paul John (1944–) Prime Minister of Australia (1991–6). Born in the working-class suburbs of Sydney, where his Irish–Catholic father was a boilermaker, he left school at 14, joined the Australian Labor Party (ALP) when he was 15 and worked as a clerk for some years before becoming a trade union research officer in 1968. A year later he entered the federal parliament as an ALP member, served briefly as a junior minister under Gough WHITLAM at the age of 31 and was appointed Treasurer when Bob HAWKE became Prime Minister in 1983. He was, with Hawke, the main policy-maker in the cabinet and pursued a programme which shocked many rank and file socialists, as it promoted a free market economy. A bitter conflict with Hawke in 1991 resulted in his taking over the leadership of the ALP and the premiership. He was the youngest Prime Minister in Australian history.

By the time of the 1993 election Labor seemed certain to be defeated, as unemployment was running at 11 per cent and the foreign debt had risen to 150 billion Australian dollars. He was saved by the Liberal Party promising to introduce an unpopular consumption tax and won the election. He continued the same economic policies he had followed as Hawke's Treasurer, and brought about closer economic and political ties with Asian countries: he tried hard to convince Australians that their future lay with Asia. Keating also brought about a historic compromise with the Aborigines, building on the High Court decision in *Mabo v Queensland* (1992), that accepted natural rights before the British settlement. Keating from 1994 enabled Aborigines to claim between 5–10 per cent of Australian territory, though this excluded land already under cultivation and did not affect the mining industry. He wanted to make Australia a republic, for which he had majority support and proposed to hold a referendum on the issue in 2001, the centenary of Australia's federation. Keating dominated parliament with his sharp wit, abrasive style and colourful language (he famously referred to his opponents as 'scumbags') but unemployment was still 8.5 per cent in 1996 and many Australians deeply disliked Keating personally. He lost the election of that year in a 5 per cent swing against Labor and resigned as leader of the ALP.

Keating, J. Edwards (1997)

Kekkonen, Urho (1900–86) Prime Minister (1950–3, 1954–6) and President (1956–81) of Finland. The son of a lumberjack, he took a law degree at Helsinki University and worked as a civil servant before entering parliament as an Agrarian Party deputy in 1936: he became a minister in the same year. At first he was anti-Soviet and was one of only two deputies to vote against ceding any territory to the Soviet Union after the Finnish–Russian War (1939–40). After Hitler invaded the Soviet Union in 1941, Kekkonen opposed the Continuation War, when the Finns fought on the side of Germany and when it was clear from 1943 that Germany would be defeated, realized the need for good relations with the USSR if Finland was to retain its independence. In 1948 he took part in the negotiations that produced the Treaty of Friendship, Co-operation and Mutual Assistance with the Soviet Union. Finland preserved a precarious independence after the war but STALIN regarded it as part of the Soviet Union's sphere of influence. No Finnish President or Prime Minister could be chosen without Soviet approval. As the Russians distrusted the Social Democrats and kept them out of office until 1966, they worked through the Agrarian Party, the only major party which would work with the Finnish Communist Party after its abortive attempt at a coup in 1948.

Kekkonen was Prime Minister in the early 1950s, serving under President Paasikivi, the architect of Finland's postwar foreign policy, which combined neutrality with close relations with the Soviet Union. He was elected President in 1956 by a wafer-thin majority after the Soviet Union intervened on his behalf. In foreign policy he pursued what became known as the 'Paasikivi–Kekkonen' line or, as it was described by some foreign critics, a policy of 'Finlandization'. This meant avoiding actions and statements likely to upset the USSR, and thus involved a measure of self-censorship. Finland joined EFTA in 1961 but followed a policy of strict neutrality, which earned Kekkonen the Lenin Peace Prize in 1980. His popularity in Finland led to special legislation which enabled him to stay in office until 1984 but, suffering from ill-health, he resigned in 1981.

Urho Kekkonen: A Statesman for Peace, K. Korhonen (ed.) (1975)

Kennedy, John Fitzgerald (1917–63)

President of the United States (1961–3). From a wealthy Boston–Irish Catholic family (his father was US ambassador to Britain from 1937–40) he graduated at Harvard, enlisted in the navy and after Pearl Harbor volunteered for duty in the Pacific, where the torpedo boat he commanded was sunk in 1943. Decorated for bravery in this incident, he suffered from chronic back pain thereafter. After the war he was elected to the House of Representatives in 1946 and to the Senate in 1952. In 1960 his youth, charm and good looks and a highly efficient political machine enabled him to secure the Democratic nomination for the presidential election. As his religion might be a handicap in the South, he chose as his running mate the Senate majority leader Lyndon B. JOHNSON from Texas. The election was one of the closest in American history: Kennedy defeated his Republican rival Richard NIXON by 118,574 votes. He was the youngest man and first Catholic to be elected President.

Foreign policy occupied most of his time. As a Senator he had attacked TRUMAN for 'losing' China by not giving enough support to JIANG JIESHI (Chiang Kai-shek) in the

CHINESE CIVIL WAR (1946–9) and had supported aid to DIEM's autocratic regime in South Vietnam. As President he believed that the US must oppose communism everywhere. He rejected EISENHOWER's caution and greatly increased the military budget. Though he knew that the 'missile gap' (the superiority the Soviet Union had in missiles) did not exist, he expanded the US missile programme: new intercontinental ballistic missiles were built and the number of nuclear-armed Polaris submarines increased. So the US could have a 'flexible response' to communist expansion he encouraged his Defence Secretary, Robert McNamara to enlarge conventional forces too. To overtake the USSR in the space race he obtained further funds for the Apollo programme to land a man on the moon (a mission achieved in 1969). To combat communism he formed the Peace Corps, volunteers to help in economic, educational and welfare programmes in the THIRD WORLD. This was a great success, unlike the ALLIANCE FOR PROGRESS, which was designed to prevent the spread of communism in Latin America by promoting economic development and democratic reform. The BAY OF PIGS INVASION of Cuba in April 1961 was intended to overthrow CASTRO but resulted in a humiliating defeat for the US. KHRUSHCHEV tried to bully Kennedy at the Vienna summit in June 1961, when he said that he would make a peace treaty with East Germany, which would end Western access to Berlin. Kennedy, invoking the DOMINO THEORY – if West Berlin fell to the communists, so would West Germany and then Western Europe – stood firm in his commitment to defend West Berlin and access to it, so Khrushchev dropped talk of a separate treaty.

More dangerous was the CUBAN MISSILE CRISIS of 1962, when Khrushchev brought the US and USSR close to nuclear war. Kennedy showed a cool nerve in dealing with the crisis. Nuclear war was avoided and Kennedy became a hero at home as he had stood up to the USSR, which had backed down.

Kennedy's greatest failure in foreign policy was in Vietnam, to which he never gave his full attention. He connived in the coup which overthrew (and killed) the unpopular DIEM and increased the number of US military 'advisers' there from 600 to 16,000, though he rejected the request of the Joint Chiefs of Staff to send regular troops there.

At home he had promised to 'get America moving again' and to extend Truman's Fair Deal but he achieved little, as he lacked adequate support in Congress: on some issues (civil rights, the welfare state) Southern Democrats would vote with Republicans. Several items of his New Frontier legislation – health insurance for the old (Medicare), federal aid for education, the reform of immigration laws – were rejected or held up by Congress. The economy was in recession in 1961 and with growth still sluggish in 1963, the president proposed tax reductions, which mainly benefited the rich. Kennedy took little action on civil rights before 1963, as he needed the support of white Southerners in Congress, so he did not attempt to pass legislation but relied on Executive Orders (which banned segregation in all new housing subsidized by the federal government), while the Attorney General (his brother Robert Kennedy) used the courts to enforce school desegregation. These actions did not satisfy blacks: Martin Luther KING accused the President of being satisfied with 'tokenism' in racial affairs. Kennedy's hand was forced by the actions of the CIVIL RIGHTS MOVEMENT which led to the Birmingham Demonstrations in Alabama. Kennedy believed that American prestige abroad suffered from segregation and feared that if nothing was done for blacks they would resort to violence. In 1963 he asked Congress to agree 'that race has no place in American life or law' and proposed a comprehensive CIVIL RIGHTS ACT which put the administration firmly behind the move for racial equality and was passed after his death.

On 22 November Kennedy was assassinated in Dallas by Lee Harvey Oswald, who was himself murdered two days later during a jail transfer. He was more widely mourned by a shocked nation than any other American President. Immediately he became a martyr, his achievements were exaggerated and he was regarded by many (though not by historians) as one of the greatest Presidents. The Warren Report decided that Oswald was responsible for the assassination and that no one else was involved. A House Committee reviewed this verdict and in 1979 came to the same conclusion.

John F. Kennedy and a New Generation, D. Burner (1988)
The Presidency of John F. Kennedy, J. Giglio (1991)
President Kennedy: Profile of Power, R. Reeves (1993)

Kenyatta, Jomo (*c.* 1897–1978) Prime Minister (1963–4) and President (1964–78) of Kenya. A Kikuyu, he was mission-educated. He worked as a clerk (1922–8) while becoming involved in Kikuyu political organizations. From 1929–46 he was in Europe (mainly in England) campaigning for African rights. When he returned to Kenya he immediately took over the national leadership. In 1953 he was sentenced on flimsy evidence to seven years' imprisonment for 'managing MAU MAU'. While in prison the founders of a new party, the Kenya Africa National Union (KANU) made him their President. KANU, whose main support came from the Kikuyu and Luo, won the 1961 elections but refused to take office until Kenyatta was released in August 1961. Thereafter there was steady progress towards independence in December 1963, with Kenyatta as Prime Minister and, when Kenya became a republic in 1964, as President. In the same year the Kenya African Democratic Union, which had support from minority ethnic groups, merged with KANU and Kenya became in effect a one-party state.

Kenyatta was at first dependent on Britain for defence and finance and called on British troops to crush an army mutiny in 1964. He allowed the US to use bases in Kenya, an unpopular move which, along with his conservative and capitalist policies, irritated radicals, as did his increasing authoritarianism and intolerance of opposition. Abroad, Kenyatta was a supporter of the NON-ALIGNED MOVEMENT and a vigorous critic of imperialism and of APARTHEID. In spite of huge problems arising from Kenya's rapid population increase and the move from countryside to towns, where there was high unemployment, Kenyatta was affectionately known as *Mzee* (old man) and revered as the father of the nation.

Kenyatta, J. Murray-Brown (1972)

Keynesianism   An economic doctrine derived from the work of the British economist John Maynard Keynes, whose most important book was *The General Theory of Employment Interest and Money*, published in 1936. Keynes was concerned at the high unemployment after the First World War which became even worse with the Great Depression beginning in 1929. He believed that unemployment could not be cured by applying classical economic theory. This said that unemployment would lead to falling wages and therefore lower costs of production, which in turn would produce a greater demand for goods and this would reduce unemployment. The government should not interfere by spending money on public works to stimulate employment, as this would divert funds to the public from the private sector. Left to itself the economy was self-adjusting and would produce full employment. Clearly that had not happened in the 1920s and 1930s. To deal with this problem Keynes devised a new economic theory, which took into account the institutional rigidities which classical economics ignored (for example, trade-union pressure might keep wages high and tariffs prevent competition). Keynes saw that a depression was caused by inadequate aggregate demand (i.e. the total spending of consumers, business and government). To counter this governments should lower interest rates (a 'cheap money' policy) and, if this did not stimulate investment sufficiently, they should substitute state action for inadequate private investment by granting subsidies or by undertaking a programme of public works, which would create employment and a demand for the products of industry. Fiscal policy is the main Keynesian tool for managing the demand for goods and services in the economy. Tax cuts will raise demand and therefore increase employment: if there is full employment and the economy is 'overheated', the government can apply the brakes by raising taxes and cutting public spending. National economies were not like households, where the books should be balanced. When the National Government of 1931 in Britain raised taxes and reduced unemployment benefit during a slump it made matters worse by reducing spending power. In a recession Keynes thought the government should deliberately run a deficit. Many regarded Keynesian economics as little different from socialism as it provided a theoretical justification for the increased role of the state in the economy, whereas Keynes favoured a mixed economy and was offering capitalism a lifeline when it appeared to be drowning.

In the US Franklin Roosevelt called for deficit spending in 1938 and Keynesianism became part of official US thinking by 1940. During the Second World War it came into its own as demand management was used to suppress private consumption and so release resources for the war effort. Raw materials were allocated to war industries, prices controlled and inflation checked by increasing taxes. In the immediate postwar decades exchange controls and the stability of the Bretton Woods system, which Keynes as the British delegate was instrumental in setting up, allowed governments to promote Keynesian programmes of growth, full employment and social welfare. The IMF and WORLD BANK were created to assist the expansion of international trade and investment. The idea that countries with balance of payments difficulties should reduce domestic demand was rejected. Instead a debtor country could seek a loan from the IMF to cover its trade deficit.

After the war there was a consensus that a return to the depression of the 1930s must at all costs be avoided, so Keynesian policies were adopted to prevent this. In the Employment Act (1946) in the US the government took responsibility for maintaining 'maximum levels of employment'. President KENNEDY cut taxes to increase economic growth when there was a deficit in the federal budget, confident that he could 'fine tune' the economy to produce full employment without inflation. In the 1970s President NIXON proclaimed that 'We are all Keynesians now' just at the time that Keynesism was beginning to unravel. It could not account for stagflation – inflation and stagnant growth – and was held responsible for some of the difficulties in the GLOBAL ECONOMY by concentrating on employment and neglecting inflation. By expanding consumption rather than savings it had denied industry the investment it needed and this had led to a declining growth of productivity. MONETARISM became popular as an alternative economic doctrine and claimed that the size of the money supply was all-important in the performance of the economy and in controlling inflation, which should be the prime economic aim of governments. Margaret THATCHER in the early 1980s, in an extraordinary reversal of Keynesianism, cut public expenditure and raised taxes in a recession.

The demise of Keynesianism was also brought about by changes in international economic affairs, when the fixed exchange rates of Bretton Woods were swept away by Nixon and replaced by floating rates; the value of national currencies would be decided by impersonal market forces. The removal of exchange and capital controls in the FINANCIAL REVOLUTION led to a huge growth of speculative currency transactions which vastly increased the power of international financial markets. The financial markets limited the room for manoeuvre of Labour governments in Britain in the 1970s by deciding what was the correct level of interest rates. Keynesianism in one country was no longer possible: high government borrowing could lead the market to take fright, sell the currency and force up interest rates.

Keynes and the Modern World, D. N. Worswick and J. Trevithick (eds) (1984)
The Political Power of Economic Ideas: Keynesianism Across Nations, P. A. Hall (ed.) (1989)

Khomeini, Ruholloh (Ayatollah) (1902–89)   Leader of the IRANIAN REVOLUTION (1978–9) and of the ISLAMIC REPUBLIC OF IRAN. Born in the town of Khomein, his father and grandfather were both SHII Islamic clergy. Khomeini studied theology at Qum, the main centre of Shii learning, where he became a teacher. He first became prominent in 1944 when he published a book attacking the policies of Riza Shah (who ruled Iran from 1926–41) but in 1946 he became a devotee of Ayatollah Borujerdi, the most learned Shii cleric. Borujerdi opposed clergy taking part in politics, so Khomeini did not take part in political activity while Borujerdi was alive, even during the turbulent years 1951–3 when the Prime Minister Musaddiq was in conflict with MUHAMMAD RIZA PAHLAVI. After Borujerdi's death in 1961 Khomeini resumed his attack on the Shah for making Iran a client of the US and for granting American advisers exemption from Iranian law: he called on the army to rise up and overthrow the royal tyranny. Following anti-government riots in 1963, in which many people were killed, Khomeini was exiled to Turkey (1964–5) and then to Najaf (1965–78), a Shii religious centre in Iraq. There he set out his ideas on Islamic government. An Islamic state, he wrote, should be based on the Quran and administered by a *faqih* (Islamic legal expert). 'It is the religious expert and no one else who should occupy himself with the affairs of government.' In Najaf and later in France (1977–8), when Saddam Hussein expelled him from Iraq, Khomeini maintained his persistent and virulent criticism of the Shah, his views smuggled into Iran on cassettes and spread through the mosque network. When the Shah was overthrown in the Iranian revolution (1978–9) Khomeini returned to Tehran to a delirious welcome. He had already appointed a pious layman, Mehdi Bazargan, as Prime Minister but did not think that much government was needed: all that was required was to apply the *Sharia* (Islamic law). There was no need for parties (all of which were abolished by 1987) or parliament. The new constitution of the Islamic Republic of Iran made Khomeini *vali faqih*, supreme guide and leader of the nation, for life. He controlled all important civil, military, judicial and religious appointments: he had unrivalled and almost absolute authority but he usually avoided interfering in the daily affairs of government, seeing himself as arbiter in conflicts among the clergy or his ministers.

He was partly responsible for bringing about the IRAN–IRAQ WAR (1980–8) by calling on the Iraqis to overthrow the secular Ba'th regime and when Iraq offered to end the war in 1982 he rejected this by demanding first the downfall of Saddam Hussein. Khomeini was therefore responsible for much of the loss of life and destruction of the economy which took place from 1983–8. His foreign policy was based on an implacable hostility to the 'Great Satan', the United States, relations with whom reached their nadir with the IRAN HOSTAGE CRISIS (1979–81). He wanted to spread the Islamic revolution far beyond Iran and called for the overthrow of Islamic regimes, particularly that of Saudi Arabia, which had close ties with the US. The Ayatollah had no success in exporting revolution to neighbouring countries, except among the Shii in Lebanon. Khomeini, believing in 'Neither East nor West', was a bitter critic too of the SOVIET INVASION OF AFGHANISTAN (1979). In 1989 he issued a *fatwa* (religious decree) condemning Salman Rushdie, a British subject, to death for his

book *The Satanic Verses* and in the same year he died, his death being greeted in Iran with hysterical expressions of grief. Incidents such as the RUSHDIE AFFAIR gave the Ayatollah Khomeini the reputation in the West of being a bloodthirsty tyrant and ISLAMIC FUNDAMENTALIST, who was determined to take his country back to the Middle Ages. In Iran he was revered as one who had successfully defied the West after centuries of humiliation and who had restored to Iran its Islamic heritage.

The Reign of the Ayatollahs, S. Bakhash (1985)
In the Name of God: The Khomeini Decade, R. Wright (1989)

Khrushchev, Nikita Sergeevich
(1894–1971)   First Secretary of the CPSU (Communist Party of the Soviet Union) (1953–64) and Prime Minister (1958–64). Born into a poor peasant family in southern Russia, he had little education before leaving the village at the age of 15 to go to a mining town, where he became a fitter. He joined the CPSU in 1918 and was a Red Army commissar during the Russian Civil War (1918–21). After the war he was a party official in Ukraine, where he impressed the first Secretary of the Ukranian Party, Kaganovich. In 1931, he followed Kaganovich to Moscow and built the underground transport system. By 1935 he was Moscow Party Secretary and played his part in STALIN's purges with thousands of victims. In 1938 he was sent to Ukraine to purge the party there: several thousand under investigation were summarily shot. Khrushchev became a full member of the Politburo in 1939, was a political officer during the Second World War and then Chairman of the Council of Ministers in Ukraine before Stalin brought him back to Moscow in 1949 and put him in charge of agriculture.

After Stalin's death he became First Secretary of the CPSU, took a leading part in having Beria executed and was then involved in a struggle for supremacy with Malenkov, which Khrushchev won when Malenkov resigned as head of the government in 1955. A group in the Presidium (the Politburo was known as the Presidium from 1952–65) led by Malenkov and Molotov tried to overthrow him in 1957 and had seven supporters in the Presidium to Khrushchev's four. He was saved as the KGB and army supported him and insisted that the matter should be discussed in a full meeting of the Central Committee of the CPSU, thus obtaining majority support for Khrushchev. Molotov and Malenkov lost their places in the Presidium but did not lose their lives, as they would have done under Stalin. In 1958 Khrushchev replaced Bulganin as Prime Minister and so held the leading posts in both party and state.

Khrushchev's joviality and peasant earthiness misled many into thinking that he was a buffoon. He genuinely wanted to improve the lot of the ordinary Soviet citizens and carried out a series of measures for their benefit: pensions and the minimum wage were increased, the housing stock was doubled, there were more medical facilities and further education and fees were no longer charged for secondary and higher education. Millions were released from the prison camps after Khrushchev's 'secret' speech to the TWENTIETH CONGRESS OF THE CPSU, which shocked so many by its denunciation of Stalin's reign of terror. Khrushchev brought this to an end and put the KGB (security police) under party control.

Agriculture was a priority, as in 1953 there were fewer cattle in the USSR than in 1913, while traction power (mechanical and animal) was only a fifth of what it was before collectivization in 1928. He wanted to increase agricultural production by investing more in machinery and fertilizers, by providing incentives (the prices paid by the state for agricultural produce trebled from 1952–9), by decentralizing decision-making and by expanding the sown area. Khrushchev provided a dynamism that had been missing before but he was capricious and often made decisions on impulse, ignoring expert advice. This was apparent in his 'virgin lands' scheme, which was to bring the steppe of

Kazakhstan and western Siberia under wheat cultivation, so that Ukraine could grow maize for cattle feed, thus increasing the meat supply. Scientists warned him of the high risk of soil erosion in Kazakhstan because of dry winds and uncertain rainfall but he went ahead and in the short-term was successful, as there was a bumper crop in 1956. By 1960, however, output had levelled off and yields were half those in Ukraine: from 1960–5 four million hectares of land in Kazakhstan were ruined and 12 million damaged. The growing of maize was no more successful, as the climate was unsuitable: of 37 million hectares sown in 1962 only seven million could be harvested ripe. The result was that in 1962 the government had to raise food prices and there were riots in the cities on a scale not seen since the civil war. The final humiliation was when Khrushchev had to import grain on a large scale from the US and Canada. A third of agricultural produce came from the 3 per cent of the sown area held as private plots by peasants.

Industrially the Soviet Union gave a misleading impression of strength when in 1957 Sputnik was launched, a satellite which orbited the earth. In 1959 a Soviet rocket reached the moon and took photographs of its dark side and in 1961 Yuri Gagarin became the first man to orbit the earth in space. These achievements appeared to show that the USSR had a lead over the US in science and technology but they used up vast resources: from 1958 the industrial growth rate declined. Khrushchev tried to promote initiative in an over-centralized system by replacing the central economic ministries by regional councils but this simply increased the provincial bureaucracy without leading to greater efficiency – the regional councils were disbanded after his fall.

In his foreign policy Khrushchev sought 'peaceful coexistence' with the Western capitalist powers, as he knew that there could be no victors in a nuclear war and he wanted to reduce the burden of arms spending. From 1953–6 there was a relaxation of international tension as he pursued a policy of DÉTENTE, helping to bring the KOREAN WAR to an end in 1953 and the INDOCHINA WAR OF INDEPENDENCE a year later. He sought good relations with China by restoring Port Arthur to it, ended the YUGOSLAV-SOVIET SPLIT by his reconciliation with TITO and signed the AUSTRIAN STATE TREATY, which provided for the independence of Austria and the withdrawal of Soviet troops, though at the same time the WARSAW PACT was formed as a counter to NATO and to protect Soviet interests in Eastern Europe. This period of *détente* came to an end in 1956 when Soviet troops crushed the HUNGARIAN RISING and when the USSR became a supplier of arms to Egypt in the SUEZ CRISIS. Relations with China deteriorated in 1960 with the SINO-SOVIET DISPUTE, when Khrushchev withdrew all Soviet and East European technicians from China. The U-2 INCIDENT resulted in Khrushchev's withdrawal from a summit meeting with President EISENHOWER and when KENNEDY became President Khrushchev put pressure on him to withdraw from Berlin (which he called 'a fishbone in the gullet') and sanctioned the building of the BERLIN WALL to stop the haemorrhage in the GDR (three million people had fled to West Germany). The most serious threat to world peace came with the CUBAN MISSILE CRISIS (1962), when there was real danger of nuclear war. Khrushchev backed down and lost much support in the Soviet leadership. He had already antagonized the armed forces by reducing them from 5.8 to 3.6 million men between 1956–60. A conspiracy among those he had promoted deprived him of all his posts in 1964, though he was given a pension and was allowed to live in Moscow.

Khrushchev and the Communist World, R. F. Miller and F. Feher (eds) (1984)

Khrushchev and Khrushchevism, M. McCauley (ed.) (1987)

Nikita Khrushchev, M. McCauley (1991)

Kim Il Sung (1912–94)   Prime Minister of the Democratic People's Republic of Korea (1948–72) and President (1972–94). Born Kim Song Ju in a peasant family he migrated to Manchuria in the early 1920s with his family, whose land had been taken by Japanese colonists. There he joined the Young Communist League in 1927, was a founder member of the Korean Revolutionary Army in 1930 and a member of the Communist Party (CP) a year later. He took the name Kim Il Sung from that of a legendary anti-Japanese hero and became a leader of guerrillas fighting the Japanese until 1942, when his unit retreated to Siberia and he came under the control of the Soviet Red Army. Returning to Korea after the defeat of Japan in 1945, he became First Secretary of the North Korean CP. In 1946 he formed the Korean Workers' Party (KWP), when the CP and other left-wing parties merged: it has ruled North Korea ever since. The USSR set up a communist state in the North which was proclaimed the Democratic People's Republic of Korea in 1948, with Kim as Prime Minister. He wanted to unite the whole of Korea (the US had set up an anti-communist regime in the South) and felt strong enough to do so, as the Soviet Union had provided him with artillery, tanks and aircraft for his powerful army. His invasion of the South began the KOREAN WAR, in which only US intervention prevented him from winning the quick victory he expected. Unable to cope with US military might, his regime was saved by MAO ZEDONG entering the war on his side.

After the war he established a ruthless dictatorship, executing many opponents in 1953 and concentrated on rebuilding the economy with Chinese and Soviet aid. He followed the Stalinist model of a command economy, with emphasis on heavy industry and the collectivization of agriculture, which was complete by 1958. As he had sealed off North Korea from the rest of the world, much of what went on in the North is unknown. Estimates of economic performance vary widely but it is beleived that North Korea had a per capita income higher than that of its communist neighbours and higher than that of the South until the late 1960s. After that the North began to fall behind the South, owing to lack of new technology and the heavy burden of a militarized state: defence expenditure officially took up 13–15 per cent of the budget, though the US estimated that the actual figure was 20–25 per cent.

Like Mao, Kim regarded himself as a political thinker and put forward the doctrine of *juche* (self-reliance), which in 1980 took precedence over Marxism as the only guiding concept of the KWP. The statue of Kim overlooking the capital Pyongyang was of suitably enormous proportions (500 feet high) for his personality cult. Kim's isolation became more complete when DENG XIAOPING restored China's diplomatic relations with the US and when in 1983 he was blamed for an assassination attempt on the South Korean President in Rangoon, a bomb killing half the South Korean cabinet. He withdrew from the Nuclear Non- Proliferation Treaty because he would not accept on-site inspection, after satellite photographs indicated that there were nuclear facilities in North Korea. The collapse of communism in the REVOLUTIONS OF 1989–91 deepened his insecurity and strengthened his determination that his son Kim Jong Il should succeed him, thus creating the first communist political dynasty.

Kim Il Sung: The North Korean Leader, Dae Sook Suh (1988)
North Korea in Transition, Chong-Sik Lee and Se-Hu Yoo (eds) (1991)

King, Martin Luther (1929–68)   A leader of the CIVIL RIGHTS MOVEMENT in the US. The son of a prominent Baptist minister in Atlanta, Georgia (who was a civil rights activist, leading campaigns for black voting rights) he followed his father in becoming a minister. While studying theology he was deeply influenced by the non-violent civil disobedience campaigns Mohandas GANDHI had organized against the British in India.

'We must meet the forces of hate with the power of love', he wrote. Before completing his doctorate in theology at Boston in 1955 he was appointed to his first ministry in Montgomery, Alabama. There he became involved in the MONTGOMERY BUS BOYCOTT and directed a year-long protest at bus segregation. The boycott ended in 1956 when the Supreme Court declared that segregation on buses in Alabama was illegal. Now well known nationally he founded the Southern Christain Leadership Conference, with its headquarters in Atlanta, which was the base for his civil rights campaigns for the next decade.

King did not direct or take part in most of the black protests of the early 1960s but his influence was extensive. The media portrayed King as controlling all forms of black protest – sit-ins, boycotts, freedom rides – but in fact he limited his active participation to a few highly publicized and orchestrated campaigns. In the 1963 Birmingham demonstrations in Alabama he achieved maximum publicity as police brutality was shown nation wide on television. The March on Washington of over 200,000 people in August of the same year was to promote civil rights legislation. Here he addressed the crowd from the Lincoln Memorial with: 'I have a dream that one day this nation will rise up and live out the true meaning of its creed – "We hold these truths to be self-evident, that all men are created equal"'. This ensured his selection as *Time*'s Man of the Year in 1963 and his award of the Nobel Peace Prize in 1964. His influence on the KENNEDY and JOHNSON administrations helped to bring about the CIVIL RIGHTS ACT of 1964. In 1965 he turned back to the South and organized the SELMA FREEDOM MARCH to the state capital of Montgomery in Alabama to demand the vote for disfranchised blacks (2.1 per cent of eligible blacks were enrolled in Selma). This provided the stimulus for the Voting Rights Act of 1965, which ended literacy tests as a prerequisite for registering voters and allowed federal officials to register voters.

From 1965 King's influence among blacks declined, as many thought that he was too conservative and too willing to compromise with whites. MALCOLM X's message of violent self-defence and the opposition of BLACK MUSLIMS to racial integration reflected the anger of northern urban blacks more effectively than King's moderation. In 1966 he was fiercely criticized by the BLACK POWER leader Stokely Carmichael. When King moved north to Chicago in 1966 to lead protests he met with an angry reception from many blacks. His support from whites declined too, as he publicly condemned US involvement in the VIETNAM WAR and as J. Edgar HOOVER and the FBI sought to discredit him. Yet he went ahead with plans for a 'Poor People's March' on Washington to protest at the economic plight of blacks. Before it took place he went in the spring of 1968 to Memphis, Tennessee to support (largely black) garbage collectors who were striking for higher pay and better working conditions. Here he was assassinated by a northern white. At the news BLACK GHETTO RIOTS took place in 125 cities in 29 states with a violence that King had long condemned: 70,000 troops were needed to suppress them. In 1986 King's birthday, 15 January, became a federal holiday.

King, D. L. Lewis (1978)
Bearing the Cross: Martin Luther King, Jr. and the Southern Christian Leadership Conference, D. Garrow (1986)
Parting the Waters: America in the King Years 1954–1963, T. Branch (1988)

Kissinger, Henry Alfred (1923–) US Secretary of State (1973–7). The son of German – Jewish parents who came to the US in 1938 to avoid Nazi persecution, he served in the US Army for part of the Second World War. In 1947 he entered Harvard University, took his doctorate in 1954 and spent the next 15 years at Harvard, lecturing and writing on international politics. His research programme on US – Soviet relations for the Council on Foreign Relations resulted in

Nuclear Weapons and Foreign Policy (1957), which criticized DULLES's concept of 'massive retaliation' and proposed a more flexible response. He directed the Harvard defence studies programme (1959–69), became a full professor in 1962 and was a defence consultant to President KENNEDY. Kissinger believed that rigid COLD WAR attitudes should be relaxed and that the balance of power was the key to international order. He sought DÉTENTE with the Soviet Union and a recognition of its strategic parity with the US, rather than looking for military superiority. Differences with the USSR should be discussed and resolved and confrontation avoided whenever possible. A moralistic approach to foreign policy and any attempt to change the internal systems of other countries should be avoided.

When Richard NIXON was elected President, Kissinger became his national security adviser and effectively displaced the Secretary of State (William Rogers) in formulating US foreign policy. He helped to define and carry out the Nixon Doctrine, which rejected the US's role as world policeman and encouraged regional powers (supported financially by the US) to take responsibility for their own security and to stem the spread of communism. Kissinger was partly responsible for the US ATTACK ON CAMBODIA, which was catastrophic for that country, while negotiating to bring about an end to American involvement in the VIETNAM WAR. His diplomacy in producing the Paris Peace Accords (1973) earned him the Nobel Peace Prize in 1973. As the President's personal emissary he went to China in 1971, where he prepared for Nixon's visit in 1972 and a volte-face in US–China relations, with the US withdrawing its objections to the People's Republic of China taking its place (previously held by the nationalist government in Taiwan) on the UNITED NATIONS Security Council. This was almost immediately followed by negotiations with the Soviet Union, which produced the SALT I agreement on limiting nuclear armaments. Kissinger's apparently spectacular successes in Vietnam, China and the USSR made him, according to Gallup polls, the most admired man in the US in 1972 and 1973.

His reputation for brilliance was enhanced and his inexhaustible energy exhibited in the shuttle diplomacy which ended the YOM KIPPUR WAR. Kissinger, Secretary of State in Nixon's second term and under President FORD, had to act quickly in airlifting military supplies to Israel after its initial setbacks, but thereafter showed a more even-handed attitude towards the Arabs. His very public shuttle diplomacy between Israel and the Arab states showed his mastery of detail, charm and endless patience in bringing about a cease-fire between Israel and Egypt and later between Israel and Syria. In 1973 he restored US diplomatic relations with Egypt (broken in 1967) after he visited SADAT in Cairo and the next year he arranged for Israeli forces to be pulled back from the Suez Canal, which could then be reopened. It was a great triumph too when the Arabs lifted their oil embargo on the US in 1974.

From 1974 his reputation waned. North Vietnam conquered the South in 1975 and communists took over both Cambodia and Laos. Congressional investigaors during WATERGATE discovered that he had ordered the FBI to tap the telephones of staff on the National Security Council, a charge he had earlier denied. It also became clear that he had attempted to prevent Chile's President, Salvador ALLENDE, from taking power and had then tried to destabilize his regime. With Ford's defeat in the presidential election of 1977 he lost control of US foreign policy. After retiring he wrote his memoirs: *The White House Years* (1979) and *Years of Upheaval* (1982)

The Price of Power: Kissinger in the White House, S. Hersh (1983)
Henry Kissinger and the American Approach to Foreign Policy, G. D. Cleva (1989)
Kissinger, W. Isaacson (1992)

Klaus, Václav (1941–) Prime Minister of the Czech Republic (1993–7). He obtained a doctorate in economics in 1967 and joined the

Academy of Sciences but after the failure of the PRAGUE SPRING he was forced to resign because of his democratic views. In 1989, as a leader of Civic Forum, he took part in the VELVET REVOLUTION and was Minister of Finance after the fall of the communist regime. A believer in MONETARISM, he was the most radical free-marketeer in the former communist countries of Eastern Europe. In his PRIVATIZATION programme 100,000 small businesses were sold and vouchers were offered to Czechs who could convert them into shares when the large state enterprises were sold. Foreign investment was encouraged and by the end of 1991 there were 3,000 joint ventures with foreign companies, notably between VW and Skoda. In 1991 Civic Forum split into the Civic Democratic Party (CDP) led by Klaus, and two other parties. The CDP won the general election of 1992, so Klaus became Prime Minister of Czechoslovakia and of the Czech Republic on the DIVISION OF CZECHOSLOVAKIA in January 1993.

With a secure majority Klaus was able to continue his economic reforms. By the end of 1993 60 per cent of Czech firms were privately owned, unemployment was low at 3.4 per cent but inflation was over 20 per cent. In the same year the Czech Republic, a model of order and stability, became a member of the UNITED NATIONS, CSCE, IMF, GATT and the WORLD BANK. Privatization was completed in 1994, inflation fell to 11 per cent and there was an increase in industrial production for the first time since 1989. In 1995 the Czech crown was made convertible and the Czech Republic became the first post-communist member of the OECD. A year later it applied for membership of the European Union. The 1996 general election deprived Klaus of his parliamentary majority (his coalition held 99 out of 200 seats) but he continued in office as head of a minority government until he resigned in December 1997.

Kohl, Helmut (1930–) Chancellor of the Federal Republic of Germany (1982–90) and of a united Germany (1990–). Born in the Rhineland–Palatinate, the son of a Roman Catholic tax officer, he joined the CDU (Christian Democratic Union) at the age of 17 before studying law and history at the universities of Frankfurt and Heidelberg. In 1959, after completing his doctorate, he was elected as a member of the *Land* (state) parliament of Rhineland–Palatinate. He was CDU leader in the region in 1963 and Prime Minister of that *Land* from 1969–76. During that time he became party leader of the CDU, was elected to the Bundestag (federal parliament), and in the 1976 election was the CDU's candidate for federal Chancellor but was defeated by Helmut SCHMIDT. He did not stand in 1980, when Franz-Josef Strauss was the CDU–CSU (Christian Social Union) candidate. Strauss's defeat enabled Kohl to recover his position and when the FDP (Free Democratic Party) withdrew from their coalition with the SPD (Social Democratic Party) and joined the CDU, Kohl became Chancellor in 1982. He called an election six months later which he won convincingly, the CDU/CSU winning 48.8 per cent of the vote, the SPD 38.2 per cent.

A huge man, affable and gregarious, Kohl was a cautious pragmatist and though he called for a *Wende* (turn-around), his economic policy continued much as before. He was not ideologically driven like THATCHER and REAGAN; he cut taxes but public expenditure was not reduced by the same amount, so there was a budget deficit until 1989. The Chancellor was careful not to offend powerful interest groups whose support he needed: large subsidies to agriculture, coal and steel therefore continued. There was little attempt to reduce the power of the TRADE UNIONS, which remained strong. There was a gradual recovery from the recession of the early 1980s, though unemployment remained high at over two million (8–9 per cent of the labour force). The 1987 election was a set-back for Kohl, as the CDU vote was the lowest since 1949 but he survived as Chancellor with the support of the FDP. Kohl continued Schmidt's policy of

locating cruise missiles in the FRG, though this became unnecessary with the INF (Intermediate Nuclear Force) TREATY of 1987. He had always been a strong believer in European integration, so that Germany would never again be a menace to its neighbours, and greatly valued the Franco-German alliance. With President MITTERRAND of France he began the European space programme EUREKA and maintained the momentum towards a united Europe by strongly supporting the Single European Act (1986), which opened the way to a single market in the EC (European Community) by 1992. He also reversed the CDU's opposition to OSTPOLITIK and gave generous credits to the GDR (German Democratic Republic: East Germany).

The EAST GERMAN REVOLUTION of 1989, when the communist regime collapsed, took Kohl by surprise. Those who wanted GERMAN REUNIFICATION assumed that it would take a long time but the movement of East Germans to the West at the rate of 60,000 a month placed a great strain on the FRG's housing and welfare systems. To stop this Kohl suggested an economic and monetary union of the FRG and GDR, which came into effect on 1 July 1990. Political union soon followed in October, after GORBACHEV approved of the change in return for large credits from the FRG. Unification was a triumph for Kohl and his Foreign Minister, Hans-Dietrich GENSCHER. In the first free elections in Germany for nearly 60 years in 1990 the SPD, lukewarm about unification, suffered its worst defeat since 1957. Kohl won handsomely, claiming that no one need be worse off from unification and that increased taxes would not be required. He greatly underestimated the costs of unification and had made his first mistake when he insisted that the conversion rate of GDR marks into DM should be 1:1. Karl-Otto Pohl, President of the Bundesbank, had wanted 2:1, as the overvaluation of the GDR mark would make the East German economy even more uncompetitive, while the increase in the money supply would lead to inflation.

Unification produced massive problems in the East. Property which had been confiscated by the communist regime was to be returned to its original owners. Two million claims, covering about half the land in the East, had been registered by the deadline of December 1992: the settlement of these claims could take up to 30 years. The uncertainty deterred investment, as East German productivity was about 30 per cent of that in the West. The difficulty arose of getting rid of uncompetitive industries without creating massive unemployment. The situation was made worse as there was a move to equalize wages in East and West by 1996, an intention which had to be abandoned, though wages continued to rise in the East far beyond productivity increases. The result in the former GDR was a fall in output of 65 per cent in 1990–1, the loss of two million industrial jobs by 1993 and of a further 750,000 in farming. Unemployment was officially 17 per cent in the East by 1992 (the real figure was probably nearer 30 per cent). The *Treuhandanstalt* was created for the PRIVATIZATION of state property in the East and sold most of the 8,000 state enterprises by the time it was wound up in 1994, but at the cost of amassing a debt of DM275 billion. To control inflation the Bundesbank raised interest rates to a postwar high of 8.75 per cent in July 1992, a policy which affected the rest of Europe, as other European central banks were forced to follow suit, and held back economic recovery. From 1991–5 economic revival in the East cost the German government DM150 billion a year, about half German tax revenues. Kohl had to renege on his tax pledges, increased income tax by 9 per cent in 1991 and imposed in 1993 a 'solidarity pact', which was a 7 per cent surcharge on income tax. There were also increases in VAT and the duty on petrol, all of which created great resentment. By 1992 there was a sharp recession in the US and a year later the worst recession in Germany since the war. Output of cars fell by 23 per cent, there were 150,000 job losses in the industry and there was a growth rate of −1 per cent. By 1994 the CDU had lost control in all but two states and the SPD had a majority in the Bundesrat, the upper house of parliament. Fortunately for Kohl the economy began to pick up in 1994 and enabled him to win an unexpected and narrow victory in the election of that year, the CDU and its FDP allies having a majority of ten seats. He continued to push for European integration and insisted that the strict conditions for a single currency imposed by the MAASTRICHT TREATY should be met.

Germany from Partition to Reunification, H. A. Turner (1992)
A History of West Germany, vol. 2, 1963–91, D. L. Bark and D. R. Gress (1993)
German Politics, 1945–95, P. Pulzer (1995)

Korean War (1950–3)   One of the most destructive and important wars of the twentieth century. Towards the end of the Second World War the Soviet Union and the US agreed to liberate Korea jointly, dividing the areas under their control at the 38th Parallel. The division of Korea was intended to be temporary but the two sides could not agree on how a united Korea was to be organized, so separate governments were established in 1948: the Republic of Korea in the South under Syngman Rhee and the Democratic People's Republic of Korea in the North under the communist KIM IL SUNG. Neither Kim nor Rhee expected the division to be permanent. Soviet troops were withdrawn from the North in December 1948 and US troops from the South in June 1949. Kim, whose army was provided with Soviet tanks, artillery and fighter aircraft, planned to unite Korea by force and was encouraged by the Joint Chiefs of Staff decision that Korea had 'little strategic value' for the US. In January 1950 Secretary of State Dean ACHESON gave a speech in which he said that the US defence perimeter in the Western Pacific ran through Japan and Okinawa to the Philippines, excluding Korea. Areas outside the perimeter, said Acheson, would have to rely on self-defence and the UNITED NATIONS. Kim, who expected a rising against Syngman Rhee's autocratic rule in the South, made the decision to attack, though it is unlikely that he would have acted without Stalin's approval. Stalin appeared to think that the fighting would be brief and that the US would not intervene but had no intention of becoming directly involved or of creating a diversion in Europe.

Kim invaded the South on 25 June 1950 and caught the US and UN by surprise, but they reacted swiftly. On the same day the UN called for the withdrawal of North Korean forces: the Soviet Union did not veto this decision, as it was absent from the Security Council as a protest at JIANG JIESHI's (Chiang Kai-shek's) regime in Taiwan representing China at the UN. President Truman, mindful he said of Manchuria (1931), Ethiopia (1935–6) and Austria (1938), when the inaction of the Western democracies encouraged aggression, applied the DOMINO THEORY to Korea and told General MACARTHUR, the Supreme Commander of the Allied Powers in Japan, to use American troops to prevent South Korea being overrun. He felt that if the communists were successful in Korea Stalin would seek to expand Soviet influence elsewhere. Having been accused of betraying Jiang and 'losing' China in the CHINESE CIVIL WAR (1946–9), Truman was determined to be tough on communism. Unless he intervened a possible third term in the White House would be impossible. On 27 June the Security Council called on the UN to provide military assistance for a Unified Command under the US and 16 nations sent forces: only those of Britain and Turkey were of any significance and they were small compared with the US contribution. The US provided nearly half of the UN forces (40 per cent were supplied by South Korea) and nearly all the naval and air forces. They were only just in time, as Kim's forces captured Seoul, the South Korean capital, and most of the South except for an enclave round Pusan in the southeast. MacArthur then carried out a bold amphibious landing in Sep-

tember at Inchon on the west coast near Seoul, far behind North Korean lines. It was remarkably successful: Seoul fell on 28 September, the US Eighth Army broke out at Pusan and the North Korean forces, caught in a pincer movement, disintegrated as they retreated north, leaving behind much of their artillery.

Truman now changed his objective. Instead of simply freeing the South he decided to move north of the 38th Parallel and unite Korea, although ZHOU ENLAI had told the Indian ambassador that a US advance would be resisted by China. This was dismissed as bluff. MacArthur captured Pyongyang, the capital of North Korea, on 19 October and informed Truman that 'the war is very definitely coming to an end shortly'. Even when he was aware of large-scale Chinese intervention in November he remained confident that the war would be over by Christmas, as the Chinese lacked air support and heavy artillery. His confidence was shattered by a massive Chinese offensive on 26 November, which halted the US advance towards the Yalu river, the border of China and Korea, and then pushed back American forces in headlong retreat. Pyongyang was recaptured on 5 December and ten days later Chinese forces were on the 38th Parallel. On 31 December the Chinese began an offensive to push the UN troops out of Korea. Seoul fell on 5 January 1951 and the Eighth Army withdrew to a line 70 miles south of the Parallel. MacArthur, his mood fluctuating between euphoria and deep depression, considered withdrawing UN forces from Korea. Truman even thought of using the atom bomb to halt the Chinese advance. This was unnecessary, as the Chinese did not have the logistical support for a prolonged offensive. The Eighth Army under General Ridgway recaptured Seoul, which changed hands for the fourth and last time in the war and advanced to the 38th Parallel. When MacArthur threatened China that it would be attacked if it did not negotiate with the UN, Truman decided that this challenge to his authority could not be ignored. With the support of Acheson, Marshall and the Joint Chiefs of Staff he dismissed MacArthur in April from all his commands and appointed General Ridgway to succeed him.

Half a million Chinese troops took part in an offensive on 22 April, came within five miles of Seoul and forced the Eighth Army to retreat 35 miles in good order. When they attacked again in May, in the last major offensive of the war, Ridgway routed them and advanced to the Parallel. Both sides were now prepared to negotiate but no agreement was reached, as many North Korean and Chinese prisoners did not want to return home. An armistice was not signed until 27 July 1953, after Stalin's death: no prisoners were to be repatriated against their will (30,000 out of 95,000 North Korean prisoners and 5,000 out of 21,000 Chinese prisoners chose to remain behind), the frontier between North and South being close to the 38th Parallel. A peace settlement has not yet been signed. South Korean casualties were over 300,000, those of the US 142,000 (including 33,000 killed). The UN Command estimated Chinese and North Korean losses at 'between one and a half and two million'. Unofficial estimates of civilian casualties are about a million in each country.

The Korean War had enormous repercussions throughout the world. South Korean independence had been preserved and the authority of the UN in resisting aggression upheld but the COLD WAR had been intensified alarmingly. China had contained the might of the US, had maintained a communist regime in North Korea and emerged with great prestige as an international power, but Acheson's hopes of the US accepting the People's Republic were dashed: in 1954 the US signed a mutual aid treaty with Taiwan and a year later Congress voted to defend the island against communist attack. Stalin's support for the North postponed DÉTENTE with

the US for another 20 years and began an arms race which the Soviet Union could not afford. The US extended the TRUMAN DOCTRINE to the Pacific by pledging US intervention against the expansion of communist rule in Asia. More aid was given to the French fighting against HO CHI MINH in the INDOCHINA WAR OF INDEPENDENCE and to the Philippines, where the communist Huk rebellion was a threat to the government. The US began its policy of containment by establishing bases throughout the world, in Morocco, Libya and Saudi Arabia and by making alliances with Australia, New Zealand and the Philippines. In a bid to strengthen NATO Acheson pressed for the rearming of Germany. One of the greatest beneficiaries of the war was Japan, whose economy began to take off with the 'Special Procurements' for US forces there. The US, anxious to make Japan a strong, democratic power, ended the OCCUPATION OF JAPAN and restored its sovereignty with the SAN FRANCISCO PEACE TREATY and integrated it into the anti- communist alliance with the JAPAN – US SECURITY TREATY. Others who benefited were dictators (BATISTA in Cuba, Trujillo in Dominica, Rhee in South Korea, Jiang in Taiwan), who could be sure of US aid provided they were anti-communist. Anti-communism became the touchstone of American policy both at home and abroad and enabled the pernicious influence of Senator MCCARTHY to spread throughout the US, diverting attention from domestic reform. The war also saw defence spending increase from $13 billion in 1950 to $50 billion in 1954 and the rise in the US of a MILITARY – INDUSTRIAL COMPLEX, which made it the most formidable military machine in the world.

Korea: The War Before Vietnam, C. MacDonald (1986)

The Korean War, B. I. Kaufman (1986)

The Korean War, W. Stueck (1995)

L

Labour Party   British political party. The Labour Party took its name in 1906, though its origins go back to the formation of the Independent Labour Party by Keir Hardie and others in 1893. Its constitution of 1918 committed it to socialism and the state ownership of the means of production. The Party Conference was the sovereign body, which determined policy, but this was dominated by the block vote of the TRADE UNIONS, which were outside the control of the party, though they were the main source of party members and funds. Conference decisions were binding on all party bodies. The Labour Party won only 57 seats in the 1918 election. Four years later it became the main party of opposition when, with 142 seats, it had more than the LIBERAL PARTY. When Baldwin surprisingly called another election in 1923 the Conservative Party lost its majority and the Labour Party under MacDonald was able to form the first Labour government, though it was dependent on Liberal support. In 1929, with rising unemployment, Labour won 188 seats and for the first time was the largest party in the House of Commons but it had still no clear majority. In the 1931 election, after MacDonald had formed a National Government with Liberal and Conservative support and been expelled from the party, Labour won only 46 seats. Clement ATTLEE became leader in 1935. In that year Labour won 154 seats and under the influence of Dalton and BEVIN moved away from its earlier pacifism to support rearmament and an end to appeasement. When the Second World War began the PLP refused to serve under Chamberlain but joined CHURCHILL's coalition government in 1940, Attlee being officially recognized as Deputy Prime Minister in 1942. Labour members of the government gained valuable ministerial experience and were able to develop policies which could be applied when the war ended. In 1945 the Labour Party surprised everyone by winning 393 seats, which gave it for the first time a clear majority (of 146) over all other parties.

The Attlee government of 1945–50 created the WELFARE STATE and nationalized about 20 per cent of British industry, but there was no overall economic plan and after 1948 little enthusiasm for further nationalization. The consensus, later known as BUTSKELLISM, which prevailed meant that the CONSERVATIVE PARTY accepted many of Labour's economic policies, while the Labour Party continued Conservative foreign policy. Attlee, Ernest Bevin and Hugh GAITSKELL all saw Britain as having a world role and were fervently pro-American, so that Gaitskell's 1951 budget hugely increased Britain's defence spending, which acted as a brake on economic development. Attlee's promotion of Gaitskell to be Chancellor of the Exchequer over the head of Aneurin BEVAN caused a split in the party which kept it out of office for the next 13 years. Gaitskell became leader when Attlee retired in 1955 and after Labour's third successive defeat in 1959 decided that the party should be modernized and abandon Marxism, as the German SPD (Social Democratic Party) was doing. He divided the party again by suggesting that Clause IV, which committed the party to the common ownership of the means of production, should be abandoned, but was unable to get his way.

Harold WILSON was leader of the Labour Party after Gaitkell's unexpectedly early death and Prime Minister when Labour won the 1964 election. He helped the old and the poor by raising pensions, family allowances and supplementary benefit. The Wilson government, however, failed to curb the power of the trade unions and had to withdraw the reforms IN PLACE OF STRIFE proposed. Defeated by the Conservatives in 1970, the Labour Party returned to power in 1974, again with Wilson as Prime Minister. When Jim CALLAGHAN replaced Wilson as party leader and Prime Minister in 1976, the strikes in the WINTER OF DISCONTENT discredited not only the unions but also the Labour Party with which they were associated. Trade unions at that time controlled 90 per cent of votes at the Labour Party Conference, elected two-thirds of the members of the National Executive Committee (NEC), sponsored many Labour MPs and contributed the bulk of party funds. They had much to do with Labour losing the 1979 election and thus opened the way for a prolonged period of Conservative rule.

In the wilderness the Labour Party lost four consecutive elections, sinking to 27.6 per cent of the vote in 1983, its lowest point since the war and was largely confined to its heartlands of the North and Scotland. Labour declined because its main source of support, workers in manufacturing industries, was greatly reduced with the collapse of old industries (textiles, steel, coal) and because several Thatcherite policies had great appeal to the electorate: the sale of council houses (58 per cent of manual workers owned their houses in 1985), the reduction of direct taxation, PRIVATIZATION as shares were sold to the public at knock-down prices which almost immediately produced a profit, and legislation to curb the power of the trade unions. However, many of Labour's troubles were self-inflicted. As the Conservative Party moved to the right, the Labour Party moved sharply to the left. Small groups of militants seized control of the constituency Labour parties and of the NEC (National Executive Committee) and committed the party to more nationalization, a new partnership with the unions, unilateral disarmament, and withdrawal from the EEC and NATO, policies which were completely out of touch with public opinion. Weakly led by Michael Foot, elected leader when Callaghan resigned, the party adopted this programme for the 1983 election, 'the longest suicide note in history', according to one Labour ex-minister. The move to the left produced another split, as four former ministers left the party in 1981 to form the SOCIAL DEMOCRATIC PARTY and took millions of Labour supporters with them, weakening the Labour Party throughout the 1980s. After the disastrous defeat in 1983 Foot resigned and was replaced as leader by Neil Kinnock. A man with impeccable left-wing credentials, he soon realized that the Labour Party would be a permanent party of opposition unless it abandoned policies the electorate disliked and adopted those it liked. He therefore began the painful process continued by John Smith and Tony BLAIR of reforming Labour's policies, which meant accepting many of Margaret THATCHER's reforms and bringing Labour's economic policies closer to those of the Conservatives. The Party Conference was emasculated and union influence reduced: the leader was put firmly in charge of deciding policy. Blair persuaded the party to abandon Clause IV. The success of New Labour was evident in the 1997 general election, when the Labour Party with 44 per cent of the vote, won 419 seats (over 100 women were elected as Labour MPs) in its greatest electoral victory ever, ending 18 years of Conservative rule. Tony Blair became the youngest Prime Minister since Lord Liverpool in 1812, committed to far-reaching constitutional reforms – elected assemblies for Scotland and Wales, the removal of hereditary peers from the House of Lords and a referendum on changing the voting system to some form of proportional representation.

The Labour Party Since 1945, K. Jefferys (1993)
The Labour Party Since 1945, E. Shaw (1996)
The People's Party, T. Wright and M. Carter (1997)

Lange, David Russell (1942–)   Prime Minister of New Zealand (1984–9). A lawyer, he entered parliament in 1977, becoming leader of the Labour Party in 1983, a year before he defeated Robert Muldoon and the National Party in the 1984 election.

Lange's main problems were at home, where foreign reserves were nearly exhausted and a run on the New Zealand dollar led to devaluation. Robert Douglas, a businessman and accountant whom Lange made Minister of Finance, decided to revive the economy by getting rid of the economic regulations which had grown up over the previous 50 years. The market not the government would make economic decisions, so he rejected the economic policies of Muldoon and of former Labour governments. The financial market was deregulated, the currency was allowed to float and all foreign exchange controls were abandoned. The tax system, based on direct taxes, was altered. The top rate of income tax of 66 per cent, reached on modest incomes, was cut to 48 per cent and later to 33 per cent. A Goods and Services tax of 10 per cent (later 12.5 per cent) was imposed to complete the biggest tax reforms since income tax was introduced in 1891. Agricultural and consumer subsidies were phased out, as were export incentives and import licences. State-owned industries (forestry, lands, coal and electricity) were told to make a profit, as one of the most regulated economies in the world became one of the most deregulated. A 'Family Care' package gave tax refunds to low-income families (mainly Maori and Polynesian) but the gap between rich and poor widened. Many traditional Labour supporters were appalled at Douglas's reforms, which pleased business and finance, and were surprised at Lange's increased majority in the 1987 election. From that time government fortunes ebbed. Lange wanted to slow down 'Rogernomics' while Douglas wanted to continue his reforms by selling off nationalized industries and by introducing a flat rate of income tax of 23 per cent. The Prime Minister refused, so Douglas wrote to him: 'New Zealand is now a country led by a Government paralysed by your inability to work with me'. He was dismissed. When Douglas was re-elected to the cabinet by the Labour caucus seven months later, Lange resigned and PRI-VITAZATION went ahead.

Revival of the Right: New Zealand Politics in the 1980s, B. Jesson, A. Ryan and P. Spoonley (1988)
The Quiet Revolution: Turbulence and Transition in Contemporary New Zealand, C. James (1986)

Lawson, Nigel, Baron (1932–)   British Chancellor of the Exchequer (1983–9). A non-practising Jew, whose grandfather had come from Latvia, he was educated at a public (independent) school and at Oxford University, where he obtained a first in politics, philosophy and economics. He then became a financial journalist and speech-writer to the Prime Minister Sir Alec DOUGLAS-HOME (1963–4) before entering parliament as a Conservative in 1974. When the CONSERVATIVE PARTY won the 1979 election and Margaret THATCHER became Prime Minister Lawson was Financial Secretary to the Treasury (1979–81) and Energy Secretary (1981–3), until he succeeded Sir Geoffrey HOWE as Chancellor of the Exchequer. MONETARISM had at first been adopted by Howe but it was Lawson who proposed the Medium-Term Financial Strategy in 1980 to reduce M3 (the money in circulation and banking deposits). This failed, as the money supply could not be controlled, and was abandoned by 1985. A fixed parity for sterling, like the old gold standard, then became the objective. Lawson therefore wanted to join the ERM (Exchange Rate Mechanism) to give Britain a stable exchange rate and lower the rate of inflation. It is 'the conquest of inflation and not the pursuit of growth and employment', he declared in 1984, 'which is or should be the objective of macro-economic policy'. Thatcher, relying on the advice of Professor Walters, an opponent of ERM, vetoed this, as it would limit the government's freedom of action on economic policy, so the Chancellor resorted to his own ERM by shadowing the Deutschmark at a parity of three to the pound.

Lawson also believed in a minimalist state, in which the role of government should be limited to 'removing controls and allowing markets to work better'. Financial deregulation, begun by Howe, was followed by a consumer boom, which sucked in imports as domestic industry had been decimated in the depression of 1979–81. In the boom, which lasted to 1989, growth rates were higher (they averaged 3.7 per cent 1984–8), living standards improved faster than at any time since the war and household borrowing escalated. There was a considerable expansion of credit cards, bank overdrafts and mortgages, which rose from £43 billion in 1980 to £235 billion in 1987. In the 1980s the real value of earnings rose by 25 per cent, of houses by 90 per cent and share values by 160 per cent. Lawson made no attempt to control the credit explosion and continued to cut the basic rate of tax from 30 per cent to 29 per cent in 1986, by another 2 per cent in 1987 and to 25 per cent in 1988, when the top rate was reduced from 60 per cent to 40 per cent. He talked of an 'economic miracle' and of success in keeping prices and interest rates down, while employment and growth rose. There was a budget surplus, partly because of higher tax revenues in the boom, the income from North Sea oil and PRIVATIZATION, and part of the public debt was repaid. Nemesis, however, was just around the corner. Inflation rose (4 per cent at the beginning of 1988, it was 10 per cent in the autumn of 1990) and by 1989 there was a record balance of payments deficit of £20 billion (4.4 per cent of GNP, as bad as in

1974). Lawson at first dismissed this as 'a blip' but then had to take action to curb demand. As raising income tax or imposing credit controls were ruled out for ideological reasons, he was left with what Edward HEATH called 'one club', interest rates. These were raised 12 times between June 1988 and October 1989, when they were 15 per cent. The result was the second slump in a decade, which proved to be the longest since the 1930s, as high interest rates hit investment, kept the exchange rate of the pound high and so damaged exports and created an added burden for mortgage holders. The Chancellor wanted the Prime Minister to get rid of Walters as an adviser. When she refused to do so he resigned in November 1989 and supported Michael Heseltine in the leadership election which took place a year later and which brought about the fall of Margaret Thatcher. He accepted a peerage in 1992.

The Economy Under Mrs Thatcher, 1979–90, C. Johnson (1991)

Lebanese civil war (1975–90)   In 1920 France created the state of Lebanon and ruled it as a League of Nations mandate through a system of 'confessionalism', by which positions in parliament, government and the civil service were allocated on a religious basis. At this time the Christian Maronites were Lebanon's largest religious community and so they dominated the state. In 1943, when Lebanon was about to become independent, the leaders of the different religious groups negotiated a National Pact, which continued the confessional system and guaranteed the Christians a majority in parliament, though the Muslims were by then probably a majority in the country. The President and top army command were Maronites, the Prime Minister was a SUNNI Muslim, the Speaker of the Chamber of Deputies a SHII Muslim and the Chief of Staff a Muslim Druze. In the 1950s under pro-Western governments Lebanon became the commercial capital and banking centre of

the Arab world. The Christian élite had great
wealth but blocked social reforms (public
health care, education and housing) which
would benefit the mainly Muslim poor. This
caused discontent, as did the political domination of Christians. An additional source of
friction was the existence in Lebanon of
large numbers (300,000 by 1972) of PALES-
TINIAN REFUGEES, who had fled there after
the first ARAB–ISRAELI WAR (1948–9) and
particularly when Palestinian guerrillas had
been expelled from Jordan by King HUSSEIN.
The Maronites wanted to get rid of the Palestinians, as their attacks on Israeli settlements
from Lebanon invited Israeli reprisals, and as
the PLO supported the Muslims and Druzes.

Full-scale civil war between Christians and
Muslims began in 1975, with the Muslims
demanding political change and the Maronites rejecting it. The Lebanese army broke
up on sectarian lines, state revenues dried up
and the government almost ceased to function. The PLO, which at first tried to avoid
becoming involved, joined in on the Muslim
side and soon controlled two-thirds of the
country. In desperation the Christians turned
to President ASAD of Syria. In 1976 Syrian
forces, acting as ARAB LEAGUE peacekeepers,
entered Lebanon, occupied half the country
and after 30,000 people had been killed,
60,000 wounded and 300,000 had fled,
arranged a cease-fire in October 1976. Syrian
intervention saved the Christians from total
defeat. This began an uneasy truce for five
years, during which the Maronites ruled the
north, the Syrian army controlled the east and
the PLO dominated the south of Lebanon.
Beirut was divided into an eastern section
controlled by the Maronites, and a western
part where the PLO and their Muslim allies
were in charge. Many towns and villages had
been badly damaged or destroyed and the
authority of the government had ceased to
exist. Sectarian militias took over local administration, collecting taxes and providing social
services.

The war became even more violent with the
Israeli invasion of Lebanon, for the first time

in 1978 and on a large scale in 1982. The
Israelis aimed to drive the PLO out of Lebanon. They succeeded, after a two-month
intensive bombardment of Beirut, which
destroyed much of the city, and withdrew
from Lebanon in 1985, except for a security
zone next to the Israeli border. The second
invasion gave rise to ISLAMIC FUNDAMEN-
TALIST groups among the Shii, particularly
HIZBULLAH, which used car bombs, suicide
attacks and the taking of hostages in its violent
anti- Christian and anti-Western campaign. A
US, French and Italian peace-keeping force
withdrew after suicide bombers destroyed the
US and French headquarters, killing over
300. Syrian forces, who had withdrawn in
1982 after being mauled by the Israelis,
returned in 1987 to restore order and stop
fighting between the Muslim Amal and
Druze militias in Beirut. In September 1988
the political system broke down completely,
as parliament could not agree on a successor
to President Amin Jumayyil, who then
departed from tradition by appointing a Mar-
onite Prime Minister, General Awn (Aoun),
the army commander. The existing Muslim
Prime Minister, supported by Syria, refused
to give way. Awn, who received arms from
Iraq, tried to expel Syrian forces and so began
a bitter conflict which destroyed much more
of Beirut before Awn was defeated in 1990.
Meanwhile the US and Saudi-Arabia had
negotiated the Taif Accords in October 1989
with the Lebanese parliament. The National
Pact was amended: there was to be equal
parliamentary representation for Christians
and Muslims in spite of Muslims being
between 60–75 per cent of the population.
The powers of the Sunni Prime Minister
were to be strengthened at the expense of
those of the Christian President but the confessional system remained. Syrian forces, with
US approval, crushed opposition to the
Accords and imposed a cease-fire. A new
pro-Syrian government began to disarm the
militias and extended its control throughout
the country, though Israel controlled the border region and continued sporadic military

actions in the south. It is estimated that 150,000 were killed in the civil war.

War and Intervention in the Lebanon, Y. Evron (1987)
The Struggle over Lebanon, T. Petran (1987)
Many Mansions: The History of Lebanon Reconsidered, K. S. Salibi (1988)

Lee Kuan Yew (1923–) Prime Minister of Singapore (1959–90). The son of a wealthy Chinese family, he was educated in English and gained first class honours in law at Cambridge University. Lee, who described himself as an 'Anglified Chinaman', returned to Singapore in 1951 and practised as a barrister before forming the socialist People's Action Party (PAP) in 1954. A year later he was elected to the Singapore Legislative Assembly and, when Singapore was granted internal self-government in 1959, became the country's first Prime Minister, a post he held for 31 years. Lee was a strong supporter of Singapore joining the Federation of Malaysia (1963) but he clashed with the Prime Minister of the Federation, Tunku ABDUL RAHMAN, who wanted to ensure that Malays dominated the new state. In 1965 Singapore was forced out of the Federation.

Lee effectively ruled a single-party state, as the PAP held all seats in parliament from 1968 to 1981, when two opposition members were elected. He promoted 'Asian values', described in a government White Paper of 1991 as 'nation before community and society above self' and 'consensus instead of contention'. Firm, paternalistic government ensured that the PAP gained control of every aspect of life: political, economic and social. PAP officials closely watched housing and clan associations, student organizations and trade unions: 90 per cent of trade union members were in the ruling party's National Trades Union Congress, headed by a government minister and run by civil servants. There were no strikes to disturb the smooth running of industry. It was impossible to start a private organization without government approval and for many years students needed a Suitability Certificate before they could enter university. 'We decide what's right', Lee said in 1987. 'Never mind what the people think'. The government alone provided economic and social services such as telephones, ports, airports, television, health services and education. Around 75 per cent of the population lived in government-subsidized housing. Much of the economy, too, was controlled by the state through government-linked companies, but Lee was careful not to take his socialism too far, as Singapore's export-oriented economy was based on investment from MULTINATIONAL CORPORATIONS.

Economic success was the great hallmark of Lee's rule. This was built on Singapore being an international entrepôt and on policies (such as tax breaks) to encourage foreign investment. In the late 1960s the state developed manufacturing and financial services. In 1960 90 per cent of manufactures were for domestic consumption: in 1993 two-thirds were exported. Half the workers in the 1980s were in foreign-owned firms, which accounted for 80 per cent of Singapore's exports. High growth rates (10 per cent each year in the 1960s, 14 per cent in the 1970s, 5 per cent in the global recession of the 1980s, 7 per cent in the first half of the 1990s) made the standard of living in Singapore the highest in Asia, apart from Japan's.

Lee made Singapore a founder of ASEAN in 1967. Strongly anti-communist, his relations with China did not improve until DENG XIAOPING began his open-door economic policy in the SPECIAL ECONOMIC ZONES, which allowed a free market and joint ventures. He remained a powerful figure behind the scenes after stepping down as Prime Minister, taking the official title of Senior Minister.

Singapore: The Legacy of Lee Kuan Yew, R. S. Milne and D. K. Mauzy (1990)

Lemass, Sean (1899–1971) Taoiseach (Prime Minister) of Ireland (1959–66). He fought in the Easter Rising (1916) and in the Irish Civil War (1922–3) on the side of those who rejected the Anglo-Irish Treaty (1921), which set up the Irish Free State without including the North. A founding member of Fianna Fail, Lemass entered the Dail (Irish parliament) in 1925 and was Minister of Industry and Commerce in various de Valera governments from 1932. A pragmatist, he differed from de Valera on economic policy. De Valera had created some of the highest tariff barriers in the world in an attempt to make Ireland self-sufficient. The result was a declining economy. When living standards were rising sharply in the West in the 1950s they were falling in Ireland: 400,000 emigrated in the 1950s.

Lemass succeeded de Valera as Taoiseach in 1959 and was the first Irish leader to recognize that Ireland needed to open up to the GLOBAL ECONOMY. He was greatly influenced by the views of civil servants, notably Kenneth Whitaker, later described by *The Irish Times* as 'the architect of modern Ireland'. Whitaker was impressed by the success of Jean MONNET's state planning in France and sought to promote foreign investment and planned growth. KEYNESIANISM was the basis for his new economic strategy. Lemass applied Whitaker's ideas. Protection was reduced, the state became more involved in industrial planning; foreign investment and export industries were encouraged by tax breaks. A rapid improvement in the economy followed. In 1960 exports exceeded the 1929 volume for the first time and by 1966 were 59 per cent above those of 1929. Agricultural output rose by 9 per cent in the 1960s but industrial output grew by 83 per cent between 1959 and 1968. Unemployment fell, as did emigration, and real incomes rose. Ireland was still economically closely attached to Britain (about half Irish exports went to Britain and half its imports came from Britain), so when Britain applied for membership of the EEC in 1961, so too did Ireland. DE GAULLE vetoed this but Lemass's export-oriented policies enabled Ireland to benefit from the world boom of the 1960s and prepared it for entry to the Common Market in 1973. He ceased to be premier in 1966 but stayed in the Dail until he retired in 1969.

Sean Lemass and the Making of Modern Ireland, 1945–66, P. Bew and H. Patterson (1982)
Sean Lemass, B. Farrell (1983)
The Best of Decades: Ireland in the 1960s, F. Tobin (1984)

Liberal Democratic Party (LDP)   The conservative party which ruled Japan continuously from its formation in 1955 until 1993. Pressure from big business and fear of a socialist resurgence prompted two conservative parties to unite and form the LDP in 1955. It followed the policies of YOSHIDA SHIGERU of concentrating on economic development and allying with the US for defence, but it was more a coalition of factions rather than a united party. In 1955 there were eight factions, based on personal or regional allegiances rather than a common policy. These factions split when a leader died. Extensive bargaining among the factions took place before party and cabinet posts could be allocated. The LDP elected its President (who automatically became Prime Minister as the LDP had a majority in the Diet) every two years and in 1971 fixed a maximum limit of two terms. The leadership of the LDP often rotated among the faction leaders.

The dominance of the LDP was largely due to the support of big business, which provided the financial backing, though its leaders pursued policies to appeal also to farmers and small businessmen. Farmers were given subsidies for rice production and vegetables, paid low taxes and were protected against agricultural imports. These measures benefited the LDP as rural constituencies were overrepresented in the Diet. Small business (in 1981 50 per cent of the work-force was in enterprises of under 30 people) were provided with cheap loans, low rates of tax and protected from the expansion of large department stores. The LDP appealed to a wider public by providing the foundations of a WELFARE STATE in health care benefits and pensions.

The LDP's share of the vote at both local and national levels declined in the 1970s, when a large number of municipalities were controlled by progressive parties. Financial abuses rocked the LDP, such as the Lockheed scandal in 1976, when Tanaka Kakuei was accused of having been paid 500 million yen by the Lockheed Company of the US to ensure that its Tristar jets were bought by a Japanese airline. In the December 1976 election the LDP failed to gain a majority in the lower house of the Diet for the first time since 1958 and did not have an overall majority again until 1986. In 1989 the LDP lost control of the upper house for the first time and in 1993 its ascendancy temporarily came to an end in the lower house, when a seven-party coalition was formed which excluded the LDP. Political instability ensured that its exclusion was brief – a year later it shared power in a surprising coalition with the Japan Socialist Party.

Party Politics in Japan, H. J. Baerwald (1986)
'The Structure and Transformation of Conservative Rule', G. Allinson in *Postwar Japan as History*, A. Gordon (ed.) (1993)
Postwar Japan 1945–95, P. J. Bailey (1996)

Liberal Party (Britain)   It is descended from the Whigs and Nonconformist radicals. Historians use the term 'Whig' or 'Liberal' to describe the same political group in the period 1832–67. Gladstone was leader of the first government (1868–74) generally called Liberal, but only with the National Liberal Federation (1877) did the structure of a mass party begin to appear. Gladstonian liberalism was committed to removing restrictions on political, religious and economic life, which involved abolishing the privileges of the Church of England and promoting *laissez-faire*. It was concerned with political rather than social reform and with 'retrenchment' in

government, which meant keeping taxes low. Gladstone split the Liberals in 1886 over Home Rule for Ireland, which kept them out of office for most of the time from 1886 to 1905.

Their overwhelming victory in 1906 began a decade of reforms, the greatest before the Second World War, which were influenced by the New Liberalism, favoured more extensive state intervention and laid the foundations of the WELFARE STATE. In 1915, during the First World War, Asquith ended ten years of Liberal rule by forming a coalition government. There has never been another Liberal administration. The Liberals divided again, disastrously, in December 1916, when Lloyd George, with the help of the Conservative leader Bonar Law, replaced Asquith as Prime Minister. About half the parliamentary Liberal Party followed Asquith into opposition. At the end of the war Lloyd George and Bonar Law decided to continue the coalition and fought the 1918 election on a common platform. The result was a massive vote of confidence in Lloyd George – over 520 coalition candidates were returned (including 136 coalition Liberals), but the Liberal Party in the country was destroyed, only 28 Asquithian Liberals winning seats. After that the Liberals never looked like becoming a party of government again. The Labour Party replaced the Liberals as the official opposition in 1922, and though the Liberals reunited again in 1923 under Asquith to oppose Baldwin's tariff reform and won 159 seats, Labour had 191. A decline followed: 40 seats in 1924 but only 12 in 1945. The Liberal Party enabled minority Labour governments to survive in 1923 and in 1929 and took part in Churchill's wartime coalition (1940–5). This was the only way Liberals could return to office.

After the war the first-past-the-post system was a considerable handicap to the Liberals and meant that the number of seats they won did not reflect the amount of their support. In February 1974 over six million people voted Liberal (19.3 per cent), yet only 14 Liberal

MPs were elected (the Conservatives with 11.8 million votes had 297 MPs, Labour with 11.6 million votes had 301). The number of Liberal MPs from 1945 to 1979 varied from 6 to 14, almost all from the South-west, Wales and Scotland. The Liberal Party did much better in local elections, winning control of numerous local authorities, and therefore tended to concentrate on 'community politics' and local issues: it backed racial and religious minorities and civil rights. The Liberal Party was a fervent advocate of proportional representation, which would greatly increase its number of MPs, but the two major parties opposed this. The best chance of a Liberal breakthrough came when it allied with the SOCIAL DEMOCRATIC PARTY in 1983. The Alliance won 7.7 million votes in the 1983 election, 25.4 per cent of the vote and only 2.2 per cent behind the Labour Party, but once again the electoral system did not reflect the voting strength of the Alliance, for whom only 23 MPs were returned. The 'mould of politics' had clearly not been broken. After the 1987 election, when it won 22 seats, the Alliance broke up, the SDP and the Liberals merging as the Liberal Democrats. They gained 20 seats with 18.3 per cent of the vote in 1992 and five years later had their greatest electoral success since 1929 (largely due to tactical voting – their share of the vote fell) when 46 Liberal MPs were returned.

Liberal Party Politics, V. Bogdanor (ed.) (1983)

liberation theology A movement among Roman Catholic clergy in Latin America which began in the 1960s. It was partly inspired by the Cuban Revolution of Fidel CASTRO but was mainly a result of the pontificate of JOHN XXIII, who called all Catholic bishops together in the Second Vatican Council (1962–5) to discuss Catholicism's role in the modern world and encourage awareness of social and economic issues. The conference of Latin American bishops at Medellín in Colombia in 1968, opened by Pope Paul VI

(the first pope to visit Latin America), declared that the Church had an 'option for the poor' and embraced the dependency theory that international capital had institutionalized poverty in South America by making the continent dependent on foreign-controlled trade and investment. This was taken up by Gustavo Gutiérrez, a Peruvian priest who published *A Theology of Liberation* in 1971, in which he argued that Latin America needed a social revolution and that violence might be required to liberate the poor. The social ownership of the means of production was called for, to end the dominance of international capitalism, which was the main cause of underdevelopment. He wanted the poor to be agents of their own liberation through *communidades de base*, grassroots communities of lay people who would act to improve social conditions. They had been organized in Brazil and approved at Medellín. Many priests took jobs in city factories and lived among the workers. Others organized religious and social activities in the shanty towns, while missionaries working in the Indian communities encouraged political action to gain land reform. Marxist ideas of class struggle, exploitation and imperialism influenced liberation theology and split the Catholic Church. Most clergy did not accept it because of its association with Marxism but some supported an armed rising and joined Marxists guerillas in the countryside.

The Church upheld human rights against authoritarian regimes in the 1970s, especially when right-wing death squads were active, and in Chile, after the fall of ALLENDE and the establishment of a military dictatorship under PINOCHET, criticized the violation of human rights there and provided relief for the destitute. In El Salvador Oscar Romero, the Archbishop of San Salvador, became increasingly outspoken in condemning deathsquads and defended the rights of popular movements to build a just society. He was murdered in 1980 as he was saying mass. Pope JOHN PAUL II criticized liberation theologians for borrowing from Marxism and forbade clergy from holding political office (some Jesuits and priests served in the SANDINISTA government in Nicaragua), but in 1986 took a more positive attitude to the base communities and said that armed struggle might be legitimate 'as a last resort to put an end to an obvious and prolonged tyranny'. The Vatican seemed to recognize that liberation theology had wide support in Latin America and that, with its Marxist elements removed, it could be a way of helping the poor. The continuing influence of the movement was shown in Brazil in the late 1980s, when the elected mayors of several important cities were from the base communities, and in Haiti in 1990, when Father Jean-Bertrand Aristide was elected President by a huge majority.

Liberation Theology, P. Berryman (1987)
Liberation Theology and its Critics: Towards an Assessment, A. F. McGovern (1989)
Liberation Theology at the Crossroads: Democracy or Revolution? P. E. Sigmund (1990)

Libya, US raids on (April 1986)   The US, convinced that QADDAFI was supporting international terrorism, considered a military strike against Libya after the terrorist bombing of Rome and Vienna airports on 27 December 1985. During a US naval exercise in the Gulf of Sidra, off Libya, which Qaddafi regarded as Libyan territorial waters, Libyan forces fired missiles at US warplanes on 24 March 1986. The US retaliated by sinking two Libyan patrol boats and attacking a missile site. On the same day US intelligence intercepted messages from Tripoli to Libyan missions in eight countries, ordering them to attack American targets. On 5 April 1986 a bomb went off in a West German discotheque crowded with US servicemen, causing 232 casualties. President REAGAN therefore ordered F1-11 bombers, using bases in Britain with the consent of Prime Minister THATCHER, to attack targets in Libya on 15 April. Three main targets in Tripoli were hit, killing or wounding 66 people: US Navy

planes bombed Benghazi barracks and airfield.

Lin Biao (1907–71)   Chinese general and politician. From a modestly affluent landholding family in central China, he went to Guangzhou (Canton) in 1925 to the Military Academy in Whampoa. A year later he took part in JIANG JIESHI's (Chiang Kai-shek's) Northern Expedition against the warlords. When Jiang turned against his communist allies in 1927 Lin joined MAO ZEDONG in the Jiangxi Soviet and from 1928–34 expanded the area it controlled and defended it against the Nationalists. When the communists were driven north by Jiang on the Long March, Lin commanded the communist vanguard and reached Yanan with the reputation of never having lost a battle. In the Sino-Japanese War (1937–45) he was badly wounded and spent 1939–42 recuperating in Russia. During the CHINESE CIVIL WAR (1946–9) he showed real brilliance as a commander, driving the Nationalists out of Manchuria and ensuring the defeat of Jiang in China. Lin captured Beijing in January 1949, Wuhan in May and Guangzhou in October.

He did not play a prominent part in the early years of the communist regime, as he suffered from prolonged ill-health, but he was steadily promoted. In 1955 he became a Marshal and member of the Politburo and joined its inner sanctum, the Standing Committee, in 1958. Lin came more into prominence when, a year later, he replaced Peng Dehuai (who had criticized the COMMUNES in the GREAT LEAP FORWARD) as Defence Minister. Following Mao, he stressed the importance of the People's Liberation Army (PLA) being loyal to the Chinese Communist Party (CCP) and compelled all soldiers to study the Little Red Book (*Quotations from Chairman Mao*). This led Mao by the end of 1963 to call on all Chinese to 'learn from the PLA' and helped to revive his fortunes after the disasters of the Great Leap Forward. Lin was a fervent supporter of the CULTURAL REVOLUTION, during which he replaced LIU SHAOQI as Mao's successor. The army was needed to restore order in 1969 and until 1971 effectively ruled China. Mao appeared to feel that the army was becoming too powerful and clashed with Lin by rehabilitating cadres who had been dismissed during the Cultural Revolution and by regarding the US as less of a threat to China than the Soviet Union, which had been involved in border clashes with China in 1969. In 1971 Lin attempted a coup to assassinate Mao and seize power. When this failed he was supposedly killed when his plane crashed in Mongolia on its way to the Soviet Union. The Mongolian government in 1990 doubted that he had been killed in an air crash there, so his death remains a mystery.

A Politico-Military Biography of Lin Piao, T. W. Robinson (1971)
The Rise and Fall of Lin Piao, J. van Ginnecken (1976)

Little Rock (1957)　　A town in Arkansas, United States where the state government defied the Supreme Court's decision in BROWN V TOPEKA (1954) that segregation of public schools was unconstitutional. When the school term began on 2 September 1957 the Governor of Arkansas, Orval Faubus, sent the National Guard to prevent nine black students entering the Little Rock High School. They were withdrawn after three weeks on the orders of a federal judge but replaced by a white mob. The mayor appealed to President EISENHOWER, saying 'the situation is out of control and police cannot disperse the mob'. The President reluctantly sent in US troops to keep order and ensure black students entered the school, telling a Southern Senator that 'failure to act in such a case would be tantamount to acquiescence in anarchy and the dissolution of the union'. This was the first time since Reconstruction that federal troops had been sent to the South to protect the civil rights of blacks. The matter did not end there, as the city voted in 1958 to close the high schools rather than keep them open on a desegregated basis. They reopened as desegregated schools in 1959 only when the Supreme Court refused to allow their conversion to private (and therefore segregated) schools.

The Little Rock Crisis, T. Freyer (1984)

Liu Shaoqi (1898–1969)　　Chairman of the People's Republic of China (1959–68). The son of a rich peasant landowner, he went to Moscow to study in 1920 and joined the Chinese Communist Party (CCP) when it was founded in 1921. On returning to China in 1922 he became the party's main labour organizer. In 1932 he joined MAO ZEDONG in the Jiangxi Soviet and became a member of the Politburo in 1934. During the Sino-Japanese War (1937–45) he worked underground to organize the party in areas under Japanese occupation before joining Mao in the communist base of Yanan. Here he became second only to Mao in importance and after the communist victory in the CHINESE CIVIL WAR (1946–9) was appointed Vice-Chairman of the People's Republic of China.

By 1956 he was Mao's heir-apparent and supported the GREAT LEAP FORWARD, but after its disastrous failure he pursued policies which were increasingly at variance with those of Mao. Liu and DENG XIAOPING reversed the Great Leap policies and reestablished central control. The functions of the COMMUNES were reduced, private plots and free rural markets allowed. Less emphasis was placed on ideology and more on expertise. All this was anathema to Mao and his radical wife JIANG QING. During the CULTURAL REVOLUTION (1966–76) Liu was accused of a 'dual track system' that restricted higher education to a privileged few and in August 1966 was named as the 'top Party person . . . taking the capitalist road'. He disappeared from public view, lost all his state and party offices in 1968 and, weakened by constant interrogations in prison and denied medical care, he died in 1969. Liu was the last major victim of the Cultural Revolution to be post-humously rehabilitated in 1980.

Liu Shao-ch'i and the Chinese Cultural Revolution, L. Dittmer (1974)

Luxembourg Compromise (1966) It created a national veto over all important decisions in the EEC (European Economic Community). In June 1965 General DE GAULLE rejected new proposals for financing the COMMON AGRICULTURAL POLICY and for majority voting on many issues. France boycotted all Council meetings in the second half of 1965 and so made it impossible for the EEC to make decisions. The Compromise allowed any state in the EEC to veto a decision if it felt that its vital interests were at stake. This prevented any significant changes in the EEC for the next 20 years. Not until the Single European Act of 1986 did members agree on a substantial extension of majority voting in order to prepare for a single market. Since then there have been few attempts to use the veto.

M

Maastricht Treaty (Treaty on European Union)   Agreed at a meeting of the European Council in Maastricht, the Netherlands, in December 1991 it came into force in November 1993, after being ratified by all 12 states of the European Community (EC). A timetable was set for Economic and Monetary Union (EMU). Controls on capital movements between member states would be abolished and their economies would begin to converge. Convergence would be measured by inflation (which must be within 1.5 per cent of the three lowest rates in the European Union, as the EC was now called), by interest rates (within 2 per cent of the lowest rates), the budget deficit (under 3 per cent of GNP), the public debt (under 60 per cent of GNP) and by foreign exchange stability (no devaluation in the last two years). For all the states which met these criteria by 1998 there would be fixed exchange rates leading to a single currency and the setting up of a European Central Bank. There was also agreement on establishing a common foreign policy and on greater co-operation to deal with immigration, the DRUG TRADE and organized crime. A Social Chapter on working conditions was removed from the treaty, as the British Prime Minister John MAJOR refused to accept it, and appeared as a separate Social Protocol, signed by the other 11 member states. Britain and Denmark were given the right to opt out of the binding final stage of EMU.

France saw the treaty as a means of influencing German financial policies, which had important effects on the French economy, and of tying down a united Germany in a European Union. Kohl regarded it as a way of achieving stability in Germany's major export markets, of preventing the resurgence of German nationalism and of reassuring Germany's partners. There were deep divisions between those (led by Britain) who did not want any further erosion of national sovereignty and those (led by Germany and France) who believed that only by making the EU a supranational community would Europe be able to compete effectively with the US and Japan. For the general public the treaty was unintelligible. Two referenda (in 1992 and 1993) were needed in Denmark before the treaty was approved, while the French voted in favour by the narrowest of margins in September 1993. By May 1998 all members, except Greece, had met the criteria for qualification to EMU, though some had done so by creative accounting and others by the PRIVATIZATION of state-owned services (the telephone service and Lufthansa in Germany).

EMU will remove some of the sovereign power of countries in the EU. They will no longer be able to print money to drive down interest rates and stimulate investment, or to devalue to help exports, and their ability to stimulate demand by deficit spending will be severely curtailed, as Germany has insisted that all members subscribe to a 'stability pact', which means that the Maastricht criteria will remain forever. At the beginning of 1999 a European Central Bank will take control of the money supply and interest rates of all countries in the EMU. For three years the euro, the new European currency, will coexist with national currencies but in 2002 all national currencies of member states will disappear. Big business has welcomed the euro, as it will do away with costly hedging operations to insure against currency fluctuations, will make international payments easier and will reduce the exchange rate risks of long-term investment. Large banks and insurance companies see a huge market, larger than that of the US, opening up with a single currency.

MacArthur, Douglas (1880–1964) One of the most distinguished soldiers in American history. The son of an American Civil War hero who became Governor of the Philippines, MacArthur graduated first in his class from West Point in 1903. Aide-de-camp to President Theodore Roosevelt (1906–7), he served in the Philippines, East Asia and Mexico, reaching the rank of major by 1917, when the US entered the First World War. He was a brave and dashing leader of the 42nd Infantry Division, being twice wounded: he ended the war as a brigadier-general. He then became superintendent of West Point and held important posts in the Philippines and the US before becoming Chief of Staff of the army, the youngest holder of that post. When his term ended in 1935 he was appointed military adviser to the Philippine government. He retired from the army in 1937 but stayed in the Philippines with the rank of field-marshal.

In 1941 he was recalled to the US army to command US and Filipino troops defending the Philippines against Japan. He fought a stubborn, defensive campaign, his troops holding out in Bataan and Corregidor until May 1942. By this time MacArthur had left for Australia, where he became Supreme Allied Commander in the South-West Pacific. He became the greatest master in the world of combined operations, skilfully co-ordinating amphibious landings with naval bombardment and air attack. He and Admiral Nimitz devised the policy of island-hopping, capturing small islands as bases and by-passing those which were larger and more heavily

defended. In this way they could cut Japanese supply routes with Southeast Asia and creep closer and closer to Japan. MacArthur was flamboyant and arrogant and disagreed with the Combined Chiefs of Staff, who gave greater priority to the defeat of Germany than to that of Japan. MacArthur became Supreme Commander of all US forces in the Pacific in April 1945. After the dropping of atomic bombs on Hiroshima and Nagasaki, MacArthur accepted the Japanese surrender on board the USS *Missouri* in Tokyo Bay on 2 September 1945. He ended the war as a five-star general.

MacArthur was Supreme Commander Allied Powers (SCAP) during the Allied OCCUPATION OF JAPAN, determined to break the power of the military–aristocratic élite which had ruled Japan before the war and make Japan a democracy. He supported the war crimes trials but opposed putting Emperor HIROHITO on trial because he wanted him to provide stability and to legitimize SCAP reforms. MacArthur played a large part in devising the democratic JAPANESE CONSTITUTION, encouraged the formation of trade unions to limit the power of big business, pushed through land reform, which transferred the ownership of land to tenants, and remodelled the education system on American lines.

When the KOREAN WAR (1950–3) began President TRUMAN sent him to Korea to prevent KIM IL SUNG overrunning the South. He was only just in time, as the North had conquered all the South except for an area round Pusan. MacArthur then carried out a bold and brilliant amphibious operation, landing well behind enemy lines, at Inchon. It was a spectacular success and led to the withdrawal of communist forces from the South. When Truman decided to overrun the North and unite Korea, MacArthur advanced north of the 38th Parallel. Even when China intervened massively in November, MacArthur was convinced that the war would be over by Christmas. His confidence was destroyed by a Chinese advance which pushed Allied troops in disarray 70 miles below the Parallel. MacArthur considered withdrawing from Korea. When he ignored the President and, pursuing his own foreign policy, threatened to attack China Truman, supported by the Joint Chiefs of Staff, dismissed him in April 1951. If he had followed MacArthur's advice he would have faced war with China (and possible Soviet intervention) which, according to Omar Bradley, 'would involve us in the wrong war, at the wrong place, at the wrong time and with the wrong enemy'. Yet 69 per cent of Americans, according to opinion polls, supported MacArthur, who received a ticker-tape welcome in New York from an estimated seven and a half million people. He tried to gain the Republican nomination for the presidential election of 1952, EISENHOWER being preferred.

The Years of MacArthur: Triumph and Disaster, 1945–64, D. Clayton Jones (1985)
Douglas MacArthur: Far Eastern General, M. Schaller (1989)
Old Soldiers Never Die: The Life of Douglas MacArthur, G. Perret (1997)

McCarthy, Joseph Raymond (1908–57)

US Senator (1946–57). The son of a farmer, he became a lawyer in 1935 and a circuit judge (1940–2) before serving in the marines during the Second World War. He called himself 'Tail-gunner Joe' and claimed that he had flown up to 30 combat missions when in fact he had not taken part in any. In 1946 he was elected as a Senator, and was soon renowned for his heavy drinking and gambling. Crude and boorish, he would probably have remained an obscure figure but for the anti-communist hysteria in the US. The fear of communism became more pervasive in 1949, when communists won the CHINESE CIVIL WAR (1948–9) and the Soviet Union exploded an atom bomb. Many Americans thought that these events could have taken place only because there were communist sympathizers in the State Department who had 'lost' China

by not giving enough support to JIANG JIESHI (Chiang Kai-shek) and that espionage had enabled the USSR to acquire atomic secrets.

McCarthy used these assumptions in February 1950 to claim that he had a list of 205 members of the Communist Party who were employed by the State Department. He produced some names of people who had been friendly to communists in the 1940s but none was a communist or was guilty of espionage. McCarthy, a loose cannon with no organization behind him, rarely followed up his charges but he put the TRUMAN administration on the defensive. His accusations were investigated by a bipartisan committee chaired by the conservative anti-New Deal Senator Tydings and were rejected as 'a fraud and a hoax perpetuated on the Senate of the United States and the American people'. McCarthy epitomized the class and regional resentments in the US. A Mid-Westerner and Roman Catholic, he detested the well-educated, wealthy and Protestant Eastern Establishment. Dean ACHESON, pilloried as the 'Red Dean of the State Department' disdainfully dismissed 'the attack of the primitives' but the KOREAN WAR (1950–3) deepened the sense of insecurity in the US and the hostility to communism. Anyone associated with the left, who supported civil rights or social justice or who criticized Jiang, was accused of being a communist. Leading Republicans, desperate for electoral success, saw how they could use McCarthy to discredit the DEMOCRATIC PARTY, which he accused of 'twenty years of treason'. EISENHOWER, the REPUBLICAN PARTY candidate in the 1952 presidential election, refused to criticize McCarthy publicly, though he despised him privately.

When Eisenhower and the Republicans won the election McCarthy did not end his crusade but extended it to other government departments and the Protestant churches, all of which, he said, were part of the 'Communist apparatus'. As Chairman of the Senate Permanent Investigating Subcommittee he investigated the influence of the Communist Party in the government and continued to rely on innuendo and guilt by association rather than firm evidence. In 1954 he took on the army, which he claimed was riddled with Reds. There was a congressional investigation, held before television cameras, in which McCarthy appeared as a mendacious, irresponsible bully. He was censured by the Senate for offensive conduct towards colleagues (not for the spurious nature of his allegations). From this time his influence rapidly declined. His alcoholism led to his death in 1957 from cyrrhosis of the liver. McCarthy had produced a climate of conformity, in which many people were afraid to express unpopular views in case they were accused of being communists, and greatly damaged the reputation of the US abroad. He had also put a strait-jacket on American foreign policy: future Presidents would have to show they were not 'soft' on communism.

The Life and Times of Joe McCarthy, T. C. Reeves (1982)
A Conspiracy So Immense: The World of Joe McCarthy, D. Oshinsky (1983)
Nightmare in Red: The McCarthy Era in Perspective, R. M. Fried (1990)

Macmillan, (Maurice) Harold, 1st Earl of Stockton (1894–1986)

British Prime Minister (1957–63). A delicate boy, who left Eton early, he was deeply affected by his possessive, domineering American mother. He gained a first class honours degree in classics at Oxford and then served in the Grenadier Guards in the First World War and was wounded three times. After the war he was aide-de-camp to the Governor-General of Canada, the Duke of Devonshire, whose daughter, Lady Dorothy Cavendish, he married on their return to England in 1920. She formed a liaison with Robert Boothby in 1929 which lasted until her death: her fourth child was Boothby's. Macmillan and his wife kept up appearances in public but in private, as Dorothy said, 'I am faithful to Bob'.

Elected as a Conservative MP in 1924, Macmillan was distressed by the unemployment of the Great Depression (1929–39) and in 1938 wrote *The Middle Way*, which combined state planning with private enterprise and accepted a mixed economy. He adopted KEYNESIANISM as a means of reviving the economy and criticized the government's domestic policy. Macmillan was a critic of the government's foreign policy too. He voted against the government in 1936 because of its failure to take action against Mussolini's invasion of Abyssinia (Ethiopia) and resigned the CONSERVATIVE PARTY whip, sitting as an Independent Conservative until Chamberlain became Prime Minister in 1937. He first became a minister under Winston CHURCHILL and in 1942 joined the cabinet as Minister Resident in North Africa, where his fluent French was useful.

The Conservatives were in opposition from 1945–51 but when Churchill became Prime Minister again he made Macmillan Minister of Housing. He acted with great panache, reduced the building standards set by Aneurin BEVAN, and built over 300,000 houses (80 per cent of them in the public sector) in 1953 and again in 1954. Following this success he moved rapidly from one post to another. He was Minister of Defence from October 1954 to April 1955, in which post he later admitted 'I was a failure', before Anthony EDEN moved him to the Foreign Office. Britain was warmly invited in June 1955 to take part in the Messina Conference to discuss closer European economic union but later withdrew, though the US encouraged British participation. 'The Empire must always have first preference', Macmillan wrote, 'Europe must come second'. After six months as Foreign Secretary he moved to the Treasury in December 1955. When the SUEZ CRISIS arose Macmillan wanted decisive action against NASSER (like Eden he regarded him as another Hitler) but the Chancellor knew that Britain could not afford it. Yet he misleadingly told the Prime Minister that there would be no real difficulty if Britain invaded Egypt. He therefore bears some responsibility for the Suez debacle and covered up British collusion with Israel in his memoirs as late as 1971. After a few days, because of the run on sterling, he advised ending the operation. The crisis brought on a collapse of Eden's health, so he resigned and it was expected that R. A. BUTLER would succeed him, but informal soundings of the cabinet showed strong support for Macmillan, who became Prime Minister.

The epitome of the Edwardian country gentleman, urbane, relaxed and witty, he appeared jovially unflappable in public though he was introspective and nervous in private. Suez had shown clearly that Britain was not in the front rank of world powers, yet Macmillan insisted on Britain keeping its own nuclear weapons (a HYDROGEN BOMB was tested in the Pacific in 1957), though these were dependent on US delivery systems. The 1957 Defence White Paper had concluded that nuclear defence would make conventional forces less necessary, so conscription was phased out and the size of the armed forces cut by half. Macmillan played an important role in negotiating the NUCLEAR TEST BAN TREATY of 1963. DECOLONIZATION was speeded up, particularly when Iain Macleod became Colonial Secretary in 1959, partly to save money but also to avoid being sucked into wars such as the ALGERIAN WAR OF INDEPENDENCE. Unlike France and Portugal, Britain wound up its empire quickly and with little bloodshed. The only unsolved problem was that of Southern Rhodesia (Zimbabwe), where there was a strong white minority. In spite of his courageous 'wind of change' speech to the white South African parliament in 1960, Macmillan did all he could to keep South Africa in the Commonwealth and when other members forced it to withdraw in 1961 bitterly attacked Canada for breaking ranks with 'the whites'.

At home some of Macmillan's reforms were unpopular, such as the drastic cutting of the railway network to reduce the losses of British Rail, and the Rent Act of 1957, which removed over 800,000 houses from rent control and allowed rent increases on those still controlled. Life peerages were introduced in 1958 and plans made to increase higher education dramatically. The University of Sussex was opened in 1961 and the go ahead was given for the new universities of York, East Anglia, Essex, Kent, Lancaster and Warwick. The Robbins Committee on Higher Education was appointed: the enlargement it recommended was accepted by the DOUGLAS-HOME government. The most contentious piece of legislation was the IMMIGRATION ACT of 1962, which restricted the number of Commonwealth immigrants, but the working class approved of it.

The economy was an intractable problem for Macmillan. Sterling crises, when it appeared that government spending was out of control, were met by rising interest rates, which increased manufacturing costs, deterred investment and made long-term planning difficult. As soon as interest rates or taxes were reduced to create a pre-election boom, imports flooded in and another sterling crisis resulted. There was a succession therefore of stop-go policies. In 1957 the bank rate was raised to 7 per cent, its highest level since 1920. Chancellor Thorneycroft in 1957 told the Prime Minister that 'With relatively few assets and large debts, we continue to live upon the scale of a great power' and wanted 'some swingeing cuts in the WELFARE STATE expenditure'. Macmillan, alarmed, would not agree, so Thorneycroft and his Treasury team resigned, a matter which the Prime Minister passed off as 'a little local difficulty'. Tax cuts in 1958 and 1959 helped to increase the Conservative majority in the 1959 election to 100, but by 1960 larger borrowing and spending had produced inflation and the boom collapsed. Disapproval of the government's economic policies was shown in the Orpington by-election in 1962, when a Conservative majority of 14,670 in 1959 turned into a Liberal majority of 7,855. The Night of the Long Knives followed, when seven cabinet ministers were dismissed, to be followed three

MAFIA (1) 255

days later by nine other non-cabinet ministers. Macmillan privately admitted that these panic measures were 'a great error' and that he was 'beginning (at last) to feel old and depressed'. During Macmillan's two administrations the standard of living rose faster than at any time since the First World War (manual wage rates were in 1964 19 per cent higher in real terms than in 1959) and unemployment was low. Yet appearances were deceptive. The British economy was growing more slowly than those of its competitors (France, Germany, Italy and Japan) and its share of world exports was falling too. Investment was low and little was done to modernize British industry.

Macmillan was surprised at the speed with which the EEC (European Economic Community) was set up and soon found that the rival group EFTA which Britain organized was no substitute for the large markets of the EEC. He persuaded the cabinet in 1961 to apply for membership. When DE GAULLE vetoed Britain's application he was mortified and was left without a strategy. 'All our policies at home and abroad,' he wrote in his diary, 'are in ruins'. The Profumo affair, when the Minister of War had to resign for being involved with a call-girl whose clients included the Soviet naval attaché, further undermined his government. He went into hospital for a prostate operation and resigned, though he remained a public figure for another 25 years, particularly as Vice-Chancellor of Oxford University. Macmillan left the Commons in 1964 and accepted an earldom at the age of 90.

Macmillan, vol. 1: 1894–1956; vol. 2: 1957– 1986, A. Horne (1988–9)
Macmillan, J. Turner (1994)
The Macmillan Years 1957–63, R. Lamb (1995)

Mafia (1)   Criminal organization in Sicily. The name first appeared in 1865 but the association to which it refers had been part of Sicilian life for centuries. As the area was neglected by mainland governments local

bosses came to dominate the regions in which they lived: it is unlikely that there was one single organization. After the unification of Italy in 1860 Mafia influence grew enormously, as every government depended on the support of Sicilian deputies controlled by the Mafia: in return the government did not interfere in Mafia activities on the island. This system ended in 1922 when Mussolini came to power. He tried to crush the Mafia and imprisoned hundreds of its less important members but was unable to break its hold on Sicilian society. After the Second World War the Mafia formed local links with the CHRISTIAN DEMOCRATIC PARTY (DC), providing votes in exchange for government contracts.

Known in Sicily, as in the US, as *Cosa Nostra* (Our Thing), it was a highly structured organization, membership of which was a lifetime commitment. At his initiation ceremony the *mafioso* had to pledge to keep certain rules, including *omerta*, the vow of silence. Death was the penalty for breaking them. Every 'man of honour' was admitted to a 'family' of about 50 members, which dominated a particular town. In Palermo there were between 30 and 50 families, which elected a Commission with authority over the whole province. The Commission did not function continuously owing to feuds among its members, particularly from 1957–63 and 1979–81, when there were vicious Mafia wars between different families. The Mafia in the US and in Sicily were distinct organizations, connected only by personal contacts. Similar but quite separate groups existed in Calabria (the '*ndrangheta*') and Naples (the *camorra*). In the late 1970s the Mafia flourished more than ever through regional government contracts, Middle Eastern arms deals and above all by having a virtual monopoly of the European heroin trade, which supplied a third of the heroin entering the US. Profits from this were estimated at $600 million a year by 1989. These were recycled into Swiss and Latin American banks, construction and legitimate businesses, the Sicilian economy depending to a large extent on this wealth, as did the Italian government: it was estimated that 30 per cent of Treasury bonds were bought with DRUG TRADE money. In 1991 the Ministry of the Interior estimated that 450 gangs were operating in Italy with 15,000 members and that a million people were involved in drug smuggling and extortion.

The *mafiosi* of Corleone, an agricultural town near Palermo, began their rise to the top of *Cosa Nostra* during a five-year civil war (1958–63) in which over 140 were killed. This struggle was the basis for episodes in Mario Puzo's novel *The Godfather*. Corleonese took over the Sicilian capital, Palermo, in the early 1980s after another round of eliminating rivals. Mafia murders – 300 a year in each of the three worst affected regions – were common but generally avoided high officials until 1979–82, when Salvatore Riina, head of the Corleonese, ordered a systematic campaign to eliminate all civil servants or politicians who got in their way. The President of the Sicilian region was killed, as were the heads of the DC and the PCI (Italian Communist Party) in Sicily and the newly appointed Prefect of Palermo, General Dalla Chiesa, who had crushed the RED BRIGADES. A new law was hastily passed to make membership of 'mafia-type associations' a criminal offence, while investigating magistrates in Palermo, the most prominent of whom were Giovanni Falcone and Paolo Borsellino, courageously collected evidence against the Mafia, using *pentiti* (repentants), such as Tomasso Buscetta, ex-*mafiosi* who were nearly always convicted murderers on the losing side in intra-Mafia warfare. In 1988 nearly 500 suspected *mafiosi* were put on trial in Palermo: 344 were found guilty. The Supreme Court in 1991 upheld the guilty verdicts, which the Mafia expected to be overturned. Its leaders then made clear that their contract with the politicians had been broken and in March 1992 murdered Salvatore Lima, Prime Minister Guilio ANDREOTTI's Mafia contact in Sicily. Falcone was assassinated outside Palermo two months later, followed by the murder of Borsellino. The national outcry against corrupt politicians who could not protect their most devoted officials led to an intensive anti-Mafia drive which resulted in the arrest of 70 leading *mafiosi*, including 'Toto' Riina, after 23 years on the run. Falcone's murder also contributed to the collapse of the old parties, especially the DC, and that in turn was a key to the successes in arresting and convicting *mafiosi*, who were no longer protected by corrupt politicians. In 1993 Andreotti was charged with colluding with organized crime. The remaining Mafia leadership appeared to be opposed to confrontation with the state. In 1996 it still ran protection rackets in all Sicilian cities, controlled the drug traffic and the labour movement, all the supermarkets in Palermo and the award of public contracts in several towns, but its leaders were being arrested and imprisoned. In September 1997 Sicilian judges handed out 24 life sentences to *mafiosi*, who included Riina and his lieutenant Leoluca Bagarella, for the murder of Falcone.

Mafia and Clientilism: Roads to Rome in Postwar Calabria, J. Watson (1988)
The Sicilian Mafia, D. Gambetta (1993)
Excellent Cadavers: The Mafia and the Death of the First Italian Republic, A. Stille (1995)

Mafia (2)   Criminal organization in the US. By 1900 in cities with large Italian populations criminal gangs had appeared, modelled on the Sicilian Mafia or *Cosa Nostra* ('Our Thing'). During Prohibition they took control of boot-legging (providing illicit liquor) and in the 1930s moved into illegal gambling and prostitution. In the 1940s they concentrated on labour racketeering and drug distribution. By 1950 two dozen syndicates ('families') had divided the US into separate areas for their criminal activities. The Kefauver Hearings in 1951–2, seen on television, publicized the Mafia's participation in interstate crime, international drug smuggling and political corruption, but from the 1920s to the late 1970s the American Cosa Nostra was virtually immune from serious prosecution. The FBI under J. Edgar HOOVER was inert, local police inefficient or corrupt.

The first legislation to combat the Mob came in 1970 with the Organized Crime Control Act. This gave witnesses protection: informers were given new identities and financial aid to relocate them. Justice Department strike forces concentrated solely on long-term investigations and the prosecution of Mafia bosses. The most important part of the Act was the Racketeer Influenced and Corrupt Organizations (RICO) section. Before this bosses could not be arrested because they did not personally commit crimes. Now connection with a criminal organization was enough for prosecution: a Mafia family's complete hierarchy could now be removed. Another RICO weapon hit at the Mafia's control of labour unions: judges could appoint watchdogs over a union and its funds. In the 1980s 23 Cosa Nostra bosses, including John Gotti, head of the Gambino family, were convicted (usually from evidence using wire-tapping). The major Mafia families, except in New York and Chicago, were eliminated or in disarray. The Mafia hold on major industries (garment-manufacturing and construction) and on the unions (the Genovese family had controlled the New Jersey Teamsters for 40 years) was broken.

Cosa Nostra lost a large share of the drug trade in the 1980s to new criminal organizations of Hispanics, blacks and Asians. In the 1990s criminals from Eastern Europe and Russia entered the US in large numbers. The US-based Russian Mafia was led by Vyacheslav Ivantsov, known as Yaponchik ('the Japanese'). Based in Little Odessa, the émigré community in Brighton Beach, New York, it has expanded into a nationwide network. Yaponchik was arrested in 1995 but had built up an organization with a turnover of billions of dollars. In addition to the ruthless Russian gangs Chinese Triads and Japanese *yakuza* have also provided competition for the American Mafia.

Busting the Mob: The United States v Cosa Nostra, J. B. Jacobs (1996)

Mahathir Mohamad (1925–) Prime Minister of Malaysia (1981–). From humble stock (his father was a Muslim schoolteacher who had migrated from India), he studied medicine in Singapore and practised as a doctor (1957–64) before being elected to parliament in 1964 as a United Malays National Organization (UMNO) member. He was expelled from the party in 1969 after accusing the Prime Minister Tunku ABDUL RAHMAN of betraying the Malay community. In 1970 he published a book *The Malay Dilemma* in which he said that the Malays were paupers in their own country: the government should protect their interests and require Chinese and Indians (about a third and a tenth of the population respectively) to absorb Malaysian culture. The book was banned by the government for increasing racial tension. He was readmitted to UMNO before the 1974 election and held various posts before becoming UMNO President and Prime Minister in 1981.

Mahathir was not an Anglophile and fervent supporter of the COMMONWEALTH like the Tunku. He resented Western influence and the patronizing attitude of white Commonwealth leaders. When the British government raised the fees of overseas students he began a 'Buy British Last' campaign in 1983: it lasted until the visit of Britain's Prime Minister Margaret THATCHER in 1988. Mahathir declared in 1981 that Malaysia's international priorities were ASEAN, the Islamic Conference Organization, the NON-ALIGNED MOVEMENT and then the Commonwealth. He introduced a 'Look East' policy, believing that Japan and South Korea provided a more relevant model for Malaysia than Western countries. Mahathir wanted Malaysia to become one of the NEWLY INDUSTRIALIZING ECONOMIES (NIEs) and an 'Asian tiger' like Singapore, Taiwan and South Korea. He invested heavily in the country's infrastructure (roads, railways, airports), launched Malaysia's first car, the Proton, in the 1980s and by encouraging foreign investment made Malaysia one of the world's largest producers of electronic equipment. Growth rates of 8 per cent in the late 1980s and early 1990s were among the highest in the world. Economic growth benefited all races and enabled Mahathir to discriminate in favour of Malays (70 per cent of places in higher education were reserved for them) without increasing racial tension.

Malaysian Politics: The Second Generation, G. Means (1991)

Major, John Roy (1943–)   British Prime Minister (1990–7). Born in London, the son of a music-hall performer who became a designer and manufacturer of garden ornaments, he lived in poverty after the collapse of the family business. On leaving school at 16 he worked as a labourer before beginning in 1963 a banking career, in which he rose to a senior position at the Standard Chartered Bank. He was elected as a Conservative MP in 1979, the year in which the CONSERVATIVE PARTY won the general election and Margaret THATCHER became Prime Minister. His first ministerial position was as Minister of State for Social Security (1986–7), followed by Chief Secretary to the Treasury (1987–9). He was then unexpectedly promoted to be Foreign Secretary when Geoffrey HOWE was removed from the Foreign Office but after only three months he went to the Treasury when Nigel LAWSON resigned as Chancellor of the Exchequer. The new Chancellor persuaded the Prime Minister to join the Exchange Rate Mechanism (ERM) in 1990, but in the same year Margaret Thatcher resigned during a leadership contest in the Conservative Party. With her backing John Major was elected as the new leader, as he seemed the best candidate to maintain party unity. At the age of 47 he was the youngest British Prime Minister in the twentieth century, though he was little known to the public

and had been in the cabinet for only three years.

Diffident and modest, he shared Thatcher's views on running the economy but avoided her strident and hectoring tone and sought genuine discussion in cabinet. His main concern was the economy, as Britain was in the worst recession since the 1930s. The unpopular POLL TAX was reduced in 1991 and replaced a year later by a Council Tax, similar to the old rates. Britain's support for President BUSH in the GULF WAR (1991) and its successful outcome brought some popularity for the Prime Minister but by the 1992 general election the LABOUR PARTY had a small but persistent lead in the opinion polls. Surprisingly, the Conservatives won the election, though they lost 40 seats and had a majority of only 21. BLACK WEDNESDAY followed in September when speculation against sterling forced Britain out of the ERM. The pound was allowed to float and in effect was devalued by 13 per cent. This was a humiliation for the government, which had strongly opposed devaluation, but was beneficial for the economy, which began to pick up. Interest rates were lowered and exports increased, but the Public Sector Borrowing Requirement was £50 billion in 1993, when there was an unpopular budget. Indirect taxes were to be increased, with higher national insurance contributions and VAT on fuel of 17.5 per cent (this was later rejected by the Commons) and there were to be cuts in public spending of £10 billion over the next three years (in defence, transport and the environment). Mortgage tax relief was reduced, as were student grants, and eligibility for welfare payments was tightened. The government's unpopularity (in the 1992 election campaign it had promised not to increase taxation) was reflected in the local elections of May 1994, when it lost 400 seats, some of them in the traditional Tory heartlands of the south: a year later it lost 2,000 seats in local government elections, its worst performance ever. Major decided to continue PRIVATIZATION by selling the coal mines and the railways, though the coal industry (one of the most efficient in Europe) had almost ceased to exist, as the privatized power companies switched from coal to gas. Railway privatization in 1996 was an extraordinary complex operation.

John Major continued to change the National Health Service in 1991 by allowing GPs to become fundholders and by compelling health authorities to operate an internal market, in which hospitals would compete with one another: they could also become self-governing NHS Trusts. He also turned his attention to the civil service, which he regarded as too big, inefficient and complacent. It was to be transformed into agencies, each with considerable autonomy, to provide services. By 1992 there were 72 agencies with 300,000 employees (over half the civil service). In an attempt to recover popularity he introduced a 'Back to Basics' campaign in 1993 to promote family values and discipline in education, but this was soon derided when ministers were discovered having extra-marital affairs.

There was a serious attempt to deal with the TROUBLES in Northern Ireland when the Downing Street Declaration was made in November 1993, but this eventually foundered when the IRA ended its cease-fire (begun in August 1994) in 1996. The European Union posed the greatest problems for the government abroad. The MAASTRICHT TREATY was the key issue. European Monetary Union (EMU) was to be set up by 1999, as was a European Central Bank. John Major was under great pressure from 'Eurosceptics' in the Conservative Party, a powerful body as the government had such a small majority, not to allow any diminution of British sovereignty. He therefore negotiated a British opt-out of EMU and of the Social Chapter (which protected the rights of workers), as he said that the latter would increase labour costs and therefore unemployment. The government signed the treaty in January 1992 but the Prime Minister was able to obtain a majority for it in parliament a year later only by

threatening a dissolution, which the Eurosceptics did not want. Relations with the EU were often stormy. The most acrimonious dispute arose over BSE ('mad-cow' disease), when the sale of British beef in the EU was banned. In retaliation Britain vetoed all European directives which required unanimity and was accused of blackmail and of attempting to paralyse the Union.

As the 1997 election approached the economy was doing well, with low inflation (2.8 per cent in 1996) and interest rates, increasing growth, falling unemployment and a stock market boom. The main problem for industry was a strong pound which made exports less competitive. Yet this increased prosperity was not reflected in the opinion polls, which gave the Labour Party an apparently commanding lead. This was confirmed in the election when the LABOUR PARTY won 419 seats and the Conservatives 165. The next day John Major announced that he would be retiring as leader of the Conservative Party.

Major: A Political Life, A. Seldon with L. Baston (1997)

Malan, Daniel François (1874–1959)

Prime Minister of South Africa (1948–54). A minister in the Dutch Reformed Church, he supported Hertzog and the National Party and was appointed editor of its newspaper *Die Burger* in 1915. He entered parliament in 1919, became a member of Hertzog's cabinet in 1924 and, as a member of the secret Afrikaner *Broederbond*, sought political power for Afrikaners and the preservation of their language and culture. When Hertzog made a coalition with Smuts in 1933 Malan refused a post in his government and a year later, when Hertzog 'fused' the National Party with Smuts's South African Party to become the United Party, Malan broke away to form the Purified National Party. The party did badly in the 1938 election but gained support during the Second World War, as there was much opposition among Afrikaners to South Africa's involvement on Britain's side. The

National Party was reunited under Malan in 1940. He fought the 1948 election on an APARTHEID programme, advocating the separation of the races, the removal of coloureds (those of mixed race) from the voters' roll and the complete domination of whites over all other races. Although he won fewer votes (37.2 per cent) than the United Party (47.9 per cent) in the election he gained a majority of seats, so for the first time South Africa had a totally Afrikaner government.

A flurry of legislation followed to reverse the relaxation of segregation which had occurred during the war. The Immorality Act (1950) extended the ban on whites marrying Africans to Indians and coloureds. All South Africans were divided by the Population Registration Act into four races: white, coloured, 'Asian' (Indian) and 'Native' (later Bantu or African). The Group Areas Act (1950) made special residential areas compulsory, so that Indian traders were moved out of the centre of Pretoria and many coloureds in Cape Town were relocated (60,000 from District Six). 'Petty *apartheid*' in the Reservation of Separate Amenities Act (1953) separated whites from all other races in transport, restaurants, sports, beaches and even park benches and post office counters. The Bantu Education Act (1951) brought all African schools under government control to ensure that Africans would be trained only for manual labour. There was no parliamentary representation at all for blacks. The Natives Representative Council, set up in 1936, was abolished and replaced, in the Bantu Authorities Act (1951), by government-approved chiefs, who would enforce government policy in the reserves. White MPs to represent Indians, established in 1946, came to an end, leaving the only non-white representation in parliament that of coloureds in the Cape. Malan wanted to end this too but did not have the necessary two-thirds majority in parliament. Enforcement of *apartheid* laws, and control of Africans moving into towns, was made easier by the Abolition of Passes and Co-ordination of Documents Act (1952), a

strange name for an Act which compelled all Africans (including women, who had been exempt till then) to carry a reference book, showing where they were employed. Opposition to *apartheid* could be speedily dealt with by the Suppression of Communism Act (1950), which gave the Minister of Justice the right to ban any person or organization he considered to be communist, a right which could be used to ban anyone opposed to *apartheid*. The Criminal Law Amendment Act (1951) provided heavy penalties for civil disobedience. Having, he thought, ensured white supremacy for the indefinite future, Malan retired in 1954.

The Making of Apartheid, 1948–61, D. Posel (1991)

'*Forty Lost Years': The Apartheid State and the National Party, 1948–94*, D. O'Meara (1996)

Malayan emergency (1948–60)   A communist insurrection in Malaya which was put down by British-led forces. In June 1948 the Malayan Communist Party, consisting almost entirely of ethnic Chinese, began attacking mine-owners, planters and officials. It wanted to destroy the Malayan economy (dependent largely on tin-mining and rubber), occupy 'liberal zones' on the model of MAO ZEDONG in China and lead a peasant revolution which would produce the withdrawal of the British and the establishment of a communist state. The guerrillas were never more than eight to ten thousand at any time. They did not have the support of the majority Malay population or of all Chinese in Malaya: at most 15–20 per cent of the population supported them. The rebels did not receive much outside help (from the Soviet Union or China) and, unlike the guerrillas in Vietnam, could be easily distinguished from the local Malay population.

To deprive the rebels of support the British established 600 large, fortified resettlement areas, with education, health and security services provided, for half a million Chinese squatters. These, combined with intelligence and police action, were successful in breaking the back of the rising by 1954, though the state of emergency continued until 1960. Up to 2,000 guerrillas carried on operating on the Malay–Thai border until 1989 when they signed a peace treaty. Some 10,000 rebels were killed during the Emergency, 3,000 Malayan police, 1,500 COMMONWEALTH troops and 5,000 civilians. The insurrection had failed but it had tied down large security forces (250,000) in a costly exercise and had delayed Malaya's economic recovery. During the rising Malaya became an independent state in 1957 under Tunku ABDUL RAHMAN.

The Communist Insurrection in Malaya, 1948–60, A. Short (1975)

Hearts and Minds in Guerrilla Warfare: The Malayan Emergency, 1948–60, R. Stubbs (1989)

Malcolm X (1925–65)   Militant black activist in the US, born Malcolm Little, the son of a Baptist preacher. In Harlem he was a pimp, male prostitute, gambler and drug dealer. In 1946 he was sentenced to ten years in prison for burglary. There his life changed, as he came into contact with the Lost–Found Nation of Islam (NOI), generally known as the BLACK MUSLIMS, led by Elijah Muhammad. He became a devotee, accepting their doctrine that all whites were devils and that only blacks can cure the evils that afflict them, and changed his name to Malcolm X, symbolically repudiating 'the white man's name' as a relic of slavery. When he was released from prison in 1952 he founded mosques for the NOI in Boston, Philadelphia and Harlem and the NOI's first nationally distributed newspaper *Muhammad Speaks*. He soon became well known through his television appearances and a spokesman for the organization, condemning leaders of the CIVIL RIGHTS MOVEMENT like Martin Luther KING because they wanted integration and were non-violent. Malcolm X believed that violence in self-defence was justified. 'There can', he said, 'be no revolution without bloodshed'.

He gradually turned away from the NOI, as he disagreed with their not taking part in politics and was disillusioned when he found that his spiritual leader Elijah had departed from the strict moral code of the NOI by fathering children by two secretaries. Malcolm's popularity threatened Elijah's leadership of the movement; he left when he found that Elijah planned to have him assassinated. In 1964 Malcolm X went on a pilgrimage to Mecca, adopted SUNNI Islam, gave up his belief that all whites were 'devils' and changed his name to El-Hajj Malik El Shabazz. He was assassinated by three members of the NOI in Harlem on 21 February 1965.

Malcolm X made a bigger impact on the black community after his death than before it. His *Autobiography*, published nine months after he was killed, provided a programme of action for black militants in the inner-cities, who looked to him rather than to Martin Luther King as a role model. The Watts riots (part of the BLACK GHETTO RIOTS) and the formation of the BLACK POWER movement took place within months of his death. Black activists in the Congress of Racial Equality and the Student Non-violent Coordinating Committee accepted many of his ideas: armed self-defence, racial pride and the creation of black-run institutions. Angry and uncompromising, Malcolm X reflected the despair of the ghettos, where he found his most devoted admirers. 'I see America through the eyes of the victim. I don't see any American dream. I see an American nightmare.'

The Autobiography of Malcolm X, A. Haley and Malcolm X (1973)

Malcolm: The Life of a Man Who Changed Black America, B. Perry (1991)

Malcolm X: In Our Own Image, J. Wood (ed.) (1992)

Mandela, Nelson Rolihlahla (1918–)

ANC leader and President of South Africa (1994–). The son of an illiterate chief with four wives in the Transkei, who was deposed by a local white magistrate for insubordination, he was brought up with a strong respect for African democracy. He was suspended from studying law at Fort Hare University College for taking part in a student protest. Moving to Johannesburg in 1941 to train as a lawyer, he founded with others the Youth League of the ANC in 1944 to press for a more militant attitude to white supremacy and succeeded when the ANC adopted its Action Programme in 1949, which supported civil disobedience. Mandela was one of those accused in the Treason Trial (1956–61) but, like all the others, he was acquitted. After SHARPEVILLE (1960) the ANC was banned, so he went to Algeria for military training and then took charge of the underground military wing of the ANC, *Umkhonto we Sizwe*, dedicated to armed struggle and greatly influenced by the anti-colonial movements in Algeria and Cuba. Arrested in 1962 and sentenced to five years' imprisonment for organizing a strike, he was charged as the leading defendant at the Rivonia trial (1964) for his role in creating *Umkhonto*. At his trial he stated his creed: 'I have fought against white domination and I have fought against black domination. I have cherished the ideal of a democratic and free society in which all persons live together in harmony and with equal opportunities'. Sentenced to life imprisonment, he spent years breaking stones on Robben Island and was treated for tuberculosis in 1984. Stubborn and headstrong, he learnt self-discipline in prison, as pressure grew for his release as the only person who could end the violence of the BLACK TOWNSHIP REVOLTS. He took part in negotiations with cabinet ministers from the mid-1980s and impressed them with his courtesy, dignity and lack of rancour.

Although he refused to renounce violence, DE KLERK released him in 1990 and he began discussions with de Klerk, BUTHELEZI and other interested parties for the transition to a government elected by all races in South Africa. While these were taking place he persuaded the ANC to suspend the armed struggle. He was elected President of the ANC in 1991 at its first national conference since 1959. Mandela was a tough negotiator and twice broke off the talks owing to the killing of ANC supporters by Inkatha members in the black townships, as he accused the security forces of being involved. During this difficult period his wife Winnie MANDELA was convicted of kidnapping and was involved in financial and sexual scandals. In May 1992 he announced the breakup of his marriage. When the first democratic elections in South Africa were eventually held in 1994 the ANC gained 62 per cent of the vote and Mandela became President.

Neither he nor the ANC, which dominated the government, had any experience of administration. The new black middle-class élite of ministers and MPs voted themselves huge salaries and appointed their relations as civil servants, state industry managers and lecturers in universities. AFFIRMATIVE ACTION, the replacement of whites by blacks in key positions, led to a massive white exodus, which increased as the crime rate soared. The government sought to bring electricity to squatter camps and remote areas and to provide clean water and decent housing, but it soon realized that it did not have the income to meet the aspirations of its black supporters. It needed foreign investment, so it abandoned socialism and adopted more conservative economic policies than those of the previous white governments: PRIVATIZATION, export-led growth, inducements for foreign capital and low tariffs. Workers suffered large cuts in real wages as the rand, the South African currency, continued to fall and put a severe strain on the government's close relations with COSATU (Congress of South African Trade Unions), which persuaded the government to retain a major share in 'privatized' industries, thus ensuring that privatization would not be successful. There was a fear that the new management of state industries would run up huge deficits so quickly that they would be unsaleable. Mandela remained a popular and charismatic figure but seemed out of his depth dealing with the complexities of the South

African economy as he approached his eighteith birthday.

Nelson Mandela, M. Benson (1994)
Nelson Mandela, M. Meredith (1997)

Mandela, Winnie (1934–) ANC (African National Congress) activist. Trained as a medical social worker, she married Nelson MANDELA in March 1958 and joined the ANC. She was an active member when it was banned in 1960, was repeatedly arrested and imprisoned and spent 17 months in solitary confinement (1969–70). Her continued defiance of the white authorities helped to keep the memory of her imprisoned husband alive. From 1977–85 she was banished from her Soweto home to the remote town of Brandfort. She approved of the 'necklace' killings in the BLACK TOWNSHIP REVOLTS and gathered round her a group of violent bodyguards, called the Mandela United Football Club, which kidnapped Stompie Seipei, aged 14, and accused him of being a police informer. He was beaten and stabbed at Winnie Mandela's home and died from his injuries. Jerry Richardson, the Football Club leader, was sentenced to life imprisonment for his murder. Winnie Mandela, charged with assault and kidnapping, was sentenced in 1991 to six years in prison but this was changed to a fine on appeal.

Winnie Mandela was reunited with her husband when he was released from prison in February 1990, but they separated in April 1992. She lost support in the ANC as a result of the trial and separation and had to give up her post as head of its welfare department. However, she remained very popular with the ANC youth and was appointed Deputy Minister for Culture, Science and Technology in the government of national unity. She was dismissed in March 1995 because of her criticism of the government and was divorced a year later.

Further revelations about her murky past arose in September 1997. One of two gunmen convicted of the murder of a Soweto doctor, Dr Asvat, claimed that he was contracted to do it by Winnie Mandela. A missing witness in her 1991 trial, Katiza Cebekhulu, a member of the Football Club, had been removed from South Africa by the ANC, so that he could not testify at her trial, and ended up in a Zambian jail before the efforts of the British MP Emma Nicholson secured his release. He claims that Winnie Mandela personally took part in the attack on Stompie Seipei.

Katiza's Journey: Beneath the Surface of South Africa's Shame, F. Bridgeland (1997)

Mao Zedong (1893–1976) Chinese communist leader and first Chairman of the People's Republic of China. Mao was the son of a peasant, who became a Marxist when working as a library assistant at Beijing University. He was a founder-member of the Chinese Communist Party (CCP) in 1921. When the CCP, on orders from the Comintern, made an alliance with Sun Yatsen's Guomindang (Nationalist Party) in 1923, Mao worked enthusiastically in the United Front in several Guomindang organizations. After visiting Hunan in 1926 Mao wrote a report on the peasant revolution there, which marked his first move away from orthodox Marxism and towards its adaptation to Chinese circumstances. Orthodox Marxists regarded the peasants as conservatives and *petit bourgeois* and thought that revolution would not originate with them but with the urban proletariat. Mao maintained that the real revolution in China, where there were few industrial workers, was taking place in the countryside and that the CCP should become involved in it. 'The Chinese revolution', he wrote, 'has only this form [a peasant revolution] and no other'.

When JIANG JIESHI (Chiang Kai-shek) turned on, and massacred, his communist allies in the Shanghai coup of 1927 and destroyed the workers' movements in the cities, the CCP was forced to seek survival in the countryside. Mao helped to form the Jiangxi Soviet and saw it expand to cover an area with a population of nine million. Jiang felt this threatened the Nationalist control of China, so he waged five extermination campaigns (1930–4) against the Jiangxi Soviet, finally forcing Mao and 80,000 followers to break out in 1934 on the Long March, which ended a year later with only 8,000 reaching the safety of Yanan in the north. During the time Yanan was the capital of communist China (1937–47), Mao established his ascendancy in the CCP as both political leader and ideologist. During this period the CCP enormously increased its membership and popularity, as it was seen as the chief opponent of Japan in the Sino-Japanese War (1937–45). In this war Mao used the tactics he had developed during Jiang's extermination campaigns, avoiding head-on conflict but tying down vast numbers of Japanese troops by guerrilla warfare behind their lines. The CCP made a second United Front with the Guomindang to fight the Japanese, but there was distrust on both sides and the CCP continued to extend its influence in north China, so that when the war with Japan ended there were about 96 million people in areas under communist control. In 1945 Jiang, recognized as leader of China by all the Great Powers, was in no mood to compromise with Mao and the CCP and refused to form a coalition government with them. The result was the CHINESE CIVIL WAR (1946–9), which ended with a crushing communist victory and the proclamation by Mao in Beijing (October 1949) of the People's Republic of China.

National unity and pride had been restored. 'Ours will no longer be a nation subject to insult and humiliation. We have stood up', said Mao. He wanted to build an egalitarian society and this meant destroying the power of the ruling landlords. This he did in the Agrarian Reform Law of 1950, which confiscated the land of the landlords (3–4 per cent of the overall population who owed 30 per cent of the land) and redistributed it to poor peasants. The power of the landlords, who had dominated China for centuries, was destroyed: about a million were executed.

He then began the gradual introduction of collectivization, beginning with mutual aid teams and leading to the creation of co-operatives, in which private ownership of land ended (except for 5 per cent of the land which peasants were allowed to retain as private plots). Collectivization was completed by the end of 1956. Industrialization was based on the Soviet model, with nationalization and an emphasis on heavy industry, organized in Five Year Plans, the first of which covered the years 1953–7. The SINO-SOVIET ALLIANCE (1950) provided Soviet technical help. From 1952, when industrial production reached prewar levels, to Mao's death in 1976 industry grew at the rate of 11 per cent per annum, the most rapid rise of any major nation in that period. China became an industrial rather than an agricultural nation, as industrial production as a proportion of the whole rose from 30 per cent to 72 per cent. This was achieved in spite of the withdrawal of Soviet technical aid in 1960 during the SINO-SOVIET DISPUTE.

From 1949–57 Mao abided by a collective leadership and sought to impose his views on his colleagues only on three occasions. In 1950, against the advice of the majority of his colleagues, he decided that China should intervene in the KOREAN WAR. This was immensely costly but it brought China security and international prestige, as he successfully pushed back US forces to the 38th parallel. His second intervention was in speeding up the pace of collectivization in 1955 and his third was in inviting criticism of the CCP in the HUNDRED FLOWERS MOVEMENT (1957). Mao's belief that the masses, if ideologically motivated, were capable of superhuman achievements resulted in the GREAT LEAP FORWARD (GLF) and the establishment of COMMUNES. During this economic disaster Mao decided that leadership should be divided into two 'fronts': he would go to the 'second front', where he could concentrate on theory and general policy and give up control of daily affairs. He therefore ceased to be Chairman of the People's Republic of China, though he remained head of the CCP. The results of this move were not at all to his liking, as he saw LIU SHAOQI and DENG XIAOPING reverse many of the policies of the GLF: Mao claimed that he was ignored and treated 'like a dead ancestor'.

He was able to recover his dominant position in 1966 only by allying with LIN BIAO and radicals such as the GANG OF FOUR, led by his wife JIANG QING. Mao feared that his life's work would be overthrown if Liu and Deng remained in control and that the revolutionary spirit must be aroused among the young, who were born after communist success in the Civil War. He used the CULTURAL REVOLUTION (CR) therefore, partly to get rid of his rivals and partly to ensure that his revolutionary legacy would be preserved. After the anarchic period of the CR (1966–9) he had to call in the People's Liberation Army (PLA) to restore order. This greatly increased the influence of the PLA and of Lin Biao, which Mao saw as a threat. As early as 1938 he had said that 'Our principle is that the Party commands the gun and the gun must never be allowed to command the Party'. When he sought to cut down the power of the army Lin Biao plotted against him and was killed in 1971 when his attempt at a coup failed. After that there was a struggle for the succession to Mao between the radicals (the Gang of Four), the moderates who had survived the CR (such as Deng) and the beneficiaries of the CR like HUA GUOFENG. Mao realized that if Deng succeeded him he would not preserve his legacy, so after the death of ZHOU ENLAI in January 1976 Deng was demoted. The Gang of Four were too unpopular to retain power so in April Mao chose Hua, who was made Prime Minister, as his successor. By this time Mao, afflicted by Parkinson's disease, could not walk and could hardly speak. He died in September.

Mao had made some monumental errors, particularly in the GLF and the CR and, in spite of his efforts to encourage mass participation, his regime was essentially Stalinist, in the monopoly of power enjoyed by the CCP and in the suppression of all opposition. Yet he had turned China from being a weak and disunited country at the mercy of foreign powers into a world power, with impressive economic growth.

Mao, Ross Terrill (1980)
The Thought of Mao Tse-tung, S. Schram (1989)
The Politics of China: The Eras of Mao and Deng, R. MacFarquhar (1997)

Marcos, Ferdinand (1917–89)   President of the Philippines (1966–86). From a wealthy family, he was accused of murdering his father's political rival in 1935. He became famous for conducting his own defence and passing the bar examinations during his long trial: he was acquitted in 1939. During the Pacific War (1941–5) he was a guerrilla fighter against the Japanese. After the war and independence for the Philippines in 1946 he was elected to the House of Representatives, then the Senate, of which he became President, before being elected President of the Philippines in 1966. He had fought the election promising land reform and economic development. There was little land reform but the economy did improve during his first term, owing to the GREEN REVOLUTION and miracle rice, a new strain with a higher yield, which made the country a rice exporter.

Marcos was re-elected President in 1969 but according to the constitution could not hold office for a third term, so in 1972 he declared martial law, jailed thousands of his political opponents (including the charismatic Benigno AQUINO), closed opposition newspapers, took control of radio and television and dismissed 150,000 civil servants. All individual freedoms were suppressed and strikes banned. Marcos did all this with the approval of the armed forces and so gave them a political role for the first time. After 1972 the government was the preserve of the Marcos family and its friends. His wife Imelda, Governor of Manila in 1975 and a member of the cabinet in 1978, often represented her husband on foreign visits. A new constitution in 1973 preserved the appearances of a parliamentary system but it was spurious, as elections were rigged and fraudulent referenda gave the President all the powers he wanted. Violent opposition to the regime appeared in risings of the Communist New People's Army (NPA) and of the Moro National Liberation army in Mindanao, during which 50,000 people were killed and half a million made refugees.

Martial law was lifted in 1981 for the visit of Pope JOHN PAUL II but there was no real freedom. Journalists who exposed government corruption were killed by unknown gunmen. The strongest opposition to Marcos now came from the Roman Catholic Church. World opinion was shocked in August 1983 when Benigno Aquino was shot dead at Manila airport. As two million people filed past his body, there were widespread protest demonstrations. An investigating commission said that 26 people, including the Chief of Staff (a cousin of Marcos) were responsible for the murder. There was further outrage when all were acquitted after a long trial.

The economy was in ruins owing to large-scale corruption and the transference of government funds into Marcos bank accounts overseas. A budget deficit of 16 million pesos in 1965 had become 7.9 billion by 1985. To finance it foreign loans rose from $600 million in 1965 to $25.6 billion in 1985. After Benigno's assassination there was a massive flight of capital, inflation and a fall in GNP in 1984–5. The NPA rising made the situation worse. To give his regime some legitimacy Marcos held a presidential election in 1986, when his opponent was Corazon AQUINO, the wife of Benigno. The National Assembly declared Marcos the winner but the Roman Catholic Bishops' Conference said that the polls were 'unparalleled in the fraudulence of their conduct'. President REAGAN, who had been a firm supporter of the anti-communist Marcos, spoke of 'widespread fraud and violence'. Both the Defence Minister and the acting Chief of Staff

resigned in protest at the rigged election and vowed to support Aquino. As a million people took to the streets the US warned Marcos against 'prolonging the life of the present regime by violence'. He was offered a safe refuge in the US in return for a peaceful hand-over of power to a new government under Aquino. The Marcos family fled to exile in Hawaii, completing a bloodless revolution of 'people's power'.

Crisis in the Philippines: The Marcos Era and Beyond, J. Bresnan (ed.) (1986)
Filipino Politics: Development and Decay, D. Wuorfel (1988)
Rebellion and Repression in the Philippines, R. J. Kessler (1989)

Marshall Plan (1947–52)   A United States project to aid the economic recovery of Western Europe after the Second World War. In 1947 the economic situation in Europe was desperate: production was low, inflation and unemployment high, starvation loomed in Germany, and in Britain in the harsh winter of 1946–7 coal supplies to industry were cut by half, food was rationed and six million were without work (twice the number at the peak of the Great Depression in the 1930s). The US saw these conditions as ideal for the spread of communism, an appraisal confirmed by the success of the French Communist Party in the elections of November 1946, when it appeared that it might win control of the government. Under Secretary of State Dean ACHESON and Secretary of State George Marshall therefore worked out a plan for European economic recovery which Marshall announced in a speech in June 1947. The Europeans were to design their own recovery programme rather than have one imposed by the US, which would fund the programme if it met with American approval. The Soviet Union was invited to take part. Ernest BEVIN, the British Foreign Secretary, was enthusiastic and with the French Foreign Minister, Georges BIDAULT, called a meeting in Paris of all European countries to consider the proposal. Molotov, the Soviet Foreign Minister, walked out, as the US insisted on the disclosure of economic information by the recipients and because the plan was incompatible with Soviet central planning. The USSR forced Poland and Czechoslovakia to reject American aid and formed their own trading bloc COMECON for Eastern Europe.

Sixteen European countries agreed in Paris to prepare a four-year plan for economic recovery. At US insistence the Western zones of Germany were included, an essential move in reintegrating West Germany into Western Europe. To administer the plan and encourage economic co-operation an organization, which became the OEEC (Organization for European Economic Cooperation) in 1948 and the OECD in 1961, was set up. Truman asked Congress for $17 billion. Eventually $13.2 billion were granted in the largest voluntary transfer of resources in history: 90 per cent of the aid did not have to be repaid. Britain ($3.2 billion and France $2.7 billion) were the greatest beneficiaries, Italy receiving $1.5 billion and Germany $1.4 billion.

Aid took the form mainly of food and raw materials. The Marshall Plan was an exceptionally far-sighted and generous measure which took 10 per cent of the US budget and 1–2 per cent of national income in its early years. It made possible the rapid economic recovery of Western Europe without demanding punitive sacrifices and provided political stability within democratic institutions. By 1950 European industrial production was 25 per cent above its prewar level. Inflation was controlled, employment increased and the trade gap with the US grew smaller. Economic co-operation in Western Europe (a prime American aim) increased through institutions such as the ECSC (European Coal and Steel Community), but the plan accelerated the division of Europe. It also bound Western Europe into a close economic and political relationship with the US.

The Reconstruction of Western Europe, A. Milward (1984)

The Marshall Plan, M. J. Hogan (1987)
The Marshall Plan and Germany, C. S. Maier and G. Bischof (eds) (1991)

Mau Mau   The name given to a Kenyan guerrilla movement organized by the Kikuyu Land and Freedom Army from 1947. Its origins lay in an acute land shortage in Kenya and resentment that blacks were not allowed to own land in the 'White Highlands', occupied by 30,000 European settlers: there were at that time five million Africans in Kenya. Kikuyu peasants, and urban workers in Nairobi, formed secret organizations bound together by oath-taking and pledged to expel whites from Kenya. There was a widespread rising by October 1952, when the government declared a state of emergency, though it did not cover the whole of Kenya: no Africans outside the central province took part in Mau Mau and many Kikuyu stood aside or fought against it. KENYATTA and other leading Kikuyu were arrested and, on spurious evidence, sentenced to seven years' imprisonment 'for managing Mau Mau'. At the height of the emergency there were 20,000–25,000 guerrillas, who were very difficult to pin down as they attacked outlying farms and Kikuyu who co-operated with the government at night and took refuge in the impenetrable forests.

To cope with the rebellion the authorities detained 80,000 Kikuyu in special camps and forcibly resettled hundreds of thousands of Kikuyu peasants in new fortified villages. The two main rebel commanders were captured and by 1956 the revolt was almost over (the state of emergency did not end until 1960), but it had taken 50,000 British troops to end the conflict. According to official figures, of those killed there were 11,503 Mau Mau, 1,920 'loyal' Africans, including about a thousand government troops, 66 British soldiers, 29 European civilians and 29 Asians. These figures exclude the thousands of Kikuyu, including women and children, who died of starvation or disease in the overcrowded, insanitary, fortified villages.

Mau Mau had suffered military defeat and failed to expel white settlers from Kenya but politically they succeeded, as they broke the British government's will to continue ruling in Kenya on behalf of a white minority which had been unable to cope with the situation. Kenya became independent in 1963. Few of those who fought in the forests with Mau Mau became leaders of the new Kenya, which was led by educated men who had remained within the two established political parties and trade unions.

Economic and Social Origins of Mau Mau, 1945–53, D. Throup (1987)
The Mau Mau War in Perspective, F. Furedi (1989)
Unhappy Valley: Clan, Class and State in Colonial Kenya, B. Berman and J. Lonsdale (1992)

May 1968   Student disturbances in France in which workers became involved and which appeared to threaten the foundations of the Fifth Republic. The students' revolt was a worldwide movement which affected other European countries, Japan, Mexico and the US, where it arose out of the VIETNAM ANTI-WAR MOVEMENT. Students were influenced by the CIVIL RIGHTS MOVEMENT in the US, by the CULTURAL REVOLUTION in China and by the PRAGUE SPRING but also had local grievances. In France the number of university students had risen to over half a million without a corresponding increase in staff or facilities. On 2 May the campus at Nanterre was closed, whereupon agitation moved to the Sorbonne. When police moved in to arrest student leaders, demonstrations spread to the Latin Quarter, provincial universities and schools. On the night of 10–11 May barricades appeared on the Paris streets in a spontaneous movement. There was no national leadership. Prime Minister POMPIDOU (against DE GAULLE's wishes) ordered the police to withdraw from the Sorbonne, which immediately became a student commune where intermin-

able meetings discussed such issues as feminism, gay rights and ecology. On 13 May workers became involved for the first time when the largest trade unions (the communist CGT and non-communist CFDT) called a one-day general strike. In Paris 800,000 students and workers demonstrated with slogans such as 'De Gaulle *au musée!*' This set off a spontaneous series of strikes in the provinces, where some workers (influenced by the student example) staged sit-ins, ignored their moderate union leaders and demanded worker participation in the running of factories. The strikes spread from the aircraft and car plants to the railways, engineering industries, department stores and civil service until ten million workers were on strike for better wages and conditions. Yet there was no revolutionary situation, as the CGT and Communist Party (PCF) were trying to control the strikes, limit the workers' demands and separate them from the middle-class students (only 2 per cent of students were from the working class) they could not control. The PCF, asking for calm, called itself 'the great and tranquil party of order'. Pompidou saw how he could split the workers from the students and brought government, employers and unions together at Grenelle. They agreed to increase wages and on a 30 per cent rise in the minimum wage, but the shop floor rejected the agreement. There was a sense of impending doom, exacerbated by the PCF call for a mass demonstration in Paris on 29 May to demand a popular government.

As Pompidou ordered tanks to the outskirts of Paris on 29 May, de Gaulle, without informing his Prime Minister, boarded a helicopter and disappeared. It later appeared that he had flown to Baden to meet General Massu, the commander of French forces in Germany. His motives remain unclear. He returned on 30 May to be greeted by a loyalist demonstration of half a million in Paris and took Pompidou's advice to call a general election. Workers began returning to work on 1 June and when the elections were held on 23 and 30 June the Gaullists benefited from popular dislike of the inconvenience caused by the disturbances and won an overwhelming majority. Edgar Faure, the Minister of Education, announced that 67 new universities were to be created and that elected student representatives would have places on the governing councils. GAULLISM, largely owing to the efforts of Pompidou, emerged strengthened from the events of May 1968.

The May Movement: Revolt and Reform, A. Touraine (1971)
Protest in Paris: Anatomy of a Revolt, B. E. Brown (1974)
May '68: Coming of Age, D. Hanley and A. Kerr (eds) (1989)

Menderes, Adnan (1899–1961)   Prime Minister of Turkey (1950–60). The son of a wealthy landowner, he trained as a lawyer but made little impression politically until he became a founder member of the Democratic Party (DP) in 1946. The DP, which called for less government interference in economic and religious affairs and for religion to be treated as a 'sacred human right', won the 1950 election with 53 per cent of the vote, a remarkable victory over the Republican People's Party (RPP), which had ruled Turkey since 1923.

Menderes dominated Turkish politics for the next ten years and continued the pro-Western policy of the previous government, sending troops to take part in the KOREAN WAR (1950–3), joining NATO in 1952 and the BAGHDAD PACT in 1955. An economic boom, helped by a succession of good harvests and an increase in world economic activity as a result of the Korean War, created unprecedented Turkish prosperity in the early 1950s. Menderes put the interests of farmers first, providing them with cheap credit. American aid was used to begin the mechanization of agriculture and increase the cultivated area by a half. Roads were built, opening up the country for the first time, and industry developed: most of the large firms at the end of the century originated in the 1950s. Menderes gained an overwhelming victory in the 1954

election but then the growth rate of the economy declined, as inflation increased and the trade gap widened: in 1958 Turkey had to seek help from the IMF. Politically Menderes had great difficulty in reducing the influence of the RPP, as its members were strongly entrenched in the army, the civil service and education. He therefore confiscated its property, took over its party newspaper and restricted the press and public meetings, giving the impression that he intended to establish a dictatorship. He departed from the secular tradition of Kemal Atatürk, the founder of the Turkish Republic, by making concessions to Muslims. The ban on religious broadcasting was lifted, religion was made compulsory in primary, and optional in secondary, schools and religious schools were allowed. These measures were very popular and were accompanied by a religious revival, though political parties based on religion remained illegal. In 1960 there were demonstrations by university students against attempts to control the activities of the RPP. The army was called in to control them and on 27 May carried out a military coup, claiming that the DP had undermined the constitution. The DP was abolished and, after a lengthy trial in which he was accused of corruption and embezzling state funds, Menderes was found guilty and hanged.

The Turkish Experiment in Democracy 1950–75, F. Ahmad (1977)
Turkey: A Modern History, E. J. Zurcher (1995)

Mendès France, Pierre (1907–82)
French Prime Minister (1954–5). The son of a cloth merchant, and a non-religious Jew, he entered parliament in 1932 as a Radical and was a strong supporter of the Popular Front, though he opposed its policy of not intervening in the Spanish Civil War. In 1938 he entered Blum's government as Undersecretary at the Treasury (the youngest member of a government in the Third Republic). During the Second World War he joined the Free

French. After the Liberation he was Minister of the National Economy in DE GAULLE'S government but resigned in 1945, as de Gaulle was not prepared to carry out the austere measures Mendès France thought were necessary. He then taught at the *École nationale d'administration*, served on the executive committee of the WORLD BANK and the IMF and represented France from 1947–51 on the Economic and Social Council of the UNITED NATIONS. He opposed France's involvement in the INDOCHINA WAR OF INDEPENDENCE (1946–54), as he said it would retard France's modernization and competitiveness. Following France's defeat at DIEN BIEN PHU in 1954 he became Prime Minister, promising to resign if he did not end the war within a month.

His government was the most dynamic and effective of the FOURTH REPUBLIC. He believed, like de Gaulle, that ministers should be appointed because of their ability and therefore ignored party leaders in choosing them. In doing so he split the parties: half the Radicals and SOCIALIST PARTY and some Gaullists supported him. Mendès France also believed that problems had to be solved, not shelved, so he personally took charge of some of the most difficult ministries, foreign affairs and then the economy. He wanted to get rid of the burdens of empire, so that more money would be available for economic modernization and for raising the standard of living. By the GENEVA ACCORDS he ended French participation in the Indochina War and followed this up by agreeing to self-government in Tunisia and began talks with Morocco (which led to independence in 1956). Algeria was a different matter. When the ALGERIAN WAR OF INDEPENDENCE began in 1954 he decided to crush the rebellion ('Algeria is France and not a foreign country') but appointed Jacques Soustelle to carry out economic and social reforms there. The same decisive approach was applied to the EDC (European Defence Community), which his predecessors had ignored. The French government had agreed to this in

May 1952 but it had not been ratified by parliament: it was denounced by the communists as anti-Soviet and by the Gaullists as it would mean a loss of French sovereignty. Mendès France, who had no great enthusiasm for it, brought it before the National Assembly, which rejected it in August 1954. He then steered through the Assembly the London and Paris agreements for the rearmament of Germany and its entry into NATO. By this time he had made many enemies and in February 1955 his government was defeated, with the help of Radical Party bosses, and he resigned.

After his fall from power he helped to form the Republican Front, which brought together non-communist parties of the left: progressive Radicals, socialists and the UDSR of MITTERRAND. This coalition formed a government under MOLLET after the 1956 election, with Mendès France as Minister Without Portfolio, but he resigned in May 1957 because of Mollet's intransigent Algerian policy. In opposition he criticized government policy in the SUEZ CRISIS, voted against the TREATY OF ROME which set up the EEC, and opposed the return to power of de Gaulle and the CONSTITUTION OF THE FIFTH REPUBLIC. Out of step with public opinion, he lost his parliamentary seat in 1958. He broke with the Radical Party in 1959, declared himself a socialist and sympathized with the striking students and workers in MAY 1968. Mendès France unsuccessfully ran a campaign against POMPIDOU and GAULLISM and then disappeared from public life.

The Fourth Republic, 1944–58, J. P. Rioux (1987)
France Since the Popular Front, 1936–96, M. Larkin (1997).

Menem, Carlos Saúl (1930–)   President of Argentina (1989–). Of Syrian descent, Menem trained as a lawyer. A fervent nationalist, he joined the traditional wing of the Peronist movement.

He was elected three times as governor of La Rioja, his home province, before he won the presidential election in 1989 as the candidate of a three-party alliance while the Peronists secured a majority in the Chamber of Deputies. A few months after assuming office in July 1989, he pardoned 210 soldiers from the 'dirty war' of the 1970s, the Junta from the FALKLANDS WAR, and the heads of three recent military risings. There was widespread outrage, but Menem maintained that such amnesties were necessary for the 'reconciliation' of the Argentine people.

The future of Argentine democracy depended on whether Menem, in contrast to Raúl ALFONSÍN, would be able to create a durable consensus regarding the measures necessary to overcome the appalling economic crisis. To general amazement, Menem, in defiance of Peronism's corporatist past, unleashed a neo-liberal programme of extensive PRIVATIZATION and public sector cutbacks in 1990. Initially, this failed to counteract the vertiginous inflation as riots, looting, as well as demonstrations by the trade unions and political opposition became widespread. However, by mid-1991 the neo-liberal economic strategy had brought inflation under control and secured major international loans. Menem's standing none the less suffered a setback as a result of the revelations concerning the breakdown of his marriage and the corruption of his wife's family and a number of ministers. However, the flamboyant Menem remained popular as long as the economy prospered, as shown by the Peronists' clear victory in the 1993 general election.

In 1994 Menem managed to revise the constitution so that he could stand for a second term the following year. To obtain the necessary two-thirds majority of the constitutional assembly, he brokered a deal with opposition leader and former President Raúl Alfonsín by which the President's powers were notably reduced. Although Menem's government limited the damage from Mexico's spectacular currency crisis of December 1994, 50 Argentine banks failed and productivity shrank, provoking strikes, riots and looting as unemployment still stood at over 18 per cent. In spite of the slump, Menem won an impressive victory in the May 1995 presidential election, while the Peronists won 10 of the 14 governorships in dispute and also improved their position in the Chamber of Deputies.

The Penguin History of Latin America, E. Williamson (1992)

Mengistu, Haile Hariam (1937–) Head of state in Ethiopia (1977–91). An obscure major when the Dergue (Armed Forces Co-ordinating Committee) overthrew Emperor HAILE SELASSIE in 1974, he skilfully eliminated his main rivals to become leader of the Dergue in February 1977. Mengistu was declared Head of State and was in effect a ruthless dictator, who routinely executed opponents and generals whom he considered had failed in operations against Tigrean and Eritrean rebels.

He faced serious threats to the integrity of Ethiopia. The ERITREAN WAR OF INDEPENDENCE had been going on since 1961, there was a rebellion in Tigre province in the north and Somali troops invaded the Ogaden in 1977. To cope with these problems Mengistu signed an agreement with the Soviet Union in 1978 for economic and military aid and also received help from Fidel CASTRO. Cuban troops enabled him to defeat the Somalis in 1978, so that he could then turn north to win back much of Eritrea with Soviet fire-power. As Soviet support declined in the 1980s the Eritreans, assisted by Tigre rebels, routed the Ethiopian army and brought the government to the point of collapse. The economy stagnated because of the war and was further weakened by natural disasters which affected much of Africa. Recurrent drought reduced agricultural production by 30 per cent and affected nine million people: over one million died in the drought of 1984–5. Mengistu responded with an enforced resettlement programme: in 1986 600,000 people were moved from the drought-stricken north and central highlands to more fertile land in the south and east. A second move, to resettle one and a half million people, began in 1988, though the UNITED NATIONS reckoned that seven million needed to be moved. In spite of the drought the population continued to grow at an alarming rate (2.9 per cent per annum) which, according to forecasts by the IMF and WORLD BANK, would make a rise in the standard of living impossible. Mengistu's greatest successes were in education and health. Literacy increased from 7 per cent to 40 per cent of the population and over half the children attended primary school (compared with 18 per cent in 1974), figures which impressed UNESCO. Access to health services rose from 15 per cent to 48 per cent of the population. In 1990 Mengistu abandoned Marxism and began to introduce a market economy. A year later rebel forces led by the People's Revolutionary Democratic Front captured Addis Ababa, overcoming a demoralized army of 350,000. Mengistu fled to Zimbabwe.

Revolutionary Ethiopia, E. J. Keller (1988)
Transformation and Continuity in Revolutionary Ethiopia, C. Clapham (1988)
The Ethiopian Transformation: The Quest for the Post-Imperial State, J. Harbeson (1989)

Menzies, Robert Gordon (1894–1978)

Prime Minister of Australia (1939–41, 1949–66). Australia's longest serving Prime Minister was a brilliant barrister before he gave up a highly successful law practice to serve in the state legislature of Victoria (1929–34): he was elected to the federal parliament in 1934. From 1934–9 he was Attorney-General and when the Prime Minister, Joseph Lyons, died, Menzies was elected leader of the United Australia Party (UAP) and was Prime Minister from 1939–41. After the 1940 election he had to rely on independents for a majority in the House of Representatives and when they withdrew their support in 1941, the Australian Labor Party (ALP) formed a new government. In 1944 Menzies

formed a new Liberal Party, which claimed to represent neither big business nor big labour but the 'forgotten people', the middle class. The Liberal Party won the election of 1949, Menzies becoming Prime Minister for a second time.

His long tenure of power was partly due to good fortune. In both the 1954 and 1961 elections the Labor Party gained more votes than the Liberal and Country parties combined but was left with a minority of seats. Menzies was helped too by the world economic boom, which maintained high commodity prices for Australia's exports. There was a growth of manufacturing (cars and consumer goods), much of which had previously been imported, and foreign investment and the standard of living of most Australians rose. A weak opposition also aided Menzies, as the ALP split (a Catholic wing broke away in 1955). Menzies pursued a moderate course at home, seeking consensus and did not change Labor's earlier policies very much. He improved some welfare provisions, the government providing free medical care for pensioners. School and university education was greatly expanded and two million immigrants were successfully absorbed. Menzies suffered a defeat when he outlawed the Communist Party in 1950. The High Court declared this illegal, so he called for a referendum on the issue, which he narrowly lost.

His staunch anti-communism was evident in his foreign policy. For defence he looked to the US, signing the ANZUS TREATY in 1951. When the KOREAN WAR began Australia was the first country to send troops to support US forces there. He also sent troops in 1955 to help fight communists in the MALAYAN EMERGENCY. Convinced that a pact wider in scope than ANZUS was needed for the containment of communism, SEATO was the result, though India, Indonesia, Malaya and Burma rejected it for strengthening neo-colonialism. This treaty was later used to justify US and Australian participation in the VIETNAM WAR: Menzies sent Australian troops there in 1965 and introduced conscription to make this possible. The Anglophile Menzies maintained close relations with Britain, allowed Britain to test nuclear weapons in Australia in 1950, hosted the first visit to Australia of a British monarch (Queen ELIZABETH II) in 1954 and supported Britain in the SUEZ CRISIS of 1956. When Britain withdrew from east of Suez, he turned more to the US, who built communications and satellite bases in Australia. Menzies announced his retirement in 1966 (he was 71), becoming Chancellor of the University of Melbourne from 1967–72.

Oxford History of Australia, vol. 5, 1942–88, G. Bolton (1990)

Meredith incident (1961–2)

It took place as part of the CIVIL RIGHTS MOVEMENT in the US. James Meredith, a young black, applied for admission to the University of Mississippi but was rejected on racial grounds. The NAACP then brought a suit in a federal court which granted him the right to enrol. When he arrived to do so he was turned away by the university authorities and by the Governor of Mississippi. A court injunction for contempt removed this barrier but a white mob prevented him entering the university. After a riot in which two people were killed and 375 wounded, President KENNEDY sent hundreds of federal marshals and 3,000 federal troops to restore order and enable Meredith to register as a student. The right of blacks to study at what had been a white university was established, as it was in the other state universities in the South in the next few years, but it was a slow process and there were only a token handful of black students at many of these universities.

military–industrial complex (MIC)

A phrase first used by President EISENHOWER in January 1961 in his farewell address: 'In the councils of government we must guard against the acquisition of unwarranted influence ... by the military–industrial complex'.

In the US the most important of the defence industry corporations produced aircraft and missiles: McDonnell Douglas, Lockheed, Boeing, General Dynamics, General Electric and General Motors. Politicians are a link between the military and industry, as they vote money for weapons in congressional committees and try to ensure that their districts and states benefit from contracts given to corporations. Lyndon JOHNSON, a Texan and Senate majority leader (1955–61) played a large part in establishing NASA at Houston, Texas. Supporters of the MIC maintain that it has stabilized the economy and has produced many inventions which have civilian uses: small transistors, hard plastics, optical fibres, lasers, computers and remote-controlled television sets. Critics say the MIC has distorted the economy by creating higher defence budgets than were necessary, that it has intensified the arms race and that it has diverted funds away from the non-defence industries and so made it more difficult for the US to compete in world markets with countries like Japan and Germany, whose defence spending is low. Japan has never spent more than 1 per cent of GNP on defence, whereas the US has allocated as much as 12.7 per cent (in 1954).

The MIC – 'the metal-eaters' according to KHRUSHCHEV – played a dominant role in the Soviet economy and kept the standard of living low for the mass of Soviet citizens. Taking 15–20 per cent of GNP it was a burden the inefficient Soviet economy could not afford and led to economic decline and the political COLLAPSE OF THE SOVIET UNION.

The Baroque Arsenal, M. Kaldor (1981)
New Weapons, Old Politics, T. L. Naugher (1989)

Milošević, Slobodan (1941–)

President of Serbia (1989–97) and of Yugoslavia (1997–). The son of a Montenegrin Orthodox priest, both his parents committed suicide. He studied law at Belgrade University and then began a successful business career, becoming general manager of Tehnogas, the state-owned gas company, and president of a Belgrade bank. At this time he was often in New York, where he perfected his English. Milošević entered politics in 1984 and succeeded his old university friend Ivan Stambolić as leader of the Serb communists in 1986, when Stambolić became President. A Stalinist, who expected unquestioning loyalty and wanted a strong centralized state, he disapproved of the 1974 Yugoslav constitution, which had given two provinces of Serbia (Kosovo and Vojvodina) considerable powers of self-government, which made them almost independent of Serbian control. Milošević promised to protect the Serb minority in Kosovo (10 per cent of the population, the rest being Albanians) against Albanian domination and became a populist demagogue, organizing massive Serb demonstrations to intimidate the Albanians. The Serb assembly in 1989 replaced Stambolić as President with Milošević, who persuaded it to approve a new constitution which ended the autonomy of Kosovo and Vojvodina. This treatment of Kosovo convinced the Slovenes and Croats that they would be better off as independent states outside a federal Yugoslavia. Milošević then changed the League of Communists of Serbia into the Socialist Party, which won multiparty elections in December 1990.

There was a crisis in Yugoslavia in 1991 as the federation began to break up when Slovenia and Croatia declared their independence in June. Milošević made no attempt to keep Slovenia within a federal Yugoslavia as few Serbs lived there, but 12 per cent of the Croat population were Serbs. He claimed that if Croatia had the right to secede from Yugoslavia, the Serbs in Croatia had the right to withdraw from Croatia. He encouraged the Serbs in Krajina and Slavonia to declare their independence of Croatia and so began the YUGO-SLAV CIVIL WAR, in which Milošević ensured that the Yugoslav National Army (JNA) supported the Serbs, as 70 per cent of its officers were Serbs or Montenegrins. Serbs seized a third of Croatia before the war temporarily came to an end in January 1992 and overran 70 per cent of Bosnia (where Serbs were 32 per cent of the population) after Bosnia-Hercegovina declared its independence in February 1992. In April Milošević was the effective ruler of the new Federal Republic of Yugoslavia, which consisted only of Serbia and Montenegro. Serbia suffered severely in the war as the UNITED NATIONS imposed a trade embargo on it in 1992 and as Milošević paid for the war by printing money, which produced hyper-inflation and destroyed much of the Serbian economy. Anxious to bring the war to an end, he accepted the plan of the Contact Group (of the US, Russia, Britain, Germany and France) which would give 51 per cent of Bosnia to the Serbs. He was furious when Milovan Karadžić, the Bosnian Serb leader, rejected this and gave no help to the Bosnian Serbs when they were driven out of Krajina in a Croat offensive in 1995. Milošević signed in Paris in December 1995 the Dayton Accords which ended the civil war and gained much of what he wanted, including a Serb area of Bosnia contiguous to Serbia itself, though he agreed to hand over the Serb suburbs of Sarajevo to the Bosnian Muslims.

UN sanctions were lifted after the Dayton Accords but this did not improve the lives of ordinary Serbs. Per capita income halved between 1987 and 1996, there was little PRI-VATIZATION, foreign investment dried up and many of the most dynamic and well-educated went abroad. There were neither jobs nor housing for the 500,000 Serb refugees from Croatia and Bosnia. Milošević's Socialist Party won the general election in 1996 but lost control of the large industrial centres in local government elections. He therefore declared these elections invalid, though he had to give way after three months of daily demonstrations by Together, the opposition coalition. After that Together fragmented in incessant bickering, which undermined the hopes for greater democracy. In Kosovo Milošević had replaced Albanians by Serbs in the police and civil service as early as 1992 and had declared

Serbian the only official language. After the civil war he tried to colonize the province with Serbs, some of them refugees from Croatia, with only limited success. The Serbian constitution prevented Milošević enjoying a third term as President, so he became President of the rump Yugoslavia instead in 1997. In September of that year his ruling alliance lost control of the Serbian parliament after elections.

miners' strikes (1972, 1974, 1984–5 in Britain)   The first strike took place when miners rejected a pay offer of 8 per cent. Flying pickets organized by Arthur Scargill, a Yorkshire miners' leader, prevented the movement of coal to factories and power stations and led the government of Edward HEATH to restrict industry to a three-day week. The strike went on till the miners were given increases of between 17 per cent and 24 per cent. This strike and its victorious outcome discredited the government and encouraged union militancy. Arthur Scargill became head of the Yorkshire miners, the largest group in the country, in 1973.

Trouble arose again in October 1973, when the National Coal Board (NCB) offered the miners a 13 per cent pay rise, the largest possible under Heath's statutory wages policy. The NUM (National Union of Mineworkers) called for an overtime ban in November and a strike in February 1974. At this Heath announced a general election, which he unexpectedly lost to the LABOUR PARTY and Harold WILSON became Prime Minister, rapidly buying the miners off. It seemed that 'the robber barons of the the system' (*Financial Times*) had brought down an elected government. When the CONSERVATIVE PARTY returned to power in 1979 its leader, Margaret THATCHER, expected another trial of strength with the unions, which she intended to crush, as she regarded them as a main cause of national decline, with their inflationary wage demands far in excess of productivity and in their resistance to technological

change. By 1984 the government was ready to take on the miners.

Nicholas Ridley, a Tory MP, put forward proposals in *The Economist* in May 1978 to deal with a miners' strike: build up coal stocks at power stations; have contingency plans to import coal; ensure power stations can switch from coal to oil; cut off money to strikers and force the union to finance them; and have a large, mobile police force ready. Thatcher carried out most of these proposals and appointed Ian MacGregor, a Scottish-American who at British Steel had turned its low productivity into almost the best in Europe, head of the NCB to reform the mining industry. Scargill, who had become President of the NUM in 1982, was an unrepentant Stalinist who had no use for democracy or parliament. 'Extra-parliamentary action', he told his union conference in 1983, 'will be the only course open to the working class and the labour movement'. Tough, energetic and an articulate mob orator, he wanted to fight the class war to bring down the government and had an exaggerated idea of his own power. When MacGregor announced in March 1984 that 20 uneconomic pits would have to close with the loss of 20,000 jobs, Scargill called the miners out on strike. He did not hold a ballot, as he feared that miners would vote against a strike. This was made clear in the nine areas which did hold a ballot: in only one, Northumberland, was there a narrow majority (52 per cent) for a strike. Scargill relied, therefore, on flying pickets to prevent the movement of coal and also to intimidate miners and their families in areas such as Nottingham, where miners continued to work. This time the police were better prepared: they had learnt from the Toxteth (Liverpool) and Brixton riots of 1981 and set up a National Reporting Centre which coordinated the activities of regional police forces and made them, in effect, a national force. Violence on the picket lines by both miners and police (10,000 pickets confronted the police at the Orgreave coking depot at Rotherham) was shown daily on television.

There was no working-class solidarity as dockers unloaded imported coal and the TRADE UNIONS, appalled at Scargill's refusal to hold a ballot, were unwilling to help. The miners' families suffered real deprivation, which they met with resilience and great fortitude, and had considerable public support. Hunger, however, drove some miners back to work and in the New Year the trickle became a flood. Scargill's refusal to compromise left the miners no way out. The strike, in which more working days were lost than in any dispute since 1926, lasted a year and ended with the comprehensive defeat of the miners.

They gained nothing from the strike. Pit closures continued at an accelerating rate, so that by the end of the decade the NUM had only 60,000 members. The miners had split, with a break-away Union of Democratic Mineworkers with 30,000 members being formed in Nottinghamshire. The Trades Union Congress was demoralized, its power ended. There were political repercussions, too. The WINTER OF DISCONTENT was exorcized and the popularity of the Prime Minister increased enormously. The Labour Party lost credibility, as its Conference supported the miners and as its leader Neil Kinnock, though highly critical of Scargill ('He's destroying the coal industry single-handed') was slow to condemn picket-line violence.

The Miners' Strike, G. Goodman (1985)
The Miners' Strike, 1984–5, M. Adeney and J. Lloyd (1987)
Scargill, P. Routledge (1993)

Mitterrand, François (1916–96)

President (1981–95) of the Fifth Republic in France. He grew up in a conservative middle-class family in the south-west and studied law and political science in Paris, where he joined the extreme right-wing *Croix de Feu*. In the Second World War he served in the army, was captured and at the third attempt escaped in 1940 to Vichy France, where he was a fervent supporter of the regime and of Marshal Pétain. He was awarded Vichy's highest honour, the *Francisque*. Fiercely anti-German, Mitterrand changed sides in 1943 and joined the Resistance, in which he acted with great bravery. After the war he was elected to parliament as a member of the UDSR (Democratic and Socialist Resistance Union) and served in 11 governments of the FOURTH REPUBLIC. As Minister of the Interior (1954–5) he was an ardent supporter of *Algérie française* and as Minister of Justice (1955–6) allowed French troops to use torture against the FLN.

When the Fifth Republic replaced the Fourth he began 23 years in opposition, of which he was the undisputed leader against what he called DE GAULLE's 'permanent coup d'état' and did remarkably well in the 1965 presidential election, when he obtained 45 per cent of the vote. In 1971 he became First Secretary of the SOCIALIST PARTY (PS) which he had only recently joined, convinced that he could win power only by a 'union of the Left'. He persuaded the Communist Party (PCF) to join him in a common programme and failed only narrowly to become President on the death of POMPIDOU in 1974, gaining 49.2 per cent of the vote to GISCARD D´ESTAING's 50.8 per cent. Mitterrand was finally successful in his bid for the presidency in 1981, when he defeated Giscard with 51.7 per cent of the vote. He immediately called for a general election in which the PS with its left Radical allies won an absolute majority of 285 seats. Four communists, for the first time since 1947, came into the government.

An aloof intellectual, withdrawn and introspective, a lover of nature, solitude and great literature, Mitterrand was also an astute, manipulative politician, known as 'the Florentine' for his Machiavellian intrigues. He wanted the government to take the lead in economic expansion by nationalizing industries, providing jobs and raising wages, thereby increasing incomes and the market for French goods. Nine of France's largest companies were nationalized, as were 36 banks; pensions, family allowances and the minimum wage were increased; the retirement age was reduced to 60, the working week by one hour to 39 hours and workers received a fifth week of paid holidays. The competitiveness of French industry was improved by three devaluations of the franc (1981–3). Mitterrand relied on the GLOBAL ECONOMY picking up but world trade fell in 1982 and there was a balance of payments disaster as imports were sucked in. Inflation remained high at 14 per cent, government expenditure rose by 11 per cent (1981–2) in real terms, the budget deficit increased and unemployment rose. The Finance Minister, Jacques Delors, announced a 'pause', which was a prelude to a remarkable U-turn and a policy of deflation. In 1982–3 there was the greatest planned reduction in purchasing power since the war, as taxes and social security contributions were raised and benefits lowered. This was successful in reducing the trade deficit by half in 1983. Laurent Fabius (the PCF left the government when he became Prime Minister in 1984) continued the austerity measures, bringing inflation down to 4 per cent by 1986 and creating a balance of payments surplus, but there was massive unemployment in the old nationalized industries – coal, steel, vehicles – and an overall figure of 10.7 per cent in 1986.

The President carried out other reforms while there was a socialist majority in the Assembly. He abolished the death penalty when a majority of the population was against doing so, extended legal aid, trebled state aid to the arts and authorized independent television channels, but he was forced to abandon his attempt to increase state control over Catholic schools when a million people in Paris demonstrated against this. His main reform was to give considerable power to the provinces. In 1982 the perfect's right to veto decisions of locally elected bodies was removed. Local affairs were handed over to 22 regionally elected councils and Corsica was given more autonomy.

As the 1986 parliamentary elections approached and it seemed clear that the socialists would lose, Mitterrand, ever the Florentine, reintroduced proportional repre-

sentation, thus enabling Le Pen's National Front to split the right and win 35 seats. The Gaullist RPF and its allies had a majority of only two, the RPF leader Jacques CHIRAC becoming Prime Minister. This raised the question of whether cohabitation (with a socialist President and conservative Prime Minister) could work. Chirac privatized some of the firms Mitterrand had nationalized but otherwise there was little change in policy, as there was a consensus on having a mixed economy with a minimum wage and social security, in retaining France's nuclear deterrent and in moving towards European integration.

In the 1988 presidential election Mitterrand, with 54 per cent of the vote, comprehensively defeated Chirac and, as in 1981, called for new elections which brought the socialists back to power, though they did not have an overall majority. Deflationary policies brought inflation down further, but unemployment remained stubbornly high at over 10 per cent and in 1993 there was a recession. The socialists were overwhelmingly defeated in the 1993 parliamentary elections and once again Mitterrand had to face cohabitation, this time with the Gaullist Edouard Balladur as Prime Minister.

Mitterrand's foreign policy was very much like that of Giscard: anti-American within limits and pro-European. He appeared the champion of the NON-ALIGNED MOVEMENT. In 1982 he made an arms deal with the SANDINISTA regime in Nicaragua, which was fighting the American-backed CONTRAS. When the GULF WAR began he reversed France's pro-Iraq policy (France had supplied Saddam HUSSEIN with arms throughout the IRAN–IRAQ WAR) by sending 10,000 French troops to join the American-led forces. Mitterrand continued Giscard's policy in Africa by sending troops to Chad to defend it against Libya and his policy in the EC of tying Germany more tightly into a united Europe. 'France is our homeland but Europe is our future', he said in 1988. He supported majority voting in the Council of Ministers rather than the veto de Gaulle had obtained in the LUXEMBOURG COMPROMISE, and was a powerful advocate of the MAASTRICHT TREATY. Mitterrand did more than any European leader except KOHL to promote European integration.

He appointed an old girl-friend, Edith Cresson, as Prime Minister in 1991, a disastrous if short-lived choice. In 1992 an operation showed that he had prostate cancer and in 1994 the details of his Vichy past became known, particularly his lasting friendship (which did not end until 1986) with René Bousquet, the Vichy chief of police who had sent thousands of French Jews to their deaths in Nazi concentration camps. It also became known in the same year that he had kept a mistress and their daughter, at public expense, in an annexe to the Elysée. Mitterrand managed to complete his term of office in May 1995 before dying later in the year. He had served longer than any elected head of state in the five French Republics since 1792. An enduring part of his legacy is the *Grands travaux* with which he lavishly adorned Paris: I. M. Pei's glass pyramid at the Louvre, the Musée d'Orsay, a gallery of nineteenth-century art, the Opéra Bastille and the Bibliothèque nationale, Europe's largest library.

The Mitterrand Experiment, G. Ross, S. Hoffmann, S. Malzachen (eds) (1987)
Mitterrand, W. Northcutt (1992)
François Mitterrand, A. Cole (1994)

Mobutu, Sese Seko (1930–97)   President of Zaire (1965–97). Baptized Joseph-Désiré Mobutu in the Belgian Congo, the son of a hotel cook, he served in the colonial *Force Publique* as a sergeant-major (1949–56), the highest post to which an African could rise, then worked as a journalist. After independence the Prime Minister, Lumumba, made him Chief of Staff but when there was a deadlock between President Kasavubu and Lumumba, Mobutu staged a military coup in September 1960, suspending all political parties. When political activity resumed

Mobutu was Commander-in-Chief of the Congolese army (1961–5) and during the CONGO CRISIS helped to end the secession of Katanga and other rebellions which were tearing the country apart. He seized power again (November 1965) after further squabbling among the politicians and made himself President and Prime Minister, a popular move as he promised a strong, united state. Political parties were dissolved, the number of provinces gradually reduced from 21 to 8, their governors appointed by Mobutu rather than being locally elected. He consolidated his dictatorship by founding in 1966 the *Mouvement populaire de la révolution* (MPR) and made it the only party in 1969. Mobutu proclaimed in 1971 his doctrine of authenticity (faithfulness to the African past), changed the name Congo to Zaire and ordered people to adopt African names, changing his own to Sese Seko. A new constitution in 1974 declared that the President was the chief officer of the party, the executive, the legislature and the judiciary. He appointed the members of all these bodies and had unchallenged authority.

Zaire, Africa's third largest state, had borders drawn up by the colonial powers without regard to ethnicity (it had over 200 ethnic groups), language, geography or other features that make a nation. The regions therefore tended to go their own way, making Zaire difficult to govern, but it was potentially an enormously wealthy country. Most mineral resources were in the east: Kasai province was rich in diamonds, Shaba in copper, cobalt (with 65 per cent of the world's known reserves), manganese and uranium. Initial economic reforms, including a massive devaluation, brought hyper-inflation under control and a growth rate of 6 per cent per annum from 1969–73, but from 1974 there was a deepening crisis and a steady economic decline, with inflation again and a huge foreign debt of $5 billion by 1980. Communications crumbled and there was destitution and despair. External factors accounted for some of this decay. The OPEC PRICE RISE of 1973 was a severe blow, there was a steep fall in the price of Zaire's main export, copper, in 1974–5 and in 1975 Zaire's main export route, the Benguela railway, was closed by guerrillas in the ANGOLAN CIVIL WAR.

Some of the damage was self-inflicted. Mobutu, with the encouragement of South Africa and the US, supported the FNLA in the Angolan Civil War and committed 2,000 troops, who were routed by Cuban and government forces. This was costly, demoralized the army and was unpopular with other members of the OAU (Organisation of African Unity). The Zairianization of the economy (1973–5), when foreign assets were seized and handed over to Zairians, was a disaster, as the new owners were not competent to run them. The state took them over in 1975, adding corruption to incompetence. As the economy disintegrated (the value of Zairian exports fell by half from 1970–5) and the foreign debt escalated, Mobutu became one of the richest men in the world, siphoning off much of the state's income for his own private use and indulging in an extravagant life-style. Vast sums disappeared in turning his home village, Gbadolite, into a city with a magnificent presidential palace and an airport with a runway long enough to take the Concorde he often loaned from Air France. His personal fortune was estimated at between $5–10 billion in the 1990s. The small élite of a hundred families he favoured was known as 'the kleptocracy'.

Mobutu was able to survive amidst the chaos surrounding him by co-option, by the ruthless elimination of opponents and by the support of foreign powers, particularly the US and France, during the COLD WAR. Politicians, denied any political power, were given a stake in the survival of the regime by appointments in the civil service, which enabled them to become rich through corruption. When this did not work, opponents were tortured, exiled or executed. Mobutu was propped up by the US to prevent further Soviet influence in Africa. 'A man of good sense', President REAGAN called him. When

rebels invaded Shaba (Katanga) from Angola in 1977–8, French and Belgian paratroops and soldiers from Morocco enabled him to survive the assault. The US and Saudi Arabia paid the bill. He repaid his backers by giving them bases in Zaire, by resuming diplomatic relations with Israel in 1982, and by approving of the annexation of the Western Sahara by HASSAN II of Morocco.

In spite of a distintegrating economy – the infrastructure (water supply, electricity, roads) collapsed, hospitals and schools closed, AIDS, cholera and bubonic plague raged unchecked and half the children under five died of malnutrition – there was no serious threat to his position until the collapse of communism and the end of the Cold War. The US (which had provided Zaire with $2 billion), France and Belgium stopped their aid and President BUSH three times asked Mobutu to stand down. He refused but was forced in 1990 to announce the end of one-party rule. He did all he could to delay and then disrupt the transition to democracy and was finally overthrown by a rising, led by Laurent Kabila, which began in the east. Kabila was supported, with arms and sometimes with troops, by Uganda, Rwanda, Ethiopia and Eritrea, all of whom accused Mobutu of supporting rebels in their own countries. In seven months Kabila advanced 1,500 kilometres (937 miles) to conquer the whole of Zaire, entering Kinshasa, the capital, in May 1997. Mobutu, absent for much of the time receiving treatment for prostate cancer in Switzerland, fled to Morocco, where he died.

The Rise and Decline of the Zairian State,
   C. Young and T. Turner (1985)
The Crisis in Zaire: Myths and Realities,
   G. Nzongola-Ntalaya (1988)

Moi, Daniel Toroitich arap (1924–)

President of Kenya (1978–). Unusually for a leading Kenyan politician, he came from a minority ethnic group, the Kalenjin. He was educated at mission schools and worked as an unqualified teacher from 1945–57, when he won a seat on the Legislative Council. In 1960 he was Assistant Treasurer of the Kenya Africa National Union (KANU) but resented the Kikuyu and Luo domination of the party, so in 1961 he joined the Kenya African Democratic Union (KADU), which represented ethnic minorities. Before independence he served in the coalition government as Minister of Education (1961–2) and Minister for Local Government (1962–3). After independence in 1963 KADU became the official opposition but a year later KANU absorbed KADU and Moi joined KENYA- TTA's government as Minister of Home Affairs from 1964–7, when he became Vice- President and one of Kenyatta's most trusted advisers. There were Kikuyu attempts to prevent him from succeeding the ageing President but he brushed them aside and followed Kenyatta as President in 1978.

He began with some popular measures, releasing political prisoners, reducing press censorship and starting a campaign against corruption, but he did not follow this through and became increasingly intolerant and authoritarian. In 1982 he made Kenya a one- party state and detained critics. By 1987 AMNESTY INTERNATIONAL was criticizing his poor record on human rights, including detention without trial and the use of torture. In 1988 parliament gave him the power to dismiss judges, thus ending the independence of the judiciary. Anyone who challenged his power was removed. There was a great scandal in 1990 when the Foreign Minister, Robert Ouko, was murdered, as many believed the government was implicated. Moi constantly rejected requests for a multi- party democracy. His strong support for capitalism, his belief that private enterprise would lead to economic growth and his sell- ing-off of state assets, such as the Kenya Commercial Bank, went down well in the US and Britain. In 1991 foreign aid was sus- pended until there were political and eco- nomic reforms and an improvement in Kenya's human rights record. Moi therefore reluctantly agreed to multiparty elections, which were held in 1992. Moi was re-elected as President with 36 per cent of the vote and KANU won 100 out of 188 seats in the National Assembly. A COMMONWEALTH monitoring group said the elections reflected 'the will of the people'. Aid was resumed in 1994 but immediately Moi reverted to repres- sion, so that Kenya's Roman Catholic bishops in a pastoral letter complained that 'Too many of our people are living in fear; it would seem there is no law, no justice, no protection, except for the powerful'. By 1996 the eco- nomy was in disarray: unemployment and crime were soaring, public services collapsing, power cuts were frequent and the auditor- general could not account for $600 million of government funds.

Decolonization and Independence in Kenya, 1940–93, B. A. Ogot and W. Ochieng (eds) (1995)

Mollet, Guy (1905–75)   Prime Minister of France (1956–7). After taking a degree in English at Lille he was a schoolteacher at Arras before turning to politics as a socialist. In the Second World War he served in the French army, was wounded and captured. Released in 1941, he took part in the Resist- ance at Arras, where he was elected mayor immediately after the war: he held this posi- tion until his death. Regarded by many as humourless and inflexible, he was an efficient organizer and in 1946 became Secretary- General of the SOCIALIST PARTY (SFIO), a post he retained until 1969. Ten years later the Republican Front of the SFIO and MENDÈS FRANCE Radicals won 170 seats. The communists had 146 seats and were eager to revive a Popular Front with the social- ists but Mollet refused, as the PCF was com- mitted to violent revolution and endorsed the Soviet Union's crushing of the HUNGARIAN RISING. He therefore formed a government with Radicals and Christian Democrats.

As Prime Minister he passed some social reforms (holidays with pay were extended from two to three weeks and state pensions were increased by adding 10 per cent to income tax and new indirect taxes) but most of his time was taken up by foreign affairs. The SUEZ CRISIS saw France and Britain humiliated but French public opinion blamed the Soviet Union and the US rather than the government. Events in Egypt convinced Mollet that only European unity could provide a counterweight to the two superpowers, so he eagerly endorsed the TREATY OF ROME, which set up the EEC. He improved Franco-German relations by returning the Saar to West Germany and had another success in the *loi cadre* of 1956, which gave universal suffrage to France's colonies (except Algeria) and made possible peaceful DECOLONIZA-TION south of the Sahara. His policy in Algeria was much less successful. He was convinced that agrarian reform was necessary there but after hostile demonstrations by *colons* greeted his visit to Algeria, he gave up any idea of land reform and turned to repression of the nationalists. His government turned a blind eye to the torture of suspects in the ALGERIAN WAR OF INDEPENDENCE (1954–62). Unable to persuade parliament to raise taxes for the army in Algeria (there were 450,000 French troops there) he resigned and looked to DE GAULLE to save the Republic from a military dictatorship. He backed de Gaulle as premier, helped to draw up the CONSTITUTION OF THE FIFTH REPUBLIC and served briefly in his cabinet. By 1962 he was trying to build up a left-wing opposition to de Gaulle, while still resisting a Popular Front with the communists, but had little success.

French Socialists in Search of a Role, 1956–67, H. G. Simmons (1970)
Ideology and Politics: The Socialist Party of France, G. Cooling et al. (1979)

monetarism   An economic doctrine, developed by Milton Friedman at the University of Chicago, which asserts that control of the money supply is a necessary and suffi-

cient condition for controlling inflation. It was a challenge to KEYNESIANISM, which dominated economic policy-making for 30 years after the Second World War. Keynesians believed that fiscal policy could reduce the level of unemployment, monetarists that the rate of unemployment was decided by structural imperfections in the labour market which government policy could not affect. Keynesians thought inflation was often the result of excess demand or high wage settlements, which could be controlled by an incomes policy, monetarists that inflation could be controlled most effectively by fixing targets for the growth of the money supply. Keynesians concentrated on reducing unemployment, monetarists on reducing inflation.

Monetarism became important in the 1970s because of rapid inflation, especially after the OPEC PRICE RISE of 1973. Keynesians thought that as unemployment rose, the rate of inflation would fall but after 1974 both rose. Consequently, monetarist arguments were more widely accepted. There were political as well as economic reasons for the appeal of monetarism. Many governments had responded to rising inflation by voluntary or statutory incomes policies but these had failed in Britain under both Conservative and Labour governments, particularly those of Edward HEATH and Jim CALLAGHAN, and TRADE UNIONS had played a part in bringing down the governments of Callaghan and of Heath. Monetarism therefore appealed to Conservatives as a way of bringing down inflation without the need for an incomes policy or confrontation with the trade unions. It was also popular with Conservatives because it provided a justification for reducing public spending and taxation and for limiting the power of the trade unions, in order to allow the market to work freely; furthermore, it enabled governments to disclaim any responsibility for unemployment.

Monetarism's impact was greatest in Britain, where it was taken up in the late 1970s by the LABOUR PARTY Prime Minister Jim Callaghan and Denis Healey at the Treasury and in the 1980s by Margaret THATCHER and her Chancellors of the Exchequer, Geoffrey HOWE and Nigel LAWSON. It fitted in well with Thatcher's desire to reduce the role of the state by PRIVATIZATION, to restrict the power of trade unions and to reduce both income tax and public spending. Lawson for a time made M3 (the currency in circulation plus bank deposits) a prime target of his economic policy but this was not successful, as he found it impossible to keep to the monetary targets he had set. By 1990 the exchange rate and interest rates were more important economic targets of the British government. Outside Britain monetarism had greatest influence with central bankers, such as Paul Volcker of the US Federal Reserve Bank, who saw the growth of the money supply as leading to inflation.

Macroeconomic Policy: The New Cambridge, Keynesian and Monetarist Controversies, K. Cuthbertson (1979)
The Rise and Fall of Monetarism, D. Smith (1987)

Monnet, Jean (1888–1979) French administrator. The son of a cognac salesman, he left school at 16 and never attended a university or *grande école*. During the First World War he organized Franco-British war supplies and was Deputy Secretary-General of the League of Nations from 1920–3. After that he was an international financier and businessman (he helped to reorganize the Chinese railways) until the Second World War, when he again worked untiringly in London and Washington to promote the Allied purchase of war material. He was a trusted adviser to President Roosevelt in drawing up the plans which made the US the 'arsenal of democracy' and built up an extensive network of personal contacts with leading American politicians, such as Dean ACHESON and John Foster DULLES, which made him very influential after the war. In Algiers in 1943 he reconciled generals Giraud and DE GAULLE and served in the provisional

government of France. He was responsible for the Monnet Plan (1946–51) for the modernization and revival of French industry, which met all its targets with considerable help from the MARSHALL PLAN.

In 1950 he suggested to Robert Schuman, the French Foreign Minister, the pooling of French and German steel production, which led to the formation of the ECSC (European Coal and Steel Community): Monnet was the first President of its High Authority. His strategy was to promote long-term goals (such as European unity) by plans to deal with immediate problems (Franco-German relations). His other great scheme was for a European Defence Community (EDC) which, like the ECSC, reflected his interest in supranational institutions. This would avoid the danger of a German national army being formed, as German units would be integrated in a European army, responsible to a European Assembly with a joint Ministry of Defence. When this scheme was rejected by the French National Assembly in 1954 he retired from public service but continued to work for European integration. He and Paul-Henri Spaak, the Belgian Foreign Minister, proposed a European Atomic Energy Community and when the Dutch suggested a Common Market, the Messina Conference was held in 1955 to discuss these proposals and led to the TREATY OF ROME in 1957. Monnet founded in 1955 the Action Committee for the United States of Europe to work for European integration. His ideas which had guided the ECSC – the transfer of powers to supranational institutions, the formation of a European judicial system and democratic control by a parliament – served as a model for the institutions of the EEC (European Economic Community). Monnet never belonged to a political party or held elective office and he refused every public honour.

Jean Monnet: The Path to European Unity, D. Brinkley and C. Hackett (eds) (1991)
Jean Monnet: The First Statesman of Interdependence, F. Duchesun (1994)

Montgomery bus boycott (1955–6)

The first major incident in the CIVIL RIGHTS MOVEMENT which resulted in the desegregation of buses in the United States. Southern blacks were greatly heartened by the BROWN V TOPEKA (1954) judgement in the Supreme Court, which declared segregation in public schools unconstitutional. They began to fight discrimination with greater determination and self-confidence, with a series of demonstrations, the most famous of which was in Montgomery, Alabama in December 1955. A black woman, Rosa Lee Parks, had refused to give up her seat to a white man in a 'whites only' section of a bus and was fined. 50,000 blacks boycotted the city buses in protest and were led by a young Baptist minister, Dr Martin Luther KING, who had been deeply impressed by Gandhi's non-violent campaign of civil disobedience against the British in India. The boycott received nationwide publicity. Blacks walked to work or arranged car and taxi pools. The non-violence of King was a sharp contrast to the attitude of the segregationists, who blew up four black churches and bombed the homes of several black ministers, including that of King. In spite of the arrest of the leaders and widespread intimidation the boycott was maintained until November 1956, when the Supreme Court affirmed a District Court ruling that segregation of bus passengers was unconstitutional. The boycott officially ended with a negotiated settlement between the city and the protest leaders in December.

The Montgomery Bus Boycott, J. Robinson (1987)

Moro, Aldo (1916–78)

Prime Minister of Italy (1963–8, 1974–6). From a middle class family, he studied law at Bari University, where he became a professor. A member of the Constituent Assembly in 1946, he was elected to the Chamber of Deputies two years later as a CHRISTIAN DEMOCRATIC PARTY (DC) candidate. He began his political career under DE GASPERI and in 1954 received his first cabinet post as Minister of Justice. Moro held further cabinet posts and became Secretary of the DC before forming his first administration in 1963.

A devout Catholic, courteous and reserved, he was a great mediator and manipulator, necessary qualities when all governments were coalitions. Fanfani had proposed an 'opening to the Left' in 1957 to include socialists in the government, but Moro was incapable of making swift decisions and it was not until 1962 that he came out in favour of a centre–left coalition, an attractive proposition as it would divide the socialists from the PCI (Italian Communist Party). He therefore included socialists in his government, but as there was a recession he said that reform was not possible until the economy improved. Even when the economy did recover strongly during his third ministry (1966–8) there was still no reform and no institution of regional government, as this would give more power to communists in the Red Belt of central Italy. His record in office was therefore not very impressive. After electoral gains by the PCI in the early 1970s he urged the DC to join in the historic compromise, an agreement with the PCI by which it agreed not to vote against DC measures and in return expected to have an informal influence on government policy.

When ANDREOTTI became Prime Minister in 1976 Moro remained a powerful figure behind the scenes and wanted to bring the PCI (the major opposition party) into the government, as he had done with the socialists in 1963. This possibility ended when Moro was kidnapped on 16 March 1978 by the RED BRIGADES. He was held in a secret hiding place for 54 days where, according to his captors, he behaved with dignity and courage. The socialists, led by CRAXI, favoured an exchange of prisoners but the PCI opposed this, as it would encourage further terrorism. When the government refused to bargain, Moro was murdered on 9 May.

Mozambican civil war (1975–92) A war between Renamo (Mozambique National Resistance Movement) and the Marxist Frelimo (Liberation Front of Mozambique) government of Mozambique but it was also, and essentially, an undeclared war of Rhodesia (until independence as Zimbabwe in 1980) and South Africa against Frelimo. Without foreign aid Renamo could not have survived. When Mozambique became independent in 1975, as a result of the PORTUGUESE REVO-LUTION of 1974, its leader, Samora Machel, expected an attack from Rhodesia and South Africa, as he helped liberation movements which sought to overthrow the Smith regime in Rhodesia and supported the ANC (African National Congress) in South Africa. Renamo had been set up by the Rhodesian intelligence service to destabilize the Mozambican government. It received arms and training from Rhodesia (and later South Africa). Its 20,000 guerrillas operated throughout Mozambique, disrupting agriculture and industry, destroying schools, health clinics, railways, oil pipelines and power stations. Renamo kidnapped foreign workers, tortured and murdered villagers, terrorizing large areas. By 1990 three and a half million people (a quarter of the population) faced starvation.

In 1990 a new constitution ended the one-party state in Mozambique and allowed a free-market economy but Renamo refused to recognize it and constantly delayed peace talks. A peace agreement was eventually signed in 1992, aided by the end of the APARTHEID regime in South Africa, which had been the main source of funds for Renamo. Free elections were held in 1994 in which Frelimo gained 44.3 per cent of the vote and had a small majority of seats (129 out of 250), Renamo winning 37.8 per cent of the vote and 112 seats. The effect of the civil war in Mozambique was devastating. An estimated one million people, nearly all civilians, were killed and half the population made dependent on food aid. The UN estimated in 1993 that 1.7 million Mozambican refugees were in neighbouring countries. The Population Crisis Committee in Washington concluded that Mozambique was 'the unhappiest nation on earth'.

Confrontation and Liberation in Southern Africa, I. Msabaha and T. Shaw (eds) (1987)
Destructive Engagement: Southern Africa at War, P. Johnson and D. Martin (1988)
Renamo: Terrorism in Mozambique, A. Vines (1991)

Mubarak, Muhammad Hosni (1928–)
President of Egypt (1981–). Trained in the Soviet Union, where he learnt Russian, as an air force pilot, SADAT made him Commander of the Egyptian Airforce, which he skilfully led during the YOM KIPPUR WAR (1973). Vice-President of Egypt from 1975, he controlled one of the most important state institutions, the security network. When Sadat was assassinated the quiet, retiring Mubarak became President, a marked contrast to his flamboyant predecessor. Tough on terrorism he had five of Sadat's assassins executed but he realized he would have to deal with Egypt's economic problems if the regime was to be stable. There were formidable obstacles to economic growth, particularly the rise of population, which increased from 40–50 million between 1980–90, necessitated food subsidies and huge food imports and contributed to a mounting foreign debt which reached $50 billion (servicing it gobbled up half of the country's foreign earnings). Mubarak did improve the infrastructure – sewerage, water, urban transport – but the public sector which produced three-quarters of industrial output was overstaffed and inefficient. The US and the WORLD BANK encouraged Mubarak to privatize the public sector but this would mean widespread unemployment and even more support for the Islamists. As oil prices collapsed in the late 1980s Egypt's economy deteriorated. Mubarak continued Sadat's foreign policy, maintaining the CAMP DAVID ACCORDS and the peace treaty with Israel, which had isolated Egypt in the

Arab world. He worked quickly to restore Egypt's leading role in the Middle East and Africa and in the IRAN–IRAQ WAR (1980–8) moved closer to Saudi Arabia and Jordan in supporting Iraq. In 1989 Egypt was readmitted to the ARAB LEAGUE. The GULF WAR (1991), which followed Saddam HUSSEIN's seizure of Kuwait, divided the Arab world again, as Egypt supported Saudi Arabia and the US and contributed 35,000 troops to the international force. Mubarak mediated between Israel and the PLO in 1993 and played an important part in bringing about an agreement, which was signed in Cairo, on self-rule in the Gaza Strip and Jericho.

The most formidable opposition to Mubarak came from the MUSLIM BROTHERHOOD and ISLAMIC FUNDAMENTALISTS. The Brotherhood was not allowed to be a political party but dominated professional organizations and supplied services for the poor – clinics, legal aid, subsidized housing and food distribution – which the government either did not provide or provided inadequately. Islamist organizations controlled the student unions and demanded Islamic law and the separation of the sexes. Islamists resorted to violence in 1992, killing 70 people, including foreign tourists. The government response was equally fierce: 29 Islamists were tried and executed in 1993 and many more were killed by security forces. Mubarak maintained a democratic façade but elections were rigged (nearly all opposition parties boycotted the 1990 election) so that the ruling National Democratic Party always had an overwhelming majority. In 1995 only one Brother was elected.

Egypt from Nasser to Mubarak: A Flawed Revolution, A. McDermott (1988)
Egypt Under Mubarak, C. Tripp and R. Owen (eds) (1989)
Mubarak's Egypt, R. Springborg (1989)

Mugabe, Robert Gabriel (1924–) Zimbabwe's first Prime Minister (1980–7) and President (1987–). The son of a labourer, he was educated at mission schools and at Fort Hare University College in South Africa. He was a teacher in Zambia and Ghana before returning home to take an active part in nationalist movements. Deputy Secretary-General of the Zimbabwe African People's Union (ZAPU) in 1962, he broke with Joshua Nkomo and joined the Zimbabwe African National Union (ZANU) as Secretary-General in 1963. In the ten years he was detained in Rhodesia (1964–74) he took correspondence courses to obtain four more degrees. After his release he escaped to Mozambique to take part in the guerrilla war against UDI (Unilateral Declaration of Independence) and Ian Smith's white minority regime. President of ZANU and commander of its military wing from 1976, his guerrilla attacks played a major part in bringing about the downfall of the Smith regime. To wage the war more effectively he formed a loose alliance with ZAPU in the Patriotic Front (1976) and attended talks in London which resulted in the Lancaster House agreement and independence for Zimbabwe. ZANU won a large majority in the pre-independence elections and Mugabe became Zimbabwe's first Prime Minister.

White settlers feared him, as he was a Marxist, had been an uncompromising guerrilla leader who had accepted the Lancaster House agreement reluctantly and had condemned whites as exploiters. He surprised them by calling for reconciliation and unity, promised not to confiscate white land and put General Peter Walls, in charge of Smith's security forces, in command of the new army, which soon included many former guerrillas. Nkomo and some of his supporters, and two whites, were included in his cabinet. He faced formidable problems. During the guerrilla war 27,500 had been killed and 750,000 displaced and there were popular expectations that the lot of the black majority would immediately improve. Racial discrimination ended, there was a rapid growth of education and health services and the Africanization of some posts as whites emigrated (between 1980–2 the white population fell by a half to 100,000), yet peasants were disappointed as the best land was still held by whites, who continued to control manufacturing industry.

External threats were another problem for Mugabe. Zimbabwe was dependent on South Africa for transport to the coast and for trade and so Mugabe, a fierce critic of APARTHEID at COMMONWEALTH conferences and supporter of international sanctions against South Africa, could not apply sanctions against it or provide bases for the ANC (African National Congress), as South Africa threatened to destabilize Zimbabwe if it did. Renamo, a rebel movement against the Marxist Mozambican government and supported by South Africa, could cut Zimbabwe's rail link with Beira. Mugabe therefore provided 10,000 troops for the Mozambican government to fight Renamo and became involved in the MOZAMBICAN CIVIL WAR. An internal threat to Mugabe was the old rivalry of Nkomo's ZAPU, with its ethnic base among the Ndebele (16 per cent of the population), with ZANU, with its Shona (71 per cent of the population) support. Nkomo was dismissed from the government in 1982. In 1987 Mugabe became President when the post of Prime Minister was incorporated in the presidency, and withdrew the 20 seats in parliament reserved for whites. He became reconciled with Nkomo when ZAPU and ZANU were united. Nkomo soon joined the cabinet and became a Vice-President.

The collapse of communism in the Soviet Union and Eastern Europe in 1990 led Mugabe to abandon plans for a one-party state. He won a resounding victory in the 1990 election and felt secure enough to end the state of emergency after 25 years. Zimbabwe had escaped the civil wars and military coups of many African states, a notable achievement for Mugabe. The economy remained a problem as inefficient state planning retarded growth and the indigenization of the economy meant the transfer of resources from whites to blacks. Populist measures such as the compulsory purchase of white-owned land in 1992 increased the government debt and did little for African farmers. Some expropriated land was given to Mugabe's political cronies. The rest was left idle and not redistributed, so that Zimbabwe became a net importer of food. A lending rate of 22 per cent and inflation of 27 per cent in 1996 deterred investment. The enormous debt of $7.6 billion (interest payments on it took 30 per cent of the budget) forced Mugabe to accept a WORLD BANK structural adjustment programme, which involved PRIVATIZATION, deregulation and devaluation. The attempt to cut the budget deficit meant that the infrastructure – roads, universities – was run down and the social services were on the point of collapse. Ian Smith had left no state debt: in 1996 Zimbabwe's debts were 130 per cent of GNP. Average wages were those of 1965, unemployment (7 per cent in 1986) was estimated at 40 per cent. Zimbabwe had become one of the world's poorest countries, with 30 per cent of the population – about ten million people-reckoned to be HIV-positive.

Zimbabwe: The Political Economy of Transition, 1980–6, I. Mendaza (ed.) (1986)

Muhammad Riza Pahlavi (1919–80)

Shah of Iran (1941–79). Educated in Switzerland and at Tehran Military Academy, he succeeded to the throne when his father Riza Shah was forced to abdicate in 1941 by Britain and the Soviet Union, who occupied Iran from 1941–6. Only 22 and inexperienced, he could not control the *Majlis* (parliament), which chose the government. After the end of the Second World War a Kurdish republic of Mahabad was proclaimed in Western Iran, with Soviet support, and there was an uprising in Azerbaijan, but both were put down after Soviet troops had left. A real threat to the Shah's authority came from his Prime Ministery Muhammad Musaddiq, who nationalised the Anglo-Iranian Oil Company. The Shah had to flee from Iran in 1953 before a coup organized by the CIA brought his return. From 1953–60 he became an absolute ruler, expanding and controlling the army and Savak, a security service which operated outside the law, torturing suspects and carrying out executions and assassinations. He exercised strict control over the press, trade unions and the judiciary, appointed ministers and intervened in all matters of government, by-passing ministers and dealing directly with generals and ambassadors. As the *Majlis* was dominated by conservative landowners who opposed reform, he ruled without it from 1961–3. In 1975 he replaced the party system by a single Resurgence Party, whose main function was to act as cheer-leader for the regime.

The Shah wanted to modernize Iran and so began what he called the 'White Revolution', paid for by burgeoning oil revenues, which rose from $1 billion dollars in 1970 to over $20 billion after the OPEC PRICE RISE of 1973, the year in which he nationalized the Western oil consortium. Literacy doubled between 1960–79 from 20 per cent to 40 per cent of the population, health care improved and infant mortality halved. The main feature of the 'White Revolution' was land reform, by which the Shah hoped to gain the loyalty of the peasants and reduce the power of the landlords. A 1961 law limited holdings to one village but peasants were not given enough land for subsistence (labourers received nothing) and to create large agro-businesses the Shah razed many villages and relocated the population. Land reform was not a success: food production declined and much food had to be imported. The Shah also tried to woo the workers, by profit-sharing schemes, and women, by giving them the vote and improving their rights in divorce. His efforts to make Iran a major industrial power led from 1973 to an enormous expansion with which the economy, with its shortage of skilled labour and inadequate infrastructure, could not cope. As imports poured in prices rose, so the government deflated the economy, bringing the boom to an end and causing widespread unemployment.

The Shah was dependent on the US for supplying his armed forces, so he joined the BAGHDAD PACT (1955) and had close relations with Israel, an unpopular move in the Muslim world. Aiming at regional hegemony, he took advantage of Saddam HUSSEIN's preoccupation with the Kurdish problem to make the Algiers Agreement (1975), which adjusted the border with Iraq to Iran's advantage. The Shah's megalomania was most apparent in the celebrations in 1971 for the 2,500th anniversary of the Persian monarchy, which he held at the ancient capital of Persepolis with great pomp and monumental extravagance, spending $200 million.

Opposition to the regime was put down with great brutality. After the arrest in 1963 of Ruhollah KHOMEINI, one of his most persistent and acerbic critics, there were large and violent anti-government demonstrations in Qum and other cities. The Shah took personal control, declared martial law and ordered his troops to 'shoot to kill'. They took two days to crush the rising, in which some religious leaders called for a *jihad* (holy war) against the Shah's un-Islamic government: at least 15,000 people were killed. Khomeini was sent into exile. There were no further major disturbances until 1977, when protests began which culminated in the IRANIAN REVOLUTION, which brought about the fall of the Shah and the establishment of the ISLAMIC REPUBLIC OF IRAN. The Shah fled, received medical treatment for cancer in the US and was then granted asylum by President SADAT in Egypt, where he died.

Iran: The Illusion of Power, R. Graham (1978)
Iran: Dictatorship and Development, F. Halliday (1980)
Iran Between Two Revolutions, E. Abrahamian (1982)

Mulroney, Brian (1939–) Prime Minister of Canada (1984–93). Of Irish ancestry, he was a bilingual native of Quebec, where his father was an electrician. He took a law degree at Laval University, Quebec and by 1977 was president of the American-owned Iron Ore Company of Canada. Elected leader of the Progressive Conservative Party in 1983, he followed THATCHER and REAGAN in calling for reductions in inflation, the state deficit and the size of the civil service and talked of the PRIVATIZATION of many state-owned corporations and of freeing the private sector from state regulation. Yet he described the social services as 'a sacred trust'. In 1984 he gained a remarkable victory in the general election, when the Conservatives won 211 seats, the Liberals 40 and the New Democratic Party 30.

During his first two years in power there were moderate reductions in inflation, interest rates, the federal deficit and unemployment but Mulroney was indecisive, often abandoning policies which generated serious opposition. In spite of campaigning for privatization, Air Canada and most state-owned corporations remained in the public sector. To consolidate Conservative support in Quebec, he gave to that province a disproportionate share of federal spending, at the expense of smaller provinces such as Newfoundland, where the unemployment rate was twice that of Quebec. In dealing with QUEBEC NATIONALISM he sought to win ratification of the 1982 constitution from Quebec, the only one of Canada's ten provinces which had refused to sign it. The Meech Lake Accord of 1987 recognized Quebec as a 'distinct society' but two provinces failed to ratify it by the 1990 deadline, because it gave a special constitutional status to Quebec. Mulroney tried again with the Charlottetown Accord of 1992, which satisfied the Quebec government but was rejected in a national referendum.

Mulroney constantly called for better relations with the US and for an open door to foreign investment. He proposed the abolition of trade barriers between the two countries in the US–CANADA FREE TRADE AGREEMENT, which was signed in 1989 after he had won an acrimonious general election on this issue a year earlier. This marked the first stage of a regional free trade bloc, which was extended to Mexico in the NORTH AMERICAN FREE TRADE AGREEMENT (NAFTA) in 1993. Mulroney became very unpopular when he introduced a value-added tax on goods and services in 1991. With mounting crime and corruption and scandals about the misappropriation of funds, he resigned in June 1993 shortly before an election in which the Progressive Conservatives were almost wiped out, their number of seats falling from 153 to two.

Mulroney: The Politics of Ambition,
  J. Sawatsky (1991)

multinational corporations (MNCs)

Organizations that are based in one country but invest and produce much of their output abroad. International companies are not new. The British East India Company was formed in 1600 and came to maintain its own armed forces and govern India, as the British South Africa Company did in Southern Rhodesia (Zimbabwe) from the 1890s to 1923. In the first half of the twentieth century Lever Brothers (now Unilever) produced goods in countries from West Africa to India, the oil companies had global interests and Ford manufactured cars in both the US and Europe.

Multinationals today are different in quantity and in the extent of their networks. They benefited from freer trade after the Second World War and from President NIXON bringing the US off the gold standard in 1971. The subsequent relaxation of exchange controls provided more liquidity and increased the flow of international capital investments, as companies were freed from the control of central banks. As multinationals competed with each other for a share of world markets, they moved investment from one country to another, helped by the INFORMATION and FINANCIAL REVOLUTIONS that had created a GLOBAL ECONOMY. Competition drove corporations to produce in regions where labour was cheap, taxes were low and there were few regulations. As labour became expensive in Japan, Japanese companies exported components to Southeast Asia, where they were assembled by cheap, female labour. MNCs often avoided trade barriers by setting up factories inside a protected area. Japanese car manufacturers invested in Britain in order to gain access to the large and lucrative market of the EEC and built factories in Mexico so they could enter the American and Canadian markets through the NORTH AMERICAN FREE TRADE AGREEMENT. Many MNCs allied with one another. The Japanese NEC helped AT&T to supply and market memory chips; Dutch Philips helped it to do the same for telecommunications and switching equipment. By 1990 Ford owned 25 per cent of Mazda and both held shares in South Korea's Kia Motors. General Motors owned half of Daewoo, the South Korean car manufacturer, and half of Sweden's Saab. Over half of US exports and imports in 1990 were transfers of goods and services within MNCs. Foreign-owned corporations also appeared in the US, where foreign investment rose from 2 per cent of the total in 1977 to 9 per cent in 1988. By 1990 they employed three million people, 8 per cent of US manufacturing workers. Over a quarter of American exports came from these companies.

MNCs did a great deal to encourage the growth of the NEWLY INDUSTRIALIZING ECONOMIES (NIEs). Japanese microwave ovens and colour televisions in 1990 were produced in Malaysia, Thailand and China. Many Mitsubishi cars, sold in the US under the Chrysler trademark, were assembled in Thailand. Seagull Technology, a California-based producer of hard disk drives, had 40,000 employees in 1990, 27,000 of them in Southeast Asia. Two hundred American MNCs employed 100,000 people in Singapore, where the largest employer was General Electric, to make electronic components for export to the US. AT&T, RCA and Texas Instruments were among the largest exporters in Taiwan. Their investments brought a higher standard of living to the countries concerned, especially when compared with the Middle East and Africa, where MNCs invested little. The downside of all this, from the point of view of American workers,

was that the relocation of American production abroad caused millions of workers to lose their jobs at home. Where other jobs were available, they were invariably in the service sector. MNCs, responsible only to their shareholders and not to national governments, were accused of exporting jobs, which reduced the bargaining power of trade unions at home and reduced domestic investment, leading to stagnation.

Strategic Partnerships: States, Firms and International Competition, L. Mytelka (ed.) (1991)
The Work of Nations, R. Reich (1991)

Museveni, Yoweri Kaguta (1944–)
President of Uganda (1986–). He studied politics and economics at Dar es Salaam University, Tanzania, where he developed his radical ideas and served briefly in Milton Obote's government before Idi AMIN seized power. In exile from 1971 he fought for Frelimo in Mozambique's struggle for independence (see PORTUGAL'S COLONIAL WARS) before building up a disciplined and effective guerrilla force in Uganda. A leading member of the Uganda National Liberation Front which overthrew Amin in 1979, he served for a short time as Minister of Defence but fell out with Obote and formed the National Resistance Army. After falling out with the other military leaders who deposed Obote in July 1985 he fought on until he entered Kampala in January 1986 and was sworn in as President.

In power he worked for national reconciliation and brought different ethnic and political groups into his National Resistance Council, but it took two years to persuade Obote's supporters to agree to a cease-fire. Since 1987 the civil war has continued in the north against the fanatical rebels of the Holy Spirit Movement, aided by the Islamist government in the Sudan and MOBUTU in Zaire. They controlled much of the north until 1997, when rebel victories in Zaire and the SUDANESE CIVIL WAR deprived them of bases and aid. Economic recovery was hindered by the civil war, by border disputes with Kenya (which interrupted the flow of imports and exports) and by the fall in the price of coffee (90 per cent of Uganda's exports) in the 1980s.

Museveni showed courage and vision to win the trust of his people and ordered the publication of a survey of Aids in 1990, which showed that one million Ugandans (6 per cent of the population) were affected. A constituent assembly, elected in 1994, decided not to introduce multiparty democracy until the year 2000 and met with the wrath of the US, which threatened to withdraw aid. Museveni argued that multiparty politics exacerbated ethnic (there are 40 ethnic groups in Uganda) and religious divisions, which had been responsible for over 20 years of bloodshed in Uganda and that Africa must be free to develop its own democratic system, based on consensus not confrontation. His popularity was confirmed in the 1996 presidential election when he received 76 per cent of the vote.

Conflict Resolution in Uganda, K. Rupesinghe (1989)

Uganda Since Independence: A story of unfulfilled Hopes, P. Mutibwa (1992)

Muslim Brotherhood Islamist party which began in Egypt and spread throughout the Arab world. Founded in 1928 by Hassan al-Banna, a schoolteacher, it wanted the *Sharia* (Islamic law) to be applied and repudiated both capitalism and Marxism. Western law, customs and education should be rejected as they were a threat to Islamic values. Mainly an urban party, strongest in Cairo and Alexandria, it had possibly half a million members (and as many supporters) at the height of its popularity in 1949. Banned from 1948–50, the Brotherhood attacked the corruption, massive unemployment and poverty which existed under King Faruq and seemed as though it would seize power, but was forestalled by the Free Officers in 1952. At first it supported NASSER but turned against him when he did not establish an Islamic government and was suppressed in 1954. In 1965 the Brotherhood

was blamed for an attempt on Nasser's life: several Brothers were executed. When SADAT became President the Brotherhood was permitted to function openly, though it was not allowed to become a political party, so Brothers stood in elections as independents or in conjunction with other parties. The Brotherhood had become a dynamic force in Egypt by the 1980s. The largest and wealthiest Islamist organization under MUBARAK, it ran an extensive network of banks, insurance companies, schools, medical and legal services. It dominated many professional associations (of lawyers, teachers, engineers) and universities and founded private mosques (40,000 out of 46,000 mosques were private in 1980 and therefore outside the control of the state).

In Syria the Muslim Brotherhood was formed in the 1930s and became a considerable political force after the BIRTH OF ISRAEL, in spite of being banned in 1963. Representing the SUNNI majority against the domination of the state by the Alawi minority (see ASAD), the *jihad* (holy war) it began against Asad in 1976 lasted four years. When several hundred Brothers were executed the protest collapsed.

Hassan al-Banna set up branches of the Brotherhood from 1945–5 in Jordan and Palestine, which thrived, particularly after the SIX DAY WAR (1967), which many Muslims saw as God punishing the Arabs for moving away from their faith. The Brothers were a powerful political force in Jordan. They were the largest single party after the 1989 Parliamentary elections. In the GULF WAR the Brotherhood supported Saddam HUSSEIN. In Palestine some Brotherhood members took part in the INTIFADA when it began in 1987 and founded HAMAS to attack Israeli targets. The Brotherhood was funded by the Saudi royal family and had close contact with Islamist movements in Pakistan and Iran.

The Society of Muslim Brothers, R. Mitchell (1969)

The Islamic Threat: Myth or Reality?, J. L. Esposito (1992)

N

NAACP (National Association for the Advancement of Colored People) US civil rights organization. Founded in 1909, when all its officers except W. E. B. Du Bois were white, it worked through the courts to bring about a gradual and orderly end to segregation and racial discrimination. It was non-violent and wanted the social integration of blacks and whites. Its greatest victory was in BROWN V BOARD OF EDUCATION OF TOPEKA (1954), a judgement which ended segregation in public schools. By the 1950s the NAACP leadership was mainly black: it had 445,000 members in 1963 and was, with the Southern Christian Leadership Conference of Martin Luther KING, the most important organization in the CIVIL RIGHTS MOVEMENT. More militant groups attacked it, the BLACK MUSLIMS for favouring racial integration and the BLACK POWER movement for its non-violence, but it continued to grow and in 1994 had 650,000 members.

Nagorno-Karabagh conflict (1988–) A dispute between the Christian Armenians and the SHII Azeris over the status of Nagorno-Karabagh, which is part of Azerbaijan though with a mainly (76 per cent) Armenian population. Open conflict began in 1990 when Armenians in Baku, the Azeri capital – there were 420,000 Armenians in Azerbaijan outside Nagorno-Karabagh – were attacked: 90 were killed and 1,500 injured (official figures). Hundreds of thousands of Armenians fled from Azerbaijan and many of the 200,000 Azeris in Armenia also took flight. After the AUGUST COUP of 1991 both Armenia and Azerbaijan became independent states as part of the CIS but their struggle continued. By the time the Russians arranged a cease-fire in May 1994 the Armenians had driven out the Azeris from Nagorno-Karabagh and occupied a buffer zone of surrounding Azeri territory, as well as a corridor across Azerbaijan from Armenia to Nagorno-Karabagh. No permanent settlement was in sight.

Wars in the Caucasus, 1990–5, E. O'Ballance (1997)

Nasser, (Nasir) Jamal Abd al- (1918–70) Prime Minister (1954–6) and President (1956–70) of Egypt. Born in Alexandria, the son of a postal clerk, he entered the Military Academy in Cairo (opened to the lower classes since the 1936 Anglo-Egyptian Treaty) in 1937. There he made friends with Anwar SADAT and other future leaders of the Free Officers. They were dismayed by the failure of the leading nationalist party, the Wafd, to end the British military occupation of Egypt. Nasser blamed the inept performance of the Egyptian army in the ARAB–ISRAELI WAR (1948–9), in which he served, on the king and corrupt politicians, and played a leading part in the coup which overthrew the monarchy and set up a republic. General Najib's removal from his key posts in the government in 1954 left Nasser, as Prime Minister and Chairman of the Revolutionary Command Council (RCC), in complete control.

Two immediate problems were the future of the Sudan, jointly ruled by Britain and Egypt, and the British military bases in the Suez Canal zone. Both were soon settled. An

Anglo-Egyptian agreement granted Sudan autonomy in 1953 and independence three years later. Nasser hoped that the Sudan would then choose union with Egypt but it opted for complete independence in 1956. Britain agreed in 1954 to remove all its troops by March 1956 but sought alternative security arrangements in the BAGHDAD PACT, which Nasser strenuously opposed. He appeared as a new leader of the NON-ALIGNED MOVEMENT in April 1955, when he attended the Bandung Conference, and in September of that year Egypt bought arms, which the West had refused to supply, from communist Czechoslovakia. This infuriated the US and Britain, who blocked a WORLD BANK loan to build the Aswan Dam, a key to Nasser's economic strategy. He therefore nationalized the Suez Canal Company, beginning the SUEZ CRISIS, in which Britain, France and Israel attacked Egypt. They were forced to abandon their assault by pressure from the UNITED NATIONS and US, so Nasser emerged as the leader of Arab nationalism and as a popular hero throughout the Middle East. For the next ten years Nasser dominated the Arab world as the main opponent of Israel, and supporter of PAN-ARABISM. The United Arab Republic (1958–61), in which Syria and Egypt united, was a step towards this goal. Nasser was an opponent of traditional regimes (Saudi Arabia and the GULF STATES) and took part from 1962–7 in the Yemen Civil War on the side of the republicans, an indecisive and very expensive intervention in which a third of the Egyptian army was involved. Committed to liberation movements in the Middle East and Africa, he gave money and arms to the FLN in the ALGERIAN WAR OF INDEPENDENCE (1954–62).

The 1956 constitution consolidated Nasser's power by setting up a system in which the President had extensive executive and legislative powers: he appointed ministers and decided policy. Nasser was elected President and the RCC was dissolved. Islam was recognized as the religion of state but in practice religious institutions were brought under state control. *Sharia* (Islamic law) courts were closed in 1956, *waqf* (religious endowments) nationalized in 1957 and al-Azhar University, the oldest seat of Islamic learning, was brought under state supervision. His failure to establish an Islamic state roused the opposition of the MUSLIM BROTHERHOOD, several of whose leaders were executed after an attempt to assassinate Nasser in 1965. He created a new mass party in 1962, the Arab Socialist Union, the only political organization allowed in Egypt. In running the economy private enterprise was at first encouraged but there was a lack of private capital, so the role of the state increased. In 1957 all banks and insurance companies were nationalized: between 1959–61 the state took control of industry, of most imports and exports, imposed high, progressive taxation and confiscated the property of many wealthy Egyptians. Land reform, begun by the Free Officers in 1952, continued. The key to the first Five Year Plan (1960–5) was the Aswan Dam, begun in 1960 with Soviet aid. Completed in 1968 it increased the arable area by 25 per cent and provided hydro-electric power for industry. Rapid industrialization saw industry's share of GNP rise from 15 per cent to 23 per cent (1952–67) but the population was rising at an unsustainable rate (from 20 million in 1952 to 30 million in 1966).

The SIX DAY WAR (1967) against Israel was a turning-point for Nasser, who bore a heavy share of responsibility for the disaster. He accepted full responsibility for Egypt's defeat and said he would resign, until millions of Egyptians poured onto the streets to dissuade him. Nasser's Arab policy changed. He accepted UN Security Council Resolution 242, which called for the peaceful coexistence of the Arab states and Israel, in return for Israel's evacuation of the OCCUPIED TERRITORIES, and withdrew from the Yemen. As the economy declined his regime and its policies were discredited. On 28 September 1970 he died of a heart attack. His successor, Sadat, abandoned many of his policies, yet his achievements were remarkable. He had asserted Arab independence from Western domination at Suez, made Egypt the leader of the Arab world, called for Arab unity and tried to create a better and fairer society for most Egyptians.

Egypt from Nasser to Mubarak: A Flawed Revolution, A. McDermott (1988)
Egypt's Uncertain Revolution Under Nasser and Sadat, R. W. Baker (1988)
Nasser, P. Woodward (1992)

nationalism   As an ideal type it is the feeling of loyalty towards a nation united by race, culture, language, history and sometimes religion. It has been the most powerful force in modern history and for some has provided an alternative faith to that of a religion. Nationalism can have a cohesive function, meeting the need to belong to a stable community in which one can take pride, and rose with compulsory mass education, which enables national traditions to be communicated to and absorbed by the population as a whole, and with the mass media (newspapers, radio, television), which bring people together and can be used as channels of propaganda. It can also be divisive and negative, leading to xenophobia and such excesses as ETHNIC CLEANSING.

The Second World War had a profound effect in arousing nationalism in Africa and Asia by providing conditions for the successful transfer of power to nationalists. The defeat of the Allied powers in the early stages of the Pacific War (1941–5) was a great stimulant to Asian nationalism, as the colonial powers were humiliated, lost their aura of superiority and were removed from the scene. After the war the INDEPENDENCE AND PARTITION OF INDIA rapidly took place and became a model for other nationalist movements in Asia. Nationalist movements arose at the same time in Africa as a reaction to Western imperialism. Western trained élites such as NKRUMAH, KENYATTA and BALEWA learnt how to form mass parties, like the Convention People's Party in Ghana

and NYERERE's Tanganyika African National Union. DECOLONIZATION produced a vast number of independent states which used nationalist rhetoric to protect themselves against neocolonialism and external economic domination by creating high tariffs around local industries.

As many African states were comparatively recent creations of the colonial powers they could not appeal to a common culture, language or civilization to hold them together. After independence, therefore, nationalism sometimes took the form of break-away movements, as in the CONGO CRISIS (1960s), when Moishe Tshombe attempted to create an independent Katanga, and in the BIAFRAN WAR (1967–72), which sought to divide Nigeria. Ethnic nationalism was a feature of the BANGLADESH and ERITREAN WARS OF INDEPENDENCE, of the effort of the TAMIL TIGERS to gain independence from Sri Lanka and of Sikh attempts to set up a separate state in Punjab.

In Europe nationalism was discredited post-1945 owing to the excesses of Hitler. The COMMUNIST TAKE-OVER OF EASTERN EUROPE meant that most of the new states formed after the First World War were under Moscow-controlled regimes, which had little independence and where nationalism was discouraged, although it did appear in the HUNGARIAN RISING (1956) and the PRAGUE SPRING (1968). Western countries looked to the multinational NATO for security and for economic prosperity to the supranational EEC (European Economic Community), in which participating nations gave up some of their sovereignty. Hence, at the same time as nationalism was arising in Africa and Asia, its importance was apparently declining in Western Europe. The GLOBAL ECONOMY also undermined the national state, which could control only a diminishing part of its own economy. MULTINATIONAL CORPORATIONS, international currency markets and the INFORMATION REVOLUTION of the satellite era took over roles previously pursued by national organizations. Some national states resisted the reduction of their powers. Margaret THATCHER played on national fears of a loss of sovereignty in trying to prevent the extension of the powers of the European Commission and of the European Parliament and called on the immense reserves of jingoism in fighting the FALKLANDS WAR. The Norwegians, determined to reject any loss of national identity, rejected membership of the European Union in a referendum. Even in the countries most in favour of European integration nationalism persisted, as the French and Germans protected their farmers through the COMMON AGRICULTURAL POLICY and imposed quotas restricting competition from Japan and the NIES (Newly Industrializing Economies). A xenophobic form of nationalism appeared with the economic recession which followed the OPEC PRICE RISE of 1973. It was led in France by Le Pen's National Front and directed at Algerian immigrants and in Germany resulted in attacks on GASTARBEITER.

The nationalism which arose in Europe in the second half of the twentieth century was, like that in parts of Asia and Africa, within states. ETA demanded a separate Basque state, the SCOTTISH NATIONAL PARTY wanted independence for Scotland and there were nationalist movements too among Flemings in Belgium, Bretons and Corsicans in France and Catalans in Spain. The most remarkable example of this phenomenon was the sudden eruption of the NORTHERN LEAGUE in Italy in the 1980s, where Umberto Bossi aimed to create a state of Padania, to include the rich North separated from the poor South. The nationalist appeal there was in an area which had never been a separate state. The COLLAPSE OF THE SOVIET UNION and the REVOLUTIONS OF 1989–91 revived nationalism in Eastern Europe, as states broke away from Soviet hegemony and became truly independent again and as the Soviet Union divided into the CIS (Commonwealth of Independent States), adding many more members to the UNITED NATIONS. There were nationalist clashes in the Caucasus, between Armenians and Azeris in the NAGORNO-KARABAGH CONFLICT and between Chechens and Russians in the CHECHNYA CONFLICT. Communist disintegration led not only to the formation of new states out of the empire created by the tsars but to further divisions within states. In the DIVISION OF CZECHOSLOVAKIA Slovaks, resenting Czech dominance in Czechoslovakia, broke away to form a separate state. Slovenia and Croatia, seeking to end Serb domination of Yugoslavia, declared their independence and prompted Serbia to begin the YUGOSLAV CIVIL WAR (1991–5). Serb nationalism, appealing to a common ethnicity, tried to create a greater Serbia by absorbing the Serb areas of Bosnia (areas which were made more homogeneous by ethnic cleansing and atrocities such as that at ŠREBRENICA), while resisting the nationalist claims of Albanians in Kosovo to be a separate state or to join Albania. Until the Second World War the national state had continuously extended its functions. At the end of the century it was on the defensive, with a world economy it could not control and with institutions (the UN, European Union, IMF, WORLD BANK) which had been created to remedy its own weakness.

Nationalism, P. Alter (1984)
Nations and Nationalism, E. Hobsbawm (1990)
Modern Nationalism, J. Hutchinson (1995)

NATO (North Atlantic Treaty Organization) Founded in 1949 to defend Western Europe against a possible communist attack. In March 1948 Britain, France, Belgium, the Netherlands and Luxembourg signed the Brussels Treaty to protect themselves against the Soviet Union and, if necessary, a resurgent Germany, but it was clear that the US was necessary for their security. The US, however, had never made a peacetime military alliance with European states. Two events in the COLD WAR in 1948 persuaded President TRUMAN that a change in

US foreign policy was needed: the CZECH COUP and the BERLIN BLOCKADE. In addition to the Brussels signatories, Canada, Denmark, Iceland, Italy, Norway, Portugal and the US signed the treaty establishing NATO in April 1949. The treaty promised mutual assistance if there was an attack on any member. Its strategic role was defensive. Greece and Turkey joined in 1952, the Federal Republic of Germany in 1955 and Spain in 1982.

NATO was the high-point of Truman's containment policy and established US military dominance in Western Europe. As the Soviet Union had a superiority of ten to one in ground forces in Europe, NATO depended on nuclear weapons for its defence and the US had no intention of sharing its control of them with its European partners. When the reduction in US military spending ended with the KOREAN WAR, NATO adopted an integrated military command under General EISENHOWER in December 1950 (all subsequent NATO commanders have been American).

There were problems within NATO. France withdrew from the integrated military command structure in 1966 because DE GAULLE resented the American domination of NATO, but it remained a member of the alliance. Greece and Turkey came into conflict over ENOSIS. In 1974 NATO managed to prevent them going to war over the issue. After the collapse of the WARSAW PACT and the REVOLUTIONS OF 1989–91, which saw the collapse of communism in Eastern Europe, several former communist states wanted to join NATO, a move strenuously opposed by Russia. Critics of the expansion of NATO say that it is no longer necessary, as there is no danger of a Russian invasion of Europe, especially after the CHECHNYA CONFLICT, and that any expansion will strengthen the non-democratic opposition to President YELTSIN in Russia. Since the end of the Cold War NATO has formed an Allied Rapid Reaction Force to take on a peace-keeping and humanitarian role in the former Yugoslavia. In February 1994 NATO forces fired their first shots in anger when enforcing the no-fly zone over Serbia imposed by the UNITED NATIONS.

NATO and the US, L. Kaplan (1988)
The Defence Policies of Nations, D. J. Murray and P. R. Viotti (eds) (1989)
The Dawn of Peace in Europe, M. Mandelbaum (1997)

Ne Win (1911–)   Burmese general and ruler of the country from 1962 to 1988. A member of the nationalist movement from his student days at the University of Rangoon (where he failed to obtain a degree), he became a close associate of Aung San, the father of Burmese independence. Born Maung Shu Maung to a Sino-Burmese family, he adopted the name Ne Win (Son of Glory) when doing military training in Japan in 1940. He returned with the Japanese army which invaded Burma in 1941. He was from 1943 Chief of Staff of the Burma National Army, which collaborated with the Japanese until 1945, when it defected to the Allies. After independence in 1948 he soon became Commander-in-Chief of the Burmese army, served briefly in U Nu's cabinet in 1950 and, at U Nu's request, was Prime Minister from 1958–60 in order to deal with communist and secessionist risings of minority peoples who wanted independence. In 1962 he seized power in a military coup, as he thought U Nu was prepared to grant autonomy to the minorities and that this would destroy the unity of Burma. The Revolutionary Council of military leaders authorized him to exercise all legislative, executive and judicial powers. Henceforth, all national and local elections were a farce, as the only party allowed was Ne Win's Burma Socialist Programme Party (BSPP), which was dominated by the military.

'The Burmese Way of Socialism' was his party's policy. All economic activity, including retail trade, was nationalized. Some 300,000 Indians and Chinese were expelled and their property confiscated. Banks, insurance companies and British businesses were nationalized but the Burmese had few management and financial skills, so shortages quickly arose, even of rice (in a country which had been a large exporter). Import-export trade and foreign investment ended. By 1970 the government was bankrupt but there was an agricultural revival in the 1970s owing to the GREEN REVOLUTION, in which new high-yield strains doubled rice production (1976–82). The rest of the economy, including oil production, was not so successful because of poor management. From 1975 Ne Win sought to finance development by foreign loans from the West, Japan and the WORLD BANK, with the result that Burma's foreign debt rose from $300 million in 1975 to $1.8 billion in 1982.

From 1963–75 Burma cut itself off from the rest of the world. Diplomats (about the only foreigners left in Burma) had to get permission to move outside the capital and Burmese citizens were not allowed to talk to foreigners. Ne Win refused to join regional associations such as ASEAN. His main problems were at home, particularly with the ethnic minorities as he would not grant them autonomy. In the 1960s the government fought Karens, Shans, Kachins and other ethnic groups, which formed a coalition, the National Democratic Front, in 1975. Since 1983 the government fought the NDF in every dry season and under Ne Win was unable to overcome it.

In 1988 the most turbulent event since independence took place in the capital. High inflation and a currency reform which wiped out the savings of the middle class led the people to take to the streets. In August security forces killed up to 10,000 protesters and, with the situation getting out of hand, Ne Win fled from Burma, leaving the country in chaos. He returned to become a prominent member of SLORC.

Burma: Military Rule and the Politics of Stagnation, J. Silverstein (1977)
The State in Burma, R. H. Taylor (1988)

Outrage: Burma's Struggle for Democracy, B. Lintner (1989)

Nehru, Jawaharlal (1889–1964)   Prime Minister of India (1947–64). Often called 'Pandit' (Hindi, 'knowledgeable'), Nehru came from a rich Brahmin family and was educated in England at Harrow and Cambridge University: he returned to India in 1914. Nehru greatly admired Gandhi. Support for Gandhi's non-cooperation movement (1920–2) led to his first spell in jail (he spent nine years there between 1920 and 1945). In 1928 he demanded complete independence for India and a year later persuaded the INDIAN NATIONAL CONGRESS to adopt this as its aim. Handsome, intellectually brilliant and charming, he became, with Gandhi's backing, the youngest President of Congress in 1929, a post he had the rare distinction of holding three times. In the 1936–7 provincial elections, held under the India Act (1935), Nehru was largely responsible for Congress gaining control of six (and eventually eight) of the eleven states of British India, but he made a great blunder in rejecting Jinnah's offer of coalition governments with the Muslim League. This turned Jinnah towards partition, to which Nehru was opposed. He withdrew from Indian provincial ministries in 1939, after the Viceroy declared war without consulting Indian opinion, and after the 'Quit India' Campaign was arrested with other Congress leaders. On his release Nehru became Congress's chief negotiator with the British and developed a close rapport with the Viceroy Mountbatten and his wife, which prepared the way for a smooth transfer of power. He reluctantly agreed to the partition of India in August 1947, as Jinnah would accept nothing else and because 'we were tired men'. Nehru then became the first Prime Minister of an independent India, a post he held until his death.

Two problems threatened the unity of the new state: the attitude of the princes and the question of language. There were 560 princely states in India, covering two-thirds of the subcontinent. In theory they could opt for independence or for union with India or Pakistan, but Nehru made it clear that he did not want any independent states in India. Sardar Patel persuaded all but three of India's princely states to join the new dominion in 1947. The Nawab of Junagadh and the Nizam of Hyderabad were Muslims with mainly Hindu subjects. When Junagadh acceded to Pakistan in August 1947 Indian troops invaded and seized the territory, as they did in Hyderabad in September 1948. The situation in Kashmir, the largest state on the Indian subcontinent, was more difficult, as the Maharajah was a Hindu with mainly Muslim subjects. There was fighting in the first of the INDO-PAKIS-TANI WARS until a *de facto* partition took place on a line held by the two sides. The Congress Party was committed to making Hindi the national language but this was spoken only in the north. Many in the south, especially in Tamil Nadu, wanted to continue using English as an official language, so Nehru, conciliatory, postponed the phasing out of English, as did his successors.

Nehru had favoured central economic planning since the 1930s and followed the Soviet model of emphasizing public sector domination of heavy industry. He restricted foreign investment to prevent MULTINA-TIONAL CORPORATIONS controlling the Indian economy and promoted import-substitution industries. In spite of an unprecedented rise of population (361 million in 1951, 439 million in 1961) per capita income rose by 30 per cent between 1951 and 1968 but economic growth was one of the lowest in Asia.

Nehru wanted social as well as political and economic change. He had often condemned India's 'caste and priest-ridden society' and in the Untouchability Act of 1955 penalized discrimination against the Harijans, though it was difficult to enforce the law as popular attitudes did not change. Women too were beneficiaries of Nehru's legislation. They were given the vote and the right to divorce. Caste barriers to marriage were removed and

female children had the same rights as males to inherit property. This legal revolution gave women equality before the law.

Nehru was his own Foreign Minister and made India a leader of the NON-ALIGNED MOVEMENT. This meant that India did not join alliances (such as the BAGHDAD PACT) sponsored by one of the superpowers and did not benefit from US aid. India remained within the COMMONWEALTH, though Nehru was a sharp critic of Britain during the SUEZ CRISIS and was the only non-aligned country to vote with the Soviet Union in the UNITED NATIONS when the USSR crushed the HUNGARIAN RISING in 1956. Sino-Indian friendship, shown at the Bandung meeting of non-aligned nations in 1955, was a key feature of his policy until 1959, when China invaded Tibet and the Dalai Lama fled to India. Thereafter relations deteriorated until India was ignominiously defeated in the SINO-INDIAN CONFLICT in 1962. A year earlier, after fruitless negotiations with the Portuguese, India annexed Goa. Nehru continued in office until he died in 1964.

Jawaharlal Nehru, S. Gopal (1990)
Jawaharlal Nehru, D. Judd (1993)
Jawaharlal Nehru, B. R. Nanda (1995)

Netanyahu, Binyamin ('Bibi') (1948–)

Prime Minister of Israel (1996–). Born in Tel Aviv, he was profoundly influenced by his father Benzion, a historian and fervent nationalist. Benzion was a follower of Ze'ev Jabotinsky, who wanted a Jewish state which covered the whole of the biblical lands of Israel, including both sides of the River Jordan, was opposed to the partition of Palestine and believed that reconciliation with the Arabs was bound to fail. Bibi served in the reconnaissance unit of the Israel Defence Forces from 1967–72 before going to the US, where he took a degree in business administration at the Massachusetts Institute of Technology in 1976. He then held management posts in the US and Israel, becoming deputy ambassador in Washington in 1982 and then Israel's ambassador to the UNITED NATIONS (1984–8). Elected to the Knesset (parliament) as a Likud member in 1983, he was Deputy Foreign Minister (1988–91) and served in Prime Minister Yitzhak SHAMIR's office from 1991–2.

When Likud lost the 1992 election and Shamir resigned as party leader a year later, Netanyahu succeeded him. He was fiercely opposed to the Oslo Accords (1993), to the creation of an independent Palestinian state, to withdrawal from the GOLAN HEIGHTS (captured from Syria in 1967) and to the evacuation of Jewish settlements in the WEST BANK. In the first direct election for Prime Minister Netanyahu narrowly defeated Peres with 50.4 per cent of the vote. Although he rarely entered a synagogue, he owed his victory to Orthodox Jews, 90 per cent of whom voted for him.

To gain a majority in the Knesset (the Labour Party had 34 seats, Likud 32 in the 120-seat parliament) he needed the support of Orthodox parties, who demanded uncompromising policies and a reversal of the PEACE PROCESS. Netanyahu therefore authorized the extension of Jewish settlements on the West Bank and postponed the withdrawal of Israeli troops from Hebron, the only Palestinian city on the West Bank that remained under Israeli control. The peace process ground to a halt and was suspended when HAMAS bombers continued their murderous activities. Netanyahu faced two irreconcilable pressures: Orthodox Jews insisted there should be no concessions to the Palestinians, while his American backers wanted to reactivate the peace process.

newly industrializing economies (NIEs)

A term applied in the late 1970s to a small group of Asian countries – South Korea, Taiwan, Singapore and Hong Kong – which were rapidly developing economically and exporting manufactured goods on a large scale. Like Japan they lacked natural resources and so concentrated on export-led growth in order to pay for essential imports of raw materials, fuel and food. They followed the path of the JAPANESE ECONOMIC MIRACLE in initially using their cheap labour in labour-intensive industries, such as textiles, in the 1960s. They attracted foreign capital in the 1970s to move to the more capital-intensive production of radios, televisions, motor cycles and ships. By the 1980s they changed again, this time into high-technology and began to compete with Japan in the production of computers. Their growth rate of per capita income averaged over 6 per cent a year from 1965–89. In the 1980s and 1990s Singapore and Hong Kong shifted to predominantly service sector industries, moving their manufacturing 'offshore', in Hong Kong's case to China.

The state played a leading role in the military dictatorships of JIANG JIESHI in Taiwan and of PARK CHUNG HEE in South Korea, providing tax incentives and subsidies for businesses and protection from foreign competition. The two countries differed in that there were many small companies in Taiwan, whereas in South Korea four huge conglomerates (Samsung, Hyundai, Daewoo and Lucky Goldstar) dominated the economy. LEE KUAN YEW in Singapore also directed economic growth. Hong Kong was the only one of the four to pursue a *laissez-faire* policy from the beginning, with minimal government spending (except on infrastructure), low taxes and the private ownership of businesses. In all cases production was geared to the GLOBAL ECONOMY. By the mid-1980s the West could no longer sell manufactured goods to Asia and faced stiff competition from the 'Asian tigers' (as well as Japan) in other markets. The relocation of manufacturing to East Asia, led by many MULTINATIONAL CORPORATIONS, was the biggest single cause of unemployment among young men between 16 and 25 in Europe and the US.

From the 1980s other countries became NIEs: Indonesia under SUHARTO, Thailand and Malaysia under MAHATHIR MOHAMAD, which became the world's largest producer of air-conditioners and a leading exporter of telephones and televisions. China, with its SPECIAL ECONOMIC ZONES, also began to industrialize rapidly in the 1980s. Several NIEs suffered a setback in 1997, when there was speculation against their currencies. The Bank of Thailand had to allow the baht to float freely in July. It plunged steeply and shares also fell. Speculators were blamed but did not create the country's problems: a current account deficit of 8 per cent of GDP, an INTERNATIONAL DEBT of $90 billion, a stock market which had fallen by two-thirds since 1974 and a banking system plagued by bad debts owing to unwise property investment. Speculation spread to other currencies, including the Malayan ringgit. The average annual growth rates of 1980–96 (7 per cent in Malaysia, 7.4 per cent in Taiwan, 7.8 per cent in Thailand) could not be maintained. The Indonesian economy imploded at the end of 1997 when its currency, the rupiah, went into free fall and many businesses went bankrupt. Even South Korea, which had been one of the most successful NIEs, was affected by bad debts and needed an international bail-out of $60 billion. It was forced to accept an IMF rescue package, which opened up its banking sector to foreign competition, raised the ceiling on foreign ownership of companies and compelled the government to abandon subsidies to favoured *chaebols* (conglomerates). The South Korean stock market fell by 42 per cent in 1997 and its currency, the won, lost nearly half its value against the dollar. Most *chaebols* were bankrupt or greatly in debt and had to sell off some of their holdings.

Asia's 'Miracle' Economies, J. Woronoff (1991)
Democracy and Development in East Asia, T. W. Robinson (1991)
The Economies of East Asian Newly Industrializing Countries, D. Chowdhury and I. Islam (1994)

Nigerian military rulers Since independence in 1960 in Nigeria, Africa's most populous country with an estimated population of 105 million in 1990, military governments have ruled for 27 years up to 1997. The military seized power for the first time in January 1966 to end a corrupt and inept government led by Sir Abubakar Tafawa BALEWA. He and the Prime Ministers of the Northern Region, Sir Ahmadu Bello, and of the Western Region, Chief Akintola, were assassinated. Most participants in the coup were Igbo officers from the Eastern Region: nearly all their victims were non-Igbos, which gave rise to fears in the north of Igbo domination of Nigeria. Surviving ministers handed over the government to Major-General Ironsi, the army commander, who had not been involved in the plot but was also an Igbo. His actions (the promotion of Igbo officers and delay in punishing those responsible for the coup) were seen in the north as complicity in the murders. In July there was a revenge coup by northern soldiers in which Ironsi and many Igbo officers were killed. General Gowon, a Christian northerner, became the new head of the military government but this was not acceptable to Lt.-Colonel Ojukwu and most Igbo, who declared the independence of the Eastern Region and so began the BIAFRAN WAR (1967–70).

After the defeat of the rebels Gowon sought reconciliation with the Igbos but was unable to run the country efficiently, as there was extensive corruption and inflation. In July 1975 he was overthrown in a bloodless coup by General Muhammed, a dynamic leader who began a ruthless and popular purge of the corrupt and inept public service. Over 10,000 civil servants were dismissed, as were many in the police and army. Muhammed announced a return to civilian rule in 1979 and became a popular hero. Nigerians were stunned by his assassination in an abortive coup in February 1976, but his deputy, Lt.-General Obasanjo, took over and continued Muhammed's policies.

Shehu Shagari won the presidential election of 1979 but all the worst features of civilian rule of the period 1960–6 reappeared and he was overthrown in 1983 in a coup, led by Major-General Buhari, which was welcomed by most Nigerians. He attacked corruption but became increasingly authoritarian, arbitrarily imprisoning opponents, and was replaced by General Babangida, who seized power in 1985. World oil prices were depressed when he took over (oil exports provided 90 per cent of Nigeria's foreign currency), so he carried out unpopular economic policies, reducing the pay of the civil service and army. He promised to hand over power to a civilian government but when elections, the fairest ever in Nigeria, were eventually held in 1993 he ordered the count to be stopped when only half the results had been declared and 'annulled' the poll. He did this because Chief Abiola, a Yoruba from the south-west, who had broken the mould of Nigerian politics by gaining support in the north, was winning. Oil workers went on strike for two months and returned to work only when the military dissolved the executive body of the whole trade union movement. General ABACHA seized power and became President in November 1993, saying his hold on power would be brief. His military dictatorship remained in control at the time of his death in 1998.

The Nigerian Military and the State, J. Peters (1997)

Nimeiri, Jaffar Muhammad (1930–)
President of Sudan (1971–85). With the economy in a desperate state and the SUDANESE CIVIL WAR at a stalemate, Colonel Nimeiri and other junior officers carried out a Military coup in 1969. Nimeiri became Chairman of the Revolutionary Command Council and Prime Minister, dissolving political parties in an attempt to end factional political strife. Committed to 'Sudanese Socialism' he nationalized foreign and domestic industries. Nimeiri's greatest achievement was to end, temporarily, the civil war which had been going on, with devastating effects on the economy, for 17 years. In 1972 he agreed to grant the south some autonomy and so there was a precarious peace until Nimeiri, under pressure from Saudi Arabia and ISLAMIC FUNDAMENTALISTS, applied the *Sharia* (Islamic law) to the whole of the Sudan, including the Christian and animist south, in 1983, thus bringing about a renewal of the civil war.

The US saw him as a most reliable ally (he reversed his policy of nationalization in 1973) in countering the threat of the Marxist Dergue in Ethiopia and of QADDAFI to US interests in the Red Sea and Horn of Africa, and provided Sudan with more US aid than any country in Africa, except Egypt, from 1980–5. Yet the economy continued to decline owing to the civil war and the huge influx of refugees from Uganda (see AMIN) and Ethiopia. Challenged by Islamic organizations he tried to gain the support of the 70 per cent of the population which was Muslim by appointing members of the MUSLIM BROTHERHOOD to posts in the cabinet. With the application of the *Sharia* traditional Islamic punishments returned – public flogging for drinking alcohol, amputation for theft and death for apostasy. He became more oppressive as unrest and strikes grew. In response to pressure from Saudi-Arabia and the US, Nimeiri dismissed all members of the Muslim Brotherhood from his government and arrested 200 of its leaders, a move that caused great anger at foreign interference in Sudanese political life and lost Nimeiri most of his remaining supporters. Nimeiri flew to Washington in 1985 to seek more US aid. In his absence his Minister of Defence led a coup which deposed him, an event which brought a million people onto the streets of Khartoum to celebrate. He was given asylum in Egypt by President MUBARAK.

Class and Power in Sudan: The Dynamics of Sudanese Politics, 1898–1985, T. Niblock (1987)
Sudan, 1898–1989: The Unstable State, R. Woodward (1990)

Nixon, Richard Milhous (1913–94)
President of the United States (1968–74). Born of

Quaker Ulster-Irish parents in a cottage without running water or electricity, he worked hard in the family store before studying law at Duke University and graduating in 1937. A naval supply officer during the Second World War, he was elected as a Republican to the House of Representatives in 1946, serving on the House Committee on un-American Activities to investigate the subversion of communists. Elected to the Senate in 1950, he became EISENHOWER's running mate in 1952 and served him faithfully as Vice-President for eight years. In 1960 Nixon lost the presidential campaign by the narrowest of margins to John F. KENNEDY and when he was defeated in the election for Governor of California in 1962 his political career seemed over. Yet after Barry Goldwater was massively defeated in the 1964 presidential election Nixon staged a come-back. As the Republican candidate in 1968 he narrowly defeated Hubert Humphrey to become President, with the smallest percentage of the national vote (43.6 per cent) since Wilson in 1912, but he failed to win a majority in either house of Congress.

Nixon had promised to end US participation in the VIETNAM WAR and this took up much of his time. In 1969 he announced the Nixon Doctrine: the US would provide security for Japan and other Asian nations by its nuclear deterrent but it would not use US troops to fight a ground war to defend other countries. The President began to pull American troops out of Vietnam and followed a policy of Vietnamization, building up South Vietnamese forces so they could fight the North on their own. To prevent North Vietnamese forces moving south along the Ho Chi Minh Trail, which went through Cambodia and Laos, Nixon escalated the war in 1970 by the US ATTACK ON CAMBODIA. This was a disastrous mistake as it failed to achieve its objective, revived the VIETNAM ANTI-WAR MOVEMENT in the US, decimated Cambodia and enabled the Khmer Rouge to take power there. By September 1972 only 40,000 US troops remained in Vietnam but air attacks

on the North increased until the Paris Peace Accords in January 1973, a deal Nixon could have had in 1969. Hailed as 'peace with honor' it was an American defeat, as all US forces were to be withdrawn from Vietnam without a corresponding withdrawal of North Vietnamese troops from the South. In just over two years the North Vietnamese overran the South and so united Vietnam as a communist country.

Both Nixon and his National Security adviser Henry KISSINGER wanted to end the policy of confrontation with the major communist powers and so pursued a policy of DÉTENTE. Nixon and BREZHNEV reached an agreement on Cuba in 1970, whereby the Soviet Union agreed not to arm Fidel CASTRO with offensive missiles and Nixon promised not to invade Cuba. Like much of his diplomacy this was a secret agreement: hardly anyone in the administration knew about it. In 1971 Kissinger went on a secret mission to China to meet ZHOU ENLAI and arranged for the President to visit Beijing in February 1972 and exchange diplomatic representatives. The US withdrew its opposition to the People's Republic of China taking up China's seat at the UNITED NATIONS, which had previously been occupied by JIANG JIESHI's (Chiang Kai-shek's) nationalist government in Taiwan. Nixon's visit to China was followed by one to Moscow, where an agreement was reached on the sale of American wheat to the Soviet Union and on the restriction of anti-ballistic systems at the SALT I talks. Rivalry with the Soviet Union in the THIRD WORLD continued in spite of détente, so Nixon became involved in the ANGOLAN CIVIL WAR by supporting the FNLA and UNITA against the Russian-backed MPLA. The US was surprised by the YOM KIPPUR WAR and had to act promptly with a massive air lift of arms to prevent an Israeli defeat. Nixon pursued the traditional US anti-communist policy in Latin America by trying to prevent Salvador ALLENDE gaining the presidency in Chile in 1970. When he failed, he allowed the CIA to destabilize the regime and exulted at Allende's overthrow by a military coup in 1973.

It seemed unlikely that there would be much domestic legislation when he became President, as he had condemned the GREAT SOCIETY and was more interested in foreign than domestic policy. Yet there was some important legislation passed between 1969 and 1975. The Democratic Congress was largely responsible for this but Nixon went along with much of it because it was popular and he was the most liberal Republican President in the twentieth century, except for Teddy Roosevelt. He even called in 1971 for comprehensive national health insurance for all, something no other President except TRUMAN had demanded. This did not pass, but Social Security benefits were increased and widened and he introduced revenue-sharing, whereby states and local districts were given a part of federal revenues to finance their own budgets. Clean air and water programmes improved the quality of both in the US. On racial issues he appealed to white Southern voters by trying to postpone desegregation of schools and busing but sought the support of blacks with AFFIRMA-TIVE ACTION programmes. Federal spending on social issues increased from $27 billion in 1969 to $64 billion in 1975.

Nixon's foreign policy affected domestic affairs. As money was printed to pay for the Vietnam War inflation increased sharply, making US goods too expensive abroad, so in 1971 the US had a trade deficit. The President responded by abandoning a fixed exchange rate for the dollar, allowing it to float and be devalued, and so destabilized the international monetary system set up at Bretton Woods in 1944. He won the 1972 presidential election with 60.8 per cent of the popular vote, more than any other presidential candidate received, except JOHNSON though the DEMOCRATIC PARTY retained its hold on the House of Representatives.

In 1972 the WATERGATE scandal began. As it developed over the next two years it became clear that the President had misused his authority to denigrate his political opponents. The affair ended with the threat of impeachment and Nixon's resignation on 9 April 1974. A month later President FORD granted him a pardon for any offences he had committed, thus preventing any prosecution for his involvement in Watergate. After his resignation Nixon had an attack of phlebitis in 1974, from which he nearly died. He then painstakingly tried, with some success, to rebuild his reputation by writing his memoirs and books on foreign policy.

Nixon: The Triumph of a Politician, 1962–72, S. Ambrose (1989)
Richard Nixon and His America, H. Parmet (1990)
Nixon Reconsidered, John Hoff (1994)

Nkrumah, Kwame (1909–72)

Prime Minister of the Gold Coast (1952–7), President of Ghana (1957–66). The son of a goldsmith, he was educated at a Roman Catholic mission school and Achimota College and was a teacher from 1930–5, when he went to the US, where he lived for ten years, studying and then teaching at Lincoln University. In 1945 he left the US for Britain, where he took part in the fifth Pan-African Congress in Manchester and worked with Jomo KENYATTA. In 1947 the founders of the United Gold Coast Convention (UGCC) invited Nkrumah to return home and be the General Secretary, but already the gap was widening between their élitist ideas and Nkrumah's vision of a populist and socialist party. In 1949 Nkrumah founded the Convention People's Party (CPP) in opposition to the UGCC. His 'Positive Action' campaign of strikes and boycotts to force the colonial government to grant independence for the Gold Coast landed him in jail for sedition. In the elections of 1951 the CPP won a majority of seats. He was released by the Governor and asked to form a government. After the CPP won further elections in 1954 and 1956 independence was granted on 6 March 1957, and the Gold Coast and British

Togoland (a UNITED NATIONS Trust Territory) became the new state of Ghana. This was a turning point in African history, as the example of Ghana, the first sub-Saharan African state to be granted independence, was rapidly followed by others.

Nkrumah regarded Ghanaian independence as the first step towards the liberation of Africa from colonialism and the unity of African people. A leading exponent pf Pan-Africanism, he entered a shortlived union of Ghana, Guinea and Mali (1958–60), and in 1958 held at Accra the first All-African Peoples' Conference, with representatives from 28 territories, many still under colonial rule. He also played a leading role in creating the OAU (Organization of African Unity) and was a fierce critic of neo colonialism and a supporter of the NON-ALIGNED MOVEMENT. Nkrumah was at first popular in Ghana and admired all over the world, but his image became tarnished as he developed a personality cult, taking the title Osagyefo ('he who is successful in war'), and established a dictatorial and corrupt regime. The Preventive Detention Act (1958) enabled him to detain anyone for up to five years without trial; the 1960 constitution, which made Ghana a republic within the COMMONWEALTH, gave Nkrumah great powers as President and in 1964 Ghana became a one-party state. Nkrumah sought to develop and diversify the economy by central government planning on socialist lines. Roads and railways were built and the Akasombo Dam, which created Lake Volta, to provide hydro-electricity. The plan was to create an industrial base for Ghana's economic growth but this was unsuccessful. The healthy Treasury surplus which Nkrumah inherited was soon dissipated, foreign loans created indebtedness and as the price of cocoa, Ghana's main export, fell by 75 per cent (1955–65) the economy collapsed. A military and police coup while Nkrumah was visiting China ended his rule in 1966. He spent the rest of his life in exile in Guinea and died in Romania where he was receiving medical treatment.

Kwame Nkrumah: The Political Kingdom in the Third World, D. Rooney (1988)
The Economy of Ghana: The First 25 Years Since Independence, M. M. Hug (1988)

nomenklatura (list of names)   The ruling group in the USSR and its East European satellites. CPSU committees kept files on all individuals suitable for public office. As a party recommendation was necessary for appointment to all important posts, the *nomenklatura* ran all institutions in the country. In 1970 in the USSR there were 250,000 *nomenklatura* in government, 300,000 in industry and agriculture and 150,000 in the universities, making a total of 700,000 (800,000 by 1982). With their wives and children they formed a ruling class of three million (1.2 per cent of the population). Members enjoyed great power, status and material privileges, which were carefully graded. Those at the top had a country *dacha*. All had access to better hospitals, special shops where foreign goods were available and schools where their children were well-educated, so they too could join the *nomenklatura*. As they wanted to retain their privileges they opposed changing the communist system. GORBACHEV found them an obstacle to reform. With the COLLAPSE OF THE SOVIET UNION many members of the *nomenklatura* used their privileged position as industrial managers to seize state assets and take part in *nomenklatura* PRIVATIZATION.

Privilege in the Soviet Union, M. Matthews (1978)
Nomenklatura, M. V. Vozlensky (1985)

Non-Aligned Movement (NAM)   A group of states, most of which were former colonies, which wanted to avoid becoming allied to either of the superpowers, the US and Soviet Union, and desired to keep out of the COLD WAR. NEHRU visited Cairo in February 1955 and agreed with NASSER to oppose all military alliances, such as the

BAGHDAD PACT and SEATO. In April 1955 29 African and Asian states met at Bandung in Indonesia and formed the NAM. Since then over a hundred states have joined: meetings have been held in various countries, decisions being reached by consensus. The desire of its members to avoid alliances with the superpowers did not mean that they could not accept aid from the US and USSR but that this aid should not affect their right to pursue their own social and economic policies. TITO was much admired for defying STALIN and accepting US aid without rejecting communism. Nasser accepted Soviet aid while persecuting communists in Egypt. NAM was committed to world peace and disarmament and particularly in its early years, promoted DECOLONIZATION and supported liberation movements. It called for self-determination in Southern Africa until Namibia was granted independence and demanded the end of APARTHEID. Hostility to Israel resulted from its demands for Palestinian self-determination and its consequent support for the PLO. NAM advocated the resolution of conflicts through the UNITED NATIONS and initiated UN Disarmament Conferences. It was especially concerned with the NORTH–SOUTH DIVIDE and wanted to change the GLOBAL ECONOMY by calling for a New International Economic Order, in which the THIRD WORLD would not be exploited by affluent capitalist countries.

The Non-Aligned Movement: The Origins of a Third World Alliance, P. Willetts (1978)
Non-alignment in an Age of Alignment, A. W. Singham and S. Hune (1986)

North American Free Trade Agreement (NAFTA) (1993)

signed by the US, Mexico and Canada. It was an extension of the US–CANADA FREE TRADE AGREEMENT, signed in 1989. Tariffs and other obstacles to the exchange of goods, services and investments were to be phased out over the next 15 years, thereby creating the world's largest free-trade zone and preparing the way for an integrated market in the Western hemisphere similar to that of the European Union in Europe.

Northern Leagues

Political movements formed in Italy in the late 1970s and early 1980s. Leagues were formed, the first in Veneto in 1979, to demand regional autonomy. They spread rapidly in the North with support from small businesses and the self-employed, who wanted lower taxes, controls on immigration, a war on crime and objected to the corrupt state run by parties based in Rome and a civil service largely staffed by Southerners. The Leagues did not want Northern profits subsidizing the inefficient South and condemned schemes such as the Fund for the South which, they said, were hijacked by the MAFIA. They wanted PRIVATIZATION of state assets and looked to Europe North of the Alps rather than Southern Italy as their hinterland.

In 1984 the Lombard League was formed with Umberto Bossi as its charismatic but erratic leader. In 1990 it won 16.4 per cent of the vote in the Lombardy regional elections. A year later Bossi persuaded various Leagues to join together with a common programme in the Northern League. The League wanted Italy to become a federation of three autonomous republics: North, Centre and South. The League won control of much local government in the North and, under a changed electoral system introduced in 1993, won 12 seats in the Chamber of Deputies in the 1994 general election. It made a pact with Silvio BERLUSCONI and formed part of his government but this soon unravelled, as the League was violently hostile to the neo-Fascist National Alliance, another of Berlusconi's partners. By 1995, with unemployment in the South 35 per cent and in the North under 6 per cent, Bossi talked of a new independent state of Padania. It seemed a formidable threat to the unity of Italy but there were considerable obstacles to such an outcome. Padania is not ethnically or linguistically different from the rest of Italy and the League has no hope of gaining a majority in parliament.

Modern Italy, 1871–1995, M. Clark (1996)

North–South divide   Refers to the division between the affluent capitalist countries of the US, the European Union and Japan and the poor, underdeveloped countries of Africa, Latin America and South Asia, which are often referred to as the THIRD WORLD. The contrast is most pronounced in Africa, which suffered from a lack of trained élites, widespread warfare, a POPULATION EXPLOSION and often a dependence on the export of one primary product.

According to a WORLD BANK survey in 1989 per capita income in sub-Saharan Africa increased by 2.7 per cent a year in the 1960s, dropped to zero in the 1970s and fell 1.2 per cent a year in the first half of the 1980s. A contributory factor to this decline was the OPEC PRICE RISE of 1973, which badly affected all African economies except those with oil (Algeria, Libya, Nigeria, Gabon, Cameroon). Landlocked, resource-poor and drought-ridden states such as Ethiopia, Sudan, Chad and Niger were in chaos. As there was a world recession the prices of African primary products fell to their lowest levels for 30 years. Unable to buy essential imports of food and oil African countries borrowed from banks and the IMF. Africa's INTERNATIONAL DEBT rose from $14 billion in 1973 to $150 billion in 1984, while the ratio of debt to GNP doubled to 40 per cent. There was extensive famine and disease and as the IMF insisted on cuts in spending and imports as a condition of new loans, there were negative growth rates in much of Africa: from −1.9 per cent in Ethiopia to −4.75 per cent in the Ivory Coast in 1994.

Latin America and the Caribbean, too, experienced rapidly rising populations and high infant mortality rates in some countries, but there were wide discrepancies in the quality of life. In Argentina the daily calorie intake was little less than in the US, whereas in Haiti 90 per cent were undernourished and suffered from parasitic diseases associated with poverty.

There has been little attempt to correct the imbalances in the North–South divide. The OAU (Organization of African Unity) called in 1973 for a New International Economic Order to produce a massive transfer of wealth from North to South: the cancellation of foreign debts, commodity price stability and the reduction of Northern protection against Southern exports. It sought the relocation of resources on the basis of need rather than of the free market and was enthusiastically supported by the NON-ALIGNED MOVEMENT and by the UNITED NATIONS General Assembly. Unfortunately there was a recession in the developed world, with rising inflation and unemployment, so the North reduced foreign aid and introduced more protective measures, so making the situation worse. Willy BRANDT, Chairman of a UN Commission on the GLOBAL ECONOMY, addressed the situation in his report *North–South: A Programme for Survival 1980*, which recommended more aid from the rich North to the poor South and in a further report in 1983 forecast 'conflict and catastrophe' unless this was done. The response of the IMF has been stabilization programmes, which in many cases have made countries poorer: GNP per head in Mozambique was $115 in 1991, $100 by 1997. Industrial production there had fallen each year since stabilization and in 1997 was half the 1990 level. The UN *Human Development Report* (1997) found that the gap between rich and poor nations was growing larger and that free markets did not apply everywhere, as the rich, industrialized countries continued to resist opening their markets to the agricultural produce and textiles of the developing world.

Structural Conflict: The Third World Against Global Liberalism, S. D. Krasner (1985)
How Can Africa Survive? J. S. Whitaker (1988)

Hunger and Public Action, A. Sen and J. Dreze (1989)

Nuclear Non-proliferation Treaty (1968)

A treaty signed by the US, the Soviet Union and Britain: it came into force in 1970. The two superpowers, the US and USSR, wanted to prevent other countries acquiring nuclear weapons. To prevent the further expansion of nuclear power, the signatories to the treaty pledged not to provide nuclear weapons, or the technology to make them, to other countries, while non-nuclear countries promised never to produce or acquire them. As with the NUCLEAR TEST BAN TREATY of 1963, the stockpiling of nuclear weapons and the development of delivery systems by nuclear powers were unaffected. A total of 97 countries had signed the treaty by the time it became operational in 1970 and 131 by 1985. China and France of the nuclear powers, India, Israel and Pakistan of the supposedly non-nuclear states, refused to sign it.

Nuclear Test Ban Treaty (1963)   Signed

by the US, the Soviet Union and Britain, it forbade nuclear tests in the earth's atmosphere, underwater or in outer space, but it did not exclude underground tests and did not limit the right to manufacture or stockpile nuclear weapons. In fact more tests were carried out in the next ten years than in the ten years before the treaty. It was therefore a small step towards arms control and DÉTENTE and was the first major agreement reached by the US and the USSR since the end of the Second World War. Ninety other countries signed the treaty between 1963–5, but not France or China.

Nyerere, Julius Kambarage (1922–)

President of Tanganyika (1962–4) and of Tanzania (1964–85). The son of a chief, he was educated at Makerere College in Uganda and Edinburgh University and taught in Tanganyika, where he become a founder member and first President of the Tanganika African National Union (TANU) in 1954. He led a vigorous but peaceful campaign for independence, TANU winning 70 out of 71 seats in the 1960 election, so Nyerere became Chief Minister, and Prime Minister when Tanganyika became independent in December 1961. He was elected President when Tanganyika became a republic later in the year. He met pressure from the trade unions for speedier Africanization by absorbing them all in an umbrella union, whose officials were appointed by the government and whose right to strike was limited. He sought to establish his authority by making his country a one-party state, which became a model of political stability in Africa. In 1964 he negotiated with Zanzibar to unite Zanzibar and Tanganika and create the state of Tanzania, becoming its first President.

Tanzania was one of the largest and poorest countries in Africa but it had a national language in Swahili (Nyerere translated some of Shakespeare's plays into Swahili) and no dominant ethnic group, so it was spared the military coups and civil wars which affected so many African states. Nyerere wanted to reduce the gap between rich and poor and set an example by living simply and paying himself a modest salary. Revered as *Mwalima* (teacher), Nyerere set out his ideals of *ujamaa*, or African socialism, in the Arusha Declaration (1967), which said that all the main banks and businesses should be in state hands and that Tanzania should not rely on foreigners but should develop by its own efforts. Nyerere, influenced by the collectivization of agriculture in communist states, wanted self-contained villages in which agriculture would be on a cooperative basis. Three million peasants were forced to move into hastily planned villages, which caused great resentment and a decline in agricultural production. Nyerere's socialist policies were not successful. State-run industries were corrupt and inefficient, while peasants were unwilling to share their resources. They were also badly hit by drought, the OPEC PRICE RISE in 1973 and the fall of world prices for their export crops, particularly coffee and cotton. The result was trade deficits, inflation, low growth and an appeal for help to the IMF, though this came in 1986 only when some socialist policies had been abandoned. Nyerere's social policies were much more successful. Almost universal primary education was established, infant mortality reduced and life expectancy increased.

As a THIRD WORLD leader, and supporter of the NON-ALIGNED MOVEMENT, Nyerere was deeply involved in DECOLONIZATION in Africa. Tanzania helped to train the Frelimo army and served as its base during the ten-year war for independence in Mozambique. Nyerere also provided training and support for the ANC in its struggle against APARTHEID in South Africa, and for the Patriotic Front, led by Nkomo and MUGABE, in its fight against the Smith regime in Rho-

desia. He opposed the brutal dictatorship of AMIN in Uganda. When Amin invaded Tanzania in 1978, Nyerere became the first African leader to defeat an African country in war. He was less successful in his Pan-Africanism. The East Africa Community, set up in 1967 to promote trade among its members (Kenya, Uganda. Tanzania), collapsed ten years later after bitter disputes between capitalist Kenya and socialist Tanzania. The Kenyan–Tanzanian border was closed for six years (1977–83). In 1985 Nyerere resigned as President, one of the few African leaders to retire voluntarily, to make way for his chosen successor, Mwinyi.

The Critical Phase in Tanzania, 1945–68: Nyerere and the Emergence of a Socialist Strategy, C. Pratt (1976)
Democracy and Dictatorship in Ghana and Tanzania, R. Pinkney (1997)

O

OAS (Organization of American States)

The main inter-American regional organization. It aimed to promote economic cooperation and development, regional security, the peaceful settlement of disputes, representative democracy and human rights. Members agreed not to interfere in the internal affairs of other states. Organized in 1948, its members consisted originally of the US and 22 Latin American countries. From 1962 former British colonies in the West Indies joined as they gained independence, though Belize and Guyana were not admitted until 1991, as they had border disputes with existing members Guatemala and Venezuela. Suriname, a former Dutch colony, joined in 1975 and Canada in 1990. Cuba was technically a member but sanctions imposed on it in 1964 were still in effect in the 1990s and effectively prevented it from participating. The OAS had 35 members in 1991.

From 1948 to the mid-1960s the US tried to make the OAS into an anti-communist alliance in the COLD WAR, whereas the Latin American Countries were more concerned with economic growth. The US linked security and economic development from 1959–65 in the ALLIANCE FOR PROGRESS and in 1965 persuaded the OAS to back US intervention in the Dominican Republic. Latin American countries became dissatisfied with US domination and its reluctance to commit significant resources to economic development and also with its intransigence over Cuba and the influence it exerted to topple ALLENDE's government in Chile in 1973. Human rights became a prime concern: an American Convention on Human Rights

was agreed in 1969 and an Inter-American Court of Human Rights was set up.

The importance of the OAS declined after 1979, as the US INTERVENTION IN GRENADA (1983) and intervention in Nicaragua against the SANDINISTA government ignored it. Latin American states worked outside the OAS and excluded the US in making their most important peace proposals, initiated by President Arias of Costa Rica. Five Central American heads of state met at Esquipulas in Guatemala in 1987 to plan political reconciliation and made it illegal for any state to assist any insurgent movement, such as the CONTRAS, in another state. In the post-Cold War era of the late 1980s the OAS revived and concentrated on economic development and social issues, as there were no political threats to the area. Problems of the DRUG TRADE, democracy and human rights were all discussed, though the US INTERVENTION IN PANAMA in 1989 showed that the US would take unilateral action when it saw fit.

Latin America, the United States and the Inter-American System, J. D. Martz and L. Schoultz (eds) (1980)
The Inter-American Dilemma, L. R. Scheman (1988)

OAU (Organization of African Unity)

Founded in 1963 when representatives of 32 newly independent African states met in Addis Ababa. Its main aim was to protect the independence and territorial integrity of member states. This meant that conflict between rival African nations should be avoided, as well as warfare between different ethnic groups within a nation (which had happened in the CONGO CRISIS), so that foreign powers would not be tempted to intervene for their own ends.

Neutrality in the COLD WAR was another aim of the OAU to avoid superpower rivalry extending to their countries. African states had taken part in the first international conference of the NON-ALIGNED MOVEMENT and the principle of non-alignment was included in the OAU charter. A primary aim of the OAU was to speed up DECOLONIZA-TION until all African states were independent and for this purpose a Liberation Committee was established, with its headquarters at Dar es Salaam in Tanzania. The Assembly of the OAU, consisting of heads of state, meets for a few days each year, the Council of Ministers twice a year, but there is no means of enforcing decisions. The resolution to sever diplomatic relations with Britain in December 1965, because of its failure to take action against Ian Smith's UDI in Rhodesia, was acted on by only ten states. The OAU is also financially weak, as most member states are poor, and it cannot compel members to pay their dues.

The OAU has had some successes, in settling a border dispute between Algeria and Morocco and in channeling military and financial aid to independence movements, such as those in the Portuguese colonies and in Rhodesia, which were themselves divided. The failures of the OAU far outweigh its successes. It has often postponed the discussion of controversial issues, so as not to split the organization. The result has been a refusal to condemn those violating human rights, such as Idi AMIN in Uganda and MENGISTU in Ethiopia. A prime purpose of the OAU was to prevent foreign powers interfering in Africa, yet African states have requested such intervention, as Ethiopia did in its clash with Somalia over Ogaden. Zaire sought French aid to crush the rising in Shaba (Katanga) in 1978. There was a general consensus in the OAU that contacts with the APARTHEID regime in South Africa should

be avoided, but this was ignored by BANDA in Malawi and HOUPHOUËT-BOIGNY in the Ivory Coast. The OAU was unable to prevent interstate wars, such as the one between Ethiopia and Somalia, or to end the civil war in the Sudan.

The OAU After Twenty Years, Y. El-Ayouty and W. Zertman (eds) (1984)

Occupied Territories Areas which had been part of the British mandate of Palestine and which were occupied by Israel as a result of the SIX DAY WAR (1997): the WEST BANK, including East Jerusalem (annexed by Jordan in 1950), and the Gaza Strip (administered by Egypt since 1949).

October Crisis (1970) Violence in Quebec which aimed to make Quebec an independent state. In the 1970 Quebec election the provincial Liberal Party under Robert Bourassa won a large majority of seats, despite a strong showing by its more nationalist rivals, the *Parti Québecois* (PQ) and the *Union nationale*. This result was rejected by extreme nationalists, such as those in the *Front de Libération du Québec* (*FLQ*). They turned from bombs, strikes, protest marches and bank robberies to kidnapping and were given tacit support by many students, workers and professional people in their campaign of terrorism. James Cross, a British trade commissioner in Montreal, was captured by the FLQ, who demanded the freeing of 'political prisoners' and half a million dollars in gold bullion. The Quebec government rejected these demands but promised safe conduct abroad for the kidnappers if Cross was released unharmed. Cross was not released by the FLQ, which kidnapped Pierre Laporte, Quebec's Minister of Labour, whereupon Bourassa asked the federal government to send in the army.

Pierre TRUDEAU, the federal Prime Minister, acted swiftly to pass the War Measures Act on 16 October, which gave unlimited powers to the federal government in a time of apprehended insurrection. The police were given wider powers to detain anyone for 21 days without charge, the FLQ was made illegal and any member could be sent to jail for five years. Protest at these measures ended on 17 October, when Laporte was murdered by the FLQ. Cross was discovered and released in early December, when his kidnappers were guaranteed a safe passage to Cuba. Later in the month those who had assassinated Laporte were captured. In the backlash at his murder the FLQ lost all support. Democratic means dominated the struggle for separation thereafter: the PQ was elected as the provincial government in 1976. The October Crisis was a major shock to all Canadians, many of whom had regarded their country as being immune to such terrorist activity.

The October Crisis, G. Pelletier

OECD (Organization for Economic Cooperation and Development)   Established to promote economic cooperation between industrial states, to coordinate aid to the THIRD WORLD and to try to resolve problems concerning world trade and economic growth. It has a professional secretariat but, unlike the European Union has no supranational institutions or a parliament responsible for supervising its activities. Originally it was founded in 1948 as the Organization for European Economic Cooperation (OEEC) to coordinate the economic rehabilitation of Europe which the MARSHALL PLAN made possible. It was in the OEEC that the Six began discussions that led to the TREATY OF ROME and the foundation of the EEC in 1957. The rise of two different trading blocs in the EEC and EFTA split the OEEC, which was refounded in 1960 as the OECD, with the US and Canada as members. Now all major industrial countries with market economies belong to it.

The OECD plays an important role in preparing for the annual economic summit of the Group of Seven industrial countries and produces authoritative reports on the economic performance of member countries. In 1990 it founded the European Bank for Reconstruction and Development. For the Third World the OECD represents the North in the NORTH–SOUTH DIVIDE. Critics accuse it of being a rich man's club, concerned only with its own selfish interests.

'First World' Relationships: The Role of the OECD, M. Camps (1975)

OPEC (Organization of Petroleum Exporting Countries)   Founded in September 1960 by Venezuela, Saudi Arabia, Iran, Iraq and Kuwait. Other states joined later: Qatar in 1961, Indonesia and Libya in 1962, Abu Dhabi in 1967, Algeria in 1969, Nigeria in 1971, Ecuador in 1977 and Gabon in 1975. Oil prices had been falling in the 1950s and in 1959 the oil companies twice cut oil prices without consulting the governments of the countries where the oil was located. OPEC was formed in response and aimed to obtain higher prices for oil, by limiting production if necessary on a quota basis, and to secure more control over their own resources from the major oil companies. In the 1960s OPEC achieved little, as some members opposed limiting their production and Libya started oil production in 1961 and so increased the supply available. Arab producers cut off exports, especially to Britain and the US, during the SIX DAY WAR (1967), but ended their boycott after a month, as they were losing revenue. In the early 1970s, with an economic boom in the industrialized countries and a sharp rise in the price of manufactured goods, OPEC wanted subtantial oil price increases but negotiations with the oil companies failed.

The YOM KIPPUR WAR in 1973 brought a change, as Saudi Arabia cut production by 10 per cent and imposed an embargo on oil to the US and the Netherlands, who were pro-Israel. Oil prices adrupled from $3.5 to $15 a barrel. The effects of the 1973 oil price shock were far-reaching. Many oil-producing states became very rich indeed: the annual revenue from oil increased between 1973–8 from $4.35

billion to $36 billion in Saudi Arabia; from $1.7 billion to $9.2 billion in Kuwait; from $1.8 billion to $23.6 billion in Iraq. Saudi Arabia, with a small population, became a major player in the GLOBAL ECONOMY: by 1975 it had greater financial reserves than the US and Japan combined, was a leading member of the IMF and the WORLD BANK and was one of the largest aid donors. As the biggest non-communist exporter of oil, it acted as a 'swing' producer for OPEC, stabilizing the international price of oil by raising or lowering output.

The oil shock of 1973 stimulated oil exploration and development outside the Middle East, especially in the North Sea, where oil extraction would have been uneconomic at pre-1973 prices. This was so successful that by 1982 Mexico and Britain were producing more oil than any OPEC member except Saudi Arabia and OPEC oil production had fallen from 90 per cent of non-communist production in 1960 to 40 per cent in 1990. Industrialized countries adopted conservationist policies and sought to use other sources of power: coal, gas, nuclear.

There was a second oil shock in 1979–80, as there was fear of a price explosion, with the IRAN–IRAQ WAR. The price of oil more than doubled from $12.5 to $30 per barrel, a price formally adopted by OPEC but it could not be sustained. Both Iran and Iraq wanted to export oil to pay for the war, and demand for oil fell in industrialized countries owing to economic recession and energy savings. Saudi Arabia lost sales heavily as it tried to keep up prices and in 1985 abandoned its role as a swing producer and competed for market share. OPEC's efforts to maintain price levels by running a cartel with production quotas for its members failed because it had no means of enforcing quotas and its members had different interests.

OPEC: The Failing Giant, M. E. Ahrari (1986)

OPEC: 25 Years of Prices and Politics, I. Skeet (1988)

OPEC price rises (1973, 1979–80)   The rise in the price of oil put some OPEC countries, particularly Saudi Arabia, among the richest countries in the world and had a marked effect on the GLOBAL ECONOMY. The golden age since the Second World War, which had seen almost uninterrupted growth and full employment, ended with recessions in 1973–5 and 1981–3. In even the strongest European economies GNP fell: in West Germany by 0.5 per cent in 1974, 1.6 per cent in 1975, 1 per cent in 1982; in Italy by 3.7 per cent in 1976, for the first time since the war. Unemployment in Western Europe, which had averaged 1.6 per cent in the 1960s, was 4.2 per cent in the 1970s, 9.2 per cent in the 1980s and 11 per cent in 1993. This weakened the position of TRADE UNIONS. Japan, too, experienced its first negative growth rate since the war in 1974–5, though it was only −0.2 per cent: its balance of payments moved from a surplus of $4.6 billion to a deficit of $10 billion in 1973. Western Europe and Japan coped well by reducing their oil consumption and there was no breakdown of the global economy as in the 1930s: economic growth continued but at a slower pace. World trade grew annually at an average of 8.5 per cent between 1963–73 but at only 3.5 per cent in the following decade. The share of advanced capitalist countries fell as that of the NEWLY INDUSTRIALIZING ECONOMIES (NIEs) increased, but the developed countries were nevertheless richer at the end of the century than they were in 1970. The oil MULTINATIONAL CORPORATIONS benefited considerably from the price rises, as they controlled the production, distribution and exploration of oil: they became the most powerful companies in the West.

Yet a price had to be paid. As the real GNP of leading industrial countries fell in the short term, a new phenomenon appeared: 'stagflation', when there was both stagnation and inflation. Countries sought means of controlling inflation, so MONETARISM replaced KEYNESIANISM as the most influential economic doctrine. As inflation was created by unbalanced budgets and excessive borrowing, the aim was to cut government expenditure, which in effect meant social welfare programmes. The WELFARE STATE began to be dismantled: beggars appeared on the streets again, sleeping in cardboard boxes, and in Britain 400,000 were officially classed as homeless in 1989. The inequality in incomes increased and there was an absolute decline in the standard of living of the poorest. In the wage sector the difference between the top and bottom 10 per cent widened by 34 per cent in Britain and 16 per cent in the US between 1979–89.

The OPEC price rises also contributed to the destabilization of the international money markets in the FINANCIAL REVOLUTION, which had begun in 1971 when President NIXON abandoned a fixed exchange rate for the dollar. The era of stability set up at Bretton Woods in 1944 ended. The OPEC countries could not spend their vastly increased wealth in the short run, so much of it returned to the West as petrodollars, was recycled to finance world trade deficits and so helped to create the INTERNATIONAL DEBT crisis. The huge amount of petrodollars in circulation stimulated speculative capital movements and further increased the instability of the international monetary system.

The countries worst affected by the OPEC price rises were those in the THIRD WORLD and in COMECON. China and the NIEs grew rapidly economically but in Africa and Western Asia growth ceased, output fell for most of the 1980s and people there became poorer. The communist states of Eastern Europe could not absorb the oil shocks, as the Soviet Union brought its oil prices more into line with world market levels, and so they lost their subsidized oil. They borrowed and by 1981 Eastern European and Soviet debt (the USSR had to pay higher prices for the Western machinery it needed) was 15 times higher than in 1970. The communist economic system, already in difficulties, could not cope with the crippling debt burden, which was partly responsible for the COLLAPSE OF THE SOVIET UNION and the REVOLUTIONS OF 1989–91.

Capitalism Since 1945, P. Armstrong, A. Glynand and J. Harrison (1991)

Opus Dei   Catholic sect, founded in Spain in 1928 by the Aragonese priest José María Escrivá de Balaguer, who ruled the movement with an iron hand until his death in 1975. The mission of Opus Dei ('the Work of God') has been to conquer and 'Catholicize' secular power by infiltrating the professional classes, especially in business, the media and education. During the early years of the FRANCO regime, Opus expanded through the backing of wealthy Catholic progressives, above all in Catalonia, while opposed from the outset by the Fascist movement, the Falange. Although Opus was recognized in 1947 as the first secular institute in the Catholic Church, it did not come to prominence until the 1950s in Spain, when it made notable advances within the Francoist political system. The major cabinet reshuffle of 1957 marked a notable shift in power away from the Falange and towards the so-called 'technocrats'. The technocrats, including not only the principal economic ministers but also López Rodó, the most powerful minister in the cabinet until 1965, oversaw the dramatic opening up of the domestic market and the subsequent transformation of the Spanish economy with the Stabilization Plan of 1959. All were members of Opus Dei. Thus Opus has combined its ultra-conservative political and theological outlook with neo-liberal economic views.

During the 1960s and 1970s Opus extended its operations to South America and parts of Europe, especially to Ireland and Italy. A notable boon for the sect was the election in 1982 of Karol Wojtila as Pope JOHN PAUL II. A close ally of Opus, he beatified the Opus founder, causing much disquiet within the Church.

Opus Dei's secretiveness and élitism, its vast, secreted wealth, and its semi-autonomous status have led many Catholics to regard it unfavourably as a Church within the Church. There is little doubt that Opus's numerical strength – it was estimated in 1996 that the sect has approximately 70,000 followers throughout the world – bears little relationship to its political and economic weight. In Spain, Opus controls many banks and businesses, including influential media outlets such as the SER radio network, and has a significant presence in education, especially in the private sector. Its waning political influence received a fillip in 1996 with the electoral victory of the *Partido Popular* (PP: Popular Party), several of whose leading figures are members of Opus Dei.

The Work of God, M. Walsh (1989)
Saints and Schemes, J. Estruch (1994)

Ostpolitik (Eastern Policy)   The attempt to improve relations between the Federal Republic of Germany (FRG: West Germany) and the communist bloc, particularly with the German Democratic Republic (GDR: East Germany). Konrad ADENAUER, Chancellor of the FRG (1949–63), claimed that West Germany had the right to speak for the whole of Germany, as it was the only democratically elected government and refused to recognize the GDR. The Hallstein doctrine isolated the FRG by refusing to have diplomatic relations with any country (except the USSR) which recognized the GDR. Bonn also caused alarm by claiming that, as there had been no peace treaty after the Second World War, the frontiers of the FRG were those of 1937, which meant that the FRG did not accept the Oder–Neisse frontier of Poland fixed after the war.

Willy BRANDT began to change all this when he became Foreign Minister (1966–9) and then Chancellor (1969–74) of the FRG. He realized that all the countries of the communist bloc wanted a recognition of the postwar boundaries in Eastern Europe and that the GDR wanted acceptance as a sovereign state, on an equal footing with the FRG.

DÉTENTE made Ostpolitik possible, as agreement with the Soviet Union was necessary before there could be any treaties with Soviet satellites. In August 1970 the FRG and Soviet Union signed a non-aggression pact, the Moscow Treaty. Both countries renounced the use of force and said that they had no claim on the territory of any other state. They pledged to regard as 'inviolable' all existing frontiers, including those between the FRG and Poland, which marked an acceptance by the FRG of territorial changes made after the war. Four months later the FRG and Poland signed the Warsaw Treaty, which recognized the Oder–Neisse frontier, though this was not finally confirmed until after GERMAN REUNIFICATION. In September 1971 there was a Four-Power Agreement on Berlin, where most of the concessions came from the USSR. It guaranteed unhindered traffic between the FRG and West Berlin and gave up the claim that West Berlin lay within the GDR and under its jurisdiction. In December 1972 the FRG and GDR agreed on a Basic Treaty, which enabled the FRG to establish formal relations with the GDR for the first time. The FRG recognized the independence of the GDR, though not its full sovereignty. Brandt's Ostpolitik was supported by the West German electorate in the general election of 1972. A year later both the FRG and GDR joined the UNITED NATIONS. The FRG recognized the borders of Czechoslovakia and established diplomatic relations with Hungary and Bulgaria. It now had formal relations with all East European countries except Albania.

Brandt claimed that he had given nothing away and had simply made agreements 'on the basis of the political situation as it exists in Europe', but critics attacked him for accepting the permanent division of Germany and the boundaries produced by aggression. He was further criticized for propping up a despotic regime in the GDR that ignored human rights. In fact the unification of Germany ceased to be an issue. Public opinion polls in the 1950s and 1960s showed that up to 45 per cent of West Germans regarded unification as the 'most important' issue of the day: from 1975 never more than 1 per cent did so. It did not become a matter of concern again until the REVOLUTIONS OF 1989–91 resulted in the collapse of communism there and made German reunification possible.

From Embargo to Ostpolitik, A. Stent (1981)
Breakthrough in the Ostpolitik, D. M. Keithly (1986)
In Europe's Name, T. Garton Ash (1993)

Özal, Turgut (1927–93) Prime Minister (1983–9) and President (1989–93) of Turkey. A pious man, never without his prayer beads, he studied electrical engineering at Istanbul University and in the 1970s worked as an economist for the WORLD BANK. In 1979 he was an adviser to the Demirel government and when this was overthrown in a military coup in 1980 he was asked to stay on as Deputy Prime Minister. He carried out economic reforms, lifting exchange controls and liberalizing trade before he resigned in 1982 over a banking scandal. A year later he was Prime Minister, as his Motherland Party, a coalition of liberal and Islamic groups, narrowly won the general election.

An admirer of Ronald REAGAN and Margaret THATCHER, he wanted a free market economy. Foreign investment was encouraged and there was a considerable improvement in the infrastructure and utilities, as telecommunications were expanded, roads and a second bridge over the Bosphorous between Europe and Asia built. Natural gas pipelines were laid between Turkey and the Soviet Union and dams were erected on the Tigris and Euphrates to double the area under cultivation in Turkey. Özal had considerable success as GNP rose by 4.5 per cent a year from 1980–5. Exports grew by 22 per cent a year from 1980–7 and their nature changed, as industry took over from agriculture: in 1979 60 per cent of exports were agricultural, in 1988 20 per cent. However, imports trebled

(1979–89) and exceeded exports. There was an inefficient state industrial sector, so Özal favoured PRIVATIZATION: little progress was made, though he did abolish government monopolies in airlines and television. The burden of all the changes fell on wage-earners, whose purchasing power declined by 47 per cent in the 1980s, as wages were frozen and prices raised by the abolition of subsidies. The IMF and WORLD BANK showed renewed confidence in Turkey and provided credits, so that the national debt grew from $13.5 billion in 1980 to $40 billion in 1989.

Özal had applied for full membership of the EC in 1987 but in 1990 the EC deferred this indefinitely, because of the high cost of integrating Turkey into the EC and because of its poor record on human rights. He nevertheless continued to pursue a pro-Western foreign policy as a member of NATO and supported the American-led coalition against Iraq in the GULF WAR (1990). He refused to become involved in the NAGORNO-KARABAGH CONFLICT, which Islamists saw as a religious struggle between Muslim Azeris and Christian Armenians, who were greatly disliked in Turkey. The Kurdish problem became more acute during his period of office, many people being killed in the numerous clashes between Kurdish rebels and the security forces. Strong measures against the political violence of ISLAMIC FUNDAMENTALISTS and of left-wing groups led to complaints about the abuse of human rights, particularly the use of torture.

Özal defied the tradition of Kemal Atatürk, the founder of the Turkish Republic, in allowing Islamic financial houses to operate and in going on a pilgrimage to Mecca in 1988, the first Turkish head of state to do so since the formation of the Turkish Republic in 1923. Özal's pilgrimage was symptomatic of the Islamic revival in Turkey, which saw Islamists holding some of the highest positions in government and even in the army. In 1989 Özal was elected President and died from a heart attack four years later.

The Making of Modern Turkey, F. Ahmad (1995)

Turkey: A Modern History, E. J. Zürcher (1995)

Turkey Unveiled: Atatürk and After, N. Pope and H. Pope (1997)

P

Palestinian refugees   About 725,000 Arabs (out of a population of 1.3 million) were driven out of Palestine during the first ARAB–ISRAELI WAR (1948–9) which saw the BIRTH OF ISRAEL. Some were forcibly ejected, others fled to avoid massacres such as that at DEIR YASSIN. Israel settled Arab villages with Jewish immigrants and took over the property of the refugees without compensation. The Israeli government ignored UNITED NATIONS demands and would not allow the refugees to return until there was a general peace settlement: as such an agreement has not beem concluded they have remained abroad, often in squalid camps. None of the neighbouring countries wanted the refugees and only in Jordan were they accepted as citizens. The cost of maintaining them was taken over by the UN Relief Works Administration (UNRWA), established in 1950, though the Arab states would not cooperate with it because this would imply a recognition of Israel's permanent existence. By 1982 relief had cost $1.5 billion, contributed mainly by the US and Britain. UNRWA registered 960,000 Palestinian refugees in 1950, 2.2 million in 1987, of whom a third were still in camps: 840,000 were in Jordan, 440,000 in Gaza, 370,000 in the WEST BANK, 280,000 in Lebanon and 260,000 in Syria. Unassimilated, their hatred of Israel remained and was demonstrated in such events as the INTIFADA.

The Birth of the Palestinian Refugee Problem, 1945–7, B. Morris (1987)

Palme, Sven Olof (1927–86)   Prime Minister of Sweden (1969–76, 1982–6). From a wealthy family, he obtained a law degree in 1951 and also took a degree in politics and economics at Kenyon College, Ohio. Palme joined the Social Democratic Party while a student. Prime Minister ERLANDER recognized his ability and made Palme his personal secretary and speech writer in 1954. Elected to parliament in 1958, he held various ministerial posts from 1963.

After the Social Democratic victory in the 1968 election Erlander resigned and Palme, his chosen successor, became party chairman and Prime Minister. He was a controversial figure who supported THIRD WORLD causes, severely criticized US policy in the VIETNAM WAR and wanted greater economic equality for women and the poor. A strong pacifist, he was active as an international statesman and was a member of the BRANDT Commission which reported in 1982 on the NORTH–SOUTH DIVIDE. At home he continued Erlander's reforms to introduce more industrial democracy by increasing workers' participation in running the companies which employed them. As inflation and taxes increased support for the Social Democrats fell away and they lost the 1976 election, after 44 years in power. They returned to office in 1982, again with Palme as Prime Minister. Owing to the high costs of the WELFARE STATE he faced a huge deficit of 13 per cent of GDP (government expenditure was 60 per cent of GDP). He therefore devalued the krona and cut public expenditure without touching basic welfare. The rapid economic growth which followed produced balance of payments and budget surpluses by 1987 but there was widespread discontent and strikes as older established industries such as steel and shipbuilding collapsed. He was shot and killed as he left a cinema in Stockholm with his wife. The motive of his murderer, who was not captured, was not clear, but in 1996 it was alleged that the South African secret services had been involved.

Party Politics in Sweden, H. Heclo and H. Madsen (1987)

Pan-Arabism   A movement which believes that all Arabs should unite to form one nation, as most speak Arabic, are Muslim and have a common culture, and that the regeneration of the Arab world can only take place through unity. It was an off-shoot of Arab nationalism. The colonial powers were blamed for artificially dividing the Arabs and arbitrarily fixing the boundaries of Arab states in order to weaken them. The BIRTH OF ISRAEL gave a great boost to Pan-Arabism as the state of Israel was formed from Arab lands only because the Arabs were not united. Pan-Arabism reached its peak in the 1950s and 1960s, when NASSER saw it as a means of asserting Egyptian leadership in the Middle East and when the Ba'th Party was a genuine pan-Arab organization, setting up branches in each Arab country. With the Ba'th Party of Syria Nasser formed the United Arab Republic in 1958 but Syria, resenting Egyptian dominance, withdrew in 1961. Further attempts at union failed and with the defeat of Arab states by Israel in the SIX DAY WAR in 1967 Nasser's leadership was discredited and Pan-Arabism lost its appeal. The ARAB LEAGUE had always rejected proposals for an Arab union and now the emphasis moved away from political union to various forms of association. The GULF WAR (1991) showed clearly the inability of Arab states to present a united front.

Islam, the People and the State, S. Zubaida (1988)

Panama, US intervention in (1989)   The Panamanian dictator General Manuel Nor-

iega had secretly supplied the CIA with information on Central America long before he came to power in 1983. President REAGAN had turned a blind eye to his drug trafficking until in February 1988 a federal grand jury in Florida indicted him of conspiring with a Colombian drug cartel to smuggle drugs into the US. The US imposed economic sanctions on Panama but Noriega remained in power. When the Panamanian presidential elections were held in May 1989 Noriega nullified the result and declared his own candidate had won. President BUSH then urged the Panamanian people to overthrow him but when an attempted coup in October 1989 failed and the plotters were executed he did nothing. Two months later the Panamanian National Assembly declared Noriega was head of state.

Noriega foolishly declared in December that a state of war existed between Panama and the US. This gave Bush the opportunity he had wanted. He ordered US marines (many from bases in the Canal Zone) to invade Panama. Resistance soon collapsed: there were only 23 American casualties but many civilians were killed and there was much damage to property, mainly from looting. A government under Guillermo Endara, the winner of the presidential election, was set up: all US troops were withdrawn by February 1990. Noriega took refuge in the Vatican diplomatic mission until he surrendered to US forces. He was taken to Miami, charged with cocaine-smuggling and money laundering and was the first ex-head of state to be convicted by an American jury in March 1991: he was sentenced to 40 years imprisonment. The US intervention was widely condemned in Latin America and by the OAS (Organization of American States) but most US citizens approved of it.

Papandreou, Andreas (1919–96)   Greek Prime Minister (1981–9, 1993–6). The son of Georgios Papandreou (Prime Minister 1944–5, 1963–5), he was arrested for Trotskyist activity as a student and emigrated to the

United States in 1938. He became a US citizen and outstanding economist, notably at the University of California, Berkeley. KARA-MANLIS, the Prime Minister, persuaded him to return to Greece in 1961 as head of the Centre of Economic Research and Planning and economic adviser to the Bank of Greece. He resumed his Greek citizenship and in 1964 became a member of Parliament and a minister in his father's Centre Union government. When the GREEK COLONELS seized power in 1967 he was arrested and allowed to leave Greece only after considerable US pressure.

When the military dictatorship collapsed in 1974 he returned to Greece and founded a new party, the Panhellenic Socialist Movement (Pasok), which he ruled with a rod of iron. He was stridently anti-American, anti-Turkish and even anti-European and talked of withdrawing Greece from the EEC and NATO and of closing American bases in Greece. As his party came closer to electoral success (it almost doubled its vote at each successive election: 14 per cent in 1974, 25 per cent in 1977, 45 per cent in 1981) his tone became more moderate. When he became the first socialist Prime Minister in Greece in 1981 there was no further talk of leaving the EEC and NATO and the American bases remained.

Although he claimed to be a Marxist there was little doctrinaire socialism in his policies. Much of the economy was already nationalized and when he extended state control it was to prevent firms going bankrupt (and hence to save jobs). Public expenditure increased from 30 per cent to 45 per cent of GNP between 1980 and 1989. Various liberal reforms were passed: civil marriage was instituted and divorce by consent; adultery ceased to be a criminal offence and the dowry system was abolished. Universities were made more democratic and a national health service was introduced but there was no full-blown WELFARE STATE, as Greece could not afford one. Greece benefited greatly from EC agricultural subsidies and in 1986 Papandreou signed the Single European Act, committing Greece to a closer union of the countries in the EC. Yet in his foreign policy he often pursued a line at variance with that of his allies. Forthright in condemning the Israeli invasion of Lebanon in 1982, he strongly supported ARAFAT and the PLO.

Papandreou became more and more autocratic. He treated parliament (which he rarely attended) with scant respect, and regularly overruled, transferred and dismissed his ministers. In 1988 there were scandals. While in a London hospital he announced that he was divorcing his American wife (they had been married for 37 years) and mother of his four children in order to marry a 34-year-old Olympic Airways stewardess. When he returned to Greece there were unprecedented financial scandals (the Bank of Crete had been defrauded of $132 million) in which he was accused of being directly involved. To add to his difficulties there was an economic crisis-a huge foreign debt, balance of payments deficit and inflation which never fell below 12 per cent in his second term. Austerity measures to deal with the problem resulted in major strikes. It was a tribute to Papandreou's charisma and confidence that three elections were needed in 1989–90 before the opposition New Democracy Party obtained a parliamentary majority. Papandreou was tried for corruption but was acquitted. In the election of 1993 Pasok won a comfortable victory and Papandreou returned as Prime Minister but he was in poor health and there were complaints that Mimi (as his wife Liani was known) had acquired too much power. He was rarely able to work more than an hour or two a day and in December 1995 began a period of four months in hospital, during which he resigned as Prime Minister.

Modern Greece, C. M. Woodhouse (1991)
A Concise History of Greece, R. Clogg (1992)

Park Chung Hee (1917–79)   President of the Republic of Korea (ROK) (1963–79). An officer in the Japanese army during the Second World War, Park then served in the

South Korean army as a Major-General during the KOREAN WAR (1950–3) and was the driving force in the military coup which seized power in 1961. There was a Five Year Plan (1962–6) to develop the economy and a new constitution in 1962, which provided for a strong popularly elected President, prior to a return to civilian government. Park, elected as President in 1963, then resigned from the army. He concentrated on economic modernization, encouraging investment in the key industries of steel, shipbuilding and petrochemicals. Park fostered the growth of the *chaebol*, the huge conglomerates, and assigned them export targets. High tariffs were combined with forced savings, direct investment in strategic sectors and almost total government control of credit through nationalized banks. Free trade zones attracted foreign capital, while exports were encouraged by tax rebates. An expansion of schools and universities produced a highly educated population: many graduates were sent to the West for advanced study. Park greatly stimulated the economy by establishing diplomatic relations with Japan in 1965 and obtaining from it a $500 million aid programme. Trade with Japan, which invested over a billion dollars in Korean shipbuilding and electronics, increased to $9 billion in 1980. Park was helped too by American subsidies of over a billion dollars in the early years of the VIETNAM WAR, when South Korea sent 300,000 troops (1965–70) to help the US in Vietnam. Exports of $40 million in 1961 rose to $15 billion in 1979, per capita income increased from $82 (1961) to $1,500 in 1979, while GNP of $2 billion grew to $60 billion (1961–79). Growth rates of 10 per cent per annum (1965–77) made the ROK a NEWLY INDUSTRIALIZING ECONOMY, second only to Japan in East Asia. Agriculture, stagnant to the 1970s, also developed owing to a price support system and investment in irrigation, fertilizers and the GREEN REVOLUTION, which made the ROK self-sufficient in rice by 1975 and brought agricultural incomes into line with those in industry.

In his highly repressive regime Park had 350,000 agents in the Korean CIA in the mid-1960s. Opponents were imprisoned and torture was routine. Park was elected President again in 1967 and in 1969 amended the constitution to abolish the two-term limit on the presidency. A new constitution in 1972 greatly increased the powers of the President: Park ruled largely by decree. He banned criticism of the government and of the constitution in 1975, but in elections to the National Assembly in 1978 the opposition gained more votes than the government. In 1979 as a world recession began, workers and students demonstrated against Park, who was killed in a botched coup by the head of his security services.

A Short History of Korea, D. Rees (1988)
The Republic of Korea: Economic Transformation and social Change, D. I. Steinberg (1989)
Korea's Place in the Sun: A Modern History, B. Cummings (1997)

PCI (*Partito Comunista Italiano*: Italian Communist Party)   Founded in 1921, it had only 25,000 members by 1926, when it was banned by Mussolini and most of its leaders were arrested. It went underground until July 1943, when its small band of professional revolutionaries led the Resistance. This enabled it to become a mass party (it had two million members in 1946) with mass organizations (trade unions, co-operatives, workers and youth organizations) to support it. Its leader after the war, Palmiro TOGLIATTI, realized that any attempt to seize power would be suicidal, as Allied armies in Italy would not tolerate this, so he worked with other parties, notably the CHRISTIAN DEMOCRATIC PARTY (DC), as a member of the government to bring about change gradually and in a democratic manner. The PCI itself was far from democratic. Organized like the CPSU (Communist Party of the Soviet Union) according to the principle of democratic centralism, real power was in the hands of the Secretariat. All decisions were made at the top and handed down to members, who had no say in reaching them: opposition to the leadership within the party was forbidden.

When the COLD WAR began the PCI was expelled from his government by DE GAS-PERI and so formed a Popular Front with the socialists, but this was never enough to bring it back into power though the PCI was consistently the second largest party in Italy. The PCI never again held posts in an Italian government. This did not mean that it was completely excluded from power, as it was successful in local politics and controlled the largest of the three trade union confederations, the CGIL. From the end of the war the PCI was dominant in the Red Belt of Emilia-Romagna in Central Italy, where there was a strong tradition of anti-clericalism (before Italian unification in 1860 it was part of the Papal States). Bologna, the largest city of the region, was a communist show-piece with its social welfare programmes, healthcare and public transport. Its communist administration was efficient, honest and never in debt.

In opposition the PCI felt that it had to support Soviet foreign policy, so it condemned the MARSHALL PLAN, and Italy being a member of the ECSC, EEC and NATO. The PCI even tried to justify the Soviet crushing of the HUNGARIAN RISING in 1956, which resulted in 400,000 members leaving the party. For the first time since the war the socialists refused to renew their pact of unity with the communists. In the same year it was thrown a life-line by KHRUSHCHEV's secret speech to the TWENTIETH CONGRESS OF THE CPSU, which criticized the abuses of the Soviet system by STALIN. Togliatti put forward his doctrine of polycentrism, which maintained that the communist movement could not be directed from a single centre (Moscow) and that there were different roads to socialism. The attitude of the PCI towards the EEC changed, as it was seen as a means of countering US influence in Europe.

Togliatti's move to free the PCI from Soviet control was continued by Enrico Ber-linguer, a leading proponent of EURO-COMMUNISM, who proposed a historic compromise with the DC, which might have led to communists holding ministerial posts again but for the murder of Aldo MORO and the SOVIET INVASION OF AFGHANISTAN. Under Berlinguer the PCI reached the peak of its popularity, winning 34.4 per cent of the vote (4 behind the DC) in the general election of 1976, but thereafter there was a steady decline. It continued to show its independence by condemning Soviet interference in Afghanistan and broke with Moscow completely when the Soviet Union crushed SOLI-DARITY in 1981. By 1985 the PCI had lost control of many cities it had gained ten years earlier and it did not appear able to address new issues – feminism, the environment, civil liberties – which were taken up by other parties. Its morale plummeted with the REVOLUTIONS OF 1989–91, which saw the end of communist regimes in Eastern Europe, and the COLLAPSE OF THE SOVIET UNION.

In 1991 it changed its name to the Democratic Party of the Left (PDS) but this split the party, 150,000 leaving to found a new party, Communist Refoundation. PCI membership in 1990 was 1.3 million, that of the PDS a year later 400,000. In the 1992 election it secured only 16 per cent of the vote, but under Massimo d'Alena it moved more towards the centre and in 1996 organized a new coalition called L'Ulivo (The Olive Tree), which named Romano Prodi, an academic economist and former CD minister, as its candidate for the premiership. The PDS had gained respectability by supporting the austerity measures which had greatly improved Italy's finances. In the election L'Ulivo won 51 per cent of the Senate seats and 46 per cent of those in the lower house and ex-communists became part of the government for the first time since 1947.

The Italian Communist Party, G. Amyot (1981)

The Strategy of the Italian Communist Party, D. Sassoon (1981)

The Italian Left in the Twentieth Century, A.
  De Grand (1989)

peace process   The search which began
after the BIRTH OF ISRAEL for a permanent
peace in the Middle East. The first Arab–
Israeli war (1948–9) ended in a truce between
Israel and its Arab opponents but no peace, as
Arab states would not recognize Israel's right
to exist. When King ABDULLAH of Jordan
sought an agreement with Israel, he was assassinated in 1951. Anti-Israel feeling among
Arabs increased after the SIX DAY WAR
(1967), when Israel retained control of the
OCCUPIED TERRITORIES. An ARAB LEA-
GUE meeting in 1967 declared, 'No negotiations with Israel, no treaty, no recognition of
Israel' and insisted that PALESTINIAN
REFUGEES had the right to return to the
lands from which they had fled or been
expelled. The UNITED NATIONS Security
Council Resolution 242 (1967) called for a
recognition of Israel by the Arabs, Israeli
withdrawal from the Occupied Territories
and a 'first settlement of the refugee problem'.
Although this was initially rejected by Syria
and the PLO, it henceforth formed the basis of
Arab demands for a peace settlement.

President SADAT of Egypt, having failed to
defeat Israel in the YOM KIPPUR WAR
(1973), sought unilaterally to make peace
with Israel, which he did in 1979, following
the CAMP DAVID ACCORDS, thus making
Egypt the first Arab country to make peace
with Israel. This was condemned by other
Arab states, as the interests of the Palestinians
and their right to a separate state had been
ignored. The peace process made little progress after 1979 under the Likud governments
of Menachem BEGIN and Yitzhak SHAMIR,
as they were opposed to the creation of a
separate Palestinian state, to withdrawal
from the Occupied Territories, to the
dismantling of Jewish settlements there and
to the return of Palestinian refugees.

The PLO meanwhile had realized that they
were more likely to obtain what they wanted
by negotiation rather than terrorism and in
1988 accepted Resolution 242 and Israel's
right to exist. A change came in 1992 when
Likud was defeated by the Labour Party in a
general election and Yitzhak RABIN became
Prime Minister. He had been a hard-liner in
dealing with the Palestinians but the INTI-
FADA convinced him that a military solution
to Israel's problems was not possible, so he
entered secret negotiations with the PLO
which produced the Oslo Accords in 1993,
when Israel and the PLO recognized each
other and laid down a timetable for gradual
Palestinian self-rule in the Occupied Territories. In 1994 Jordan became the second
Arab country to make peace with Israel.
Rabin paid with his life for accepting the
partition of Palestine, when he was assassinated by a Jewish extremist in November 1995.
By this time Israel had withdrawn from the
Gaza Strip and part of the WEST BANK but
the peace process suffered a setback in 1996
when Binyamin NETANYAHU became Prime
Minister at the head of a Likud government.
Opposed to the creation of a Palestinian state
and dependent on Orthodox parties for his
majority in the Knesset (Israeli parliament)
he outraged Arabs by extending Jewish settlements in the West Bank. The peace process
came to a halt in 1997 when HAMAS suicide-
bombers continued to wreak havoc in Israel,
though the US, Israel's main supporter,
worked hard to revive it.

Building a Palestinian State, G. E. Robinson
  (1997)

Pearson, Lester Bowles (1897–1972)
Prime Minister of Canada (1963–8). He lectured in history at the University of Toronto
(1924–8), after studying there and at Oxford
University. In 1928 he joined the foreign service, worked in the Canadian High Commission, London (1935–41), was ambassador to
the US (1945–6) and Secretary of State for
External Affairs (1948–57) in the ST. LAUR-
ENT government. During the SUEZ CRISIS
(1956) he helped to create the UN Emergency

Force which separated Egyptian and Israeli forces, for which he was given the Nobel Peace Prize in 1957, the first Canadian to be so honoured. In 1958 he succeeded St. Laurent as head of the Liberal Party and was leader of the opposition in parliament until 1963, when the Liberals defeated the Conservatives under DIEFENBAKER in the election of that year and Pearson became Prime Minister.

QUEBEC NATIONALISM was an increasing problem for the government. Pearson responded by setting up the Royal Commission on Bilingualism and Biculturalism (1963–71) to suggest a federal policy to promote the equality of 'the two founding races'. Its interim report in 1965 declared that Canada 'is passing through the greatest crisis in its history' as Francophone (French-speaking) Canadians suffered from enormous disadvantages. It called for both French and English to be official languages in the federal government and in the provinces of Ontario, Quebec and New Brunswick. The Pearson government tried to reduce tension by creating a fairer balance between Anglophones (English-speaking Canadians) and Francophones in the federal civil service. Pearson also did much to improve social services, passing the National Medicine Act (1965) to provide joint federal – provincial finance for medical insurance for all Canadians.

Canada, 1957–67, J. Granatstein (1986)
The Life of Lester Pearson, vols 1 and 2, J. English (1989, 1992)

Peres, Shimon (1923–)   Prime Minister of Israel (1984–6, 1995–6). Born in Poland, he emigrated to Palestine in 1934 and lived on a *kibbutz* before attending Tel Aviv, Harvard and New York universities. In 1947 he joined *Haganah*, the Israeli defence force, and fought in the War of Independence (1948–9) which brought about the BIRTH OF ISRAEL. He so impressed BEN-GURION that he made Peres head of the Israeli navy at the age of 25. From 1952–65 he held posts in the Ministry of Defence, increased Israel's arms and aircraft production and began its nuclear research programme. In 1965 he resigned from Mapai, the leading left-wing party, to join Ben-Gurion's breakaway Rafi Party. This was unsuccessful electorally so Peres began its merger with Mapai and another left-wing party to form the Israeli Labour Party in 1968. Back in office as Minister of Transport (1970–4) and of Defence (1974–7), he was elected Chairman of the Labour Party in 1977 when Yitzhak RABIN resigned owing to financial irregularities. Labour lost the election of 1977 so Peres was leader of the opposition to Menachem BEGIN's Likud government during the Israeli invasion of Lebanon in 1982. He wanted a more conciliatory approach to the Palestine problem than that of Likud.

The 1984 election produced a hung parliament, so Peres made an unlikely coalition with Yitzhak SHAMIR, now the leader of Likud. Peres was to be Prime Minister for two years with Shamir as Deputy Premier and Foreign Minister: the roles would then be reversed for the following two years. As Prime Minister he withdrew Israeli forces from Lebanon in 1985 and took tough measures to reduce the inflation rate of 400 per cent by cutting subsidies and phasing out expensive projects, such as the Lani fighter aircraft. He succeeded in reducing inflation to under 20 per cent yet foreign debt and defence expenditure took up 60 per cent of the budget. In 1988 Likud gained a narrow electoral victory and the coalition was renewed, with Peres again as Deputy Premier. He was dismissed in 1990 when Likud ruled without the aid of the Labour Party and led the opposition till 1992, when Rabin replaced him as leader of the Labour Party, renewing their bitter personal rivalry which went back to 1974.

In the same year Labour won the election and Peres became Foreign Minister, playing an important role in negotiations with the PLO and Yasir ARAFAT which led in the Oslo Accords (1993) to the gradual extension of self-rule to the Palestinians in the OCCU-PIED TERRITORIES, seized after the SIX DAY WAR in 1967. A year later he made a peace treaty with Jordan. He shared the Nobel Peace Prize with Arafat and Rabin in 1994. When Rabin was assassinated in November 1995 he again became Prime Minister. His chances of winning the first direct election for Prime Minister were ruined by HAMAS suicide-bombers who killed 62 Israelis. Binyamin NETANYAHU narrowly won in 1996, thus completing Peres's dismal record of fighting five general elections and losing them all.

Perón, 'Evita' (Maria Eva Duarte de) (1919–52)

Argentine politician and social reformer. The illegitimate child of a large, poor family in Buenos Aires province, Eva Duarte left home at 15 for Buenos Aires with aspirations as an actress. There she became a star of radio soap operas and was waiting for her breakthrough in films when she met Colonel Juan PERÓN, the director of the Secretariat of Labour and Welfare under the military regime, and became his lover and in October 1945, his wife.

Following Juan Perón's presidential victory in February 1946, Evita gradually assumed a central political role within the regime, even though she held no official position. Her stirring oratory and populist instinct not only helped cement the support of the trade unions, but also that of the *descamisados* (literally, 'shirtless'), or urban poor, who acclaimed her as the 'Madonna de América', their personal protectress. While Evita's own origins undoubtedly enhanced her appeal with the working classes, it won her the undying hostility of the upper classes. She also established and directed a charitable organization, the Fundación de Eva Perón, that became such a major provider of social welfare, including hospitals, housing, schools and hostels, that it virtually paralleled the state's welfare system. Consequently Evita's work with the trade unions and poor can be seen as a continuation, and extension, of that originally undertaken by her husband, as well as a perpetuation of the traditional politics of patronage. Evita was also instrumental in

securing, in 1947, the vote for women. As president of the Peronists' women's organization, she played an important role in re-electing Perón in 1951 with a massive female vote.

Her death from cancer in 1952 was a grave blow to Juan Perón and weakened not only Perón's support among the working classes but also his popular appeal. Evita's charisma, reforming achievements and early death converted her into a mythical figure, a sort of secular saint and national legend.

Eva Perón: The Myth of a Woman, J. M. Taylor (1979)
Evita, M. Navarro (1981)

Perón, Juan Domingo (1895–1974)

President of Argentina (1946–55, 1973–4) and founder of the Peronist movement. Having entered the army at the age of 16, Perón was eventually appointed a lecturer in military history at the Argentine Staff College in 1930. He later served as military attaché in Chile. During the late 1930s and early 1940s he travelled to Italy, Germany and Spain, learning a great deal at first hand about Fascism.

A participant in the coup of 1943, Perón, now a colonel, was rewarded with the directorship of the Secretariat of Labour and Welfare. The coup was to transform Perón's life. He built up the trade unions and improved their benefits in exchange for their loyalty, thereby creating a powerful mass following. This provided Perón with the springboard for his subsequent rise, as he first became Minister of War and then, in July 1945, Vice-President. Widespread disquiet within the established parties at Perón's fast-growing, potentially Fascist, power led to his arrest by the military junta three months later, but a mass demonstration organized principally by the trade unions on 17 October 1945 prompted his release. The Peronist movement had been born. A few days after his release, Perón married his mistress, the actress Eva Duarte. The following year, in

February 1946, he was elected President with 54 per cent of the vote.

Over the next decade Perón was to forge the Peronist movement out of dissident members of the Radical Party, nationalists, Catholics and the trade unions, particularly the General Confederation of Labour. The two pillars of the regime were the army, whose loyalty (once it had been purged) was assured through the granting of numerous privileges, and the trade unions. The movement therefore ranged from the extreme left to the extreme right of the political spectrum. Peronism was fervently nationalist (Perón was the first President to claim the possession of the Falkland Islands, or Malvinas) and populist with Fascist features (such as the personality cult and the subordination of civil society to the state). Instrumental in promoting the regime's social programme and maintaining the loyalty of the trade unions was Eva Duarte de PERON (Evita).

In keeping with his ultra-nationalist and populist rhetoric, Perón nationalized many leading industries, boosted the import-substitution businesses, and achieved a limited redistribution of wealth while developing the WELFARE STATE.

The death of Evita in 1952 was a major blow to Juan Perón as it undermined his general popularity, in particular his relationship with the trade unions. Increasingly severe economic problems and mounting opposition, particularly from the Catholic Church and the army, further eroded his support, as did the mounting contradictions of the Peronist movement's heterogeneous social base. Following the abortive coups of 1953 and June 1955, Perón was finally toppled by the army in September 1955 and fled into exile.

In exile (located in FRANCO's Spain from 1960 onwards), Perón was to exercise a powerful influence on events in Argentina. Though the Peronist movement had been declared illegal, he was still able to disrupt successive military regimes. This was due to his continuing hold over the trade unions and other groups, and the creation of new forces

such as the Montoneros (an urban guerrilla group dedicated to the armed struggle), as well as the sacred memory of Evita. Eventually, in 1972, Perón was permitted to return to Argentina, regaining the presidency the following year, at the age of 77, with over 60 per cent of the vote.

The greater heterogeneity of the Peronist movement as a result of the changes over the last two decades resulted in bitter in-fighting, especially between the revolutionary Montoneros, whom Perón was now determined to stamp out, and the reformist old guard. By the time Perón died in July 1974 the movement had become engulfed by schisms, the economy had run into serious difficulties after the OPEC PRICE RISE and the death squads had emerged.

Perón's Argentina, G. I. Blanksten (1974)
Perón: A Biography, J. A. Page (1983)
Resistance and Integration: Peronism and the Argentine Working Class, 1946–1976, D. James (1988)

Pinochet Ugarte, Augusto José Ramón (1915–)   Dictator of Chile (1973–90). From the port town of Valparaíso, Pinochet was the son of a dock clerk.

Commissioned in 1936, be rose to become, under President ALLENDE, commander-in-chief of the armed forces and a cabinet member in August 1973. Soon afterwards he organized the coup of 11 September 1973, which ended four decades of Chilean democracy, and took command of the ruling junta.

Pinochet's overriding aims once in power were to destroy the left and to implement an uncompromising neo-liberal economic policy in order to reduce radically the role of the state. At least 10,000 alleged left-wingers were therefore murdered during the dictatorship's first year, while many thousands more were jailed, tortured and exiled. Political activity in general was banned and severe censorship imposed. On the economic front, Pinochet first returned all properties expropriated under Allende to their former owners.

From 1975 the junta then applied MONE-TARISM and the shock treatment outlined by the Chicago school to bring under control the soaring inflation of the Allende years. What followed was South America's most radical experiment in neo-liberal economics, absent from South America since the 1920s, as the public sector and WELFARE STATE were devastated by the PRIVATIZATION of state enterprises, the liberalization of trade, the undermining of the trade unions, the slashing of public spending, and severe cut-backs in the social services. As a result, between 1976 and 1981 the economy expanded at 8 per cent a year and inflation was greatly reduced (from 600 per cent in 1973 to 31.2 per cent in 1980), while unemployment and inequality grew markedly as the boom benefited the upper, and, to a lesser extent, the middle classes, at the expense of the working classes.

Taking advantage of the economic 'miracle', Pinochet, who had hitherto ruled Chile by decree, tried to give his regime a measure of political legitimacy through a new constitution. Duly ratified in a heavily skewed plebiscite, the authoritarian constitution banned Marxist parties while allowing Pinochet to remain in office until 1989, when a second plebiscite would provide him with the opportunity for another eight years in power. However, in 1981–2 the economic bubble burst, through a combination of the international recession and a debt crisis, resulting in the worst downturn in Chilean history as the foreign debt soared to $17 billion. By 1985 the economy had largely recovered, the growth rate reaching 5–6 per cent, the highest level in the region. Yet nearly half the population still lived in poverty in 1988 while the top 5 per cent took 80 per cent of the national income. The regime faced increasing criticism in 1986 from the Catholic Church, the international community (including even the USA), as well as being under assault from guerrillas.

The 1988 plebiscite, designed as a further step in the legitimation of Pinochet's rule by approving his candidacy for the presidency, saw the dictator defeated by a 17-party coalition of left and centre parties that favoured the complete reinstatement of parliamentary democracy. The same coalition also triumphed in the congressional and presidential elections of the following year and assumed power in March 1990, Patricio Aylwin of the Christian Democrats being made President. Pinochet, claiming that his mission had been fulfilled, relinquished power reluctantly. However, he retained his position as commander of the army.

Pinochet subsequently became the spokesman for the army's outrage at the findings of the National Commission for Truth and Reconciliation of 1990–1, which concluded that the military dictatorship had pursued a 'systematic policy of extermination' against the opposition. However, the government refused to act on the Commission's investigations. Pinochet himself stayed on as head of the army until 1998.

Chile: The Pinochet Decade, P. O'Brien and J. Roddick (1983)

Pinochet: The Politics of Power, G. Arriagada (1988)

The Struggle for Democracy in Chile, P. W. Drake and I. Jaksic (eds) (1996)

Plaid Cymru (Party of Wales)   Welsh nationalist party. Unlike Scotland, Wales did not have its own distinctive political institutions at the end of the nineteenth century: English laws applied to Wales and the Church of England was the established religion. Plaid Cymru (PC) was formed in 1925 to seek independence for Wales and put great stress on defending Welsh language and culture, which were declining. In 1901 51 per cent of the people in Wales spoke Welsh but by 1971 this had dropped to 21 per cent, mainly in the rural areas of North and West Wales. Welsh nationalism was conservative and traditional, built round the chapel and with a strong sense of community. In the mainly English-speaking and increasingly secular parts of Wales, PC's promotion of the Welsh language was a serious political handicap, as it meant that its electoral appeal was confined to the Welsh-speaking areas. English-speakers feared that PC wanted to impose the Welsh language on them. PC was aware of this and so in the 1960s tried to widen its support by taking up economic issues. Its vote increased and in 1974 it won three seats for the first time in a general election, though the working class of South Wales continued to vote for the LABOUR PARTY.

'Scottish and Welsh Nationalist Parties since 1945', J. Kellas in *UK Political Parties Since 1945*, A. Seldon (ed.) (1990)

PLO (Palestine Liberation Organization)

A movement formed in 1964 to bring together various Palestinian groups who wanted to free Palestine from Israeli control. Its charter called for a 'democratic and secular Palestine' which should include all the territory (including the state of Israel) held by Britain as a mandate under the League of Nations. It therefore called for the 'elimination of Israel'. In its early years the PLO commanded little respect and met considerable hostility from some Arab states, Jordan resenting its claim to authority over the Palestinians living in Jordan. After the SIX DAY WAR (1967) the PLO realized it could not rely on Arab states to defeat Israel, so power passed to al-Fatah, which took control of the PLO in 1968–9 and made Yasir ARAFAT chairman.

Al-Fatah began guerrilla warfare against Israeli settlements from Jordan, which had the longest frontier with Israel and the largest Palestinian population. King HUSSEIN regarded the PLO as a threat to his kingdom and in Black September 1970 the Jordanian army attacked the PLO and evicted it from Jordan. The PLO moved its base to Lebanon, on Israel's northern frontier, from where raids and Israeli retaliation took place as in Jordan. The PLO became caught up in the LEBA-NESE CIVIL WAR in 1975, in which the Syrians and Israelis took part. In 1976 the Syrians

defeated the PLO but allowed it to continue its operations against Israel in the south. The Israeli invasion of Lebanon in 1982 was an attempt to crush the PLO. Defeated in the south the PLO was pushed back to Beirut from where, after two months of fierce fighting, it agreed to withdraw. When Israel withdrew from Lebanon, the PLO resumed activities in the south on a reduced scale. President ASAD of Syria expelled Arafat from Lebanon in 1983, so the PLO moved its headquarters to Tunis.

Various affiliated groups of the PLO, such as PFLP (Popular Front for the Liberation of Palestine), carried out attacks on Israeli targets outside the Middle East, often independently of the PLO. There were assassinations of Israelis and the taking of hostages but the events which gained most media attention for the PLO were the hijackings of civil aeroplanes. Israeli athletes were killed at the Munich Olympic Games (1972), an Italian liner, the *Achille Lauro*, was hijacked in 1973 and there were terrorist attacks on Rome and Vienna airports in 1985.

In 1974 the PLO was recognized by the ARAB LEAGUE as the sole representative of the Palestinian people and became a member of the League: a month later Arafat addressed the UNITED NATIONS, which gave the PLO observer status. The UN General Assembly affirmed Palestinian rights to independence and the right of PALESTINIAN REFUGEES to return to their homes and property. By this time the PLO leaders realized that the most they could hope for was a Palestinian state based on the Israeli OCCUPIED TERRI-TORIES of the WEST BANK and Gaza, but they would not gain this until they accepted Resolution 242 of the UN as a basis for negotiations. Not until 1988 did the PLO accept 242, the UN partition plan of 1947 (see ISRAEL, BIRTH OF) and Israel's right to exist. It also renounced terrorism. The INTI-FADA, violent demonstrations against Israeli rule, had already begun in Gaza and the West Bank with the support of the PLO. In 1990 the PLO supported Saddam HUSSEIN in the

GULF WAR, as he linked Iraq's future withdrawal from Kuwait with that of Israel from the occupied territories. This caused the GULF STATES to withdraw financial aid from the PLO.

Secret Israeli–Palestinian talks began in 1992 on an 'interim self-governing authority' in the occupied territories. Agreement was reached with the Oslo Accords in August 1993 on the PLO taking control of Gaza and Jericho by April 1994: there would be a transitional period of local self-government on the West Bank. The contentious issues of Israeli settlers and Jerusalem were left to be decided later. Arafat accepted Israel's right 'to exist in peace and security' and called for an end to the *intifada*, while Israel recognized 'the PLO as the representative of the Palestinian people'. Implementation was slow and very difficult but in September 1995 agreement was reached for Israel to withdraw gradually from the rest of the West Bank, a process which should be completed in 1999. The success of the Likud Party in Israel's 1996 general election and the appointment of Binyamin NETANYAHU as Prime Minister produced a severe obstacle to the implementation of the PEACE PROCESS, which ground to a halt in 1997.

The Palestine Liberation Organization, H. Cobban (1984)
The PLO, A. Gresh (1986)
The PLO under Arafat, S. Mishal (1986)

Pol Pot (1928–98)   Prime Minister of Kampuchea (Cambodia) (1975–9). Born Saloth Sar, the son of affluent peasants, he won a scholarship to study in Paris in 1948. There he joined the Cambodia section of the French Communist Party. He failed his engineering course and returned to Cambodia in 1953. When the INDOCHINA WAR OF INDEPENDENCE ended a year later he became fiercely anti-Vietnamese because the VIET MINH accepted an independent Cambodia without insisting on any role for the Khmer Rouge (Cambodian communists). From 1955–63 he

was a schoolteacher in Phnom Penh, becoming leader of the Khmer Rouge in 1962. He took refuge from the persecution of communists by Prince SIHANOUK by retiring to the safety of the mountainous north-east and during the VIETNAM WAR sought support from the Viet Minh for a rising against Sihanouk. His request was rejected because Sihanouk allowed HO CHI MINH to use part of Cambodia as a sanctuary for the VIET CONG and as a supply route to South Vietnam. During the guerrilla warfare against Sihanouk which began in 1968 he took the name Pol Pot. The opportunity for increasing his power base came with the US ATTACK ON CAMBODIA and US support for the unpopular Lon Nol regime, which unseated Sihanouk in 1970. The devastation caused by the US bombing of Cambodia greatly increased support for Pol Pot, who now had aid from North Vietnam, as Lon Nol had close relations with the US. Lon Nol was defeated by the Viet Minh in 1975, when Pol Pot became Prime Minister of the Democratic Republic of Kampuchea (DRK).

For the next four years Pol Pot carried out a draconian policy which was unparalleled in its brutality. Anyone who had worked for the Lon Nol regime, who had previous contact with Vietnam, was foreign educated (apart from Pol Pot himself and his close associates) or an intellectual was executed. Money, markets and religion were abolished, all Vietnamese were expelled and all citizens were moved from the towns into the countryside. Over three million people were forced to move, partly because of an ideological commitment to a state in which there would be only one class of peasants and workers, partly to disrupt social networks from which opposition groups might arise. In the countryside villages had to be self-sufficient: no one (except Khmer Rouge cadres) was allowed to move from one village to another. The penalty for disobeying orders was death. People were transferred to underpopulated areas in the north and east, where they had to carve fields out of the forests in malarial areas unsuited to rice production. Others had to work 18 hours a day on mass construction projects (dams and irrigation channels). Death from disease and starvation amounted to 80 per cent of the population in some areas. It is estimated that one and a half million people died in four years (1975–9). Agricultural production did increase under the Khmer Rouge but it was used to buy Chinese weapons, not to feed the starving. Pol Pot considered all opposition as treason. An attempt to replace him as leader in 1976 resulted in the first of a series of bloody purges within the party, in which thousands were tortured and killed. As relations with Vietnam deteriorated in 1978 Pol Pot decided that cadres in the east, in contact with Vietnam, were disloyal and so systematically killed them. His paranoia led him to mount attacks in Vietnam. These brought about the VIETNAMESE OCCUPATION OF KAMPUCHEA, which rapidly ended Pol Pot's rule and that of the Khmer Rouge.

Pol Pot returned to the Thai border where, succoured by the Thai government and China, he had to co-operate with non-communist opponents of Vietnam such as Sihanouk. He announced his retirement as military leader in 1985 but remained a powerful and feared figure in the Khmer Rouge. He is thought to be responsible for the Khmer Rouge accepting the political settlement of 1991 brokered by the UNITED NATIONS, for its boycott of the 1993 elections and for the military challenge to the government set up after that. As thousands of guerrillas defected to the government the Khmer Rouge disintegrated, leaving Pol Pot with only 2,000 followers in northern Cambodia. In June 1997 he ordered the execution of his former security chief, Son Sen, with his wife and family, and a month later was tried by his former commander in a classic CULTURAL REVOLUTION show trial, where successive speakers denounced him before a crowd of 500 villagers. Scarcely able to walk, he was sentenced to life imprisonment. The UN Human Rights Commission described his crimes as 'the worst to have occurred anywhere in the world since Nazism'.

Cambodia 1975–8: Rendezvous with Death, K. D. Jackson (1989)
Brother Number One: A Political Biography of Pol Pot, D. Chandler (1992)
The Pol Pot Regime 1975–9, B. Kiernan (1996)

Polisario   A Sahrawi liberation movement which aims to make the Western Sahara an independent country. The Western Sahara, an inhospitable desert area with a population of 250,000 nomadic Sahrawis, has the world's largest phosphate deposits (estimated at 1.7 trillion tons) and rich fishing off its Atlantic coast. It was a Spanish colony from 1884–1976 and though the UNITED NATIONS has called for a referendum on self-determination since 1966, FRANCO agreed that when Spain withdrew in 1976, two-thirds of the territory should go to Morocco and a third to Mauritania. The International Court of Justice said in 1975 that Morocco had no rights of sovereignty there.

Polisario was formed in 1973 and when Spain pulled out immediately proclaimed the new state of the Sahrawi Arab Democratic Republic. This became a member of the OAU (Organization of African Unity) in 1984, whereupon Morocco and Mauritania had to fight a war against 12,000 Sahrawi guerrillas, an economic burden which was too great for Mauritania, which withdrew from its part of the area, which Morocco proceeded to occupy. HASSAN II, King of Morocco, built at enormous expense one of the most extravagant feats of military engineering, a wall of sand, 12 feet high and 2,000 miles long, to keep guerrillas out of Morocco. Planned with US help, it is protected by barbed wire, fortifications, minefields and electronic surveillance and is manned by 150,000 troops. The Sahrawis were given military, diplomatic and logistical support by Algeria and QADDAFI in Libya. Algeria also provided shelter for over 100,000 Sahrawi refugees. In 1988 Polisario and Morocco accepted a UN plan for a referendum but President BUSH was reluctant to put pressure on Morocco, as Hassan provided troops for the US-led coalition in the GULF WAR. Morocco, exhausted financially by the war, agreed on a cease-fire with Polisario in 1991 but refused to withdraw and postponed the date of the referendum indefinitely. The Western Sahara is the UN's last major DECOLONIZATION problem.

Western Sahara: Roots of a Desert War, T. Hodges (1983)
The International Dimensions of the Western Sahara Conflict, Y. Zoubir and D. Volman (eds) (1992)

poll tax (community charge)   A local government tax imposed by the government of Margaret THATCHER in 1988–90. The CONSERVATIVE PARTY had long wanted to alter local government finances and get rid of the rates, which charged households according to the value of their property. Thatcher therefore declared that the community charge, a flat-rate tax to be paid by every adult, would be the flagship of her legislative programme after her victory in the 1987 election. She disliked the rates, as the poor often paid no rates at all yet made the greatest use of the social services. She also thought that the poll tax would make the poor vote more 'responsibly' at local elections for low-spending councils. Under the rating system they could vote for high-spending (Labour) councils because they did not have to pay for any of the services provided. Her officials and several ministers were opposed to the tax but only Nigel LAWSON spoke out against it. It was therefore introduced in Scotland in 1988–9 and in England a year later.

There was an immediate outcry, and widespread rioting because the greatest beneficiaries, as in so many of the tax changes introduced by the Conservatives, were the wealthy, an objection which many Conservatives shared. Some 38 million people were to pay the poll tax (14 million paid rates), so administration costs doubled but non-

payment was the most difficult problem: by early 1991 £1 billion was unpaid. Local authorities had therefore to increase the tax for those who were paying to cover the shortfall or to bring non-payers to court, a costly and cumbersome process with which the courts would not be able to cope. The tax was a disaster for Mrs Thatcher as it destroyed her authority, made her a political liability (by the spring of 1990 opinion polls put the Conservatives at under 30 per cent, 20 points behind the LABOUR PARTY) and contributed to her downfall. When John MAJOR replaced her as Prime Minister he decided to abandon the poll tax and in 1993 replaced it by a council tax which was similar to the old rates.

Pompidou, Georges (1911–74)   Prime Minister (1962–8) and President (1969–74) of France. The son of schoolteachers, he was a brilliant student at the prestigious *Ecole normale supérieure*. In 1944 he joined DE GAULLE's staff and his provisional government and became a member of the Gaullist party RPF when it was formed in 1947. Pompidou joined the Rothschild Bank in 1955 and within a year was its managing director. He returned to politics in 1958 when de Gaulle became President of the Fifth Republic and was the main French negotiator of the Evian agreements which ended the ALGERIAN WAR OF INDEPENDENCE (1954–62). He was invited by de Gaulle to become Prime Minister in 1962, though he was unknown to the public and was not an elected deputy or top civil servant. As Prime Minister he was overshadowed by de Gaulle until MAY 1968, when student demonstrations and worker strikes left the President disorientated. Pompidou coolly took charge of the situation, split the workers from the students in the Grenelle agreements and persuaded de Gaulle to call an election, which gave the Gaullist UDR a majority in the National Assembly (the UDR won 293 seats, its allies 64 and the opposition 127). Yet de Gaulle dismissed him in July, as he blamed Pompidou for making concessions to the workers. When de Gaulle resigned in 1969 Pompidou won the presidential election as the Gaullist candidate.

In office Pompidou was more affable and approachable than his remote predecessor and surprisingly interfered more than de Gaulle in government affairs. De Gaulle had restricted presidential initiatives to the 'reserved area' of defence and foreign policy: Pompidou extended them to economic and social matters. He saw his prime task as that of modernizing French industry. France had overtaken Britain in industrial output and in its standard of living in 1967 and continued its rapid growth under Pompidou. Pompidou adopted a Sixth Economic Plan in 1971, with massive investment in nuclear power, telecommunications and computerization. Industrial growth of 5.5 per cent a year created full employment: the real wages of workers rose by 35 per cent between 1969–73, making France more prosperous than ever before. As part of the modernization process Pompidou wanted to develop the infrastructure of communications. In 1967 France had only 500 miles of motorways. The President encouraged the private sector to become involved and in 1970 the *autoroute du Sud* (Paris–Lyon–Marseille) was completed and the *Boulevard Périphérique*, the ring road round Paris. He also gave Paris one of the best public transport systems in the world. The Métro was extended, rolling stock renewed and a new Regional Express Network linked the suburbs with Paris. The telephone system was also dramatically improved. Pompidou's ideas on urban renewal met with much less enthusiasm, as they involved building skyscrapers and dreary, dormitory new towns. His own monument was the Georges Pompidou Centre or Beaubourg, an enormous glass and tubular structure, which was a centre for modern art with a vast exhibition space. When it was opened in 1977 it immediately became the biggest tourist attraction in Paris.

Pompidou's foreign policy was, with one major exception, a continuation of that of de Gaulle. He maintained the general's nuclear deterrent, his anti-American stance and his pro-Arab policy, selling Mirage jets to Libya while maintaining an arms embargo on Israel. He also opposed any strengthening of the powers of the European Commission and rejected the political integration of European countries, but he differed from de Gaulle in approving the admission of Britain, Denmark and Ireland into the EEC. The OPEC PRICE RISE of 1973 was a great shock to France, where inflation doubled in 1973–4, and marked the beginning of a recession which Pompidou did not live to see. He was diagnosed as having leukaemia but continued to carry out his duties until the day before he died in April 1974.

Policy-making in France from de Gaulle to Mitterrand, P. Godt (ed.) (1989)
France Since the Popular Front, 1936–96, M. Larkin (1997)

population explosion   It took thousands of years for the earth's population to reach an estimated one billion by 1825. In the next 100 years it doubled to two billion and from 1925 to 1976 doubled again to four billion. By 1990 it was 5.3 billion and was expected to be eight or nine billion by 2025. The average world annual population growth from 1970–5 was 1.7 per cent but this covered wide divergences: 0.2 per cent in Europe, 3 per cent in Africa. The African population increased by 2.6 per cent a year in the 1960s, 2.9 per cent in the 1970s and over 3 per cent by the late 1980s, a doubling in size every 22 years, the biggest rate in the world. Some African countries showed a staggering increase: between 1960 and 1990 Kenya's population quadrupled from 6.3 to 25.1 million, that of the Ivory Coast from 3.5 to 12.6 million. Africa's population (including the North) rose from 281 to 647 million in that time. Yet the largest absolute increase was in Asia, though the rate was slowing down there. Of the 923 million increase in the world in the 1980s, 517 million took place in Asia (146 million in China, 166 million in India). Africa and Asia have increased their share of world population from 63.7 per cent (1950) to 71.2 per cent (1990).

The population explosion was made possible by public health schemes such as immunization promoted by the WORLD HEALTH ORGANIZATION, which reduced infant mortality and increased life expectancy, and in some areas by the GREEN REVOLUTION, which led to an increase in food production and a fall in the price of basic foods. The WORLD BANK said that from 1953–85 the price of rice fell by 42 per cent and of wheat by 57 per cent. Rapid urbanization in the THIRD WORLD, with all its attendant problems of overcrowding and crime, was one effect of the population increase. Another was to widen the NORTH–SOUTH DIVIDE and increased immigration, as countries with few resources could not feed adequately or employ the extra people. Population growth also contributed to ENVIRONMENTAL DISASTERS: the overgrazing of the African savannah, the destruction of the Amazon rain-forests and the salinization of land from India to Kazakhstan. It also led to serious conflict over water rights in the Middle East, as Jordan, Syria and Israel quarrelled over the water in the Jordan and Litani valleys.

In the developed countries (Western Europe had a fifth of the world's population in 1950 and a sixth in 1985), where birth rates were low because of economic security, female education and the availability of contraception, there was a fear of being outnumbered in certain areas by immigrants, which led to restrictive IMMIGRATION ACTS in Britain and France. There was concern too in the most populous country of all, China, which had 20 per cent of the world's population but only 7 per cent of its farmland. MAO ZEDONG had welcomed a large population but as fears grew that China would not be able to feed itself, the most draconian family planning system in the world was introduced: each family was limited to one child. By 1992 the Chinese birthrate had fallen to 19 per thousand (when it was 29 in India and an average of 37 in other developing countries) and its fertility rate to the replacement level of 2. Malthusian predictions that population increase will exceed the means of subsistence have not so far come about (except in Sub-Saharan Africa) but there is a general agreement that the projected growth cannot continue with current levels of consumption.

The Population Explosion, P. Ehrlich and A. H. Ehrlich (1990)
The State of the World Population, N. Sadik (1990)
Living Within Limits, G. Hardin (1993)

Portugal's colonial wars (1961–75)

When Britain, France and Belgium were pulling out of their African colonies in the late 1950s, Portugal was strengthening its control in Mozambique, Angola and Guinea-Bissau. This was partly for economic reasons. The oil, diamonds and coffee from Angola made a significant contribution to the Portuguese budget and encouraged Portuguese settlers to go to Africa: in 1974 there were 330,000 in Angola, 200,000 in Mozambique. The colonies were also a protected market for Portuguese exports, especially textiles and wine. Political considerations also played their part. 'Africa', wrote Caetano, who succeeded SALAZAR in 1968, 'is for us a moral justification and a *raison d'être* as a power. Without it we would be a small nation; with it we are a great power'. African grievances were long-standing: they were denied education and the right to form trade unions, were compelled to grow cash crops at the expense of food and were subject to forced labour. The wars, which began in Angola in 1961, in Guinea-Bissau in 1963 and Mozambique in 1964, were soon caught up in the COLD WAR, with each of the factions being supported by a foreign power.

The revolution which began in the cotton fields of northern Angola in 1961 was a Bakongo movement, inspired by the independence of the Belgian Congo (Zaire) nine months earlier. There was a different type of rising in the capital Luanda, where educated Africans resented their jobs in government service being taken by Portuguese immigrants. These early revolts, in which there were atrocities on both sides (about 20,000 Africans and 700 whites were killed), were easily put down. A weakness of the rebels was that there were two (later three) parties which were divided geographically and ethnically and which fought each other as well as the Portuguese. The FNLA (National Front for the Liberation of Angola), led by Holden Roberto, was based among the Bakongo people in the north and supported by MOBUTU of Zaire. Jonas Savimbi's UNITA (National Union for the Total Independence of Angola), which broke away from the FNLA in 1965, was strong among the Ovimbundu people of the south and east. The Marxist MPLA (Popular Movement for the Liberation of Angola), led from 1962 by Agustinho Neto, appealed for national rather than ethnic support, its main followers coming from urban Angolans round Luanda, *mesticos* (of mixed race) and Kimbundu people. The MPLA operated from Zambia, with the help of Kenneth KAUNDA, after it became independent in 1964, and received aid too from the Soviet Union and Tanzania, but the liberation movements were not strong enough to defeat the Portuguese, so a stalemate developed.

In Guinea-Bissau the rebellion was led by Amilcar Cabral and the PAIGC (African Party for the Independence of Guinea and Cape Verde). Operating in terrain (marshes and forests) suitable for guerrilla warfare, with the support of the local population and of Sékou Touré in neighbouring Guinea and supplied with arms by the Soviet Union, it was able to take control of two-thirds of the country by 1973.

The Portuguese army suffered significant defeats too in Mozambique, in spite of the sophisticated equipment supplied by NATO countries. The rebellion began there in 1964 when Samora Machel invaded with 250 men from Tanzania. Inspired by NKRUMAH and NYERERE, Frelimo (Front for the Liberation of Mozambique) had been set up in 1962 and sent its first recruits for guerrilla training to Algeria and Egypt a year later. The movement received support from the OAU (Organization of African Unity), Tanzania, Zambia, the Soviet Union and East European countries. In the areas it controlled Frelimo set up its own administration, schools and health services, to win the support of the local population, but rivalries within the movement weakened it: its leader Eduardo Mondlane was assassinated by a parcel bomb in 1969. From 1969–70 the Portuguese mounted Operation Gordian Knot to wipe out Frelimo's hold on northern Mozambique. Many Frelimo bases were overrun but the Portuguese army was exhausted by the effort, while Frelimo was able to use bases in Zambia to open up a new western front in Tete province. The Rhodesian railway to Beira was cut and Frelimo was able to provide bases for ZANU (Zambian African National Union) guerrillas to attack the Smith regime in Rhodesia. As Frelimo moved south and occupied a third of Mozambique, General Spinola realized that Portugal could not win the war and in *Portugal and the Future* wrote that the African wars were holding up Portuguese economic development, isolating it internationally and 'will finish by leading our country into revolutionary disintegration'. On 25 April 1974 junior and middle-ranking officers led the PORTUGUESE REVOLUTION which overthrew Caetano and aimed at DECOLONIZATION; the independence of Guinea-Bissau was granted in September 1974, of Mozambique and Angola in 1975.

Mozambique: From Colonialism to Revolution, A. Isaacman and B. Isaacman (1983)
The Decolonization of Portuguese Africa, N. MacQueen (1997)

Portuguese revolution (1974–6)   By the time António de Oliveira SALAZAR was incapacitated by a stroke in 1968, the foundations of the *Estado Novo* ('New State') dictatorship created by him in the 1930s were crumbling. This was partly due to the dramatic economic and social changes of the 1960s, including the shift of the workforce from the land to the cities, mass emigration, the expansion of the tourist industry, and the diversification abroad of Portuguese finance and industry, but above all to PORTUGAL´S COLONIAL WARS, which had been raging in Africa since the early 1960s. Junior and middle-ranking officers, who, radicalized by the conflict in Africa, had organized the Armed Forces Movement (MFA), overthrowing the regime in a coup on 25 April 1974. When the tanks trundled into central Lisbon, they were welcomed by euphoric crowds.

Over the next two years the 'Revolution' was to be characterized above all by a series of struggles within the army. Following the coup, the MFA established the Committee of National Salvation (JSN), made up of seven top-ranking officers, in order to legitimize the movement. Presided over by the monocled General António de Spínola, a hero of the colonial conflict who had none the less done more than anyone to call into question its continuity by advocating a political solution, the JSN proceeded to dismantle the institutions of Salazar's Estado Novo, introduce basic democratic freedoms, enact an amnesty for political prisoners, and initiate a debate on the future of the colonies. Spínola, who commanded a majority in both the JSN and the provisional government, also set about building up his support within the country at large with a view to filling the political vacuum that now existed with a Western-style parliamentary regime that removed the military from politics but established him as the DE GAULLE of Portugal. However, the MFA resented Spínola's right-wing populism as well as disagreeing over the future of the colonies: whereas the general sought to perpetuate Portuguese rule through a colonial federation, the MFA favoured DECOLON-IZATION, which it proceeded to implement. Spínola resigned on 30 September 1974, the new cabinet containing seven instead of one MFA officers as well as the politically radical Colonel Vasco Goncalves as Prime Minister.

Following Spínola's fall, the MFA began to contemplate a more durable political role for itself, resulting in the transfer of the executive powers of the JSN to the MFA-dominated Council of Twenty. The ongoing debate over the future of the regime, and the role of the MFA within it, divided the MFA between a left-wing, focused on the Prime Minister Vasco Goncalves, the supporters of Spínola on the right, and, finally, a faction under Major Melo Antunes, who aspired to a socialist regime within a Western-style parliamentary democracy.

An attempted coup by Spínola and his supporters in March 1975 led to their elimination from the political scene as the general fled to Spain. The MFA therefore shifted to the left, declaring itself a 'national liberation movement' and centralizing power in the Council of the Revolution, as reflected in the large-scale nationalization of industries, banks and insurance companies. The MFA was trying to create a populist, left-wing regime rooted in the masses, but independent of the emerging political parties, which it saw as rivals. A number of popular, spontaneous mobilizations were encouraged from above, such as factory takeovers, the formation of neighbourhood committees, and land occupations in the south, which gave the transition from the Salazar dictatorship to democracy its revolutionary tone.

Elections for a constituent assembly were allowed to go ahead by the MFA, but on the condition that the civilian political parties accepted a supervisory role for the MFA over the next three to five years. Most of the parties, including the Socialist Party under Mário Soares, defended the establishment of a liberal parliamentary regime, while the communists aligned themselves with the left-wing of the MFA. The desire of the electorate, over 90 per cent of which turned out to vote, for moderate change was reflected in the support for the Socialist Party (37.9 per cent) and the

Popular Democratic Party (26.4 per cent). By contrast, the pro-Soviet Communist Party garnered a mere 12.5 per cent. Much as the MFA had feared, the moderate political parties now competed with it for power. During the 'Hot Summer' of 1975 a struggle was unleashed between the socialists, in alliance with military moderates under Major Melo Antunes, and the increasingly communist-dominated government.

In July 1975 the moderates, including the socialists, left the government in protest at the communists' influence, only for the new, and fifth, provisional government to be even more closely associated with the Communist Party. As a result, the faction under Major Antunes, known as the Group of Nine, demanded that the links between Prime Minister Goncalves and the communists be severed. Given that the Group of Nine now enjoyed widespread support within the MFA, Goncalves and the other radicals backed down. The socialists and social democrats therefore formed a government on 19 September 1975, with the communists in opposition. Thus the MFA finally supported the establishment of a liberal parliamentary democracy and the armed forces withdrew from the political arena.

On 25 November 1975 the radical left, including Goncalves, attempted to seize power. The abortive coup, which had brought Portugal to the brink of civil war, marked the end for the radicals and the final triumph of the Group of Nine. In June 1976 Colonel Ramalho Eanes, who had overseen the defeat of the 25 November 1975 uprising, was elected President, while Mario Soares became Prime Minister of the first constitutional government the following month. The moderates' anti-communist strategy had triumphed, not least through the vigorous backing of the US and EEC, which together had provided Portugal with $272 million in emergency aid in October 1975.

Although the 'Portuguese Revolution', which had transformed the country, was undoubtedly shaped by popular mobilizations and the political parties, it was not the outcome of a mass revolutionary upsurge, but an élitist affair determined largely by factional struggles within the armed forces. Despite this, less than 20 people lost their lives during the events of 1974–6, in contrast to over 200 during the civilian-dominated TRANSITION in Spain.

Portugal, T. Gallagher (1983)
Portugal, W. C. Opello (1991)
The Making of Portuguese Democracy, K. Maxwell (1997)

Prague Spring (1968)   The attempt by Dubček and other reformers to establish 'socialism with a human face' in Czechoslovakia. The reform movement originated within the Czechoslovak Communist Party (CCP) in the early 1960s as the economy was declining: in 1963 there was a negative growth rate. Reformers such as Ota Šik persuaded the Party Congress in 1966 to combine central planning with features of the free market but the NOMENKLATURA dragged their heels and little was done. This convinced some that economic reform was impossible without political reform. Slovaks too wanted change, as they felt that nearly all key positions in the republic went to Czechs.

In January 1968 Novotný was replaced as head of the CCP by Alexander Dubček, First Secretary of the Slovak CP, though Novotný retained his post as President of Czechoslovakia. Censorship ended in March, so free expression was possible for the first time in 20 years; the victims of GOTTWALD's purges of the 1950s were rehabilitated and Novotný gave up his remaining post as President. The CCP published its Action Programme in April, which talked of 'a new, profoundly democratic model of Czechoslovak socialism'. Dubček's ideas drew on those of Nagy in Hungary and anticipated those of GORBACHEV. The CCP should retain its leading role but it had to justify this by 'winning over all workers by persuasion and example'. Instead of unthinking obedience 'each member of the Party ... has not only the right but the duty to act according to his conscience'. Decision-making should be decentralized and works councils in industry elected. Freedom of association and expression was to be guaranteed and citizens would have the right to travel abroad. There was to be genuine equality between Czechs and Slovaks. Dubček was anxious to avoid Nagy's mistakes, so stated that Czechoslovakia's membership of the WARSAW PACT and alliance with the Soviet Union were 'the cornerstone of Czechoslovak foreign policy'.

These reforms caused great concern in the USSR and its East European satellites, particularly in East Germany and Bulgaria. There were demands that the CCP should control the media and non-communist organizations and threatening Warsaw Pact manoeuvres took place in Czechoslovakia in June and July. Soviet leaders were particularly worried about the extraordinary Congress of the CCP, due to be held in September, as they feared that even more radical reforms (such as the demand for independent political parties) would be put forward then. Fearing that Dubček had lost control of the situation 500,000 troops, mainly Soviet but with small contingents from East Germany, Poland, Hungary and Bulgaria, invaded Czechoslovakia on 21 August in the largest military operation in Europe since the Second World War. The forces used were twice as large as those used in the HUNGARIAN RISING (1956). There was no violent resistance: between 80 and 200 people were killed. The Czechoslovak leaders were taken, almost as prisoners, to Ukraine. The Soviet Union wanted to impose a puppet government, as it had done during the Hungarian Rising of 1956, but could not find anyone to lead it. Dubček and other leaders were therefore freed and returned to their former positions but they had to give up their reforms. The BREZHNEV DOCTRINE was announced in *Pravda* on 26 September to justify Soviet interference and to warn other satellites not to step out of line. Gradually, reformers were removed from the Presidium of the CCP, which led the student Jan

Palach to immolate himself in Prague's Wenceslas Square on 16 January 1969. In April Dubček was replaced as First Secretary of the CCP by Gustav HUSÁK. 'Normalization' had begun.

The Slovaks benefited from the Prague Spring, as in January 1969 Slovakia became a republic of equal status with the Czech lands in the federal republic. The overall failure of the reforms, however, showed the narrow limits within which Soviet satellite states would be allowed to move. The long-term impact was felt most by reformers in the Soviet Union. Gorbachev drew many lessons from the Prague Spring, including his determination not to use force in Eastern Europe, a decision that made possible the REVOLUTIONS OF 1989–91.

The Czechoslovak Experiment, 1968–9, I. Svitak (1971)
Reform Rule in Czechoslovakia: The Dubček Era 1968–9, G. Galia (1973)
Soviet Intervention in Czechoslovakia, 1968, J. Valenta (1979)

PRI (*Partido Revolucionario Institucional*: Institutional Revolutionary Party)

The dominant political party in Mexico from 1929 to the end of the twentieth century. Founded in 1929 as the National Revolutionary Party by President Calles, a revolutionary general, it provided a long period of political stability through its emphasis on equality and basic welfare for the poor and the common citizenship of all ethnic groups. It absorbed about 400 liberal and socialist parties which had arisen during the Mexican Revolution and also the civil service and armed forces. The party became synonymous with the state and adopted the colours of the Mexican flag. It won every presidential and state election, had an overwhelming majority in both houses of Congress and controlled most officials down to the municipal level. In 1938 President Lázaro Cárdenas reorganized the party and renamed it the Mexican Revolutionary Party, dividing it into four sections (military, agriculture, labour and popular) so that it represented society as a whole and so that the party could control competing sections within a single movement. Miguel Alemán, the first civilian President, carried out a further reorganization, dropped the military sector and gave the party its present name. The three sections became the Confederation of Mexican Workers, the National Peasant Confederation and the National Confederation of Popular Organizations for government employees and professional groups, including the army. The PRI distributed patronage profusely through its control of the many state industries and this led to endemic corruption. Other parties could make little impact as the PRI had effective control of all institutions of state, television and radio and most of the press.

The PRI used the phrase 'electoral alchemy' to refer to the dishonest practices it used to win every election by a huge majority (until 1988). In the 1976 presidential election López Portillo stood unopposed as the PRI candidate and claimed 98.7 per cent of the vote. Subsequent elections showed a drop in support for the PRI until in 1988 Salinas obtained only 50.7 per cent of the vote in the presidential election and the PRI gained 51.9 per cent in the congressional election, the opposition claiming that they were rigged. The palpable loss of support occurred because in the 1980s growth rates were near zero and real wages fell 40 per cent. There was also a conflict within the party between the *politicos* (the old party managers) and the younger *tecnicos* (technocrats), who wanted to modernize the economic system. Cuauhtémoc Cárdenas, son of Lázaro, formed a democratic movement within the party before forming his own Party of the Democratic Revolution (PRD), which attracted wide popular support, as did PAN (*Partido de Acción Nacional*), which appealed to business. Opposition parties began to win seats in Congress in the late 1970s, won their first Senate seats in 1988 and first state governorship in 1989. By 1990 the PRI's corporate machinery was breaking down, as the Peasant Confederation broke away to ally with the PRD. Salinas himself recognized that Mexico could not remain a state where power was monopolized by one party and by PRIVATIZATION removed the patronage on which the PRI had relied. The PRI suffered electoral defeat in the mid-term elections of July 1997, when it lost control of the lower house, holding 239 out of 500 seats. It was still the largest party and controlled the Senate but it also lost control of Mexico City, the capital, where Cárdenas was the first directly elected mayor, with twice the number of votes of his PRI rival.

privatization　The sale of nationalized industries to the private sector. This was pioneered in Britain by the governments of Margaret THATCHER, though privatization was scarcely mentioned in the CONSERVATIVE PARTY manifesto of 1979. In her first administration (1979–83) the aim in the nationalized industries was to reduce the subsidies they required by setting strict financial limits. There were some modest privatizations, of British Aerospace, British Cable and Wireless and the National Freight Company, but a more systematic programme was not worked out until her second administration (1983–7). Privatization then became a central feature of her programme and the part for which she became renowned abroad. Thatcher saw both economic and political advantages in privatization. The state would save money by not paying subsidies, which it was believed prevented industries becoming competitive. The money thus saved and the revenue raised by selling nationalized industries could be used to cut income tax and to reduce the PSBR. There was also the benefit to the government as it was no longer responsible for determining wages, which in the private sector could be left to market forces: this would avoid confrontation with the TRADE UNIONS. A political benefit was the creation of a property-owning democracy which would support the Conservatives and force the

LABOUR PARTY to embrace the market economy and abandon nationalization, as this would alienate millions of small shareholders.

The large-scale privatization of British Airways, the Trustee Savings Bank, British Gas, Rolls-Royce, Rover, Jaguar and BP took place, raising the number of shareholders from three million in 1979 to eleven million in 1991 and bringing into the Treasury £24 billion by 1987. The share of public corporations in the economy was cut by half to 5 per cent of GDP. These sales were very popular as shares were sold at below market prices; buyers could therefore sell quickly and make a handsome profit (the value of British Telecom shares, for example, went up by 91 per cent in the first week). Another form of popular capitalism was the sale of council houses. The Housing Act of 1980 gave council tenants the right to buy their houses and, as with the other privatizations, they were sold at less than their market value, because of discounts given to tenants based on the length of their residency. By 1990 20 per cent of council houses had been sold and this too had a political pay-off. At the time of the 1987 election 57 per cent of working-class households were owner-occupied; 44 per cent voted Conservative, 32 per cent Labour and 24 per cent Liberal/SDP.

By the end of the decade privatization was less popular, as it was seen in many cases that a public monopoly had simply become a private monopoly: what was good for shareholders (higher profits) was not good for consumers (higher prices). To protect the interests of the public regulatory bodies had been set up but they did not prevent 80 per cent of the population opposing the privatization of the water companies in 1989. The privatization of the railways, rushed through in 1996–7 before a general election, was widely considered over-elaborate, even chaotic, and was also unpopular. The privatization of some industries benefited the consumer: the prices charged by British Telecom fell in real terms by 35 per cent by 1997. Other privatizations did not: water companies made £10 billion profit (by 1997), yet water bills rose by a third in real terms.

Privatization was regarded abroad as a great success and was widely copied. Jacques CHIRAC used British privatization as a model when he privatized French state banks and other businesses from 1984–6, but it was not only in countries with conservative regimes that privatization was admired. Socialist regimes in Portugal, Spain, Australia and New Zealand went in for privatization, as did the ex-communist countries of Eastern Europe after the REVOLUTIONS OF 1989–91. In Hungary 1,600 new companies were created from nationalized industries in 1988–9, though the pace was slower in Poland and Russia, in spite of Boris YELTSIN's acceptance of the market economy. Privatization was carried out in Singapore, Malaysia and Korea, and in Latin America, in Chile, Brazil and Mexico. Only in Africa was progress towards privatization very slow.

Privatization in Western Europe, V. Wright (ed.) (1994)

Q

***

Qaddafi, Muammar (1942–) Head of state in Libya (1969–). A Bedouin, he was politically active at school, from which he was expelled for organizing a demonstration against the monarchy. Qaddafi then joined the army and was trained at the Benghazi Military Academy, passing out as an officer in 1966. Opposed to the monarchy, which he saw as subservient to British and American interests, he formed a Free Officers movement (in imitation of that in Egypt which had deposed King Faruq), which carried out a coup in 1969 when King Idris was in Turkey.

A Revolutionary Command Council (RCC) of 12 members, with Qaddafi as its chairman, took over control of the country, ended the defence agreements with Britain and the US and their bases in Libya, closed the churches and introduced Islamic laws which forbade alcohol and gambling and imposed penalties of amputation for theft and stoning for adultery. Greatly influenced by NASSER and the Ba'th Party, Qaddafi's ideas were an amalgam of Arab nationalism, socialism and Islam. He saw himself as a new Mahdi (Divinely Guided One), sent to lead the Islamic world. His ideas were most fully developed in the *Green Book* (green is the colour of Islam) where he put forward a Third Universal Theory, in opposition to communism and capitalism. It involved handing over power to the people in a *Jamahiriya* (state of the masses). Political parties were banned, as they represented sectional interests. All Libyans were members of a local Popular Congress which elected delegates to a General People's Congress (the equivalent of a parliament), which was the

ruling body and replaced the RCC in 1977, though all major decisions were made by Qaddafi himself. In the new economic system private shops and factories were abolished, and foreign companies nationalized. Workers were encouraged to take over businesses, students replaced diplomats at embassies abroad and untrained people moved in to run government departments. The result was chaos: most goods were unobtainable, except on the black market. By 1988 Qaddafi had to admit that his new system was not working. Private shops were encouraged to reopen and revolutionary committees were deprived of most of their powers. Qaddafi's development plans (there were three between 1973 and 1989) were more successful. In a country of over a million square miles, of which only 2 per cent is arable, the greatest project was to pump water from beneath the southern desert to the coast, where most of the three to four million population lived. The vast oil revenues (which rose to $22 billion in 1980 before declining to $6 billion in the early 1990s) gave Libya the highest per capita income in Africa ($8,800 in 1989) and enabled Qaddafi to provide education, roads, free health and social services, a minimum wage and a guaranteed right to work.

From the moment he seized power Qaddafi was involved in disputes with other Arab leaders. He organized an unsuccessful coup against President NIMEIRI of the Sudan in 1975, fought a brief frontier war with Egypt in 1977, was implicated in the assassination of SADAT in 1979 and supported KHOMEINI in the IRAN–IRAQ WAR (1980–8). An inveterate opponent of Arab monarchies, which he regarded as un-Islamic, he backed an attempt to overthrow King HASSAN II of Morocco in 1974, and in 1979 financed the seizure of the grand Mosque, Mecca, hoping that this would bring down the Saudi royal family. Qaddafi's subversive activities were not confined to other Arab states. He supported Muslim minority movements in the Philippines and Thailand, gave aid to AMIN, backed the northern Muslims in the Chad Civil War (in order to occupy the Aouzou strip on the border of Libya and Chad) and spent huge amounts of money in black Africa, especially in Nigeria and Rwanda, in attempting to convert Christians to Islam. Qaddafi blamed European imperialism, the US, neo-colonialism and Israel for all the ills of the Arab world and so gave help to militant causes everywhere. From the mid-1970s Qaddafi supplied the IRA with arms, money and explosives: the seizure of £15 million of arms in the coaster *Eksund* by French customs officers in 1987 led to the exposure of Libya's terrorist connections in Europe as a whole. President REAGAN condemned him as 'the leading international terrorist and criminal' and in 1986 ordered US RAIDS ON LIBYA by aircraft. Qaddafi did more than anyone to identify Islam in the Western mind with terrorism, particularly when Libya was held responsible for the bomb which exploded on Pan Am flight 103 over Lockerbie in Scotland in 1988. The US and Britain persuaded the UNITED NATIONS to impose sanctions on Libya in 1992 because Qaddafi refused to extradite two Libyans suspected of being responsible, though Libya's main export, oil, was unaffected.

Libyan Politics, Tribe and Revolution, J. Davis (1987)
The State and Social Transformation in Tunisia and Libya, L. Anderson (1987)
The Green and the Black: Qadhafi's Policies in Africa, R. Lemarchand (ed.) (1988)

Quebec nationalism   A variety of movements wishing to protect the distinctive-

ness of the Canadian province. Some Quebec nationalists wanted greater autonomy within the Canadian federation, others an independent state separated from the rest of Canada. The dominant ethos in Quebec was Catholic, conservative and agrarian until the 1950s, when a substantial middle class of intellectuals and professional groups grew up. This wanted to get rid of the clerical control of education and the social services and to end the domination of Anglophones (English-speaking Canadians) in the economy and civil service. Francophones (French-speaking Canadians) felt discriminated against: in the 1950s they formed 25 per cent of the population, yet held only 10 per cent of the top posts in the federal civil service. They also felt threatened by Canada's increasing population (from 11.5 to 22 million between 1941–76), as the Francophone birthrate declined.

In 1960 the Liberals came to power in Quebec under Jean Lesage, who introduced a Quiet Revolution (1960–6) against US and English economic and cultural domination. The provincial government took direct control of education and social services from the Catholic Church, created a network of state enterprises and demanded changes in the Confederation that would give Quebec greater revenues and jurisdiction. This did not go far enough for radical nationalists, who wanted immediate independence. Some nationalists resorted to violence and in 1963 there were several bombing incidents. Lesage and the Liberals were defeated in the 1966 Quebec election by the *Union Nationale*, led by Daniel Johnson. 'What we must claim and obtain for Quebec', he declared, 'is recognition as a national state'. He was encouraged in this by General DE GAULLE's visit to Montreal's Expo 1967 when, speaking from the balcony of the City Hall in Montreal, the general called '*Vive le Québec libre*'. In 1967 René Lévesque, unable to persuade the Liberal Party to support Quebec nationalism, left it and formed his own *Parti Québecois* (PQ), which called for a new relationship between Quebec and the rest of Canada:

sovereignty–association (equal status with the federal government for Quebec). It seemed to have little chance of success when, in the 1970 Quebec election, the Liberals obtained a large majority, the PQ winning only seven seats.

The year 1970 was a violent one in Canada, when extreme nationalists turned from bombs, protest marches and bank robberies to kidnapping in the OCTOBER CRISIS. Prime Minister TRUDEAU responded energetically to crush those responsible. The PQ lost support, but with high unemployment in Quebec it recovered to win control of the Quebec legislature in 1976 and soon passed measures to make French the only official language in Quebec. Lévesque held a referendum in 1980 on 'sovereignty–association' but 60 per cent of the Quebec electorate voted against it.

The federal government had consistently opposed Quebec independence, but at the same time tried to reassure Francophones that they would not be treated as second-class citizens and that their language would have equal status with English. Lester PEARSON had set up a Royal Commission on Bilingualism and Biculturalism (1963–71) which recommended that both English and French should be official languages throughout the federal civil service and in business. This became law in the Official Languages Act of 1969. Trudeau, from Quebec himself, was opposed to giving special status to Quebec but sought in revising the constitution in 1982 to add a Charter of Rights which would protect the interests of Francophones. Quebec did not sign the new constitution, so MULRONEY began new negotiations which in 1987 produced the Meech Lake Accords, which recognized Quebec as a 'distinct society'. This was accepted by Quebec but it never became law, as two provinces had refused to ratify it by the 1990 deadline because it gave preferential treatment to Quebec. Another attempt at a settlement was made in the Charlottetown Agreement of 1992, which gave greater autonomy to Quebec, but this was rejected in a nationwide referendum by 54.4 per cent to 44.6 per cent. These failures to amend the constitution in ways that would satisfy Quebec led to a revival of the PQ and of Quebec separatism. A referendum in October 1995 rejected independence for Quebec by the slimmest of margins and prevented, at least temporarily, Canada being thrown into confusion, as an independent Quebec would split the rest of Canada into two unconnected pieces, leaving two million Canadians in the Atlantic provinces isolated from Ontario and the West.

Quebec: Social Change and Political Crisis, K. McRoberts (1988)

R

Rabin, Yitzhak (1922–95) Prime Minister of Israel (1974–7, 1992–5). Born in Jerusalem (his mother was Russian, his father American), he took part in the Allied invasion of Syria in 1941 against the Vichy French. From 1943–8 he commanded a Palmach (the commando unit of the Israeli defence force) brigade and in the War of Independence (1948–9) directed the defence of Jerusalem and fought against Egypt in the Negev. After the war he continued with his army career, graduating from the British Staff College in 1953 and becoming Chief of Staff (1964–8). In that post he worked out the strategy (rapid deployment of reserves and the destruction of enemy aircraft on the ground) which was so successful in the SIX DAY WAR (1967). In 1968 he retired from the army and was ambassador to the US from 1968–73. There he built up a close relationship with President NIXON and his national security adviser Henry KISSINGER, which led to the US giving increased economic and military aid to Israel. Elected to the Knesset (Israeli parliament), he joined Golda Meir's government and when Meir suddenly resigned in 1974 Rabin beat his rival Shimon PERES to became leader of the Labour Party and Israel's first native-born Prime Minister.

A cautious pragmatist, dour and determined, he made two military disengagement agreements as a result of Kissinger's shuttle diplomacy, by which Israel pulled out of part of Sinai in return for massive American aid and a guarantee of Israel's oil supplies, though there was no full peace agreement with Egypt as he was not prepared to give up the whole of Sinai. With a reputation as a hawk in security matters, he ordered the Entebbe raid in Uganda in July 1976 to free Israeli hostages seized by Palestinians. In 1977 he stepped down as Labour Party leader because of a breach of currency regulations and was replaced by Peres. In the Labour–Likud coalition of 1984–90 he was Minister of Defence and arranged for the withdrawal of Israeli troops (except in the security zone next to the Israeli border) in the LEBANESE CIVIL WAR. He was also responsible for Israel's brutality in dealing with the INTIFADA.

In 1992 he replaced Peres as leader of the Labour Party and became Prime Minister again when Labour won the election in the same year, after three defeats under Peres. He was more flexible than Yitzhak SHAMIR, who did not want to give up any of the OCCUPIED TERRITORIES seized in the Six Day War. The PEACE PROCESS, the attempt to make a settlement with the Palestinians about the WEST BANK and Gaza, moved very slowly and was interrupted by tough Israeli action against HAMAS bombers who wanted to disrupt the negotiations. Attacks on northern Israeli settlements by HIZBULLAH led in 1993 to the most severe Israeli air and artillery attacks on Lebanon since the Israeli invasion of Lebanon in 1982. A breakthrough came in September 1993 when Israel and the PLO both recognized each other and established a timetable for gradual Palestinian self-rule in the occupied territories. Peres, his Foreign Minister, was responsible for the Oslo Accords, but without Rabin's approval there would have been no agreement. This was a major turning-point in the history of the Middle East, as Israel was accepting the partition of Palestine. For these agreements Rabin, with Peres and Yasir ARAFAT, was awarded the Nobel Peace Prize in 1994. Rabin also indicated in 1994 that he would be prepared for a full withdrawal from the GOLAN HEIGHTS in return for a peace settlement with Syria. Israel militarily withdrew from the Gaza Strip and Jericho in May. In 1994 he made a peace treaty with Jordan ending a state of war which had existed for 46 years. Rabin made a further agreement in September 1995 to withdraw gradually from the rest of the West Bank, excluding the areas of Jewish settlement, by 1999. The deep divisions in Israeli society between those who did not want to give up any of the occupied territories and those, like Rabin, who regarded them as an economic, political and military burden, led to Rabin's assassination by an Israeli student on 4 November 1995.

Rafsanjani, Ali Akbar Hashemi (1934–)

President of Iran (1989–97). The son of a moderately wealthy farmer, he studied theology at Qum under KHOMEINI and followed him in his opposition to MUHAMMAD RIZA PAHLAVI. Rafsanjani continued to work against the Shah after Khomeini was exiled in 1964 and was imprisoned several times, though he managed to make a considerable fortune from land speculation. In 1978 he helped to organize the demonstrations which produced the IRANIAN REVOLUTION (1978–9) and the fall of the Shah. In the ISLAMIC REPUBLIC OF IRAN which followed Khomeini's return, he was involved in purging opponents of the regime as deputy Minister of the Interior before becoming Speaker of the Majlis (parliament) in 1980, a position which made him the most powerful figure in Iran after Khomeini. In 1986 he was involved in secret diplomacy with the US which erupted in the IRAN–CONTRA AFFAIR. As acting Commander-in-Chief (1988) he persuaded Khomeini to bring the IRAN–IRAQ WAR (1980–8) to an end. After the death of Khomeini in 1989 he was involved in a power struggle with Islamic radicals which he won by being elected President of Iran with enhanced powers, as the post of Prime Minister was abolished.

A pragmatist, he wanted to end open hostility to the West, as Iran needed Western aid to recover from the devastation of the war, but he was constrained by the radicals, who were determined to prevent Iran from becoming again dependent on the US. He nevertheless reduced support for HIZBULLAH in the LEBANESE CIVIL WAR and put pressure on Islamic militants there to release Western hostages. Rafsanjani condemned Saddam HUSSEIN's invasion of Kuwait but kept Iran neutral in the GULF WAR. The collapse of the Soviet Union after the AUGUST COUP of 1991 enabled him to extend Iranian influence to the newly independent states of Central Asia and the Caucasus. He would not get politically involved in Central Asia, as this would deflect him from economic recovery at home, and did not take the side of the SHII Azeris in the NAGORNO-KARABAKH CONFLICT between Armenia and Azerbaijan, as the Armenians were hostile to Turkey, Iran's rival in the region. Iran was in a strong position as it could provide access to the sea for the landlocked states of the area: Rafsanjani gained a considerable success when Azerbaijan decided to send its oil pipeline through Iran rather than through Russia or Armenia. At home his policy of PRIVATIZATION and the reduction of subsidies was opposed by Ayatollah Kamenei, Khomeini's successor as Supreme Leader. The economy was severely depressed and corruption widespread, with the rial in September 1994 worth one fortieth of its pre-revolution value. Inflation was crippling for the salaried middle- and working classes. Government-sponsored bodies such as the Foundation for the Disinherited were a dead weight on the economy, which attracted little long-term investment because of the insecurity. Rafsanjani had to cope with deepening disillusionment with the regime, which prompted the pious former Prime Minister, Mehdi Bazargan, to say that the

Islam which has prevailed since the Iranian Revolution has caused many Iranians to lose their faith completely.

Rákosi, Mátyás (1892–1971)

Head of the Hungarian Communist Party (1945–55). Taken prisoner by the Russians in the First World War, he became a Bolshevik before returning to Hungary in 1918. There he was a founder member of the Hungarian Communist Party and commander of the Red Guard in Bela Kun's Soviet Republic (1919). After its fall he escaped to the USSR, where he worked for the Comintern. In 1924 he returned to Hungary but was arrested a year later and imprisoned from 1925–40. Expelled to the Soviet Union in 1940 he was sent back to Hungary with the Red Army in 1945 to prepare the country for an eventual communist takeover.

Intelligent, cynical and ruthless, he followed what he called 'salami tactics', removing one group after another, slice by slice, from the coalition government which ruled Hungary at the end of the war, until he was ordered by STALIN in 1947 to stop the 'parliamentary pirouetting' and take over complete control. Opposition parties were banned and in 1948 Rákosi forced the Social Democrats to merge with the communists. A devoted Stalinist, he copied the Soviet model in forcing the peasants into collective farms and in producing a Five Year Plan, which aimed to make Hungary into a 'country of steel and iron'. Peasants were given high compulsory delivery quotas, while the state paid low prices for their produce, with the result that their standard of living fell by 30 per cent between 1945–52. All private firms and banks were nationalized. Workers' production norms were raised and their wages reduced, so their living standards plummeted too. By 1953, with an inefficient, centralized economy and high military expenditure, Hungary was almost bankrupt.

Such a system survived only by terror, which was harsher than in other East European countries. There was a series of SHOW TRIALS, which ended in leading communists such as László Rajk, the foreign minister, being executed. Between 1949–53 750,000 (out of a population of 10 million) were investigated, of whom 150,000 were sent to prison or concentration camps. The atmosphere of terror pervaded every aspect of life, so that parents dared not reveal their true beliefs even to their children. In the thaw which followed the death of Stalin in 1953, the Soviet leaders told Rákosi that he had mismanaged the economy and relied too much on terror. They forced him to give up his post as Prime Minister to Imre Nagy but he remained First Secretary. As tension continued in Hungary, and as KHRUSHCHEV was reconciled to TITO, Rákosi was removed at Soviet insistence from all his party and governmental positions. He retired to the Soviet Union, where he lived for the rest of his life.

Rawlings, Jerry (1947–)

Head of state in Ghana (1979, 1981–). Son of a Scotsman and a Ghanaian, he was commissioned as an officer in the Ghanaian Air Force in 1969. As a Flight-Lieutenant he led junior officers and NCOs in a coup against the military government in June 1979, promising to restore civilian government after an election. There was wide support for the coup and a desire to end the corruption and incompetence of the professional middle classes and army who had run the country. As chairman of the Armed Forces Revolutionary Committee Rawlings acted decisively: eight military leaders were tried and executed, a popular move in Ghana but condemned abroad. People's Courts confiscated the assets of profiteers and corrupt officials. In September 1979 Rawlings handed over power to a civilian government and retired from the armed forces in November.

As the economic situation continued to deteriorate and there were corruption scandals, Rawlings seized power again in December 1981 but this time did not promise to return to civilian rule. The constitution was abolished, parliament dissolved and political parties banned. The country was run by the Provisional National Defence Council (PNDC), of which Rawlings was chairman, and which included civilian officials. Mass participation at the local level was popular but this popularity did not last, partly because of events beyond government control. In 1982–3 a severe drought led to food shortages and price increases and in 1983 the Nigerian government expelled a million Ghanaians. The result was misery, starvation, disease and increased crime. There were attempted coups for which 34 people were executed (1984–7) and university students went on strike. Rawlings responded with repression, detaining political opponents and tightly controlling the press. Close relations and trade agreements with the communist Eastern bloc and Cuba had strained relations with the US, whose support was needed if Ghana was to obtain loans from the IMF and WORLD BANK. These were obtained but at the cost of austerity budgets in 1983–4, which caused much suffering in the form of high unemployment, fuel prices and sales taxes. There were several devaluations of the currency (in 1988 it was two per cent of its 1982 value) but slowly the economy recovered: cocoa production, which accounted for two-thirds of Ghana's foreign earnings, doubled from 1983–9. In 1992 Rawlings was elected President again with 58 per cent of the vote.

The Struggle for Popular Power – Rawlings: Saviour or Demagogue? Z. Yeabo (1992)
Death and Pain: Rawlings' Ghana, M. Adjei (1994)
Democracy and Dictatorship in Ghana and Tanzania, R. Pinkney (1997)

Reagan, Ronald Wilson (1911–) President of the United States (1981–9). The son of a shoe salesman, he graduated in economics at Eureka College, Illinois in 1932. After being a radio sports announcer he moved to Hollywood in 1937 and began a 30-year career in films (he made 50) and television. He married the actress Jane Wyman and, after their divorce, married another actress Nancy Davis in 1952. During the Second World War he served in the Army Air Corps, rising to the rank of captain. Reagan was six times President of the Screen Actors Guild, becoming an outspoken anti-communist and leaving the DEMOCRATIC PARTY in 1963. In 1967 he became Governor of California, a post he held for two terms (1967–75). In 1968 and 1976 he unsuccessfully sought the presidential nomination of the REPUBLICAN PARTY but succeeded in 1980, when in the presidential election he easily defeated Jimmy CARTER, whose popularity had plummeted in the IRAN HOSTAGE CRISIS. At 69 he was the oldest President ever elected. The Senate also gained a Republican majority. He survived an assassination attempt in 1981 to triumph in the 1984 presidential election, when he won all states except Minnesota and DC: every section of the community, except blacks, preferred him. Reagan gained 59 per cent of the popular vote.

A man of great charm with a self-deprecating sense of humour, he showed great skill in winning support of Congress for his conservative domestic policy. He aimed to reduce the part government had played in managing the economy since Roosevelt. 'Government is not the solution to our problem. Government *is* the problem', he said in his inaugural. He wanted to cut taxes, federal spending and business regulations. His tax policy was based on supply-side economics: the belief that high rates of taxation discourage enterprise, saving and investment and that the economy would be stimulated by cutting taxes. In 1981 he reduced the top rate of tax from 70 per cent to 50 per cent, capital gains tax by a third and also reduced business and inheritance taxes. This produced a sharp fall in tax receipts but in 1986 he continued to lower taxes by reducing the highest rate from 50 per cent to 27 per cent and by decreasing the number of tax brackets from 14 to 2.

Much of the tax burden was transferred to higher Social Security payments. The federal budget increased every year under Reagan, as military spending increased enormously, but the rate of increase for domestic spending was sharply curtailed. Social security, Medicare and farm subsidies were not affected but many of JOHNSON'S GREAT SOCIETY reforms were impaired. Spending on food stamps, low-income housing, child-assistance benefits and child day care increased at a lower rate than before in the belief that welfare encouraged people to be idle and created a dependent underclass. Federal spending fell from 24.4 per cent of GNP to 22.15 per cent. PRIVATIZATION of federal facilities was considered but only CONRAIL (a freight railroad), the Alaska railroad and a few airports were sold to the private sector. The banking, oil-drilling and transport industries were deregulated but otherwise federal regulations continued to increase. The power of the TRADE UNIONS declined even further under Reagan, particularly when the air-traffic controllers went on strike in 1981. The President dismissed them all and so destroyed their union. By 1990 only 16 per cent of workers were union members, the lowest figure since the 1920s.

Partly due to the huge increase in defence spending (40 per cent in real terms from 1981–3) the 1980s saw the biggest peacetime economic expansion in American history. Real economic growth averaged 3.8 per cent in the Seven Fat Years (1983–9), during which inflation fell from 12 per cent in 1980 to under 4 per cent in 1984 and remained there to the end of the decade. The economy grew by a third and 19 million new jobs were created, though employment in manufacturing fell by 6 per cent (1980–90). The US led the GLOBAL ECONOMY in the 1980s, especially in computers. In 1990 the US had two-thirds of the world market in software and 70 per cent in leading edge microchips. Over half the world's personal computers were in the US in 1990. The US was the only major industrial nation to increase investment as a share of

GNP and to reduce unemployment. The downside of the boom, a result of cutting taxes at the same time as defence spending massively increased, was the creation of enormous budget deficits. In 1983 the budget deficit was $195 billion, so heavy borrowing, notably from Japan and Germany, where interest rates were low, was needed to cover it. From being the world's largest creditor in 1980, the US became the world's largest debtor ten years later. A national debt of $1 trillion in 1980 trebled by 1992. 'We are in a real sense living on borrowed money and time', said Paul Volcker of the Federal Reserve Bank in 1985. As the foreign-owned share of manufacturing doubled (from 5.2 per cent to 12.25 per cent between 1977–87) and as 20 per cent of all US bank assets were owned by foreigners in 1988, the US was paying $248 billion in servicing its debt in 1990, more, according to the *Wall Street Journal*, than 'the combined amounts that government spends on health, science, space, agriculture, housing, the protection of the environment and the administration of justice'.

Reagan's foreign policy was dominated by his relations with the Soviet Union, which he described as the 'evil empire'. With a deep-seated hostility to communism, he at first rejected CARTER's policy of DÉTENTE, as he believed that the US had fallen behind the USSR in both conventional and nuclear weapons. He wanted to restore America's superiority, so it could negotiate arms control from a strong position. In 1981 he began the greatest military build up in history when he ordered production of the neutron bomb. SDI (Strategic Defence Initiative) followed in 1983, the most expensive weapons system ever, and in the same year he began deploying cruise missiles in Western Europe. Relations improved after GORBACHEV came to power. A real success came with the INF (Intermediate Nuclear Force) TREATY of 1987, which for the first time reduced the number of nuclear weapons. Better relations were apparent too when he agreed with Gorbachev in

1988 that Cuban troops would leave Angola and that Namibia should become independent, though he continued to dabble in the ANGOLAN CIVIL WAR by supplying arms to UNITA. He also supplied Stinger shoulder-fired anti-aircraft missiles to Afghan rebels fighting against the Soviet-backed government.

Central America and the Caribbean appeared to the President to present a communist threat. Here he abandoned Carter's policy of refusing military aid to governments with poor human rights records. El Salvador, Honduras and Guatemala all had brutal military regimes but Reagan supported them as they were anti-communist. As left-wing rebels in El Salvador, supported by CASTRO and the SANDINISTA government of Nicaragua, controlled a quarter of the country, Reagan gave substantial military and economic aid to the government and sent military advisers. In Nicaragua the Sandinistas had overthrown the vicious SOMOZA regime in 1979. Reagan regarded Nicaragua as another Cuba, a Soviet beachhead from which revolution could spread throughout Latin America. In 1981 he ordered the CIA to train and arm counter-revolutionaries (CONTRAS), who then attacked Nicaragua from Honduras. Congress imposed a ban on military aid to the Contras in 1984, so the administration sought to help them in a devious plot, the IRAN–CONTRA AFFAIR. The US INTERVENTION IN GRENADA was another example of Reagan's obsession with communism in the Caribbean.

The most spectacular failure of Reagan's foreign policy came in the Middle East. He saw Israel as the country most likely to keep Soviet influence out of the area, so he gave tacit support to the Israeli invasion of Lebanon in 1982. After the Sabra and Shatila massacres in 1983 a UNITED NATIONS force was sent to keep the warring factions apart. The Pentagon wanted US troops withdrawn but Reagan refused until a suicide bomber killed 241 Americans on 23 October 1983 at the Marine barracks in Beirut. He then removed

them. The most damaging episode was the selling of arms to Iran in the hope that this would secure the release of American hostages in Lebanon. This contradicted Reagan's assurance that he would never negotiate with terrorists and produced barren results. The confusion in American foreign policy was further increased when the President, at the same time as he was supplying arms to Iran, effectively took the side of Iraq in the IRAN–IRAQ WAR by protecting the oil tankers of Kuwait, Iraq's ally, in the Persian Gulf.

When Reagan's second term ended he remained extremely popular, in spite of the Iran-Contra Affair and the US's colossal debt: 68 per cent of Americans approved of his overall performance. In November 1994 he announced that he was suffering from Alzheimer's disease.

Looking Back on the Reagan Presidency, L. Berman (ed.) (1990)

Ronald Reagan and the American Presidency, D. Mervin (1990)

President Reagan: The Role of a Lifetime, L. Cannon (1991)

Red Brigades (*Brigate Rosse*: BR)   Italian left-wing terrorist organizations. Formed in October 1970, they described themselves as 'autonomous workers' organizations', prepared for a violent, armed struggle to overthrow the bourgeois state, as legal opposition had been unsuccessful. Most of the original members were working class or lower middle class, though some had a university education and many had strong Catholic backgrounds. Their inspiration and model came from such Latin American guerrilla movements as the TUPAMAROS and the wartime Resistance movement of 1943–5.

Kidnapping took place and in 1977–8 a new phase, the 'strategy of annihilation'. Members of the professions ('servants of the state') were indiscriminately attacked in an attempt to terrorize the ruling élite and disrupt the state. Members of the CHRISTIAN DEMOCRATIC PARTY were among the chief targets, culminating in the kidnapping and murder of Aldo MORO in 1978. This caused widespread revulsion – hundreds of thousands demonstrated against the BR, making them more isolated. Tough anti-terrorist laws were passed increasing police powers and a new anti-terrorist squad led by General Dalla Chiesa was formed. As the terrorists became more demoralized, *pentiti* (repentants) provided information in return for reduced prison sentences. This enabled police to break up most BR 'columns' in 1979–80. The BR remained an occasional nuisance but had failed in all their aims.

The Red Brigades and Left-Wing Terrorism in Italy, R. Catanzaro (1991)
The Politics of Left-Wing Violence in Italy, 1969–84, D. Moss (1989)

Republican Party   US political party. The party originated in opposition to the Kansas–Nebraska Act (1854), which allowed slavery in the new Western territories. In 1860 Lincoln extended the party's appeal by promising high tariffs and subsidies for a transcontinental railroad, which businessmen liked, and free homesteads (farms), which attracted Western farmers. Republican support was therefore strongest in the Mid-West and New England: the slave-holding South was almost solidly Democratic. The Republicans' first success in a presidential election was in 1860, when Lincoln became President. This precipitated the American Civil War, during which the Republicans were the party of Union and denounced the Democrats as traitors. After the Civil War, Radical Republicans imposed Reconstruction on the South, which left it embittered for decades.

From 1868 to 1933 there were eleven Republican and only two Democratic Presidents, though Congress was often in Democratic hands. During this time the Republicans, known as the Grand Old Party (GOP), became increasingly identified with big business, supporting high tariffs and opposing labour unions, and claimed much of the credit for the prosperity which accompanied America's rise to become the major industrial power in the world. A split between Theodore Roosevelt and William Howard Taft enabled the Democratic Woodrow Wilson to become President in 1913. Republicans presided over the boom of the 1920s, the greatest so far in American history, but made no attempt to control the speculation which led to the Wall Street Crash of 1929 and the Great Depression. Republican Presidents Coolidge and Hoover had benefited from the boom: now they were blamed for the depression, and Hoover was overwhelmed in the presidential election of 1932 by the Democrat Franklin D. Roosevelt. He won the support of blacks, industrial workers, farmers, much of the middle class and the South, which kept the Republicans out of office for the next 20 years.

The GOP regained the presidency with EISENHOWER in 1953, and won seven out of twelve presidential elections from 1952–96 (Eisenhower 1952 and 1956, NIXON 1968 and 1972, REAGAN 1980 and 1984, BUSH 1988), though it did not control Congress for 40 years, from 1954–94. It held the Senate from 1953–4, 1981–6 and 1995, the House of Representatives from 1953–4 and 1995. Eisenhower represented the moderate wing of the Republican Party, though his policies were conservative: less government regulation of the economy, lower taxes for the rich and resistance to civil rights legislation. Republican success was due to the conversion of the white South to the GOP. In 1964 Barry Goldwater was annihilated in the presidential election by Lyndon JOHNSON but, apart from his home state of Arizona, all the five states that he carried were in the Deep South, four of which had never voted for a Republican presidential candidate since Reconstruction. The identification of Northern Democrats with the CIVIL RIGHTS ACTS of 1964–5 and the judicial decisions of the WARREN court destroyed the hold of the party on the South, as white Democratic segregationists changed over to the Republicans.

The balance of power in the party began to shift from the Northeast and Mid-West to the South and West. The Western states, particularly the key states of California, were nearly always Republican after 1968. In the South and West there were powerful interests (oil, mining, large-scale farmers) who wanted less government interference, but most voters were appalled by the BLACK GHETTO RIOTS, the crime and drugs of the big Eastern cities. Racial hostility was a powerful determinant of electoral behaviour and benefited the Republicans. The culmination of Republican success in the South came in 1994, when a majority of Southern Congressmen elected were Republicans. The GOP controlled Congress for the first time since 1954, with a Senate majority leader Trent Lott from Mississippi and the Speaker of the House Newt Gingrich from Georgia.

Turning Right in the Sixties: The Conservative Capture of the GOP, M. C. Brennan (1995)
Storming the Gates: Protest Politics and the Republican Revival, D. Batz and R. Brownstein (1996)

Reuther, Walter Philip (1907–70)   US trade union leader. He worked in a factory at the age of 16 and in 1926 went to Detroit, where he became a foreman in the Ford Motor Company but was dismissed in 1932 for trade union activity. From 1933–5 he was in Europe studying working conditions and worked for a time in a Soviet car plant, an experience which gave him an undying hatred of communism. On returning to Detroit he led sit-down strikes which made the United Auto Workers (UAW) a power in the automobile industry. He was President of the union from 1946 until his death.

Reuther was not a typical semi-literate union boss but an articulate social visionary. At one time a socialist, he rejected socialism in the 1940s as impracticable in the US, but he believed that labour must take the lead in improving the lives of blacks and other poor people. In 1952 he became President of the Congress of Industrial Organizations (CIO) and worked hard to rid it of corruption, racketeering and communists. He led the CIO into a merger with the AMERICAN FEDERATION OF LABOR (AFL) in 1955 and was Vice-President of the AFL–CIO. Reuther negotiated benefits for union members such as a guaranteed wage, annual salary rises linked to productivity, cost-of-living increases and pension, health and welfare benefits. He was a fervent supporter of the CIVIL RIGHTS MOVEMENT (he took part in the march on Washington in 1963) and had considerable influence in the DEMOCRATIC PARTY, but he fell out with George Meany, President of the AFL–CIO, for being dictatorial, too conservative, lukewarm to civil rights and inactive in seeking to attract unskilled workers and employees in the South. Reuther took the UAW out of the AFL–CIO in 1968 (it was readmitted in 1981) and briefly affiliated with another large union, the Teamsters (1969–73). He was killed when his chartered plane crashed in fog.

revolutions of 1989–91   The collapse of communism in Eastern Europe. The peacetime dissolution of the communist bloc was a great surprise, as it took place when communist parties were still in control of the media, the army and the secret police. Equally surprising was that the communists gave up power peacefully, except in Romania and Yugoslavia. There were particular reasons in each country for the collapse but two events above all others prepared the way: Mikhail GORBACHEV's becoming General Secretary in 1985 of the CPSU (Communist Party of the Soviet Union) and the rapid decline of the East European economies. Gorbachev wanted co-operation not confrontation with the US, as the arms race, particularly after SDI, was too costly for the USSR and prevented the modernization of its economy. Long-range missiles meant there was no need for a buffer zone in Eastern Europe, which was an economic burden to the Soviet Union. The

SOVIET INVASION OF AFGHANISTAN had shown Gorbachev that there was no point in trying to prop up unpopular communist regimes, so he made clear that the BREZHNEV DOCTRINE no longer applied and that it was to be replaced by what the Soviet spokesman Gennady Gerasimov called the Sinatra Doctrine: 'I did it my way'. 'What the Poles and Hungarians decide', Gorbachev said in July 1989, 'is their affair but we will respect their decision whatever it is'. The economic decline of Eastern Europe had begun in the mid-1970s after the OPEC PRICE RISE of 1973, but it was masked at first by Western loans. Capitalist countries coped with the rise by rapid technological change and computerization, but the centrally controlled communist economies were too cumbersome to adapt successfully and could not compete either with the cheap production of the NEWLY INDUSTRIALIZING ECONOMIES (NIEs) of the Pacific rim. Consequently there was a general fall in living standards: real wages declined in Poland by 17 per cent (1980–6), in Yugoslavia by 25 per cent and in Hungary by 15 per cent.

The revolutions began in Hungary, where there was pressure for change from within the Hungarian Socialist Workers' (communist) Party (HSWP) by 1985 and enthusiastic support for Gorbachev's GLASNOST and perestroika. Western-style banking was introduced in 1987, income tax in 1988, full repatriation of profits for foreign investors in 1989 and foreign trade was liberalized, so moves towards a market economy were taken while the communists were still in power. In January 1989 the party called the HUNGARIAN RISING of 1956 'a popular uprising' and not a counter-revolution as hitherto, thus undermining its own legitimacy. A month later a multiparty system was allowed and the leading role of the communist party abandoned. The HSWP dissolved itself in October and re-formed as the Hungarian Socialist Party but by the end of 1989 it had only 120,000 members. The reformers led by Imre Pozsgay thought they could win the parliamentary elections held in March/April 1990 but they received only 8.5 per cent of the vote, a drastic indication of the people's rejection of communism.

In Poland General JARUZELSKI persuaded the Central Committee to begin round table talks with the opposition. They began in February 1989 and set a precedent which was followed in nearly all communist states, thus beginning the dismantling of communist power in a peaceful way. SOLIDARITY was legalized in April. Its success in the June elections was followed by a non-communist Prime Minister in Mazowiecki, who proceeded to dismantle the communist system and return to a market economy. The German Democratic Republic (GDR: East Germany) appeared to be unaffected by Gorbachev's reforms but the EAST GERMAN REVOLUTION of 1989 brought an end to the communist regime there and soon led to GERMAN REUNIFICATION. The fall of the BERLIN WALL on 9 November affected Bulgaria, where hundreds of thousands of demonstrators demanded an end to communist rule. The Central Committee forced ZHIVKOV to retire and agreed to a multiparty system. Opposition groups joined in the Union of Democratic Forces (UDF) and demanded round-table discussions, supported by large demonstrations and strikes. In April 1990 the Communist Party changed its name to the Bulgarian Socialist Party (BSP), which in the June elections retained power with 47 per cent of the vote. As the economy continued to decline, prices increased dramatically when subsidies were withdrawn. In a further election in October 1991 the UDF formed a government which for the first time since 1944 did not contain any communists. The VELVET REVOLUTION in Czechoslovakia was deeply influenced by the massive but peaceful demonstrations which took place in Leipzig and other cities in the GDR and by the breaching of the Berlin Wall on 9 November. After that progress was swift. By the end of the year Václav HAVEL was President and rapidly established a democratic system and a market economy.

Romania and Yugoslavia were the only countries where violence accompanied the revolutions. CEAUŞESCU ignored the disturbances in Eastern Europe and was confident enough to leave for a visit to Iran in December 1989. Spontaneous anti-government demonstrations began in Timisoara but spread to Bucharest when Ceauşescu returned. Fighting took place when the Securitate (secret police) fired on demonstrators and continued until Ceauşescu was captured and shot by the army on Christmas Day. A National Salvation Front was formed by former communists who were able to retain power by winning the elections of May 1990. Fighting took place in Yugoslavia when Slobodan MILOŠEVIĆ, the President of Serbia, decided that if he could not hold the Yugoslav Federation together with Serbia as the dominant state, then a Greater Serbia, which would include the Serbs in Croatia and Bosnia, should be formed. This was unacceptable to Franjo TUDJMAN, the Croatian President, and so the YUGOSLAV CIVIL WAR began in 1990 and was to continue for the next five years. Isolated Albania was the last country to be affected by the revolutions of 1989. Not until the fall of Ceauşescu were there anti-government demonstrations, but it was a year before opposition parties were legalized and multiparty elections were not held until March 1991. The communist Albanian Party of Labour won these with 60 per cent of the vote but discontent continued as there was high unemployment and a food shortage, so in June a government of national unity, which included some opposition members, was formed. As thousands fled from Albania by sea, parts of the country slipped from government control. The communists were finally removed from power when the Democratic Party won the election in March 1992.

Surge to Freedom: The End of Communist Rule in Eastern Europe, J. F. Brown (1991)
Eastern Europe in Revolution, I. Banac (ed.) (1992)

Why Did the Socialist System Collapse in Central and Eastern Europe? The Case of Poland, the Former Czechoslovakia and Hungary, J. Adam (1996)

Rome, Treaty of (1957)   Signed by France, Germany, Italy and the BENELUX countries it created the EEC (European Economic Community). The treaty was more a statement of objectives than a series of detailed regulations, which were worked out later. The removal of tariffs between the member states to create a common market in manufactured goods was to take place in three stages of four years each, beginning in 1958. There was to be a common tariff on imports into the EEC and the treaty said that there should be a progressive abolition of restrictions to provide services, especially finance, insurance and banking, within the EEC, though there was little progress in this direction for the next 25 years. A free market for labour within the EEC, a COMMON AGRICULTURAL POLICY (CAP), a social fund and European Investment Bank were also envisaged.

The administrative structure owed much to that of the ECSC (European Coal and Steel Community). A supranational Commission was the executive of the EEC. Its main role was to initiate policy but all major decisions were taken by the Council of Ministers, which represented national governments and was answerable to them. The Commission did not report to the European Parliament and was in effect the legislature of the EEC. The European Parliament was not a legislative body and has never passed a law. It had to be consulted by the Council of Ministers, which could then ignore it. It was the only elected body in the EEC but had no powers of taxation or control of spending, though in theory it could reject the Community budget as a whole. The parliament was more a talking-shop than an effective institution. The European Court of Justice regarded the treaty as if it were a European constitution in deciding on the legality of the Commission's directives and insists that Community law must override the national law of a member state where they conflict. The Treaty of Rome was adapted by the MAASTRICHT TREATY.

The Government and Politics of the European Community, N. Nugent (1989)

Rosenberg case (1951)   A trial for espionage in the United States. Julius Rosenberg, a US army engineer and life-long communist, was accused with his wife Ethel and other of passing information to the Russians in 1944–5 about the building of the atom bomb. The Rosenbergs insisted on their innocence but all were found guilty by a jury in 1951 and were given long prison sentences, except for Julius and Ethel Rosenberg, who were sentenced to death, as they had refused to co-operate with the prosecution in exposing Soviet espionage. After appeals failed they were executed in the electric chair in June 1953. The trial took place at the height of the anti-communist hysteria which made Senator MCCARTHY a national celebrity. Ethel's conviction was considered controversial, as she had played only a minor part in the conspiracy and because it appeared that her indictment was an attempt to pressurize her husband into confessing. They are the only Americans executed for espionage.

We Are Your Sons, R. Meeropol and M. Meeropol (1975)

Rushdie affair   Salman Rushdie, a British author born a Muslim in Bombay who had rejected his faith, was sentenced to death in a *fatwa* (religious decree) on 14 February 1989 by Ayatollah KHOMEINI, who declared his book *The Satanic Verses* blasphemous. Muslims throughout the world had been outraged as Rushdie portrayed the Prophet Muhammad, thinly disguised as Mahmoud (meaning false prophet) as an unscrupulous lecher who duped his followers and included in the Quran certain verses which were the work of

the devil: the satanic verses. Prostitutes were given the same names as Muhammad's wives. The symbol for their seclusion and protection, 'The Curtain', was made into the image of a brothel, which men circumambulated, just as pilgrims do at the holy shrine of the Kaaba in Mecca. Copies of the book were burned in Bradford, England and in many parts of the world. The Secretary-General of the Islamic Conference called on all 45 members to ban the book and boycott the publishers. Britain broke off diplomatic relations with Iran after the *fatwa* but these were restored in September 1990, when the British government acknowledged that *The Satanic Verses* offended Muslims and said it had no wish to insult Islam. The *fatwa* remained.

The Rushdie Affair: The Novel, the Ayatollah and the West, D. Pipes (1990)

Rwandan massacres   At independence in 1962, 85 per cent of the population of Rwanda were Hutus, dominated by the Tutsi minority which had been favoured by the Belgian colonial rulers. A Hutu rising in late 1963 overthrew Tutsi rule and resulted in 20,000 Tutsi deaths and 250,000 fleeing to Uganda. In 1972, in the neighbouring state of Burundi, a violent Hutu revolt was savagely repressed by the Tutsi-dominated army in which thousands were killed while many fled for safety to Rwanda. The ethnic tension in Rwanda in the late 1980s and early 1990s was exacerbated by the increasing population, pressure on the land and the collapse of coffee prices, resulting in an economic crisis which the WORLD BANK and IMF (International Monetary Fund) demanded should be dealt with by austerity measures and reforms to government. In October 1990 Tutsis of the Uganda-based RPF (Rwanda Patriotic Front) invaded Rwanda to overthrow the one-party state of the Hutu President Habyarimana, who had seized power in a military coup in 1973. French, Belgian and Zairean troops helped the Rwandan army to repel them but as the civil war continued a million people fled to Uganda and Tanzania to avoid the fighting. French troops withdrew in February 1993 and there was pressure on Habyarimana from within his own party for multiparty elections. In August 1993 Habyarimana and the RPF signed the Arusha Accord in Tanzania to end the civil war: there was to be a transitional government, which would include the RPF, before a general election. A small UNITED NATIONS force arrived to help implement the Accord.

Habyarimana, under pressure from some in his own party who did not want to surrender power, delayed enforcing the Arusha Accord and was summoned by African leaders to Dar es Salaam, where he grudgingly agreed to implement the agreement. On 6 April 1994, on his way home, Habyarimana's plane was hit by a rocket over Kigali (the Rwandan capital) airport, killing all on board. The government blamed the RPF, the RPF accused hard-liners in Habyarimana's party. Immediately the Presidential Guard and the *Interahamwe* (those who attack together), a youth militia formed by the President and fiercely loyal to him, began to murder Tutsis and Hutus who had opposed the President. Hutu civilians were compelled to murder their Tutsi neighbours and in ten weeks between

500,000 and a million Tutsis were massacred. The UN force was ineffectual in preventing the atrocities. The RPF resumed the civil war, carried out retaliatory murders, and gradually conquered most of the country by 1994, so that between two and three million Hutus (out of a population of just over seven million) fled to makeshift camps in neighbouring Tanzania and Zaire, where they faced hunger and disease. This created one of the most severe refugee problems since the Second World War.

Hutu leaders and *Interahamwe*, responsible for the genocide of the Tutsis, took control of the camps and used them as bases from which to attack Tutsis in Zaire and Rwanda. Some 300,000 Banyamulenge, Tutsis who had lived in eastern Zaire for 200 years, fought back vigorously and drove hundreds of thousands of Hutus from the camps further into Zaire, greatly exacerbating the problem of feeding them. They also contributed to the success of Laurent Kabila's rebellion, starting in eastern Zaire, which overthrew MOBUTU in 1997.

The Rwanda Crisis: History of a Genocide, G. Prunier (1995)
Rwanda: Genocide in the Twentieth Century, A. Destexhe (1996)

S

Sadat, Muhammad Anwar al- (1918–81)
President of Egypt (1970–81). From a humble
background (his father was a clerk) he entered
the Military Academy in 1936 and was commissioned two years later. Opposed to British
bases in Egypt and the corrupt regime of King
Faruq he joined the Free Officers and after
the coup of 1952, which deposed Faruq,
became a member of the Revolutionary Command Council. NASSER never gave him ministerial office but he held various posts and in
1969 was appointed Vice-President. This
enabled him to become President on Nasser's
death, though many expected him to be a
figurehead only.

He rejected such expectations in 1971 when
he dismissed the 25,000 Soviet advisers in
Egypt and moved closer to the US. Sadat
made an alliance with Syria and in October
1973 surprised Israel by attacking it in the
YOM KIPPUR WAR. There had been no
decisive success for either side when a cease-
fire was made, which enabled Sadat to claim
victory and restore the prestige of the Egyptian army. After the war Sadat renewed diplomatic relations with the US, broken seven
years earlier, and through KISSINGER's mediation made two agreements with Israel: in
January 1974, whereby Israeli forces would
withdraw from the east bank of the Suez
Canal and in September 1975, by which the
Israelis withdrew behind the Mitla and Geddi
passes in Sinai. These agreements enabled
Egypt to clear and reopen the Suez Canal by
June 1975 and to recover the oilfields in Sinai,
both important sources of revenue. Sadat
wanted to go further and end the Arab–Israeli
conflict, which he regarded as a necessary

condition for economic recovery. He loved
the dramatic gesture, which drew worldwide
attention to him, and on 20 November 1977
flew to Israel and addressed the Knesset, the
Israeli parliament. This move, admired in the
West, angered Arab states, who regarded it as
a step towards a separate peace with Israel.
Subsequent negotiations, mediated by President CARTER, produced the CAMP DAVID
ACCORDS in September 1978, for which
BEGIN and Sadat were awarded the Nobel
Peace Prize. Peace between Israel and Egypt
was finally signed at the Treaty of Washington in March 1982. As a result Egypt was
expelled from the ARAB LEAGUE and was
isolated in the Arab world, losing the financial
support of the oil-rich states of Saudi-Arabia
and Kuwait. The US stepped in and provided
Egypt with more aid than the rest of Africa
and more than any other state except Israel.

Sadat's closer alignment with the West
produced a modest change in political life.
Censorship was lifted and a controlled multiparty system allowed, Sadat forming his own
party, the National Democratic Party, though
real power remained in the hands of the President and the electoral system ensured that
his party dominated parliament. His economic policy of *infitah* (opening) was designed
to attract foreign investment by granting tax
concessions but most of this went into construction, tourism and services rather than
industry. High inflation, a large trade deficit
and mountainous foreign debt were accompanied by a fall in the real wages of workers and
serious riots in 1977, the worst since 1952,
when the government reduced food subsidies.
The rapid rise of population, for which there

was no employment, added to Sadat's problems. Arrogant and autocratic, he turned to Islam to make himself more popular, called himself 'the Believer President', and allowed the MUSLIM BROTHERHOOD, suppressed by Nasser, to function openly. By 1977 Islamic organizations were very critical of him. They disliked his support for MUHAMMAD RIZA PAHLAVI, Shah of Iran and his condemnation of the IRANIAN REVOLUTION as a 'crime against Islam', for the Camp David Accords and for his pro-Western economic policies. New, secret ISLAMIC FUNDAMENTALIST groups called for a jihad (holy war) against Sadat. On 6 October 1981 he was assassinated by Islamists in the army, who were passing before him in a parade to mark the anniversary of the Yom Kippur War. By this time his popularity in the West as an enlightened leader was in marked contrast to his growing unpopularity in Egypt, where he was known as 'Pharaoh'.

Man of Defiance: A Political Biography of Anwar Sadat, R. Israeli (1985)
Egypt's Uncertain Revolution Under Nasser and Sadat, R. W. Baker (1988)
Egyptian Politics Under Sadat, R. Hinnebusch (1988)

St. Laurent, Louis Stephen (1882–1973)
Prime Minister of Canada (1948–57). Bilingual (his father was French-Canadian, his mother of Irish descent), he rose from the humble background of his father's country store to read law at Laval University, Quebec, where he became Professor of Law in 1914. He did not enter politics until 1941, when the Prime Minister Mackenzie King sought a replacement for his faithful French-Canadian ally, Ernest Lapointe, who had died. St. Laurent, Minister of Justice and Attorney-General, supported King's war effort, including the unpopular introduction of conscription in 1944. As a reward King made him Secretary of State for External Affairs in 1946. When King retired in 1948 St. Laurent became Liberal Party leader and Prime Minister.

After the communist seizure of power in the CZECH COUP of 1948, St. Laurent broke with King's policy of 'no commitments' and played a prominent role in the formation of NATO. He supported the intervention of the UNITED NATIONS in the KOREAN WAR (1950–3) and in the SUEZ CRISIS (1956), helping at that time to keep India and Pakistan in the COMMONWEALTH. At home a considerable achievement was the entry of Newfoundland (attracted by social welfare programmes, trade and investment) into the Canadian Confederation as its tenth province. Another major success was the agreement in 1954 with President EISENHOWER to build the St. Lawrence Seaway from Montreal to the Great Lakes, thus enabling deep-water ships to reach Chicago and other Lake ports. It was opened in 1959. St. Laurent tried to unite and develop Canada by equalizing provincial revenues, by extending old age pensions to all over 65 and by expanding university education. The right of appeal from the Supreme Court to the Judicial Committee of the Privy Council in London was ended. The Liberal Party was narrowly defeated in the 1957 general election by the Conservatives under John DIEFENBAKER. St. Laurent retired and was succeeded as Liberal leader by Lester PEARSON.

Louis St. Laurent, D. Thomson (1967)

Sakharov, Andrei Dmitrievich (1921–89)
Soviet nuclear physicist and dissident. The son of a physicist, he was born in Moscow and graduated at Moscow State University. Sakharov became involved in nuclear research and played a leading part in developing the hydrogen bomb, tested in 1953. For this he was admitted, by a rare unanimous vote, to the prestigious Academy of Sciences at the age of 32. He received many honours but became worried about the genetic effects of radioactive fall-out and helped to persuade KHRUSHCHEV to make the partial NUCLEAR TEST BAN TREATY OF 1963. In the 1960s Sakharov came into conflict with the govern-

ment by supporting the PRAGUE SPRING in 1968 and by publishing abroad an essay *Progress, Coexistence and Intellectual Freedom*, in which he predicted the integration of the communist and capitalist systems and criticized the persecution of dissidents: 18 million copies were sold in the West. After his wife died of cancer Sakharov gave all his savings to charity. In 1970 he successfully campaigned for the release of the scientist Zhores Medvedev from a psychiatric prison and a year later married the human rights activist Yelena Bonner. For his campaign for human rights in the USSR he was awarded the Nobel Peace Prize in 1975 but he was not allowed to leave the country to accept it. Sakharov supported the national minorities (Jews, Germans, Tatars) who wanted to return to their homeland and monitored the observance in the USSR of the HELSINKI FINAL ACT. When he denounced the SOVIET INVASION OF AFGHANISTAN (1979) as 'a monstrous error' and called for an international boycott of the Olympic Games due to be held in Moscow in 1980, he was arrested by the KGB and exiled to Gorky (Nizhni Novgorod), where he was isolated and kept under strict surveillance. He was freed by GORBACHEV in 1986, returned to Moscow and was elected to the USSR Congress of People's Deputies in 1989, becoming, with his immense moral authority and fervent humanitarian beliefs, one of its leading figures. Sakharov had long suffered from heart problems and died suddenly a few months later.

Memoirs, A. D. Sakharov (1990)

Salazar, António de Oliveira (1889–1970)

Dictator of Portugal (1932–68). From a devoutly Catholic and conservative family of lowly peasant origins in northern Portugal, the withdrawn and studious Salazar was educated at a seminary, nearly entered the priesthood, but eventually became a lecturer in financial law at the élitist University of Coimbra.

Under the military dictatorship established after the coup of 1926, Salazar rose fast because of his alleged financial expertise, first as Minister of Finance in 1928, and then as Prime Minister in July 1932, a post he retained until 1968. In the early 1930s Salazar laid the foundations of the Estado Novo ('New State'), an authoritarian and corporatist regime with Fascist features that was formally dedicated to 'God, Country, and the Family'. Unlike the Fascist states, the Estado Novo did not mobilize the masses, the oddly reticent and reclusive Salazar (never marrying), being intimidated by crowds. Outwardly modest and self-effacing, Salazar none the less possessed the absolute inner conviction that he alone could chart Portugal's destiny.

Socially the Salazarist system was rooted in the Church, the industrial and financial oligarchy, the civil servants that staffed the state bureaucracy, the smallholding peasantry of the north, and the big landowners of the south, while being ultimately guaranteed by the army and the notorious, Gestapo-trained secret police known, from 1945, as the International Police for the Defence of the State (*Policia International de Defensa do Estado*, PIDE), with its nationwide network of informers. Opponents of the regime were tortured, imprisoned and sometimes murdered. Even the unemployed could be dragooned into forced labour camps.

Salazar's longevity as leader was partly due to the deliberate curtailment of potentially threatening social and economic change: hence economic power was overwhelmingly concentrated in the hands of a few fabulously wealthy families (ten families absorbed over 50 per cent of the national wealth), while education, despite Salazar's own rise to power via learning, was actively discouraged, as a means of social control (in 1970, 25.8 per cent of Portuguese over the age of ten were illiterate). Stability lay too in the maintenance of the police state, a strict balancing of the budget, the privileged lifestyle of the armed forces' upper ranks, and Salazar's deftness at playing the regime's various interest groups off against one another.

During the Spanish Civil War (1936–9) and the Second World War (1939–45) Salazar adopted a stance of ostensible neutrality (though in fact sending General FRANCO troops during the Spanish conflict). Afterwards, Salazar's anti-communism and the Azores' strategic importance resulted in US backing for the regime, thereby ending its international isolation and guaranteeing its continuity. Portugal was therefore a founding member of NATO in 1949 but kept out of the UNITED NATIONS on account of the regime's authoritarianism until 1955.

The fact that not even opponents from the armed forces could unseat the civilian dictator, whether by means of a coup (there were 12 attempted risings against Salazar) or presidential elections, demonstrated the extent to which Salazar had, by 1945, subordinated the armed forces to his civilian authority. A serious threat emerged in 1958 in the shape of the charismatic and outspoken General Humberto Delgado, who not only promised to remove Salazar if he won the presidential election, but also attracted massive popular support. Consequently the election result had to be rigged in favour of the official candidate (direct presidential elections were subsequently abolished), while the maverick Delgado was exiled and eventually murdered by the PIDE in Spain in 1965.

The Salazar regime never had to face an effective opposition, but its foundations were none the less visibly crumbling during the dictator's last decade in power. The dramatic shift of workers from the land to the cities (the agricultural population plummetted from 50 per cent of the workforce to under 30 per cent during the 1960s) undermined the closed and conservative social basis of the regime. Massive emigration, which stood at 1.5 million in 1975, also provided many Portuguese with greater wealth and expectations, as did the huge expansion of the tourist industry in the 1960s. The Salazar regime was shaken above all by PORTUGAL'S COLONIAL WARS, which broke out in 1961. Salazar, who never visited Africa, stubbornly refused to relinquish the colonies, despite the damaging cost of the war to the Portuguese economy (up to 45 per cent of the national budget was spent on the war). The political radicalization of the armed forces was a further, eventually fatal, consequence of the African wars.

Salazar suffered a stroke in 1968 that incapacitated him. His dictatorship collapsed overnight with the PORTUGUESE REVOLUTION of 1974–6.

Salazar and Modern Portugal, H. Kay (1970)
Portugal, T. Gallagher (1983)
Portugal, W. C. Opello (1991)

SALT (Strategic Arms Limitation Talks)

Held from 1968 to 1970 by the US and the Soviet Union to limit their nuclear arsenals. Both President NIXON and Leonid BREZHNEV saw the benefits to be gained from reduced military expenditure and that neither side could win a nuclear war. The first agreement (SALT I) took place after tortuous negotiations in 1972. It froze for five years the number of land-based intercontinental ballistic missiles (ICBMs) that each side could deploy at 1,054. There was a moratorium on the construction of submarine-based missiles, leaving the Soviet Union with 950 and the US with 656.

By 1970 the two superpowers had a rough parity in nuclear forces. This meant that they were in a state of 'mutually assured destruction' (MAD) in a nuclear war, a situation which provided security as in any attack the other power would have enough nuclear forces left to retaliate. This balance could be destroyed by the anti-ballistic missile (ABM) systems being developed, which would destroy incoming missiles before they reached their target. An impenetrable ABM system would allow a superpower to make a first strike without fear of retaliation. SALT I therefore included an ABM Treaty, which limited each side to 100 ABMs. This reduced the incentive for a first strike and recognized that it was in the interests of both sides to preserve the nuclear balance. The SALT I agreements were observed beyond their expiry date while SALT II negotiations took place.

The SALT II agreement, signed in 1979 by Brezhnev and President CARTER, limited each side to 2,400 ICBMs, of which no more than 1,320 could have multiple warheads. This was little different from the existing and planned deployments by both sides. The US Senate did not ratify the treaty because of the SOVIET INVASION OF AFGHANISTAN but both sides kept to its terms until President REAGAN breached its ceiling in the mid-1980s. The SALT negotiations were succeeded by START (Strategic Arms Reduction Talks).

Salvadorean civil war (1981–92)   The origins of the war lay in a repressive military regime, which had controlled El Salvador since 1931, and in the deprivation of the peasantry in a country where a small oligarchy of landowners owned most of the land. In the 1970s Catholic priests, influenced by LIBERATION THEOLOGY, and revolutionary groups worked among the peasants and urban poor. The army responded by organizing death squads to murder priests and opposition leaders or add to the number who 'disappeared'. In 1980 gunmen shot and killed the Archbishop of San Salvador, Oscar Romero, who had criticized the death squads, as he was saying mass. Troops fired into the crowd gathering at his funeral killing many and soon the countryside was in revolt. Five revolutionary groups united in the *Frente Farabundo Marti para la Liberación Nacional* (FMLN) and began military operations in January 1981. The US, anxious to avoid another Nicaraguan Revolution (1979), in which the left-wing SANDINISTAS had seized power, provided finance and training for the military regime, which became the third largest recipient of US aid after Israel and Egypt. At first the guerrillas had some success until air power forced them onto the defensive, though they expanded their operations from five provinces to all 14 by 1988.

The first civilian President in 53 years, José Napoleon Duarte, was elected in 1984, promising economic reforms and peace negotiations. He provided neither in one of the most corrupt governments in Salvadorean history. Death squads continued to operate, there was no land reform and the economy declined. In 1989 he lost to ARENA, a right wing party, whose leader and new President, Alfredo Cristiani, promised peace, but increased repression of the trade unions convinced the FMLN that he was not serious. It therefore opened the largest offensive of the war. In 1990 there was a return to negotiations under UNITED NATIONS auspices, the FMLN insisting on a large reduction in the size of the army. The US, no longer fearful of the spread of communisum after the COLLAPSE OF THE SOVIET UNION and the defeat of the Sandinistas in the 1990 Nicaraguan election, joined the strong international pressure for an agreement, which was reached on all issues, the war ending in February 1992. A total of 75,000 had been killed and a million peasants displaced during the war.

A Decade of War: El Salvador Confronts the Future, A. Sundaram and G. Gelber (eds) (1991)

Revolution in El Salvador: Origins and Evolution, T. S. Montgomery (1992)

San Francisco Peace Treaty   Signed in September 1951, it came into effect in April 1952. A treaty signed by Japan and 48 other countries by which Japan regained its independence and the OCCUPATION OF JAPAN ended. The Soviet Union refused to sign as on the same day the JAPAN–US SECURITY TREATY was endorsed and so the USSR remained technically at war with Japan. John Foster DULLES had led the US negotiating team on behalf of President TRUMAN. He had attended the Paris Peace Conference after the First World War and was convinced that the harsh terms imposed on Germany had resulted in the Second World War. Dulles therefore ensured that Japan was granted generous terms. It gave up all claims to its former empire: Korea, Taiwan, the Pescadores, the Kuriles, South Sakhalin and the Pacific islands which it had received as mandates of the League of Nations after the First World War. Japan also agreed not to demand compensation for the victims of the atom bombs dropped on Hiroshima and Nagasaki. It was not required to pay punitive reparations, though it did agree to pay compensation to certain countries.

Sandinistas   A revolutionary movement (*Frente Sandinista de Liberación Nacional*: FSLN) in Nicaragua, named after the national hero Augusto César Sandino, who had fought against US marines and been murdered by Anastasio SOMOZA. The FSLN, led by Marxists inspired by the Cuban Revolution, was formed in 1961 to overthrow the Somoza dictatorship but had little success and many setbacks until 1978, when it joined with other opposition groups in a civil war which ended in 1979 with the flight of Anastasio Somoza Debayle. A coalition government was set up which included the Conservative Party leader Violeta Chamorro and three LIBERATION THEOLOGY priests, though the dominant influence was the FSLN. Freedom of the individual and of the press was decreed, the death penalty abolished and the National Guard, Somoza's power base, abolished. It was replaced by a Sandinista-controlled military and police, devoted to the revolution. The ruling junta nationalized all the Somoza family assets (43 per cent of the economy) and carried out an agrarian reform to give land to peasant co-operatives, but there was no limit on the size of private holdings and no further nationalization. However, the promised elections were delayed and in 1980 two leading moderates, including Violeta Chamorro, resigned from the junta because it had moved too far to the left.

Somoza had left Nicaragua with debts of $1.5 billion and a ruined economy which desperately needed US aid. As the Sandinistas devoted their scarce resources to a successful literacy drive and to health – infant mortality was halved by 1985 – the country could not afford to pay for such programmes and for essential imports, so the debt rose to $3.5 billion. The situation was made much worse by the civil war in which the CONTRAS, supported by the US, fought the government. Defence took up 40 per cent of the budget by 1984, when 400,000 people had been displaced by the war. The Roman Catholic hierarchy, which had supported the Sandinistas in the late 1970s, withdrew its support. In 1993 Pope JOHN PAUL II visited Nicaragua, condemned liberation theology and ordered priests to break with the government. The Sandinistas responded to growing opposition by increasing repression. The FSLN was organized as a Leninist-type party, disciplined and hierarchical, with power centralized in a nine-member National Directorate, whose members held key positions in the army and government. Other party leaders were appointed by the Directorate, which tightened its political control by banning opposition rallies and imposing censorship. Yet the Sandinistas had a mass following from landless peasants and organized labour and in the 1984 election, the first since the revolution, their candidate Daniel Ortega, with 63 per cent of the vote, was elected President and the FSLN won 61 out of 86 seats in the National Assembly.

The US's hostility to the Sandinistas increased, as they joined the NON-ALIGNED MOVEMENT, refused to condemn the SOVIET INVASION OF AFGHANISTAN and supported the rebels in the SALVADOREAN CIVIL WAR. In 1986 President REAGAN imposed an economic embargo on Nicaragua, declaring that it was an 'extraordinary threat' to US security, thus forcing the Sandinistas to depend even more on Soviet and Cuban aid. The civil war ravaged the economy, devastating the sugar and cotton lands and reducing production to half that of 1979. The government printed money to pay for the war, with the result that inflation reached 14,000 per cent in 1988 and real wages fell by 93 per cent between 1981–9. In 1988 Ortega introduced a free market and austerity programme, ending most state subsidies, freeing wages and prices. A year later the budget was cut by 44 per cent, 30,000 public employees were dismissed and the currency was devalued. The government, which had closed the Catholic Church's radio station and the opposition newspaper *La Prensa*, held between four and seven thousand political prisoners. President Arias of Costa Rica persuaded other Central American leaders to co-operate to bring about peace without consulting the US. Ortega agreed to an election in 1990, which the US thought would be rigged but which produced a victory for Chamorro's coalition of 14 parties. Ortega became leader of the opposition, though the FSLN with 40 per cent of the vote was the largest party and retained control of the military and the trade unions. After its defeat the FSLN underwent a critical self-examination, admitting that it had been internally undemocratic and had sometimes abused its power. In open elections for all party posts below the Directorate most leaders were replaced and in 1991 the FSLN adopted a more democratic constitution.

The End and the Beginning: The Nicaraguan Revolution, J. A. Booth (1985)

Sandinistas: The Party and the Revolution, D. Gilbert (1989)

The Undermining of the Sandinista Revolution, G. Prevost and H. E. Vanden (eds) (1997)

Schmidt, Helmut (1918–) Chancellor of the Federal Republic of Germany (FRG: West Germany) (1974–82). The son of a schoolmaster, he studied at the University of Hamburg and served in the German army during the Second World War. After the war he joined the SPD (Social Democratic Party) and, with his energy and intelligence, rose rapidly in the party and served as a minister in the city-state of Hamburg before becoming Willy BRANDT's Defence Minister (1969–72) and then Finance Minister (1972–

4). When Brandt was forced to resign in 1974 Schmidt succeeded him as Chancellor.

A highly cultivated man (he is an accomplished pianist), who speaks English fluently, he continued Brandt's policy of OSTPOLITIK, which had produced better relations with the Soviet Union and Eastern Europe, and signed the HELSINKI FINAL ACT in 1975. Security was a major concern, as the USSR had installed SS-20s (medium range nuclear missiles) in Eastern Europe. Although the German army had half a million troops in 1975, the FRG was still dependent on the US nuclear umbrella. Schmidt persuaded NATO to embark on the 'twin-track' approach to the Soviet Union: install cruise and Pershing missiles in Western Europe but offer to withdraw these if the SS-20s were withdrawn. This policy achieved its aim (after Schmidt had ceased to be Chancellor) with the INF (Intermediate Nuclear Force) TREATY of 1987. This emphasis on nuclear missiles for defence (Schmidt wanted arms reduction not an arms race) was unpopular in the FRG and led to a series of 'peace rallies', the biggest anti-military protest since the 1950s: 650,000 attended the final demonstration in Bonn. Schmidt was one of the few statesmen to follow the US in boycotting the Moscow Olympic Games in 1980 after the SOVIET INVASION OF AFGHANISTAN.

The Chancellor had to cope with the OPEC PRICE RISE in 1973, which ended the prolonged postwar boom. The floating of the dollar in 1971 by President NIXON had also destabilized the financial markets and produced inflation. There was a depression in which unemployment and inflation rose: production declined in 1975 for the first time since the currency reform of 1948. Schmidt saw currency stability as his prime objective and, with the French President Valéry GISCARD D´ESTAING, persuaded the EEC to create a stable European currency zone by adopting the European Monetary System. The FRG recovered more quickly from the recession than other European countries. Inflation was 3 per cent in 1978, the lowest level in Western Europe, while exports expanded to the highest levels yet by 1979. One effect of the oil price rise was that Schmidt's government turned increasingly to nuclear power for energy. By 1980 14 nuclear power stations were in operation and 12 were under construction. As the public became aware of the problem of disposing of radioactive nuclear waste, which remained toxic for thousands of years, the GREEN PARTY was formed and the Chancellor lost some support. A second rise in oil prices in 1979–80 resulted in another recession. The growth rate fell (1980–2), there was a balance of payments deficit in 1980 and there were nearly two million unemployed (a record level) in 1982, though once again the FRG did better than other European countries.

In the 1976 election the SPD vote fell by 3.3 per cent; that of the CDU rose by 3.8 per cent. The CDU was the biggest party in the Bundestag but Schmidt remained in power, as he had a majority of ten with his FDP partners. He regained some prestige with his effective handling of the BAADER–MEINH-OFF GROUP. Its leaders were arrested and in 1971 the hostages in a hijacked plane were freed in a commando raid in Somalia. The 1980 election saw a recovery in his position which gave his coalition a majority of 45, but with the recession of 1980 his allies began to desert him. The state's share of GDP had risen from 39 per cent to 48 per cent between 1969 and 1979. The FDP wanted state expenditure to be reduced and proposed cuts which included social security benefits. When Schmidt rejected these demands in 1982, his FDP ministers resigned and the FDP moved back to an alliance with the CDU. A 'constructive vote of no confidence' took place successfully for the first time and Schmidt was replaced as Chancellor by the CDU's Helmut KOHL. In 1983 Schmidt became the publisher of the newspaper *Die Zeit*.

Helmut Schmidt, Helmsman of Germany, J. Carr (1985)

Germany from Partition to Reunification, H. A. Turner (1992)
German Politics, 1945–95, P. Pulzer (1995)

Scottish devolution   There was little interest in Scotland in having a separate parliament until the 1960s, when the SCOTTISH NATIONAL PARTY (SNP) began to gain support and won its first seat at Westminister. Edward HEATH responded to the rise of Scottish nationalism by committing the CONSERVATIVE PARTY to an elected Scottish assembly (the Kilbrandon Report recommended this in 1973) in its election manifestos of 1970 and 1974. The LABOUR PARTY won the election of 1974, so it was Jim CALLAGHAN who decided to act on the Kilbrandon Report, partly to gain SNP support for his minority government. However, the proposals were so watered down that no effective assembly was possible: the Scottish parliament in Edinburgh was to have no powers of taxation and its decisions could be vetoed by the Secretary of State for Scotland. When the bill was passed amendments ensured that there would not be a Scottish parliament at all, as 40 per cent of all on the register (not 40 per cent of voters) had to approve in a referendum of such an assembly. In the referendum 51.6 per cent of those voting supported a Scottish parliament but this was only 32 per cent of those on the register and so did not meet the threshold. When Margaret THATCHER won the election of 1979 all idea of devolution was dropped, though support for it increased in Scotland in the 1980s because she was seen by many to be insensitive to Scottish issues, particularly in her decision to impose the POLL TAX there a year earlier than in England.

Tony BLAIR revived the idea of devolution after the Labour victory in the 1997 election (in which the Conservatives lost all their seats in Scotland), as part of his proposals for sweeping constitutional reform. The government published a White Paper on devolution in July, which proposed a Scottish parliament which would be able to pass legislation relating to health, education, local government, transport, economic development, agriculture, fisheries and the police. Westminster would retain sovereignty – Scotland would remain part of the United Kingdom and the Scottish parliament would not be able to make Scotland independent – and powers concerning the constitution, foreign policy, defence, national security and social security. Scottish MPs at Westminster will continue to take part in all proceedings there but a Boundary Commission, to report in 2007, will review (and almost certainly reduce) the number of seats held by Scottish MPs in the House of Commons. If a referendum approved of a Scottish parliament, it would be elected in 1999 and meet in 2000. If the Scots approved of tax-raising powers for a Scottish parliament, it would be able to raise the basic rate of income tax by up to three pence in the pound. The White Paper met the demands of many nationalists, as it proposed a Scottish parliament independent of the House of Commons, with real powers, though it went only part of the way for the SNP, which wants complete independence. In the referendum in September the Scots voted decisively for home rule and by an unexpectedly large majority for a parliament with tax-raising powers, 74.3 per cent voted for a Scottish parliament and 63.5 per cent for it to be able to raise taxes. All 32 of the local authorities voted overwhelmingly for a Scottish parliament and only two voted against tax-raising powers.

Scottish National Party (SNP)   Since the Act of Union (1707) Scotland has retained several of its own institutions: Scottish legal and educational systems, the Presbyterian Church of Scotland as the Established Church and the 'royal burghs' (local authorities). These kept alive a sense of national identity on which the SNP (formed in 1928 as the National Party of Scotland to promote Scottish self-government – it merged with the Scottish Party in 1934) was able to build. At

first it had little appeal and in 1955 obtained only 12,112 votes (0.5 per cent of the total). Its fortunes increased with the decline of Scotland's traditional industries in the 1960s, which brought rising unemployment and the feeling that the remote British parliament in London was indifferent to Scotland's fate. The SNP overturned a large LABOUR PARTY majority in a by-election at Hamilton, Lanarkshire in 1967 to secure its first MP and won its first seat in a general election in 1970 with 11.4 per cent of the vote. Its confidence grew with the discovery of North Sea oil off the Scottish coast, as it appeared now that Scotland could be economically independent of England and prosperous. Support for the SNP doubled between 1970 and 1974: in the February election of that year it won seven seats with 21.9 per cent of the vote, which increased to 11 MPs and 30.4 per cent of the vote in October.

Jim CALLAGHAN, as head of a minority Labour government in the late 1970s, needed SNP support to stay in power, so he promised a SCOTTISH DEVOLUTION bill. When a referendum in Scotland in 1979 failed to meet the requirements of the bill the SNP promptly withdrew its support from the minority Labour government, which had then to face an election in 1979 which it lost. In that election the SNP vote fell to 17.3 per cent and its MPs were reduced to two, which increased to three in 1987 and six in 1997. After Tony BLAIR won the general election of 1997 he held a referendum on the setting up of a Scottish parliament. This was approved massively by the Scottish people, a result welcomed by the SNP (which had campaigned for a 'Yes' vote), which saw it as the first step towards an independent Scotland.

'Scottish and Welsh Nationalist Parties since 1945', J. Kellas in *UK Political Parties Since 1945*, A. Seldon (ed.) (1990)

SDI (Strategic Defense Initiative)   Announced by President REAGAN in March 1983 and called Star Wars by the press, it was designed to provide an effective anti-ballistic missile system in space by using satellite-launched lasers or particle beams to destroy missiles in flight. Reagan said it was purely defensive but GORBACHEV maintained that it was a 'first strike' weapon which could be used offensively against targets on land. Critics said that it would violate the ABM (Anti-ballistic Missile) Treaty of 1972 (part of SALT I), which restricted the US and Soviet Union to building no more than two ABM sites and would undermine the concept of deterrence based on mutually assured destruction (MAD), as it would allow a first strike to be delivered behind a space shield which would prevent any retaliation. It would effectively make the Soviet Union's nuclear arsenal useless and would restore to the US the dominance it had enjoyed in the 1950s. Many scientists doubted whether it could ever be effective but the USSR could not take the risk and so increased its military spending to unsustainable levels, thus contributing to the COLLAPSE OF THE SOVIET UNION. On 13 May 1993, after spending $30 billion on its development, the Pentagon announced that further research on SDI would be discontinued.

SEATO (Southeast Asia Treaty Organization) (1954–77)   An alliance for the containment of communism. After the French defeat in the INDOCHINA WAR OF INDEPENDENCE (1946–54) and the communist victory in the CHINESE CIVIL WAR (1946–9) the US was greatly concerned about the spread of communism in Southeast Asia. John Foster DULLES, the US Secretary of State, wanted to prevent this, and particularly communist expansion in Vietnam, Cambodia and Laos. He therefore organized a Collective Defence Treaty, which was signed in Manila in September 1954 by the US, Britain, France, Australia, New Zealand, Pakistan, the Philippines and Thailand. The signatories agreed to help each other if any of them was attacked or weakened by internal subversion:

the poorer members would receive economic assistance from the richer. SEATO did not take part in the VIETNAM WAR owing to disagreement among the allies but slowly developed counter-insurgency techniques which were applied in Thailand and the Philippines. It failed to contain communism and after the US pulled out of Vietnam Pakistan withdrew in 1973, France in 1974 and SEATO was disbanded three years later.

SEATO: The Failure of an Alliance Strategy, L. Buszynski (1983)

Second Republic (Brazil) (1946–64)   A new constitution in 1946 replaced the *Estado Novo* (New State) of Getúlio Vargas by representative democracy, with a President elected for five years who could not stand for a second consecutive term. In fact there was considerable continuity with the *Estado Novo*, as the lines of development followed after the Second World war were those laid down by Vargas in the 1930s. The state continued to take the lead in import-substitution industrialization and the 1943 Labour Code was maintained, giving many benefits to workers: an eight-hour day, paid holidays, the right to strike, minimum wages and health and safety regulations, though these did not apply to the exploited agricultural labourers. Enrico Dutra (President 1946–51) relaxed import and exchange controls to attract foreign investment but like Vargas was an economic nationalist, who nationalized most of the foreign-owned railway network and enlarged the huge Volta Redonda steelworks to make the country self-sufficient in heavy industry.

Vargas became President for the third time in 1950, though this was the first time he had been directly elected. Chosen on a nationalist and pro-labour ticket, he soon found that foreign investment (of which nationalists disapproved) was needed for continued industrialization. He wanted a partnership with US companies for oil exploration but Congress vetoed this. Faced with a huge INTERNATIONAL DEBT, he asked Oswaldo de Aranha to reduce it. Aranha's austerity measures produced strikes and a conflict with the Minister of Labour, João Goulart, whom Vargas dismissed. This annoyed the trade unions so in 1954 Vargas announced that the minimum wage would be doubled, thus antagonizing the industrialists. The armed forces stepped in and gave Vargas an ultimatum – resign or be removed. On 24 August 1954 he committed suicide by shooting himself.

Juscelino Kubitschek (President 1956–61), of Czech descent, found the economy in chaos but rejected deflation and went for growth, promising 'fifty years of development in five'. His main project was the building of a new capital, Brasilia, 600 miles north-west of Rio de Janeiro in the almost uninhabited state of Goías. Soon renowned throughout the world for its modern architecture, particularly that of Oscar Niemeyer, it aimed to open up the hinterland. It did eventually produce economic growth in Goías and Matto Grosso but in the short term immediately added enormously to the state debt.

Kubitschek's successor as President. Jânio Quadros, resigned after only seven months and was followed by his populist Vice-President, João Goulart, backed by the nationalists and the trade unions but distrusted by the armed forces and the right. When Congress passed a law restricting the remittances of foreign companies to 10 per cent of their investment capital, foreign investment declined. Goulart therefore printed money to pay for development, with the result that inflation reached 65 per cent in 1962. There was a run on the currency and strikes and food riots as living standards plummeted. Goulart then set about creating a mass following for himself. He was a wealthy rancher and no revolutionary but his proposal to nationalize the oil industry, expropriate the large estates and legalize the Communist Party alarmed the middle class and industrialists. On 31 March 1964 a bloodless military coup ended his presidency and began a period of Brazilian military rule. Goulart took refuge in Uruguay.

Politics in Brazil, 1930–64, T. E. Skidmore (1967)
The Brazilian Economy: Growth and Development, W. Baer (1989)
Brazil: Politics in a Patrimonial Society, R. Roett (1992)

Selma Freedom March (1965)   A march to protest at the intimidation which prevented blacks from voting in Dallas County, Alabama. Selma, a city of 29,000, had 15,000 blacks of voting age, of whom only 355 were registered to vote. Martin Luther KING chose Selma as he thought whites would resist violently and that this (through television) would draw attention to his cause and force the government to act. Sheriff Jim Clark, like 'Bull' Connor in the Birmingham demonstrations of 1963, was expected to overreact, which he did. King decided to lead a protest march from Selma to the state capital of Montgomery, 56 miles away, where the participants would petition Governor Wallace to protect blacks who wanted to register to vote. When the march began on 7 March, there followed one of the most vicious assaults in the history of the CIVIL RIGHTS MOVEMENT. Troopers attacked the demonstrators with tear gas, while Clark and his men used bull whips and rubber tubing wrapped in barbed wire. All this was seen on national television. From that time it was clear that Congress would have to act: on 15 March President JOHNSON asked it for a strong new voting rights law. On 17 March a judge rejected Wallace's request for a ban on the march and ordered state and local officials not to interfere with it. The march, led by King, began again on 21 March and was successfully completed on the 25th. It played a great part in securing passage of the Voting Rights Act of 1965 (see CIVIL RIGHTS ACTS), though Johnson knew that the right of blacks to vote would not affect the deep-seated racism and discrimination in the South. In 1994 the average household income of blacks in Selma was $9,615, of whites $25,580: over half the blacks in the area lived in poverty.

Sendero Luminoso (Shining Path)   A Marxist guerrilla movement based in the Indian peasant communities of Ayacucho province in Peru. Founded in 1960 by Abimael Guzmán, a university professor of philosophy at the University of Ayacucho, it was the most radical and ruthless guerrilla movement in Latin America. Its ideology was a mixture of Marxism, Maoism, *indigenismo* (which rejected European influence and wanted to revive the cultural heritage of the Indian peoples) and of the ideas of José Carlos Mariategui, the founder of Peruvian communism who sought a return to the Inca system of co-operative agriculture. It was at its most active in the 1980s. It assassinated politicians and local officials but also leaders of the left in trade unions and peasant organizations which did not co-operate with it. Sendero controlled large rural areas and many towns in the south and central highlands. Its 'armed strikes' in the cities succeeded in intimidating both the authorities and the local population: it regularly cut off the electricity supply to the main cities, including the capital Lima. DRUG TRADE barons financed it in return for protection but it was involved in a bloody conflict with another revolutionary movement, MRTA (*Movimiento Revolucionario Tupac Amaru*), which competed with it for territory and drug money.

In their drive against Sendero the security forces committed atrocities and, according to human rights organizations such as AMNESTY INTERNATIONAL, were responsible for over half the 25,000 deaths during the struggle. Their greatest success came in 1992 when Guzmán and 20 leading members of Sendero were captured. Guzmán was sentenced to life imprisonment and though Sendero attacks continued, its number of activists declined from a peak of 10,000 to under 1,000. In 1994 Guzmán called on his followers to make peace.

Militarism and Politics in Latin America: Peru from Sanchez Cerro to Sendero Luminoso, D. M. Masterson (1991)

The Shining Path of Peru, D. S. Palmer (ed.) (1992)

Senghor, Léopold Sédar (1906–)   President of Senegal (1960–80). The son of prosperous Catholic parents, he was educated at mission schools and at the University of Paris. He was the first African to gain an 'aggregation' degree. From 1935–9 he was a secondary school teacher in France, where he taught in *lycées* (grammar schools) from 1935–9. In Paris he became a close friend of the West Indian poet Aimé Césaire: they both wrote poetry in French and devised the idea of *Négritude*, which they described as 'the affirmation of the values of African culture'. Senghor joined the French army when the Second World War began, was captured by the Germans and was in a prisoner of war camp from 1940–2. Released, he joined the Resistance (1942–4) and after the war was elected in Senegal as a Socialist Party deputy (1946–58) to the French National Assembly. He took part in the formation of the French Union in 1946 and ten years later opposed, as did Sékou Touré in Guinea, the *loi cadre*, as it split French West Africa into too many small, weak states, which were bound to be dependent on France. Senghor formed his own political party in 1948, the Bloc *Démocratique Sénégalais* which, under various names, has dominated Senegalese politics since its electoral victory of 1951. Senegal joined Mali in the Mali Federation in 1959 but Senghor withdrew from it a year later, when Senegal became independent with himself as President.

His rule was authoritarian. He banned some political parties and absorbed the rest by 1966 into his own governing party and nationalized major industries. There was considerable unrest in 1968 among workers and students after a wage freeze: only the presence of French troops prevented a revolution. Senghor responded to further unrest in 1973 by imprisoning students and banning trade unions. Senegal's economy was mainly dependent on the export of one crop, ground-nuts, and this was badly affected from 1968 by the Sahelian drought. Senghor borrowed from the WORLD BANK and IMF but this added the problem of indebtedness to Senegal's other problems. Friendly relations with France, which provided financial and technical aid and was granted a military base at Dakar, account for the regime's extraordinary longevity. Senghor resigned as President in 1980 (the first African leader since DECOLO-NIZATION to do so voluntarily) to be followed by his chosen successor, Abdou Diouf. In 1984 he was the first African to be admitted to the *Académie Française*.

Black, French and African: A Life of Léopold Sédar Senghor, J. G. Vaillant (1990)

Shamir, Yitzhak (1915–) Prime Minister of Israel (1983–4, 1986–92). Born in Poland, he studied law at Warsaw University and, after emigrating to Palestine in 1935, at the Hebrew University, Jerusalem. In 1937 he joined Irgun Zvai Leumi, a terrorist organization, but left it in 1940 to become a leader of the even more extreme Stern Gang, and was associated with the assassination of Lord Moyne, British Minister of State in Cairo, in 1944. Arrested by the British in 1946, he escaped to France and did not return until the BIRTH OF ISRAEL in 1948. From 1955–65 he worked for Mossad (Israeli Intelligence) mainly in Europe and became its head. He then pursued a business career before being elected to the Knesset (Israeli parliament) in 1973. From 1977–80 he was Menachem BEGIN's choice as Speaker of the Knesset, though he opposed the CAMP DAVID ACCORDS (1978), as they involved returning Sinai to Egypt. Foreign Minister from 1980–3 he became head of the Likud Party and Prime Minister when Begin resigned in 1983.

In the 1984 election no party gained a majority, so Shamir made a coalition with Shimon PERES and the Labour Party by which Peres would be Prime Minister for two years with Shamir as Deputy Premier

and Foreign Minister: for the following two years the positions would be reversed. In the 1988 election Likud gained only a small majority, so Shamir once again made a coalition with Labour with himself as Prime Minister. In 1990 he fell out with Peres, who supported the US proposal for an Israeli–Palestinian peace conference which Shamir opposed, and for the next two years ruled without Labour, in alliance with extreme right-wing and religious parties. Shamir wanted a Greater Israel stretching 'from the Jordan River to the Mediterranean Sea'. He helped his Housing Minister, Ariel Sharon, in bringing about the most extensive expansion of Jewish settlement in the WEST BANK and Gaza, territory occupied by Israel after the SIX DAY WAR (1967). During the GULF WAR he did not retaliate when Saddam HUS-SEIN directed Scud missiles at Tel Aviv and Haifa, as this would have blown apart the Allied coalition against Iraq.

After the war the Americans were anxious to settle the Palestinian problem by calling for Israeli–Palestinian talks. Shamir was opposed to the creation of a separate Palestinian state in the OCCUPIED TERRITORIES and refused to negotiate with the PLO and Yasir ARAFAT. The American Secretary of State James Baker was alarmed at Jewish settlement on the West Bank and at Shamir's handling of the INTI-FADA (which caused many teenage deaths) as they were obstacles to peace. In 1991 he persuaded Egypt, Syria, Lebanon and Jordan (with some Palestinians attached to the Jordan delegation) to take part in a conference to bring peace to the Middle East based on Resolution 242 of the Security Council of the UNITED NATIONS, which the PLO had accepted in 1988. Shamir, under intense US pressure, agreed to take part but negotiations were soon deadlocked over procedural issues. It was clear that as long as Shamir was Prime Minister no progress would be made, but he was defeated in the 1992 election and the Labour Party returned to power. He then revealed that he had planned to drag out the talks for ten years. In 1993 he gave up the leadership of Likud.

Sharpeville African township south of Johannesburg in South Africa. When the ANC (African National Congress) announced a series of one-day marches against the pass laws (all black South Africans had to carry an identification card) the PAC (Pan-Africanist Congress) called for a more sustained campaign: demonstrators should refuse to carry passes and should present themselves at police stations, inviting arrest. During a peaceful march to the police station at Sharpeville on 21 March 1960, the police panicked and fired on the crowd: 69 people were killed, many shot in the back, and 186 wounded. There were strikes throughout the country but there was no real threat to white supremacy. VERWOERD's government arrested the leaders of the ANC and PAC and banned both organizations: repression practically destroyed the African resistance movement. Universal condemnation of the massacre led to demands at the UNITED NATIONS for sanctions against South Africa but these were vetoed by Britain and the US, who continued to invest in South Africa. The 'stability' which followed the repression helped to produce a decade of unparalleled economic growth. The fierce criticism by members of the COMMONWEALTH of Sharpeville in particular and APARTHEID in general led Verwoerd to withdraw from that organization in 1961.

Black Politics in South Africa Since 1945, T. Lodge (ed.) (1983)

Shevardnadze, Eduard (1928–) Soviet Foreign Minister (1985–90, 1991) and head of state in Georgia (1992–). The son of a Georgian schoolteacher, he entered Tbilisi Medical College to become a doctor but after joining the CPSU in 1948 he was offered a post in the Komsomol (Communist Youth League). This began his political career, which saw him rise through the party hierarchy to become Minister of the Interior (1965–72) in Georgia, where he made a reputation by fearlessly exposing corruption which went to the top of the party hierarchy. He was appointed First Secretary of the Georgian Communist Party in 1972 and held this post until 1985 when GORBACHEV, an old friend, unexpectedly brought him to Moscow as Foreign Minister of the USSR and a full member of the Politburo.

He helped to end the COLD WAR by stopping Soviet intervention in the AFGHAN CIVIL WAR and by supporting Gorbachev's efforts to make arms reduction treaties with the USA. He broke the impasse in arms reduction negotiations by consenting in 1989 not to link arms reductions with the ending of SDI and in 1990 agreed with NATO on convential arms ceilings in Europe. Such views roused the hostility of nationalists and the MILITARY–INDUSTRIAL COMPLEX. In December 1990 he resigned because he felt that Gorbachev was making too many concessions to the conservative communists and nationalists and warned of an impending dictatorship, nine months before the AUGUST COUP of 1991.

In 1991 there was chaos in Georgia, where Zviad Gamsakhurdia was elected President. He began a civil war by taking military action against separatists in South Ossetia (where the inhabitants wanted to join the Russian Republic) and provoked armed resistance in Abkhazia by trying to abolish its autonomous status. By January 1992 law and order had collapsed throughout Georgia and military opponents of Gamsakhurdia had taken over the country. They invited Shevardnadze to return. He agreed if elections were held for a parliament and for a Chairman of parliament, who would in effect be the state President. In October he was overwhelmingly elected as Chairman but chaos continued as 200,000 refugees fled from Abkhazia to Georgia. Abkhazia, aided by arms from Russia, was effectively lost in 1993, when Georgia seemed about to collapse. Shevardnadze went to Moscow and obtained Russian support in ending the civil war, in return for Georgia joining the CIS and allowing Russian military bases in Georgia. There was a fragile truce in

Abkhazia in 1994 and in 1997 Shevardnadze and the Abkhazian leader Ardzinba met and agreed to settle their differences peacefully, but huge obstacles remained to a permanent resolution of the conflict, such as the return of the refugees and whether Abkhazia should remain an autonomous province of Georgia or be independent.

The Wars of Eduard Shevardnadze, C. M. Ekedahl and M. A. Goodman (1997)
'Success Story', J. F. Matlock *New York Review of Books*, 25 September 1997

Shii (Shia)   A minority group (about 15 per cent) of Muslims. Shii means 'party' and refers to Muslims who believe that the imamate (the temporal and spiritual leadership of Islam) belongs to Ali (the Prophet Muhammad's cousin, husband of his daughter Fatima and father of the Prophet's only grandchild) and his descendants. The most important group is the 'Twelver' Shiis, who believe that there were 12 Imams (Ali and his descendants) after the Prophet: the twelfth did not die but disappeared and one day will return. 'Twelver' Shiism has been Iran's state religion since the sixteenth century. The Ayatollah KHOMEINI believed that mullahs (Shii learned in Islamic law) were entrusted by the invisible Imam with responsibility for the whole community and should return it to an ideal Islamic state. Shii practice is much the same as that of SUNNI Islam, as it is based on the same sources: the Quran, the *hadith* (traditions of the Prophet) and the *Sharia* (Islamic Law). Shiis differ from Sunnis in that their religious activities (theological colleges and welfare organizations) are not under the control of the state and their clerics are ranked and given titles, such as Ayatollah (sign of God). Shiis are the largest group in Iraq (about 55 per cent) and Lebanon and form about a quarter of the population in Saudi Arabia and a fifth in Pakistan.

Introduction to Shi'i Islam, M. Momen (1985)

show trials (1949–52)   Public trials of leading communists in Eastern Europe, which resembled those in the Soviet Union from 1936–8. TITO's break with Moscow in 1948 led STALIN to believe that there were internal enemies in all the 'fraternal' communist parties of Eastern Europe, who must be exposed and punished, so he ordered a purge. Hundreds and thousands of party members, whose numbers had increased astronomically since 1945 (the Polish CP had 20,000 prewar members, 1.3 million in 1948; the Hungarian CP 3,000 members in 1945, 1.2 million in 1949), were dismissed, but the terror reached its peak when party leaders were tried. Particularly suspect were those who had served in the International Brigades in the Spanish Civil War, communists who had spent the war at home or in London rather than in Moscow, or who had any contact with Tito. Jews too were distrusted, as Israel had sided with the US. Communists who rejected the Stalinist model of industrialization were accused of 'bourgeois nationalism' and of following the 'national path to socialism'. The trials were scripted: victims had to rehearse their answers to questions numerous times before the public trial.

The first major trial to take place was in Albania in May 1949, when a former Minister of the Interior, Koci Xoxe, was accused of wanting to unite Albania with Yugoslavia and was executed. The most important of the anti-Tito trials, and a model for those to follow, was that of László Rajk in Hungary, who had been a member of the International Brigade in Spain and confessed to having been a US and French agent at that time. He was hanged in october 1949. Traicko Kostov, who had been in contact with Yugoslav partisans in the Second World War, was executed in Bulgaria in December 1949. In Czechoslovakia GOTTWALD was slow to begin a witch-hunt but eventually the most murderous of the show trials was organized in Prague by the Russians. Eleven of the fourteen accused were Jews, including Rudolf Slánský, the General Secretary of the party, who was alleged to be an American agent working for the Israelis while at the same time serving Tito. Eleven of those tried were executed in December 1952. The death of Stalin brought a change of attitude in the USSR and an end to the show trials, though Patrascanu was shot as late as 1954 in Romania.

The only countries in the Eastern bloc which did not stage major show trials were East Germany and Poland. Leading communists there were put on trial, such as GOMULKA, who had rejected the collectivization of agriculture and had to admit to 'nationalistic and right-wing mistakes'. They were imprisoned and disgraced and not executed.

The Czechoslovak Political Trials 1950–4, J. Pelikan (1971)
Show Trials: Stalinist Purges in Eastern Europe 1948–54, G. H. Hodos (1987)

Sihanouk, Norodom (1922–)   King of Cambodia (1941–55) and then, at various times, Prime Minister, President and king again. He has been the dominant figure in Cambodian politics from the mid-1940s. When the French returned to Cambodia (part of Indochina in the French Empire) after the Second World War he demanded independence. The French, in serious difficulties in the INDOCHINA WAR OF INDEPENDENCE (1946–54) agreed to this in 1953, so Sihanouk became a hero. The GENEVA ACCORDS (1954) required elections to be held in Cambodia in 1955, so Sihanouk abdicated in favour of his father, became Prime Minister and Foreign Minister and formed his own political party, the Popular Socialist Community (Sangkum). This won all the seats in the National Assembly in the rigged elections of 1955. From then until 1970, with Sangkum the only party allowed to contest elections, Sihanouk ruled as a dictator.

His main aim, with traditional enemies Vietnam and Thailand on either side, was to keep out of any regional conflict which would threaten Cambodia's independence. During the VIETNAM WAR (1960–75) the North Vietnamese used the Ho Chi Minh trail through Cambodia to provide the VIET CONG in South Vietnam with arms and set up a communist headquarters in Cambodia. Sihanouk, to prevent the VIET MINH from supporting the Khmer Rouge (Cambodian Communists), turned a blind eye and in 1965 broke off diplomatic relations with the US. In 1970 the army, in a US-backed coup led by Lon Nol, overthrew Sihanouk when he was abroad.

The coup threw Sihanouk into the arms of the communists. He went to Beijing, were he called for a United Front with the Khmer Rouge and formed a government-in-exile. As the Khmer Rouge gained control of the Front, Sihanouk was left as a powerless figurehead. When the Khmer Rouge under POL POT defeated Lon Nol and changed the name of Cambodia to Kampuchea, Sihanouk lived in the capital Phnom Penh under house arrest. Six of his fourteen children and several grandchildren were killed by the Khmer Rouge. He was released in 1979 when the VIETNAMESE OCCUPATION OF KAMPUCHEA took place and formed another government-in-exile, which included the Khmer Rouge, in 1982. After the Vietnamese withdrew from Cambodia in 1989 preparations were made, under UNITED NATIONS auspices, for a peace agreement which was signed by all factions in 1991. Sihanouk was elected President of Cambodia's Supreme National Council. After elections in 1993 the National Assembly voted to restore the monarchy and he became king again but he had no real power. By this time his health was poor and he received treatment in Beijing for prostate cancer.

Sihanouk, M. Osborne (1994)

Sino-Indian dispute (1962)   A conflict over two areas of the Sino-Indian border which had not been agreed in a formal treaty and where the maps used by each side differed considerably. In the east is an area of 35,000 square miles called the North-East Frontier Agency (NEFA), which is shown as part of

China on Guomindang maps but has never been administered by China. In the west is the Aksai-Chin plateau, mainly desert and uninhabited, which India claimed as part of Ladakh. It was shown as part of British India on maps of the Raj but was never administered by Britain or by India after independence.

Trouble arose as a result of the Tibetan revolt against China in 1959, when India discovered that China had built a road through western Tibet and across the Aksai-Chin plateau. China said that the border, never defined, should be fixed by negotiation and proposed a compromise which would give the Aksai-Chin to China and NEFA to India. The Indians would not accept this and in 1962 attacked Chinese troops in NEFA. The Chinese reacted forcefully and won an overwhelming victory, leaving India humiliated and bitter. They expelled India from the whole of the disputed area but did not go beyond the territory China claimed. China then announced a cease-fire and handed NEFA to India, thus giving India two-thirds of the disputed territory. There was no agreed settlement and Sino-Indian relations remained sour for the next 20 years.

India's China War, N. Maxwell (1970)

Sino-Soviet dispute (1956–89)   It arose out of ideological differences between China and the Soviet Union and out of different perceptions of their national interest. MAO ZEDONG had differed from STALIN since the 1920s in asserting the need for a mass-based rural revolution in China, but it was not until KHRUSHCHEV's secret speech to the TWENTIETH CONGRESS OF THE CPSU that the rift opened. Mao was furious that he had not been told in advance and had further cause for complaint when Soviet leaders criticized the GREAT LEAP FORWARD and the formation of COMMUNES. In 1959 Khrushchev reneged on an agreement to provide China with technical data on the manufacture of an atom bomb and in 1960 withdrew all Soviet technicians and their blueprints from

China: 300 industrial projects had to be abandoned.

China and the USSR differed too on foreign policy. Khrushchev's policy of peaceful coexistence and his statement that 'war is not fatalistically inevitable' between communist and capitalist states irked the Chinese, who felt that it was better to 'resist imperialism firmly and bury it' rather than 'to be afraid of sacrifice and to capitulate'. There was further acrimony when there was a SINO-INDIAN DISPUTE and fighting between India and China in 1962 over their border. Khrushchev refused to support China's claims, gave generous credits to India and described the fighting as 'stupid'. In the same year the Chinese condemned the Soviet withdrawal of missiles during the CUBAN MISSILE CRISIS as shameful capitulation. The NUCLEAR TEST BAN TREATY (1963) was to Mao simply an attempt to stop China becoming a nuclear power.

Tension continued under BREZHNEV. China condemned the WARSAW PACT invasion of Czechoslovakia to end the PRAGUE SPRING in 1968 as aggressive imperialism and regarded the BREZHNEV DOCTRINE as one that could be used against it. In 1969 there was a series of border clashes with the Soviet Union, which built up large military forces on the Chinese frontier. As Chinese relations with the US improved in the 1970s, the Soviet Union moved closer to Vietnam, whose relations with China deteriorated. After the death of Mao DENG XIAOPING sought better relations with the USSR so that he could concentrate on modernizing the economy. ANDROPOV and particularly GORBACHEV responded positively. Soviet troops were withdrawn from the Chinese frontier and from Afghanistan, trade was increased and in 1989 Gorbachev visited Beijing to normalize relations.

Sino-Soviet Relations, T. Hart (1987)

Sino-Soviet Treaty (1950)   It established a 30-year alliance between China and the

Soviet Union. STALIN had done little to help the communists during the CHINESE CIVIL WAR (1946–9) but the imposition of a US trade embargo on China in November 1949 compelled MAO ZEDONG to look to the USSR for economic help. Mao went to Moscow (his first visit outside China) and after tough negotiations concluded the treaty. Each side would aid the other if attacked by Japan or countries in alliance with Japan. This seemed unlikely, as Japan was disarmed after the Second World War and its constitution prevented it from having armed forces, but it was understood that the Soviet Union would support China if it was attacked by the US. Mao received a modest loan of US$300 million (repayable at 1 per cent interest per annum) with which to buy Soviet machinery. In return Mao had to accept the concessions JIANG JIESHI (Chiang Kai-shek) had made in a treaty with Stalin in 1945: he recognized Outer Mongolia (a Soviet satellite) as independent, allowed the Soviet Union the use of naval bases at Lushun (formerly Port Arthur) and Dairen and joint Sino-Soviet administration of the Chinese Eastern Railway across Manchuria. KHRUSHCHEV gave up these concessions, apart from the one referring to Outer Mongolia, in 1954.

The alliance appeared one-sided in the USSR's favour but it may have deterred the US from attacking China during the KOREAN WAR (1950–3). Soviet assistance in China's first Five Year Plan helped to build 100 industrial plants. Thousands of Soviet experts were sent to advise the Chinese, Chinese students were sent to the USSR for training and the Five Year Plan was based on the Russian model, with a concentration on heavy industry, so Soviet influence in China was considerable in the early 1950s. Tensions soon arose, however, which led to the SINO-SOVIET DISPUTE.

China's Role in World Affairs, M. Yahuda (1978)

Six Day War (5–10 June 1967)   A war in which Israel attacked Egypt, Syria and Jordan. Arab states had never made peace with Israel since the ARAB–ISRAELI WAR of 1948–9. Al-Fatah attacked Israeli targets across the frontier from Jordan in November 1966, but it was the actions of President NASSER of Egypt which made war inevitable. On 18 May 1967 he asked the UNITED NATIONS to withdraw from Sinai, where they were stationed on the Israeli border. He then moved his troops into Sinai and closed the Straits of Tiran to Israeli shipping. On 30 May King HUSSEIN of Jordan signed a defence pact with Egypt, which already had one with Syria. As the UN was clearly not going to take any action to open the Straits the Israeli Defence Minister, Moshe DAYAN, persuaded the Israeli cabinet to authorize a pre-emptive strike.

The outcome of the war was decided in the first three hours on 5 June as Israeli planes attacked all 17 Egyptian airfields, destroying 300 of their combat aircraft on the ground. The Jordanian airforce was annihilated and the Syrian suffered such heavy losses that it took no active part in the war. Israel later claimed that it had destroyed 418 Arab warplanes for the loss of 27 of its own. Israel now had air superiority, which it used to devastating effect in attacking Arab armour. On 6 June Israel captured the Gaza Strip and advanced into Sinai, defeated seven Egyptian divisions and reached the Suez Canal by 9 June. Jordan too was rapidly defeated on 7 June, losing the old city of Jerusalem and the WEST BANK and accepted the UN's demand for a cease-fire, which Egypt also agreed to on 8 June. Israel could now turn on Syria, which had confined itself to artillery bombardments. Israeli troops stormed the GOLAN HEIGHTS which overlooked Israel and advanced 30 miles (48 km) into Syria, which accepted a cease-fire on 10 June.

This remarkable and crushing victory left Israel in control of Sinai, the Gaza Strip, the West Bank, the whole of Jerusalem and the Golan Heights. It was now the dominant power in the Middle East with troops on the east bank of the Suez Canal. A problem Israel created for itself was that it had half a million resentful Arabs to control in the conquered territories. Egypt had suffered a terrible disaster: its economy was badly affected by the loss of its oilfields in Sinai and by the closure of the Suez Canal; its prestige had plummeted, as had its claims to be leader of the Arab world. Another result of the war was an intensification of the PALESTINIAN REFUGEE problem: 300,000 Palestinians fled from the West Bank across the Jordan, while 100,000 Syrians left the Golan Heights. The great powers now became more involved in the Middle East. The prestige of the Soviet Union, the supplier of arms to Egypt and Syria, declined, while the US saw in Israel a country which could prevent the spread of Soviet influence in the Middle East and so for the first time supplied Israel with arms and aid on a massive scale. The Arab states, as in 1948, refused to make peace or recognize the state of Israel and rejected direct negotiations.

The Sandstorm, D. Kimche and D. Bawley (1968)

SLORC (State Law and Order Restoration Council)

A military junta which seized power in Burma (Myanmar from 1989) in September 1988. It disbanded the People's Assembly and governed under martial law. In the brutal repression which followed up to 3,000 pro-democracy demonstrators were killed. The junta decided to hold elections in 1990 for an assembly which would draw up a new constitution but before the election placed under house arrest the leaders of the opposition, including AUNG SAN SUU KYI. In the elections the opposition National League for Democracy (NLD) won 80 per cent of the seats. SLORC refused to accept this and has not allowed the representatives to meet. All leaders of the NLD were detained and Suu Kyi remained under house arrest.

SLORC differed from the previous military dictatorship of NE WIN in that free enterprise replaced socialism as the government ideology. South Korea, where military leaders such as PARK CHUNG HEE worked closely with business corporations, is their model. Korean, Thai and Japanese investors have taken part in joint ventures to develop Myanmar's abundant natural resources, especially oil. The French company Total is building a billion dollar pipeline to carry Burma's natural gas to Thailand. Forced labour is used on a massive scale to build the infrastructure (roads and railways) for tourism and foreign investment. Large licence fees help SLORC to build up foreign reserves and to acquire more arms with which to consolidate its position, but investors are cautious because of unrest, particularly from the ethnic minorities seeking autonomy or independence. SLORC became heavily involved in the DRUG TRADE (half the world's heroin supply comes from Burma). The UNITED NATIONS Commission on Human Rights reported in February 1996 on SLORC's violations: 'Torture, summary and arbitrary executions, forced labour ... and oppression of ethnic and religious minorities'.

Burma: The Challenge of Change in a Divided Society, P. Carey (ed.) (1997)

Social Democratic Party (SDP)

British political party which rose and fell in the 1980s. Roy Jenkins in his Dimbleby lecture in November 1979 said that as the LABOUR PARTY moved to the left and the CONSERVATIVE PARTY under Margaret THATCHER moved sharply to the right the centre was unrepresented. Labour went even further to the left at its party conference in 1980, when withdrawal from the EEC, nuclear disarmament and more nationalization became party policy. An electoral college was to be set up to choose the party leader and in January 1981 the structure of the college was announced: 40 per cent of the vote was to go to the trade unions, 30 per cent to the constituency parties and 30 per cent to the Labour MPs, who would therefore lose control over choosing their leader. All this was too much for the

'Gang of Four', Labour ex-ministers Roy Jenkins, David Owen, Shirley Williams and William Rodgers, who launched the SDP in March 1981. By the end of the year 28 Labour MPs and one Conservative had joined the party. The SDP agreed to an alliance with the LIBERAL PARTY, whereby the two parties would not compete with each other nationally but would field only one candidate, either Liberal or SDP, in each constituency. A Gallup poll in December 1981 indicated that the Alliance had 50 per cent support, Labour and the Conservatives trailing with 23 per cent each.

A new force in British politics appeared to have arrived but the SDP lacked constituency roots. Its middle-class leaders did not attract traditional Labour voters and the FALKLANDS WAR deprived it of the initiative and of publicity. Even so, it did well in the 1983 election with 25.4 per cent of the vote, only two points behind Labour (27.6 per cent) but the first-past-the-post system gave Labour 209 MPs and the Alliance 23. Many sought a merger of the two parties but Owen, who had replaced Jenkins as leader of the SDP in 1983, strongly opposed this. In the 1987 election the Alliance vote fell 3 per cent to 22.5 per cent and it had one less seat. The pressure for a merger, still resisted by Owen, now became intense. A ballot of SDP members showed 57 per cent were in favour: the Liberal Party Conference in 1987 voted by 998 votes to 21 to merge. Owen resigned as SDP leader while Steel arranged for the SDP and Liberals to join as the Social and Liberal Democrats (which soon became the Liberal Democrats) in March 1988. Owen continued to lead a rump of the SDP but it performed disastrously in the 1990 local government elections, when it won only five seats and the Liberal Democrats 669. Owen disbanded the party, whose two remaining MPs were defeated in the 1992 election.

SDP: The Birth, Life and Death of the Social Democratic Party, I. Crewe and A. King (1995)

social market economy   The economic system developed in the Federal Republic of Germany (FRG: West Germany) after the Second World War by Chancellor ADENAUER's Economic Minister Ludwig ERHARD. He rejected the planned economy and nationalization which the SPD (Social Democratic Party) wanted, as he thought that this would give rise to a large bureaucracy, which would eat up resources needed for investment. Erhard wanted industry to be privately owned with the market setting price and wage levels but also wanted a WELFARE STATE to protect the interests of the workers and to give them a stake in the new economic system. Businesses were therefore freed from the restrictions imposed by the Third Reich and the Allied occupation authorities, but at the same time social insurance covered the old, the disabled and the unemployed. There was a comprehensive system of health care, family allowances, government assistance with rents for the poor and for the building of houses. To correct inequalities resulting from the war (millions of Germans had come as refugees to the FRG from former German territory seized by Poland and the Soviet Union) burden-sharing legislation in 1952 transferred resources to those who had suffered most.

Another aspect of the social market economy was to bring the TRADE UNIONS into a co-operative partnership with employers. Unions were organized so that one union represented a whole industry. This avoided rivalries between competing unions, simplified bargaining with employers and strengthened the unions. Seventeen industrial unions formed the German Trade Union Federation (DGB: *Deutscher Gewerkschaftsbund*) which took some responsibility, with the state and the employers, for decision-making in the policy of co-determination (*Mitbestimmung*). This was introduced by the British in the Ruhr: workers in the coal and steel industries were given half the seats on supervisory boards, though management had the casting vote. It was extended to all coal and steel companies with over 1,000 employers by the Co-determination Law of 1951. In 1976 this was extended to all firms with over 2,000 employees. Many employers bitterly opposed co-determination, yet it made German firms more competitive, as workers were fully informed about investment decisions and the introduction of new technology. Workers' Councils were also formed (in 1952): they had no decision-making powers but had to be consulted and informed about plans which affected employees. In return for power-sharing workers had to accept limits on their freedom of action. Many disputes were settled by labour courts: while this was happening workers could not strike and all strikes needed a three to one majority in favour in a ballot. Unions had to accept the free market and abandon the class struggle, so they saw their role as increasing benefits for workers within the market economy. As unions had such an important role in the social market, conservative CDU (Christian Democratic Union) governments found it very difficult to reduce their powers or cut the welfare system: all CDU cabinets contained at least one trade union representative. The social market economy, with its elaborate checks and balances to defuse conflict and promote co-operation, played a key role in the WIRTSCHAFTSWUNDER (economic miracle) in the FRG.

The Social Economy of West Germany, G. Hallett (1973)
The Politics of the West German Trade Unions, A. S. Markovits (1986)
Industrial Relations in West Germany, V. Berghahn and D. Karsten (1987)

Socialist Party (France)   In 1905 some Marxist groups coalesced to form the SFIO (French Section of the Workers' International) which sought the public ownership of the means of production. Led by Jean Jaurès, it loyally accepted the directive of the Second International (an organization founded in 1889 in which all socialist parties were repres-

ented) that it should not take part in bourgeois governments, though its revolutionary rhetoric was at variance with its democratic practice, which sought to attain power peacefully through parliament. By 1914 a million working-class voters supported it. In the mid-1930s the Fascist threat persuaded communists, socialists and radicals to join together in a Popular Front, which won the 1936 elections. Léon Blum therefore became the first socialist Prime Minister in France and in his short-lived administration brought the Bank of France under state control and introduced the 44-hour working week and paid holidays.

Socialists were members of many governments in the FOURTH REPUBLIC, sharing power with the PCF (Communist Party) until 1947 and then from 1947–53 as a 'third force' (opposed both to GAULLISM and the PCF) in alliance with the Radicals and MRP (a Christian Democratic Party). They nationalized some industries and helped to set up the WELFARE STATE and the ECSC (European Coal and Steel Community), following the lead of Robert Schuman and Jean MONNET. The SFIO went into opposition in 1952 for the first time since the war but returned to power under Guy MOLLET four years later. Mollet signed the TREATY OF ROME setting up the EEC (European Economic Community) but had a disastrous foreign policy, being partly responsible for the SUEZ CRISIS and for escalating the ALGERIAN WAR OF INDEPENDENCE (1954–62), a war which tore France apart. With its support declining precipitately the SFIO lamely voted for DE GAULLE to be given special powers and so brought the Fourth Republic to an end.

The Gaullists dominated the Fifth Republic until 1981 and kept the socialists out of office. In 1969 the SFIO changed it name to the PS (Socialist Party) and acquired a new leader, François MITTERRAND, who revived the moribund party by uniting the left. In 1972 he agreed on a common programme (much of which was carried out from 1981–3 when Mitterrand was President) with the PCF. By the time the communists withdrew from this agreement in 1977 the PS had made gains at their expense and attracted more votes than the PCF. In 1981 Mitterrand won the presidential election and the PS topped the poll in the parliamentary elections, so the socialists were in power for the first time in the Fifth Republic. At first the PS carried out a programme of nationalization and increased welfare expenditure, but as inflation and unemployment increased during the recession, Mitterrand did a U-turn to a SOCIAL MARKET ECONOMY. The socialists and their allies were narrowly defeated in the 1986 parliamentary elections, so Mitterrand had to cohabit with a Gaullist Prime Minister, Jacques CHIRAC, for two years until the socialists regained control of the Assembly. Economic problems, however, continued and in the 1993 elections the PS suffered a crushing defeat and Mitterrand had once again to cohabit with a Gaullist Prime Minister, Edouard Balladur. Socialists lost the presidency too when, after Mitterrand's term of office expired in 1995, Chirac won the presidential election. The Socialist Party took advantage of Prime Minister Juppé's unpopularity in seeking to cut back the social security system and bounced back in the 1997 general election, which President Chirac called unnecessarily. The Socialists and their allies won 253 seats (up from 63) to become by far the largest party. Their leader Lionel Josepin was the new Prime Minister.

The Long March of the French Left, R. W. Johnson (1981)
The French Socialist Party, D. S. Bell and B. Criddle (1988)
The French Socialists in Power, 1981–6, T. R. Christopherson (1991)

Solidarity   Polish workers' movement. It began as a trade union movement in August 1980, when workers at the Lenin Shipyard in Gdansk went on strike, led by Lech WALESA. Solidarity became a vast organization of ten million members from different social groups (manual and skilled labourers, teachers, doctors, lawyers, engineers), with branches throughout the country. In March 1981 there were demands for a general strike, and there was a danger that BREZHNEV would intervene, as he had done to crush the PRAGUE SPRING in 1968. This was avoided owing to pressure from President CARTER and as General JARUZELSKI, Prime Minister since February 1981 and Communist Party (CP) leader in October, proclaimed martial law in December, arrested Solidarity's leaders and abolished the union.

Solidarity went underground and did not surface again until 1988 when, with the economic situation deteriorating again (there was a huge foreign debt and large price rises), there were two waves of strikes. Though Solidarity was not responsible for them, the government agreed to round-table talks with Solidarity which began in February 1989. Solidarity was legalized in April and a new electoral law agreed for elections in June. The Communist Party was guaranteed 65 per cent of the seats in the Sejm (parliament) but, for the first time in communist Eastern Europe, the anti-communist opposition could compete for the remaining 35 per cent. There was also to be a Senate where the seats were open to all parties, and a President of the republic. Solidarity won a huge victory in the elections, gaining 92 out of 100 Senate seats and 160 out of 161 Sejm seats available. After this humiliation for the communists, a government was formed by the Catholic layman Tadeusz Mazowiecki of Solidarity, the first non-communist prime minister in Eastern Europe since 1948, an event which helped to bring about the collapse of other communist governments in the Soviet bloc.

Solidarity was now a political party as well as a trade union, but its free market reforms were unpopular, as they led to rising prices, unemployment and a falling standard of living. The differences between Walesa and the Solidarity intellectuals led to acrimonious exchanges and the destruction of Solidarity's unity, when Walesa formed his own party, the Centre Alliance. The presidential elections, which Walesa won in 1990, completed the break-up of Solidarity, as there were two candidates from the movement, Walesa and Mazowiecki. The political groups which split from Solidarity were no longer directly connected with the trade union, whose membership had fallen from ten million in 1980 to two million ten years later.

Solidarity bounced back in the 1997 general election to secure, with its allies, 34 per cent of the vote, beating the ruling ex-communist Democratic Left Alliance, with 26.5 per cent. Pro-welfare, it was committed to help the poor and halt 'dishonest' PRIVATIZA-TION, but it was deeply conservative on moral issues and there was an undercurrent of anti-Semitism in its propaganda.

The Birth of Solidarity, A. Kemp-Welch (ed.) (1991)
Breaking the Barrier: The Rise of Solidarnosc in Poland, L. Goodwyn (1991)
Professionals, Power and Solidarity in Poland, M. D. Kennedy (1991)

Solzhenitsyn, Aleksandr Isayevich (1918–)
Soviet novelist, historian and dissident. Born in the south Caucasus after his father was killed in an accident, he was brought up at Rostov on Don, where he graduated in mathematics and physics. While a student he became a Marxist. He served in the Red Army from 1941, becoming an artillery captain. He was a model Soviet citizen until 1945, when he was arrested and sentenced to eight years in prison for criticizing STALIN in private correspondence. His years as 'a special assignment prisoner' in an institute for scientific research were later described in *The First Circle* (1968). In 1953 he was exiled 'in perpetuity' to Kazakhstan, where he worked as a schoolteacher and survived cancer to tell his story in *Cancer Ward* (1968). These semi-autobiographical novels could not be published legally in the USSR. Amnestied in 1956, he moved to central Russia and was admitted to the Writers' Union in 1962, the year in which *One Day in the Life of Ivan*

Denisovich (a novella about life in a prison camp) appeared in the journal *Novy Mir* (New World). KHRUSHCHEV sanctioned its publication after hearing extracts read out to him, which misled him into thinking that the story celebrated 'honest toil' by prisoners who were loyal to the communist system. He soon changed his mind but not before hundreds of thousands of copies had been sold. Expelled from the Writers' Union in 1969, Solzhenitsyn was awarded the Nobel Prize for Literature in 1970. For publishing in Paris in 1973 the first part of the *Gulag Archipelago*, which was a description of the prison camp system from its beginnings under Lenin, interspersed with his own reminiscences and those of other inmates, he was expelled from Russia and deprived of his Soviet citizenship in 1974.

He settled in Vermont, USA in 1976, where he remained in self-imposed isolation until he returned to Russia in 1994. His experience of the USA did not make him a democrat. He disliked its materialism and thought that the multiparty system led to the abandonment of principle in the search for political gain. His long essay *Rebuilding Russia*, published by two Soviet newspapers in 1990, attacked both the Soviet and Western parliamentary systems and looked forward to a religious and national revival. He seemed to favour an authoritarian state but it was not clear how this could be reconciled with the freedom of speech and conscience which he vehemently demanded.

One Day in the Life of Ivan Denisovich, A. Solzhenitsyn (1963)
Solzhenitsyn, M. Scammell (1984)
Solzhenitsyn's Challenge to Russia and the West, J. P. Willerton, *International Journal of Social Economics* (1993)

Somalia, UN intervention in (1992–5)
When Siad Barre was overthrown in 1991 no single faction could control the country, which fell apart in inter-clan fighting. In December the OAU (Organization of African Unity) asked the Security Council of the

UNITED NATIONS to consider the crisis in Somalia. Somalia, awash with weapons provided by the superpowers during the COLD WAR, had become a wasteland: by 1992 50,000 had been killed, a million had fled as refugees to Ethiopia and Kenya. Drought also caused mass starvation, in which 300,000 died.

In January 1992 the Security Council imposed an arms embargo and in April authorized the use of troops to escort humanitarian supplies. President BUSH in November said that the US would be prepared to command and control an operation to ensure the delivery of supplies, whereupon the Security Council authorized member states 'to use all necessary means'. This was the fourth time the Council had authorized military enforcement, the others being in the KOREAN WAR (1950), the CONGO CRISIS (1960–5) and the GULF WAR (1991). Instead of mediating at the request of the parties concerned, the UN was intervening to restore peace as well as to deliver humanitarian aid.

Some 37,000 troops from 22 countries opened up roads to the interior and aid flowed in, but when the UN tried to disarm the warlords there was violent resistance: 25 Pakistani troops were killed by General Farah Aidid's forces in June 1993. The UN declared that he was an outlaw, but attempts to capture him suffered from confusion as to who was in charge of UN units. The US Quick Reaction Force operated independently of the UN commander and on 3 October lost 18 Rangers and two helicopters in fighting Aidid: between 200 and 300 Somalis were also killed. The bodies of the dead Americans were paraded through the streets and shown on television. President CLINTON was not prepared to take casualties, so on 7 October he announced that US forces would be withdrawn by the end of March 1994. The hunt for Aidid was called off. The last UN forces pulled out in March 1995, leaving Somalia to anarchy, clan warfare and economic collapse. Aidid was killed in the continuing civil war in August 1996.

Seeking Peace from Chaos: Humanitarian Intervention in Somalia, S. M. Makinda (1994)
Learning from Somalia: The Lessons of Armed Humanitarian Intervention, W. Clarke and J. Herbst (eds) (1997)

Somoza   The family who ruled Nicaragua as a dictatorship from 1936 to 1979. Anastasio Somoza García (1896–1956), the son of a Conservative senator and coffee planter, had his further education in the US, where he learnt fluent English. He married into the wealthy Debayle family and in 1933 became the first Nicaraguan commander of the National Guard (GN), founded by the US in 1925 when it was occupying the country. US marines left in 1933 and a year later Anastasio treacherously murdered Augusto César Sandino, the guerrilla leader and national hero who had fought against the Americans and with whom he was negotiating. He seized power in 1936 and after an eight-day civil war ruled Nicaragua as his private fiefdom. '*Nicaragua es mi finca*' (Nicaragua is my farm), he declared. A pliant tool of the US, he received the warm support of successive American Presidents while using the GN (a combined army and police force) as his power base and building up vast landholdings. He was killed by a gunman in 1956, his son Luis (1922–67) becoming President a year later. Educated at Louisiana State University, he benefited from ALLIANCE FOR PROGRESS loans and US investment, so that Nicaragua's GNP rose by 6.2 per cent a year in the 1960s. However, only the landed oligarchy benefited (Nicaragua depended on exports of coffee and cotton) and as imports rose faster than exports there was a large foreign debt. When Luis died from a massive heart attack he was succeeded by his brother Anastasio Somoza Debayle ('Tachito') (1925–80), head of the GN.

'Tachito' made it clear that Nicaragua did not belong to the NON-ALIGNED MOVEMENT but was 'totally aligned with the

United States'. American aid and support therefore continued, much aid and investment enriching the Somoza family. While agricultural production increased faster than in any other Central American country, the number of landless labourers grew enormously as the vast estates became even bigger. Somoza and his cronies were the only ones to benefit from the earthquake which destroyed much of Managua, the capital, in 1972 as they appropriated aid and bought up land cheaply. The Somoza family businesses included ports, the state airline, merchant shipping, hotels, newspapers, radio and television, banks and chemical factories. The estimated wealth of the Somoza family in 1979 was $1 billion.

Opposition grew in the 1970s from the SANDINISTAS, the Catholic Church, businessmen and the Conservative Party, led by the Chamorros. The turning-point came in 1978 when the editor of *La Prensa*, Pedro Joaquín Chamorro, who criticized the regime in his newspaper, was shot and killed by an unknown gunman. 'Tachito' was blamed and faced simultaneous attacks of the Sandinistas from the north and a democratic opposition front, sponsored by Costa Rica and Panama, from the south. There was the first mass uprising against the regime when people from the urban slums joined the rebellion. The GN retaliated by massacring thousands. AMNESTY INTERNATIONAL said that in some areas all males over 14 were systematically murdered. There were spontaneous anti-Somoza risings, with Mexico, Venezuela, Costa Rica and Panama supplying the rebels. President CARTER called an emergency meeting of the OAS (Organization of American States) to urge the formation of an inter-American force to stop the fighting, but was rebuffed. For the first time since it was formed in 1948 the OAS rejected a US proposal to intervene in an American state. Somoza fled on 17 July 1979 and settled in Paraguay, where in 1980 a bazooka shell destroyed his armour-plated car and killed him.

Soviet Union, collapse of GORBACHEV'S GLASNOST helped to bring this about as it enabled the nationalities in the Soviet Union to push for independence. The first move came in the Baltic states, which had been independent between the two world wars. Estonia claimed economic autonomy in 1987 and a year later its sovereignty, which meant that the laws of the republic had precedence over those of the Union. In 1989 Lithuania and Latvia also claimed sovereignty. Lithuania took the lead in 1990 by declaring its independence in March, followed by Estonia and Latvia in August. Soviet forces struck back in January 1991 by attacking the television centre in Vilnius, killing 13 people, but Gorbachev was not prepared to allow a bloodbath and, with Soviet involvement in Afghanistan in mind, called off the assault. The REVOLUTIONS OF 1989–91 in Eastern Europe also had an exhilarating effect in the USSR, as national independence seemed possible. Georgia, after a referendum of 99 per cent in favour, declared its independence in April 1991. Boris YELTSIN, Chairman of the Russian Supreme Soviet, had taken a step towards independence by calling in May 1990 for Russian sovereignty, including ownership of its natural resources, and an independent foreign policy, measures passed by the Russian parliament in June.

With the Union about to break up Gorbachev made a desperate effort to keep it together by negotiating a new Union treaty, which would give real economic and political sovereignty to the republics. Six republics (the Baltic states, Georgia, Armenia and Moldavia) refused to take part in a referendum on this issue, but 75 per cent in the other republics voted in favour of it in March 1991. The 'Nine Plus One' (the nine republics and Gorbachev) agreement in April committed those republics to a new union treaty: defence, foreign policy, energy and communications would be run 'jointly' by the Soviet government and the republics. In all other matters the republics would run their own affairs. The treaty was to be signed on 20 August. This was too much for the hard-liners in the CPSU, the Soviet army and the KGB, who saw the treaty as one further step towards the disintegration of the Soviet Union. To prevent this happening they staged the AUGUST COUP. Its failure precipitated the disintegration it sought to avoid and was followed by all the republics declaring their independence by 16 December. The leaders of the three Slav republics (Russia, Ukraine, Belarus) met on 7–8 December, determined to destroy the USSR and deprive Gorbachev of his power base. They declared that the USSR no longer existed as 'a geopolitical reality'. The three republics joined together in the CIS (Commonwealth of Independent States) and were soon joined by eight non-Slav republics. On 31 December 1991 the USSR officially ceased to exist. All its ministries and embassies abroad came under Russian control.

From Union to Commonwealth, G. Lapidus et al. (1992)
The End of the Soviet Empire, H. Carrière d'Encausse (1995)

Space exploration   The investigation of the universe beyond the earth's atmosphere by manned and unmanned spacecraft. Rockets were an important development in military technology during the Second World War, the Germans using V2 rockets to attack London. After the war they were used to launch earth satellites, the first being the Soviet Sputnik in 1957, which began the space race. The Sputnik was little more than a radio transmitter but artificial satellites soon grew in size and sophistication. The Americans sent their first satellite, Explorer 1, into orbit in 1958. The Soviet Union gained another first in 1961 when it launched the first man, Yuri Gagarian, into space to orbit the earth, showing that a safe return to earth was possible and that the problems of weightlessness could be overcome. The US followed in 1962 with an orbital space flight by John Glenn. In the mid-1960s both the US and USSR put two or three spacemen on one

flight, docked with unmanned vehicles and for the first time astronauts floated freely in space outside the spacecraft.

President KENNEDY, shocked that the Soviet Union was ahead in the space race, allocated more resources to NASA (National Aeronautics and Space Administration) and promised that the US would be the first to land a man on the moon. This duly took place in 1969, when Neil Armstrong and Edwin Aldrin landed there three years after the first Soviet soft landing on the moon by an unmanned satellite. Almost the entire surface of the moon was photographed in 1966–7. In 1972 US astronauts spent 72 hours on the moon but after this the US abandoned its moon landing programme and concentrated on sending unmanned satellites into outer space and on building a space station to be put into permanent orbit around the earth. In the 1970s the US produced the space shuttle, an extraordinary reusable vehicle that lifts off like a rocket and lands like an ordinary plane: shuttles were used to repair satellites orbiting the earth. Soviet and American spacecraft met and docked in space for the first time in 1975.

Planetary exploration began when the Soviet Union took pictures of the far side of the moon in 1959. The US sent Mariner 2 past Venus in 1962 and in the 1980s probes reached Jupiter, Saturn, Uranus and Neptune. Other countries joined in space exploration: the European Space Agency (ESA), China and Japan launched satellites and the ESA and Japan built planetary probes. A robot landed on Mars in July 1997 and showed how the solar system can be surveyed safely and robotically. Such advances have made a space station an out-of-date concept.

Space exploration has had significant results. It has contributed to the INFORMATION REVOLUTION, as satellites make it easier for broadcasters to beam their programmes round the world and much more difficult for governments to control them. They are also invaluable in weather forecasting, topographical and geological surveys and in gathering military intelligence, which enabled the US and USSR to understand each other's military capabilities. Satellites were at the core of President REAGAN's SDI or 'Star Wars'. One of the most important effects of space exploration has been the acquisition of a much more detailed knowledge of the universe. Surveys have been made of all the planets from Mercury to Neptune and of many of their satellites. Probes sent to other planets in the solar system and the Hubble telescope (1990) in orbit in space can pick up signals from distant galaxies and even pictures of deep space and of the Big Bang that created the universe.

SPD (*Sozialdemokratische Partei Deutschlands*: Social Democratic Party)

German political party. It originated as a Marxist working-class party in 1875 and in the late nineteenth century was the largest and best organized of all the European socialist parties: by 1912 it had 110 seats in the Reichstag, more than any other party. It was the largest party again during the Weimar Republic but controlled the government only from 1928–30. The SDP was the only party to vote, courageously, against the Enabling Act (1933) which gave Hitler dictatorial powers. After the Second World War it expected to do well, as it was the only party with a creditable anti-Nazi record, but it was consistently outvoted by the CDU (Christian Democratic Union) and was in danger of becoming a permanent opposition party with the support of no more than a third of the electorate. It acquired the reputation of being a party that always said no. The SPD opposed the currency reform of 1945 and ERHARD's WIRTSCHAFTSWUNDER (economic miracle). It also opposed the ECSC (European Coal and Steel Community) and rearmament and did not show how it would provide for German security.

At the local level the SPD often did well and dominated some state and municipal governments. In office it behaved pragmatically, avoiding talk of Marxism and the class struggle. As its old base of blue-collar workers declined it needed to turn itself (as the CDU had done) into a broad-based People's Party (*Volkspartei*) and bring its radical rhetoric more into line with its moderate practice. It did this at Bad Godesberg in 1959, when Marxist theory and the class struggle were abandoned and the SPD claimed that democratic socialism sprang from Christian ethics and humanism. Instead of demanding nationalization and government planning, the SPD accepted private enterprise and the SOCIAL MARKET ECONOMY. 'As much competition as possible, as much planning as necessary', it declared. Anti-clericalism, which had lost it many votes, was rejected and the social mission of the churches accepted. Its old defence policy (a neutral Germany with no nuclear weapons) was also modified, as there was no longer opposition to rearmament for national defence or to NATO.

The new policies enabled the SPD to narrow the gap with the CDU and in 1966 it formed a coalition with the Christian Democrats, the first time the SPD had been part of a German government since 1930. In 1969 the SPD changed coalition partners to the FDP (Free Democratic Party) and remained in office until 1982 under Chancellors BRANDT and SCHMIDT. Deep divisions in the party appeared when Schmidt supported the deployment of nuclear missiles on German soil. As the rank and file members of the party became more radical and anti-American, the FDP members of the coalition were increasingly unhappy and in 1982 transferred their allegiance to Helmut KOHL and the CDU. The SPD had an opportunity to recover power with the EAST GERMAN REVOLUTION of 1989 but was reluctant to accept GERMAN REUNIFICATION and was rejected by the voters in the first general election in a reunited Germany in 1990. Some consolation was provided by its success in the *Land* (state) parliaments, which gave the SPD control of the *Bundesrat* (the upper house of the German parliament).

Parties, Opposition and Society in West Germany, E. Kolinsky (1984)
A History of German Social Democracy, Part 2, S. Miller and H. Potthoff (1986)
The German Social Democrats Since 1969, G. Braunthal (1994)

special economic zones (SEZs)   Areas of China which aimed to attract foreign investment and technology and produce goods for export. In 1980 four SEZs were set up: Shenzhen bordered Hong Kong, two were in Guandong province not far from Hong Kong, while the fourth was on the coast of Fujian opposite Taiwan. They were based on similar zones in the NEWLY INDUSTRIALIZING ECONOMIES (NIEs). They gave incentives to foreign investors: accessibility, as they were all on or near the coast, a cheap and obedient labour force and preferential tax rates. They were also designed to improve the quality of Chinese goods by the transfer of skills and modern technology. The SEZs were very successful in producing growth rates higher than in the rest of China and in offering higher wages and better living conditions. Trade and investment could be carried out there on the initiative of the local government and without authorization from Beijing. Businesses made their own investment, production and marketing decisions and foreign ownership was legalized. Boom towns soon arose and in 1984 14 new SEZs were created. Shanghai became an SEZ in 1990: when 23 major cities in inland China were also designated SEZs in 1992 they ceased to be 'special'.

It was not long before attendant problems appeared. Investment of $5.2 billion by 1988 and nearly 6,000 joint ventures with foreign companies was lower than expected, as the workforce was unskilled, quality standards poor, management was often inefficient and productivity low. The SEZs sucked in imports, which exceeded exports (in 1988 Chinese exports were $47 billion, imports $54 billion). There was also monumental corruption and smuggling and social problems, such as an increase in crime and prostitution. Conservative veterans in the Chinese Communist Party (CCP) were alarmed at the reappearance of capitalism in China but the SEZs survived, because they had the support of DENG XIAOPING and of senior officials, who obtained lucrative jobs there for their children. The SEZs were needed if Hong Kong was to be successfully integrated into China (most of the capitalists who invested in Shenzhen came from Hong Kong) and if Taiwan was to be tempted to become part of China.

Shanghai with an official population of 13 million has become the centre of the economic revolution in the 1990s, when it grew economically at 14 per cent a year. In the 1980s heavy industry (steel and textiles) predominated but in the next decade it became a global financial and trading centre, with new technologies such as computers and biotechnology. The Japanese firm NEC agreed to build there a $1 billion microchip plant to open in 1999. NEC will have management control but will own less than a third of the firm. China will gain some of the best semi-conductor manufacturing in the world. For a few years before HONG KONG RETURNED TO CHINA in 1997 mainland companies bought into key strategic industries in Hong Kong: telecommunications, airlines, power and gas. Such activities have made China a global player. According to the WORLD BANK the Chinese economy in 1992 was second only to that of the US and by 2020 will be larger. In Hong Kong and Shanghai China will have two of the most important stock exchanges in the world.

China Opens its Doors: The Politics of Economic Transition, J. Howell (1993)
Growing Out of the Plan: Chinese Economic Reform 1978–1993, B. Naughton (1995)
Ideology and Economic Reform Under Deng, 1978–93, Z. Wei-Wei (1996)

Srebrenica   Town in Bosnia where one of the worst atrocities of the YUGOSLAV

CIVIL WAR took place. In 1993 Resolution 819 of the UNITED NATIONS set up 'safe havens' in Goražde, Žepa and Srebrenica, Muslim towns surrounded by the Serbs, in order to protect the inhabitants there. By 1995 there was 40,000 people in the Srebrenican enclave. On 30 May the Security Council of the UN published a document written by Yasushi Akashi, the UN's civilian head in former Yugoslavia, saying that the UN should pull out of the 'safe havens' in the east of Bosnia. This gave a signal to the Serbs that they could take Srebrenica and the UN would do nothing. On 6 July Serb artillery started pounding the area. The Dutch commander of the UN troops there asked for air strikes but Akashi refused. The Dutch troops surrendered their weapons and vehicles to the Serbs and even their blue UN helmets, which could then be used by the Serbs to persuade the Muslims to surrender. Srebrenica fell on 11 July and the massacre of Muslim males in the area began. The Red Cross reported that between six and eight thousand people were unaccounted for: on 10 August the US ambassador to the UN showed the Security Council photographic evidence of mass graves on the outskirts of the town. The Bosnian Serb leader Radovan Karadžić and General Ratko Mladić were indicted for war crimes at Srebrenica by the international war crimes tribunal in the Hague. The incident dealt a fatal blow to UN peace-keeping.

Srebrenica: Analysis of a Massacre, J. Honig and N. Both (1996)
Srebrenica: The Darkest Scenario, F. Westerman and B. Rys (1996)
A Soft Area: Srebrenica, D. Rohde (1997)

Stalin, Iosif Vissarionovich (1879–1953)

General Secretary of the CPSU (1922–53). Stalin, 'man of steel', was the name he adopted in 1912. He was born Dzhugashvili, the son of a Georgian shoe-maker, and was one of the few Bolshevik leaders to come from the working class. He was expelled from the Tiflis (Tbilisi) Orthodox seminary in 1899 for his Marxist activities and became a full-time revolutionary in 1901. He was arrested six times between 1902 and 1913 and twice escaped from internal exile. He was in exile in Siberia from 1913–17 and returned to Petrograd after the February Revolution. After the October Revolution he joined the Politburo when it was formed in 1919. A post which was to be crucial in his rise to power was that of General Secretary of the CPSU, to which he was appointed in 1922. In this position he chose secretaries who headed local party organizations: they elected delegates to party conferences, who in turn elected the party's Central Committee, Politburo and Secretariat. As General Secretary Stalin came to control all these bodies. Lenin regretted Stalin's accretion of power and in a secret memorandum of 4 January 1923 suggested that Stalin should be removed as General Secretary. He planned to work with Trotsky to out Stalin at the Party Congress, which was to meet in April, but on 9 March Lenin had his third stroke, from which he never recovered. This and the unpopularity of Trotsky, who was Lenin's obvious successor, saved Stalin. On Lenin's death in January 1924 Kamenev and Zinoviev persuaded the Bolshevik Central Committee to suppress Lenin's memorandum and supported Stalin against Trotsky. Stalin was a superb tactician, with a sharp eye for the weaknesses of others. He used his position of General Secretary first to isolate his rivals and then to secure their dismissal. He allied with Bukharin to force Trotsky, Kamenev and Zinoviev out of office and then turned against Bukharin. From 1929, when Trotsky was forced to leave Russia, Stalin was in a dominant position, though this did not become unassailable till the murder of Kirov in 1934.

Stalin realized that the Soviet Union was far behind its capitalist rivals economically and, as he feared attack from the Western powers, decided that this gap would have to be closed quickly. In 1924 he put forward the idea of 'Socialism in one country', by which he meant that Russia could become strong by its own efforts. He began a period of rapid industrialization through the Five Year Plans, which were successful in making the USSR one of the greatest industrial powers in the world. To finance this industrialization he introduced the collectivization of agriculture, though at enormous cost in the murder or deportation of the *kulaks*. Such policies could only be carried through by centralizing power and by establishing a dictatorship. One-party rule had been set up by Lenin but Stalin carried this much further by establishing personal control of the party, the government and the secret police and by using the latter to remove, not enemies of the regime, but former Bolsheviks. All who had disagreed with Stalin or whom he regarded as in any way a threat to his position were eliminated in the Great Purges. These did enormous damage to every sector of Soviet society and especially to the armed forces, whose officer corps was decimated. This almost led to the Soviet Union's defeat when Germany invaded in 1941.

In the mid-1930s, responding to the rise of Nazism and militarism in Japan, Stalin sought alliances with the Western democracies in the name of 'collective security' and ordered European communist parties to support democratic governments through Popular Fronts. The Western democracies were shocked when he abandoned his anti-Nazi stance and made the Nazi–Soviet Pact in 1939. This advanced Soviet borders in Poland, Finland and Romania and enabled Stalin to annex the Baltic republics. He then had two years to rearm before the German onslaught in Operation Barbarossa (1941). This caught him by surprise, as he refused to heed warnings of German plans to attack. The Soviet Union managed to survive this partly by good luck (Japan did not attack in the east), partly owing to Hitler's mistakes in diverting troops from the attack on Moscow to the southern and northern fronts and partly because Russia was able to develop its industry beyond the Urals, out of reach of the Germans: 1,500 individual enterprises and ten

million people were moved from west to east, so that in the last two years of the war the USSR was producing more tanks, guns and aircraft than Germany. The costs were enormous – 20 million Russian dead and widespread devastation – but the USSR emerged from the war as one of the two superpowers. In 1945 Stalin's prestige and popularity had never been higher. In 1941 he had become Prime Minister (a post he held until his death) and Commander of the armed forces. In 1943 he took the title Marshal and in 1945 that of Generalissimo. He had been a dominant figure at Allied conferences at Tehran (1943), Yalta (1945) and Potsdam (1945).

In 1945, when Stalin's prestige and popularity were at their height, the 'cult of personality' (which involved extravagant praise for everything the 'great father' did) attributed all Soviet achievements to his genius and inspiration. With 25 million people homeless, factories and infrastructure destroyed, the task of reconstruction was daunting. There were no foreign loans for the huge investment programme and massive defence expenditure imposed a further burden. Defence swallowed up 20 per cent of the budget in the 1940s, a much higher proportion than in the West. The privations of the 1930s would have to continue in the 1940s and 1950s. Stalin based his Five Year Plan (1946–50) on earlier ones, concentrating on heavy industry with consumer industries and agriculture neglected. By 1953 coal and steel output were double that of 1940, though real urban wages reached the level of 1928 only in 1952. Peasant incomes were squeezed, as delivery quotas and taxes increased and as currency reform in 1947 wiped out nine-tenths of their savings: farmers' incomes in 1949 were only 50 per cent of those in 1928, before collectivization. Private plots (1–2 per cent of the land) provided nearly half the vegetables and over two-thirds of the country's meat and milk in 1950. In 1953 the Soviet Union had fewer head of cattle than in 1916, to feed a population between 30 and 40 million larger. KHRUSHCHEV said that the countryside looked as if the Tatar hordes had just passed through.

Stalin's foreign policy was dominated by the need for security. He had no master-plan for the COMMUNIST TAKEOVER OF EAST-ERN EUROPE but seized opportunities as they arose to extend Soviet influence. He accepted Finnish neutrality rather than risk a conflict with the US, kept out of the GREEK CIVIL WAR, gave little help to MAO ZEDONG in the CHINESE CIVIL WAR and was unenthusiastic about the SINO-SOVIET TREATY of 1950. As the COLD WAR developed, particularly after the TRUMAN DOCTRINE (1947) promised aid to countries resisting communism, he set up the COMINFORM. The YUGOSLAV-SOVIET SPLIT of 1948, when he broke with TITO, led to the SHOW TRIALS in the communist states in Eastern Europe (which Stalin instigated). COMECON was set up in 1949 to facilitate Soviet control of their economies, a belated response to the MARSHALL PLAN. The attempt to push the Allies out of Berlin failed in the BERLIN BLOCKADE (1948–9) and was unable to prevent the formation of the Federal Republic of Germany (West Germany). Western opinion thought that Stalin was behind the KOREAN WAR (1950–3) but this seems unlikely. He assented to North Korea's attack on the South but made it clear to KIM IL SUNG that he would not take part, although the Soviet Union seemed stronger than ever with its own atom bomb in 1949. Stalin's paranoia resulted in further purges. After the sudden death of Zhdanov in 1948 the leading officials of the Leningrad Party organization were executed but blood-letting was now sporadic. In 1953 a Doctors' Plot was uncovered in Moscow, where nine doctors (most of them Jewish) were accused of murdering Zhdanov. Khrushchev was convinced that this was simply the first step to eliminate leading Bolsheviks such as Molotov and Malenkov. This was prevented when Stalin had a stroke in March and died four days later.

Soviet Politics 1945–53, T. Dunmore (1988)

Stalin in Power, R. C. Tucker (1990)
Stalin: Triumph and Tragedy, D. Volkogonov (1991)

START   Strategic Arms Reduction Talks were proposed by President REAGAN in 1982 and were to replace the SALT (Strategic Arms Limitation Treaty) talks. They differed from previous negotiations as they were designed to reduce the number of nuclear weapons rather than place an upper limit on them. Progress was held up as GORBACHEV insisted until 1987 that no agreement could be made until the US abandoned SDI (Strategic Defense Initiative). Agreement was finally reached in July 1991 by President BUSH and Gorbachev to reduce each side's long-range nuclear weapons by 50 per cent but was followed shortly afterwards by the COLLAPSE OF THE SOVIET UNION, which left Russia, Ukraine, Belarus and Kazakhstan each holding nuclear weapons. Boris YELTSIN sought their return to Russia and also wanted further reductions on nuclear weapons. In January 1993 a START II Treaty was signed by Yeltsin and Bush which, over the next decade, would cut the nuclear warheads of Russia and the US to between 3,000 and 3,500. Implementation depended on the ratification of START and the NUCLEAR NON-PROLIFERATION TREATY (1968) by the successor states to the Soviet Union which had nuclear weapons. All agreed in principle to return these weapons to Russia or destroy them by the end of the century.

Sudanese civil war (1956–)   Sudan is the largest country in Africa (2.5 million square km) with an Arab, Muslim North and an African South, which is Christian or animist. When independence came in 1956 Southerners wanted separation from the North or a federation in which they would have considerable self-government. They got neither and found that most government positions in the South were held by Northerners. This caused resentment and fear of Muslim domination and led to an army mutiny in the South which began the civil war. Northerners in the South were murdered but by October the government had recovered control. The military regime of General Abboud (1958–64), which tried to impose Islam on the South, was disastrous for Southerners. They were forced to change Christian names to Arab ones, Arabic was the only language used in the administration, teaching in Southern languages was forbidden and Christian missionaries were expelled. The civil war was resumed therefore in 1962 and *Anyanya* ('snake-poison') was formed to fight for the independence of the South, and set up an alternative administration in the areas it controlled. In 1971, with the economy collapsing and perhaps a million people already killed in the civil war, NIMEIRI staged a military coup and determined to end the war. He reached an agreement with the rebels in 1972, granting autonomy to the South, and allowing Christian missions to return. There was an uneasy peace until 1983, when Nimeiri imposed the *Sharia* (Islamic law) throughout the Sudan.

The civil war resumed, with Colonel John Garang, a Southern Christian, forming the Sudan People's Liberation Army (SPLA), supported by Ethiopia, Libya, Israel and Cuba. Renewed war meant the abandonment of work on the oilfields in the South and the flight of a million refugees to the North. Drought and famine made the situation in Sudan worse, as did the influx of refugees (estimated at 600,000 by 1991) from Ethiopia and Chad. The UNITED NATIONS estimated the death-toll from the war between 1983 and 1989 at half a million.

A coup by military Islamists, led by Brigadier al-Bashir in 1989, marked a return to strict Islamic practices. Since then all aspects of life in the North have been dominated by the only legal political party, the National Islamic Front (NIF), led by Dr Hassan al-Turabi, a multilingual Islamist, with law degrees from the University of London and the Sorbonne in Paris. Members of the NIF held all senior posts in the army, police and civil service, with the result that hundreds of senior officials and army officers went into exile, most of them to Egypt. Khartoum became a centre for ISLAMIC FUNDAMEN-TALISTS as Turabi set up camps to train Islamists for military action in other African countries. In 1993 the US put Sudan on its list of countries supporting international terrorism and two years later Eritrea and Uganda broke off diplomatic relations with Sudan for supporting rebels in their countries. Egypt blamed Sudan for the attempted assassination of President MUBARAK in Addis Ababa in September 1995.

Internationally isolated, the Sudanese government had at first considerable success in the civil war which escalated after the 1989 coup and in which atrocities were commonplace. The government was aided by splits in the Southern opposition, as the Southern Sudan Independence Army (SSIA) broke away from the SPLA. The SSIA wanted complete independence for the South, whereas Garang still officially wanted a united Sudan but with a change in the internal balance of power, so that the domination of the African South by the Arab, Muslim North would be ended. Turabi also benefited from the end of the MENGISTU regime in Ethiopia in 1991. The NIF managed to conquer most of the South before there was a remarkable recovery by Garang, who reconquered much of it. In 1995 he agreed with the Northern opposition to form the National Democratic Alliance (NDA), so that Northern forces would be over-stretched coping with rebels in both North and South. The civil war became a huge and open-ended drain on the North's resources, so that in June 1997 the NIF offered the South 'self-determination', which they had sought for 40 years. It was also promised a referendum in four years' time to decide whether to remain in a united Sudan or to secede from it.

Sudan After Nimeiri, P. Woodward (ed.) (1991)

Civil War in the Sudan, M. Daly and A. A. Sikainga (eds) (1993)

War of Visions: Conflict of Identities in the Sudan, F. M. Deng (1995)

Suez Crisis (1956)   In the 1950s NASSER antagonized Britain, France and Israel, who colluded to attack Egypt in an attempt to overthrow him. Nasser, strongly opposed to colonialism, alienated the French by supporting the Algerians in the ALGERIAN WAR OF INDEPENDENCE. He was also hostile to the BIRTH OF ISRAEL. In 1955 he set up guerrilla bases in Egypt, from which Israel could be raided, and closed the Straits of Tiran to Israeli shipping, thus denying it access to African and Asian markets. Nasser announced a huge arms deal with Czechoslovakia in September 1955, to the alarm of the US, but it was the events related to the building of the Aswan Dam which brought the crisis to a head. The dam in Upper Egypt would increase Egypt's cultivated area by 30 per cent, enable it to prevent floods and droughts and would supply hydro-electric power for industrialization. It was announced in December 1955 that the WORLD BANK would provide a loan of $200 million, to which the US and Britain would add $70 million, for the construction of the dam, but in July 1956 DULLES, the US Secretary of State, said that the deal was off. A week later Nasser announced that Egypt had nationalized the Suez Canal and that revenue from it would finance the building of the dam. Full compensation was promised to the Canal's owners (mainly British and French) but three months of diplomacy failed to persuade Nasser to accept multinational control of the Canal, through which most Middle East oil shipments passed. EDEN, the British Prime Minister, compared Nasser to Hitler and was determined that he should not be appeased as Hitler had been at Munich in 1938. He decided that Nasser could not be allowed 'to have his thumb on our windpipe' and that he must be 'destroyed'. At first he hoped for American support but President EISENHOWER, in an election year, was opposed to

European colonialism and did not want to push the Arabs into the arms of the Soviet Union. 'I must tell you frankly', he wrote to Eden on 2 September, 'that American public opinion flatly rejects the thought of using force'.

Israel saw an opportunity of ending the Egyptian blockade of the Straits of Tiran and of striking at the guerrillas and so colluded with France, who devised a plan which was put to Britain in October. The Israelis were to attack Egypt and when they had seized most of Sinai, Britain and France would order both sides to withdraw from the Canal, so that an Anglo-French force could occupy and 'protect' the Canal. Britain accepted the plan and on 29 October Israel invaded Sinai. On 30 October Britain and France gave their ultimatum, which Egypt rejected, so on the 31st British and French planes destroyed most of the Egyptian airforce on the ground. An invasion fleet from Cyprus arrived at Port Said on 5 November and, aided by paratroopers, captured the city and advanced along the Canal, which the Egyptians had blocked by sinking ships in it. The US had not been informed of the attack and led the condemnation of Britain and France at the UNITED NATIONS. The Soviet Union, at first occupied by the HUNGARIAN RISING, joined in by saying that it was 'fully resolved to crush the aggressors and to restore peace in the Middle East'. In Britain public opinion generally and the CONSERVATIVE PARTY almost solidly supported the government. The LABOUR PARTY was prepared to use force only if it was sanctioned by the United Nations and bitterly attacked Eden's handling of the crisis. There was a run on the pound, which the US would do nothing about until the invasion ended. Britain and France, therefore, agreed on 6 November to the UN call for a cease-fire.

The consequences of the crisis were far-reaching. Britain and France, as allies of Israel, were regarded as anti-Arab and lost influence in the Middle East. Britain's greatest friend there, Nuri al-Said in Iraq, paid for his friendship with his life in a coup nearly two years later. The failure of the British action, and the condemnation of many COM-MONWEALTH leaders such as NEHRU, led Eden to resign in January 1957. Britain's dependence on the US was now clear, a fact recognized by MACMILLAN, the new Prime Minister, who lost no time in restoring good relations with the US. France's failure at Suez helped to bring about the fall of the FOURTH REPUBLIC, the return to power of DE GAULLE and the granting of Algerian independence in 1962. Many Frenchmen were convinced that Britain and the US could not be relied on and that France should therefore develop its own deterrent and become more closely involved in Europe: in 1957 France became a founder member of the EEC. Instead of toppling Nasser the crisis greatly increased his prestige in the Arab world. Egypt accepting a Syrian request for political union in the United Arab Republic in February, 1958. Israel also benefited. It withdrew, under US pressure, from Sinai in March 1957, only after gaining unrestricted passage through the Straits of Tiran. There was also a great reduction in raids from the Gaza Strip until the mid 1960s. The Soviet Union was another beneficiary, as it was seen by Arabs as a friend and soon became a major provider of arms to Egypt, Syria and Iraq. In October 1958 it agreed to help in building and paying for the Aswan Dam. The USSR was now a major rival to the US in the Middle East, a position it retained until the early 1970s. The response of the US was the Eisenhower doctrine, which offered assistance to any Arab state threatened by communism.

Britain and the Suez Crisis, D. Carlton (1988)
Suez 1956: The Crisis and its Consequences,
   W. R. Louis and R. Owen (eds) (1989)
The Suez Crisis, K. Kyle (1991)

Suharto (1921–)   President of Indonesia (1968–98). In the Javanese tradition he had only one name. The poorly educated son of a peasant, he served in the Dutch colonial army

and in 1943 joined the Indonesian army set up by the Japanese. He fought against the Dutch and after independence rose to become a general and head of the Strategic Command. It was troops from this unit which put down the attempted coup (in which six generals were killed) in 1965, organized by dissident elements in the army and the Indonesian Communist Party (PKI). Staunchly anti-communist, he encouraged the slaughter of PKI members which followed. It is estimated that as many as half a million people were killed in the worst bloodbath in Indonesian history, during which the PKI was destroyed. President SUKARNO's power was fatally weakened, as the PKI had provided him with mass support, so Suharto seized the opportunity to take over control gradually. In 1966 Sukarno gave him supreme authority to restore order; a year later the People's Consultative Assembly relieved Sukarno of all his posts. Suharto became acting President and in 1968 President, a position to which he was regularly re-elected.

The New Order he set up aimed to control the population rather than mobilize it, as Sukarno had done. State surveillance of the people reached down into every village. Power, centred round the President, was placed in the hands of a small group of senior officers and civilians who were Western-trained. Golkar, the army's body established in 1964 for organizing functional groups, was made into a machine for winning parliamentary elections and was highly successful, winning the 1971 and later elections. Other parties were rationalized after the 1971 election: nine parties were reduced to two, one representing Muslims, the other Christians and secular parties. They were never able to challenge Golkar, the Muslims gaining 30 per cent of the vote in 1978 and less afterwards, the secular parties winning about 15 per cent. When an opposition figure with popular appeal appeared, as Megawati Sukarnoputri (daughter of Sukarno) did in 1997, she was effectively banned from public life. Democracy was a façade, as parliament had no real power. It did not draft legislation and had no say in deciding policy: it was simply a rubber stamp for endorsing the government's actions. In the presidential elections there was only one candidate.

Economic and political stability were the main objectives of Suharto's government. Economic recovery was vital, as in 1965 inflation was 650 per cent, so Suharto cut government expenditure and attracted foreign investment by giving legal and financial incentives. Indonesia's major creditors – Japan, the US, Australia – co-ordinated the flow of aid. Inflation was reduced to single figures by the early 1970s and there was a sustained period of economic growth, which averaged 4.3 per cent per annum from 1965–88. Indonesia was fortunate in being the largest Asian oil producer and so benefited from the OPEC PRICE RISE of 1973. Two-thirds of the state's revenue came from oil and gas at the beginning of the 1980s. The state dominated the economy through state-owned enterprises and by controlling investment until the economic deregulation of 1988, which encouraged private development, foreign investment ($4.5 billion in 1995) and the growth of the Jakarta Stock Exchange. Suharto tried to gain popular support by improving education, health and welfare services and the infrastructure of roads, electricity supply and telecommunications. Absolute poverty, as defined by the WORLD BANK, declined from 70 per cent of the population in 1965 to 15 per cent 20 years later, in spite of the population increasing from 48 million to 182 million (1971–90).

In foreign policy Suharto did not attempt to play a role on the world stage as Sukarno had done and reversed many of Sukarno's policies. He quickly ended the confrontation with Malaysia and broke off diplomatic relations with China, because he said that Beijing had supported the attempted coup by the PKI: they were not restored until 1990. Better relations with his Southeast Asian neighbours led to Indonesia becoming a founding member of ASEAN in 1967. There were closer relations too with the US, which replaced the Soviet Union as a provider of arms. Condemnation was provoked throughout the world by the invasion and annexation of EAST TIMOR in 1975–6, during which a conservative estimate is that 60,000 people were killed, a tenth of the population.

As corruption spread throughout the system, the President was accused of running the nation's affairs for the personal profit of himself and his family. There was concern too about the denial of human rights and the use of torture. Yet Suharto's dictatorship remained remarkably stable, until the collapse of the economy in 1997–8 which brought about his enforced resignation.

Suharto and his Generals, D. Jenkins (1984)
The Army and Politics in Indonesia, H. Crouch (1988)
Indonesian Politics Under Suharto, M. R. J. Vatikiotis (1995)

Sukarno (1902–70)   President of Indonesia (1945–68). Born in Java, the son of a schoolteacher, he went to Dutch language schools, where he showed a remarkable facility for learning languages. He joined the nationalist organization Sarekat Islam, graduated as an engineer and in 1927 founded the Indonesian Nationalist Party (PNI). Charismatic and a gifted orator who could move mass audiences, he addressed meetings throughout Java calling for independence and non-cooperation with the Dutch on the lines of Gandhi's campaign against the British in India. In 1928 the PNI adopted the Indonesian language (based on Malay, widely used as a lingua franca) as a means of uniting the hundred ethnic groups in the Dutch East Indies. He was imprisoned in 1930 and then spent most of the time until 1942, when the Japanese arrived, either in prison or internal exile. During the Second World War he and other politicians worked with the Japanese and gained valuable administrative experience. Almost immediately after the Japanese surrender in 1945 Sukarno proclaimed the independence of Indonesia, with himself as President, but four and a half years of conflict were needed before the Dutch withdrew, leaving Indonesia as a sovereign state.

For the next seven years Indonesia struggled with a Western-style democracy. Endemic political instability (28 parties were represented in parliament) enabled the President, whose position was largely ceremonial, to play a more active role. He took advantage of revolts in 1956–7 in Sulawesi and Sumatra, put down by the army, to proclaim martial law and end democratic government. Sukarno handed government over to a National Advisory Council, consisting of functional groups, with himself as Chairman.

In foreign policy Sukarno at first followed the lead of NEHRU and joined the NON-ALIGNED MOVEMENT. His prestige increased enormously in 1955; he was seen as a leader of the THIRD WORLD at the Bandung Conference when he acted as host to 29 Afro-Asian nations. When the Dutch refused to hand over Irian Jaya (Western New Guinea) to Indonesia, he announced a new course. Dutch businesses were taken over and most Dutch were expelled from Indonesia. The Dutch handed over the territory in 1963. This made Sukarno, as a great crusader against colonialism, a hero in Indonesia. He did not have the same success when he tried similar tactics in the confrontation (1963–6) with Malaysia. Not only was he unsuccessful but he ruined the Indonesian economy.

He had no knowledge of economics or interest in economic development and saw inflation rise to 650 per cent in 1965. The Soviet Union provided him with arms and $2 billion of economic aid by 1965, the year Sukarno cut his links with the capitalist world by withdrawing from the IMF and WORLD BANK. He also announced an anti-imperialist axis with China, North Vietnam and Cambodia. Sukarno had moved very close to the PKI, on whom he relied for a mass following (it had three million members) to counter the influence of the army. On 3 September 1965 the PKI and some army officers staged a coup in which six generals were killed. Nasution, the army commander, survived, as did General SUHARTO, commander of the Strategic Reserve in the capital. His troops crushed the rebellion by 20 October. PKI leaders and up to half a million of their followers were killed or imprisoned. This began Sukarno's downfall. Suharto became Acting President in 1967 and replaced Sukarno as President a year later. Sukarno, in ill-health and embittered, lived under house arrest until his death.

Sukarno, J. D. Legge (1973)
Modern Indonesia: A History Since 1945, R. Cribb and C. Brown (1995)

Sunnis The largest group of Muslims (about 80 per cent). They share with SHIIS a belief in the Quran, the *hadith* (traditions of the Prophet Muhammad), and the *Sharia* (Islamic law) but differ from them in believing that the *umma* (Muslim community) can choose the ruler of Islamic society, who need not be descended from the Prophet's family. Unlike the Shiis, Sunni religious activities are under the control of the state and their clergy are not given religious titles.

T

Taft–Hartley (National Management Relations) Act (1947)   It curtailed the power of the TRADE UNIONS in the United States. Strikes had increased markedly in 1946, when 5.6 million workers were involved, more than ever before. This created widespread public resentment. The Republican Congress passed the Act to redress the balance of power between employers and workers, which the Wagner Act (1935) had tipped in favour of the unions. The emphasis was on the right not to join a union. The closed shop was outlawed and the union shop (in which a union represented all workers) allowed only when state law permitted it and when the majority of union members voted for it. 'Unfair' union practices, such as sympathetic strikes and boycotts, were forbidden and unions were made responsible for breaches of contract and for acts of violence committed by members during strikes. The automatic deduction of union dues from wages and union contributions to political parties were also forbidden. Unions had to register and their officials had to take a non-communist oath. Strikes by government employees were made illegal: other strikes could take place only when a majority of workers had voted for them. Unions had to give 60 days' notice before striking and the President could order an 80-day cooling-off period for strikes endangering national health or safety. Trade unions denounced the Act as a 'slave labour act'. President TRUMAN, anxious to win back the union support he had lost, vetoed the bill but Congress passed it again over his veto. It has remained substantially unchanged.

Taliban   An Islamic group which fought in the AFGHAN CIVIL WAR and conquered most of the country by 1997. It was founded in 1994 by a senior mullah from Kandahar, Muhammad Omar Alchund, who had been a field commander during the SOVIET INVASION OF AFGHANISTAN. He drew his forces from refugees, mainly Pushtuns, in Pakistan. The Taliban had a collective leadership in which much authority was delegated to local commanders. Its main funds came from Saudi Arabia, the United Arab Emirates and Bahrain. The Taliban were educated in Quranic schools in a rigid form of SUNNI Islam and they imposed a harsh regime in the areas they conquered. The *Sharia* (Muslim law) was stricly applied: thieves had limbs amputated and adulterers were stoned to death. Women were forced back into purdah and were not allowed to mix with men outside their immediate family. They were forbidden to work, except in hospitals and clinics and then only with women. Girls were denied education and outside the home women had to wear the traditional *burqa*, which covered them from head to foot and had a netted slot over the eyes. Articles of Western depravity such as television sets were destroyed.

The Taliban had remarkable success in defeating the other guerrilla groups which fought one another after the Soviet occupation ended. Backed by Pakistan, they controlled two-thirds of the country by the autumn of 1996. They captured the capital, Kabul, in September. In May 1997 they took Mazar-i-Sharif in the North, the only large city which had remained outside their control. Their victory was the result of an alliance with

Uzbeks who had defected from the army of General Dostum, but when the Taliban tried to disarm their allies there was renewed fighting in which they were pushed out of Mazar-i-Sharif.

Tamil Tigers   The Liberation Tigers of Tamil Eelam are a group of Tamils in Sri Lanka who want a separate state in the North and East of the country. Tamils, who formed under 30 per cent of the population of Sri Lanka, felt that the governments of Solomon and Sirimavo BANDANARAIKE had discriminated against them by promoting Sinhala as the official language (Sinhalese and Muslims form 70 per cent of the population) and Buddhism as the national religion. Anti-Tamil riots in 1977, 1981 and 1983, in which the militant JVP played a leading role, were the severest the country had seen. Most Tamils were not violent but the Tigers waged guerrilla warfare against the government and initially used bases in the South Indian state of Tamil Nadu. The Tigers effectively controlled the Jaffna peninsula in the North of Sri Lanka and from 1984 increased their attacks on unarmed Sinhalese, carrying out bomb attacks in Colombo.

The Indian government became involved when the Indo-Sri Lankan Accords were made in 1987 by Prime Minister Rajiv GANDHI of India and President Jayawardene of Sri Lanka. An Indian peace-keeping force, initially of 7,000 troops, was to be sent to the Jaffna peninsula to end hostilities there. The Tigers were to hand over all their weapons and Tamil and English were to have equal status with Sinhala as official languages. The Accords met with violent protests from the Sinhalese majority and could not be implemented as the Tigers would not surrender their arms. Indian troops (100,000 by mid-1988) therefore attacked the Tigers' strongholds in the Jaffna peninsula, forcing them into the tropical forests, where they continued the struggle. When the last Indian troops left Sri Lanka in 1990, the Tigers took control of much of the territory in the North and East which the Indians had vacated. The Tigers were widely believed to be responsible for the assassination by a suicide bomber of Rajiv Gandhi in 1991. As the government continued its offensive against the Tigers in 1995, capturing their capital in Jaffna, the Tigers blew up oil storage tanks in Colombo and made suicide bomb attacks there. Government optimism that the civil war (in which 43,000 people were killed between 1983 and 1996) would soon be over was destroyed in July 1996, when the government suffered its worst defeat of the war when a military base in the north-east was overrun and 1,000 troops were killed by the Tigers.

Sri Lanka: Ethnic Fratricide and the Dismantling of Democracy, S. J. Tambiah (1986)
The Break-up of Sri Lanka: The Sinhalese–Tamil Conflict, J. Wilson (1988)

Tangentopoli (bribe city)   A name applied to Milan in the late 1980s but which referred more generally to the pervasive corruption in Italy since the Second World War. Bribery permeated every level of society. Shopkeepers bribed tax collectors, patients bribed doctors to obtain bogus certificates which would qualify them for disability pensions (four million Italians out of a population of 58 million obtained such pensions): bribes were needed even to get a telephone installed. State-controlled industries and development funds were a valuable source of patronage. No contracts were signed for public works without substantial bribes (*tangenti*) to the politicians concerned. Carlo Di Benedetti, the head of Olivetti, admitted paying billions of lira in bribes because of 'the systematic extortion imposed on the business community by Italy's political parties'. CHRISTIAN DEMOCRATIC PARTY (DC) politicians were the main beneficiaries of such a system, as they dominated postwar governments. Other parties joined in. The Socialist Party (PCI) was a junior partner in most governments after 1963. Its cabinet members demanded bribes before acting to save Venice from flooding and took millions of dollars from relief funds for Bangladesh, Somalia and Senegal. There was consternation too at the way European Union funds for the relief of poverty disappeared into the pockets of Italian politicians and how COMMON AGRICULTURAL POLICY payments were claimed on behalf of farmers who did not exist. Some of the corruption was connected with organized crime, as one of the chief recipients of the government Fund for the South was the MAFIA, which controlled the construction and other industries which obtained government contracts.

Magistrates anxious to probe into political corruption found parliament imposed restrictions on their activities, as hundreds of deputies and senators used their parliamentary immunity to avoid investigation and possible prosecution. Magistrates had a powerful weapon against those who were not politicians as anyone could be imprisoned while an investigation was going on: this was widely used to obtain confessions. From 1992 magistrates in Milan in operation Clean Hands uncovered a vast web of corruption, the leading magistrate Antonio Di Pietro becoming a national hero. The Socialist leader and former Prime Minister Bettino CRAXI, charged with corruption when his parliamentary immunity expired, was sentenced to eight years in prison and fled to Tunisia before his appeal could be heard. Leading figures from other parties, notably Giulio ANDREOTTI, were also indicted. By mid-1993 magistrates had requested the lifting of parliamentary immunity on 395 deputies and senators (a third of the total).

Tangentopoli led to the collapse of the political parties which had ruled Italy since the war. The Socialist vote fell in 1994 to 2.2 per cent, that of the DC (which changed its name in 1994 to the Popular Party) to 11.1 per cent. Top civil servants and businessmen went to prison (or committed suicide) while awaiting trial: by 1994 3,000 had been charged. Silvio BERLUSCONI tried and failed to stop the anti-corruption trials when he was Prime Minister in 1994 and when he was himself indicted used all his power as a media mogul to discredit Di Pietro and brought about his resignation. As many Italians in politics, business and the civil service were threatened by the Clean Hands drive, Berlusconi had much support. The civil service protected its own. According to Di Gianbattista, the President of Italy's Public Accounting Office, a quarter of civil servants found guilty of serious crimes were not disciplined. At the beginning of 1996 not one of the politicians, civil servants and businessmen shown to be corrupt was in jail as, owing to the cumbersome nature of the Italian judicial system, appeals can last for seven years and only 5 per cent of cases investigated reach the trial stage.

The Crisis of the Italian State: From the Origins of the Cold War to the Fall of Berlusconi, P. McCarthy (1995)
Italy: The Unfinished Revolution, M. Frei (1996)

technological revolution The application of science-based inventions to industry and daily life has been the most important source of economic growth since 1945. It not only improved old products but also created new ones. Some new products (plastic and artificial fibres such as nylon) appeared before the Second World War, but it was the war which acted as a great stimulus to invention in producing radar, the jet engine, the atom bomb, early computers used in code-breaking and the ideas and techniques which were the basis of the INFORMATION REVOLUTION and of the electronics industry. All these inventions were later adapted for civilian use. The COLD WAR soon followed the end of the war, so vast sums of money continued to be spent by Soviet and American governments on the MILITARY–INDUSTRIAL COMPLEX and SPACE EXPLORATION, which also provided spin-offs for civilians: hard plastics, optical fibres, sensing devices.

Transport was revolutionized by the jet engine, developed most successfully by Boeing. Gas turbines, produced in the 1960s, made aircraft more powerful, quieter and cheaper to run, while the wide-body design allowed more passengers to be carried. A huge aerospace industry arose, which employed 823,000 people in the US in 1989, with a further 540,000 working in air transport. Air travel became an essential part of the GLOBAL ECONOMY. The motor industry too expanded rapidly and eventually spread worldwide through firms established by MULTINATIONAL CORPORATIONS. The isolation of villages ended and suburbanization began. Farming was transformed by mechanization, particularly the use of tractors: five million in 1950, 22 million in 1980.

The electronics industry was the basis of much of the change taking place in industry and daily life. Scientists at the Bell laboratories in the US introduced in 1947 the first semiconductor, the transistor. Smaller than the valve, lighter and more reliable, it used less power and generated less heat. It was used widely and made possible the portable radio and compact hearing aids. Missile systems developed by the superpowers stimulated the miniaturization of components and led to great advances in computer technology. In 1971 the first micro-chips appeared, integrated circuits mimicking a computer's central processing unit, and were used in pocket calculators, digital wrist-watches and desk-top computers. Developments in electronics have been at the heart of the information revolution. By 1985 the electronics industry was the largest manufacturing industry in the US.

Mechanization and computerization affected most industries. Computercontrolled robots assemble many parts of motor cars, and some trains run without drivers. Factories have computerized systems of 'just in time' deliveries of components which eliminate the need for large warehouses. In heavy industry, such as electricity generation or steel production, sophisticated control systems monitor and automatically adjust the process in ways which would have needed many skilled employees in the past. Hospitals

and medical practice use increasingly complex and computerized equipment. Retailing has been mechanized by the automated scanning of bar-codes which adds up the purchases and tells the operator how much change to give.

Biotechnology is another new industry which has arisen during the technological revolution. Recombinant DNA techniques, which combine genes from one species with those of another, were recognized as practicable in 1973 and by the 1990s were widely used in medicine and agriculture.

Daily life has been transformed by new technology, even in the THIRD WORLD, where the transistor radio can reach the remotest village because of the miniature long-life battery. In European homes many items which are taken for granted – the television, the fridge – hardly existed in 1945. The microwave, camcorder, central heating timer, burglar alarm and self-focusing camera have all appeared since that date, all reliant on micro-chip technology. Vinyl LP records (which played for an hour instead of the eight minutes of the old 78s) were introduced in 1948 and were followed by cassettes (which could record voice or music) in the 1960s and compact discs, which used laser technology, in the 1980s.

The technological revolution has created jobs in new industries but these, except for the service industries, require highly skilled and comparatively few workers. In the late 1980s Nippon Steel with Inland Steel of the US built a cold-rolling mill in Indiana, which cut the time needed to produce a coil of steel from 12 days to one hour, but the whole plant was run by a small team of technicians. Automated cash-points and vending machines replace human beings by machinery, thus contributing to DEINDUSTRIALIZATION.

The Globalization of Production and Technology, J. Howells and M. Wood (1993)

Tet offensive (January/February 1968)

An attack in South Vietnam by VIET CONG and VIET MINH troops under the command of General GIAP during the VIETNAM WAR. The surprise assault took place during the Tet lunar New Year holiday: 100 towns were attacked, including the capital Saigon and 36 out of 44 provincial centres. In Saigon the presidential palace, the airport and the head-quarters of the general staff were raided and the American embassy penetrated. Hanoi believed that there would be a massive rising in the South against President Thieu's puppet government and that the South Vietnamese army would collapse. None of this happened. Hue, where 3,000 people were executed, was captured and held for three weeks but else-where communist gains were recaptured within two or three days. The offensive was a complete military disaster: 45,000 out of 80,000 communist troops were killed, whereas US losses were just over a thousand and those of the South Vietnamese army 2,000. The Viet Cong was almost wiped out, so that most of the fighting had henceforth to be carried out by troops from the North, who were not able to mount another large-scale offensive until 1972.

Tet was nevertheless a turning-point in the war, as it was a great psychological victory for the communists. American public opinion was shocked that US intelligence did not know about the coming attack and at the ability of the Viet Cong to strike anywhere in the South. As victory, it seemed, was impos-sible, the VIETNAM ANTI-WAR MOVE-MENT gained more support. President JOHNSON, shaken by Tet, announced on 31 March that bombing of the North would be suspended and offered peace talks, which were to drag on for another five years. He also announced that 'I shall not seek and I will not accept the nomination of my party for another term as your President'.

Thatcher, Margaret Hilda (1925–), Baron-ess   British Prime Minister (1979–90). The daughter of a grocer who was a Metho-dist lay preacher, she lived above the family shop in Grantham, Lincolnshire. Margaret

Roberts went from a local grammar school to Oxford University to read chemistry. In 1951 she married a businessman, Denis Thatcher: their twins, Carol and Mark, were born two years later. She studied law, qualified as a barrister and in 1959 was elected to parlia-ment as a Conservative MP. When Edward HEATH became Prime Minister (1970–4) he appointed her as Minister of Education, where she was a big spender (the education budget rose from 4 per cent 6 per cent of GNP) and abolished more grammar schools than any of her predecessors: she approved all but 310 of the 3,420 schemes for comprehens-ive education submitted to her. A year after the defeat of the CONSERVATIVE PARTY in the 1974 election she stood as a candidate in a leadership election for the Conservatives. She was not expected to win but polled 130 votes to Heath's 119 and so became Leader of the Opposition. In the 1979 general election the Conservatives gained 43.9 per cent of the vote to the LABOUR PARTY's 36.9 per cent and had 70 more seats than Labour: Thatcher became Prime Minister, the first woman to hold that office in Britain.

A dedicated politician, she had no hobbies, hardly ever took a holiday and was endlessly busy, surviving on very little sleep. She rejected the BUTSKELLISM which had pre-vailed since the war, as consensus politics simply diluted truth with error, maintaining that she was 'not a consensus politician or a pragmatic politician' but 'a conviction politi-cian'. Her convictions were those of the Man-chester School of the 1840s: the belief in a minimalist state (as far as the economy was concerned), which should not interfere in the workings of the free market. The frontiers of the state should be pushed back and all restrictions on enterprise abolished. Moder-ates and doubters she dismissed as 'wets', 'not one of us', but as wets dominated the party in 1979 she had to include many of them in her first cabinet. She did not feel secure enough to begin weeding them out until September 1981. The FALKLANDS WAR (1982) added immensely to her authority and guaranteed victory in the 1983 election. The Conservative vote was lower (42.4 per cent) than in 1979, but the vagaries of the British electoral system gave the Conservatives 387 seats, an overall majority of 144.

The Prime Minister abandoned KEYNES-IANISM, the dominant economic philosophy since the war, and took up MONETARISM, the belief that control of the money supply is all that is needed to control inflation. Unfortunately, the money supply could not be controlled, so monetarism was abandoned. There were two depressions in the 1980s, one at the beginning fuelled by Chancellor HOWE's budgets, the other at the end of the decade made worse by the LAWSON budget of 1988. In between there was a boom which Chancellor Lawson hailed as an 'economic miracle', when growth rates reached nearly 5 per cent but the average growth between 1979 and 1990 was 1.8 per cent a year, a very poor performance (the average growth from 1970–9 was 2.4 per cent). A quarter of Britain's manufacturing industry was destroyed in the recession of 1979–81, with the result that manufacturing output in 1990 was only 6 per cent higher than in 1979. In this period manufacturing grew in the US by 35 per cent and in Japan by 58 per cent. Investment was lower in 1990 as a percentage of GDP than it was in 1979, the only OECD country in which this was the case. Britain at this time enjoyed the benefits of North Sea oil, which brought billions of pounds to the Exchequer and ensured that there were no balance of payments problems for most of the decade. Oil money largely went into foreign investment, which increased from £2.7 billion in 1975 to £90 billion a decade later, when Britain was second only to Japan in its overseas portfolio. Unemployment was a persistent problem, reaching the official figure of 3.1 million in 1986, but as the government changed the way of calculating the figure, always in a downward direction, the number of unemployed was probably 3.8 million. The state's role in the economy was diminished by PRIVATIZA-TION, whereby most nationalized industries

were sold to the private sector. The 'big-bang' (27 October 1986) ended the old restrictive practices in the Stock Exchange and replaced brokers milling around the floor of the Stock Exchange with dealers sitting in front of computers.

Thatcher was determined to crush the TRADE UNIONS, which had brought down the Heath government in 1970 and that of Jim CALLAGHAN in 1979. She blamed them for the inefficiency of British industry with their restrictive practices and overmanning and for the relative economic decline of Britain by their wildcat strikes and inflationary pay settlements. A step by step approach was adopted by Jim Prior and Norman Tebbit. A series of Acts from 1980–4 made secondary picketing (not at the place of work) illegal, removed the legal immunities of trade unions except in a trade dispute (they would be liable for damages in a political strike), required secret ballots every five years for the election of union officials and ballots to decide if members wanted unions to fund political parties (i.e. the Labour Party). The real test came with the MINERS' STRIKE of 1984–5, for which the government had carefully prepared and which saw the comprehensive defeat of the miners. It was followed by the defeat of the newspaper printers, whose restrictive practices prevented the use of modern technology. Rupert Murdoch installed computerized technology for Times Newspapers at a new, fortified plant at Wapping in the London docklands. This strike too, after much violence on the picket lines between printers and police, was defeated: new working practices and machinery were introduced. The government's trade union legislation was very popular but it did not affect wage settlements, which continued to run ahead of productivity.

After the trade unions, the Prime Minister wanted to tackle local government. Since the Municipal Corporations Act of 1835 local authorities had been elected with responsibility for providing certain services and with the right to raise their own revenue through local taxes. As it believed in market forces, the government wanted to relieve local authorities of many of their functions and hand them over to the private sector: privatization at the local level. It therefore mounted a sustained attack on local government, deciding how much local authorities could spend and how much they could raise in local taxes. Government grants to councils were reduced yearly, yet they were not allowed to increase the rates as they wished because the Rates Act (1984) permitted the government to 'cap' rates (i.e. impose maximum rate levels). The independence of local authorities was drastically reduced and they were further undermined as much local government work was transferred to unelected quangos appointed by the government. Polytechnics were removed from local authority control, schools were given financial inducements to opt out of their charge. Councils were forced to sell many of their houses and were not allowed to use the proceeds to build new ones. Funds for housing were given to housing associations instead of local councils. The Greater London Council and Metropolitan authorities were simply abolished without consultation and in 1987 the POLL TAX (community charge) was introduced, though all local authorities said it was unworkable. It was also highly unpopular and was soon abandoned. The market system was imposed too on the National Health Service (NHS), as hospitals had to compete with one another for the patients of fund-holding GPs. Thatcher claimed that the NHS was 'safe in our hands' but it was partly dismantled as many dentists refused to take NHS patients. Under Thatcher the rich got richer and the poor became poorer, largely as a result of a move from direct to indirect taxation. Thatcher was opposed to a 'dependency culture' and the 'nanny state'. From 1988 the social security system changed, loans from a Social Fund replacing National Assistance, but there were no loans for those unable to repay them. Some 700,000 lost their housing benefits and 16–18 year olds were unable to claim unemployment benefit. Beg-

gars reappeared, sleeping on the streets, as poverty in Britain increased in the 1980s from 5 million to 6.6 million (EEC figures) and crime by 79 per cent. An underclass emerged which rioted in Bristol in 1980, in Brixton (London), Toxteth (Liverpool), Moss Side (Manchester) in 1981, in Handsworth (Birmingham) and Tottenham in 1985. Lord Scarman reported on the Brixton Riots of 1981, 'the like of which had not previously been seen in this century in Britain', yet those in Toxteth two months later were even worse.

Thatcher's foreign policy was based on the 'special relationship' with the US. This had more meaning than usual as the Prime Minister had a very close rapport with President REAGAN, whose views she shared. There was a setback when the US INTERVENTION IN GRENADA took place in 1983 without the US consulting or even informing Britain beforehand. Thatcher soon overcame her outrage and allowed the US to keep cruise missiles in England: in return she received Trident missiles for Britain's nuclear submarines. In 1988 she gave permission for the use of British bases in the US RAIDS ON LIBYA, which led QADDAFI to supply arms to the IRA. The special relationship did not outlast Reagan, as President BUSH regarded Germany as the most important European power. Her other main preoccupation was the EEC (European Economic Community), particularly Britain's contribution to the EEC budget, which was far in excess of any benefits received from it. By persistently and loudly demanding 'our' money, she obtained a considerable reduction, at the cost of icy relations with Helmut SCHMIDT and Valéry GISCARD D´ESTAING. Howe, as Foreign Secretary, persuaded her to sign the Single European Act (1988), though it committed Britain to what she had always opposed: closer integration and a loss of sovereignty. Both Lawson and Howe pressed her hard to join the ERM (Exchange Rate Mechanism) but she resisted until John MAJOR became Chancellor of the Exchequer. She disliked the Rhodesia settlement which ended Ian Smith's UDI and created Zimbabwe, as it left a left-wing black government in control. Thatcher treated most COMMON-WEALTH leaders, who greatly disliked her tabloid chauvinism, with disdain and refused to impose sanctions on the APARTHEID regime in South Africa. In Northern Ireland she showed considerable statesmanship in making the ANGLO-IRISH AGREEMENT in 1985 with Garret Fitzgerald, which recognized for the first time since 1922 the direct interest of the Irish government in the North.

Margaret Thatcher was an imperious figure who surprised and amused journalists by her use of the royal 'we' ('we have become a grandmother'). The Conservative vote at 42.3 per cent in the 1987 election was almost identical with that of 1983 and she had a comfortable majority, but there was a massive decline in her popularity as boom turned to bust (the stock market crash of October 1987 wiped 24 per cent off stock prices) and with the poll tax. Divisions within the cabinet became clear with the resignation of senior figures such as Chancellor Lawson and Deputy Prime Minister Howe. His resignation speech in November 1990 was a devastating critique of her diplomatic style and of her anti-Europeanism and seemed to invite a challenge to her leadership. This was taken up by Michael Heseltine. In the first ballot Thatcher was just short of being an outright winner, gaining 204 votes to Heseltine's 152, but she had lost the support of two-fifths of Tory MPs and was advised by her cabinet colleagues that she would not win the second round. She therefore resigned, not because of parliamentary or electoral defeat but owing to dissent within the Conservative Party.

Margaret Thatcher was the first British Prime Minister to win three successive general elections since Lord Liverpool in 1812–27 and was the longest continuously serving Prime Minister in the twentieth century. The political scene had been transformed by privatization, changes in trade union law and local government, and the introduction of market forces into the WELFARE STATE. There was a new consensus in politics very different from the Butskellism of the past: the Labour Party accepted much of the Conservative agenda, such as its trade union legislation and privatization. She had no doubt at all about her own importance. 'Thatcherism is not for a decade', she declared triumphantly in 1990, 'It is for centuries'. Later more sober counsels prevailed. 'In politics there are no final victories', she wrote in her memoirs. She retired from the Commons in 1992 and accepted a life peerage.

The Thatcher Effect, D. Kavanagh and A. Seldon (eds) (1989)
The Economy Under Mrs Thatcher, 1979–90, C. Johnson (1991)
One of Us, H. Young (1991)

Third World   A term which some see as referring to all countries which were not part of the First (capitalist) World or the Second (communist) World. Others see it as having a French origin, derived from the Third Estate, which before the French Revolution referred to all social groups who were outside the privileged First and Second Estates (clergy and nobility). In both cases it refers to the vast majority of poor and underdeveloped countries (several of which formed the NON-ALIGNED MOVEMENT) in Africa, Asia and Latin America. Some historians reject the term altogether, as it is not a precise analytical concept and hold that it is meaningless to group together countries as disparate as Egypt and Liberia. Willy BRANDT, former Chancellor of the Federal Republic of Germany, preferred to speak of the NORTH–SOUTH DIVIDE, but this too has been criticized as imprecise and misleading.

Inside the Third World: The Anatomy of Poverty, P. Harrison (1993)

Tiananmen Square massacre (June 1989)
The use of the People's Liberation Army (PLA) by the government to crush the pro-democracy movement in Beijing. Widespread student discontent throughout China came to

the surface the day after HU YAOBANG died on 16 April 1989. In the next few days thousands of people gathered in Tiananmen Square to demand freedom of the press and of speech. Around 600,000 gathered on 22 April for Hu's official funeral ceremonies. Similar demonstrations took place in Shanghai and other cities. ZHAO ZIYANG, General Secretary of the CCP, attempted conciliation but DENG XIAOPING decided to use force, believing (with the CULTURAL REVOLUTION in mind) that concessions would simply produce further demands and end in chaos.

Martial law was declared by Li Peng, the Prime Minister, and by 20 May there were a quarter of a million troops in and around Beijing. When they attempted to move they were surrounded by huge crowds and on 21 May a million people in Beijing demonstrated against the imposition of martial law. While the government failed to take any effective action factories, government ministries and CCP organizations came out in support of the students. Troops withdrew to the city limits on 22 May and it seemed that the people had won. Zhao was dismissed from the Politburo Standing Committee on 24 May. On the 27th student leaders were prepared to end their occupation of the square but a militant minority prevented this. A 30-feet high plaster statue of a woman (like the Statue of Liberty in New York) holding aloft in her hands the torch of freedom, was erected in the Square on 29 May and revived the student movement. The rise of a militant workers' movement that declared its support for the students was a further threat to Deng's regime, which feared the rise of a SOLIDARITY-type movement in China. Many party, army and government members were defecting to the students, as hostility to the regime swept through the major cities. Deng therefore obtained the consent, sometimes reluctant, of his military commanders for an attack on central Beijing, which took place on 3–4 June. Between 600 and 1,200 people, including 39 students and some soldiers, were killed (and between 6,000–10,000 civilians injured)

as troops fought their way to the Square. There was no massacre of students in the Square itself: the 3,000–5,000 students remaining were allowed an orderly and peaceful evacuation. Local authorities in other cities brought the democracy movement to an end without bloodshed, even though there were massive demonstrations protesting at the massacre in Beijing.

Large-scale arrests resulted in 35 people in five cities, mainly workers and unemployed, being tried and publicly executed for violence (there were no students or intellectuals among this number). Zhao lost all his party posts, JIANG ZEMIN (Deng's choice) becoming General Secretary. The CCP had lost its legitimacy, central control over the provinces had been weakened and there were deep divisions in the PLA. These were the longer term effects of the massacre. Economic sanctions were imposed by some foreign governments but these lasted only a short time, as few countries would put principle before profit and China's market was potentially enormous. It remained to be seen whether, as Deng believed, rapid economic growth could continue without any political change.

China's Search for Democracy: The Student and Mass Movement of 1989, S. Ogden, K. Hartford, L. R. Sullivan, D. Zweig (eds) (1991)
Quelling the People, T. Brook (1992)
The Legacy of Tiananmen, J. A. R. Miles (1996)

Timor, East, Indonesian seizure of (1975–6)

At the end of the Second World War Timor was handed back to its former colonial powers, the Netherlands in the West and Portugal in the East. West Timor became part of Indonesia when the Dutch East Indies acquired its independence in 1948, the East remaining under Portuguese control until the PORTUGUESE REVOLUTION of 1974, after which Portugal virtually abandoned its colony. A left-wing party Fretilin (Revolutionary Front for an Independent East Timor) soon took control of almost the whole country and in November 1975 declared the independence of the Democratic Republic of East Timor.

Concerned that an independent East Timor would encourage secessionist movements elsewhere in Indonesia and that it would serve as a base for communist subversion, the Indonesian government invaded East Timor in December. The UNITED NATIONS called on Indonesia to withdraw but SUHARTO ignored the call, as he had the support of the US. Indonesia annexed the territory in June 1976. Fitful guerrilla warefare by Fretilin continued in the mountains, though this was not a serious threat to Indonesian control. Many villages were resettled as a counter-insurgency measure and this led to famine in which perhaps 100,000 died (out of a population of 650,000). The UN Human Rights Commission noted 'extrajudicial killings, disappearances, torture and arbitrary detention'. Fretilin suffered a major blow when its military commander was captured in 1992 but Indonesia has failed to win the loyalty of the indigenous people, in spite of the government spending more per capita on state aid to East Timor than on any other part of Indonesia except Irian Jaya (West New Guinea). Cardinal Belo, head of the Catholic Church in East Timor, and José Ramos Horta were awarded the Nobel Peace Prize in 1996 for their defence of human rights in East Timor.

East Timor: Nationalism and Colonialism, J. Joliffe (1978)

Tito, Josip Broz (1892–1980)   General Secretary of the Communist Party of Yugoslavia (1937–80), President of Yugoslavia (1953–80). Born into a peasant family in Croatia (which was then part of the Austro-Hungarian Empire) he began his adult life as a GASTARBEITER working in Germany. In the First World War he served in the Austro-Hungarian army as a sergeant, was taken prisoner on the Eastern Front in 1915 and when released in 1917 joined the Red Guards in

Siberia. When he returned to Yugoslavia in 1920 he was a communist. He joined the Communist Party of Yugoslavia (KPJ) and worked as a trade union organizer. Imprisoned (1928–34) for organizing demonstrations against the Yugoslav government, he adopted the pseudonym Tito. With his fluent German and Russian, Tito worked for the Comintern (Communist International) in Europe and benefited from the decimation of the KPJ leadership in STALIN's purges to become General Secretary of the KPJ. A faithful Muscovite, he welcomed the Nazi–Soviet Pact (1939) and turned against the Nazis only when they invaded the USSR in 1941. Though the KPJ at this time had only 12,000 members, he formed the Partisans to resist the German occupation. For much of the war the Partisans competed with a second resistance movement, led by Draža Mihajlović, backed by Yugoslavia's monarchy in exile but support for him was confined to Serbs. Tito, on the other hand, stressed the national character of the Partisans, who welcomed Croats, Serbs, Muslims and Jews. Tito's promise of a classless society, with social and economic equality, also attracted many people. The turning-point for Tito came in 1943, when the British switched their support from Mihajlović to him. He occupied western Yugoslavia and the Dalmation coast and in 1944 went on the offensive, tying down 21 German divisions. As the Germans withdrew to avoid being cut off by the Russians advancing into Hungary, Tito was able to establish communist power throughout Yugoslavia by May 1945.

Tito consolidated his control by one of the most ruthless purges in Eastern Europe, during which thousands were executed. The secret police, he said, had 'to strike terror into the bones of those who do not like this kind of Yugoslavia'. Opponents – middle class liberals and democrats – were eliminated. At first a Stalinist economic system was imposed, with a Five Year Plan (1947) which concentrated on heavy industry and central direction of the economy. The property of large estates and of the Church was given to the peasantry. Ethnic conflict, particularly between Serbs and Croats, had disfigured the prewar monarchy, so Tito set about building a multinational Yugoslavia, in which each region would have considerable autonomy. In 1946 he made Yugoslavia into a federal state of six equal republics (Slovenia, Croatia, Bosnia and Hercegovina, Macedonia and Serbia) and two autonomous areas (Vojvodina, with a Hungarian minority, and Kosovo, populated mainly by Albanians – both were in Serbia). Tito's independent foreign policy brought about the YUGOSLAV–SOVIET SPLIT in 1948. The split prepared the way for Tito to pursue a Yugoslav 'road to socialism', rejecting his earlier Stalinst economic model. Self-management of factories was introduced but a greater boost to the economy came from tourism, as the Adriatic coast was developed, and from the remittances from the million Yugoslavs who worked in Germany. In 1965 30 laws, known as 'the Reform', were passed to provide the fabric of a market economy. There was to be limited private employment, the abolition of most price controls and in 1967 foreign investment was allowed up to 49 per cent of total capital and foreign investors could export their profits. Foreign loans too made the 1970s a prosperous decade for most Yugoslavs. Decentralization was extended from economics to politics in the 1974 constitution, which recognized the sovereign status of the republics, gave the autonomous provinces of Vojvodina and Kosovo more freedom from Serbian control and granted the republics the right to veto legislation passed by the federal assembly. This stimulated regionalism and economic disunity, as each republic sought to develop its own industries and each republican section of the League of Yugoslav Communists (LYC), as the KPJ was known from 1952, acted independently of the federal LYC. Yugoslavia was, therefore, already beginning to break up. The only thing that kept it together was Tito.

Relations with the Soviet Union were renewed in 1955, when KHRUSHCHEV apolo-gized for the break of 1948: Tito took a pro-Soviet line in the HUNGARIAN RISING (1956) and advised Dubček against political liberalization during the PRAGUE SPRING (1968). Tito became the only European leader of the THIRD WORLD and the NON-ALIGNED MOVEMENT in 1953. At the time of the SIX DAY WAR he supported NASSER and broke off diplomatic relations with Israel and in the same year his recognition of East Germany led West Germany, a major economic support, to break off diplomatic relations with Yugoslavia.

Like other leaders of the communist bloc, such as CEAUŞESCU, Tito promoted a cult of personality and had a sybaritic taste for palaces, hunting lodges, Adriatic islands and 32 residences for his personal use, as well as two ocean-going yachts and his luxurious blue train. In his last years the economic decline of Yugoslavia was evident: industries were inefficient and money borrowed from abroad was used to pay workers more rather than to improve productivity. Ethnic tensions were not far below the surface, as the richer provinces of Slovenia and Croatia resented their profits going to the support of Macedonia, Montenegro and Kosovo.

Tito's Flawed Legacy: Yugoslavia and the West 1939–84, N. Beloff (1985)
Tito: Yugoslavia's Great Dictator: A Reassessment, S. K. Pavlowitsch (1992)
Tito and the Rise and Fall of Yugoslavia, R. West (1996)

Togliatti, Palmiro (1893–1964) General Secretary of the PCI (Italian Communist Party) (1926–64). Born in Genoa, the son of a schoolmistress and a petty clerk, he won a scholarship to the University of Turin in 1911 and joined the Socialist Party in 1914, but his real political education began when he came under the influence of Antonio Gramsci after the First World War. Both were founder members of the PCI in 1921, Togliatti becoming its leader when Gramsci was arrested in 1926. The party went underground with the rise of Mussolini and Togliatti left for Moscow where, astute and cautious, he survived the purges of the 1930s and rose to be Vice Secretary of the Comintern. In 1937 he was sent by the Comintern to take charge of communists fighting in the Spanish Civil War and remained there until 1939.

He returned to Italy in 1944 and concentrated on liberating Italy rather than on formenting revolution. Communists were the strongest force in the Resistance and some wanted to seize power but the pragmatic Togliatti realized that Allied troops in Italy would not allow this and pursued a policy of gradualism and compromise, working in the government with bourgeois parties such as the CHRISTIAN DEMOCRATIC PARTY (DC). He accepted the Lateran Treaty of 1929 (which recognized Roman Catholicism as the state religion) as part of the new constitution and as Minister of Justice (1945–6) made no attempt to reform the judiciary. His aim of a lasting coalition of the mass popular parties (the PCI had two million members in 1946), which would carry out major social reforms, came to an end with the COLD WAR and the dismissal of the communists from his government by DE GASPERI in 1947. Togliatti then worked for an electoral victory by allying with the socialists in a Democratic Popular Front, but this obtained only 31 per cent of the votes in the 1948 general election.

In opposition Togliatti had to follow the Soviet line in foreign policy and opposed MARSHALL PLAN aid, membership of NATO and of the EEC (European Economic Community), while trying to maintain an Italian road to socialism outside Soviet control. His opportunity came with KHRUSHCHEV's secret speech to the TWENTIETH CONGRESS OF THE CPSU in 1956. Togliatti took a more radical approach than other Western communist leaders and criticized Khrushchev for not going far enough. Why, he wanted to know, had STALIN been able to act as he had done? Togliatti decided that the Soviet model should not be obligatory for other communist parties and put forward his idea of polycentr-

ism, demanding 'full autonomy for ... communist parties' and national roads to socialism, thus becoming a precursor of EUROCOMMUNISM. He still felt the need to support Soviet foreign policy and justified the crushing of the HUNGARIAN RISING (1956) but with DÉTENTE he was able to be more independent and refused to condemn China in the SINO-SOVIET DISPUTE. He died at Yalta, where he had gone to meet Khrushchev, from a cerebral haemorrhage. Though more admired than loved (he was arrogant and sarcastic), a million people attended his funeral in Rome, a tribute to the man who had changed the PCI from a small group of militants into the largest communist party in Western Europe.

The Strategy of the Italian Communist Party,
   D. Sassoon (1981)

Tonkin Gulf Resolution (August 1964)

On 2 August 1964 an American destroyer was attacked by North Vietnamese gunboats in the Gulf of Tonkin, off the North Vietnam coast, when it was collecting intelligence after a South Vietnam commando raid. The destroyer, accompanied by another warship, returned to the same area where, on the night of 4 August, the North Vietnamese allegedly launched another attack. It was not certain that such an attack had taken place but President JOHNSON used the incident to ask Congress for powers 'to take all necessary measures to repel any armed attack against the forces of the United States'. The House of Representatives voted in favour of the Resolution by 416 to nil, the Senate by 88 votes to 2. The Resolution enabled the President to begin bombing North Vietnam, with whom the US was not at war, and to send large numbers of ground troops to South Vietnam, so considerably escalating the VIETNAM WAR. The Resolution was repealed in 1971.

Truth is the First Casualty: The Tonkin Gulf Resolution, J. Goulden (1969)

The Gulf of Tonkin Resolution, J. Galloway (1970)

trade unions Organizations of workers to improve wages and working conditions. The first 30 years after the Second World War marked the high point of trade union power, in spite of isolated legislation such as the TAFT–HARTLEY ACT (1947) in the US, which weakened labour unions by outlawing the closed shop and unfair union practices such as sympathetic strikes. To combat this the AMERICAN FEDERATION OF LABOR, which represented craft unions, combined in 1955 with the CIO (Congress of Industrial Organizations), representing unskilled workers in mass production, to form the AFL-CIO. Mass-production industries such as cars, steel and shipbuilding formed a favourable environment for union organization and collective bargaining. Full employment in the postwar boom made unions powerful and able to ensure social services and pensions for their members. In West Germany the SOCIAL MARKET ECONOMY established by Ludwig ERHARD brought trade unions into a cooperative partnership with employers and the government. Unions there were large and covered a whole industry, thus avoiding rivalries between competing unions and strengthening the unions in wage bargaining. German unions accepted the free market and flexibility in internal labour markets and were largely responsible for the industrial harmony that prevailed there. They were able to preserve jobs and contain inflation by accepting restraint in wage increases, which did not exceed the rise in productivity. Social Democracy in Scandinavia also gave a powerful voice to the unions, which accepted high taxation in return for WELFARE STATE benefits. In Britain too the unions were a formidable force, particularly when the LABOUR PARTY was in power, as they provided most of the funds for the party, sponsored many Labour MPs and had a block vote at the annual Labour Party Conference. The close connection of the TUC (Trade Union Congress) and the Labour Party did not, however, produce industrial harmony, as there was a craft union tradition in Britain with hundreds of small unions competing with one another and quarrelling over demarcation disputes. A minor quarrel between two small unions could paralyse a whole industry. The number of days lost in strikes in Britain was only slightly lower than in France or Italy, where unions were much weaker, the number of workers in the most powerful French union CGT falling from five million to 1.6 million between 1945–58. In 1968 75 per cent of French workers were not in unions. In the communist bloc trade unions were of little importance, being simply 'transmission belts' for the directives of the CPSU and other communist parties.

The postwar boom came to an end with the OPEC PRICE RISE of 1973 and with it there was a decrease in trade union power. The numbers in trade unions fell as MULTINATIONAL CORPORATIONS moved jobs to countries where labour was cheap and taxes low. As the old mass-production industries declined in Western Europe and the US, they were replaced by the service sector, where jobs were generally unskilled and poorly paid. DEINDUSTRIALIZATION meant the loss of 2.8 million jobs in US manufacturing in the 1980s and more in the 1990s. Around 35 per cent of non-agricultural workers were members of labour unions in the US in 1945, 14.6 per cent in 1997. The percentage was as high as that only because the public sector – federal and state civil servants, municipal employees – was heavily unionized: in the private sector only 10 per cent of workers were members of a union. Trade union power reached a low point in the US when President REAGAN declared a strike by the Professional Air Traffic Controllers' Association illegal and wiped out the union. Cuts in jobs, pensions and health coverage for workers followed in the next 15 years. In Japan, 56 per cent of the labour force were union members in 1947, 24 per cent in 1992. Trade unions lost two-thirds of their members in France between 1974 and 1993, when only 9 per cent of workers were in unions. In Britain the number of workers in trade unions fell from 13 million in 1979 to 7.2 million, under a third of all employees, in 1997 and, as in the US, most were in the public sector, where unionization was 61 per cent (21 per cent in the private sector).

With the TECHNOLOGICAL REVOLU-TION fewer workers were needed on the shop floor, while competition in the GLOBAL ECONOMY forced governments to concentrate on lowering inflation rather than on maintaining full employment. High unemployment became a permanent feature of Western economies, further weakening the trade unions. In Britain there was a deliberate attempt to reduce union power, which was blamed for industrial anarchy and Britain's lack of competitiveness. Harold WILSON's Labour government tried, and failed, to limit union power with IN PLACE OF STRIFE (1969). Overmighty unions succeeded in bringing down the governments of Edward HEATH in 1974 and of Jim CALLAGHAN in the WINTER OF DISCONTENT (1979), but this created an anti-union backlash which Margaret THATCHER was able to use to pass legislation to reduce union influence and to win comprehensively in the MINERS' STRIKE of 1984. At the end of the twentieth century trade unions were everywhere in decline, in spite of the Teamsters' success in the US after a two-week strike in August 1997, the greatest trade union victory for two decades.

Workers in Industrial America, D. Brady (1980)
Trade Unions, C. Crouch (1982)
Trade Unions and Politics, K. Coates and T. Topham (1986)

Transition, the   The peaceful transition in Spain between 1976 and 1978 from the dictatorship of General FRANCO (1939–75) to a democratic parliamentary monarchy.

Once General Franco died on 20 November 1975 the overwhelming majority of Spaniards, including not just the opposition to the dictator but many of his former supporters too, expected the authoritarian regime to be replaced by a more democratic one, but it was unclear what shape this would take, or how it would be achieved. The first government appointed by King JUAN CARLOS, who had been made head of state two days after Franco's death in accordance with the law of 1969, was headed by the former Francoist Prime Minister Carlos Arias Navarro. A grey and uninspiring character, Arias Navarro was too deferential towards the hard-line Francoists, dubbed 'the Bunker', and too hostile to the opposition to achieve meaningful political reform. In July 1976 the king, in collaboration with his key adviser, Torcuato Fernández Miranda, replaced Arias Navarro with the surprise choice of the relatively unknown Francoist functionary, Adolfo Suárez. He combined all the qualities required to transform the dictatorship from within: the knowledge and trust of an insider along with the will and pragmatic sense necessary to undertake its reform, as well as considerable charm and political ability.

Suárez's first task was to dismantle the political system inherited from the Franco dictatorship. This he did by persuading the Francoist Cortes, or legislature, to dissolve itself. Thus, one year after the dictator's death, his own Cortes committed collective suicide by passing in November 1976 the Law for Political Reform. This law, which established the sovereignty of the people, introduced political pluralism and replaced the Francoist political system with a democratically elected bicameral legislature, was the first major triumph of the Transition. The strategy may have been designed by the king and Fernández Miranda but it had been carried out with extreme skill by Suárez. The Prime Minister had managed to win over both the army and the bulk of the Francoists. In the public referendum on the law in December the government won an overwhelming endorsement with 94 per cent of the vote. Over the next few weeks the hard-line right unsuccessfully attempted to derail the Transition through a campaign of violence, which it hoped would force the army to intervene.

The next challenge for Suárez was to incorporate the democratic opposition to the dictatorship into the new political framework. Now that he had disarmed the old regime, Suárez's was able to negotiate with the opposition from a position of strength. Although the left had always defended the idea of a *ruptura*, or complete break, with the old regime, Suárez's *fait accompli* in dismantling the dictatorship's political system through co-operation rather than confrontation forced it to embrace the idea of reform. It was in any case clear that an attempted *ruptura* would probably have resulted in widespread social conflict and the eventual intervention of the army. By ceding control of the transition process to Suárez, the democrats accepted that the country would continue to be run in the meantime by politicians from the Franco regime. Suárez set about integrating the opposition by organizing the first democratic elections in Spain in over 40 years. The final step on the road to the democratization of the dictatorship was the legalization on 9 April 1977 of the PCE (Spanish Communist Party), the old regime's most redoubtable enemy.

The general election of June 1977 further consolidated the regime by marking the triumph of moderation: the moderate right, in the shape of the Prime Minister's *Unión de Centro Democrático* (UCD: Central Democratic Union), outstripped the Francoist right of Fraga's *Alianza Popular* (AP: Popular Alliance), while the moderate left, in the form of Felipe GONZALEZ's PSOE (*Partido Socialista Obrero Español*: Spanish Socialist Workers' Party), defeated the PCE. The raison d'etre of the democratically elected Cortes was to draw up a new constitution, while the UCD government focused on the twin threats of the economic crisis and the escalating terrorism of the Basque separatist group ETA

(*Euskadi Ta Askatasuna*: Basque Homeland and Freedom). Against a background of world recession and soaring oil prices, the post-Franco economy was characterized by diminishing investment, balance of payments deficits, mounting inflation, and, worst of all in the circumstances, fast-rising unemployment. Spanish democracy might be seriously limited by the economic crisis. Suárez eventually reacted to the situation by agreeing in October 1977 upon a plan of action, the so-called Moncloa Pacts, in collaboration with the other political parties. This was above all a deal between the government and the left, whereby the unions would moderate their wage demands in exchange for social and fiscal reforms.

Co-operation was also the hallmark of the deliberations that led to the passing of the constitution on 31 October 1978 by both chambers of the Cortes. The most novel feature of the constitution, which defined Spain as a 'social and democratic State' within the political framework of a parliamentary monarchy, was the division of the state into regional or autonomous governments. This was designed largely to placate the regional aspirations of the Basques and Catalans, leading opponents of the Franco regime, and overcome the shortcomings of the dictatorship's heavily centralized state. In the referendum held five weeks later, 87.9 per cent of the voters backed the new constitutional arrangement. Formally, the Transition was over, though the consolidation of democracy in Spain would take several more years.

The Transition was enormously facilitated by the profound economic and social changes of the 1960s and 1970s. The moderation of the opposition, especially the PCE and the *Comisiones Obreras* (communist trade unions), and even the Church, also made a fundamental contribution to its passage. Undoubtedly the shadow of the Civil War (1936–9), when the democratic Second Republic was torn apart by fratricidal conflict, loomed large. Given that the Transition was based on reform rather than rupture, and concerned only the political system, it was inevitable that many institutional pillars of the old regime, such as the Civil Guard and army, were left almost entirely untouched. Still, the largely peaceful transformation of a dictatorship into a parliamentary democracy by means of the old regime's own legal channels had no contemporary precedents.

Spain: Dictatorship to Democracy, R. Carr and J. P. Fusi (1979)
The Transformation of Spain, D. Gilmour (1985)
The Triumph of Democracy, P. Preston (1986)

Troubles, the   The violence in Northern Ireland which began in 1968. Ever since the division of Ireland in 1921 into a mainly Protestant North and a Catholic Irish Free State (which became the Republic of Ireland in 1949), the Protestants in the North had been determined to maintain their ascendancy. They did this by discriminating in houses and jobs in favour of Protestants and by gerrymandering local boundaries, which gave Protestants a majority in the local government of Londonderry, a predominantly Catholic area. In 1967 Catholic nationalist and republican leaders formed the Northern Irish Civil Rights Association (NICRA), inspired by the CIVIL RIGHTS MOVEMENT in the US, to campaign against discrimination. People's Democracy was formed in October 1968 by students at the Queen's University, Belfast, as a radical, socialist offshoot of NICRA. It became the principal initiator of violence in the North, seeking revolution and confrontation as it marched into Protestant areas and helped to destroy the moderate centre in Ulster politics. People's Democracy was at the centre of nearly every violent confrontation between civil rights demonstrators and the unionists, backed up by the RUC (Royal Ulster Constabulary). On 4 January 1969 there was a civil rights march (based on Martin Luther KING's SELMA FREEDOM MARCH in 1965) from Belfast to Londonderry, organized by People's Democracy. It

was attacked outside Derry by a Protestant mob wielding cudgels: the RUC gave the marchers no protection. Later that day the RUC and 'B' Specials (Protestant special constabulary) went on the rampage in Derry's Catholic Bogside. In retaliation the inhabitants sealed off the Bogside, making it a 'No-Go area' and called it Free Derry.

These events broke up the alliance which Terence O'Neill, the Northern Ireland Prime Minister, was promoting between the moderates in both communities. James Chichester-Clark replaced O'Neill as Prime Minister in April 1969 and tried to reduce tension by introducing reforms Catholics had long demanded to end discrimination in housing, jobs and local government, but the reforms came too late. There was serious rioting in the summer of 1969, which the RUC was unable to contain, so Chichester-Clark asked for British troops to be sent to Northern Ireland, initially to protect the Catholic population, for the first time since 1922. The IRA became involved in defending the Catholic ghettos and in December 1969 the Provisional IRA split from the Official IRA and thereafter played a leading part in the conflict between Catholic and Protestant. The situation deteriorated further in 1971 when the British government of Edward HEATH allowed the security forces to move into Catholic areas in the search for arms: 300,000 houses were searched between 1971–8. Many Catholics were now convinced that the IRA offered their best protection. Heath allowed internment without trial for suspected terrorists: it lasted until December 1975, during which time 2,108 people were interned. This was another disastrous policy, which thrust Catholics into the arms of the IRA. Hatred of the army, seen as a tool of the unionists, increased even more after Bloody Sunday (30 January 1972), when 13 Catholic demonstrators were shot and killed by British troops in Londonderry. 1972 was the most violent year of the Troubles.

With the situation in the North deteriorating rapidly, Heath decided in 1972 to prorogue the Protestant-dominated Northern Irish parliament at Stormont and impose direct rule from London. Willie Whitelaw, the Secretary of State for Northern Ireland, wanted to involve the Catholics in running the North by power-sharing. The Constitution Act of 1973 set up an elected unicameral assembly, from which an executive was to be appointed by the Secretary of State. Brian Faulkner, the leader of the Ulster Unionist Party, supported this but in doing so split his party, as many members had no intention of sharing any power with Catholics. The SDLP (Social Democratic and Labour Party), a mainly Catholic party formed in the North in 1970 to promote change by democratic and peaceful means, also approved. A significant development took place in December 1973 when the Irish government became directly involved in the North. At a meeting of the British and Irish governments at Sunningdale, Berkshire, the Irish government agreed that Northern Ireland would remain part of the United Kingdom until the majority decided otherwise. A Council of Ireland was to be set up with certain executive functions and anti-terrorist co-operation between North and South was to be improved. The Sunningdale Agreement was anathema to the unionists, who did not want any involvement of the Republic's government in the affairs of the North. In January 1974 the Northern Ireland executive, which included representatives of Faulkner's Unionists and of the SDLP, took office but it was brought down after only five months by the Ulster Workers' Council (UWC), founded by the three main Unionist parties and Protestant terrorist groups: the UDA (Ulster Defence Association, the largest Protestant paramilitary force) and the UVF (Ulster Volunteer Force). It called a strike in May which paralysed the province – the Unionist members of the executive resigned and the first attempts at power-sharing ended. During the strike the Troubles spread to the South: car bombs in Dublin and Monaghan killed 27 people. They moved to England too when in November 1974 19 were killed by an IRA bomb in a pub in Birmingham.

Successive British governments have since then tried to contain terrorism on both sides while seeking a political solution. The death of ten IRA prisoners in 1981 from a hunger-strike in the Maze prison, Belfast, meant reconciliation was even more unlikely. The government of the Republic again became involved in the North by the ANGLO-IRISH AGREEMENT of 1985, but this horrified the unionists. A stalemate ensued. The 'temporary' direct rule from England became permanent and it was clear that there could be no peace in Northern Ireland without the IRA taking part. John Hume of the SDLP worked tirelessly with Gerry Adams of Sinn Fein and negotiated with the British and Irish governments to bring about the Downing Street Declaration of December 1993, signed by John MAJOR and Albert Reynolds. This promised the inclusion of Sinn Fein in all-party talks about the future of Northern Ireland when IRA violence ended. The IRA declared a cease-fire in August 1994 and in February 1995 there was a Framework Agreement between the British and Irish governments, which was to be the basis of negotiations. It proposed a legislative Assembly for Northern Ireland elected by proportional representation, with Assembly Committees, formed in proportion to party strengths, to head the executive departments of the Northern Ireland Office. A weighted majority would be needed to pass contentious legislation, thus in effect giving the nationalists a veto. There would also be a North–South body, like the Council of Ireland proposed at Sunningdale in 1973, to have 'executive functions' over water, European Union programmes and culture. The two governments would make proposals to harmonize fisheries, industry, transport, energy, health, education and economic policy. All decisions would require the agreement of both sides. The proposals were based on power-sharing and on establishing an all-Ireland body, both of which the Unionists had always rejected. Little progress was made in meeting nationalist aspirations and on 9 February 1996 the peace ended in spectacular fashion by the explosion of a massive bomb, which caused extensive damage and killed two people, in London's dockland. The peace process, popular throughout the North, thus ended and there were few further initiatives from Major's government, which relied on Ulster Unionist votes in the Commons.

When Tony BLAIR became Prime Minister in 1997, after a LABOUR PARTY victory in the general election, he was determined to revive the peace process and offered to include Sinn Fein if the IRA renewed its cease-fire. Unlike Major he set a timetable for the talks to end in May 1998 and did not make the decommissioning of IRA weapons a precondition of Sinn Fein participation in the talks. In July 1997 the IRA restored its cease-fire, thus making all-party talks possible on the basis of the Framework Agreement of 1995. An agreement was reached in April 1998 by which, subject to approval in a referendum, the Irish government would give up its territorial claim to Northern Ireland, there would be elections in June for a Northern Ireland Assembly, with legislative and executive (but no tax-raising) powers, a North–South body would be set up and the British government agreed to release within two years all prisoners linked to organizations observing the cease-fire. The referendum in May in the North produced a 71 per cent yes vote (on an 81 per cent turn out). Catholics overwhelmingly supported the Agreement; Protestants were more evenly divided. There was a huge majority for the Agreement in the Irish Republic. In the June 1998 elections for the 108-seat Northern Ireland Assembly, the UUP was the largest party with 28 seats (the Democratic Unionist Party, opposed to the Agreement, won 20 seats), the SDLP winning 24 and Sinn Fein 18. Around 75% of voters supported parties in favour of the Agreement and so indicated that the vast majority of people in Northern Ireland wanted an end to the Troubles.

Northern Ireland Since 1968, P. Arthur and K. Jeffery (1988)
The Irish Troubles: A Generation of Violence, 1967–92, J. B. Bell (1993)
Northern Ireland: A Chronology of the Troubles 1968–93, P. Bew and G. Gillespie (1993)

Trudeau, Pierre Elliott (1919–) Prime Minister of Canada (1968–79, 1980–4). Born and raised in Quebec, a millionaire by inheritance, he took degrees in social sciences and law at Canadian, American and European universities. Fluent in both French and English, he was one of the progressives who wanted to overthrow the traditional conservative élite in Quebec. He was a founder of *Cité Libre* in 1950, a secular publication which sought to replace the influence of the Catholic Church by that of the state. From 1951–61 he practised law, specializing in labour and civil rights cases and supported Jean Lesage's Quiet Revolution (1960–6) in Quebec. He was assistant Professor of Law at Montreal University from 1961–5, when he was elected to the Canadian House of Commons as a Liberal. As Minister of Justice in the PEARSON government he liberalized the criminal code, legalized abortion, contraception and homosexual acts between consenting adults and made divorce easier. When Lester Pearson retired in 1968, Trudeau defeated several Anglophone ministers to become leader of the Liberal Party and convincingly won the election of that year.

Trudeau was opposed to QUEBEC NATIONALISM, as it would split the federal state and lead, he thought, to a semi-Fascist regime in Quebec but, a French Canadian himself, he realized that the aspirations of Francophones should be met. As English was the principal working language of the civil service he passed the Official Languages Act in 1969, which recognized both French and English as official languages. This was not enough for extreme nationalists, who resorted to kidnappings in the OCTOBER CRISIS of 1970, which the Prime Minister dealt with firmly. Having promised a Just Society, he expanded unemployment insurance in 1971 to cover everyone. He also tried to minimize the disparities between regions, and so defuse agitation, by providing basic income support for all who needed it, including the self-employed. Some communities, especially in the Maritimes and Quebec, were supported for months at a time by this, but the result was a huge rise in federal deficits by the late 1970s. Trudeau pursued an independent foreign policy and intensely annoyed the US by recognizing the People's Republic of China (and so withdrawing recognition of Taiwan) and by cutting Canada's contribution to NATO forces in Europe.

With a decline in the economy and rising unemployment, support for the Liberals declined. In the 1972 election they won 108 seats, the Conservatives 109, leaving the balance of power with the National Democratic Party (NDP), which won 30 seats. Trudeau remained as Prime Minister but had to adopt policies of which the NDP approved. Income tax was cut, old age pensions increased substantially and government oil-pricing policy sheltered Canadians from the OPEC PRICE RISE of 1973. Yet these measures did not satisfy the NDP, which withdrew its support. This forced an election in 1974, which the Liberals won with 140 seats, to the Conservatives 95 and the NDP 16. Apart from a six-month period in 1979–80, Trudeau was to remain in power for the next decade.

The main problem he faced was that of the constitution, which he wanted to amend to reassure those in Quebec that the federal government would look after their interests. He wanted to include a Charter of Rights, which would guarantee the use of two official languages in the legislatures and courts of Quebec, Manitoba and New Brunswick and in all federal institutions and services and would give the right in all provinces to education in either language. There was also the question of 'patriation' (that the British parliament should give up its right to amend Canada's constitution, a right inserted in the Statute of Westminster (1931) at the request of Ontario and Quebec). In 1981 the Canadian House of Commons approved the constitutional reforms, as did nine of the ten provinces (the exception being Quebec) and in 1982 the British parliament gave up its right to legislate for Canada. This still left unresolved the question of Quebec's acceptance of the changes. In 1984 Trudeau suddenly announced his retirement and returned to law practice in Montreal.

The New Democrats, 1961–86, D. Martin (1986)
The Outsider: The Life of Pierre Elliott Trudeau, M. Vastel (1990)
Trudeau and Our Times, vol. 1, S. Clarkson and C. McCall (1990)

Truman, Harry S. (1884–1972)   President of the United States (1945–53). Born in Missouri, he could not afford to go to college and so worked on the railroad, as a bank clerk and then as a farmer from 1906–17. He served in the artillery in France in 1918 as a captain and after the First World War unsuccessfully ran a haberdashery business. He had joined Kansas City's Pendergast organization before the war and with the backing of its political machine he was elected to the county court (an administrative agency) in 1922 and as presiding judge in 1926. For the next eight years he was Jackson County's chief administrator. He entered the Senate in 1935 as a Democrat, supported Roosevelt's New Deal and caught the attention of party leaders as head of a committee investigating the national defense programme in the Second World War. Relentless yet fair, he exposed enormous waste and fraud in defence contracts. He was chosen as running-mate for FDR, whom he hardly knew, in the 1944 election, as many DEMOCRATIC PARTY bosses were hostile to Vice-President Henry Wallace, whom they regarded as too liberal. When Roosevelt died in 1945 Vice-President Truman automatically became President.

Forthright, approachable and modest, he was the first modern American President without higher education. International relations dominated his presidency. The Second World War was still going on and though decisions concerning the defeat of Germany and the establishment of the UNITED NATIONS had already been taken, Truman ordered the atom bomb to be dropped on Japan, convinced that this would end the war quickly and save the lives of numerous American servicemen, who would have been killed in an invasion of Japan. As the COLD WAR began, he followed the containment policy proposed by George Kennan to prevent further Soviet expansion and provided aid to Greece and Turkey in 1947 in what became known as the TRUMAN DOCTRINE. There was a possibility of communist successes in Western Europe through the ballot box (the French and Italian communist parties were both strong) as European economies seemed about to collapse. To prevent this Truman offered aid in the MARSHALL PLAN, which marked the beginning of West European economic resurgence. When STALIN probed Western resolve in the BERLIN BLOCKADE Truman supplied Berlin with food and fuel by air until Stalin called off the blockade. He acted against the advice of the State Department (which wanted friendly relations with Arab states because of Middle Eastern oil) in immediately recognizing the state of Israel, when this was proclaimed in 1948.

So far Truman's foreign policy had been remarkably successful but in 1949 there were two major set-backs: communists won the CHINESE CIVIL WAR (1946–9), forcing JIANG JIESHI (Chiang Kai-shek) to flee to Taiwan, and the Soviet Union exploded an atom bomb earlier than expected. Truman's response was to approve US membership of NATO and to order the development of the HYDROGEN BOMB and a review of defence policy. The report NSC 68 (National Security Council Paper number 68) in 1950 was a key document of the Cold War and advocated that the US should unilaterally defend the non-communist world and that this would involve, for the first time, a massive build up of US

military strength in peace-time. Defence expenditure would have to rise from $13 billion a year to $50 billion (a figure reached in 1952). The KOREAN WAR (1950–3), during which US armed forces vastly increased, saw Truman move from containment to liberation, as he sought to conquer the communist North and so unite Korea. This was a disastrous move, as it brought in China which pushed back US and UN forces to the South and produced a stalemate.

At home Truman showed a less sure touch than in his foreign policy. The expected depression after the war did not take place but there was inflation and industrial unrest. Around 4.6 million workers were on strike in 1946, more than ever before in US history, as workers sought pay increases to cover the higher cost of living. Truman took over the railroads and mines, asked Congress for legislation to call-up the strikers and obtained an injunction against the United Mine Workers, which was heavily fined by a federal court. All this infuriated organized labour. In the election for Congress in 1946 the President's unpopularity resulted in the REPUBLICAN PARTY winning control of both houses for the first time since 1930. Republicans in Congress severely cut public expenditure, reduced taxes and ignored Truman's requests for social welfare legislation. They also passed the TAFT–HARTLEY ACT in 1947 to curb the power of the TRADE UNIONS. The President vetoed it to mend his fences with labour but it was passed again over his veto. Truman, whose family had supported the Confederate cause, was the first President to support civil rights legislation. He did this from conviction but also from self-interest, to win the black vote. The President issued executive orders to end racial discrimination in appointments to the civil service and to end segregation in the armed forces. He also used the Justice Department to support the NAACP's attempts to challenge the legality of segregated housing, education and transport. All this was very unpopular with conservative Southern Democrats. By the time of the 1948 election the Democratic Party was falling apart. The left broke away to support the candidate of the Progressive Party, Henry Wallace, whom Truman had dismissed as Secretary of Commerce for criticizing the administration's anti-Soviet foreign policy. Thirty Southern Democrats (known as the Dixiecrats) objected to the civil rights platform of the Convention and put forward their own candidate, Strom Thurmond, for the presidency. All the polls indicated a Republican victory but, while the Republican candidate and Governor of New York Thomas E. Dewey waged a bland campaign, Truman made 350 speeches in a 'whistle-stop' tour of 31,000 miles, attacking the 'do-nothing' Congress. He won and the Democrats regained control of Congress.

In his second term Truman tried to carry out his programme of social reform including medical insurance for all, which he called the Fair Deal. He met with only limited success, as Southern Democrats allied with Republicans to prevent civil rights measures becoming law, while powerful pressure groups ensured that other reforms were rejected. Much of the President's time was taken up in dealing with espionage and anti-communism. The Alger Hiss Case showed that communists had held high office in the State Department, while the admission of the British atomic scientist Dr Klaus Fuchs that he had provided the USSR with atomic secrets between 1943–7 led to the trial of his American accomplices. Some of them were convicted: two, Julius and Ethel ROSENBERG, were executed in 1953. These cases, and the Korean War, gave Senator Joe MCCARTHY the nationwide audience he needed for his splenetic anti-communist campaign, often waged in front of the television cameras, which adversely affected the lives of many innocent people and produced a hysterical reaction in which few dared to question the Senator from Wisconsin.

Truman chose not to stand for re-election as President in 1952. He had made that office stronger, using the veto more than all but two other Presidents, sending troops to Korea and

Europe on his own authority and dismissing the popular Douglas MACARTHUR for challenging the authority of the President. Yet he was not a popular President and suffered for a war in Korea he did not win and the popular fear that there were communists who held high government posts. He was rejected by his own party and seen by some (and later revisionist historians) as one whose policies had done much to bring about the Cold War. His reputation began to revive shortly after his death. Forty years later he had become a hero to most Americans and was regarded as a most successful President, an opinion he shared when he said, on leaving the White House, that he had prevented the repetition of the mistakes between 1919–41 that were responsible for the Second World War.

The Harry S. Truman Encyclopedia, R. S. Kirkendall (ed.) (1989)
Truman, D. McCullough (1994)
Man of the People, A. L. Hamby (1996)

Truman Doctrine   A policy put forward by President TRUMAN in 1947 to stop the spread of communism. On 21 February 1947 Britain imformed the US that it could no longer help the Greek government fighting communists in the GREEK CIVIL WAR (1944–9) and that it would withdraw its 40,000 troops there. Britain also said that it would end its aid to Turkey, pressurized by the Soviet Union to share its control of the Dardanelles. Dean ACHESON, US Under Secretary of State, persuaded Truman that the US should act promptly to fill the vacuum and apply the containment policy. On 12 March Truman asked Congress for $400 million to help Greece and Turkey and spelled out the Truman Doctrine: 'I believe that it must be the policy of the United States to support free peoples who are resisting attempted subjugation by armed minorities or by outside pressures'.

George Kennan thought the approach was too open-ended, as it committed the US to support any country in the world threatened by communism. There was the problem too of persuading a Republican Congress to ratify the policy. Acheson did this by propounding a version of the DOMINO THEORY. If Greece fell to the communists, so would Turkey, and the Soviet Union would take control of the Dardanelles, giving it access to the Middle East and its oil. Only the US could stop the Soviet Union. Congress gave Truman the money he wanted, so the US intervened in the internal affairs of other states outside North and South America for the first time in its history. Later Presidents used the doctrine to justify their own foreign policy initiatives: JOHNSON in Vietnam (1964–7), CARTER in the Persian Gulf (1980) and REAGAN in Central America (1983).

Tudjman, Franjo (1922–)   President of Croatia (1990–). Born in Zagorje, the same wine-growing region as TITO, he joined the Partisans in the Second World War and became a communist: Tito thought so highly of him that he put him in charge of personnel and promotions in the Yugoslav People's Army (JNA). In 1961 he became the youngest general in the country and seemed to have a brilliant future, but in 1963 he moved to the Institute of War History in Zagreb and there became a Croatian nationalist. In 1971 he and others proposed a new Croat constitution, which would make Croat the sole official language and would give Croatia greater self-government. As this would set off a chain reaction in the other provinces of Yugoslavia, Tito purged the leaders of the movement and imprisoned many, including Tudjman. He was imprisoned again in 1981 in the first major political trial since Tito's death.

In 1990 there were elections in all the provinces of Yugoslavia. Tudjman formed his own party, the Croatian Democratic Union (HDS), and campaigned on a nationalist platform, promising to put an end to the over-representation of Serbs (12 per cent of the population) in government. The HDS obtained 42 per cent of the vote and two-thirds of the seats in the Croatian parliament. Tudjman became President of Croatia. Instead of conciliating the Serbs he antagonized them by making Croat the only languge of administration, by dismissing Serbs employed by the state and by adopting for the Croatian flag the red and white checkerboard shield used by the Ustasha, the puppet government set up by the Nazis in the Second World War, which had massacred thousands of Serbs. Tudjman was cautious in making Croatia independent, as he knew that his forces were no match for the well-armed JNA, but he could not afford to be left behind by Slovenia, so both provinces declared their independence in June 1991. The Krajina Serbs immediately declared their own independence within Croatia and so began a war in which Croatia lost a third of its territory by the time this phase of the conflict ended in January 1992. In 1993 he fought his former allies, the Muslims, in Bosnia and indulged in the ETHNIC CLEANSING from which the Croats had suffered in Krajina. This was one of the most vicious episodes in the YUGO-SLAV CIVIL WAR. He finally made his peace with the Muslims in March 1994 and agreed with them to form a confederation. Tudjman meanwhile was quietly building up his armed forces, trained by ex-US generals and equipped with weapons bought on the black market. In May 1995 he surprised everyone by attacking and overrunning Serb-held Western Slavonia and in August routed the Serbs and drove them out of Knin and Krajina. He was now a Croat hero, though Eastern Slavonia (with its oil) still remained in Serb hands. He was a signatory to the Dayton Accords, negotiated under US auspices, which brought the war to an end in 1995, giving to the Bosnian Croats 21 per cent of Bosnia.

Tudjman continued with his aggressive nationalist and authoritarian policies after the war was over. His Croat Democratic Union lost the local elections in Zagreb in

October 1995 but he refused to accept an opposition mayor, so the administration was paralysed. He blocked the return of Serb refugees to Krajina, provided for in the Dayton Accords, obstructed the investigation of war crimes committed by Croats and supported Croats in Mostar who refused to accept a newly elected council in June 1996, as it had a Muslim majority.

Croatia: The Rebirth of a Nation, M. Tanner (1997)

Tupamaros Uruguayan guerrilla movement. Inspired by the guerrilla victory of Fidel CASTRO in Cuba, it was formed in 1963 and derived its name from Tupac Amaru, an Indian Chieftain who had led a massive rising of Andean communities against the Spaniards in the eighteenth century. Its leader, Raúl Sendic, had worked as a lawyer among the impoverished cane cutters of the north but the Tupamaros soon became an urban guerrilla movement (half the population of Uruguay lived in the capital city of Montevideo). At first it used the proceeds from robberies to distribute food to the poor, but as the economic crisis got worse after 1968 it extended its activities to kidnapping. Right-wing Uruguayan politicians were captured and held in 'people's prisons'. In 1971 the army was given the task of wiping out the Tupamaros. It tortured prisoners to gain intelligence and in 1972 a leader of the movement defected and gave the security forces the information they needed to eliminate the Tupamaros. Sendic and other leaders were captured later that year. The movement was crushed in 1973, the year in which the military took over. When civilian rule returned in 1985 all imprisoned Tupamaros were released. They then announced that they were taking up non-violent politics and formed a political party.

Latin American Revolutionaries: Goals and Methods, M. Radu and V. Tismaneanu (1990)

Twentieth Congress of the CPSU (1956)

The occasion on which KHRUSHCHEV attacked STALIN. Khrushchev had been involved in Stalin's reign of terror but apparently was not aware of the full extent of this until 1954–5, when he was deeply shocked. The Presidium (Politburo) agreed that the report of an investigating commission could be given only in a closed session of the CPSU, which should not be made public. Khrushchev saw that he could discredit his rivals, more deeply involved in the terror than he had been. He quoted from Lenin's 'Last Testament', in which Lenin had criticized Stalin and recommended that he should be removed from his post as General Secretary of the CPSU. He went on to imply that the murder of Kirov in 1934 was on Stalin's orders and that 'cruel and inhuman tortures' had been used to obtain confessions during the purges. Of 139 members of the Central Committee 98 had been arrested and shot in 1937–8. Khrushchev condemned Stalin for his refusal to heed early warnings of an impending German attack in 1941 and blamed him for the USSR's defeats in that campaign. Khrushchev rejected the idea that there was bound to be war between capitalist and communist countries ('War is not fatalistically inevitable') and said that there were different ways of moving from capitalism to communism, including free elections. The text of the speech was not published in Russia until 1988 but an abridged version was issued in Belgrade in 1956 and a full version in Washington. It had a marked effect in Eastern Europe, where expectations of change were raised, and contributed to events in Poland, when Khrushchev had unwillingly to accept GOMULKA as head of the Polish Communist Party, and to the HUNGARIAN RISING, which was put down by Soviet troops.

U

U-2 incident (May 1960)　　The shooting down of an American U-2 reconnaissance plane near Sverdlovsk in Russia. The US had carried out 20 such flights since 1956, which could not be shot down as their altitude was beyond the range of Soviet fighters and of surface to air missiles (SAMS). The U-2 could fly up to 80,000 feet (15 miles) and had cameras which could photograph newspaper headlines ten miles below. Each flight had been authorized by the President and had provided valuable evidence that the USSR did not have a lead in missiles. The U-2 plane was shot down on 1 May by a SAM missile because it had lost height owing to engine trouble. When the Soviet Union announced its success on 5 May the State Department at first said that it was not a spy plane and had lost its way. KHRUSHCHEV then triumphantly produced the pilot Gary Powers and his photographs of military installations. President EISENHOWER on 11 May admitted that he had authorized the flight because he needed to prevent another Pearl Harbor, when Japan attacked the US in 1941 without warning. When the Paris summit meeting opened on 16 May Khrushchev demanded an apology before discussions could begin and, as Eisenhower refused, he stormed out of the meeting and blamed the US for its failure. U-2 flights over the USSR were discontinued and were soon unnecessary, as from 1961 satellites orbiting the earth took over their functions. Gary Powers was sentenced to ten years in jail but was exchanged for a Soviet spy in 1962.

Mayday, M. Beschloss (1986)

UDI (Unilateral Declaration of Independence)　　The attempt of the Rhodesian Front (RF) to set up a white supremacist government in an independent Rhodesia (Zimbabwe). When the CENTRAL AFRICAN FEDERATION broke up in 1963, Zambia and Malawi quickly gained independence. The 250,000 white settlers in Southern Rhodesia, who had been self-governing since 1923, also demanded independence but the British government would not grant this until there was majority rule for the four million Africans. This was not acceptable to the white settlers, whose government banned the black National Democratic Party, though this was re-formed as the Zimbabwe African People's Union (ZAPU). Joshua Nkomo's leadership produced a split in the party when the Revd Ndabaningi Sithole and others withdrew from ZAPU to form the Zimbabwe African National Union (ZANU). Both ZAPU and ZANU were banned and in 1964 its leaders were imprisoned, where they were to remain for ten years. The RF, which was run largely by a handful of white farmers, decided that the only way to maintain white supremacy was to declare independence. In Britain the general election of 1965 produced a LABOUR PARTY victory but its majority was so small that strong action against the settlers was politically difficult. Harold WILSON, the British Prime Minister, assured them that he would not use force, so on 11 November 1965 Ian Smith, the Rhodesian Prime Minister, rejected British authority and declared UDI. Not one country recognized the new regime.

The British government reluctantly asked the UNITED NATIONS to apply economic sanctions to Rhodesia but South Africa and the Portuguese government in Mozambique helped Rhodesia to evade them and other governments did not always enforce them. They had, therefore, little effect and even stimulated industry in Rhodesia, as new industries arose to provide goods which could no longer be imported. As the British would not use force, ZANU and ZAPU decided to begin guerrilla warfare. The first clash occurred in 1966 but failed miserably.

In 1972 ZANU, whose members received training and arms from Algeria, Ghana, China and Czechoslovakia, began a new phase in the guerrilla war. ZAPU, with its base in Zambia, also built up its military wing, trained and equipped by the Soviet Union, but did not take much part in the war until the late 1970s. The Portuguese collapse in Mozambique in 1974 changed the whole situation, as guerrillas could now infiltrate the whole long Rhodesian frontier with Mozambique. Sithole, Nkomo, MUGABE and other black leaders were released. Mugabe replaced Sithole as leader of ZANU in 1976 and the two liberation movements joined together in a loose alliance, the Patriotic Front (PF), as guerrilla activity spread throughout the country. About 10 per cent of the population was resettled in 'protected' villages, where they could not help the rebels, while Rhodesian forces raided guerrilla bases in Zambia and Mozambique. Many white farmers abandoned their land, as the government gave up trying to control the rural areas and Smith had to rely increasingly on African soldiers for his army. The cost of the war was too great for Rhodesia. Smith at last realized that a black government was inevitable but hoped to keep real power in white hands by negotiating with moderate African leaders, as VORSTER, the South African Prime Minister, had advised him to do. In 1978 he agreed with Bishop Muzorewa and Sithole on a new constitution, which would provide black majority rule and a black Prime Minister, but with whites retaining control of the army, police and civil service. In the elections of April 1979

under this 'internal settlement' Muzorewa won a large majority, though Africans were unable to vote for the Patriotic Front. Margaret THATCHER, the British Prime Minister, wanted to recognize the new regime but, under pressure from African heads of state at a COMMONWEALTH Conference in Lusaka, agreed to call all parties to a constitutional conference at Lancaster House in London. Smith, confident that Muzorewa would win an open election, agreed to take part. At the conference UDI was abandoned, and it was agreed that there should be a cease-fire, that the guerrillas (122,000) should be disarmed and demobilized and that there should be elections to form a government leading to independence. Whites were guaranteed for seven years 20 out of the 100 seats in the legislature. The two sections of the PF fought the elections separately. ZANU, which had played the major part in the guerrilla war and had spread its influence widely, received 63 per cent of the vote and 57 out of 80 African seats; ZAPU had 24 per cent of the vote and 20 seats. Muzorewa was humiliated, winning only three seats, while Smith won all 20 seats reserved for whites. Robert Mugabe became President of an independent Zimbabwe (as Rhodesia was now called) on 18 April 1980.

The Struggle for Zimbabwe, D. Martin and P. Johnson (1981)
Challenge to Imperialism: The Frontline States in the Liberation of Zimbabwe, C. Thompson (1985)

Ulbricht, Walter (1893–1973) First Secretary of the communist Social Unity Party (SED) in the German Democratic Republic (GDR) (1950–71). The son of a Saxon tailor, he completed his training as a cabinet-maker before joining the German Social Democratic Party in 1912. He served in the army in the First World War and became a member of the Communist Party soon after it was formed in 1918. Ulbricht became a full-time party employee and sat in the Reichstag as a communist deputy from

1928–33. When Hitler came to power he went to the Soviet Union, returning to Germany in 1945 to re-establish the communist party there. A poor orator and colourless personality, he was an excellent organizer. When the SED was formed Ulbricht was a leading figure in it long before the GDR was formed in 1949. Then as General Secretary (changed to First Secretary in 1954) he established communist control of East Germany through the NOMENKLATURA (the privileged élite he placed in the top party and government jobs) and the Stasi, the secret police which eventually kept files on over six million people and had a network of nearly two million informers. Ulbricht adopted the Soviet system of democratic centralism: all decisions were made by the Politburo, which the parliament then confirmed. No dissent was allowed. The public was indoctrinated in Marxism through state control of the media and education. In 1960 Ulbricht became Chairman of the Council of State and head of the armed forces, thus combining leadership of the government and of the party.

Economic policy was based on that of the Soviet Union. Industry was nationalized, agriculture collectivized and production targets were set by Five Year Plans. The government fixed prices and wages. There was a concentration on heavy industry at the expense of consumer goods and considerable dislocation as large reparations were paid to the USSR and as trade, which had been mainly with Western Europe, moved to the East: by 1954 75 per cent of the GDR's trade was with the communist bloc. The economic revival was impressive, as by 1953 production was 108 per cent of the 1936 level, in spite of the GDR receiving no MARSHALL PLAN aid. After the death of STALIN in 1953 the new Soviet leaders wanted less repressive policies and were considering replacing Ulbricht. The east German rising of 1953, when half a million people went on strike and 51 were killed, paradoxically saved Ulbricht, as his removal would have been regarded as a sign of weakness. The Soviet Union came to his assistance

militarily but also by ending reparations, writing off the GDR's debt and by giving large-scale credits. The GDR, which had been part of the Soviet economic system through membership of COMECON since 1950, joined the WARSAW PACT in 1955. The haemorrhage of skilled workers to the West was ended in 1961, when Ulbricht obtained KHRUSHCHEV's approval to build the BERLIN WALL.

A New Economic System was introduced in 1963, which gave factories greater independence and judged them according to profitability, not the quantity of goods produced. In the 1960s the GDR became the strongest state in the Eastern bloc, with a standard of living higher than in the Soviet Union. By 1969 14 per cent of households had a refrigerator and washing machine and two-thirds had a television set. Ulbricht sent troops to join in the invasion of Czechoslovakia to end the PRAGUE SPRING in 1968 and made the GDR into a model 'people's democracy', unswervingly loyal to the Soviet Union. Yet within three years Ulbricht had lost the support of his Soviet sponsors, as he had made clear his dislike of the improved relations between the USSR and West Germany. He was allowed a dignified retirement. In 1971 he requested to be relieved of his position as head of the SED owing to ill-health. He died in obscurity two years later.

The GDR: The History, Politics, Economy and Society of East Germany, E. Schneider (1978)
The GDR: Moscow's German Ally, D. Childs (1988)
Germany from Partition to Reunification, H. A. Turner (1992)

United Nations (UN)   The organization which replaced the League of Nations at the end of the Second World War. The structure of the UN was worked out by the Big Four (US, USSR, Britain and China) in 1944 and approved at Yalta (February 1945) after the Russians had inserted a veto for the permanent members of the Security Council. The

UN's aim was 'to save succeeding generations from the scourge of war [and] reaffirm faith in fundamental human rights'. The Charter, however, prohibits intervention 'in matters which are essentially within the domestic jurisdiction of any state', thus making it impossible to enforce human rights. To safeguard peace the UN can impose economic sanctions or intervene militarily with forces provided by the member states. The Charter was adopted by 51 nations at San Francisco in June 1945: by 1997 there were 185 members. No state has been expelled from or has left the organization.

The main bodies in the UN are the General Assembly, the Security Council, the Secretariat and the International Court of Justice. The General Assembly, which meets for the last quarter of every year, approves the budget, calls international conferences, adopts resolutions and oversees the work of many subsidiary organizations. The Security Council, responsible for maintaining international peace and security, had originally 11 members: five permanent members, who were victors in the war (the US, USSR, Britain, France and China, though China was represented until 1971 by the Nationalist government on Taiwan) and six others elected for two years by the General Assembly. In 1965 the number was increased to 15, ten of them elected: its decisions require a vote in favour by nine members. Each of the permanent members had a veto. The Council meets frequently and can take 'action with respect to threats to the peace . . . and acts of aggression': its decisions are binding on all UN members. In the 1990s there have been moves to increase the number of permanent members and particularly to include two of the economic superpowers, Japan and Germany, a move supported by President CLINTON in 1992. The International Court of Justice in the Hague consists of 15 judges elected by the Assembly and the Council for nine years and considers cases brought to it by states. The Secretariat, with 16,000 officials in New York and 50,000 elsewhere, is the UN's civil service, headed by the Secretary-General. There have been seven Secretaries-General in the twentieth century: Trygve Lie (Norway, 1946–53), Dag HAMMARSKJÖLD (Sweden, 1943–61), U Thant (Burma, 1961–71), Kurt Waldheim (Austria, 1971–81), Javier Perez de Cuellar (Peru, 1982–91), Bhoutros Bhoutros-Gali (Egypt, 1992–6) and Kofi Annan (Ghana, 1996–). The UN has numerous specialized agencies such as the WORLD BANK, IMF (International Monetary Fund), the WORLD HEALTH ORGANIZATION, the Food and Agriculture Organization and UNESCO. UNRWA (Relief and Works Agency) provides support for PALESTINIAN REFUGEES who fled during the ARAB–ISRAELI WARS. GATT (General Agreement on Tariffs and Trade) is closely linked to the UN. These agencies have benefited millions in the THIRD WORLD. For the first 45 years the COLD WAR prevented the UN taking action on many major issues, as the great powers used their veto. By the end of 1989 the Soviet Union had vetoed 114 resolutions (103 of them before 1966), as it regarded the UN as an American-dominated assembly. With DECOLONIZATION Third World countries, many of whom took their lead from the communist bloc, formed a majority in the Assembly, so all US vetoes (67 to 1989) took place after 1965. Britain has vetoed 30 resolutions, France 18 and China 3. Decisive UN action was possible in the KOREAN WAR as the Soviet Union withdrew from the Security Council at the time in protest at Taiwan representing China and so could not use its veto. To get round the use of the veto the General Assembly passed the Uniting for Peace Resolution in 1950, which enables debates to be transferred from the Council to the Assembly. It was used in 1956 during the SUEZ CRISIS, when the Assembly called for an immediate cease-fire and the withdrawal of forces from the Canal. Britain and France, largely because of US pressure, agreed to abide by the resolution. However, when the Assembly called for the withdrawal of Soviet troops during the HUNGARIAN

RISING it was ignored. The Uniting for Peace Resolution was also used to transfer debate on the OCCUPIED TERRITORIES to the Assembly after the SIX DAY WAR (1967) and to pass pro-Palestinian resolutions.

Economic sanctions have rarely been used by the UN and have had little effect. They were first used in 1966 against Rhodesia after Ian Smith's UDI (Unilateral Declaration of Independence) but South Africa ensured they were ineffective: the final settlement of the dispute and the independence of Zimbabwe owed nothing to the UN. An arms embargo was imposed on South Africa in 1977 with minimal results and there were sanctions too on Iraq after its invasion of Kuwait, but the GULF WAR began before they could bite.

The UN necessarily played a role in the Middle East when Britain handed over its Palestinian mandate. It then incredibly approved of a partition, which resulted in the BIRTH OF ISRAEL, against the wishes of two-thirds of the population. When Israel in the Arab–Israeli wars enlarged the territory awarded to it the UN issued Resolution 242 in 1967, which acted as a benchmark for all subsequent conflicts in the area. The UN also introduced peace-keeping forces, multinational forces under UN command, originally in 1956 to keep Egyptian and Israeli forces apart after the Suez crisis. These were successful only as long as both sides wanted them: shortly after Egypt asked for them to be removed in 1967 the Six Day War began. The Gulf War (1991) was the second occasion the UN was involved in a major war but like the first (the Korean War), it was really an American war in which the US provided most of the armed forces and all the commanders. After the defeat of Saddam HUSSEIN the UN imposed punitive terms on Iraq under Resolution 687: nuclear and chemical disarmament with verification on a long-term basis, reparations financed by income from controlled oil exports and economic sanctions until Iraq complied with the resolution.

Most UN activity took place in the ex-colonial world, though where the superpowers were directly involved, as in the VIETNAM WAR, the UN kept out. In Africa it had a very mixed record. It was deeply involved in the CONGO CRISIS (1960–5), prevented the secession of Katanga and therefore the break-up of the Congo (Zaire), but the UN was put under great stress as KHRUSHCHEV accused Hammarskjöld of taking a pro-Western line. The UN had little success in bringing the ANGOLAN and MOZAMBICAN CIVIL WARS to an end, as the superpowers supported different parties, until the Cold War ended. Its Rome peace accord in 1992 ended the war in Mozambique which had been going on for 16 years. The peace held and in 1994 the first democratic elections were held there. In Angola the peace agreement soon broke down. The most ignominious failures of the UN occurred in the UN INTERVENTION IN SOMALIA and in Rwanda, where the UN became a passive accomplice to genocide. A peace-keeping force of 2,500 was sent in November 1993 and was warned by moderate Hutu officers that extremists planned to eliminate the Tutsis. When the RWANDAN MASSACRES began the UN did nothing, when prompt action could have saved the lives of a million people. A similar abject fiasco took place in Bosnia during the YUGOSLAV CIVIL WAR, when UN forces allowed the Serbs to massacre the male population in the 'safe haven' of ŠREBRENICA. UN troops were humiliated as some were taken hostage. The UN's self-denying ordinance was overturned after the Gulf War when the Security Council took action in Iraq, against the wishes of the government, to protect the Kurds in the north by creating a 'no-fly' zone.

United Nations, Divided World: The UN's Role in International Relations, A. Roberts and B. Kingsbury (eds) (1988)

From Cold War to Hot Peace: UN Interventions 1947–94, A. Parsons (1995)

The United Nations and Changing World Politics, T. Weiss, D. P. Forsythe and R. A. Coate (1996)

US–Canada Free Trade Agreement (FTA) (1989)   In the 1950s and 1960s the US was the focal point of Canada's foreign trade. By 1960 70 per cent of Canada's imports and 75 per cent of its foreign investment came from the US: 60 per cent of Canada's exports went to the US (75 per cent by 1987). One half of Canada's manufacturing industry was American-owned and an increasing proportion of Canada's natural resources. In the 1980s there was considerable pressure from the US to get rid of all tariff barriers between the two countries but much of the impetus of the FTA came from Canada, which relied on American markets. All tariff barriers were to be removed and non-tariff barriers (concerning services and investment) reduced. By 1990 a third of all US investment abroad was in Canada: the US traded more with the province of Ontario than with Japan, while Canada invested more in the US than the Japanese. FTA was the first step towards a regional economic bloc, which was extended to Mexico in the NORTH AMERICAN FREE TRADE AGREEMENT (NAFTA) in 1993.

Trading with Canada: The Canada–US Free Trade Agreement, G. R. Winham (1988)
Making Free Trade Work: The Canada–US Agreement, P. Morici (ed.) (1990)

V

---

velvet revolution (1989) A phrase used by Václav HAVEL to describe the peaceful demise of communist rule in Czechoslovakia. This was precipitated by the REVOLUTIONS OF 1989–91, which saw the end of communist regimes in Poland and Hungary and the collapse of the BERLIN WALL.

On 20 November 200,000 filled Wenceslas Square in Prague, chanting 'Now is the time'. Huge crowds gathered there on each of the following nights, and there were similar massive demonstrations in provincial cities such as Brno and Bratislava demanding an end to one-party rule. On 24 November the Central Committee of the CP narrowly decided not to use the army against the demonstrators. The divided communist leadership, influenced by the round-table negotiations in Poland between the CP and SOLIDARITY, began negotiating with the opposition on 26 November and on the 29th deleted from the constitution the reference to the party's leading role. A government of National Unity was formed on 10 December, with most of its members from the pro-democracy Civic Forum and other non-communist parties. HUSÁK resigned as President. On 28 December Alexander Dubček, hero of the PRAGUE SPRING in 1968, became Chairman of the Federal Assembly, which elected Havel as President on the 29th. 'The end of communism took us all by surprise', he said. He moved rapidly to dismantle the communist system. Around 1,600 political prisoners were freed, the secret police disbanded, freedom of the press and of association guaranteed. Václav KLAUS, the Finance Minister, rejected central planning and moved towards the free market and capitalism. In the June 1990 elections Civic Forum and PAV (Public Against Violence, a Slovak organization) were victorious. The communists, with 13 per cent of the vote, were the only major party not included in the new government.

Verwoerd, Hendrik Frensch (1901–66)

Prime Minister of South Africa (1958–66). An immigrant from the Netherlands when he was two years old, he was educated in South Africa and Germany before becoming professor of psychology and later of sociology at Stellenbosch University. In 1936 he protested against the admission of German Jewish refugees into South Africa. He left university life in 1937 to be editor of *Die Transvaler*, a new National Party newspaper. A republican and member of the *Afrikaner Broederbond*, a secret society to promote Afrikaner culture and political power, he built up support for the National Party in the Transvaal and was openly pro-German during the Second World War. He failed to be elected for parliament in 1948 but was appointed to the Senate and in 1950 became Minister of Native Affairs in MALAN's government. In this office he was responsible for much APARTHEID legislation, such as the Bantu Education Act (1953). Verwoerd believed that giving Africans higher education 'misled them by showing them the green pastures of European society in which they are not allowed to graze', so the Act provided for Bantu education to be in the vernacular, with an emphasis on manual training.

When he became Prime Minister in 1958 he was the dominant personality, with the sharpest intellect, in parliament. He softened the language of *apartheid* to make it more acceptable without changing the fundamental concept. '*Apartheid*' became 'separate development', 'Natives' were 'Bantu', but Verwoerd maintained that racial separation should be rigidly maintained: any change would endanger the whole system, as one concession would lead to another and eventually to black majority rule. As the main architect of *apartheid* he had rejected the idea of independence for the African reserves in 1951 but by 1959 he was talking of independent homelands (BANTUSTANS) as the goal of separate development. The Promotion of Bantu Self-Government Act (1959) set up eight *Bantustans* (later increased to ten), with limited powers of self-government but there was no possibility of their being viable economically and they simply became dumping grounds for the Africans white South Africa did not need as cheap labour. The SHARPEVILLE massacre in 1960, when 69 unarmed demonstrators against the pass laws were shot and killed by police, was universally condemned but did not deflect Verwoerd from his rigid adherence to *apartheid*. ANC and PAC leaders were arrested, their organizations banned and black opposition almost wiped out.

The 1960s was a decade of great prosperity for white South Africans, who gave much of the credit to Verwoerd. In 1960 he began cutting South Africa's ties with Britain, when a decimalized currency of rands and cents replaced sterling. He held a referendum (which he narrowly won) in the same year as to whether South Africa should be a republic and withdrew from the COMMONWEALTH in 1961 owing to its condemnation of *apartheid*. For Afrikaners, who felt that South Africa was free for the first time, Verwoerd was a hero, though he wanted white unity, which he thought had been prevented by the loyalty of English-speakers to the British crown. Verwoerd had survived an assassination attempt in 1960, when a mentally unstable white farmer shot him, but was not so fortunate in 1966, when he was stabbed to death by a parliamentary messenger, later declared insane.

Verwoerd, A. Hepple (1967)
Malan to De Klerk, R. Schrire (ed.) (1994)
Forty Lost Years: The Apartheid State and the Politics of the National Party, 1948–1994, D. O'Meara (1996)

Viet Cong (Vietnamese communists)
The name given by Ngo Dinh DIEM to those who formed the National Liberation Front in 1960 to oppose his dictatorial government in South Vietnam. They fought during the VIETNAM WAR on the same side as the VIET MINH.

Viet Cong, D. Pike (1966)

Viet Minh
A shortened form of *Vietnam Doc Lap Dong Minh Hoi* (League for the Independence of Vietnam), formed in southern China in 1941 by HO CHI MINH and Vo Nguyen GIAP. Several disparate groups (socialists, communists, nationalists, Catholics) took part in the coalition but the Communist Party had control. It aimed to free Vietnam from Japanese control and then gain independence from France. It fought successfully in the INDOCHINA WAR OF INDEPENDENCE (1946–54), after which it controlled North Vietnam. During the VIETNAM WAR (1960–75) it linked up with the VIET CONG and reunited the country in 1975.

The Viet-Minh Regime, B. Fall (1954)

Vietnam anti-war movement
The most extensive protest movement in American history. It was at first confined to students and began soon after President JOHNSON ordered the bombing of North Vietnam in March 1965. It was strong in only a few élite campuses such as Berkeley until the late 1960s: only 2–3 per cent of college students called themselves activists between 1965–8

and 20 per cent took part in anti-war demonstrations. These increased when the President committed large numbers of American troops to Vietnam. As costs and casualties rose the protests became more confrontational in 1968, with students burning their draft cards. From 1969–71 there were massive demonstrations, with over 600,000 marching on Washington in November 1969. The movement was no longer confined to students, with blacks and war veterans taking part, as many did not think that the war could be won after the TET OFFENSIVE of 1968. The US ATTACK ON CAMBODIA in 1970 increased the unrest. On 4 May at Kent State University four students were shot and killed by the Ohio National Guard. This spread the protests to other universities, many of which had not been previously involved. Students went on strike in 350 campuses and two million (a quarter of the total) took part in demonstrations. The National Guard was called out in 16 states and on 21 campuses: 75 colleges and universities had to close for the rest of the academic year. The anti-war movement declined in 1971 when President NIXON suspended the draft and began to withdraw US troops.

Millions of Americans, many of them working class, had been outraged by the demonstrations, as they regarded students as a pampered and privileged élite, many of whom avoided military service (most students were automatically deferred until mid-1968). Polls showed that 58 per cent of Americans blamed the students for the Kent University deaths, while only 39 per cent opposed the invasion of Cambodia.

Who Spoke Up? American Protest Against the War in Vietnam, 1963–75, N. Zaroulis and G. Sullivan (1984)

Campus Wars: The Peace Movement at American State Universities in the Vietnam Era, K. Heineman (1993)

Vietnam War (1960–75)   A war between North and South Vietnam in which the US became heavily involved, fighting its longest war and suffering its first defeat. At the end of the INDOCHINA WAR OF INDEPENDENCE (1946–54) the GENEVA ACCORDS stipulated that elections should be held in 1956 throughout the country and that Vietnam would then be reunited. The unpopular regime of Ngo Dinh DIEM in the South knew that the communists were likely to win free elections there and so refused to hold them. He was supported by President EISENHOWER, worried about the spread of communism after the communist victory in the CHINESE CIVIL WAR (1946–9) and after communist aggression in the KOREAN WAR (1950–3). He was determined to maintain the containment policy and put forward the DOMINO THEORY, that if Vietnam fell to the communists, so would the rest of Southeast Asia. In 1960 South Vietnamese communists (VIET CONG) formed, with other groups opposed to Diem, the National Liberation Front, to reunite Vietnam by stirring up unrest in the South and by waging guerrilla warfare against the Diem regime. HO CHI MINH, communist leader of North Vietnam, supported this. DE GAULLE had told KENNEDY (elected President of the US in 1960) not to get involved in Indochina: 'You will sink step by step into a bottomless military and political quagmire, however much you spend in men and money'. Yet Kennedy increased the number of American advisers to Diem from 600 under Eisenhower to 16,000 by 1963, though he rejected the Joint Chiefs of Staff request to send regular troops there.

JOHNSON, who succeeded as President when Kennedy was assassinated in 1963, did not want to escalate the war, as he was more concerned with domestic reform and his GREAT SOCIETY, but he could not afford to be seen as soft on communism. TRUMAN had been accused of 'losing' China by not giving enough support to JIANG JIESHI (Chiang Kai-shek): LBJ was determined not to 'lose' Vietnam. The US connived in a coup in which the repressive Diem was overthrown and murdered in November 1963. The following year, following an attack by North Vietnamese gunboats on an American destroyer in the Gulf of Tonkin, the President was given *carte blanche* to wage the war as he saw fit by the TONKIN GULF RESOLUTION in Congress. Although the VIET MINH had taken little part in the insurrection in the South, LBJ ordered full-scale bombing of the North in February 1965, after the Viet Cong attacked an American airbase at Pleiku. He hoped that American combat troops would not be needed, but the bombing did not affect morale in the North and led to regular Viet Minh troops crossing into the South. On 1 April 1964 the President authorized the use of American troops in offensive operations: there were 25,000 US troops in Vietnam in November 1964, a number which rose inexorably to 543,000 by April 1969. (Australia and New Zealand also sent some troops, as did Thailand, the Philippines and South Korea.) Another effect of bombing the North was that the Soviet Union, which had been largely uninvolved in the war, now sent huge amounts of modern equipment, including SAMs (surface to air missiles), to the North. The VIETNAM ANTI-WAR MOVEMENT began with demonstrations in Washington, where students regarded the US as an oppressor rather than a liberator. Dissatisfaction grew as it appeared that the US could neither win nor end the war. Official optimism that the war was going well was shattered by the TET OFFENSIVE in January 1968, when over 100 targets in the South were attacked. Tet was a military disaster for the Viet Cong, but it was a psychological success. It convinced most Americans that the war could not be won and persuaded LBJ not to seek re-election.

NIXON was elected President but was no more willing than Johnson to be 'the first American President to lose a war'. He wanted to get out of the war but on what he saw as honourable terms. He therefore pursued a policy of Vietnamization: American troops were gradually withdrawn but aid to the South Vietnamese army was increased so that it could survive on its own and bombing

of the North was intensified. The main infiltration route from the North (the Ho Chi Minh Trail) went through Laos and Cambodia, so Nixon decided on a US ATTACK ON CAMBODIA in May 1970. This had a devastating effect on Cambodia but failed to destroy communist supply routes. In February 1971 South Vietnamese forces, with US air support, invaded Laos. This too was unsuccessful and had equally disastrous consequences. The North showed it was capable of mounting a major campaign when in March 1972 it launched a three-pronged attack against Hue in the north of South Vietnam, Kontum in the centre and Saigon in the south. This was repulsed, with enormous losses, by US Air Force backing for the South Vietnamese army. KISSINGER resumed talks with the North, which was under pressure to make a settlement from both the Soviet Union and China, which wanted better relations with the US. An agreement was finally reached in the Paris Peace Accords in January 1973, when the US agreed to withdraw its troops from the South and stop bombing the North. The few remaining American troops were withdrawn but the war continued. As US aid was reduced, morale in the South declined and when the North attacked in force in 1975 the South's army disintegrated. Saigon fell on 30 April, with hundreds of thousands of Vietnamese who were on the losing side left to face 're-education' in concentration camps. Phnom Penh, the Cambodian capital, had already fallen to the Khmer Rouge on 17 April, while the coalition in Laos gave way to a communist government. Some 58,000 US servicemen had been killed and 300,000 wounded of the three million who fought in Vietnam. South Vietnam military casualties were 225,000 killed, 570,000 wounded; those in the North an estimated 660,000 killed. Civilian casualties were calculated at 300,000 killed in the South, 65,000 in the North.

The war did not have the dire effects on the strategic balance of power in the COLD WAR which had been predicted. Cambodia and

Laos now had communist governments as well as Vietnam but the other dominoes did not fall. The rest of the countries of Southeast Asia remained non-communist, friendly to the US and created ASEAN. Vietnam was devastated, as the US dropped on it three times the tonnage of bombs deposited by American bombers in the Second World War. Defoliants, designed to remove cover for the Viet Cong, destroyed the productivity of the soil as well as forests. There were marked effects in the US too, as $150 billion were spent on war expenses. As money was printed to pay for the war there was a sharp increase in inflation which undermined the dollar and destabilized the international monetary system. US goods became too expensive abroad, so in 1971 the US registered its first trade deficit of the century. In 1971 Nixon abandoned a fixed exchange rate for the dollar and with it the Bretton Woods agreement of 1944 which had brought so much prosperity. Stagflation, a stagnant economy with inflation, affected the US in the 1970s, enabling Germany and Japan to benefit by capturing US markets. The war also produced cynicism about the government (reinforced by WATERGATE): there was a huge credibility gap between optimistic official statements and the reality shown on television. A distaste arose for foreign entanglements that threatened to revive the interwar isolation and was at first to inhibit activity in the GULF WAR and later in the YUGOSLAV CIVIL WAR.

The Second Indo-China War, W. S. Turley (1986)
America's Longest War: The United States and Vietnam 1950–75, G. Herring (1986)
The Vietnam Wars 1945–90, M. B. Young (1991)

Vorster, Balthazar Johannes (1915–83)

South African Prime Minister (1966–78) and President (1978–9). Born in the Cape, the son of a wealthy sheep farmer, he studied at Stellenbosch University, where VERWOERD was one of his lecturers, and became a lawyer.

During the Second World War he was interned for supporting Germany and for sabotage as a member of the *Ossewabrandwag* (Oxwagon Firewatch), which wanted a totalitarian Afrikaner republic. He entered parliament in 1953 and as Minister of Justice (1961–6) showed that he was a harsh and uncompromising upholder of white supremacy. Vorster increased the number of police, built up a vast network of informers and gave the police powers to detain people without trial, thus avoiding any intervention by the law-courts. By crushing black opposition after the SHARPEVILLE massacre Vorster gained the reputation of being a tough leader and this enabled him to succeed Verwoerd as Prime Minister in 1966. In fact, Vorster was less rigid than Verwoerd in the application of APARTHEID and alienated Afrikaner extremists by agreeing to have black diplomats in South Africa, talking of real independence for the BANTUSTANS, accepting the idea of Namibian independence and moving away from rigid segregation in sport. He tried to establish better relations with African states but failed, owing to the intervention of South African troops in the ANGOLAN CIVIL WAR and the repression which followed the Soweto riots when he banned BLACK CONSCIOUSNESS organizations and many individuals. Vorster resigned a year after an overwhelming election victory because of a political scandal involving one of his ministers, Connie Mulder, but became State President. He had to resign that office too in 1979, when his own involvement in the 'Muldergate' scandal became known. In retirement he was a fervent supporter of white supremacy, criticized BOTHA's ending of 'petty apartheid' and gave some support in 1982 to Treurnicht's breaking away from the NP to form the Conservative Party.

The Militarization of South African Politics, K. Grundy (1986)
Malan to De Klerk, R. Schrire (ed.) (1994)
Forty Lost Years: The Apartheid State and the Politics of the National Party, 1948–1994, D. O'Meara (1996)

W

Walesa, Lech (1943–) President of Poland (1990–5). Brought up on a poor farm, he left home at the age of 16 to become an electrician and later went to Gdansk, where he worked in the Lenin Shipyard. He was a strike leader in 1970–1, when GOMULKA fell from power, and was dismissed in 1976 for protesting that the concessions made to workers in 1970 were not being observed. Unemployed for four years, he climbed over the shipyard gates (in an incident which has become part of Polish folk lore) to join workers occupying the yard when there was further unrest in 1980. Walesa took charge of the strike, which spread along the Baltic coast, and formed an Interfactory Strike Committee, with representatives from 200 factories, which became the trade union SOLIDARITY. Demanding the right to strike and to form an independent trade union, Walesa negotiated with the government, which accepted Solidarity's right to exist, though forbidding it 'to play the role of a political party'. Walesa ran the union in an autocratic manner – when negotiating with the government he decided what should be done without consulting his colleagues or the rank and file – and lost some popularity as, convinced that Poland's weak economy could not stand continual strikes, he spent a lot of time persuading workers to go back to work.

In 1981 General JARUZELSKI declared martial law, arrested Solidarity leaders and made the union illegal. Walesa was detained for nearly a year and after his release appeared as the government's most uncompromising opponent. He was awarded the Nobel Peace Prize in 1983 but did not play a major role in Poland again until 1988, when there were further widespread strikes and disturbances following food price rises. Jaruzelski held round-table talks with Walesa and other Solidarity leaders, legalized the union and agreed to elections in 1989 which were a triumph for Solidarity and Walesa and led to the first non-communist Prime Minister in Eastern Europe since 1948, Tadeusz Mazowiecki. He was from Solidarity's intellectual wing, which increasingly differed from the poorly educated Walesa, whom they saw as an authoritarian figure, who wanted a strong executive presidential system built around himself. In 1990 Walesa deliberately split Solidarity by forming his own party, the Centre Alliance, to support him in the presidential elections, in which he was opposed by Mazowiecki. Walesa won the election in December 1990 and so became the first freely elected President in Poland since 1922, but his addiction to free-market economics was unpopular with Poles, who saw their standard of living decline as unemployment rose. An erratic and authoritarian President, he was seen by many, with his undignified manner and ungrammatical Polish, as unsuited to lead the country. In the presidential election of November 1995 Walesa was narrowly defeated (he received 48 per cent of the votes) by the ex-communist minister Aleksander Kwasniewski.

Warren, Earl (1891–1974) Chief Justice of the US Supreme Court (1953–69). The son of a railroad worker, he graduated as a lawyer and was a district attorney before becoming Attorney-General in California

(1939–43). In 1943 he was elected for the first of a record three terms as Governor of California (1943–53). He was the unsuccessful REPUBLICAN PARTY candidate for Vice-President in 1948 and sought the presidential nomination in 1952 before backing Dwight D. EISENHOWER. 'Ike' made Warren Chief Justice in 1953, but later thought that this was the worst mistake of his presidency, as the Chief Justice consistently supported individual rights against government infringements. President JOHNSON appointed him to head the Warren Commission to investigate the assassination of President John F. KENNEDY, which established that Lee Harvey Oswald was solely responsible.

The 'Warren Court' made rulings, many written by the Chief Justice himself, which produced significant changes in American life, particularly affecting civil rights, education, police procedures and legislative appointments. The decision BROWN V BOARD OF EDUCATION (1954) declared segregation in public schools unconstitutional and was a landmark in civil rights legislation. It was followed up by a Court order in 1958 ordering immediate desegregation at LITTLE ROCK, Arkansas. Two further rulings in 1962–3 concerned education: prayers and Bible-reading in public schools violated the constitutional principles of the separation of church and state, the Court declared. Public schools must not show the slightest preference for any form of religion. The Court threw its full weight behind the CIVIL RIGHTS MOVEMENT. In 1963 it ruled on the sit-ins, when blacks were refused service at 'whites only' lunch counters, declaring that local laws upholding segregation on private business premises were unconstitutional. *Cox v Louisiana* (1964) reversed the conviction of black demonstrators who had refused to disperse when ordered by the police. The justices said that breach-of-the-peace laws could not prevent peaceful assembly. The Court quickly approved of the CIVIL RIGHTS ACTS of 1964–5 and in LOVING V VIRGINIA (1967) declared laws banning marriage between people of different races illegal. In *Jacobellis v Ohio* (1963) the Supreme Court did much to liberalize censorship in saying that sexual material which 'has literary or scientific or artistic value' cannot be called obscene. The Supreme Court revised criminal procedure in *Miranda v Arizona* (1966) by saying that police must tell suspects that they can remain silent, that statements they make can be used against them and that they have the right to consult a lawyer before they are questioned. The justices also ruled on the reappointment of electoral areas in *Reynolds v Sims* (1964). They declared that both houses of state legislatures should be appointed according to 'one person one vote', which meant that electoral districts should be equal in terms of voters, thus ending the long-standing over-representation of rural areas.

Warsaw Pact (1955)   A military alliance of the USSR, Albania, Bulgaria, Czechoslovakia, the German Democratic Republic (GDR), Hungary, Poland and Romania. It was signed only nine days after the Federal Republic of Germany (West Germany) joined NATO: it provided for defence against any armed attack in Europe and for non-intervention in the affairs of member states, a proviso ignored in 1968 when Warsaw Pact forces invaded Czechoslovakia to bring to an end the PRAGUE SPRING. Its headquarters were in Moscow and its Supreme Commander was always a Russian. The Pact was a counter to NATO and enabled the Soviet Union to station Soviet troops in member states. In 1956 the Soviet Union crushed the HUNGARIAN RISING to prevent Hungary leaving the Pact. Albania withdrew in 1968 and the GDR in August 1990, just before GERMAN REUNIFICATION. The *raison d'être* of the Pact disappeared with the end of the COLD WAR and the REVOLUTIONS OF 1989–91, which saw the collapse of communism in Eastern Europe. It was dissolved by its members in July 1991.

The Warsaw Pact, R. A. Remington (1971)

Watergate   The biggest political scandal in the US in the twentieth century. On 17 June 1972 police arrested five men who had broken into the DEMOCRATIC PARTY headquarters in the Watergate complex in Washington, DC to install electronic bugging devices. All were employed by the Committee to Re-elect the President (CREEP), whose chairman was President NIXON's former Attorney General, John Mitchell. The President announced on 29 August that 'no one in the White House staff... was involved in this very bizarre incident'. The matter aroused little public interest and did not affect Nixon's popularity in the presidential election, which he won by an enormous margin.

All those charged with the break-in were tried before Judge Sirica in January 1973 and found guilty and in February the Senate appointed a committee under Sam Ervin to investigate the Watergate affair. A month later one of the burglars, James McCord, broke his silence and said that the aim of the break-in was to disrupt the Democratic George McGovern's presidential campaign and that John Mitchell was 'overall boss'. Two of the President's closest advisers, John Ehrlichman and Bob Haldeman, resigned on 30 April as did the President's counsel, John Dean. In May a special prosecutor, Archibald Cox, a Harvard law professor, was appointed and the Ervin committee began its hearings. These went on till August and revealed that some of Nixon's closest associates had planned the break-in and had then conspired to cover up their involvement. Eventually over 20, including Mitchell, Haldeman and Ehrlichman, were convicted and jailed.

The Senate investigation and two journalists on the *Washington Post* uncovered evidence of presidential misdeeds which were unrelated to Watergate but seriously damaged his reputation. Nixon paid federal taxes of $800 on a salary of $200,000 in 1970–1 (in 1974 he agreed to pay back $444,000 in taxes); he spent public money on his private houses and dropped anti-trust suits against certain corporations in return for campaign contributions. In June 1973 Dean told the Ervin committee that the President himself had been involved in the cover-up about the break-in. Proof of this appeared possible when a White House official revealed in July that all conversations in the President's office had been taped since 1970. Cox and Ervin immediately subpoenaed them, whereupon Nixon refused to release the tapes on the grounds of 'executive privilege'. October was an eventful month in the Watergate affair. Nixon ordered the dismissal of Cox, causing a public outcry, and handed over some tapes to Judge Sirica, but parts had been erased. The Judiciary Committee of the House of Representatives then began to consider whether to impeach the President. In July 1974 the Supreme Court ordered Nixon to hand over all necessary tapes and the House Judiciary Committee recommended his impeachment for obstructing justice, abuse of power and refusal to comply with the Committee's subpoenas. On 5 August Nixon, in accordance with the Supreme Court ruling, made public a tape containing imformation 'at variance... with my previous statements'. It showed that six days after the break-in he had ordered the FBI to halt its investigation into that event. Most of his remaining support in Congress now disappeared and so, with his conviction on impeachment charges certain, he resigned on 9 August, the first President to do so. Gerald FORD was sworn in as the new President and, a month later, pardoned Nixon for all the offences he had committed. A short-term effect of Watergate was that the Democratic Party won control of Congress in 1974 and the presidential election two years later. It also led Congress to re-assert its authority: the War Powers Resolution of 1973 forbade the President to commit US troops without consulting Congress.

The Wars of Watergate: The Last Crisis of Richard Nixon, S. Kutler (1990)
Nixon, Ruin and Recovery, 1973–90, S. Ambrose (1993)

Welfare State   A state in which the government provides social services, such as education, health, housing and insurance for sickness, unemployment and old age. Bismarck in the 1880s was an unlikely progenitor of the Welfare State with his State Socialism. In the first decade of the twentieth century his lead was followed by other countries such as New Zealand, when Richard Seddon was Prime Minister, and Uruguay, which Batlle y Ordóñez made into the first Welfare State in Latin America.

In Britain some welfare services were provided in the nineteenth century by the state (compulsory elementary education from 1880) and others by local authorities (gas, water, electricity, sewerage, transport) but it was the Liberal governments of Campbell-Bannerman (1905–8) and Asquith (1908–16) which first made a sustained effort to provide a range of social services which laid the basis of the Welfare State. The causes of poverty were attacked by setting up trade boards to deal with low pay in certain industries, by providing old age pensions, by labour exchanges, by unemployment and health insurance, to be paid for largely by graduated taxation. The New Liberalism rejected Gladstone's view of a minimalist state and sought more state intervention, as did the LABOUR PARTY, but up to 1939 welfare was largely restricted to the poor. During the Second World War an enlarged role for the state in providing welfare was accepted by both the main political parties and was expressed in the Beveridge Report (1942), which recommended welfare benefits 'from the cradle to the grave', where all would be treated equally. This was the time when the term 'Welfare State' was first widely used.

At the end of the war there was a widespread desire to erase the memory of the Great Depression (1929–39) and to erode the appeal of the Soviet Union and communism. The first ATTLEE government (1945–50) established the Welfare State in Britain with the National Insurance Act, which provided benefits for the sick, disabled and unemployed and old age pensions for all (for men at 65, women at 60). The National Health Service made available free medical and dental services. The CONSERVATIVE PARTY accepted, and even claimed credit for, the Welfare State in a consensus with the Labour Party which later was known as BUTSKELLISM and which survived till the late 1970s. Other European countries soon followed the British example as they became economically prosperous in the 1950s, though welfare schemes varied considerably, both in what they covered and in how they were funded and administered. In Britain and the Scandinavian countries the state was the main source of funds, employers and employees contributing smaller amounts, whereas in France, Italy and Germany the state paid considerably less. Employers in France and Italy paid two-thirds of the cost, in Britain 20 per cent. Social measures were operated by the state in Britain; in Scandinavia unemployment insurance and health care (except in Sweden) were run by non-governmental institutions. Free medical care for all insured people existed in Britain, Germany, Italy and Spain, but in France, Scandinavia, Belgium and Switzerland sick people had to pay between 10 per cent and 25 per cent of the costs. Old age pensions, low in Britain, high in France and Italy, were available at different ages: 65 for men and 60 for women in most countries but 60 for men in France and Italy (where women were granted a pension at 55), 67 in Sweden and 70 in Norway. In the Soviet Union peasants were excluded from most services until 1965.

There was much greater resistance to state welfare schemes in the US. President TRUMAN's Fair Deal was torn apart by Congress, though President JOHNSON had more success with his GREAT SOCIETY which, he said, 'demands an end to poverty and racial injustice'. Medicare and Medicaid gave some medical services to the old and the poor. There were state-controlled social security schemes in many THIRD WORLD countries but they were restricted to those in regular paid employment: soldiers, civil servants, professional groups and workers in essential services such as railways and mines. Domestic and agricultural workers and the self-employed were excluded. This was a regressive system, as contributions were paid by all tax-payers but the benefits went to a small, well-paid urban minority. The Welfare State greatly improved the health of recipients (there was a fall in infant mortality and an increase in life expectancy) and considerably expanded opportunities in higher education, as many more universities were built. It was also very popular, as its benefits were universal. Even those who in principle opposed high taxation and state expenditure were strongly in favour of services from which they gained personally.

The world recession which followed the OPEC PRICE RISE of 1973 made the Welfare State more difficult to fund, as higher unemployment reduced the state's income from taxation at the same time as it increased its expenditure on social services, particularly unemployment benefits. The New Right criticized the Welfare State on both economic grounds (the burden of high taxation and the disincentive of universal and generous benefits) and for moral reasons (the 'nanny state', it was said, produced a 'dependency culture'). The Conservative regimes of Margaret THATCHER in Britain and of Ronald REAGAN in the US tried to reduce government expenditure by such measures as PRIVATIZATION and by reducing the amount spent on the Welfare State. There was a move away from universal provision to targeting groups most in need, the indexation of benefits was reduced, the rules for eligibility were tightened and charges were introduced or raised. In the US President CLINTON promised in 1992 to 'end welfare as we know it' and signed a Republican Welfare Reform Act in 1996 which reduced benefits for 13 million Americans, nine million of whom were children. Yet even in Britain the state spent more on the Welfare State in real terms, largely because of the cost of high unemployment, because a larger proportion of the population

was old and unproductive and because Medical Advances – new drugs, equipment and treatment – were extremely expensive. By the late 1980s most major European countries were spending 40–50 per cent of GNP on social services: it was not clear whether resources could ever keep up with demand.

Comparative Social Policy and the Third World, S. MacPherson and J. Midgley (1987)
Modern Welfare States: Politics and Policies in Social Democratic Scandinavia, E. S. Einhorn and J. Logue (1989)
The Development of Welfare States in Europe and America, P. Flora and A. J. Heidenheimer (eds) (1991)

West Bank (of the River Jordan)   An area which was part of the territory allocated to Arabs by the UNITED NATIONS partition plan of 1947. After the first ARAB–ISRAELI WAR (1948–9) King ABDULLAH of Jordan annexed the West Bank, but it was seized by Israel in the SIX DAY WAR (1967) and became part of the OCCUPIED TERRITORIES. Jewish settlements began there under Labour governments and greatly accelerated when Likud became the leading party in government in 1977. By 1995 1.2 million people lived in the area, including 120,000 Jewish settlers who aroused considerable Arab opposition so that the INTIFADA, which began in Gaza, spread to the West Bank. By the time of the Oslo Accords (1993) half the territory was in Jewish hands. Two years later the PLO signed an agreement with Israel for the withdrawal of Israeli troops from seven cities but the victory of Likud and Binyamin NETANYAHU in the 1996 Israeli general election halted the PEACE PROCESS, as many in his cabinet were opposed to Arab rule in the West Bank.

Whitlam, Edward Gough (1916–)
Prime Minister of Australia (1972–5). The son of a senior civil servant, he served in the Royal Australian Air Force during the Second

World War, graduated in arts and in law at Sydney University and practised as a lawyer before entering parliament in 1952. After the massive defeat of the Australian Labor Party (ALP) in the 1966 election, Whitlam became its leader in 1967. He lost the 1969 election (in spite of a 7 per cent swing to Labor) but widened the basis of the ALP, which was no longer simply a party of the industrial working class, by promoting policies which appealed to white collar workers and the young. Labor had shed its nationalization and 'white Australia' policies by the time he became leader. A witty and fluent speaker with an imposing presence (he was 6 ft 4 inches tall) he dominated parliament as opposition leader.

Labor won the 1972 election, so Whitlam became the first Labor Prime Minister since Chifley in 1949. He had been elected on a reform platform and wanted a more just and humane society, in which wealth would be distributed more evenly. In his first month of office he pushed through a remarkable series of reforms: conscription was ended, the case for equal pay for women was reopened before the Arbitration Commission, the imperial honours system was abolished, military aid to South Vietnam was ended and diplomatic relations were opened with communist China. In the 18 months of his first administration an unprecedented number of bills were passed. Tariffs were reduced by 25 per cent, university fees abolished, public servants were given large pay increases. Spending on education increased too, as Colleges of Advanced Education were built in every state, new universities were opened and the arts and culture subsidized. Farmers lost their fertilizer subsidies. Whitlam also lowered barriers to Asian and African immigration.

All his reforms could not be carried out as the ALP did not have a majority in the upper house, the Senate, which blocked measures to reform industrial relations and the electoral system. To deal with this opposition he asked the Governor-General to call new elections in 1974 for both the House of Representatives and the Senate. The ALP was returned to power in the lower house but was still without a majority in the Senate. Reforms continued with Medibank, which gave a free health service for Australians, wage indexation and a Racial Discrimination Act. Papua New Guinea, Australia's only significant colony, was granted independence. Whitlam decided on a Keynesian solution to stagflation and increased government expenditure by 32 per cent, spending more on health, education, urban and regional affairs. Critics accused him of irresponsibility. In October 1975 Malcolm FRASER, the newly elected leader of the Liberal Party, said that the opposition (which controlled the Senate) would not pass the budget until the government agreed to a general election. Whitlam rejected this ultimatum whereupon, in one of the most extraordinary incidents in Australian history, the Governor-General Sir John Kerr (a Whitlam appointee) unexpectedly intervened, dismissed Whitlam (the first time a Governor-General had removed an elected Prime Minister), made Fraser the Prime Minister of a caretaker government and called for new elections. By 1975 the postwar boom was ending, following the OPEC PRICE RISE of 1973 and Britain's decision to join the EEC. Inflation was 17 per cent, there was a large trade deficit and unemployment was at a postwar high of 5 per cent. The ALP lost the election in the worst defeat for a government since federation (the Liberal–Country Party alliance won 91 seats in the House of Representatives, the Labor Party 36). Whitlam remained its leader until 1977, when he resigned after a second electoral defeat. He retired from politics in 1978, became a lecturer in politics and international relations at the Australian National University at Canberra and from 1983–8 was Australia's representative at UNESCO. As an elder statesman he was highly regarded even by people who had not voted for him and his opinions were sought on a wide range of issues.

Oxford History of Australia, vol. 5, 1942–88,
   G. Bolton (1990)

Wilson, (James) Harold, Baron (1916–95)

British Prime Minister (1964–70, 1974–6). The son of an industrial chemist in Yorkshire, he won an exhibition to Oxford, where he gained an outstanding first in politics, philosophy and economics. He remained in Oxford after his degree as a lecturer in economics, became a Fellow of University College and seemed destined for an academic career. During the Second World War he worked in the civil service as a statistician on wartime planning, joined the LABOUR PARTY and in 1945 became an MP. He rapidly advanced under ATTLEE to become President of the Board of Trade at the age of 31, the youngest cabinet minister since Palmerston. His period there is best known for the 'bonfire of controls' he made. When Sir Stafford Cripps resigned as Chancellor of the Exchequer in October 1950, the post did not go to Wilson but to his rival Hugh GAITSKELL. A year later Wilson resigned (along with Aneurin BEVAN) because he said that the country could not afford the huge increase in defence expenditure which Gaitskell introduced in his budget. From that time Wilson was regarded as a Bevanite and man of the left, though in fact he was more of a centrist, whose prime concern was to maintain the unity of the Labour movement. He voted for Gaitskell in the leadership contest of 1955, yet ran unsuccessfully against him as the left's candidate in 1960. On Gaitskell's death in 1963 Wilson, again with the support of the left, was elected leader of the Labour Party. He was a brilliant leader of the Opposition, incisive and witty and completely overshadowed the Prime Minister, Sir Alec DOUGLAS-HOME, in the Commons. Labour narrowly defeated the CONSERVATIVE PARTY in the 1964 election, so Harold Wilson found himself Prime Minister. A further election in 1966 gave Labour 48 per cent of the vote and a comfortable majority of 98.

Faced with an economic crisis and a balance of payments deficit of £800 million, the largest since the war, Wilson rejected devaluation, as the Labour Party had devalued in 1949 and so missed an opportunity to make British exports more competitive. This was an enormous error, as it made significant economic growth impossible and in the end devaluation could not be avoided. Far from deflating, the Chancellor of the Exchequer, Jim CALLAGHAN, increased pensions and social security benefits and paid for them by increasing taxation and surcharging imports. This led to a run on the pound, so the bank rate was raised to 7 per cent. Wilson had to turn to the US for support in defending the pound. A loan of $3 million was arranged with central banks. Yet after a seaman's strike, which crippled exports for six weeks, the pound was at last devalued in 1967 from 2.80 pounds to the dollar to 2.40 and a phased withdrawal of British forces from east of Suez began. Britain's second application to join the EEC was vetoed by DE GAULLE later in the year. When Roy Jenkins became Chancellor his 1968 budget was the most deflationary since the war and took £900 million out of the economy by increasing taxes on petrol, alcohol and tobacco, and continued this in 1969. The balance of payments moved into surplus in 1969 and an even bigger surplus in 1970, as exports were cheaper after devaluation, but growth from 1964–70 had averaged only 2.7 per cent a year, much less than that of Britain's competitors.

Wilson tried to limit the power of TRADE UNIONS, which were seen by the public as being largely responsible for Britain's relative economic decline, and so Barbara Castle produced a White Paper IN PLACE OF STRIFE, but this had ignominiously to be abandoned owing to the opposition of the trade unions and many Labour MPs. The government also failed to reform the House of Lords (a bill to do this was withdrawn in 1969 because it was not assured of a majority), local government and the civil service.

The Wilson administration's greatest successes were in education and in liberalizing society. The Education Secretary Anthony Crosland announced in 1965 that the tripartite system of R. A. BUTLER's 1944 Education Act would be replaced by comprehensive schools, which would be attended by all pupils. By 1970 there were a thousand comprehensives, attended by 30 per cent of all secondary school pupils. As the grammar schools were shut down, education for the privileged élite in public (fee-paying) schools was allowed to continue. Following the Robbins Report of 1963, which asked for a doubling of students in higher education by 1968, nine new universities were built in the 1960s and the older ones greatly expanded. Crosland also commissioned 30 polytechnics to provide a wider range of courses than the universities and to concentrate on teaching rather than research. By 1968 Robbins's target had been met. Another innovation, in which Wilson took a personal interest, was the Open University, founded in 1969. This was for older students who had not gone to university but who could now take a degree by correspondence course (some instruction was given on radio and television) and was a great success. At the Home Office Jenkins supported bills which ended capital punishment, allowed abortion, homosexual acts between consenting adults in private and divorce by mutual consent. The voting age was lowered from 21 to 18 in 1969, an Ombudsman was appointed to investigate complaints about the action of government departments, a Rent Act fixed fair rents for private tenants and gave greater security of tenure and a Redundancy Payments Act gave compensation to workers made redundant. The IMMIGRATION ACT of 1968 restricted further immigration from the COMMONWEALTH but there was a genuine attempt to improve the lot of coloured immigrants who were already settled in Britain. Race Relations Acts of 1965 and 1968 set up a Race Relations Board to resolve racial disputes without going to the courts and banned discrimination in housing, education and other services. There was therefore plenty of legislation in Wilson's governments to make Britain a more civilized society.

In foreign policy Wilson continued along the lines laid down by earlier Conservative administrations. The Anglo-American alliance was the centrepiece. DECOLONIZATION continued, Zambia, Malawi and Malta gaining independence in 1964, Gambia and Singapore in 1965, Barbados, Botswana, Guyana and Lesotho in 1966. Britain's decline as a world power was evident in the INDO-PAKISTANI WAR in 1965: the Soviet Union, not Britain, brought the two countries together at Tashkent to settle their differences. In the BIAFRAN WAR (1967–79) Wilson supported the Nigerian government, but it was events in Rhodesia following Ian Smith's UDI in 1965 which were most intractable. Wilson encouraged Smith's intransigence by saying that he would never use force and made himself look ridiculous when he said that sanctions would work in weeks rather than months. The APARTHEID regime in South Africa ensured that sanctions were easily avoided.

By 1970 the economy had improved owing to the devaluation of 1967 and Jenkins's austere budgets, and Labour was ahead in the opinion polls. Wilson was shocked, therefore, to lose the election to Edward HEATH and the Conservatives, who had a majority of 38. As leader of the Opposition again he was nothing like as effective as he was in 1963–4, but he bounced back in 1974 when Heath unexpectedly failed to gain a majority in the election. Wilson formed a minority government and promptly gave the miners the large pay rise they were demanding and so ended the three-day week and the state of emergency Heath had declared. With the crisis over, Wilson held another election in October 1974 which left him with an overall majority of three. Stock markets were collapsing and prices rising throughout the world after the OPEC PRICE RISE of 1973. Wilson put his faith in the Social Contract with the TUC, which he hoped would replace conflict with co-operation. In return for repealing Heath's Industrial Relations Act, the unions were expected to accept voluntary wage restraint. It did not work out like that. The trade unions used the miners' 'special case' to push up the 'going rate' for wage increases, which rose by 19 per cent in 1974 and 23 per cent in 1975. In spite of Healey's 'rough and tough' budget of 1975, which raised income tax and indirect taxes, the pound fell by a third in 1975 and Wilson found December 'the most hectic and harrowing month I experienced in nearly eight years as Prime Minister'. A loan was negotiated with the IMF but in return for massive cuts in public expenditure. The Prime Minister defused the issue of EEC membership, which threatened to divide the Labour Party. He pacified the left by holding a referendum in 1975, in which 67 per cent voted in favour of remaining in the Common Market. Wilson surprised everyone by resigning in 1976 shortly after his sixtieth birthday. His departing honours list gave awards to unsuitable cronies, one of whom ended up in jail for fraud. He remained in the Commons for another seven years before accepting a life peerage. There was a sad physical and mental decline in his last years with Alzheimer's disease.

Harold Wilson, B. Pimlott (1992)
The Wilson Governments, 1964–70, R. Cropey,
    S. Fielding and N. Tiratsoo (eds) (1993)
Harold Wilson, P. Ziegler (1993)

Winter of discontent (1978–9)   The time when the TRADE UNIONS in Britain brought the Labour government to its knees. Harold WILSON and Jim CALLAGHAN had pursued an incomes policy, with the co-operation of the TUC (Trades Union Congress), since 1975 but this had led to a reduction in the standard of living of many workers. When Callaghan announced in 1978 that there would be a further stage in which the rise in incomes would be limited to 5 per cent (inflation was running at 8 per cent) the TUC would not accept it. In November 1978 a strike by Ford workers, the pace-setters, began and lasted for nine weeks until they accepted a 17 per cent pay rise. Petrol tanker and long-distance lorry drivers went on strike in the New Year and settled for 17–20 per cent on 19 January, but the most serious and

damaging strikes were those of the lowest paid workers in the public sector. Over a million local government manual workers went on strike, closing hospitals, schools and social services. Most of these events were shortlived and in limited areas (gravediggers went on strike in Liverpool) but they received national attention on television and in the newspapers. As rubbish piled up in the streets, the media portrayed the strikers as callous and selfish. The government appeared paralysed and took no initiative. Public opinion turned against the trade unions and the government: a Gallup poll in February 1979 put the CONSERVATIVE PARTY 20 per cent ahead of Labour (three months earlier it had been five points behind). When the local government workers accepted a rise of 9 per cent plus a pound a week the strikes came to an end but the damage had been done.

The Labour Party had always had close links with the trade unions, which provided it with funds, block votes at Labour Party Conferences and sponsored many Labour Party MPs. This connection now became an electoral liability: a vote for Labour appeared to be a vote for industrial anarchy and the tyranny of the trade unions, which were seen as far too powerful. They were to be one of the chief victims of the Winter of Discontent, as they ensured a Conservative victory in the 1979 election and a government which reduced the powers of the unions in ways undreamt of a decade earlier.

Wirtschaftswunder (economic miracle)
The revival of the Federal Republic of Germany (FRG) from the devastation of the Second World War to become the leading European economy by 1961. The recovery began with the currency reform of 1948 (see GERMANY DIVIDED) and the removal of most price controls which brought a flood of goods onto the market. The exchange rate of the new Deutschmark (DM) was fixed at 4.2 to the American dollar, an undervaluation which soon enabled the FRG to build up its

exports. The economy was aided by the creation of an autonomous central bank (which became the Bundesbank in 1957), with a statutory obligation to maintain a stable currency and with control over the money supply and interest rates. Other banks too played a large part in economic revival by investing heavily, the Deutsche Bank becoming part owner of many leading firms, such as Bayer, Bosch, Siemens and VW. Large-scale American aid in the MARSHALL PLAN and the demand engendered by the KOREAN WAR (1950–3) also helped industry. The need for a highly trained workforce was met (until the BERLIN WALL was built in 1961) by a flood of refugees from the German Democratic Republic (GDR: East Germany), but the *Wirtschaftswunder* owed most to Ludwig ERHARD, Chancellor ADENAUER's Economics Minister (1949–63), who freed industry from the restrictions imposed by the Third Reich and by the Allied occupation authorities and established a SOCIAL MARKET ECONOMY. Huge sums were spent by the government on railways and urban commuter systems to provide an infrastructure for industry and large sums were spent too on education and on research and development. The WELFARE STATE, which was an essential part of the social market economy, and the power given to the TRADE UNIONS by the policy of co-determination, produced a contented workforce, so there was co-operation rather than confrontation between workers and managers and few strikes.

Less than half of German industry had been destroyed in the war and only 5 per cent was taken as reparations: the rest was rebuilt using the latest US technology, which gave German industry an edge over that of its competitors (British industry continued to use old, outmoded machinery). The production of cars increased 27-fold between 1949–66, so that the FRG produced ten times as many vehicles as the whole of Germany in 1937. Steel output, which hardly existed in 1946, soon became the largest in Europe, producing 34 million tons in 1960. The chemical

and electrical industries were also the largest in Europe. Although the Allies had split up IG Farben (the largest of all German firms in 1930) into three parts (Bayer, BASF and Hoechst), each of them became bigger than the parent company. With an average economic growth each year in the 1950s of 7.5 per cent, which almost wiped out unemployment, the FRG was the powerhouse of Europe and played a leading role in the formation of the ECSC (European Coal and Steel Community) and the EEC (European Economic Community). Industrial production increased six-fold from 1949 to 1966 and, as tight monetary policies prevented inflation, exports rocketed. From 1952 the FRG had a trade surplus and by 1960 was second only to the US in world trade. The FRG built up one of the world's largest currency reserves, making the DM a reserve currency, constantly revalued. This was a remarkable achievement for a country which had lost 40 per cent of its territory and 35 per cent of its population as a result of the war and the division of Germany.

The Americanization of West German Industry, 1945–73, V. Berghahn (1986)
The Political Economy of West Germany, 1945–85, J. Leaman (1988)
The West German Economy, E. Owen Smith (1994)

women's liberation   As early as 1792 Mary Wollstonecraft in *Vindication of the Rights of Women* had demanded that women should receive the same opportunities as men in education, work and politics, but in the nineteenth century nearly all women were under the control of men. With industrialization they had more opportunities for employment in textile factories, as secretaries (after the invention of the typewriter) and as shop assistants, but most of these jobs were unskilled and poorly paid. The growth of elementary education provided schoolteaching as a respectable occupation for unmarried, middle-class women. Women gradually gained more legal rights (to property, for example) in the late nineteenth century in Western Europe and access to higher education and the professions, where they formed an extremely small minority. FEMINIST MOVEMENTS concentrated on obtaining the vote for women, an object which had been achieved in most of Western Europe and the US by 1939. The Second World War extended this to many countries where women did not already have the vote: France, Italy, Japan, Belgium and Eastern Europe. Women in Africa eventually received the vote with DECOLONIZATION. By the 1960s women had the vote almost everywhere, except in some Islamic countries and Switzerland, the last European country to give the vote to women in 1971.

In the 1960s there was a second wave of feminist activism which arose out of the CIVIL RIGHTS MOVEMENT and the VIETNAM ANTI-WAR MOVEMENT and reached a peak from 1969–73, when there were hundreds of women's organizations and scores of periodicals. Some of this activity was concerned with sexual freedom and the right of women to control their own bodies. There was a demand for education about birth control, safe contraception and legal abortion. These demands were met in several countries in the 1960s and 1970s. The contraceptive pill was widely available by 1965 in Western Europe, except in some Catholic countries such as Ireland. Abortion was allowed in Britain in 1967 if two doctors said it was needed on medical or psychological grounds and the Family Planning Act enabled local authorities to provide advice on birth control. In the US the Supreme Court decision *Roe v Wade* in 1973 guaranteed women a 'constitutional right' to abortion, a decision greeted with dismay by the Roman Catholic Church and fundamentalist Protestants, who allied with conservative politicians in an attempt to have the decision overturned. They failed when the Supreme Court in 1992 narrowly upheld *Roe v Wade* but violent picketing and attacks on abortion clinics made implementation of the act difficult. In Britain the situation was different – 81 per cent in an opinion poll in 1991 said that women should make their own decision on abortion. Abortion was illegal in Ireland, where the Catholic Church prevented any change in the law, so many Irish women came to Britain for abortions.

After the war vast numbers of women entered the labour market in the US. In 1940 25 per cent of women, mainly young, unmarried and poor, worked outside the home, a similar proportion as in 1910. By 1970 women were 43 per cent of the total workforce and married women workers outnumbered single ones: the greatest growth was taking place among well-educated, middle-class wives. In 1980 only 15 per cent of American families (compared with 70 per cent in the early 1950s) consisted of a father who worked and a mother who stayed at home. Yet women were discriminated against in employment: they were in low-paid jobs in the service sector or doing clerical jobs and were paid less than men in the same work. There were few women in top jobs – in 1970 under 5 per cent of managers and executives were women. Liberation meant not only an end to discrimination but child-care facilities, which would make it easier for married women to work. Congress passed a law to provide these in 1972 but President NIXON vetoed it as a threat to the family. Yet women's legal position in the workplace improved significantly. The CIVIL RIGHTS ACT (1964) outlawed discrimination in employment on grounds of sex as well as of race. The Equal Pay Act of 1972 prohibited sex discrimination in federal-supported educational programmes and expanded the jurisdiction of the Equal Employment Opportunities Commission to include local government. By the mid-1970s AFFIRMATIVE ACTION programmes were helping women more than blacks. Yet equal pay legislation did not affect the low pay in jobs classed as female. The 'feminization of poverty' (a term first used in 1978) took place as women were increasingly among the poor, assigned most of the unpaid work such as child care and care for the elderly in their families and often worked in sweatshops. Two-thirds of minimum-wage workers were women in 1989. Even when they worked outside the home, they were held responsible for most household chores: washing and ironing, cleaning and cooking.

The situation of working women in Britain was similar to that in the US. In 1951 they formed 31 per cent of the workforce, little more than in 1911, but this had risen to 43 per cent by 1980. As in the US, working women had to cope with household chores, too. Around 63 per cent of working women in 1980 were in jobs done mainly by women, where the pay was low. Few women held highly paid jobs: only two senior managers out of 590 in British Rail in 1984 were women. In the civil service in 1987 women were 76 per cent of low-level administrative assistants and only 4 per cent of those in top grades. Only 1 per cent of bank managers, 2 per cent of accountants and university professors and 5 per cent of architects were women in 1978. Opportunity 2000 aimed to obtain more prominent positions for women. Betty Boothroyd in 1992 became the first woman Speaker of the House of Commons and the LABOUR PARTY adopted women-only lists of candidates, only to find them declared illegal as they contravened sex discrimination legislation. Like women in the US British women benefited from some legislation. The Labour government in 1975 passed the Sex Discrimination Act and Equal Pay Act. The Employment Protection Act gave women paid maternity leave, made dismissal on grounds of pregnancy illegal and required employers to give a mother her job back after the birth of her child. The government also created an Equal Opportunities Commission, based on that in the US. Some of the legal gains women had made were whittled away by Conservative governments in the 1980s and 1990s. The 1986 Wages Act removed half of workers from the protection of Wages Councils, which fixed minimum rates in low-paid industries. With PRIVATIZATION and the spread of con-

tract work, workers lost their legal protection, sick pay and pensions as many workers were classed as part-time. By 1990 80 per cent of low paid, part-time workers were women. Wage Councils were abolished completely in 1993, so there was no regulatory mechanism to prevent wages being pushed down.

In Japan too women at work were badly treated. The 1947 Labour Standards Law guaranteed equal access for employment opportunities to women and equal pay for equal work but there were ways round the law. Women were expected to leave work on marriage or the birth of their first child. If they returned it was to part-time employment, as they had lost their seniority and status. Japanese women in employment grew from four million in 1953 to 13.5 million in 1980, but there were gender differences in pay as companies structured their pay and promotion according to continuity of employment. Discrimination against women affected higher education too: in 1990 33 per cent of males went to university but only 15 per cent of females. Even when they graduated their prospects were not bright: in 1985 over 70 per cent of Japanese firms refused to employ female graduates on the grounds that they would marry and have children. In 1989 only 8 per cent of managers were women.

In communist states women worked in order to survive, so there were almost as many women as men in the labour-force. They gained social security and reproductive rights but, like women in the West, had to look after the home and children as well. Professions which they dominated, such as medicine, lost status and income. In the THIRD WORLD most women had no rights and in countries where ISLAMIC FUNDAMENTALISTS were dominant they were rigorously segregated from men and forced into obscurity. At the end of the twentieth century women's liberation could claim some successes, particularly in the Western liberal democracies, but even there it faced formidable obstacles in seeking to end discrimination.

Power and Prejudice: Women and Politics,
  A. Coote and P. Patullo (1990)
Women in Britain Since 1945, J. Lewis (1992)
A Century of Women, S. Rowbotham (1997)

World Bank (International Bank for Reconstruction and Development)   An agency of the UNITED NATIONS. Proposed at Bretton Woods (1944) to lend money for development, it became an intermediary between advanced industrial and developing countries and decided what economic policies should be followed in many countries. It is almost entirely an American creation (every President is a US citizen, appointed by the White House) and derives its equity from the capital of its shareholders (155 in 1996) and borrowing on the world market. Its first task was to rebuild the European economies ruined in the Second World War before turning to the needs of developing countries which were regarded as credit-worthy, where it promoted large-scale, capital-intensive projects in the infrastructure: power plants, roads, railways, dams. These were regarded as a prerequisite for successful economic development.

There was a major change of policy in the 1970s under Robert McNamara. The World Bank, sensitive to the NORTH–SOUTH DIVIDE as exemplified in the BRANDT Report of 1977, established a Special Fund to help the least developed countries with debt relief and moved to projects with simpler technology. The new object was to reduce poverty and inequality. McNamara took up the cause of the 'bottom 40 per cent', the one billion people thought to be living in absolute poverty. There was massive lending for rural development, population planning, health, water, sanitation and the provision of services for squatters in slums. In the 1980s there was an attempt to change the thinking in developing countries by 'structural adjustment' programmes, whereby countries would open up their protected economies to international competition, reduce government intervention and promote the PRIVATIZATION of state enterprises.

The INTERNATIONAL DEBT crisis showed just how little control the Bank had. Most of its THIRD WORLD members were heavily in debt in the 1980s, so that its flow of money to them shrank and then turned negative. The Bank, like the IMF, often took out more from countries in repayments than it put in through new loans. These negative transfers made the Bank appear a burden rather than a benefit to poor countries. It failed to increase productivity and reduce poverty in the 1970s and in the 1980s its adjustment programmes were not sustainable economically, socially or politically. The Bank was also criticized for the ENVIRONMENTAL DISASTERS produced by some of the projects it funded, such as the destruction of the Amazonian rain-forest. Yet it remained the main source of development loans and after the REVOLUTIONS OF 1989–91 became involved in reviving the economies of the ex-communist states of Eastern Europe and of the CIS (Commonwealth of Independent States).

The World Bank made an astonishing *volte-face* in policy in 1997 when it abandoned its long-standing support for minimal government in favour of a new model based on a strong and vigorous state. Its report said that the role of government had been vital in making possible the 'dazzling growth' of the NEWLY INDUSTRIALIZING ECONOMIES (NIEs) of Asia and it now laid down that the key tasks of government included investment in social services, providing a welfare safety net, protecting the environment, establishing the rule of law and tackling corruption. Markets and governments were seen as having complementary roles.

*Aid and Power: The World Bank and Policy-
  Based Lending*, 2 vols, P. Mosley, J. Harrigan and J. Toye (1991)
*Banking on the Poor: The World Bank and
  World Poverty*, R. L. Ayres (1993)
*Master of Illusion: The World Bank and the
  Poverty of Nations*, C. Caufield (1997)

World Health Organization (WHO)   An agency of the UNITED NATIONS with its headquarters in Geneva. Founded in 1948, it was to monitor and collect statistics on world health, advise developing regions on health care and co-ordinate national efforts to eradicate diseases. Its achievements were modest until the 1970s, when it established effective health services in deprived regions. The WHO took the lead in fighting epidemic diseases and had a major success when it eradicated smallpox in the decade 1967–77, the first disease to be eliminated by human effort. In 1980 a comprehensive programme of immunization, begun in 1974, aimed to get rid of other killer diseases: tuberculosis, measles and polio. Inoculation quadrupled in ten years with remarkable results. In India and Indonesia the rate of measles/TB inoculation rose from 0.1 per cent in 1980 to 96 per cent in 1990. An exception was the Soviet Union, where immunization levels declined from 95 per cent to 68 per cent in the same period. In 1988 the WHO declared its aim of eradicating polio, leprosy and tetanus (which affect 30 million people) by the year 2000. As part of its war on disease the WHO attacked the causes of disease (polluted water, poor sanitation and hygiene) and in the 1980s provided 1.6 billion people in the developing world with safe water. WHO activities tend to mirror the balance of power in the NORTH–SOUTH DIVIDE. The eradication of smallpox was carried out at the request of the US, which largely funded and staffed the programme. The global programme on AIDS (acquired immune deficiency syndrome) is also sponsored by the US, where there are many cases. The effect of the WHO campaigns has been to increase life expectancy sharply, from 42 to 70 years (1948–90) in China and East Asia. This has contributed to the POPULATION EXPLOSION and all the attendant problems which this has produced.

Y

Yeltsin, Boris Nikolaevich (1931–) President of Russia (1991–). Born in the Urals into a poor family, he graduated from the Ural Polytechnic Institute and worked as a construction engineer before joining the CPSU in 1961 to further his career. Impulsive and energetic, he became head of the Sverdlovsk Party organization (1976–85) before, benefiting from GORBACHEV's reforms, he was moved to Moscow as First Secretary of the party there and a candidate (non-voting) member of the Politburo. Passed over for promotion in 1987 (he did not become a full member of the Politburo) he turned against Gorbachev and said that two years of perestroika had achieved nothing. He was dismissed as First Secretary in November, and in February 1988 ceased to be a member of the Politburo.

Yeltsin found a new power base for himself in the Russian Supreme Soviet (parliament). He was narrowly elected Chairman in May 1990 and called for Russian sovereignty, which included ownership of its natural resources and the primacy of its legislation over that of the USSR. The Russian parliament passed these measures in June and Yeltsin resigned from the CPSU. In June 1991 a presidential system was established in Russia and Yeltsin was elected President with 57 per cent of the vote, the first Russian leader to be democratically elected. He was now the most powerful figure in the Soviet Union after Gorbachev, whose reputation was destroyed by the AUGUST COUP of 1991. Yeltsin's finest hour was when, with great courage, he led the opposition to the coup and ensured its failure. He used his enormous prestige to

humiliate Gorbachev. He was still prepared to negotiate a new political union for the USSR but Ukraine's declaration of independence in December forced him to bring about the COLLAPSE OF THE SOVIET UNION, which was followed by the formation of the CIS (Commonwealth of Independent States). He also persuaded the Russian parliament to give him emergency powers for a year so that he could push through economic reforms and made Yegor Gaidar, a free market economist, Deputy Prime Minister (Yeltsin was Prime Minister as well as President).

Yeltsin was now in an immensely strong position as head of by far the largest state in the CIS, but he failed to consolidate his power by forming a political party and soon found himself in confrontation with the Russian parliament over economic policy. Gaidar's freeing of prices in January 1992 led to an enormous increase in unemployment and in the cost of living, putting at least 50 per cent of people below the poverty level. A 'red and brown' alliance (of communists and nationalists) was formed against him. In December 1992 Yeltsin was unable to make Gaidar his Prime Minister and was forced by parliament to accept Viktor Chernomyrdin instead. An attempt to impeach Yeltsin narrowly failed and there was disagreement within the government, as Vice-President Rutskoi opposed Gaidar's reforms. In September 1993 Yeltsin suspended Rutskoi and dissolved parliament. Many deputies rejected this and passed a resolution making Rutskoi President instead of Yeltsin. This confrontation ended in violence in October 1993, when Yeltsin ordered the army to bombard the White House in

Moscow, where the parliament sat. Yeltsin's victory was a Pyrrhic one, as it destroyed his democratic credentials and as the December elections left him with only minority support in the new parliament, the revived communists and nationalists such as Zhirinovsky doing well. The elections of December 1995 were a further blow to Yeltsin. Our Home is Russia, the party of his Prime Minister Chernomyrdin, received under 10 per cent of the vote, the communists being the most successful party with 22 per cent.

After the demise of the Soviet Union Russia took its seat on the Security Council of the UNITED NATIONS and was in charge of nearly all the armed forces of the CIS. Good relations with the 'near abroad' (other republics in the CIS) proved difficult, as there was fear of Russian domination, particularly when Russian troops intervened in Moldova to support Russian settlers in the Dniester region. Strife with Ukraine over control of the Black Sea fleet and the Crimea (populated mainly by Russians but given to Ukraine in 1954) was avoided, as Yeltsin seemed satisfied with the granting of regional autonomy to the Crimea and accepted joint ownership of the Black Sea fleet. Yeltsin wanted to continue Gorbachev's good relations with the West: in April 1992 Russia joined the IMF, though this occasioned much domestic criticism, which was renewed when Yeltsin reluctantly accepted in 1997 that Poland, Hungary and the Czech Republic would join NATO. Yeltsin's greatest difficulties remained at home. In the CHECHNYA CONFLICT he showed a distaste for compromise and a willingness to use force, which was applied so incompetently that his popularity plummeted. Yet his overriding problem was that of the economy. The freeing of prices in 1992 had destroyed one foundation of state control of the economy but another remained: the state ownership of industry. PRIVATIZATION began in October 1992 but was criticized as 'NOMENKLATURA privatization' by which communist managers turned their control of state enterprises into their own private ownership. Around 18,000 of Russia's large

firms (and most small businesses), covering 80 per cent of employment and manufacturing, were privatized from 1992–5, though the largest and most powerful enterprises (as in oil and electricity) were excluded. Private firms lacked elementary skills in marketing and financial management and, according to the Russian National Survey, got rid of 23 per cent of their employees (1993–6), operated at half capacity and so became even more inefficient. Workers were worse off, their wages being paid late or not at all. From 1993 to 1996 Russian industrial output fell by a third, as many firms were part of the MILITARY–INDUSTRIAL COMPLEX which the government could no longer afford to maintain and other businesses relied on the sales and supply networks shattered by the collapse of the Soviet Union. Business suffered too from high federal and local taxes, the vast number of permits needed to do anything and from the arbitrary power and corruption of civil servants, which made it almost impossible to run a business legally. Crime was pervasive and vicious: 9 out of 30 top officials in the Russian Business Roundtable, an organization of leading executives, were assassinated in 1995. Agriculture continued to be neglected. State farms were technically transferred to private ownership in 1992 but there was no practical way individual members of a collective farm could exercise their property rights. The government was inept in collecting taxes, enforcing contracts and protecting the weak, whose social services had all but disappeared. State pensions were often long overdue.

Yeltsin spent much time in hospital in 1994–5 as a result of his excessive drinking and heart problems. He won the presidential election of 1996 with 54 per cent of the vote in the second round, 14 per cent more than his communist rival Zyuganov, largely because he controlled the media and had the support of the popular ex-general Lebed. He survived a multiple heart by-pass operation shortly afterwards, from which he made a slow and arduous recovery.

The Reincarnation of Russia Struggling with the Legacy of Communism, 1990–4, J. Lowen-hardt (1995)

Russia in Transition: Politics, Poverty and Inequality, D. Lane (ed.) (1996)

Kremlin Capitalism: The Privatization of the Russian Economy, J. R. Blasi, M. Krou-mova and D. Kruse (1997)

Yom Kippur War (1973)

An ARAB–ISRAELI WAR. As Israel continued to occupy the territories it had conquered in the SIX DAY WAR (1967) Presidents SADAT of Egypt and ASAD of Syria realized that they could not recover their lost lands through diplomacy alone. In 1972 Sadat decided to go to war and made a secret agreement with Syria to attack Israel on the Day of the Atone-ment (Yom Kippur), the holiest day in the Jewish calendar. Sadat knew that he was un-likely to win a prolonged war against Israel but reckoned that with superior numbers and firepower the Egyptians could win an early battle which would create the conditions for superpower intervention.

Egypt and Syria attacked Israel simultane-ously on 6 October 1973 and caught the Israe-lis by surprise. Initially the Egyptians, well-equipped with Soviet weapons, had great suc-cess. Under the protective shield of SAM missile batteries, which neutralized the super-iority of the Israeli Air Force, they put 75,000 men and 800 tanks across the Suez Canal, overran the fortified Bar Lev line and estab-lished strong bridgeheads on the east bank of the Canal. They then intended to wait for an Israeli attack and fight a defensive battle but, to take the pressure off the Syrians on the Golan Heights, they made the mistake of advancing deep into Sinai on 4 October and so had to fight the sort of fluid battle they had sought to avoid. They were now beyond the protection of the SAM missiles and by eve-ning had lost 300 tanks and were in retreat. The Israelis, aided by a massive airlift of sophisticated weapons from the US, followed up their success and in a brilliant manoeuvre

on 15 October, a force led by Ariel Sharon crossed to the west bank of the Canal in a gap between two Egyptian armies and established a bridgehead. Breaking out of this the Israelis came within 50 miles (80 km) of Cairo before the UNITED NATIONS arranged a cease-fire which was sponsored by the US and Soviet Union, on 22 October.

The Syrian attack on the Golan Heights was not as well-planned as the Egyptian cross-ing of the Canal but it nevertheless nearly succeeded. The two Israeli brigades defend-ing Golan were almost wiped out in two days, but they inflicted heavy losses on the Syrians and gave time for Israeli reinforcements to arrive. The Syrians breached the Israeli defences but were too exhausted to exploit their gains. Jordan, Iraq and Morocco all sent troops to help the Syrians but to no avail. Syria accepted a cease-fire on 22 October.

The war ended with Israel in a very strong position but its losses were heavy. It admitted losing 115 aircraft (it lost only 27 in the Six Day War), though the Americans thought the number was nearer 200. 2,521 Israeli soldiers had been killed, 7,056 wounded and the myth of Israeli invincibility destroyed. Israeli public opinion was shocked and blamed the Labour government of Golda Meir and especially the Defence Minister, Moshe DAYAN. The Labour Party, which had ruled the country since the BIRTH OF ISRAEL, now began a steady decline which ended with the right-wing Likud Party winning the election of 1977. Israel had come close to defeat and so decided that its armed forces must be superior to those of all the Arab countries combined. It therefore vastly increased its spending on the armed forces, with US aid. The war made Sadat a hero in Egypt and restored the honour of the Egyptian army. Egypt gained as KIS-SINGER began his tireless shuttle diplomacy which in 1974–5 produced Israeli withdrawals from the Canal, which was reopened in June 1975, and part of Sinai, which enabled Egypt to recover its oilfields. One effect of the war had repercussions throughout the world. On

20 October OPEC had banned oil exports to the US. Although the ban was lifted in March 1974, there was a massive OPEC PRICE RISE which badly affected industrial countries but was a devastating blow in the THIRD WORLD.

October Earthquake, Z. Schiff (1974)
No Victor, No Vanquished: The Yom Kippur War, E. O'Ballance (1978)

Yoshida Shigeru (1878–1967) Prime Minister of Japan (1946–7, 1948–54). The most powerful Japanese politician during and immediately after the OCCUPATION OF JAPAN. Born in Tokyo, he graduated at Tokyo University and then joined the Foreign Ministry. He was Deputy Foreign Minister (1928–30) and then ambassador to Italy (1930–2). An outspoken critic of the military in the 1930s, the army blocked his appointment as Foreign Minister and so he became ambassador to Britain (1936–8). In 1945 he was briefly imprisoned for advocating Japan's surrender, as he feared that if the war continued there would be a left-wing revolution. When the war was over and SCAP (Supreme Commander Allied Personnel – General MACARTHUR) ruled Japan, Yoshida became Foreign Minister and when the US prevented Hatoyama Ichiro from holding public office for supporting the prewar military regimes, Yoshida took over from him as leader of the Liberal Party and as Prime Minister after the elections of 1946.

A conservative politician, he reluctantly accepted the reforms proposed by SCAP, as he believed that co-operation with the US would ensure stability, economic help and a wealthy market for Japan's foreign trade. His support for the JAPANESE CONSTITUTION was crucial in ensuring its approval by the Diet in 1946. When the COLD WAR intensified the US wanted Japan to build up its armed forces and join in the struggle against communism abroad. Yoshida did not want this, as he feared a resurgence of the military and popular opposition to rearmament. He

was prepared to give up Japan's independence in foreign policy in order to obtain American military protection and economic aid. In 1950 he offered military bases in Japan to the US in return for a peace treaty and the end of the Occupation. He proposed that the JAPAN–US SECURITY TREATY should be signed at the same time as the SAN FRANCISCO PEACE TREATY and agreed to nearly all American demands. The US forced him to impose a trade embargo on China and to accept the regime of JIANG JIESHI (Chiang Kai-shek) in Taiwan as the legitimate government of China, a move which ensured bad relations with the People's Republic of China for the next 20 years. Yoshida also had to agree to a limited military programme of 180,000 troops in a Self-Defence Force (DULLES had wanted 350,000). Conservatives were dismayed that the elections of 1952–3 produced no dominant party and feared that the left would unite and win the next election. As Yoshida opposed the merger of his pacifist conservatives with the militant Hatoyama faction (rehabilitated in 1951), he was forced out of office at the end of 1954. The next year conservative groups united to form the LIBERAL DEMOCRATIC PARTY, with Hatoyama as its first leader and Prime Minister. Yoshida retired but continued to exercise considerable influence as an elder statesman. The policies he had pursued in office established the guidelines for subsequent Liberal Democratic governments.

Empire and Aftermath: Yoshida Shigeru and the Japanese Experience 1878–1954, J. H. Dower (1979)
Winners in Peace: MacArthur, Yoshida and Postwar Japan, R. B. Finn (1992)

Yugoslav civil war (1991–5) It began as an attempt to preserve Yugoslavia as a unitary state but soon became, for Slobodan MILO-ŠEVIĆ, a means of creating a Greater Serbia. In December 1990 there was an overwhelming majority for independence in a referendum held in Slovenia. On 26 June 1991

Slovenia declared its independence and faced an assault by the Yugoslav National Army (JNA), but few troops were involved and on the third day of the ten-day war Serbia withdrew its support from the JNA's attempt to hold Yugoslavia together, so that it could concentrate on Croatia. Slovenia therefore became independent with remarkably little bloodshed: the JNA suffered 44 casualties, the Slovenes a handful.

Milošević was prepared to let Slovenia go (there were few Serbs there) but not Croatia, which also declared its independence. In Croatia about 12 per cent of the population was Serb, centred in Krajina, on Croatia's border with Bosnia, and in eastern Slovenia, contiguous to Serbia. Milošević did not dispute Croatia's right to secede from Yugoslavia but said that Serbs in Croatia had the same right to withdraw from Croatia (though he did not allow the same right to Albanians in Kosovo, which was part of Serbia). Well-organized Serb paramilitary forces in Croatia, aided by volunteers from Serbia and the artillery of the JNA, seized as much territory as they could from the poorly armed Croats. In the process ETHNIC CLEANSING began, as Croats were massacred, their homes burned and vast numbers were forced to flee to Croat-held areas. The war was no longer about preserving the integrity of Yugoslavia but creating independent Serb enclaves which could later join Serbia. As a third of Croatia was taken by the Serbs the EC tried to mediate but one truce after another was broken. In September 1991 the EC and then the UNITED NATIONS imposed an arms embargo on Yugoslavia but this helped the Serbs, who controlled the Yugoslav weapons factories and the heavy armour of the JNA. A month later the JNA bombarded the medieval town of Dubrovnik and the Dalmatian coast, aiming to destroy Croatia's lucrative tourist trade. By January 1992 both sides were exhausted and so this phase of the war came to an end, as the EC recognized the independence of Croatia and Slovenia.

A new area of conflict now arose in Bosnia and Hercegovina, where 44 per cent of the population was Muslim, 34 per cent Serb and 17 per cent Croat. When Bosnia declared its independence in February 1992, the leader of the Bosnian Serbs, Radovan Karadžić, immediately proclaimed a separate Serb state in Bosnia. The Bosnian Muslims, denied arms by the embargo on Yugoslavia, were no match for the armed might of the Serbs and the JNA, who soon overran 70 per cent of Bosnia, extending their ethnic cleansing and accompanying atrocities to the areas they conquered. As Milošević supported the Serbs, Franjo TUDJMAN, the Croat leader, aided the Muslims but at the same time seized part of Bosnia for Croatia and in April–May 1993 fought against the Muslims in central Bosnia. Not until 1994 did the Bosnian Muslims and Croats end their fighting and agree to form a federation.

The UN had sent a Protection Force (UNPROFOR) to Bosnia in February 1992 but it had no artillery, heavy armour or close air support: it was to hold a line separating Serb-held areas from the rest of Croatia. Later, when fighting extended to Bosnia, it was to negotiate with the Serbs to send aid convoys to areas, such as Sarajevo, cut off in the fighting. They were humiliated by the Serb commander, General Mladić, who seized much of the aid. UN/EC negotiators Lord Owen and Cyrus Vance produced the Vance–Owen plan in January 1993 to divide Bosnia into ten provinces, defined mainly on ethnic grounds, but this was rejected by the Bosnian Serbs, as they would have to give up much of the territory they had seized. In April 1993 ŠREBRENICA, a Muslim town surrounded by Serbs, was declared a 'safe area' by the UN, as were Sarajevo, Tuzla, Bihać, Žepa and Goražde. The deep divisions in NATO and the UN (the US wanted an end to the arms embargo on Bosnia and tougher action against the Serbs who were bombarding the civilian population of Sarajevo, whereas Britain was opposed to any further action) meant that nothing was done as half the population of Bosnia were driven from their homes and many were massacred. In July 1994 the Contact Group (Russia, US, Britain, France, Germany) proposed that Muslims and Croats should have 51 per cent of Bosnia, Serbia 49 per cent. In spite of Milošević supporting this, the Bosnian Serbs rejected it. When NATO planes did strike at Serb military targets in May 1995, the Serbs seized hundreds of UN peace-keepers as hostages. They were eventually released but to prevent future outrages Britain and France decided to set up a 10,000-strong Rapid Reaction Force with artillery and tanks. A further humiliation for the UN occurred in July 1995 when Mladić seized the 'safe areas' of Srebrenica and Žepa. UN soldiers looked on as Muslim men, who had surrendered, were selected for execution. Tadeusz Mazowiecki, the chief UN human rights investigator in the former Yugoslavia, resigned in disgust at UN conduct over the fall of Šrebrenica.

The war changed course in July 1995 as the Serbs attacked another 'safe area', Bihać. This gave the Croats a perfect excuse to resume fighting. For the past three years they had been building up a formidable army by buying arms on the black market and by using retired US generals to train it. In two days they recovered Western Slavonia and then struck at Knin and Krajina. They met little resistance as the Bosnian Serbs and Milošević failed to aid their fellow Serbs and now the ethnic cleansing of Serb areas took place. By September the 70 per cent of Bosnia held by the Serbs had been reduced to 55 per cent. The US took the lead in NATO air strikes on the Serb military infrastructure throughout Bosnia, bombing air defence systems, ammunition factories and communications. For the first time NATO intervened on a massive scale to bring an end to the conflict. The UN, sidelined, decided to pull out completely. President CLINTON wanted to bring an end to the war before the presidential elections in 1996, so Richard Holbrooke, his Assistant Secretary of State for European Affairs, busily moved around the former Yugoslavia

persuading all parties to make peace, which they agreed to after talks at Dayton, Ohio. Bosnia was to be divided into three areas: a Serb republic with 48 per cent of the territory, a Croation section with 21 per cent and the rest was to be held by the Bosnian Muslims. The Serb area was in two parts (one next to Serbia and Montenegro), connected by the Posavina corridor in the north. Most of the Bosnian Croat area was next to Croatia, but there were some enclaves in Muslim territory. The Muslim areas were the most fragmented: their capital of Sarajevo was surrounded by Serbs and separated from Goražde by 25 miles (40 km) of Serb territory. Muslims in central Bosnia were separated from the Bihać pocket in the north-west by Croats and were landlocked. In theory the Bosnian and Croatian sectors were united in a federation but in practice the Croatian police and army in Bosnia were linked to those in Croatia. There was much illusory idealism in the peace – Bosnia was supposedly a united country in which all refugees would be able to return to their former homes but ethnic cleansing, coupled with the fear and loathing of one group for another, made this unlikely. Some 60,000 NATO troops were to be deployed for a year to enforce the peace terms.

Europe's Backyard War, M. Almond (1994)
The Death of Yugoslavia, L. Silber and A. Little (1995)
Yugoslavia's Bloody Collapse: Causes, Course and Consequences, C. Bennett (1995)

Yugoslav–Soviet split (1948–55)   TITO had spent the Second World War in Yugoslavia and had freed most of the country from German occupation without outside assistance. He was therefore self-confident and independent of Soviet control. STALIN expected Yugoslavia to concentrate on agriculture and accept Soviet economic domination but Tito devoted only 6 per cent of investment to agriculture in his Five Year Plan which began in 1947. However, it was over foreign policy that the major rift with Stalin arose. Tito occupied Trieste and so was in conflict with Italy: Stalin ordered him out, as he was not prepared to risk another war. Stalin also disapproved of Tito's support for the communists in the GREEK CIVIL WAR and of his talk about a Balkan federation, which Yugoslavia would lead. He insisted that Yugoslavia should consult the USSR on all foreign policy questions and vastly over-rated his authority when he said: 'I will shake my little finger and there will be no more Tito'.

In 1948 Yugoslavia was expelled from the COMINFORM, a break which resulted in a savage purge of the Communist Party of Yugoslavia, during which 50,000 were tortured and killed, accused of putting the interests of the Soviet Union before those of Yugoslavia. The split also enabled Tito to pursue a Yugoslav 'road to socialism' by introducing self-management of factories. After the break with Stalin Tito was supported economically by the US, who gave him $2.7 billion of non-repayable assistance between 1951–60, more than US allies Greece and Turkey received: this saved Yugoslavia from economic collapse. In return Tito made an agreement with Italy about Trieste and withdrew his support from the Greek communists. Relations with the Soviet Union were renewed in 1955, when KHRUSHCHEV apologized for the breach of 1948.

Stalin Against Tito: Cominformist Splits in Yugoslav Communism, I. Banac (1988)
Western 'Containment' Policies in the Cold War: The Yugoslav Case, 1948–53, B. Heuser (1989)

Z

Zhao Ziyang (1919–) Prime Minister of the People's Republic of China (1980–7) and General Secretary of the Chinese Communist Party (CCP) (1987–9). From a landlord family, he joined the Communist Youth League as a schoolboy in 1932 and the CCP six years later. During the Sino-Japanese War (1937–45) and the CHINESE CIVIL WAR (1946–9) he organized communist guerrilla bases. After the communist victory he was transferred to Guandong province, where he later became Party Secretary. He vigorously implemented the Agrarian Reform Law (1950) and after the failure of the GREAT LEAP FORWARD (1958–60) supported the reforms of LIU SHAOQI. During the CULTURAL REVOLUTION (1966–76) he was publicly humiliated by Red Guards and forced to walk through the streets of Guangzhou wearing a dunce's hat. He then spent a brief spell in Inner Mongolia before he was rehabilitated in 1973 with the help of ZHOU ENLAI.

His career really took off when he was sent to Sichuan, the largest province in China and one of the most prosperous, as Party Secretary in 1975. There he reversed the policies of the Great Leap Forward and of the Cultural Revolution by authorizing 15 per cent of the land to be farmed privately and its produce to be sold on the open market. This produced a spectacular leap in production. He also showed considerable flexibility in running state industries: plant managers were given financial autonomy and allowed to combine with other enterprises. Workers were rewarded with bonuses for high production. Industrial production in Sichuan increased by 80 per cent between 1976–9. DENG XIAOP-

ING was from Sichuan and when he returned to power in 1977 brought about the rapid rise of Zhao: membership of the Politburo in 1979, of its influential Standing Committee in 1980 and in the same year he replaced HUA GUOFENG as Prime Minister. Like HU YAOBANG and Deng he promoted the economic modernization of China, advocating 'any structure, system, policy or measure' which would increase production. He extended his Sichuan policies to the whole of China, giving self-management to thousands of enterprises and enabling peasant families to increase their control of agriculture. Zhao set the pattern for China's future economic development and brought about a high growth rate, though his advocacy of SPECIAL ECONOMIC ZONES brought about a clash with Li Peng who favoured a more cautious, government-controlled course. When Hu Yaobang was disgraced in 1987, Zhao replaced him as General Secretary of the CCP, giving up the premiership to Li Peng. He seemed destined to be Deng's heir but fell from grace during the student demonstrations in Beijing two years later. The CCP was split between reformers like Zhao, who wanted dialogue and a compromise with the students, and conservatives such as Li, who did not want to make any concessions. Deng supported Li, who crushed the demonstrations in the TIANANMEN SQUARE MASSACRE. In June 1989 Zhao was dismissed.

Zhivkov, Todor (1911–) General Secretary of the Bulgarian Communist Party (1954–89). An uneducated peasant, he became a printer and joined the Communist

Party in 1932. He took part in the small parti-
san movement during the Second World War
and in the coup which brought the Fatherland
Front coalition to power in September 1944.
This included several parties but the communists controlled the key ministries of internal
affairs and justice. Zhivkov was in charge of
the reign of terror which liquidated communist opponents: official figures gave 2,138
death sentences and 10,000 imprisoned but
there were many more victims of the regime.
In the Communist Party Zhivkov rose
rapidly, as a member of the General Committee (1948), of the Politburo (1951) and General Secretary (1954). In 1962 he became
Prime Minister and so controlled both government and party. A new constitution (1971)
made the Council of State the main policy-
making body: Zhivkov was its President.

Zhivkov wanted Bulgaria to have 'a common circulatory system' with the Soviet
Union and so slavishly copied the Stalinist
economic system, with collectivization of
agriculture and an emphasis on heavy industry. The Bulgarian economy was closely tied
to that of the Soviet Union, importing Russian oil and iron ore and exporting agricultural produce and manufactured goods. He
created a successful computer industry by
making agreements with Hitachi and Toshiba
(the Soviet space programme used Bulgarian
computers) but as the price of Soviet oil rose
from 1975 Zhivkov had to borrow more. By
1989 Bulgaria had a debt of $10 billion and the
economy was in decline. Zhivkov twice
offered, to KHRUSHCHEV and BREZHNEV,
to give up Bulgaria's independence and make
it part of the USSR but his offers were
rejected. In his foreign policy Zhivkov was a
faithful ally of the Soviet Union: a member of
COMECON and of the WARSAW PACT, Bulgaria joined in the invasion of Czechoslovakia
which ended the PRAGUE SPRING in 1968.

The Bulgarian population was generally
docile: there were no major strikes. The
main domestic problem. Zhivkov faced he
created himself, by forcing the Turks (10 per
cent of the population) to emigrate or assim-

ilate. He closed Turkish schools in 1958 and
arranged for Turkey to take 130,000 Bulgarian Turks between 1968 and 1978. In 1984 he
decided to end the Turkish problem once and
for all: Turks had to adopt Slav names, the
Turkish language was forbidden in public and
circumcision (required by Islamic custom)
was banned. These measures led to a further
emigration of Bulgarian Turks, and were
unpopular with many of his colleagues. Zhivkov ignored GORBACHEV's perestroika and
GLASNOST and became increasingly out of
touch, even with members of his own party.
The day after the BERLIN WALL was breached (9 November 1989) members of the
Central Committee forced him to give up his
posts. In 1992 he was sentenced to seven
years' imprisonment and fined a million dollars for embezzlement and corruption but,
owing to his age, he did not go to prison.

*Todor Zhivkov: Statesman and Builder of New
  Bulgaria*, R. Maxwell (ed.) (1985)
A Short History of Modern Bulgaria, R. J.
  Crampton (1987)
Bulgarian Politics, Economics and Society, R. J.
  McIntyre (1988)

Zhou Enlai (1898–1976)   Prime Minister
of the People's Republic of China (1949–76)
and Foreign Minister (1949–58). Born into a
gentry family, he went to Japan as a student
but returned in 1919 after the anti-Japanese
May Fourth Movement. In 1920 he was in
France where he became a Marxist and joined
the Chinese Communist Party (CCP),
founded in 1921. Returning to China in 1924
he soon held a key position in the United
Front of communists and nationalists as a
political commissar at the Military Academy
at Whampoa, headed by JIANG JIESHI
(Chiang Kai-shek). He organized the workers'
militia, which secured Shanghai for the
advancing nationalist army in 1927. When
Jiang turned on the communists, Zhou narrowly escaped execution. In 1931 he joined
MAO ZEDONG in the Jiangxi Soviet, a com-
munist-controlled area and was Chairman of

the CCP Military Committee, a position he gave up in favour of Mao during the Long March (1934–5), on which the communists survived nationalist attacks only by retreating north to Yanan. When Jiang was kidnapped at Xian in 1936 by some of his own troops, who wanted him to fight the Japanese rather than the communists, Zhou obtained his release and negotiated with Jiang another United Front against Japan. For the next few years he was the liaison between communists and nationalists. Following the communist victory in the CHINESE CIVIL WAR (1946–9) and the foundation of the People's Republic of China, Zhou became its first Prime Minister, a post he retained until his death.

Charming, persuasive and pragmatic, Zhou survived all purges in the party leadership and was compared to a 'willow branch', strong but flexible and able to bend before the wind. Zhou, by knowing when to yield and when to stand firm, avoided the disgrace which befell leaders such as LIU SHAOQI and LIN BIAO during the CULTURAL REVOLUTION. While being faithful to Mao, Zhou sought to prevent the worst excesses of Mao's leadership. He prevented the complete breakdown of government and the destruction of the CCP during the Cultural Revolution and tried, not always successfully, to prevent the humiliation of party officials by the Red Guards. From 1971 he attempted to restore political stability and brought back DENG XIAOPING into the leadership but he was faced with the unremitting hostility of the GANG OF FOUR, led by Mao's wife JIANG QING, who wanted to maintain the radical policies of the Cultural Revolution. Zhou, like Deng, thought that expertise rather than ideological correctness was needed for economic development and promoted export-led growth and the importation of technology from the capitalist world.

As Foreign Minister (1949–58) his patience, negotiating skills and his command of detail were much in evidence. He aimed to restore China's international prestige and in 1950 negotiated the SINO-SOVIET TREATY, though he was unable to prevent this unravel-ling in the SINO-SOVIET DISPUTE. Similarly his warm relations with Jawaharlal NEHRU, who was persuaded to accept China's occupation of Tibet in 1950–1, did not survive the SINO-INDIAN DISPUTE (1962) over borders. Zhou tried to promote solidarity among the communist states on China's border. He helped KIM IL-SUNG to revive North Korea's shattered economy after the KOREAN WAR (1950–3) and built a road and rail network in Guangxi province in order to send supplies to HO CHI MINH, fighting the French in the INDOCHINA WAR OF INDE-PENDENCE (1946–54). Zhou negotiated skil-fully the GENEVA ACCORDS (1954) to end this war and obtain independence for North Vietnam. He was prominent at the Bandung Conference (1955) in Indonesia of the NON-ALIGNED MOVEMENT, which followed heightened tension after the formation of SEATO and the US defence treaty with Tai-wan, where Jiang and the nationalists had fled. Even after he ceased to be Foreign Min-ister Zhou retained control of foreign affairs: he carried on secret negotiations with Henry KISSINGER in 1971 which led to President NIXON's visit to China in 1972, a remarkable turnabout in foreign policy. His *rapproche-ment* with the US enabled the People's Republic of China to obtain representation in the UNITED NATIONS (China had been represented there by the Guomindang gov-ernment in Taiwan) and to take a permanent seat in the Security Council.

Zhou Enlai struggled with cancer for three years before he died. His death was followed by unprecedented demonstrations of public grief in Tiananmen Square, Beijing and in other major cities in China.

Zhou Enlai, D. Wilson (1984)
Zhou Enlai and the Foundations of Chinese Foreign Policy, Kuo-Kang Shao (1997)

Zia ul-Haq, Mohammad (1924–88)

President of Pakistan (1978–88). From a middle-class family, he served with British forces in Southest Asia during the Second World War and was commissioned in 1945. When the INDEPENDENCE AND PARTITION OF INDIA took place in 1947 he joined the Pakistan army and fought in the INDO-PAKISTANI WARS of 1965 and 1971. He was promoted above more senior officers by Zulfikar Ali BHUTTO to become Chief of Staff in 1976 and a year later led a bloodless military coup. Zia promised elections for October and a return to civilian rule but on 1 October he postponed the elections indefinitely, the first of many broken promises. Bhutto was tried for incitement to murder an opponent in 1974 and was sentenced to death. In spite of appeals for clemency from heads of government from all over the world, Zia refused to commute the sentence and Bhutto was hanged in April 1979.

Zia became President in 1978 and made the country's laws conform to the *Sharia* (Islamic law). Islamic punishments – flogging, amputation and hanging for 'major' crimes such as theft, drinking alcohol and adultery – were introduced, bank interest was abolished and fasting during Ramadan was made compulsory. Western-style democracy was declared un-Islamic. In an attempt to control Western, secular influence, schools teaching in English were told to use Urdu. Islam played a large part in Zia's foreign policy too. After the SOVIET INVASION OF AFGHANISTAN in 1979 Pakistan became the main base for *Mujahidin* guerrillas fighting against the Russians and the communist government in Kabul. Zia was the recipient of huge amounts of American aid as the COLD WAR was extended.

He amended the constitution to give himself more powers and in 1985 lifted martial law and the state of emergency (which had existed since 1969). This enabled Benazir BHUTTO to return to Pakistan in 1986 to be greeted by enormous crowds as a hero on her four-week tour of the country, when she demanded the holding of national elections and an end to military rule. Violent clashes between different ethnic groups (Pathans, Biharis, Punjabis and Sindhis) in Karachi posed another threat to Zia: the strife in Sind is primarily between Pathans and Sindhis on one side and Bihari refugees from India. In 1988 he dismissed the National Assembly and provincial assemblies and the cabinet, claiming that it was weak and incompetent and unable to control the escalating violence in Sind. There was no return to martial law and political parties were not banned. It is not clear what Zia intended to do next as he was killed in an air crash in August 1988. Sabotage was suspected.

The Military and Politics in Pakistan 1947–86, H. A. Rizvi (1986)
Pakistan: The Continuing Search for Nationhood, S. J. Burki (1991)

Zionism   A movement for the foundation of a Jewish state in Palestine, the historic homeland of the Jews. It looked back to the days of the kings of Israel, when Mount Zion had been the site of the fortress of Jerusalem. Zionism arose as a result of the anti-Semitism and persecution of Jews in Russia and Eastern Europe in the late nineteenth century. Theodor Herzl, a Viennese journalist, made Zionism into a political movement when he published *The Jewish State* in 1896 and a year later organized the first Zionist Congress at Basle in Switzerland which established the World Zionist Organization (WZO). Many prominent European Jews did not support Zionism, as they were assimilated in the countries where they lived, but the movement received a great boost during the First World War when the British government issued the Balfour Declaration, which favoured the establishment of a Jewish home in Palestine. The Israeli state, proclaimed in 1948 (see ISRAEL BIRTH OF), realized the Zionist dream. Some Jews, including BEN-GURION, thought that there was no longer need for a Zionist movement but the WZO continued to exist, raising money for Jewish immigration to Israel and lobbying (very successfully in the US) on behalf of Israel.

A History of Zionism, W. Laqueur (1972)